A Survey of Hinduism

A SURVEY OF HINDUISM

Klaus K. Klostermaier

Second Edition

State University of New York Press

Published by
State University of New York Press, Albany

Printed in the United States of America

For information, address State University of New York Press,
State University Plaza, Albany, N.Y., 12246

Production by Marilyn P. Semerad
Marketing by Nancy Farrell

Library of Congress Cataloging-in-Publication Data

Klostermaier, Klaus K., 1933–
A survey of Hinduism / Klaus K. Klostermaier. — 2nd ed.
p. cm.
Includes bibliographical references and index.
ISBN 0–7914–2109–0 (hc. : alk. paper). — ISBN 0–7914–2110–4 (pb. : alk. paper)
1. Hinduism.
BL1202.K56 1994
294.5—dc20 93–46778
CIP

10 9 8 7 6 5 4 3

Contents

List of Figures vii

List of Photographs ix

Preface to Second Edition xi

Note on Pronunciation and Use of Sanskrit Words xiii

Introduction 1

PART I. HINDUISM: DEVELOPMENT AND ESSENCE

1. India and the West 17
2. The History and Development of Hinduism 30
3. Hindu *Dharma*: Orthodoxy and Heresy in Hinduism 49
4. Revelation and Scripture in Hinduism 65
5. *Itihāsa* and *Purāṇa*: The Heart of Hinduism 81
6. The Bhagavadgītā 99
7. The World of the Hindu 112
8. The Many Gods and the One God of Hinduism 130

PART II. *TRIMĀRGA*: THE THREE HINDU PATHS TO LIBERATION

9. The Path of Works: *Karmamārga* 155
10. Purity and Merit: The Twin Concerns of *Karmamārga* 170
11. The Hindu Sacraments: The *Saṃskāras* 183
12. The Path of Knowledge: *Jñānamārga* 193
13. *Ātman* and *Brahman*: Self and All 204
14. Karma, *Vidyā, Mokṣa*: Liberation from Rebirth 212
15. The Path of Loving Devotion: *Bhaktimārga* 221
16. Lord Viṣṇu and His Devotees 239
17. Śiva: The Grace and the Terror of God 261
18. Devī: The Divine Mother 278
19. Mudalvan, Murugan, Māl: The Great Gods of the Tamils 294

PART III. THE STRUCTURAL SUPPORTS OF HINDUISM

20. The Divine Presence in Space and Time: *Mūrti, Tīrtha, Kāla* 311
21. The Hindu Social Order: *Caturvarṇāśramadharma* 333
22. The Professional Religious: *Saṃnyāsa* 345
23. *Strīdharma*: The Position of Women in Hinduism 361
24. Hindu Structures of Thought: The *Ṣaḍdarśanas* 377
25. Hindu Logic and Physics: *Nyāya-Vaiśeṣika* 387
26. Hindu Psychology and Metaphysics: *Sāṁkhya-Yoga* 397
27. Hindu Theology, Old and New: *Pūrva Mīmāṃsā* and Vedānta 408

PART IV. THE MEETING OF EAST AND WEST IN MODERN INDIA

28. Hindu Reforms and Reformers 429
29. Mahātmā Gandhi: A Twentieth-Century Karmayogi 447
30. Hindu Nationalist Politics and Hinduism as A World Religion 461

Chronology 477
Maps 490
Notes 493
Glossary 591
Abbreviations Used 615
Bibliography 617
Index 675

List of Figures

2.1	Prehistoric rock paintings and drawings from Bhimbhetka	35
2.2	Seals and figurines from the Indus civilization	37
4.1	Sage Vyāsa dictating Mahābhārata to Gaṇeśa	72
7.1	Purāṇic world model	119
7.2	The map of the Purāṇic world model	120
7.3	*Amṛtā manthana*: The churning of the Milk Ocean	128
9.1	Vedic fire sacrifice	158
11.1	Some *saṃskāras*	184
15.1	The nine degrees of devotion	230–31
15.2	Implements used for daily *pūjā*	235
16.1	Viṣṇu in human form	243
16.2	Nammālvār	253
17.1	Śiva *trimūrti* from Elephanta	264
18.1	*Devī Mahiṣāsuramārdiṇi*: The Goddess slaying the buffalo demon	280
18.2	Śrī Rāma *yantra*	287
20.1	*Vāstu-puruṣa maṇḍala*	318
20.2	The pattern of a *Vāstu-puruṣa maṇḍala*	319
20.3	Diagram of *Padmagarbha* maṇḍala of the Bṛhadeśvara Temple	320
27.1	Ādiśaṅkara	414
27.2	Rāmānuja	418
27.3	Madhva	424
28.1	Rāmakrishna Paramahaṃsa	439
1	The Hindu calendar	480–81

List of Photographs

1 Temple scene in Mathurā xiv
2 Ancient Śiva sanctuary beneath an old pipal tree 40
3 Nāga, Khajurāho twelfth century 42
4 Agni, Khajurāho twelfth century 135
5 Kubera, Khajurāho twelfth century 136
6 Śiva Sadāśiva, Mahārāṣṭra, Heras Institute Bombay 142
7 Viṭhobhā (Viṣṇu), Mahārāṣṭra, Heras Institute Bombay 144
8 Durgā, Khajurāho twelfth century 148
9 Playing Kṛṣṇa's flute in Sevākuñj 233
10 Platform for *rasa-līlā* dance in Sevākuñj, Vrindāban 238
11 Varāha *avatāra*, Khajurāho twelfth century 242
12 Keśighāṭ in Vrindāban, where Kṛṣṇa subdued the demon Keśi 247
13 Viṣṇu Upendra, Khajurāho twelfth century 250
14 Śiva Taṇḍava, Khajurāho twelfth century 272
15 Śiva Bhairava, Mahārāṣṭra, Heras Institute Bombay 276
16 Lakṣmī, Khajurāho twelfth century 284
17 Kālī, Bengal, Heras Institute Bombay 290
18 Sundaramūrti, South India, Heras Institute Bombay 303
19 Outer hall in a South Indian temple 322
20 Śiva Kānphaṭa, Mahārāṣṭra, Heras Institute Bombay 355
21 Memorial for a *satī* 373
22 Ramaṇa Maharṣi 441

Preface to the Second Edition

Recent events in India — the agitation for the "liberation" of the legendary birthplace of Rāma in Ayodhya, the destruction of the Babri Masjid on December 6, 1992, and the widely reported Hindu-Muslim riots in dozens of cities and towns—have drawn the world's attention to Hinduism, the religion under whose banner an increasing number of political activists battle for hegemony on the South Asian subcontinent.

Almost as a byproduct of the news about communal riots and fanaticism, information about the world's largest democracy, its cultural diversity, its economic potential, its rich traditions and its treasures of art is thrown in. The certainty of a growth in power and influence of Hinduism, and the possibility of an emergence of a Hindu theocracy on the Indian subcontinent are reason enough to expect more and more people outside India to evince an interest in the history and present shape of Hinduism.

A Survey of Hinduism is attempting to offer both historical information and an insight into the contemporary situation in India. Reviews of the first edition, which appeared in 1988, were encouraging and it was particularly gratifying to see reviewers in India, Hindus themselves, approve of my presentation. I am grateful to SUNY Press for offering me now the opportunity to bring out a second edition. For extensive comments and suggestions I have to thank Swami Dayananda Bharati, Sri S. Vidyasankar, Dr. D. Raghavan, Sri M. P. Pandit, Profs. Joel Brereton, Leona Anderson, V. Narayan, and H.-W. Gensichen, to mention only a few. In response to suggestions I have added chapters on *Strīdharma* and on Mahātmā Gandhi, and have made major changes in several other chapters. The revision also allowed me to make reference to new literature; an astonishingly large number of both general and specialized books on Hinduism have appeared in the past five years. An extended visit to India in January–February 1992 in connection with lecture invitations and a research project supported by the Social Sciences and Humanities Research Council of Canada enabled me to renew old contacts and establish new ones. I am grateful to SSHRCC as well as to the University of Manitoba, which granted me a year's administrative leave to work on my project.

I wish to thank especially Dr. Jhash (Santiniketan), Dr. Devadoss (University of Madras), Dr. Janaki (Kuppuswami Research Institute), and Dr. Srivatsa Goswami (Vrindaban Research Institute) for their invitations and discussions. As always, I found India immensely exciting and challenging and hope to have communicated something of that excitement and challenge in my writing.

Winnipeg, August 1993

Note on Pronounciation and Use of Sanskrit Words

As a rule the Sanskrit vowels have the same value as Italian vowels; a line above a vowel means a length: *ā* = *aa*. Consonants correspond, with some exceptions, to the English consonants. Among the more notable differences are aspirate consonants. For example, *th* is not pronounced like the English *th* in *theater* but is a double consonant like the *t-h* in *hot-house*. *J* and *C* and their aspirates are pronounced like *dsh*. There are different *t*/d sounds (indicated by dots underneath the letters) for which there are no exact equivalents in English. *Ś* and *ṣ* are pronounced like *sh*. Although the English does not have some of the consonants indicated by diacritics (usually a dot above or below the consonant) the diacritic has been retained for the sake of correct rendering of the words (in Sanskrit the word meaning may be quite different if the *d* is exchanged for a *ḍ*, or *t* for a *ṭ* etc.). *Ṛ*, *ṛ* are pronoucned *ri*.

In a work meant not primarily for the specialist in the field, Sanskrit words are rendered normally in their uninflected stem forms rather than with their nominative case endings (e.g., *hetu* for *hetuḥ*; *maṇḍapa* for *maṇḍapam*) Words, like *karma* and *yoga* that have become part of the English vocabulary have been left in the customary form of writing. I have also followed the common practice of adding an English plural -*s* to Sanskrit words (neither separating the -*s* through a hyphen, as is done nowadays in some scholarly journals nor using the grammatically correct plural formations; therefore, I have rendered the plural for *Purāṇa*(m) as *Purāṇas*, and not *Purāṇa*-s or *Puraṇā(ṇi))*. Indian names have usually been left as they were found in the documents quoted; no attempt has been made either to transcribe them correctly or to provide them with diacritics. Tamiḷ names and words have not been consistently transliterated according to the most recent conventions; for the sake of easier identification the Sanskritized form of some names has been retained (e.g., Sundaramūrti instead of *Cuntaramūrti*). In the bibliography Indian names have usually been dealt with as if they were European names. This technically is not always correct (e.g., Śastri and Iyengar are really titles and not proper names), but it makes it easier to identify authors.

1 Temple scene in Mathurā

Introduction

> Among all the great religions of the world there is none more catholic, more assimilative, than the mass of beliefs which go to make up what is popularly known as Hinduism.
>
> —W. Crooke[1]

Most of India's nearly 900 million people call themselves Hindus.[2] In addition, some 20 million Hindus are settled all over the world, substantial numbers of them in North America. Hindu gurus have become very visible in the West during the past few decades as promoters of a faith that many young Westerners adopted as their own. Hinduism is not only one of the numerically largest but also the oldest living major tradition on earth, with roots reaching back into the prehistory of humankind. It has preserved beliefs and practices from times immemorial, and it has developed under the influence of many other traditions.

For many centuries India had been a distant and mysterious land to Westerners. Since the Age of Discovery, and it is an interesting coincidence that the discovery of America took place as the result of Europe's search for India, India has become increasingly familiar to the West. The West realized that India had more to offer than spices and markets, and in turn India gave up its initial reserve opening up its treasures of literature and culture to Western scholars. India's ancient heritage is readily accessible today.

Hinduism, although offering many striking parallels to other great religions, nevertheless cannot be easily compared to any of them. That has as much to do with its history as with its present adherents, with the way religion has been conceived in India and the way it is understood today in the West. Hinduism, although certainly circumscribing Indian religiosity, has many specific historico-cultural and socio-political dimensions. It both represented and always found itself in a situation of cultural and religious pluralism. Hinduism has aroused the curiosity not only of scholars of religion but equally that of sociologists and anthropologists, political scientists and archeologists, philosophers and historians, not to forget the philologists who were the first to get seriously interested in Hindu literature. We must remind ourselves, however, that Hinduism was not created by its sages and saints primarily to provide material for doctoral dissertations for European and American scholars or to enable anthropologists and sociologists to do their field work but for the physical and spiritual sustenance of its population: it was meant to interpret reality to Hindus, to make life more meaningful to them, to provide them with a theoretical and practical framework for their individual and corporate existence, to educate them intellectually and morally, and finally, to fulfill their longing for ultimate freedom and salvation.

In contrast to Ancient Greece and Rome, whose classical literatures and traditions have been the major inspiration of Western humanities, but whose modern successor nations have little in common with them, India is a modern country in which much of the ancient tradition is still alive. It is alive not only in the age-old rituals that continue to be performed, or in the popular stories from Epics and *Purāṇas* that are still enjoyed by contemporary audiences in theaters and films, but also in the structure of its society and many of its laws, in its institutions as well as in its popular customs. It would be wrong, however, to portray Hinduism as a relic of a fossilized past, a tradition unable to change, a museum exhibit that must not be touched. Quite the contrary. Hinduism in its long history has undergone many changes, it is rapidly adapting to modern times and constantly bringing forth new movements and taking new directions. Hinduism has always been more than mere religion in the modern Western sense and it aims at being a comprehensive way of life as well today, a tradition by which people can live.

Many Westerners who come to India experience what has been called a *culture-shock*. That has not so much to do with the difference in living standards between India and the West, a difference that is rapidly diminishing, but rather with a different kind of logic of life. Hinduism is built on basic assumptions different from those of the West. Once these are accepted, it appears as logical and as consistent as any other tradition.

The bewilderment of Westerners who come into contact with living Hinduism may also have to do with the available literature on Hinduism. Much of it is devoted to some kind of orchid collecting, not to a description of the real landscape. Much popular writing about India either attempts to shock the reader by reporting bizarre happenings and describing sinister characters or to romanticize a country and civilization so delightfully different from our own. Much scholarly writing focuses on the past of India: the literary and architectural monuments, the practices and institutions of classical India. A great amount has been written, and continues to be written, on Vedic ritual and ancient Indian kingship, topics no doubt of great historic significance but of very marginal relevance today. Similarly, many a book on Hindu mythology, on the gods and goddesses of India, which is coming out, more often than not does not attempt to tell the reader how contemporary Hindus understand these and how and why they worship them, but frequently tries to prove a Freudian, a Jungian, or another psychological or anthropological thesis, playing around with structuralist, functionalist, or other theoretical models that are clever and appear plausible to Western intellectuals, but explain little and often distort a great deal of Hindu reality. Given the enormous mass of writings associated with Hinduism it is very easy to find supportive quotes for every thesis. It is another question whether the thesis would be acceptable to Hindus and whether it fits the context in India. Hindu resentment against the "endless psycho-analyzing of our Gods, Goddesses and heroes" erupted in February 1991 in one of the unlikliest of places, in the Department of South Asian Studies at the University of California at Berkeley.[3] Individual American scholars were criticized for considering Rāma a symbol of "the type of Indian son who makes a passive homosexual identification with his father" or taking Gaṇeśa as "example of a story representing the primal Oedipal triangle of a son, father and mother."

Here the attempt is made to describe Hinduism as the living tradition of the Hindus; a tradition with its own logic and with a purpose of its own. The intention is to portray Hinduism in such a way that contemporary Hindus would be able to recognize themselves in it and outsiders would be helped to understand something of this tradition that is alien to them but that they wish to come to know and that they will encounter on a visit to India.

The method adopted in this Survey of Hinduism obviously has something to do with the purpose of the book. The idea is to offer correct information on Hinduism as a whole and also to make a modern Westerner understand some of its meaning. As for information, this has to be selective. Hinduism is simply too large a subject to be exhaustively dealt with in a volume this size and too much has been written about it, which need not be repeated but can be referred to. As for understanding, this can, obviously, be communicated only to the extent that it is available. Understanding usually takes the form of translating something unknown into known categories. The choice of the categories into which one translates is crucial and cannot be totally arbitrary. Understanding in a nonelementary sense happens within certain systematic contexts, operating with certain presuppositions and identifying certain structures.[4] Thus an interpretation of a phenomenon like Hinduism in modern Western categories takes place within a given philosophical or theological, a sociological or an anthropological, a historical or political framework. These frameworks facilitate the integration of information but they also may hinder us from seeing the specifics and those aspects for which there is no parallel. As L. Dumont has remarked: "Hindu religion, or philosophy is at least as all-embracing in its own way as any sociological theory may be."[5]

In some areas of interpretation of Indian history as a whole and its intellectual and religious history in particular a notable rift has emerged between "Western" and "Indian" scholars. There is no doubt that some early Western scholarship on India was influenced not only by prevalent European historical and philological methodologies but also by colonial interests and that some of these attitudes still linger on. There is equally little doubt that some Indian scholarship was motivated by an urge to prove the correctness of popular traditions or by an effort to establish intellectual priority or moral superiority. Over and above such unscholarly tendentiousness and prejudice there is, of course, a cultural context that influences both the choice of topics and the aim of investigations. A typical "Western" investigator may consider his or her task accomplished if a text has been philologically and grammatically analyzed. A typical "Indian" scholar would identify with the issues with which the text is dealing, would possibly take sides, and argue for a particular school of thought. Whereas the former would be satisfied with a purely historical account of religious notions, the latter would internalize them and see their existential implications. As an "insider-outsider" I have attempted to pay attention to both concerns, fully aware of the fact that it is not always possible to avoid taking sides.

Intentionally I did not choose the framework of any one particular contemporary Western academic discipline.[6] That made my task at one and the same time easier and more difficult: easier because I did not have to justify with the concepts of a particular discipline what obviously does not fit into its schema;[7] more difficult because the range of phenomena to be dealt with becomes so much larger, the choice of vocabulary more problematic, and the risk of transgressing beyond one's competence so much greater.

The study of other cultures is no longer just the hobby of a few leisured academics; it has or should become a major component of general education. The world of the 1990s is connected through multiple networks of trade and commerce, political and military alliances, and through large scale migrations of populations. If we consider each other as belonging to the same human family we cannot consider cultures and races eternally immovable barriers. Nor can we ignore them. We can penetrate them and enter into an exchange. I agree with L. Dumont that "cultures not only *can* be made to communicate, they *must*."[8] Through that communication we will doubtlessly also become capable of sharing other cultures' viewpoints, seeing their logic from within, and valuing as precious what was merely exotic to us before; we will not only learn about Hinduism, but also learn from Hinduism.

Hinduism, as a way of life embraces virtually all aspects of culture. This survey focuses on those aspects of Hinduism that are "religious" in a more specific sense, without either leaving out or completely separating from it other aspects of life that in the West are no longer connected with religion. Hindu religion has, in spite of its all-inclusive character, a metaphysical core, and there is no denying the fact that it provided a religious interpretation to the whole of life. Hinduism always left much freedom to its adherents to choose among many options and exerted, except in matters that had to do with sectarian disciplines and caste rules, little pressure on its followers. India has always held a great variety of races and cultures within its boundaries, varieties of languages, traditions, gods and cults. In spite of the emergence of all-India expressions of Hinduism, such as Vaiṣṇavism and Śaivism, the regional roots of particular branches of these are very much in evidence and local practices vary markedly from one place to the other. At all times the flexibility of Hinduism also showed in the very obvious difference between theory and practice; a difference that makes it all the more unlikely to understand Hinduism by merely paying attention to its verbalized theory without having observed its living practice.

Serious Western study of India began as Sanskrit philology with the establishment of chairs for Sanskrit in major European universities in the early nineteenth century. It concentrated on classical drama and epics, on Vedānta, Veda, and grammar, and eventually on the Prakrits, which were part of the Sanskrit dramas and are also the canonical languages of the Buddhists and Jains. The study of modern Indian languages and especially the study of South Indian languages developed only very recently in the West, and with it the interest in popular religion, the *Purāṇas*, and mediaeval literature in Indian vernaculars. There would be few Indianists today who doubt the importance of these languages and literatures for an understanding of almost all aspects of Indian culture. But work is still scarce. Many more Western scholars know Sanskrit than Tamil, and again there are many more translations of ancient Pāli and Ardhamāgadhī works available than of medieval or modern Hindī, Marathī, or Bengālī texts. It is encouraging to see that the younger generation of Indianists, especially in North America are devoting their talent and energies to translating such vernacular literature.[9]

Nobody will deny the importance of knowing Sanskrit and the intrinsic value of Sanskrit literature for Indian studies. After all, Sanskrit was the language of Brahmin scholarship for more than 2,000 years and Sanskrit literature constitutes an irreplaceable treasure-house of the literary achievements of many generations of Indian poets, scholars, and thinkers. One must not forget, however, that several times in Indian history successful attempts were made to break the monopoly of Sanskrit learning by expressing important ideas and lofty thoughts in other languages. An impressive vernacular literature has developed that embodies and further develops the ancient culture and by virtue of being vernacular reaches a much larger strata of the population. Thus the Hindī re-creation of the *Rāmāyaṇa*—Tulasīdāsa's free rerendering of Vālmīki's Sanskrit work in the mediaeval Hindī *Rāmcaritmānas*—has become immensely more popular than the Sanskrit original, and it has influenced the thoughts and values of a much larger number of people. Contemporary translations of epics and *Purāṇas* in Indian vernaculars and religious journals in Hindī, Marathī, Gujarātī, Bengālī, Tamiḷ, and so forth reach a much wider audience than the classical Sanskrit treatises. To some extent modern vernacular religious literature keeps repeating and exposing the content of the classical texts. But it is not *mere* repetition and exposition. A popular religious journal in modern Hindī like *Kalyāṇ*, which has a monthly circulation of over 175,000, also deals with contemporary problems and offers a fairly faithful mirror of recent developments within Hinduism. It is not only simple folk who write letters and express their religious sentiments in journals like this, also scholars and religious leaders address a large readership through this medium.

As a young man and as a student of Indian religions at a European university, I made a quite deliberate decision not to write anything on Hinduism unless I had seen Indian reality for myself and experienced Hinduism *in loco*. Looking for an opportunity to immerse myself in the Hindu milieu I accepted an invitation from the late Swami Bon Maharaj to join his Institute of Indian Philosophy in Vrindāban, Uttar Pradesh. Vrindāban has meanwhile become quite well-known due to the spread of the Hare Krishna movement and their preaching of Caitanya Vaiṣṇavism. The sojourn in Vrindāban, the daily experience of a vibrant and intense Hinduism, the many contacts with pious and learned Hindus intensified my motivation to read and study the sources.[10] Vrindāban is a small town, and surrounded by numerous villages, largely untouched by modern developments. I moved from there to Bombay, a modern metropolis, the most Westernized of India's big cities. Hinduism is flourishing also in Bombay, and I learned to appreciate the new ways in which it appears and the appeal it has for sophisticated modern people.[11] A year spent in Madras opened my eyes to the quite distinct Dravidian tradition within Hinduism, a tradition whose distinctiveness is emphasized also through contemporary political developments.

Life in India, for most people, is quite unromantic. To provide for the daily necessities, be it in the villages or in the big cities, is for the majority of Indians an exhausting, competitive task. In India, as most everywhere, there is poverty, unemployment, disillusionment among the youth; there are natural calamities and social tensions, language riots and religious confrontations. To experience all this for ten years has a sobering effect on one's youthful enthusiasm and prevents one from unduly romanticising India, present or past. But living in India nevertheless also makes one aware of the reality of a great old civilization, of the influence of great figures and movements from the past and the present, of the pervasive presence of religion in all aspects of daily life, for better or worse. No amount of reading texts can replace the immediacy of recognition given through an encounter with a *samnyāsi* who has spent a lifetime in pursuit of *mokṣa*. No theory of art can do what a visit to a place like Elephanta or Ajanta does to a sensitive person. No description can adequately express the sensation of participation in a major temple feast in a place like Madurai or Tirupati.

Over 80 percent of India's population is Hindu. With an estimated 900 million Indians, that leaves a considerable number of non-Hindus who in some way or other interact with the Hindu majority.[12] The largest group, no doubt, are the Muslims. Even after partition, which was intended to give to Indian Muslims a homeland of their own in Pakistan, some 120 million Muslims can be found in India. The coexistence of this large minority with the Hindu majority is an uneasy one: centuries of conflict have created a permanent, latent tension that, at the slightest provocation, flares up into a riot, often with great loss of life and property on both sides. The Sikhs, for long counted as part of Hinduism, are now asserting their own religio-cultural identity. They constitute only about 2 percent of India's population. They are strongly concentrated in the Punjab where they claim to have a majority. Not all Sikhs are convinced that they need a separate Khalistān but the more extremist faction does not shy away from terrorism and murder to press the claim. About the same number of Indians are Christians, around 14 million, divided into a great many different churches and denominations. There are about 3 million Buddhists, 2 million Jains, a few hundred thousand Parsis and Jews—all of them with a long Indian history of their own.

The tribals, officially now called *ādivāsīs,* original inhabitants of the country, make up a sizeable minority of over 45 million. They comprise hundreds of different groups, strongly concentrated in Central India, but to be found throughout the subcontinent. They are in varying degrees influenced by Hindu culture and often have lost their own languages but they, in turn, have greatly contributed to the development of Hinduism. Many castes, especially among the lower ones, were formed by assimilating tribes to Hinduism. Much of the local tradition of Hinduism can be linked to tribal origins: tribal forms of deities merged into larger Hindu gods, tribal places of worship and sacred spots were taken over by Hinduism as *tīrthas* and places where Hindu temples were built.[13] In a countermove to the so-called Sanskritization, a term coined by M. N. Srinivas to describe the trend among low castes and tribals to heighten their status by employing brahmin priests and by adopting high-caste rituals, a reassertion of tribal culture is taking place in India. To some extent this is the result of a deliberate policy encouraged by the central government, to protect the cultures of the tribes. It also is a reaction against what tribals perceived to be Hindu aggressiveness and exploitation. It is worth noting that tribals are in the forefront of India's ecological movement; they initiated the Chipko movement and launched massive protests against the Narmada development scheme.

Furthermore, an estimated 100 million Indians are and are not Hindus. These are the people whom Gandhi had called *Harijan,* "God's People," and who were otherwise known as outcastes. Strictly speaking they had no right within traditional Hindu society, but they lived with it and functioned at the margins of it.[14] They even patterned their own society along caste structures, observing higher and lower, clean and unclean among themselves. Under Dr. Ambedkar, himself a Māhār, member of a scheduled caste, several million outcastes abandoned Hinduism and adopted Buddhism as their religion. But most stayed within Hinduism. The Indian government made special provisions for the "scheduled castes" by reserving places in schools and positions in government for them. Some have done fairly well economically, the majority, however, lives on the margins of Hindu society; quite literally so. Atrocities against Harijans are still quite commonplace and a caste-Hindu backlash is noticeable against what is seen as "pampering" of the "scheduled castes" by the government. In connection with recommendations on their behalf by the Mandal Commission, this lead to riots and self-immolation by caste-Hindus some years ago.

A writer on the history of Hinduism can choose an agreed upon periodization of Indian history as basic plan. Someone dealing with Hindu philosophy has a convenient traditional schema to follow. Similarly, someone studying Hinduism from a sociological point may either choose to follow the topicalization of a particular school of thought or adopt the traditional Hindu categorization. If one entertains the ambition to deal with Hinduism as a whole, comprehensively, historically and topically, philosophically and sociologically, one has to find one's own disposition and must justify it before one's readers. Here is the outline of the book, its basic plan. The first part of the book attempts to lay the groundwork by briefly describing the history of the relation between India and the West, the development of Hinduism, the criteria by which Hinduism defines itself over against other traditions, the basic writings that possess canonical value, the common world-view, and the accepted theology underlying Hinduism. The second part deals with Hindu religion in the more specific sense. Adopting the time-honored *trimārga* scheme, it describes the path of work, knowledge, and loving devotion. The most salient features of each are presented in some detail, especially those features prominent in contemporary Hindu practice and theory. The third part attempts to identify the structural supports of Hinduism: supports that include the physical reality of India, sacred time and space, the fixation of thought in recognized systems, and social order. The fourth part deals with the changes brought about in Hinduism by its encounter with the modern West. It led to reforms within Hinduism and the development of Hindu nationalism. To counterbalance the impression left by recent events, involving radical politicized Hinduism, I inserted a chapter on Mahātmā Gandhi as a model Hindu of the twentieth century. Although necessarily not exhaustive, the sketch of Hinduism offered within this survey aims at presenting a recognizable likeness of Hinduism. The chronology is designed to highlight certain events and persons and also to allow the reader to retrace the historic sequence and locate dates mentioned in the book itself. The glossary should serve as a mini-dictionary for Indian terms used and found necessary in describing Hinduism. The bibliography lists the sources and provides titles for more detailed and more advanced reading; it is, however, not to be considered exhaustive in any area and the mention or lack of mention of a work should not be interpreted as a value judgment.

India is a large country containing a considerable portion of the earth's present population. India's civilization in all its aspects—material, intellectual, artistic, spiritual—is a major component of world civilization and has been so for the past 5,000 years at least. Learning about it widens our horizons and makes us better understand what it means to be human.

The world civilization now forming would be much the poorer if it left out the contributions that India has been making and continues to make. India is rapidly also becoming a modern power and a major factor in world affairs.

Hindī religious books often end with a *kṣamā-prārthana*, a statement in which the writer requests his readers' indulgence for the shortcomings of his book. It may be appropriate to begin the book with such a *kṣamā-prārthana*. It is not directed so much at those who look for information about Hinduism in this book but at those about whom the book is written. The very idea of writing, as an outsider, about the life and religion of a people as large and ancient as the Hindus, requires, I believe, an apology. Others have done it before, of course. That says nothing about its appropriateness. Quite articulate critiques of Western "Orientalism" has been voiced by Orientals and Westerners alike. Orientalist constructions of India[15] have evidently much to do with constructions of reality in general undertaken by the systematizing Western mind. Sociological, psychological, economical, and historical constructions of Europe or America fall into the same category. Such attempts reveal an attitude that is communicated together with the very idea of "science" and "scientific." Basically it consists of the assumption that the "scientist" knows better and, eventually, will know it all.

Hindus are quite capable of speaking for themselves. This is acknowledged in this survey by letting Hindu voices speak for Hinduism and by keeping outsiders' voices and interpretations to a minimum. Hinduism for me is not a 'case' to be studied and brought within preformed and preset categories (taken from Western culture) but an expression of human nature and culture to be accepted on its own terms.

Part I

Hinduism: Development and Essence

The vastness and heterogeneity of Hinduism offers enormous challenges to every description. Although a great many questions regarding the history and development of Hinduism are still open and the traditional Hindu neglect of chronology makes it often impossible to date persons or literary works within less than a 500 year margin, the chapter dealing with these matters was one of the easier ones to write: there are, after all, names and books, coins and monuments, noticeable periods and styles that one can get hold of and that are, essentially, factual. It is more difficult to present the essentials of Hinduism in a noncontroversial manner. The question "What are the Essentials of Hinduism?" will receive as many different answers as people one asks. Many Hindus presume that whatever their thoughts on God, world, and humankind are must be Hinduism. Others draw the boundaries so narrowly on the basis of caste and ritual purity that relatively few would qualify. Questions of orthodoxy had to be answered by those who were responsible for maintaining a distinct Hindu tradition vis-à-vis breakaway movements from within and assaults from without. The answers given here to the question as to who is orthodox and who is heretic may not be acceptable to all. But they represent authoritative opinions and should convince the reader that, contrary to some popular assumptions shared by some liberal Hindus and non-Hindus alike, Hinduism is not simply the sum total of all other religions and the doctrinal tolerance of Hinduism has definite limits.

The identity of Hinduism rests on the particular revelation on which the Hindu tradition believes itself to be grounded. A revelation, by its very nature, is specific and cannot be derived from general principles or from commonly accessible facts. The Vedas and the other books held sacred as scriptures by Hindus differentiate Hinduism from other religions possessing their own specific holy books, and they permit us, at least in a negative way, to define the essentials of Hinduism over against what is not Hinduism.

Acceptance of the Veda as revealed scripture is certainly the most basic criterion for anyone to declare oneself a Hindu—the preferred self-designation of Hinduism in Indian languages is *Vaidik dharma,* the religion of the Veda—but there is another genre of literature that has shaped the minds and hearts of present day Hindus much more profoundly: the two great epics Mahābhārata and Rāmāyaṇa, and the voluminous Purāṇas, the true bibles of Hinduism. It is typical for Hinduism to have not one but eighteen such scriptures, accepted by the followers of the various great sects. They exalt Viṣṇu, Śiva, Devī to the highest position; they contain the colorful myths for which Hinduism is famous; they instruct their readers in matters of worship and hygiene, promise health, wealth, and eternal salvation to all who recite them. The *itihāsa-purāṇa* literature is enormous—it has hardly any parallel in another culture. Not all Hindus can be expected to be fully acquainted with it, though many know surprisingly much from it.

There is one book, however, that virtually all Hindus know and many recite daily by heart: the Bhagavadgītā, the Song of the Lord. It has become a classic also in the West; scores of translations in English and other European languages are available. It is a Kṛṣṇa book, but it articulates much that is typical for all of Hinduism, and it contains advice and opinion that most Hindus accept as expressing their own aspirations.

The relative geographic isolation of the Indian subcontinent facilitated the development over long periods of time of a civilization little influenced from the outside. Cosmological and other ideas developed and found fairly universal acceptance throughout India. Together these could be termed the *Hindu world picture.* The Hindu world-view appears in a number of variants but it also shows a surprisingly large number of common features—features distinctive enough to set it off against the world-views of other civilizations.

All observers, including Hindus themselves, would describe Hinduism as polytheistic. Nowhere else in the world do we find such a profusion of gods and goddesses, divine beings and demons, ramifications of genealogies of gods, and manifestations of the divinity in human and animal forms. But that is only the surface of Hinduism, the colorful appearance of a tradition that has enormous depths. Although Hinduism could never be conceived as a parallel to biblical or Islamic monotheism, it has developed its own sophisticated notions of the unity of the highest principle, and many forms of Vaiṣṇavism, Śaivism, or Śāktism have theologies in which One

Supreme Being is given the title and role of Lord, or Mistress, the creator, sustainer and destroyer of the whole universe, and the savior of those who believe in him or her.

1 India and the West

India has created a special momentum in world history as a country to be searched for.

—G. W. F. Hegel[1]

Since the beginning of recorded history, the West has been fascinated by India.[2] From Classical Antiquity, countless fanciful tales and amusing fables circulated throughout Europe, concerning India's peoples, its animals and plants, its sun and rains, its mountains and rivers; and these continued to be retold until the late Middle Ages. But not all was fancy and fable. Accurate descriptions of certain parts of India were given in ancient times by writers who had either accompanied Western adventurers or who had traveled there on their own initiative, for purposes of trade or simply out of curiosity.

EARLY CONTACTS BETWEEN EAST AND WEST

The greatest single impetus in this direction in Antiquity was the invasion of India by the armies of Alexander the Great in 327–326 B.C.E. More than one eyewitness described the battles Alexander fought, the rivers he crossed and the cities he conquered, the allies he won and the kings he defeated. The newcomers were awed by the heat of the Indian plains, the great numbers of war elephants, the enormous size of the population, and the curiosity of their customs and manners. Even then, the wisdom of Indian holy men was proverbial; accordingly, one of the first things Alexander did on entering India was to call upon and converse with some of these "gymnosophists"; this in spite of the fact that they were instrumental in encouraging Indian resistance against the Macedonian invasion.[3] The Greeks seem to have admired the brusque and incisive manner of these men, and so famous did they become that eventually Alexander asked one of them (whom the Greeks called Kālanos) to succeed his preceptor Aristotle as his constant companion and counselor. This "naked wise man" seems to have been a Jain *muni* of the *Digaṃbara* sect: he was to end his life voluntarily on a pyre, having discovered that he was suffering from an incurable disease.[4]

The early mediaeval Alexander romance contains an exchange of letters between Alexander and an Indian king called Dindimus in which Alexander asks for, and receives, information about the Brahmins. "We Brahmins," the king writes, "lead a pure and simple life; we commit no sins; we do not want to have more than what is reasonable. We suffer and sustain everything . . . " In short, the Brahmins lead an ideal life, they can teach wisdom and renunciation. In his reply to Dindimus Alexander recognizes that "only the Brahmins are good people."[5] This high opinions of Brahmins is still noticeable in the eighteenth century, when Lessing in his *Nathan* proclaims that only at the Ganges can one find morally perfect people.

For several centuries a lively commerce developed between the ancient Mediterranean world and India, particularly the ports on the Western coast. The most famous of these ports was Sopāra, not far from modern Bombay, which was recently renamed Mumbāī. Present day Cranganore in Kerala, identified with the ancient Muziris, claims to have had trade contacts with Ancient Egypt under Queen Hatsheput, who sent five ships to obtain spices, as well as with ancient Israel during King Solomon's reign. Apparently the contact did not break off after Egypt was conquered by Greece and later by Rome. According to I. K. K. Menon, "there is evidence of a temple of Augustus near Muziris and a force of 1200 Roman soldiers stationed in the town for the protection of Roman commerce."[6] Large hoards of Roman coins were found also on the East Coast, near today's Mahabalipuram; a sign of commerce with Roman traders, who must have rounded the southern tip of India to reach that place. Taprobane, identified with today's Śrī Laṇka, plays a major role in ancient accounts of India—an island described to be even more wonderful and exotic than India herself. The kings of Magadha and Malwa exchanged ambassadors with Greece. A Maurya ruler invited one of the Greek Sophists to join his court, and one of the greatest of the Indo-Greek kings became famous as the dialogue partner of the great Buddhist sage Nāgasena,[7] while in the opposite direction, Buddhist missionaries are known to have settled in Alexandria, and other cities of the Ancient West.[8] These early contacts were not limited to the exchange of pleasantries; one Greek ambassador went so far as to erect a Garuḍa column in honor of Vasudeva, while Greek epic poetry was translated into Indian languages and heard with appreciation in the court of Broach. The celebrated collection of Indian animal fables, the *Pañcatantra,* found its way into the West in a variety of translations and adaptations, including a version of the life of Buddha that resulted in the creation of the legend of Saint Josaphat.[9]

It is evident, then, that Indian thought was present in the fashionable intellectual circuit of ancient Athens, and there is every reason to suppose that Indian religious and philosophical ideas exercised some influence on early and classical Greek philosophy.[10]

Interest in India increased considerably during the time of the Roman emperors. During the time between the reign of Augustus and that of Caracalla, East-West commerce flourished. A colony of Indian merchants is known to have existed in Alexandria; and under Augustus, Claudius, and Antoninus Pius, Indian embassies visited Rome. At least one celebrated Greek philosopher, the neo-Pythagorean Apollonius of Tyana (first century C.E.), is reputed to have visited India to improve his knowledge of Indian wisdom.

Both Greeks and Romans habitually tried to understand the religions of India by trying to fit them as far as possible into Greco-Roman categories. Deities in particular were spoken of, not in Indian but in Greek terms and called by Greek names. Thus Śiva was identified as "Dionysos," Kṛṣṇa (or perhaps Indra) as "Heracles." The great Indian epics were compared to those of Homer. Doctrinally, the Indian concept of transmigration had its counterpart in the *metempsychosis* taught by Pythagoras and Plato; nor was Indian asceticism altogether foreign to a people who remembered Diogenes and his followers.[11] According to one persistent legend, Jesus spent the time between the twelfth and thirtieth years, a period of his life about which the Gospels are silent, in India, studying with Buddhist *bhikkus* and Vedāntin *ācāryas.*[12]

Towards the end of the second century C.E., Tertullian, a Christian writer, defended his fellow believers from the accusation that they were "useless and should therefore be exterminated" by stating that the Christians were "neither Brahmins, or Indian gymnosophist, forest-dwellers or withdrawn from life," but that they participated fully in the public and economic activities of Rome.[13] Some centuries later, the writer of the treatise *De moribus Brachmanorum* (originally thought to have been written by Ambrose of Milan, now considered to be the work of Prosper of Aquitania) has high praise for the Brahmins, who could serve, he says, as exemplars to Christians.[14]

With the victory of Christianity in the West and the simultaneous decline of the Roman Empire and still more with the Arab conquest of the Near and Middle East, the West lost contact with India; all that remained were faint and often distorted memories of India as a land of fabulous riches, exotic creatures, and a fantastic religion. However, the Arab conquest of India once more intensified exchange between India and the West, a West over which Arab influence was also now becoming more deeply felt.[15] Alberuni, a Muslim traveler who visited India between 1017 and 1030 C.E., gave an admirably comprehensive account of many aspects of India's culture, including a fairly detailed summary of some important works of religious literature, unknown to the West until then.[16] It was through the Arabs that Indian learning reached the West, particularly in the fields of medicine, mathematics, and astrology. Indeed, the Indian decimal system and its symbols became known in the West as "Arabic numerals."

The great merchant-adventurer Marco Polo (1254–1324 C.E.) visited and described a number of places in India that he had seen, but his accounts were not usually taken seriously by his contemporaries, who considered him to be something of a storyteller rather than a serious topographer.[17] It was the search for India which led Cristopher Colombus to the discovery of America in 1493. To this very day we call the original inhabitants of America *Indians* and find it often awkward to specify whether we mean "American Indians" or "Indian Indians." The West's contact with India intensified after Vasco da Gama's historic voyage around the cape of Good Hope in 1498, which led to an increased interest in India by the European powers. Together with the generals and the merchants came Christian missionaries. Some of them became interested in India's local religions and, though frequently showing a heavy apologetic bias, the works produced by some seventeenth and eighteenth century missionaries provided much useful material about India.[18] Of particular interest, both to their contemporaries and to us today, is the work of some artists of the eighteenth century who traveled through India and left vivid sketches and paintings of life and country. William Hodges[19] spent three years in India between 1780 and 1784, most of them in Banaras, which offered vast scope to his pen and brush. He was one of the few white men to ever see a *satī* performed,[20] leaving a moving description. Between 1785 and 1788 he published *Select Views in India*. His slightly younger contemporaries Thomas and William Daniell, famous for their paintings of Indian landscapes, traveled in India between 1786 and 1793 and inspired an Indian fashion in architecture in Britain.

BEGINNING SCHOLARLY INTEREST IN INDIA

By the middle of the eighteenth century, European scholars were starting to get interested in India's literature; but they were initially severely handicapped because of the Brahmin's reluctance to teach Sanskrit to *mlecchas* (foreigners) or to allow them to read their scriptures. The German philosopher Arthur Schopenhauer (1788–1860), whose enthusiastic praises of the Upaniṣads are frequently cited, had to rely on a Latin translation made by Anquetil du Perron from a Persian version made by Prince Dara Shikoh of the original Sanskrit text!

During the first half of the eighteenth century J. E. Hanxleden wrote the first Sanskrit grammar under the title "Grammatica Granthamia seu Samscrdumica."[21] It was never published, but was put to use by J. P. Wessdin (Fra Paolino de St. Bartolomeo), who wrote two Sanskrit grammars and some quite informative works on India toward the end of the eighteenth century.[22] The greatest incentive to the scholarly study of India's history and culture was, however, provided by the British administration, which encouraged research and the publication of materials pertinent to its own purposes.[23] Typically, the first Sanskrit works to be translated into English were the Hindu law codes which the British officials needed to know. The British East India Company commissioned a group of Indian *paṇḍits* to compile a compendium of current Hindu law from the numerous original sources. The resulting work, named *Vivādārṇavasetu,* had first to be translated into Persian before an English translation could be made. It was published in 1776 by the East India Company under the title *A Code of Gentoo Law.*

The first Englishman to have a good knowledge of Sanskrit was Charles Wilkins, whom Warren Hastings (then governor general of Bengal) had encouraged to study with the Brahmins in Banaras. In 1785 he wrote an English translation of the Bhagavadgītā, followed two years later by a translation of the *Hitopadeśa.* His Sanskrit grammar, which appeared in 1808, became the basis for all later work.

One of the most important figures in European Indology was Sir William Jones (1746–1794) who had acquired a good command of Persian and Arabic before coming to India in 1783, where he immediately took up the study of Sanskrit. One year later he founded the Asiatic Society of Bengal, which was soon to become the leading center for the publication of text editions and translations of important Hindu sources. Jones translated the *Manusmṛti* and published it in 1794 under the title *Institutes of Hindu Law, or the Ordinances of Manu.*[24] After Jones's untimely death the work was continued by Thomas Colebrook, who edited and translated numerous Sanskrit works. As professor of Sanskrit at Fort William College Calcutta he wrote in 1798 a four volume series entitled *A Digest of Hindu Law on Contracts and Successions,* which consisted of translations of legal materials collected by a group of Indian *paṇḍits.* Less interested in literature and poetry than in more scholarly Hindu works on law, arithmetics, astronomy, grammar, philosophy, and religion, he was the first Western scholar to provide correct and precise information about the Veda in his paper "On the Vedas, or Sacred Writings of the Hindus," Roberto de Nobili's *Ezour Vedam* being exposed as a fraud.[25]

Another Englishman, Alexander Hamilton, who had studied Sanskrit in India and was detained in Paris on his way back to England on account of Anglo-French hostilities, became instructor to the first generation of French and German Sanskritists, for whom university chairs were established in the first half of the nineteenth century. Although thus far those in continental Europe who wished to study Indian culture had had to rely on French and German translations of English versions and monographs, they now could draw upon the resources of their own scholars, who began to produce text editions and original versions. August Wilhelm von Schlegel, the brother of the poet Friedrich Schlegel, became the first professor of Sanskrit at the newly established university of Bonn in 1818. A. L. Chézy, the first French Sanskrit scholar, held the chair at the Collége de France in Paris.[26] Franz Bopp, a fellow student of Schlegel's at Paris, became the founder of comparative philology and linguistics.[27]

Although the East India Company did not allow Christian missionaries into its territories and maintained a policy of religious noninterference, Western Christians considered India a mission field and tried to employ Indian studies for this purpose. Missionary activities on East India Company territory began in 1813, though William Carey had been at work in Serampore (Srīrampur), a Danish settlement near Calcutta, since 1800. A further important step was taken in 1830, with the opening of Scottish missionary Alexander Duff's school in Calcutta. In the same year the famous

Sanskritist H. H. Wilson became the first holder of the Boden professorship in Oxford, founded "to promote the translation of the Scriptures into Sanskrit, so as to enable his countrymen to proceed in the conversion of the natives of India to the Christian religion." Both H. H. Wilson (1832–1860) and his successor to the chair, M. Monier-Williams (1860–1888), engaged in lexicographic work to lay the foundations for Bible translations, which were soon made into the main languages of India.[28]

Following the historical trend that dominated in European scholarship in the nineteenth century, French and German scholars concentrated on studying the Vedas, the oldest document of Indian religious literature. Some of the students taught by Eugéne Burnouf at the Collége de France later attained lasting eminence as Vedic scholars. One of these was Rudolph Roth, who together with Otto Böthlingk edited the seven volume *St. Petersburg Wörterbuch* (1852–1875), which remains unsurpassed.[29]

Friedrich Max Müller became the most famous of them all. The son of the poet Wilhelm Müller, he earned fame through his monumental edition of the *Ṛgveda with Sāyana's Commentary* (1849–74). Of even greater significance than his Indological work is the fact that due to his wide general education and interests he became the founder of Comparative Religion as a scholarly discipline. Perhaps the crowning achievement of his life's work was his editorship of the fifty volumes of the *Sacred Books of the East* (1876–1904).[30] Müller did not find in his native Germany the support for his studies offered by England, which subsequently became the main center of Indian studies and libraries.

An astonishingly large number of brilliant scholars devoted themselves in the decades that followed to the study of India's past. Indology became a respected discipline at most major European universities, and scholars produced a steady stream of critical text editions, translations, monographs, and dictionaries.[31] They even impressed the traditional Indian paṇḍits by their learning, and soon the first Hindu scholars arrived to study in European departments of Sanskrit to familiarize themselves with the scholarly methods developed in the West. Recognized Indian scholars, especially those proficient in English, were invited on lecture tours through the West and were thus given opportunity to explain authentically the traditions of India to an attentive but often misinformed audience.[32]

In the United States the popular philosophers Ralph Waldo Emerson (1803–1882) and Henry David Thoreau (1817–1862) were the first to show some serious interest in Indian thought, especially in Vedānta. The first to teach courses in Sanskrit was Isaac Nordheimer, who offered a course at the City University of New York as early as 1836. Edward Eldridge Salisbury introduced Sanskrit at Yale in 1841, and the prestigious American Oriental Society was founded in 1842. Though Indologists form only part of its membership, its journal and its monograph series are the major organ for classical Indian studies in the United States. Since the latter half of the nineteenth century several outstanding Sanskritists have taught and worked in the United States: Charles Rockwell Lanman (1850–1941), one of Rudolph Roth's students, became the founder-editor of the Harvard Oriental Series. His *Sanskrit Reader* is still in use. J. H. Wood's (1864–1935) translation of the major commentaries and glosses to Patanjali's *Yogasūtra* is still widely referred to. Maurice Bloomfield (1885–1928) emerged as one of the major vedic scholars of his time; his *Vedic Concordance*, a monumental work, has been recently reprinted. Edward Washburn Hopkins's (1857–1932) books on the Mahābhārata are still authoritative on many points. Robert Ernest Hume (1877–1948) has deservedly gained fame for his translation of the *Thirteen Principal Upaniṣads* which has seen many reprints. Franklin Edgerton's (1885–1963) *Bhagavadgītā* has been acknowledged as the most scholarly translation to date.[33]

Today all Western countries have university departments and research institutes in which advanced studies in Indology, including religious and philosophical Hinduism, are being undertaken. An impressive percentage of scholars referred to in this book are native Indians who enjoy the added advantage of working with materials from their own traditions. It almost goes without saying that India is today once more the leading country in Indian studies, both in the traditional way of learning as represented by the paṇḍit-schools and in the modern methods, as initiated by Western scholars and continued and refined by Indian academicians. Indian universities publish numerous scholarly journals in English and in this way contribute to the West's understanding of Indian traditions.

SCHOLARLY AND EXISTENTIAL INTERESTS

Early Western interest in Indian studies was kindled, on the one hand, by the requirements of the British administration in India and, on the other, by the predominantly historical and philological interests of Western scholars, trained in their own classical Greek and Latin traditions. More recently the accent has shifted to the contents of Indian philosophical and religious literature. The attitude of classical Western Indology had been that of strictly objective scholarly research; the professionals often frowned upon people who tried to identify themselves with certain positions of the Indian tradition on which they worked. The great works of this period, like Christian Larssen's monumental *Indische Altertumskunde* or Friedrich Bühler's *Grundriss der indoarischen Philologie und Altertumskunde* dealt with India as the established classical scholars had dealt with ancient Greece and Rome. For all their enthusiasm in their professional studies (which centered on India's classical past) these scholars did not give up their typically Western way of thinking. By their own choice they remained outsiders, fulfilling their calling as scholars according to the Western ideal, sometimes even refusing, as Max Müller did, to pay a visit to India.

The social and spiritual convulsions of our time, beginning with the First World War, together with the renewed self-consciousness of the generation that had experienced the Indian Renaissance, have made many of our contemporaries more ready to listen to what India has (and always had) to say. There was a remarkable growth of interest in Buddhism in the early 1920s. On a more scholarly level, a great stimulus for Indian studies was provided by the first East-West Philosophers' Conference organized by Charles A. Moore (1901–1967) in Honolulu in 1939. Subsequent meetings have been attended also by a considerable number of eminent scholars from India.[34]

It is not easy to analyze the reasons for this new development. The contemporary West no longer has a unifying world-view, a commonly accepted religion or philosophy of life as basis for the solution of its social or psychological problems and as sustenance in times of crisis. The experiences of the last fifty years have undermined the naive optimism that had grown from a faith in unlimited technological progress. Having witnessed a complete breakdown of much that was taken for granted in former times, we are now faced with a deep-rooted insecurity and probably the irreparable loss of the authority of those institutions that for centuries had provided Westerners with a firm frame for their life and thought. An increasing number of people are opening to the suggestion that they might replace some traditional Western values and attitudes, which have proven short lived and self-destructive, with Eastern modes of thought, which have nourished cultures that have endured for thousands of years.[35] Slowly, however, the realization is also dawning that a mere replacement of one set of ideas and values by another would help us as little as did the timid or arrogant aloofness of former times.

Patterns of partnership are beginning to dominate in international relations, a partnership that includes dialogue on all levels, allowing differences—even of a basic nature—to coexist without interrupting communication. Much of what we find in Hinduism has no counterpart in the West. Hindu thinkers have anticipated ideas and developed theories in many areas that have only recently begun to be explored in the West. In the analysis of language, in the technicalities of hermeneutics, in the methods of psychosomatic activation, and last but not least in philosophical and religious speculation and spiritual training, Hindu India is centuries ahead of the West. Western thinkers, through their study of Indian philosophies and religions have "discovered a new technical philosophy of undreamed-of complexity and ingenuity" and this contact has "expanded the imagination, increased the number of categories, made possible new studies in the history of logic, revealed new sensations and has driven the mind back to its origin and out to its possibilities."[36]

INTERPRETING HINDUISM IN WESTERN TERMS

Early Western Indologists used to deal with everything that concerned India. Meanwhile the field has grown to such an extent that specialization has become necessary both for the sake of the integrity of research and for the sake of students interested in Indian studies. Even within the specialized field of Hinduism one has to narrow down one's enquiry to either a particular school of thought, a period, or even a single person. Nevertheless, to assign the correct place of one's particular research within the larger framework of Hindu culture, one must reach out and familiarize oneself with other aspects and the history of the total phenomenon.

There is a certain temptation for Westerners who study Hinduism to follow through vaguely familiar thoughts and complete them according to their own thought models. We have to resist this temptation because all further interpretation is based upon principles that have been borrowed from elsewhere. We have to take seriously the historicity of each tradition, not only in the vaguely idealistic (and ultimately unhistorical) Hegelian sense, but in its own exact and precise historical factuality. Hinduism is what it is today because it has developed that way through its own history. It is not necessarily what we would like or wish it to be. History always offers several alternatives for the development of a certain idea; this development depends on circumstances and unforeseeable factors that translate one of these possibilities into historical fact. Western approaches to reality, the compartmentalization of knowledge into such categories as science and arts, philosophy and theology, sociology and psychology do not coincide with Indian approaches and their specific avenues of enquiry.[37] Despite more than 150 years of diligent work by a handful of devoted scholars on many essential points we have not yet reached a verbal understanding. Western languages have no adequate translations for many of the key terms in philosophical and religious Sanskrit texts. Ananda Coomaraswamy, who must have suffered quite acutely under this situation, stated: "Asiatic thought has hardly been, can hardly be presented in European phraseology without distortion and what is called the appreciation of Asiatic art is mainly based on categorical misinterpretations."[38] Misunderstandings are thus bound to happen even with the best of intentions (and even good intention cannot always be taken for granted). To try to avoid some misunderstandings, the following representation of Hinduism uses original terms wherever practicable.

At some later state we may be able to discover for ourselves that Hinduism and Western religions do not differ so much in the answers they give to similar problems, but in the problems they consider relevant. Problems that never occur to the Westerner may be of the utmost significance for the Hindu. Hinduism is not just a variant of Western religion; the very structure of Hinduism is different. Scholars like Betty Heimann,[39] Heinrich Zimmer,[40] Maryla Falk,[41] Rene Guénon,[42] Stella Kramrisch,[43] and Wendy O'Flaherty,[44]—Westerners well-grounded in their own traditions—have made structural studies of Hinduism that presuppose not only specialized Indological expertise but also a comprehensive general knowledge and a great deal of empathy. We must not expect everything we find in Hinduism to fit into the frame of our present knowledge. Modern science cannot be adequately explained in the terminology of mediaeval philosophy of nature; equally, Indian philosophical and religious thought cannot be satisfactorily reproduced using our current Western idiom. Translations of authoritative Hindu literature are always interpretations, for better or for worse, according to the insight of the translator. This is true for the translations of many a European philologist with an insufficient philosophical background (not to mention those "translators" who, ignorant of the original languages, simply restyle an existing translation in the fashion and idiom of the day). This applies still more to some Indian translators who are unfamiliar with the real meaning of the Western terminology they frequently use. And occasionally a translation can be more tendentious than an original work, if it is meant to support the particular viewpoint of a particular proselytizer. In those points that are really crucial, the meaning of a text cannot be found without a thorough study of the sources in the original languages within their original context. The literary sources of Indian philosophy and religion, moreover, are quite frequently written in such a concise and condensed style that a student cannot even understand them grammatically without oral instruction and commentary. Furthermore, the same terms are used in different senses by different systems. There are also frequent indirect quotations from and references to writings with which the Indian expert is familiar but that a Western reader without a competent guide would overlook.[45] It is from learned Hindus that a Western student of Hinduism has to learn how to read and to understand Hindu sources: the premises they work with, the axioms they take for granted, the problems they consider relevant.

Although India and the West quite obviously and visibly differ from each other, as every casual visitor of India will notice, one ought to beware of the dichotomization of East and West along the lines of spiritual vs. materialistic, or collective vs. individualistic, or archaic vs. modern. Whether it has to do with more recent developments or with a better knowledge of both East and West than previously available, it appears that all these characteristics are fairly evenly distributed throughout East and West, and one will, in all likelihood, have to choose others, if one wishes to insist that the "East is East and West is West" and so forth. Indians have made some major contributions to contemporary modern science and technology, and Westerners have been recognized by their Indian colleagues as specialists in Sanskrit learning and commended for their genuine understanding of Hindu culture. It is, in all likelihood, less a question of fundamental differences but of mutual recognition and learning from each other in the interest of developing a truly cosmopolitan civilization.

ENCOUNTERING HINDUS AND HINDUISM

A book can never replace the experience of the living encounter, but it can prepare the ground for it. Thorough familiarization with the background of the dialogue partner is the first requirement for a meaningful encounter. It goes without saying that no claim can be made to an exhaustive treatment or to an interpretation that would not show shortcomings due to personal limitations. There are, even now, subtle and highly competent Hindu philosophers whose teaching is virtually inaccessible to those who have not undertaken the necessary training. And there are millions of Hindus who practice diverse archaic cults and ceremonies, rationalizing in their own peculiar ways the effectiveness and meaning of what they are doing. If we are to understand Hinduism as it is and not to construct to our own purposes an artificial Hindu religion that we are able to manipulate, we have to be open to the whole panorama of phenomena that together constitute the living tradition of Hindu India.

More and more Hindu gurus and swāmīs in ochre robes are coming to Europe and America to lecture, to collect funds, to establish centers, and to launch religious movements adapted to the Western mind. The quite phenomenal expansion of Mahesh Yogi Maharishi's Transcendental Meditation Society, the success of Swami Bhaktivedanta's International Society for Krishna Consciousness, and the mass pilgrimages of planeloads of Americans to Balyogeshwar Guruji's camp are not merely the result of smart organization and cleverly manipulated publicity; they also reflect an obvious need on the part of many people in the West, especially among the young. By now a number of Westerners have been initiated into Hindu orders and are recognized, also by Indians, as legitimate teachers of Hinduism. In the new Hindu movements they hope to find what they have missed in their synagogues and churches: practical guidance in self-discovery, an integrated worldview, systematic training of psychic powers, emotional satisfaction, and perhaps, true mystical experience. It would be very sad if Hindu propaganda in the West were to lead only to the establishment of a few Hindu sects and if the great opportunity for the growth of new and genuinely modern forms of spirituality by entering into dialogue with the still living Western religious tradition were missed. Such an encounter would certainly prove beneficial to both partners; it may even be necessary for them if they are to survive as interpreters of the meaning of life in a time of confused and disintegrating local traditions.

2 The History and Development of Hinduism

> Thus I saw the moving drama of the Indian people in the present, and could often trace the threads which bound their lives to the past, even while their eyes were turned to the future. Everywhere I found a cultural background which had exerted a powerful influence on their lives.
>
> —Jawaharlal Nehru[1]

Every living tradition—and the Hindu tradition perhaps more than others—is profoundly shaped by its own history. Through that history even those features that the tradition itself considers to be nonhistorical are strongly affected. Attempts to describe the "essence" of Hinduism in terms of absolute doctrinal formulations must fail simply because they neglect the historical dimension and the development that has led to those beliefs. As J. C. Heesterman has said,

> Tradition is characterised by the inner conflict of atemporal order and temporal shift rather than by resiliance [sic] and adaptiveness. It is this unresolved conflict that provides the motive force we perceive as the flexibility of tradition. Indian civilization offers a particularly clear case of this dynamic inner conflict. The conflict is not just handled surreptitiously by way of situational compromise. Once we look beyond the hard surface of the projected absolute order, it appears subtly, but no less effectively, to be expressed by the same scriptures that so impressively expound the *dharma*'s absoluteness.[2]

ORIGINS OF HINDUISM

It is impossible to give a precise definition of Hinduism or to point out the exact place and time of its origin. The very name *Hinduism* owes its origin to chance; foreigners in the West extending the name of the province of Sindh to the whole country lying across the Indus River and simply calling all its inhabitants *Hindus* and their religion *Hinduism*. Hindus, however, appropriated the designation and use it themselves today to identify themselves over against, for example, Muslims and Christians. In spite of the impossibility of defining it, the term can be meaningfully employed. Contemporary Hinduism preserves many elements from various sources, differently emphasized in various parts of the country and by individual groups of people. Roughly speaking we may identify four main streams of tradition that have coalesced to form Hinduism:

1. The traditions of the original inhabitants of India, whose stone-age culture has been traced back about half a million years[3] and some of whose practices and beliefs may still be alive among the numerous tribes of *ādivāsīs*;[4]
2. Influences from the so-called Indus civilization, which was rediscovered only half a century ago and which extended over an area of more than 800,000 $km.^2$ in Northwestern and Northern India;[5]
3. The very old and highly developed Dravidian culture, represented by the Tamils today and possibly preserving certain features of the Indus civilization;[6]
4. Vedic religion, codified in India by Aryan settlers, and spread throughout the greater part of India by conquests and missionary movements.[7]

Later invasions, and contacts with the Muslims and the modern world, have again contributed to the development of certain ideas within Hinduism. Despite the frequency with which Indian patterns of life have been disrupted, we nevertheless find that India is "a country of enduring survivals,"[8] an open-air museum of the history of religion and culture. A continuing Indian tradition underlies the attempts to define the Hindu identity in terms of religion.

The most common description which Hindus give to their religion is *sanātana dharma*, "eternal religion," a term that has several overtones.[9] It presupposes that the Vedic Sanskritic tradition is *the* religion; it also gave rise to exclusivist tendencies with Hinduism. Śaṅkara reestablished in the ninth century *sanātana dharma* against the heresies of Buddhism and Jainism in India and sent out his missionaries to spread the pure doctrine all over India. The claim to be defenders of *sanātana dharma* was also made by schools of thought hostile to Śaṅkara. In modern times movements like the Ārya Samāj, which considered popular purāṇic Hinduism to be a corrupt form of the true religion, tried to reestablish a purely Vedic *sanātana dharma.* In contemporary Hinduism we find attempts to widen the circle of *sanātana dharma,* or Hinduism, so as to embrace also the Jainas, Buddhists, Sikhs, and all the sects of Hinduism.

Most Hindus prefer even now to define their religion in a more restricted fashion, and they call themselves *Śaivas, Vaiṣṇavas, Śaktas,* or whatever group they belong to. There are others who feel the need to define the unity underlying the nationhood of India in terms that would allow Hindus to transcend sectarian boundaries within India and at the same time distinguish them from the followers of other traditions. A collection of statements on the topic Essentials of Hinduism by some thirty prominent Hindus, which appeared about fifty years ago, shows as many different standpoints without allowing one to single out any specific characteristics of Hinduism.[10] V. D. Savarkar, for many years the chief ideologist of the Hindu Mahāsabhā, distinguished *Hindudharma,* Hinduism that defies definition, from *Hindutva,* Hindudom, a more inclusive term. Hence he wrote:

> A Hindu is one who feels attachment to the land that extends from *Sindhu* to *Sindhu* (sea) as the land of his forefathers—as his Fatherland; who inherits the blood of the great race whose first and discernible source could be traced by the Himalayan altitudes of the Vedic *Saptasindhus* and which assimilating all that was incorporated and ennobling all that was assimilated, has grown into and come to be known as the Hindu people; and who, as a consequence of the foregoing attributes, has inherited and claims as his own the Hindu *saṅskṛti,* the Hindu civilization, as represented in a common history, common heroes, a common literature, a common art, a common law and a common jurisprudence, common fairs and festivals, rites and rituals, ceremonies and sacraments.[11]

Hindutva has in recent years become a political issue of the first magnitude—few of those who propose or oppose it may know about its origin. Even less modest is the description of the "indefinable Hindu" given by the former RSS (Rāṣṭrīya Svayamsevak Sangh = National Volunteer Association) leader M. S. Golwalkar.

> We the Hindus, have based our whole existence on God. . . . In a way, we are *anādi,* without a beginning. To define such a people is impossible, just as we cannot express or define Reality because words came into existence after Reality. Similar is the case with the Hindu people. We existed when there was no necessity for any name. We were the good, the enlightened people. We were the people who knew the laws of nature and the laws of the Spirit. We built a great civilization, a great culture and a unique social order. We had brought into actual life almost every thing that was beneficial to mankind. Then the rest of humanity was just bipeds and so no distinctive name was given to us. Sometimes in trying to distinguish our people from others we were called the 'enlightened', the *Āryas,* and the rest, the *Mlecchas.* When different faiths arose in foreign lands in the course of time and those alien faiths came in contact with us, then the necessity for naming was felt.[12]

The RSS has risen to prominence in the last decade and its present leaders command a large following both among RSS members and outside.

More specific is the definition given to Hinduism by the Viśva Hindū Pariṣad, the World Council of Hindus, which was founded in 1964 and held "a historic assembly" during the *Kuṃbha Melā* at Prayāga (Allahabad) in January 1966. There the attempt was made to formulate something like a basic creed to which all Hindus could subscribe, devise some common rites, and develop a canon of holy books to give visible unity to Hinduism.[13]

THE ANTECEDENTS OF HINDUISM

Definitions of Hinduism, even in a very vague form, have usually taken their inspiration from Vedic religion. Recently, however, the great importance of the other streams of Indian tradition have gained more attention. Therefore D. D. Kosambi remarks:

> It is still not possible to establish a general sequence of development from the stone age down in the most densely settled areas, namely the Punjab, the Gangetic basin, the coastal strip of the peninsula. There were notable intrusions in each of these regions. Yet India shows extraordinary continuity of culture. The violent breaks known to have occurred in the political and theological superstructure have not prevented long survivals of observances that have no sanction in the official Brahmin works, hence can only have originated in the most primitive stages of human society; moreover the Hindu scriptures and even more the observances sanctified in practice by Brahmanism show

> adoption of non-brahmanic local rites. That is, the process of assimilation was mutual, a peculiar characteristic of India.[14]

Nobody has as yet interpreted the religious significance of the prehistoric cave paintings (Figure 2.1) at Bhimbetka (ca. 30,000 B.C.E.) that were discovered only in 1967, and we do not know whether and how the people who created these are related to present-day populations of India.[15] The religions of most of the Indian *ādivāsīs* of today show strong Hindu influences; but some more or less universal Hindu beliefs like rebirth and transmigration of the *jīva* from animal to human existence probably originated among the autochthonous populations.

For over a century most Indologists assumed that the Āryans, the people connected with Vedic religion, invaded India around 1500 B.C., coming from the general direction of today's Iran-Afghanistan. The closeness of the language of the Avesta and the Ṛgveda, the similarity of the ritual, especially of the fire sacrifice and the pattern of social organization suggested a common origin of Vedic Indians and Avestan Iranians. Archeological as well as linguistic evidence was marshalled to support the argument that the ancestors of these two people, the Proto-Āryans, invaded Iran and India from a Central Asian or Southern Russian home.[16] When, in the first half of our century the remnants of Mohenjodaro and Harappa were excavated, the ruined cities of the Indus valley were adduced as a further argument for the thesis, that it was the vigorous seminomadic Āryans who destroyed the decadent city-civilization of the Harappans. Numerous references in the Ṛgveda to the destruction of fortresses and the release of waters by Indra were interpreted as reminiscences of the struggles of the Āryans against the Dasyus, dark-skinned original inhabitants of India, linked with the Indus civilization. Early dating of the Indus civilization—a peak between 2500 and 1700 and a rather rapid decline and complete disappearance by 1500 B.C.E.—seemed to neatly fit the Vedic chronology established by Max Müller. Meanwhile, both the spatial and the temporal extent of the Indus civilization has expanded dramatically on the basis of new excavations and the dating of the Vedic age as well as the theory of an Āryan invasion of India has been shaken. We are required to completely reconsider not only certain aspects of Vedic India, but the entire relationship between Indus civilization and Vedic culture.

To begin with, the continuingly expanding finds relating to the Indus civilization (see Figure 2.2) not only suggest a geographical

Figure 2.1 Prehistoric rock paintings and drawings from Bhimbhetka

overlap between the areas occupied by the Indus people and the Vedic Āryans, but also continuity between Indus and Vedic civilization.

One of the most intriguing pieces of evidence is afforded by the dating of the disappearance of the River Saraswatī, along whose riverbed most settlements mentioned in the Ṛgveda as well as a great many Indus civilization sites have been found. The course of the former Saraswatī has been located by aerial infrared scanning, and it has been determined that it ceased to carry water around 1900 B.C.E. If, as Müller suggested, the "Āryan invasion" took place around 1500 B.C.E., it does not make much sense to locate villages along the banks of the by then dried-up Saraswatī.

Also, no evidence has been found of any large scale violent conflict as a reason for the demise of the Indus civilization. Although there may have been conflicts in the vast area covered by the Indus civilization between component groups and nations, there is no reason to assume that the end of the Indus civilization was brought on through an outside invasion. Skeletal studies appear to indicate that the people of the Indus civilization belonged to the same diverse racial stocks as the present population of Northwest India. Also: evidence is mounting that the excavations conducted in Dwarka, dated around 1500 B.C.E. and traditionally related to Kṛṣṇa's kingdom, pertain to the "Vedic" period containing palaces and temples constructed of solid stone and exhibiting a high degree of technical skill and artistic accomplishment.

Geological research[17] indicates that major upthrusts took place in Northern India in the recent past, causing displacements of rivers, raising the level of many localities in Northern India and generally causing major disruptions, one of which might have been the desiccation of the Indus area and the creation of the Rajasthan desert. Geographers locate the mouth of the Saraswatī River near the Rann of Kutch, adjacent to the Thar desert, which was a fertile and well-irrigated part of the Indus–early Vedic civilization.

Astronomical evidence, for long available but usually discounted by historians, is also being refined and confirmed, suggesting not only the fairly detailed and accurate knowledge of sidereal movements possessed by Vedic Indians, but allowing us to set precise dates to certain passages in the Ṛgveda.

In addition, "decoding" of the Ṛgveda as recently advocated by S. Kak[18] would radically change the very way we read texts like the Ṛgveda. It would also explain why the *ṛṣis*, the sage-poets of ancient India, set such great store by exactly memorizing the texts,

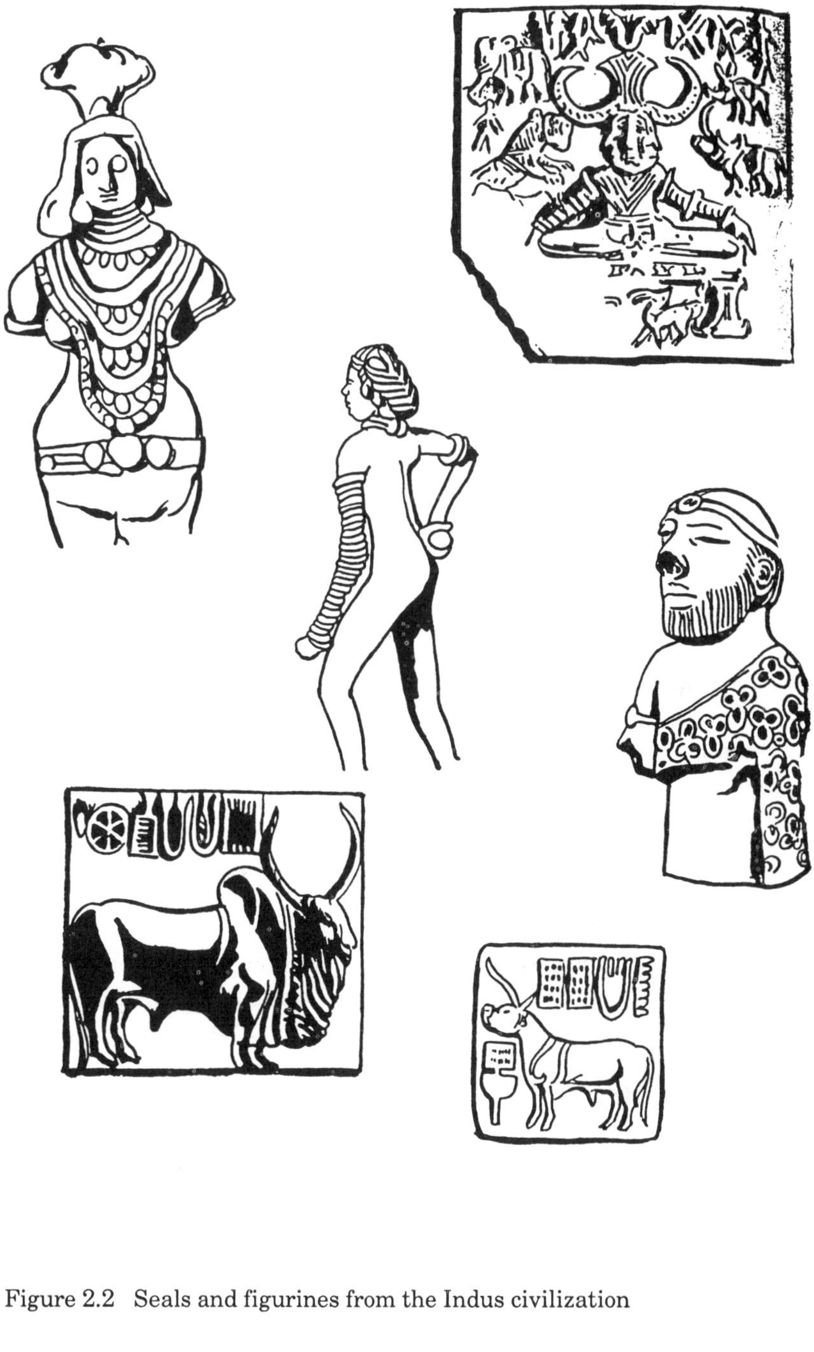

Figure 2.2 Seals and figurines from the Indus civilization

and why they insisted on absolute and faultless precision in the performance of the Vedic sacrifices, reenactments of the movement of the heavens and the principal means to assure the harmonization of the world here with the world beyond. We can be certain that these first efforts to get away from a historicist-humanistic Western reading of the Vedas will be followed by more detailed analyses and probably by quite startling discoveries about the character and content of Vedic civilization.

The certainty seems to be growing that the Indus civilization was carried by the Vedic Indians, who were not invaders from Southern Russia but indigenous for an unknown period of time in the lower Central Himālayan regions. The Indus civilization did not die a sudden death but, like the contemporary civilizations of Mesopotamia and Egypt, succumbed to a variety of influences, the most important ones probably being climatic changes, with many of its elements continuing in the more recent civilization of these areas.

S. C. Kak, summing up a wide range of arguments from astronomy, population studies, and internal literary evidence, concludes that

> by the middle of the fourth millennium B.C.E. the Indo-European and the Dravidian worlds had already interacted and met across North-West India and the plateau of Iran. . . . The Indo-European world at this time must already have stretched from Europe to North-India, and just below it lay the Dravidian people. The interaction for centuries between these two powerful peoples gave rise to the Vedic language, which, though structurally Indo-European, was greatly influenced by the Dravidian language. The Vedic civilisation was a product of the civilisation of these two peoples as was the Harappan civilisation.[19]

Working on the assumption that the Harappans spoke a Sanskritic language, Kak attempted a decipherment of the Indus script coming to the conclusion that most seals mention names of owner (in genitive case) and numerals, indicating a commercial use of the seals. Going further than Kak, David Frawley[20] describes the religion of the Indus valley civilization as "Vedic," assuming that the brick platforms found there were used for Vedic *yajñas,* that the famous "Śiva-Pasūpati-Seal" not only indicates the presence of Śaivism but also the practice of Yoga, and that it represented possibly the cradle of civilization, and certainly a type of "religion-based" culture typical of ancient civilizations in general.

Both Kak and Frawley point out that the ancient Vedic-Harappan civilization was not entirely homogenous, that, considering the vast area it covered, local variants as well as local conflicts developed, and that the wars described in the Ṛgveda, to the extent they are references to real wars and not metaphorical descriptions of natural or spiritual events, may well have taken place between various clans of Vedic Āryans and need not have involved "Harappans" as a hostile group.

Another opinion links the ancestors of the Tamils to Mohenjo-Daro and Harappa: the ancient Dravidians are supposed to have migrated south and settled in today's Tamilnādu, preserving the heritage of the Indus culture, its myths and its gods, which again found their way back into the Brahmanic religion through the Purāṇas, Saṃhitas, and Āgamas.[21]

Āryan society appears at a very early stage to have had a hierarchial structure with *brahmins* and *kṣatriyas* competing for the first place, *vaiṣyas* constituting the bulk of independent farmers, cattle breeders, artisans, and traders, and the *śudras* provided services of all kinds. Outside this structure there existed the indigenous, tribal population that became partly assimilated in the course of time. Also slavery seems to have been known in ancient India.[22] The brahmins were the custodians of the *yajña*, the all-powerful sacrifice. The hymns and rites connected with it were handed down orally from generation to generation, jealously guarded from outsiders. Whereas brahmanic religion knew neither temple nor image, the religious tradition preserved in the epics and Purāṇas, with its *mūrtis* and *maṇḍirs*, its miracles and myths, became more popular, assimilating, transforming, and often replacing Vedic religion, The Vedic sacrifices continue to this day in one form or another, and Vedic ritual is observed by most Hindus on ceremonial occasions.[23] But on the whole the epic and purānic forms of Hinduism, often with a strongly local accent, prevail and dominate the Indian religious landscape. Purānic accounts mention one Ṛṣi Agastya, an Āryan missionary who was responsible for the hinduization of South India. Hindu influence spread further to South East Asia and Indonesia during the "Golden Age" of India.[24] Although for several centuries Buddhism and Jainism were the religions that claimed the most followers and enjoyed the patronage of the most powerful rulers, a Hindu renaissance, under the Guptas in North India and the Pallavas in the South, all but swept away these "heretical" movements and established Hindu supremacy both in cultic form and religious speculation.[25] The Brahmins,

2 Ancient Śiva sanctuary beneath an old pīpal tree

while upholding Vedic tradition, especially in Vedāntic philosophy, successfully catered to the people by assuming the lead in the various great sects of the Śaivas, the Vaiṣṇavas, and later the Śāktas. There were regular missionary movements within India, and books like the Bhagavadgītā, the Rāmāyaṇa (especially in Tulasīdāsa's version), and the Bhāgavata Purāṇa were widely disseminated. Geographically, Śaivism predominates in South India; Vaiṣṇavism prevails in the North; whereas Bengal, Assam, and Orissa are strongly Śākta. But in most places followers of different Hindu traditions live side by side.

However, frictions were not unknown between different groups of Hindus, and Indian history knows of Śaiva kings persecuting Vaiṣṇavas and Vaiṣṇava rulers exiling followers of other faiths.[26] Indeed some of the sectarian scriptures are venomous and malicious in their abuse of countersects,[27] and quite often regional and local differences are also very marked.[28]

In trying to take account of the factors that helped shape Hinduism we must not forget the physical and geographical reality of India![29] For the Hindu the very concrete land of *Bhārata* is Holy Land, and certainly the landscape has for thousands of years been the fountainhead of religious inspiration, too. The mighty mountain ranges of the Himalayas, unconquered for thousands of years, its peaks clad in eternal snow, the powerful rivers that nourish, and quite often ravage, the country, the vast seas surrounding it, the immense plains with their murderous heat in summer, the huge bright stars and a moon almost as luminous as the sun, an abundance of species of plants and animals, the hot, dusty summers and the cloud-heavy monsoons—all these have fired the spirit of a multiracial population, gifted with a vivid imagination, active emotion, and sharp intelligence, combined to produce the multicolored flower garden of Hinduism.

Hinduism is very much tied to specific places and local traditions. The towns and districts associated with certain *avatārs* are the Holy Land for the followers of particular sects and the destination of countless pilgrims.[30] The great rivers are also holy rivers because their waters purify from all their sins those who bathe in them.[31] All over India certain trees receive worship, either as manifestations of Viṣṇu or Śiva in the form of the *tulasī* or *uḍuṃbara,* or after being sanctified through ceremonies, like the marriage of trees, or by having shrines established beneath them.[32] Other local sanctuaries, certain images, the tomb of a renowned yogi, or the memorial of an especially conspicuous occurrence (often a stone

3 Nāga, Khajurāho twelfth century

with a peculiar shape or with some strange imprints) form centers for pilgrimages in smaller provinces. Some mountains and hills, foremost amongst them Kailāsa and Aruṇācala, have been considered sacred from time immemorial. It is India as a geographic entity that offers the occasions of sanctification; only in India are cows, snakes, rats, and vultures sacred; only in India do ascetical and religious practices lead to salvation. Ancient India singled out *Madhyadeśa,* the heartland of India, as the really holy land; beyond its boundaries salvation could not be gained.

This feature must be borne in mind if we wish to understand the real Hinduism. The attempted universalization of Hinduism as we find it in Vivekananda or Radhakrishnan is largely the result of their Western and Christian training.

CHANGE AND DEVELOPMENT WITHIN HINDUISM

New ideas and problems continually stimulated the growth of new developments within Hinduism. In recent times the most powerful of these new ideas has been nationalism, which has become an integral part of modern Hinduism. The great national philosophers proclaim an identity of nationalism and Hinduism: Hinduism, they say, is the raison d'être of India.[33] Hinduism is becoming an ideology of Indian nationhood for a variety of groups, the common bond of the culturally and linguistically divergent parts of India. Even those secular politicians of India who dissociate themselves from the Hinduism of the temples and the pilgrimages, from *paṇḍas* and *sādhus,* give their nationalism a religious halo. The idea of India as *Bhārat-Mātā* stands for the sanctity and inviolability of the territory of India. Jawaharlal Nehru, the great humanist and sometimes caustic critic of Hinduism, wrote in his will that he did not want any religious ceremonies to be performed after his death; he did wish, however, that part of his ashes be scattered over India and into the Ganges. Hinduism traditionally does not recognize the borderlines within which religion in the West has been confined for some centuries—politics, social structures, hygiene, science—everything is assimilated and considered part of the divine reality.

The intrusion of the West into traditional India has also created enormous problems for Hinduism. There are those who want to turn the clock back and purge India of all that is has learned from the West in the past 200 years. There are those who naively fail to see any problem at all and simply identify Marx, Freud, and Einstein with some *avatāra* of Viṣṇu. But there are also intelligent and sensitive people in India, who suffer under the cultural schizophrenia and try to find ways to a new sanity. A. D. Moddie in his book *Brahmanical Culture and Modernity* seems to offer a good analysis, when he writes: "Ours is the problem of a painful transition, made more painful by resistances to a modern aesthetic and industrial culture by Brahmanical minds, smug with a moral and hierarchical superiority of the past and out of touch with the practical and attitudinal needs of the present . . . we are striving today for the most strategic thing in our time, a new identity for ourselves and the world . . . it is no less than an identity with the spirit of the age, the fulfillment of a new *karma* . . . "

More concretely, he pinpoints the areas of tension between the "brahmanical" and the "modern" mind thus:

> The Brahmanical attributes in this context are of the old society, traditional, caste-dominated, hierarchical, authoritarian, village and land-based. That culture is status-oriented and it inherently shuns change, social and technological. . . . What is written on the *patra* is naively to be assumed law, life and reality. The modern or industrial culture is essentially international, not village or caste-based in its social motivations. It is scientific, rational, it is achievement-oriented and it acknowledges not a hard hierarchy but a mobile elite of intellects, skills, and, yes—wealth.

Moddie thinks that the Hindus are held back from readily and freely accepting the modern culture by their religious traditions, which have become instincts. "The formidable law of Karma and the theory of re-incarnation induce little sense of obligation and achievement this side of death. Generations of belief in a long cycle of existences produces a degree of fatalism, a deep belief in *bhāg* . . . this life is dismissed as *māyā* or *līlā*, a play of the gods, or a *jāl* in which one is entrapped. Why strive in an illusion?"[34]

A Westerner who has had occasion to witness the rise of the new castes in industrial societies, of status-oriented thinking and bureaucratic hierarchies would not, perhaps, follow Moddie in his praise of the modern or industrial culture. Perhaps this is a stage all mature societies reach once technological innovation has ceased to be the primary force of social transformation. Our society, dominated by management hierarchies and trade-union conservatism, may in many ways become more rigid within the next generation than we would like it to be.

Hindus are quite often diametrically opposed to one another on very basic issues, but in an almost indefinable way they remain

Hindus, in spite of the complexity of their several peculiarities and prejudices, which as a people they will hardly be able to shed or to radically alter.[35] Much of Hinduism may be mere tradition and many Hindus may disown conventions they have been brought up with, yet Hinduism as a whole shows amazing life and vigor. It is and remains one of the world's great living religions, undoubtedly challenged by modernity, but also reinforced by it. If Hinduism follows the path outlined by S. Radhakrishnan, shedding its sectarian and narrowly dogmatic aspects, it may become even more appealing to modern people, not only in India but also in the West; it may also at the same time become even more difficult to define than even before.[36]

While many Indians, especially in the big cities and in professions that demand a modern, "Western" orientation, may be secularized and largely westernized, one should not believe that it is only the backward traditionalists, the small-town businessmen and *paṇḍits* who keep Hinduism alive in our time. Among the spokespersons for contemporary Hinduism there are extraordinarily intelligent, highly educated, and politically astute men and women who are nonetheless modern for being Hindu.

The great strength of Hinduism has at all times been its capacity to absorb and assimilate ideas from many different sources without giving up its own peculiar fundamental orientation. Though Jainism and Buddhism originally broke away from the brahmanic-vedic community, the religion that finally emerged as Hinduism during the Gupta restoration showed features of Buddhism and Jainism and was thus able to exert an almost universal appeal on the people of India. This quite often implied a somewhat radical reorientation. Despite the practice of animal sacrifice and meat eating in the Vedic religion, the new Hinduism that emerged as Vaiṣṇavism adopted the Jain principles of the rejection of animal sacrifice and dietary vegetarianism, and the Buddhists are considered to have been instrumental in providing it with the doctrinal superstructure of repeated *avatāras*. Also it is not unlikely that Judeo-Christian influences were at work during the first centuries of the Christian era, molding certain aspects of Hinduism. During the time of the Roman emperors, when anti-Semitic laws forced Jews from the heartlands of the Roman Empire, to emigrate, a considerable number of Jews settled on the West Coast of India. There is a group of Black Jews in South India who must have intermarried with the local population. In addition the Bene Israel, a group of white Jews who preserved their racial purity, are established in several major centers, including Bombay, where they have two synagogues.[37] It is impossible to determine to what extent these longtime residents, belonging to a different religion, have influenced Hinduism in the localities where they have been in contact. According to an old tradition of the Christians in Kerala, Thomas, one of the Twelve Apostles of Jesus, preached his faith along the Malabar coast in South India and was martyred close to the modern city of Madras.[38] The Mar Thoma Christians maintain that he preached the Gospel in Northern India, too, even in the famous university town of Taxila, and that he established several churches on the banks of the River Yamunā. Despite strong arguments that suggest a link between the Syrian Christians of India and Nestorian communities in Asia Minor in the fourth century, it is not impossible that some Christians were already living in Malabar before that. These South Indian Christians maintained their numbers largely unchanged throughout the centuries, and they lived in peace with their Hindu neighbors and had their own caste structure. Some scholars have attempted to link certain forms of Vaiṣṇavism (the worship of the infant Kṛṣṇa and certain peculiarities of Madhva's theology, e.g., his belief in being Vāyu's, the "spirits" incarnation and his doctrine of predestination) to Christian influences.[39]

There had always been a quite lively exchange between Greece and Northern India and the commerce in ideas must have been mutual: Indians not only gave of their religion and philosophy but also received. Those channels of communication did not break when the Arabs conquered the Middle East. Settlements of Arab merchants in Indian seaports were quite common in pre-Muslim times. It is again a quite well-founded suggestion that during the first centuries of the Muslim era an Arabic version of the Gospel stories was brought to India and was assimilated by various groups.[40]

The contact of Hindus with Islam resulted not only in a relatively large number of (sometimes forced) conversions but also in friendly and fruitful exchange on a broad level. Several of the Muslim rulers were impressed by, and sympathetic to, the Hindu sages and scholars. Some, like Akbar, went so far as to provoke a reaction from a Muslim orthodoxy afraid that the Muslim faith might suffer through the acceptance of Hindu ideas. A considerable number of Hindus, however, found Islamic ideas worth considering and adopting, and new movements sprang up in which Hindus and Muslims felt equally at home. Kabir, the Muslim weaver, attracted Hindus into his *panth*; and Gurū Nanak, the Hindu, wanted his Sikhism to be a universal religion, embodying the best of both the Hindu and

Muslim tradition. The development of *bhakti*, especially in North India, with its emphasis on the Oneness of God and exclusive love of Him, the equality of all worshippers before Him, and its insistence that basic human virtues rather than wealth or status are the signs of true religiosity, may be linked directly to influences from Islam.

The European invasion, beginning with the Portuguese occupation of Goa, also had its religious impact on Hinduism. The first Portuguese missionaries not only succeeded in getting legislation passed that forced non-Christians either to become Christians or to emigrate and had Hindu temples destroyed, but also rebaptized thousands of (in their opinion) schismatic Christians, thereby splitting the Indian Christian community into feuding Latin and Syrian factions.[41] Protestant missions, under the Danish Lutherans, the British Anglicans, the American Baptists and Methodists, and numerous others, set out to shepherd Indians into their different churches, sometimes in the process implanting into their proselytes not only an aversion to their Hindu past but also a hatred of rival Christian factions. Except for a few courageous attempts by individuals, who often enough had to defend themselves against attacks from within their own churches, the Christian missions in India tragically ignored India's indigenous religion. Hindus like Raja Ram Mohan Roy, Keshub Chunder Sen, Swami Vivekananda, and (to a certain degree) Mahātmā Gandhi and Sarvepalli Radhakrishnan tried to integrate what they found most attractive in Christianity into their own vision of Hinduism.[42] Mainly the ethics of the Gospels and the social concern of the Christian missionaries found the approval of modern Hindus and evoked in them the desire to develop their own religion in these areas. Swami Vivekananda, one of the most influential Hindus around the turn of the century, attempted to reawaken the pride of Hindus in their own tradition, institutionalizing these new features in his Ramakrishna Mission. Although the Ramakrishna movement is not considered an orthodox *saṃpradāya* by the more conservative Hindus, it has nevertheless captured the imagination of a great many modern and progressive Hindus and is held to be a nonsectarian and universal expression of a new and reformed Hinduism that at the same time preserves the best of the ancient tradition.

Recent attempts—beginning with Brahmabhandav Upadhyay—to articulate a "Hindu-Christianity," to introduce Hindu rites and scriptures into Christian worship and daily life may result in a new form of Hinduism as well as Christianity.[43]

Despite its openness for many influences and the considerable changes that it has undergone throughout the ages, Hinduism is not simply the sum total of all other faiths or a conglomerate of diverse beliefs. There is a distinct character, an unbroken tradition and a unifying principle that allows Hinduism to be faithful to itself while inviting others to share whatever treasures they may possess. In all the historic encounters between Hinduism and other religions Hinduism has always emerged the stronger and richer and succeeded in absorbing the other elements.

3 Hindu *Dharma*: Orthodoxy and Heresy in Hinduism

> All those traditions and all those despicable systems of philosophy which are not based on the Veda produce no reward after death; for they are declared to be founded on darkness. All those (doctrines) differing from (the Veda) which spring up and (soon) perish, are worthless and false, because they are of modern date.
>
> —*Manusmṛti* XII, 95

Translations can sometimes be quite revealing. If we try to find an Indian synonym for the term *religion* (admittedly difficult to define even within the Western tradition!), we have to choose from a variety of terms, none of which coincides precisely with our word. The most common and most general term is *dharma*, today usually translated as "religion."[1] Another important aspect of religion is expressed by the term *sādhana*, frequently rendered in English as "realization." In its sociological sense *religion* may often have to be understood as *saṃpradāya*, mostly (and erroneously) translated as "sect," which describes the great Hindu traditions of Vaiṣṇavism, Ṣaivism, and Ṣāktism and their subdivisions. The term *mārga* ("path") is also frequently used as synonymous with "religion" in the sense of a path to salvation. Thus the *tri-mārga* scheme organizes the entire range of religious affiliations into *karma-mārga*, *bhakti-mārga*, and *jñāna-mārga*: the path of works, the path of loving devotion, and the path of knowledge, respectively. The representation of Hindu religion will differ again according to the affiliation of the writer with regard to caste or position in society; thus a brahmin householder will offer a different presentation of religion from that of a *samnyāsin,* who has given up all caste affiliation and all ritual.

THE MEANING OF *DHARMA*

Dharma, etymologically from the root *dhṛ-,* "to sustain" or "to uphold," has been given diverse meanings in various Indian schools of thought. At one end of the spectrum we have the grammatical or logical use of the term *dharma* as merely an element of a word or a proposition.[2] At the other end is the onto-cosmological interpretation of *dharma* as that "which gives sustenance to the universe or the universal principle of all things."[3] Generally, however, it is used with reference to 'religion' in the specific sense of socio-ethical laws and obligations. P. V. Kane thinks that *dharma* is "one of these Sanskrit words that defy all attempts at an exact rendering in English or any other tongue."[4] He eventually circumscribes the term by saying that it comprises "the privileges, duties and obligations of a man, his standard of conduct as a member of the Āryan community, as a member of one of the castes, as a person in a particular stage of life."

Manusmṛti, the laws of Manu, the most important authority on the subject, identifies the sources of *dharma* as "the Veda in its entirety, the traditions (*smṛtis*) fixed by men conversant with the Vedas, the customs of righteous people and one's own conscience (*ātmanastuṣṭi*)."[5] The promise is held out to the man who follows all the rules laid down in Manu's law book that "he will obtain fame here on earth and supreme bliss beyond."[6] The same book also condemns as *nāstikas,* those who place their own reasoning above the authority of tradition.[7] *Nāstika* is normally translated as 'atheist', though it does not quite correspond to its English equivalent.[8] In India followers of atheistic systems like that of the Sāṁkhya are *āstikas* or orthodox, because they do not explicitly question or reject the Vedas; whereas Buddhists and Jains or the followers of any non-Vedic religion are *nāstikas,* including also the solidly materialistic and hedonistic Lokāyatas. The *dharma* of the *Manusmṛti* is also geographically defined:

> The land between the two sacred rivers Sarasvatī and Dṛṣadvatī, this land created by divine powers is the Brahmavarta. The customs prevailing in this country, passed on from generation to generation, that is called the 'right behaviour' (*sadācarā*). From a brahmin born and raised in this country, all men should learn their ways. The country where the black antelope naturally moves about is the one that is fit

for sacrifice—beyond is that of the *mlecchas* (the barbarians, the unclean!). A twiceborn (viz. a Brahmin, a Kṣatriya, a Vaiśya) should resort to this country and dwell in it; a Śudra, however, may, for the sake of gaining his livelihood, live anywhere.[9]

From the point of view of content this *dharma* comprises social classification and the division of society into four *varṇas*, each with its particular functions and rights; the whole complex of sacrifices and rituals; the *saṃskāras*, performed at the critical periods of life; marriage laws, right of succession, the regulation of the relationship between men and women, parents and children, teachers and pupils; the definition of sin and atonement, pilgrimages and vows, feasts and celebrations—including the myths concerning the creation of the universe, transmigration, and final emancipation.[10]

Because, according to Hindu tradition, Manu is the mythical ancestor of all of humankind, his ordinances are *manava dharma* or 'the law of humankind', *sanātana dharma,* or 'eternal' and 'natural' religion. Modern Hindu scholars try to justify this claim in terms of the many religions and systems of law prevailing in the world as well as to specify how it relates to Hindu law. Thus Śṛī Narāyanjī Purusottama Sangani explains:

Upon which as a fundament everything is built and which gives to the whole world its order, that which provides one in this world with blessed peace and in the next with supreme bliss and helps to attain to complete emancipation, that is *sanātana dharma,* the eternal religion. It is of the nature of God, because it has developed through God himself. As God has no beginning, middle or end, so the *sanātana dharma* has no beginning or end. It is beginningless, of hoary antiquity, always the same, in it there is no development or change. This religion is from God and therefore God is its Lord.[11]

He continues to state in detail that this religion of humankind exists in a general form, comprising the duties of firmness, forgiveness, restraint, abstention from stealing, purity, control over the senses, forbearance, knowledge, truth, and freedom from hatred and anger, and in a specific form as absolute truth "revealed only to Hindus, different according to the *catur-varṇa-āśrama* scheme of life." The concept of *svadharma* is a very crucial one: *dharma* is right conduct not in a general moral sense but specified for each caste and each situation in life. Time and again the rule laid down in the Bhagavadgītā is quoted: "It is better to fulfil one's own duties (*dharma*), however imperfectly, than to do that of another, however perfect it may be."[12]

Thus dharma presupposes a social order in which all functions and duties are assigned to separate classes whose smooth interaction guarantees the well-being of society as a whole, and beyond this maintains the harmony of the whole universe. Dharma has its roots in the structure of the cosmos, and the socio-ethical law of humankind is but one facet of an all-embracing law encompassing all beings. Hence we can also appreciate the frequently quoted maxim: "The 'law' when violated destroys—when preserved protects: therefore *dharma* should not be violated lest the violated *dharma* destroy us."[13] Thus dharma, at least theoretically, is its own justification: dharma does not depend on a personal authority that could also make exceptions and pardon a transgressor; it is inherent in nature and does not allow modifications. Dharma guarantees the continued existence of India; the *avatāras* appear to rescue dharma from corruption and thus restore the country. In the strictest and fullest sense dharma coincides with Hinduism. That did not prevent certain developments from taking place within what was considered 'law' in Indian history, nor did it exclude the treatment of many moral questions on a rational and universal basis.[14]

THE WEIGHT OF *DHARMAŚĀSTRA*

Dharmaśāstra as a literary genre is undoubtedly the largest in the whole of Indian literature.[15] This is due to both the importance of the subjects dealt with under it and the inherent difficulty of applying its principles to concrete instances. According to Indian tradition dharma is hidden and had to be revealed by competent persons. Because dharma was supposed to be the overarching rule of life, everything came under its purview and great care had to be taken to find expressions of dharma in particular circumstances. The universal nature of dharma also explains the absence of the division between a "religious" and "secular" sphere, so fundamental to the modern West.

The meaning of the word *dharma* has undergone many changes in the course of the millennia,[16] and its revival in the context of today's *Hindu jagaran* is felt as a threat by Indian secularists. As D. Derret[17] points out, dharma is not the result of theoretical or logical conceptualization but of experience lived through by several generations and interpreted in the spirit of these experiences. It is very malleable and beyond the grasp of outsiders, who do not share this life experience. It is group centered and group oriented. It is based on notions of authority, duty, consensus. It is in many ways the very opposite of "law" as understood in the modern West, with its emphasis on equality, rights, and majority votes.

Though from an absolutist, Vedāntist standpoint good and evil are relative, the two sides of one coin as it were, the *dharmaśāstra* tradition of India has laboured continuously to separate sharply dharma from *adharma*, to spell out quite unambiguously what *righteousness* and *unrighteousness* mean and what they lead to.

Thus the fourth century logician Vātsyāyana analyzed the elements of both in the following manner: *adharma* as well as dharma depends either on body, or speech, or mind. Unrighteousness related to the body is threefold: violence, theft, and unlawful sexual indulgence. Correspondingly righteousness connected with the body consists in charity, succor of the distressed, and social service. The vices originating from speech are telling lies, caustic talk, calumny, and absurd talk. The corresponding virtues of speech are veracity, talking with good intention, gentle talk, and recitation of scriptures. *Adharma* connected with the mind is threefold: illwill, covetousness, and irreligiosity. Dharma originating in the mind is kindness, disinterestedness, and faith or piety.[18]

Patañjali's *Yogasūtras* offer a less systematic, but more popular series of virtues necessary for the attainment of peace of mind and are an exposition of dharma under the two categories of *yama* and *niyama* (restraints and observances). The *yama* comprise nonviolence, veracity, abstinence from theft, continence, and abstinence from avariciousness; and the *niyama*, purity, contentment, ritual actions, study, and 'making the Lord the motive of all action'.[19] Through these and similar analyses of dharma there emerges quite clearly the universal validity of dharma, though its motivation and particular application may be typically Hindu. The voluminous dharmaśāstra literature that has developed over the centuries contains as well as casuistry and local law, much that has been at the center of ethical reflection in the West, too.[20] As liberal forces in the West fought to change laws, which were defended by conservative institutions as divine or natural laws, so modern Hindus have often found the custodians of dharma obstructing the path toward social justice and progress.[21] The defenders of the traditional law allowed the burning of widows, the frequently inhuman ways in which the upper castes treated the outcastes, the superstitions and vices of the past. For this reason many of those who fought for a better lot for the masses became bitter enemies of the established order. In recent times voices could be heard from within the tradition advocating reform without overthrowing the entire structure. "Hinduism is not a static structure, but a dynamic force" wrote A. S. Altekar, adding:

> Unfortunately, the truth of this proposition is not sufficiently realized by the Hindus themselves. The orthodox Hindu believes that Hinduism is once and for all time fashioned by the pristine *śāstras* of hoary antiquity; the educated Hindu is not sufficiently acquainted with the history of his culture and religion to know their true nature. It was a dark day when the non-official change-sanctioning authority, the Daśavara Pariṣad of the Smṛti, was replaced by a government department presided over by the Minister for Religion. For, when Hindu rule came to an end in the thirteenth century, this department also disappeared, and during the last 600 years Hinduism has remained more or less static. With no authoritative and intelligent agency to guide him, the average Hindu believes that religious beliefs, philosophical theories and social practices current in the twelfth century comprise the whole of this tradition and it is his conviction that these beliefs and practices are sanctioned by the scriptures (which he does not understand), and that to depart from them is an unpardonable sin. This utter and pitiable ignorance of the real nature of Hinduism is at the root of the amazing opposition which measures like the Hindu Code have evoked in the recent past even in educated circles.[22]

There is no doubt that 'modernity' has made inroads into traditional Indian dharma, and a respected authority like Laxman Shastri Joshi finds that "the moral foundations of Indian society appear to be crumbling rapidly."[23] He sees, to his distress, that "nationalism appears to be taking the place of the old socio-religious consciousness" that he considers "not a healthy product of the new human civilization." He takes a bold stance, however, when he declares: "The need has arisen today for laying the foundations of a new ethics without invoking the aid of collectivity, God or any supernatural or transcendental principle. We need an ethics that will give man the confidence in his powers of creating his own social existence. . . . Morality is the beauty of human existence, it is the rhythm of human life."

Reflections about dharma do not, however, remain in the sphere of ethical theory, they enter into very practical issues: laws for the new Indian republic that would be binding for all the diverse groups of Hindus, who had so far been following a multitude of traditional laws sanctioned by various *śāstras*, and 'codes of conduct' for all those who engage in public activities. India in fact abrogated traditional law in certain sectors, when it declared 'untouchability' to be abolished and discrimination on account of caste to be punishable. As daily life shows in countless instances, the transition is not easy and can by no means be considered to have been completed.[24]

We shall have constant need to refer to dharma when describing the various aspects of Hindu life and doctrine. A few other key concepts for the understanding of religion in the Indian sense will be introduced at this juncture.

REACHING INDIVIDUAL PERFECTION THROUGH *SĀDHANA*

Sādhana, derived from the root *sādh-*, "to finish" or "to accomplish," denotes the "means of realization." One who practices a *sādhana* is a *sādhaka,* a word closely related to the word *sādhu,* the "just man" or "saint." Although dharma is imposed on persons by nature or society, they are free to choose their own *sādhana.* Therefore, although there is basically only one dharma, there are countless *sādhanas,* which differ considerably and essentially. They are connected insofar as according to the classical *caturvarnāśrama* scheme the last stage in the life of a Brahmin was to be that of *samnyāsa,* the life of the wandering ascetic, wholely dedicated to *sādhana,* the pursuit of complete emancipation. The scheme has been departed from quite frequently even in former times; in fact any man or woman can become a member of a *saṃpradāya* (a religious order) and practice the *sādhana* that agrees with his or her condition.[25] Though the classical schema of the three ways is usually applied, there are in fact many more ways; almost every sect and subsect has its own ideas about *sādhana.* All agree, however, in the basic conviction that one is not born free but must liberate oneself through discipline. The analysis of the nature of bondage determines also the nature of the *sādhana*: for the followers of Śaṅkara, bondage consists of an illusion about the real nature of the Self; for the followers of Rāmānuja it is forgetfulness of the Lord; for many *bhakti* schools it is a wrong emotional attitude toward world and God; and for *śakti* schools a separation from the Mother. *Sādhana* entails bodily as well as mental and spiritual practices. It is usually practiced under the guidance of a guru, through whom the disciple has to search and whom he or she has to serve. The general name for the ascetic practices is *tapas,* literally, "heat." Some of those practices must go back to prehistoric times: ancient Vedic texts already use the term and sometimes the creation of the universe itself is ascribed to *tapas*. *Tapas* may mean anything, from real self-torture and record-breaking austerities to the recitation of sacred syllables and the chanting of melodies. Fasting, *prāṇayama* (breath control), *japa* (repetition of a name of God or a short *mantra*), and study of scriptures are among the most common practices. At the *melās* one can observe other varieties of *tapas*: lying on a bed of thorns or nails, prolonged standing on one leg, lifting one arm for years till it is withered, looking straight into the glaring sun for long hours, and similar sportive feats. Many ascetics keep silence for years. This is one of the most powerful means of storing up spiritual energy. Although perhaps under Christian influence the practices associated with *sādhanas* are often associated with theistic ideas not very different from the ideas of the value of voluntary suffering and self-mortification, originally they had nothing to do with either ethical perfection or pleasing God. *Tapas* used to be seen as psychophysical energy, the accumulation of which determined one's position in the universe. The aim, therefore, was to reach a higher position with greater power through *tapas*. There are numerous stories in Indian literature about forest hermits who had accumulated so much *tapas*, that the gods, and even the highest among them, Indra, became afraid of losing their positions. The gods usually sent to the ascetic as their ultimate weapon a bewitchingly beautiful heavenly damsel to confuse his thoughts or a rude fellow to make him lose his temper in an outburst of anger, thereby burning up all his stored up *tapas* energy. The ascetic would then have to start afresh, unless he decided to embrace another vocation. If a man had gathered enough *tapas* he could compel a *deva* to appear before him who would have to offer him an absolutely effective boon, opening up infinite possibilities for the imagination of authors and poets. The boons are limited by the power of the god, and the *tapasvīn* has to make the right choice. If the god is not quick witted enough, the ascetic who called him can also turn the boon against the god. The gods, therefore, usually grant boons with built-in precautions, stipulating the conditions under which the boon will be effective.

A telling story is that of Vikra, who, after practicing severe *tapas* for many years, called on Śiva, asking him to grant the boon, that whosoever's head he would touch, that man should die instantly. Śiva laughingly granted the boon, realizing his folly only when Vikra chased his wife and him, to try out the new art. Śiva in his despair sought refuge with Viṣṇu, asking for advice. Viṣṇu, cunningly, induced doubt in Vikra. Śiva, he told Vikra, cannot always be taken seriously. He might have been joking or lying—so better try it first on yourself. Vikra did so, and thus killed himself with the boon he had received. The story has as its main theme the superiority of Viṣṇu over Śiva, who has to appeal to Viṣṇu to save his life.

ORTHODOXY BATTLING HERESY

This incident reveals something of the rivalry that exists between the different *saṃpradāyas*, the various churches and sects of Hinduism. The great majority of Hindus belong to either Vaiṣṇavism, Śaivism, or Śāktism; all of them have countless subdivisions, springing from local traditions, cults, and a great many religious teachers.[26] Between them there had often been competition for the dominance of Viṣṇu, Śiva, and Devī; not seldom also intolerance and fanatical zeal. In the nineteenth century the *Kumbha Melās*, the occasions when a large number of *sādhus* of all *saṃpradāyas* congregate, witnessed regular battles between Śaivas and Vaiṣṇavas, in which many lost their lives.[27] The immediate reason for the quarrels was usually a question of precedence in the ritual bath at the most auspicious time, but there always lurked a much larger and more important issue: the right belief! Vaiṣṇavas are absolutely sure that Viṣṇu alone is the Lord and that placing Śiva above Viṣṇu is the grossest heresy and unbelief. And Śaivas, of course, know that only Śiva is the Great Lord, whom all must adore and serve and for whose glory they spend themselves. The *Liṅgapurāṇa* promises Śiva's heaven to one who kills or tears out the tongue of someone who reviles Śiva.[28] The Vaiṣṇava scriptures contain not only barbed stories, such as the one about Vikra, but also venomous invectives against all who do not follow Viṣṇu.[29] Considerable friction existed also between the followers of these purānic traditions and the orthodox vedic Brahmins. The Pañcarātrins, one of the prominent sects of Vaiṣṇavas, were labeled great sinners, whose existence was the result of killing cows in some former birth. They were accused of being absolutely non-Vedic; further, it was held by the orthodox, that the literatures of the Śāktas, Śaivas, and Pañcarātras were for the delusion of humankind.[30]

Both Śaivas and Vaiṣṇavas considered the "atheistic" Buddhists and Jains their common enemy.[31] Numerous are the historical instances of persecution of people who refused to conform to the idea of orthodoxy that demanded the acknowledgment of brahmanical authority and Vedic revelation.[32]

Some authors seem to think that the reception of Buddha among the *avatāras* of Viṣṇu would express a spirit of tolerance. But the way in which this Buddha-*avatāra* is described in the *Viṣṇupurāṇa*, and the general Hindu attitude of considering both good and evil as coming from the same Supreme Being, would suggest that we have here an early and unmistakably hostile Hindu text dealing with Buddhism.[33]

Buddha is introduced as one of many forms of the *māyā-moha* (delusive power) of Viṣṇu: he engages in what may be termed psychological warfare against the *daityas* on behalf of the *devas*, who have come to take refuge with him. He is sent to destroy the enemies of the Vaiṣṇavas from within. He is characterized as *raktāṃbara*, dressed in a red garment, as *mṛdvalpamadhurākṣara*, speaking gently, calmly, and sweetly. The teachings, which he communicates for the self-destruction of the *daityas*, considered as pernicious and heretical by the Hindus, are

1. The killing of animals for sacrifices should be discontinued.
2. The whole world is a product of the mind.
3. The world is without support.
4. The world is engaged in pursuit of error, which it mistakes for knowledge.

As a result of this teaching the *daityas* abandoned the dharma of the Vedas and the *smṛtis*, and they induced others to do the same. The same *māyā-moha* of Viṣṇu had appeared before Buddha as "a naked mendicant with shaven head and a bunch of peacock feathers in his hands," and he would appear again as the preacher of the Cārvāka doctrines.

The *Viṣṇupurāṇa* calls the Ṛk, Yajus, and Sāmaveda the "garments" of a man: a man is naked if he goes without them. The *daityas*, seduced by Buddha are in such a position. Whereas the *devas* were unable to dislodge the *daityas* before, they now defeat them: "The armor of dharma, which had formerly protected the *daityas* had been discarded by them and upon its abandonment followed their destruction."

The *Viṣṇupurāṇa* follows up the story of the defeat of the *daityas* by establishing general rules concerning the treatment of heretics. The text calls them naked, in tune with the aforementioned idea, and sinners. The criterion of orthodoxy is behavior in conformity with the rules laid down for each one of the four *āśramas*. There is no fifth *āśrama*, the text categorically states.

Our Purāṇa shows special concern for the conscientious performance of the daily rites prescribed for the householder; the most prominent features of Buddhists being the neglect of them. A neglect of the daily rites for a year is considered so grave a sin that there is no expiation for it: "There is no sinner upon earth more culpable than one in whose dwelling the *devas*, the *rsis*, the *pitṛs*, and the *bhūtas* are left to sigh without an oblation."

The *Viṣṇupurāṇa* suggests complete excommunication of the Buddhists: all social contact must be broken, even looking at a heretic necessitates lengthy expiations. The Hindu who dines with a Buddhist goes to hell. Buddhists are to be considered as unclean, whatever their caste affiliation may have been. Not only is the Hindu told to have nothing to do with the Buddhist, he must discourage the Buddhist from associating with him: if a heretic observes a faithful one in his rituals, these remain without fruit.

To illustrate its teaching the *Viṣṇupurāṇa* tells the story of king Śatadhanu and his pious wife: the mere conversation of the king with a *pāṣaṇḍa* suffices to let him be reborn as a dog, a wolf, a vulture, a crow, and a peacock before assuming a human body again. The instrument of his salvation is his wife who looked away from the heretic when the king conversed with him and thus remained undefiled.

According to an old tradition it was Śaṅkarācārya who tried to reconcile the rival Hindu churches in the eighth century by introducing the so-called *pañcāyātana-pūjā*, the simultaneous worship of Gaṇeṣa, Sūrya, Viṣṇu, Śiva, and Devī, explaining that all deities were but different forms of the one Brahman, the invisible Supreme Being.[34] That this attempt was not well received by all those who clung to the idea of one God is illustrated by a story in which the followers of Madhva, the "Hammer of the Jainas," explain their master's negative relationship to Śaṅkara and his followers:

> The demon Manimat was born as the illegitimate child of a widow and was therefore called Śaṅkara. He studied the *śāstras* with Śiva's blessings and the depraved welcomed him. He really taught Buddhism under the guise of Vedānta. He seduced the wife of his Brahmin host and used to make converts by his magic arts. When he died, he asked his disciples to kill Satyaprajñā, the true teacher of Vedānta; the followers of Śaṅkara were tyrannical people who burnt down monasteries, destroyed cattle and killed women and children. They converted Prajñātīrtha, their chief opponent, by force. The disciples of Prajñātīrtha, however, were secretly attached to the true Vedāntic

doctrine and they made one of their disciples thoroughly learned in the Vedic scriptures. Acutyaprekṣa, the teacher of Madhva, was a disciple of this true type of teacher, who originated from Satyaprajñā. Madhva was an incarnation of Vāyu for the purpose of destroying the false doctrines of Śaṅkara, which were like the doctrines of the Lokāyatas, Jainas and Pāśupatas, but were more obnoxious and injurious.[35]

The same Śaṅkara is said to have had the Kārpātikas whipped because they were not vedic. He founded the Daśanāmi order and established *maṭhas* at four strategic points in India, allocating to each a quarter of India for missionary purposes. Śaṅkara, as described in the *Digvijaya*, 'the conquest of space', conformed to the current idea of the *ācārya*, the 'doctor' who had to be able to defend his own position against all objections and to defeat his opponents in public debate.

Though quite often the existence of "six viewpoints," accepted as orthodox, is taken as a sign of doctrinal tolerance within Hinduism, each author necessarily identifies himself with one of them and tries to prove the others either wrong or defective. The decision, to call a system orthodox or heretical, is often based on subjective criteria and sectarian affiliations. Thus Mādhava, a fourteenth century Advaitin, arranges his *Sarvadarśaṇasaṁgraha*, the summary of all systems, in such a way that each following system cancels out the preceding one; in the end Advaita Vedānta, as expounded by Śaṅkara, emerges as the only truth.[36] Thus the Cārvākas, unabashed materialists and hedonists and enemies of the vedic-brahmanic religion, are defeated by the Buddhists, who in turn are proved wrong by the Jainas. These have to give way to the Rāmānujists, who in turn are superseded by the followers of Madhva. Four schools of Śaivism, the Pāśupata, the Śaiva, the Pratyabhijñā, and the Raseśvara systems, cancel each other out successively. The truth of the next, the Vaiśeṣika system, is overthrown by the Naiyāyikās, who suffer defeat at the hands of the Mīmāṁsakas. These in turn have to give way to the followers of Pāṇini, who are ousted by the Sāṁkhya system. The Yoga system finally comes closest to the truth, which is fully present in Śaṅkara's Advaita Vedānta.

The *Brahmasūtra*, as understood by Śaṅkara, is largely a refutation of non-Vedāntic systems of thought. Not only does it reject the four major schools of Buddhism but also Sāṁkhya and Bhāgavatism. Śaṅkara explains the need for the exposition of *brahman* knowledge by stating that "there are many various opinions, partly based on sound arguments and scriptural texts and partly on fallacious arguments and scriptural texts misunderstood. If a man would embrace one of these opinions without previous consideration, he would bar himself from the highest beatitude and incur grievous loss."[37]

Synopses of the various systems from other standpoints will choose a different sequence to prove their views right—the accusation hurled against rival sects of not being Vedic or being ignorant of the correct methods of interpretation of texts results either in the insinuation that the doctrines in question reveal crypto-*nāstikas* or in the 'tolerant' opinion that the others have some glimpses of truth mixed with untruth, while the system held by the writer is the whole and sole truth.

Religious Hinduism is unanimous, however, in rejecting—in addition to Buddhism and Jainism—the system known as Cārvāka or Lokāyata, a solidly materialistic system that, as part of India's 'realistic' philosophical tradition, has also engaged the attention of Western scholars more recently.[38] The previously mentioned Mādhava writes that he thinks most of his contemporaries in fourteenth century India to be Cārvākas, regarding wealth and pleasure as the only aim in life and living according to the motto: "As long as you live enjoy yourself—nobody can escape from death. Once this body is consumed by fire—how will you ever return?" The only reality they acknowledge is material: the four elements—earth, water, air, and fire—together with their combinations. The so-called spirit of man is only a byproduct of these, similar to the emergence of alcohol in the fermentation of certain substances. Man's soul dies with the body. They even quote scripture to corroborate their theories: "Arising from out of these elements, one also re-enters into them. When one has departed, there is no more knowledge," says the *Bṛhadāraṇyaka Upaniṣad*.[39] Wisdom consists of aiming at the maximum enjoyment with the least trouble and avoiding grief. To the more pious contemporaries who ask why one should go to such lengths in organizing sacrifices and religious celebrations, they coolly reply: religion is of use only for the priests as their means of livelihood; the Vedas are full of untruth and contradictions. The Vedic paṇḍits defeat each other, and the authority of the way of knowledge is canceled by those who advocate the way of works. The Vedas are nothing but the incoherent rhapsodies of swindlers and impostors. It is difficult to surpass the cynicism of the Cārvākas, as illustrated in the following quotation from an otherwise lost work by a certain Bṛhaspati:

> There is no heaven, no spiritual liberation, nor any soul in another world. The good deeds of the various classes do not leave any trace. The *agnihotra*, the three Vedas, the *samnyāsin*'s three staffs, the ashes on one's body are all inventions, made for gaining a livelihood by those who lack vigour and intelligence. If an animal slaughtered in the *jyotiṣṭoma* goes to heaven, why does the sacrificer not immediately kill his father? If *śraddha*, the sacrifice for the deceased, does profit the dead, then the traveler does not need to take any provisions on his journey. If sacrifice nourishes the beings in heaven, why not those who stand on a rooftop? Let a man enjoy his life and let him eat *ghī* even if he has debts. Once the body is burnt, how should he return? Why does one who leaves his body not return for the sake of his relations? I tell you why: all these ceremonies are without value, they have been introduced by the Brahmins for the sake of gain. The authors of the three Vedas were frauds and humbugs. The well-known formulae of paṇḍits, priests and their like, the obscene ritual prescribed for the queen in the *aśvamedha* were all invented by rogues and demons.[40]

Like almost everything else in Hinduism, so also the dichotomy between orthodox and heretics operates differently on different levels. On one level—the level of caste-regulated behavior—the distinction between *āstika* and *nāstika* is quite clear. *Nāstikas* are excommunicated. On another level—the level of personal religiosity and devotion—the distinction is blurred; as caste is not observed in the gatherings of *bhaktas*, so *bhakti* religion offers salvation also to those who are *nāstikas*. It introduces, however, its own criteria for excommunication: sins against the name are unforgivable.

The two levels on which Hinduism moves, not only the level of the absolute and the relative, are in constant interaction. The observation of caste rules and Vedic propriety alone would not qualify a person for salvation by Viṣṇu—one needs to be elected by him, an election that has to be earned through acts of devotion and service—but it is insisted upon also by Vaiṣṇava writers. However, and here we again switch levels, the perfect one, the saint, the guru, can take liberties with rules and regulations: divine licence suspends human law. And again, in a devotional context a person may be considered a saint, a soul close to God, and he or she still may be denied those rights that come from observing caste regulations.

Hindus are used, of course, to compartmentalizing society and accepting a corresponding compartmentalization of right and wrong behavior. The devotee, in *satsaṅg*, moves temporarily into another society: the caste of the believers that operates under its own laws. The termination of the *satsaṅg* brings about the termination of this status: one moves back into the caste one was born into.

Though it may be impossible to establish criteria of "orthodoxy" that would find acceptance by all Hindus, it would not be correct to conclude that such an idea is absent from Hinduism and that we have to substitute for it instead an idea of "orthopraxy."[41] Doctrinal issues have been discussed by Hindus throughout the ages with tenacity and also with the understanding that an aspect of absolute truth always reflected in any particular religious doctrine. There has never been one central authority in Hinduism strong enough to decide the issue categorically, but the numerous heads of the various Hindu churches have nevertheless established very rigorous canons from within which their understanding of orthodoxy is defined.[42] Thus they clearly determine which books have to be considered as revelation, which authors may be used as commentators, and which line of tradition must be followed. Students of religion in traditional institutions were not supposed to read other books or to listen to any other teacher. This often makes them incapable of appreciating or understanding any version of Hinduism that differs from their own; even today the debates between paṇḍits of different schools are often quite acrimonious and filled with narrow-minded attempts to 'defeat' each other. It is somewhat amusing to hear American Hare Krisna followers repeat the traditional Caitanyite arguments against Advaita, of which they probably know very little. The more recent history of Hinduism is also fraught with intolerance: the Ārya Samāj and its offspring, the Hindu Mahāsabhā and the Rāṣṭrīya Svayamsevak Saṅgh, have intimidated and often provoked non-Hindus. They have been responsible for numerous Hindu-Muslim riots, for atrocities in the name of the true religion, and finally, for the assassination of Mahātmā Gandhi, whom they considered an enemy of Hinduism. The *"Hindutva"* agitation, leading up to the infamous destruction of the Babri-Masjid in Ayodhya and the subsequent riots in many places have opened the eyes of many to the large potential of intolerance present in today's political Hinduism.[43]

In a nonviolent, but nevertheless very effective, way the caste *pañcāyats* and the leaders of *saṁpradāyas* have always exercised control over their members, carefully watching them and enforcing their views of orthodoxy, if necessary through imposition of penances or expulsion from the community. Hinduism may appear to be very vague and extremely tolerant to the outsider, but the insider must conform to very precise regulations of life within the group. *Svadharma,* everyone's peculiar set of duties and obligations, orders and restricts each person's life. Those who have achieved freedom from social duties by choosing *samnyāsa* must conform to the precise rules of their own particular *sampradāya,* if they do not want to risk being reprimanded by zealous colleagues. When *sādhus* meet they first ask one another about the *sampradāya* and their guru; quite often they remonstrate with one another, pointing out violations of rules and customs. As long as someone lives with a guru he or she has to serve the guru conscientiously and loyally, without showing any sign of an independent opinion. For many the guru represents God himself: to contradict him or her would be blasphemy; blind faith and unquestioning service are considered to be the way to eternal bliss; and the attitude of certain *gurus* towards the rest of humanity consists, at an advanced age, of a mixture of limitless arrogance, naive self-deceit, and megalomania, not unfrequently supported by European and American admirers.

Rivalries between different denominations of Hinduism in our time often acquire political overtones. Thus a recent takeover of the Vaishna Devī shrine by an independent board supported by the governor of Kashmir resulted in a bitter exchange between Karan Singh, the president of the Virāṭ Hindū Samāj, and the governor, Jagmohan. Karan Singh accused Jagmohan of being an Ārya Samājist, and as such being against image worship, whereas he himself defended the rights of the Dharmarth Trust that is "responsible for the advancement and promotion of Sanātana Dharma."[44] In early 1993 members of the RSS who had been in the forefront of the Ayodhya agitation forcibly installed Rāma pictures in Kṛṣṇa temples and disturbed a popular Kṛṣṇa festival in Kerala.[45]

4 Revelation and Scripture in Hinduism

> Let Scripture be your standard for laying down what should be done and what should not. Knowing what the rules of Scripture have determined, do your work in this world.
>
> —*Bhagavadgītā* XVI, 24

No other living tradition can claim scriptures as numerous or as ancient as Hinduism; none of them can boast of an unbroken tradition as faithfully preserved as the Hindu tradition. The sources of Hinduism are not only historical materials to be worked up by the scholar of antiquity; they have been recited and studied by the faithful throughout the ages. The reading of a Hindu religious scripture in a worship setting always is carried out with some kind of solemnity. To ward off all unfavorable influences and create an auspicious disposition, a so-called *maṅgala-śloka* is recited before the text proper begins, hymns of praise and devotion to a number of deities, to the guru, and to the text to be read. Time, place, and the external circumstances of the recitation are regulated, and the reading itself is usually done in a prescribed recitative.[1] It is essential to observe all these rules in order to obtain the fruits of the reading, which are quite often spelled out concretely at the end of the book itself.[2] The reading is not terminated abruptly either. The last sentence is read twice, thus indicating the end of the reading. The gods who were addressed in the beginning are now implored to forgive all inattention, disrespect, and incorrect or imperfect reading; this is the so-called *aparādha kṣamā pañca stotra,* marking the conclusion of the recitation. The book of scripture itself is always treated with reverence; it is never laid on the bare floor and is carefully guarded against all disrespect. In former times Hindus did not allow people from low castes, or foreigners, to read or to possess their sacred books; nowadays anyone can buy printed copies (and quite often translations also) of the Hindu scriptures in a book-store. Though secular Western scholarship has begun to analyze and dissect the Hindu scriptures, Hindus continue to regard them as revelations,[3] given to their ancestors as special privilege; and they resent the secularist view that sees in them only ancient literature. Before the sacred lore was written down it existed for untold centuries as an oral tradition handed down from generation to generation.[4] It was committed to writing only at a relatively late period in its history—and even now the proper study consists in memorizing the texts. The authentic Hindu tradition consists of that chain of authorities in which the oral tradition has been kept alive.[5]

Not all the various sacred books of the Hindus are considered to hold the same degree of revelation. The Indians developed at an early age a precise and widely accepted theological epistemology, according to which all authoritative literature is categorized. The *prasthāna trayī*, the triad of instruments for the attainment of religious knowledge for the sake of salvation, consists of *śruti, smṛti,* and *nyāya* or *pramāṇa*. From Śaṅkara (8th century C.E.) onward these were identified by the Vedāntins with the Upaniṣads, the Bhagavadgītā, and the *Brahmasūtra*. Other schools such as the Mīmāṁsakas would not agree with this. As the different branches of Hinduism differ in their ideas concerning orthodoxy and heresy, so they differ also in their recognition of certain classes of scriptures and their relative position in this scheme.

REVELATION PROPER: *ŚRUTI*

Śruti means literally that which has been perceived through hearing; it is 'revelation' in the most immediate sense. As a technical term it constitutes the scriptures with the highest theological value, containing supreme and undebatable authority. *Śruti* may be commented upon, but it can never be questioned. In theological debates discussion is carried on only for the purpose of establishing the meaning of *śruti*. Hārīta, an author of an early *dharmasūtra*[6] holds the opinion that *śruti* is of two kinds, the Vedic and the Tantric or Āgamic. He thereby acknowledges that in his time the non-Vedic traditions had become powerful enough to claim a position equal to that of the Veda, which originally had held this title exclusively. Even now the *sanātanists*, the followers of the Vedic dharma, refuse to acknowledge the Āgamas, the Scriptures of the

Vaiṣṇavas, Śaivas, and Śāktas as *śruti*. This is a rather unrealistic position, since for more than a thousand years Hindu religion has been much more influenced by the Āgamas than by the Vedas, and even the acknowledged *ācāryas* of Vedānta accepted the Āgamas and shaped their interpretation of vedic texts accordingly.[7]

For all practical purposes, then, we have to accept two mainstreams of *śruti*, though no Hindu will allow that all the scriptures accepted by the one or the other Hindu *saṁpradāya* are revelation and therefore are of any consequence to him.

The Veda, sacred knowledge, comprises several categories of literature: saṃhitās, *brāhmaṇas*, *āraṇyakas*, and (early) upaniṣads. According to Jan Gonda their final codification took place in pre-Buddhist times (ca. 600 B.C.E.) after hundreds of years of oral transmission.[8] The earliest part, the Veda in the strict sense, is divided into four saṃhitās or collections: *Ṛgveda*,[9] a collection of more than a thousand hymns addressed to various gods; *Sāmaveda*,[10] a collection of extracts from the former with the appropriate musical instructions for recitation; *Yajurveda*,[11] the book of Vedic ceremonies; and *Atharvaveda*,[12] a heterogeneous collection of hymns and spells. The four Vedas are neither sacred history nor doctrine; they are the instruments for the performance of the *yajña*, the sacrifice that stood at the centre of Vedic religion.[13]

Traditional scholars correlate the secular learning of the Hindus as *Upavedas* or supplementary knowledge with the four Vedas: *Arthaveda*, the science of statecraft and politics with the Ṛgveda; *Gandharvaveda*, music and the fine arts with the *Sāmaveda*; *Dhanuṣveda*, the art of archery (and warfare in general) with *Yajurveda*; and *Ayurveda*, medicine and biology, with the *Atharvaveda*.[14]

Despite the existence of four Vedas, the Ṛgveda occupies a special position as *śruti*. Because of the importance given to the exact wording, to the very sounds and syllables of the text itself, a series of auxiliary sciences for the study of the Veda, the *Vedāṅgas*, came early into existence as an essential part of the Brahmin's training.[15] Among them *Śīkṣa* deals with the precise and faultless pronunciation; *Kalpa* discusses the details of ritual; *Vyākaraṇa* is the study of grammar, including some linguistics and philology; *Nirukta* treats the etymology of unusual and rare words; *Chaṇḍa* specializes in the explanation and practice of verse meters; and *Jyotiṣa* teaches planetary science, astronomy and astrology together, which was (and is) the instrument for determining the right moment for religious acts.[16] Though the *Vedāṅgas* are not part of the *śruti,* they are indispensable for those who have to perform Vedic rituals.

The thoroughness of these auxiliary sciences is quite extraordinary: to hand down the text of the hymns of the Ṛgveda orthologically, special mnemonic and reading techniques were developed. In addition to memorizing the text of the saṃhitās, the Vedic student had to learn the *pāda-patha* (the "word text," where the words were given in their original and complete form), the *krama-patha* ("step text," where each word was connected both with the preceding and the following word), the *jaṭa-patha* ("braided text," involving a reverse recitation), and the *ghana-patha* ("dense text," involving a complicated series of combinations and retro-combinations of words). A class of works called *Pratiśākhyas* described all the grammatical changes necessary for constituting the *saṃhitā* text out of the *pāda-patha.*[17]

The hymns themselves were never simply read out, but they had to be recited in an exactly prescribed pitch. Through Vedic recitation "brahmins gain merit and perfection and contribute to the sacred order of the universe."[18] Although the text of the Ṛgveda remained unchanged throughout India for thousands of years, different styles of recitation developed and were preserved in different parts of the country. The recitation had to be accompanied by precisely studied movements of the right arm and of the fingers according to accent and pitch. A young Brahmin had to go through many years of intensive training before he was qualified to officiate at a sacrifice. Because it was believed that a single mispronounced syllable could spoil the entire costly arrangement, extreme care was taken to perfect the Brahmin's training. Harsh punishment awaited the offender: a Brahmin who read the Veda without the correct movements of the hand faced expulsion from his caste; one who did not pay attention to the exact length of the syllables, to cadences and tunes, was threatened with being reduced to ashes and being reborn as a vile animal. The effect of the mantra was supposed to depend on its correct pronunciation rather than on the meaning of a sentence or the action of a deity. The *Śatapatha Brāhmaṇa* contains a telling myth: Tvaṣṭṛ, whose son Viśvarūpa had been killed by Indra, is about to conjure up, with a soma-libation, *Vṛtra indraśatruḥ,* the one who cannot fail to kill Indra because in him all the powers of the *devas* are combined. Because of a wrong accent in the infallible mantra, the one who was destined to kill Indra is destined—unfailingly—to be killed by Indra.[19] This belief in the literal efficacy of the mantra was analyzed and systematized in one of the recognized orthodox schools, the *Pūrva Mīmāṁsā.*

The *Brāhmaṇas,* a voluminous collection of writings, deal mainly with explanations of the sacrifice and contain early versions of many myths. They are also considered part of *śruti.*[20] The *Āraṇyakas,* the forest treatises, and the Upaniṣads. The two latter classes of writings are sometimes intermingled,[21] and they contain similar materials. The Upaniṣads are also called the Vedānta, the end of the Veda: they mark the latest part of the Veda, and they are regarded as the end and aim of the Veda. Within *śruti* a twofold division obtains: *Karmakaṇḍa* and *Jñānakaṇḍa.* The Vedic *Saṃhitās* and the *Brāhmaṇas,* which center around the sacrifice, make up the "part of action," systematized by *Pūrva Mīmāṃsā;* the *Āraṇyakas* and the Upaniṣads, with their emphasis on speculation and intuitive knowledge, form the *Jñānakaṇḍa,* the part of wisdom. This has found its systematic development in the numerous schools of Vedānta philosophy. The most authoritative Vedāntins quote from about 15 Upaniṣads; the popular modern editions contain 108 Upaniṣads.[22] Besides these at least 100 more Upaniṣads have been composed in recent centuries; even today certain sects and schools mold their teachings in the form of a Upaniṣad to lend it greater authority with the orthodox.[23] Each one of the Upaniṣads belongs to one of the Vedic Saṃhitās; thus there are *Ṛgveda Upaniṣads, Sāmaveda Upaniṣads* and so on. Among the Saṃhitās again, different traditions are distinguished, pointing out the fact that Vedic religion developed within, and was handed over by, a number of families, each of which kept its own particular traditions and rites within the general frame of Vedic religion.[24] The Upaniṣads in their imagery show quite clearly the specific family relationship. Thus the *Bṛhadāraṇyaka Upaniṣad,* belonging to the white *Yajurveda,* begins its cosmogonic and soteriological speculations with a metaphorical explanation of the horse sacrifice, which is the specific symbol of the white *Yajurveda* and treated prominently in the *Śatapatha Brāhmaṇa,* which belongs to the same school. The Upaniṣads contain a good deal of 'mystical' practice and theory, but they have also numerous allusions to the rites and ceremonies of the Vedas.

The later Upaniṣads are compendia of doctrines of various schools of Hinduism and really belong to the Āgamas, a class of literature considered as authoritative and as ancient as the Vedas by the followers of Vaiṣṇavism, Śaivism, and Śāktism; that is, by the majority of Hindus.

The term *āgama*, Scripture, is often used to denote all writings considered revealed by the Hindus. More specifically the term is used in connection with non-Vedic scriptures, considered to be revelation by particular Hindu sects. Thus we have traditional lists of 108 *Pañcarātra* or Vaiṣṇava Āgamas (also called *Saṃhitās*), 28 Śaiva Āgamas, and 77 Śākta Āgamas (also called *Tantras*). Each of these sects has numerous subsects and the recognition of a scripture depends on one's affiliation with one of them.[25] In the most specific sense the scriptures of the Śaivites are called *āgamas*. They normally consist of four parts, called *jñāna* or knowledge, *yoga* or concentration, *krīya* or rituals, and *cārya* or rules for daily life. The last two parts are considered to be the most important and are usually the most extensive, because they affect worship and life in a major way. This class of scriptures had been for a long time neglected by Western scholars. After the pioneering work of O. Schrader,[26] others followed, and a steady stream of text editions and translations has been appearing lately. The Āgamas have been found important not only as sources for the beliefs and practices of the sects by which they have been adopted as scriptures but also for the study of the cultural history of India. They often contain detailed information on temple building, image making, and performance of public festivals. According to G. S. Murti:

> The *Āgama* is fundamentally a *Sādhana Śāstra* . . . it prescribes a particular way of life and a practical course of self-discipline in conformity with the theoretical teachings of its philosophy. It also governs, to a considerable degree, the forms of worship performed in the temples and the forms of rituals performed in the homes. . . . For the past hundreds of years the Vedic sacrifices or *yajñas* have largely given place—specially in South India—to resplendent rituals of temple-worship based on the Āgamas . . . [27]

The Purāṇas, another large class of sacred books of Hinduism, about which more detail is provided in the next chapter, are considered scripture too by some Hindu sects. Thus Vaiṣṇavas would quote the *Viṣṇu Purāṇa* and the *Bhāgavata Purāṇa* side by side with the Upaniṣads as equal in authority. Puraṇās as well as āgamas make claims to be direct revelations of the god with whom they are affiliated and contain numerous passages in which the Supreme God is the speaker and promulgator of commands. The more general Hindu practice would assign them a place within *smṛti*.[28]

The Bhagavadgītā has acquired a special position within Hinduism: it calls itself an Upaniṣad, claiming the authority of the *śruti.* It no doubt comes from the Vedānta tradition, but it also shows strongly Āgama influences; traditional authorities of Vedānta philosophy consider it as the *smṛti-prasthāna.*

In between *śruti* and *smṛti* come the numerous sūtras, short compendia summarizing the rules concerning public sacrifices (*Śrautasūtras*), domestic rites (*Gṛhyasūtras*), and general religious law (*Dharmasūtras*)—collectively called the *Kalpasūtras.* Because they do not usually contain new revelation, they are not quoted in doctrinal arguments.[29]

SACRED TRADITION: *SMṚTI*

Smṛti, literally, "that which has been remembered," tradition, constitutes the second highest religious authority. The term *smṛti* is used in either a narrower sense, comprising only the *Dharmaśāstras,* or in a wider sense, including *Itihāsa* and Purāṇa. The *smṛtis* in the narrow sense are associated with family traditions within Vedic religion. Their rules are therefore not always identical and in case of doubt each Brahmin was bound to follow his own *smṛti* rather than any other authority. The *smṛtis* as we have them today must have been preceded by centuries of development: the many references to former law givers and scholars establish again an unbroken succession of *dharma.*[30]

Among the *smṛtis* the *Manusmṛti* occupies a special place and has been more widely accepted than any other such code. Manu is considered to have been the ancestor of the entire human race and the lawgiver for all humankind; he did not make the law but promulgated the revealed dharma as it applied to different classes of society. The castes and the regulation of life according to the *caturvarṇāśrama* scheme are connected with creation itself, the description of which forms the first part of the book. After dealing with what one expects from a law book—rules for castes, duties of individual classes of people, civil and criminal law, sacrifices and atonements—the book concludes with an excursus on transmigration and supreme bliss.[31] Although it certainly allows us glimpses of social life in ancient India we must bear in mind that such books often do not reflect the actual conditions but an ideal aimed at by the authorities.[32] Among the numerous other *smṛtis, Yajñavalkyasmṛti* and *Viṣṇusmṛti* deserve special mention. The latter already includes a Vaiṣṇava interpretation of dharma.[33]

For daily life *smṛti* is often of greater importance than *śruti*; it affects the life of every Hindu in many details. The most orthodox Hindus are called the *smārtas,* followers of tradition, which still influences Indian society to a very large degree.[34] A good deal of the material of both *śruti* (in the Vedic sense) and *smṛti* has been incorporated into *Itihāsa-Purāṇa,* literally, "ancient history." It comprises the two great epics, the Mahābhārata and the Rāmāyaṇa and the 18 *Mahāpurāṇas;* some schools claim the title also for a large number of so-called *Upapurāṇas.*[35] Because these books are written in a more popular style, containing many stories and examples, they have found a place in the heart of the Indian masses and even today probably exert a much greater influence on the mind and imagination of the majority of Indian people than any other literature. The Mahābhārata and the 18 *Mahāpurāṇas* are said to have been composed by Vyāsa Kṛṣṇadvaipayana, the same *ṛṣi,* who according to tradition, compiled the Veda in response to revelation (see Figure 4.1). This enhances the authority of these books as sources of religion and law. It is in the Purāṇas, however, that the split between the various branches of Hinduism becomes most pronounced, and many chapters in them are narrowly sectarian in character.[36]

Figure 4.1 Sage Vyāsa dictating the Mahābhārata to Gaṇeśa

The core of the Purāṇas may well be as old as the Vedas; we read in some Upaniṣads that Purāṇas were narrated during the protracted sacrifical sessions. The Purāṇas quite frequently contain the full or expanded versions of myths alluded to in the Vedic hymns, and tales of heroes and gods even antedating the Veda may have been preserved in them. Attempts to reconstruct the Ur-Purāṇa or the "Original Purāṇa Saṃhitā" have not been very successful, and therefore scholars have concentrated on studies of the *Vāyu-Purāṇa* as most probably containing most of its ancient form.[37]

The texts of the epics and Purāṇas that we have in our printed editions has been fixed only between the fourth and the tenth centuries C.E., but the materials contained in them belong very often to a much earlier period. The Purāṇas have been long neglected by modern scholars; only recently has their value as sources for historical and geographical information been vindicated. For a knowledge of popular Hinduism as it is and has been for some centuries, they are indispensable.

Itihāsa and Purāṇa have, in the course of time, absorbed almost the entire religious literature, including the philosophical speculation of the *darśana,* so that the average pious Hindu could claim to have *śruti* and *smṛti,* and *nyāya*—the whole religion—while reading a Purāṇa.

THE INTERPRETATION OF THE REVEALED WORD: *PRAMĀṆA*

Nyāya or *pramāṇa,* logical argument or rational proof, is the third avenue of religious knowledge in Hinduism. *Nyāya,* too, is used in a general sense of logical proof and as the specific name of a school of thought which specialized in logic and epistemology.[38] All Hindu theologians clarify at the beginning of their treatises their evaluation of the traditional six modes of knowing, determining which of them they consider as means for religious knowledge. These modes are *pratyākṣa* or sense perception, *anumāna* or inference, *śabda* or authority (especially of scriptures), *upamāna* or analogy, *arthāpatti* or hypothetical supposition, and *abhāva* or nonperception. Religious knowledge derives mostly from *śabda,* the Word. Centuries before the West had developed its own brand of linguistic analytical philosophy, Indian theologians had evolved the most subtle philosophy of language, in whose controversies many interesting problems of a theological nature are raised. As T. R. V. Murti says: "Indian philosophy has rightly considered language and thought as intimately related. The *Nyāya-Vaiśeṣika* is essentially a philosophy of *padārtha,* the meaning of words. As in Aristotle, here also categories of language are categories of Being. . . . Both the *Pūrva* and *Uttara Mīmāṃsā* do not profess to be anything more than an exegesis of the Revealed Word (the Veda)."[39] The most important contributions to the elucidation of the Word have been made by the *Pūrva Mīmāṃsā* and the grammarians. For the Brahmanical tradition language itself is of divine origin, the Spirit descending and embodying itself in phenomena, assuming various guises and disclosing its real nature to the sensitive soul.[40] The *Mīmāṃsakas* analyze the problem: What makes a word meaningful? They found as answer that it is the connection of the word with *akṛti,* the Uncreated Idea that as such is incomprehensible and never exhausted by the individual word. *Śabda* is in this form ever-present and eternal. We do not always perceive it, because its perception depends on its manifestation through the physical word sound. If it were not eternal the word could not be understood every time it is uttered. The word we speak and hear is only a partial manifestation of an eternal, meaningful reality; it is not produced by our utterance. Because the word is not an effect, it is not perishable either.[41]

The school of Pāṇini, the grammarian, developed this *śabda* philosophy further in the theory of *sphoṭa.* Etymologically *sphoṭa* means a boil that, when opened, suddenly ejects its contents. Applied to the problem here, it illustrates the fact that the meaning of a word appears suddenly after the syllables have been pronounced—none of the individual syllables conveys either part or the whole of the meaning. Thus they say: "The eternal word, called *sphoṭa,* without parts and the cause of the world, is verily Brahman. Thus it has been declared by Bhartṛhari: 'Brahman without beginning or end is the indestructible essence of speech—it shines forth in the meaning of all things and out of it comes the whole world'!"[42] Ultimately, according to this school, all words denote the Supreme Brahman, and they maintain that "he who is well-versed in the Word-Brahman attains to the Supreme Brahman."[43] Language had been one of the main concerns of Indians throughout the ages. Pāṇini in the fourth century B.C.E., wrote "the first scientific grammar," unsurpassed as a single-handed achievement even today. His *Aṣṭādhyāyī*[44] introduces a perfect phonetic system of the Sanskrit alphabet, offers an astonishingly complete analysis of the contemporary linguistic materials, and is the first work to trace words to a limited number of verbal roots.[45] There were grammarians before him as his references reveal, and there followed others, notably Kātyāyana and Patañjali[46] to complete and develop the work. Similarly the Dravidians occupied themselves with linguistic studies of which the *Tolkāppiam* is particularly renowned for its age and its perception.[47] Language itself, and not only the scriptures, was considered "divine," an attribute that even extended to the characters in which it was written.[48] Learning the language, especially studying grammar, was considered a spiritual discipline.

VEDIC INTERPRETATION

It is in the study of the Veda in the strict sense, that Western and Indian scholarship disagree most sharply. Modern Western Veda scholarship was initiated by Eugéne Burnouf in Paris (1801–1852) and reached a first peak in the work of his two pupils Rudolph Roth (1821–1895) and Friedrich Max Müller (1823–1903). Roth provided the educated European public with the first detailed and accurate knowledge of the Veda but he also held on to European aims in the study of the Veda: according to him the study of the Veda was not meant "to ascertain the meaning which Sāyaṇa or Yakṣa attributed to the hymns"[49] but to read the hymns as "lyrics" separate from the "theological" background. Friedrich Max Müller was the first to edit and see the entire Ṛgveda Saṁhitā published together with Sāyaṇa'a commentary; and he received respect from the Indian paṇḍits for this. His translations, however, were "Western" in outlook and intention. Among Western scholars R. Pischel (1849–1908) and K. F. Geldner (1852–1921) were the only ones to consider the "Ṛgveda as a purely Indian document to be interpreted, not with the help of comparative linguistics or mythology, but with the later, even classical literature of the subcontinent."

There are, by now, several complete translations of the Ṛgveda into Western languages. Each of them is unsatisfactory.[50] Jan Gonda considers the Ṛgveda an "untranslatable corpus" and concludes:

> The distance in time, space and cultural environment between the authors of the Veda and modern Indologists, the incompleteness of our sources, the reinterpretation suggested by the Indian traditionalists and the prejudices and limitations of modern scholarship itself have contributed to a deplorable state of affairs. The very plurality of meanings so frequently given in our dictionaries show that a modern lan-

> guage cannot in many cases offer one single equivalent of an ancient Indian term . . . [51]

According to traditional Indian rules the Veda could be interpreted in three ways, the choice of alternatives being left to the interpreter. Thus one could understand the hymns as relating to either sacrificial rites (*adhiyajña*) or to deities (*adhidaivata*) or the Self (*adhyātma*). To explain the widely divergent interpretations of the Veda—some modern Hindus believe that the Vedas contain the principles of nuclear physics or that Western scientific progress was due to the "stealing of the Veda" from India in the nineteenth century—it may be helpful to remember with R. N. Dandekar that "though the Veda was regarded as the final authority, complete freedom was allowed in its interpretation."[52]

In the period of perhaps close to 4000 years since the hymns of the Veda came into existence, and through which the text has been preserved with unparalleled fidelity, the meaning given to the words of the Veda has undergone several drastic changes. The very use of the word *vid*, from which the name *Veda* is derived, in the hymns themselves suggests that the Vedic texts were "viewed as being verbal expressions of sacred knowledge."[53] The hymns describe and praise the (Vedic) gods, whom to know was the privilege of the Āryans, and whose worship secured their protection. Speaking was considered a very important activity, and addressing the gods counted as prerogative of the highest class of people, the Brahmins, who took the very name of their *varṇa* from the designation of the sacred word. *Brahman*, derived from the root *bṛh* = to grow, to become great, was originally identical with the Vedic word that makes people prosper: words were the principal means to approach the gods who dwelled in a different sphere. It was not a big step from this notion of "reified speech-act" to that "of the speech-act being looked at implicitly and explicitly as a means to an end."[54] In RV 3, 53 Viśvamitra claims that his powerful words (*brahman*) protect his Bhārata clan, in contrast to the speakers of false speech, the non-Āryans, whose words are like a milkless cow and bear neither flowers nor fruit;[55] the Veda is the source of everything good and beneficial. No wonder, because the "gods themselves created the godly speech."[56] Vedic prayer, *brahman*, reified and personified, resulted in the figures of the creator god Brahmā and later in the Upaniṣadic notion of Brahman as the metaphysical principle of everything and the hidden ground of reality.[57] The word—*vāc*, of feminine gender—appears in the famous *Vāk-sūkta* of the *Ṛgveda* (10.125) as the Goddess singing her own praises as sustainer of the gods and preserver of the world. When the texts of the Veda were used exclusively in the context of the Vedic sacrifice (*yajña*) the sacrifice was considered the source of the (by now established collections) three Vedas and were used instrumentally as part of the mechanism of the sacrifice, for which it did not matter what intrinsic meaning the words had. Kautsa, a teacher mentioned in the *Nirukta* by Yāska (ca. 500 B.C.E.), a work devoted to an etymology of Vedic words that were no longer understood by ordinary people, held that the word of the Veda was no longer understood as meaningful 'normal' speech but as a fixed sequence of sounds, whose meaning was obscure beyond recovery. Although the text itself was preserved through a variety of mnemonic devices (*vikritis* = modifications), the preservation of meaning obviously was more difficult. The difficulty had much to do with changing paradigms of thought. Because writing was considered sacrilegious, efforts were made to transmit the sounds of the text in their proper sequence without paying as much attention to its understanding.

Subhash C. Kak, a computer engineer by profession, has recently come up with a fascinating "decoding" of the Ṛgveda that might have immense implications for our understanding not only of the Ṛgveda. According to him "the *Ṛgveda* is a Stonehenge in words," an astronomical code. By using clues from the *Śatapatha Brāhmaṇa* that refer to the "Veda as an altar of words" and comparing instructions for the building of Vedic fire altars with astronomical data, he arrived at startling conclusions concerning the observational skills of the Vedic Indians and the astronomical information contained in the Ṛgveda as a whole and in some hymns in particular. In his opinion "altars were man's way of trying to reach the sky. So is this book. Its entire makeup represents space and sky. It is clearly a symbolic altar."[58] Kak believes that the astronomical paradigm was lost about 3000 years ago and replaced by a different one, which made it impossible to recognize the astronomical information contained in the Ṛgveda.

The effort of the grammarians went in the direction of preserving and interpreting the Vedic texts for ritual application, not for cosmological understanding. Patañjali, the author of the Mahābhāṣya, declares *veda-rakṣa*, preservation of the Vedic text the first and foremost task of Sanskrit grammar. Its second most important task was to supply rules for the modification of Vedic texts in ritual settings. The duty of Brahmans was to study the text and learn its proper pronunciation. A purely instrumental use of the Veda was promoted through *Mīmāṁsā*. As M. M. Deshpande has it: "The Vedas have come a long way from being living speech-acts of certain Āryan priests of ancient India, and the Indian tradition now reveres them mostly as preserved sacred texts which are chanted in ritual performances and which remain only in a theoretical sense that basic texts of modern Hinduism."[59]

THE POWER OF THE REVEALED WORD

Words of blessing and curses were always taken seriously by the Hindus; an almost material substantiality was attached to them, which would bring about their realization almost automatically. The mantra, used in connection with the Vedic sacrifice, works without fail. The Word is a power that makes the gods subject to human will. "Brahman is the word," and the Brahmin is the keeper and lord of it. Speech itself was addressed as a deity as early as in the time of the Ṛgveda.[60] In later Hinduism the body of a divinity was considered to consist of mantras, which are identical with cosmic processes. No sacrifice could be performed without words. The *Atharvaveda* has mantras for and against everything: mantras to cure fever and illness, to awaken love and affection, to raise enmity and hatred and to make sick and kill an enemy. Tantric Hinduism operated with esoteric syllables that were meaningless for the non-initiate but full of significance and power for the one who had received *dīkṣā*.[61]

The most famous, most powerful and most mysterious of all mantras is OM [AUM], also called *prāṇava*, the ur-mantra. Many expositions have been brought forward, none of them fully convincing. The texts that speak of OM suggest that it has to be understood from within the context of the mantra-theory. A mantra need not have an intelligible word meaning; it is the sound equivalent of some reality and at the same time the medium by which this otherwise transcendent reality is reached. OM is not a concept of something but it is the *śabda-brahman*, the Supreme Being in the form of sound. It is the primeval sound, the medium between pure, spiritual *brahman* and the concrete material world. The *Chāṇḍogya Upaniṣad* calls OM the *all-word*.[62] Through the identification of important concepts and beings the mantra OM, otherwise empty, is filled with concepts and meaning. The recitation of OM, on the one hand, reduces all beings into the nothing of OM, "the image of the supreme reality." On the other hand, the recitation makes OM itself meaningful without, however, identifying it with any particular being. The *Māṇḍukya Upaniṣad* identified AUM with the four stages of consciousness: *A* stands for the waking state, *U* for dream, *M* for deep sleep; *AUM* in its totality corresponds to *turīya*, the transcendent state. There is no logical proof for the statement 'Om is Brahman'[63]—it is *śruti*, revelation! "OM—this syllable is the whole world. Its further explanation is: the past, the present and the future—everything is just the word OM. And whatever else that transcends threefold time—that too is just the word OM. . . . OM is the *ātman*."[64] OM stands at the beginning of every hymn and every religious action, as well as of every recitation of a sacred text. With OM everything comes to a conclusion.

Because the sacred texts themselves have the quality of mantras, the opinion could develop that it is ultimately unimportant whether their meaning is understood or not. Many Brahmins who traditionally function at the occasions where the recitation of Vedic mantras is required do not really understand their meaning. The blessing derived from scripture does not depend on its comprehension, as the example of the *Śrīmad Bhāgavata Mahātmya* explains:

> He who daily recites the *Bhāgavata*, with the uttering of every single letter gathers as much merit as he would get by the gift of a brown cow. He who daily listens to half or even a quarter of a verse from the *Bhāgavata* gathers merit as from the gift of a thousand cows. It is better to keep half or quarter of a verse from the *Bhāgavata* in one's house than a collection of hundreds and thousands of other holy books. The glorious and holy *Bhāgavata* confers long life, freedom from disease and good health. He who recites it or listens to it is freed from all sins. To the man who prostrates before a copy of the *Bhāgavata* I give wealth.[65]

True to this interpretation, rich merchants arrange frequently for the reading of holy books over loudspeaker systems. Hired Brahmins recite the whole book without interruption. Hardly anyone listens—it is enough to recite the text faithfully to gain merit.

The whole life of a Hindu is enveloped in mantras. According to the most orthodox rules the conception of a child is supposed to be accompanied by the recitation of mantras; mantras are spoken over the expectant mother before birth; birth itself, name giving, initiation and marriage, purification and temple visits, death and cremation, all have to be performed with mantras. At the time of initiation an ascetic receives his personal mantra, whispered into the ear by the guru. This will be *his* mantra, his *daimonion* through which he distinguishes himself from others, it is a name that nobody knows but he and his master. He is not permitted to divulge this secret word unless he himself has to give *dīkṣā* to a disciple. Many Hindus carry mantras written on tiny pieces of paper in small capsules of copper, silver, or gold, fastened to arm, leg, or neck to protect themselves from certain illnesses or as a safeguard against the evil eye.

Time and again this faith in the effectiveness of the mantras leads to scurrilous happenings. Some years ago a businessman had lodged a complaint with the police against a *sādhu* who had boasted of a miraculous mantra through which he could double any given amount of money. With great expectations the businessman gave the holy man 2000 rupees. The *sādhu,* however, disappeared with the amount before he had doubled it.[66]

The understanding of Scripture as mantra[67] should, however, obscure neither the importance of the understandable content nor the tremendous effort of countless generations of Hindus to derive meaning from it and build up a coherent system of philosophico-religious thought. The desire for comprehension led at a very early stage to the elaboration of the sūtras, in which the essentials of certain branches of knowledge are condensed and systematized. One of the most important works of this kind are the *Brahmasūtras,* also called *Vedāntasūtras,* a compendium of 550 short statements that purports to render pithily the rich content of the main Upaniṣads. In it the attempt is made to expurgate the contradictions between different Upaniṣadic doctrines.[68] The voluminous commentaries written in the course of centuries upon this text are the main works of Vedānta. Similarly there are sūtras and *bhāṣyas* in all the other areas of Hindu thought. The desire to understand and to grasp the meaning of revealed truths has helped to produce some of the most penetrating works of philosophical theology. All questioning has definite limits; to question too much is to destroy the foundation upon which one stands and that alone allows one to engage in meaningful conversation.

5 *Itihāsa* and *Purāṇa*: The Heart of Hinduism

Śruti and *smṛti* are the two eyes of *dharma,* but the *Purāṇa* is its heart—on no other foundation does it rest but these three.

—*Devibhāgavata Purāṇa* XI, 1, 21

Itihāsa, (hi)story, is the collective term for the *Rāmāyaṇa* and the Mahābhārata, in Western publications usually called the *Great Epics.*[1] Related to them in character and importance are the Purāṇas, "ancient books," of which usually eighteen are accepted as *Mahāpurāṇas,* scriptures of the major Hindu traditions. The *Itihāsa-Purāṇas* are often called the *fifth Veda,* the Holy Book of the mass of people who were not entitled to study the four Vedas. Western scholarship has for a long time played down the importance of the *Itihāsa-Purāṇas,* partly because of their largely mythological contents, partly also because the existing texts and editions offered such a bewildering variety of readings, claiming ancient origins for obviously very recent interpolations and on the whole lacking the unity of theme and structure of epic or historical works in the Western sense. Indian tradition has always claimed great antiquity and authority for these writings; and though the more critical approach of modern Indian scholarship[2] has had to dismantle some of the cherished legends surrounding these books, it has tended on the whole to reinforce the traditional view and lent it greater importance.[3] As in several areas studied before, in the field of *Itihāsa-Purāṇa* studies, too, one has to respect the typically Indian character of this literature and its subject matter in order not to approach it with models of epics or history taken from elsewhere. The *Itihāsa-Purāṇas* are in a very real sense the heart of Hinduism, with all their strengths and weaknesses. Although the core of the *Itihāsa-Purāṇas* may possibly go back to the seventh century B.C.E., it is much more popular and much more alive today in India than any folk literary tradition of Europe.

Indian languages are strongly influenced by the vocabulary and the imagery of the *Itihāsa-Purāṇa*; the numerous rewritings of these texts in the Indian vernaculars are quite often the first major literary works in those languages. They have shaped Hindu religious and theological terminology and have become the medium for imparting secular knowledge as well. They are the source for much of Indian sociology, politics, medicine, astrology, geography and so on. Reading the *Itihāsa-Purāṇa* one can recognize the character of the Indian people, enlarged, typified, idealized—true in an uncanny sense. The persons described, their wishes and fantasies, their joys and sorrows, their emotions and ideas are much closer to the India of our own time than the venerable age of the books would suggest. Many Indians bear the names of the heroes and heroines of the *Itihāsa-Purāṇa*; most of them are familiar from early childhood with the stories contained in them, stories that combine entertainment with moral education. School readers in the Indian vernaculars are full of tales from them. Countless films and dramas take their subjects, often with very little modification, from these ancient books. Even simple people in the villages can speak with such enthusiasm and earnestness about Rāma and Sītā, about Kṛṣṇa and Arjuna, Hanuman and Rāvaṇa, Bharata and Lakṣmana that one realizes that contemporary India also identifies with the tradition expressed in the *Itihāsa-Purāṇa*. Broadcasting and television, printing presses and professional *Kathā* performers, films and musicals keep this "true history of India" alive, "history not of events, but of the urges and aspirations, strivings and purposes of the nation."[4] Whatever critical literary scholarship may or may not find out about the texts and their history, Hinduism without them would not be what it is. Anyone interested in the real religion of the Indian people today would find in the *Itihāsa-Purāṇa* the source for all aspects of the contemporary living religion of the masses.

THE GREAT EPIC

> The *Mahābhārata* represents a whole literature rather than a single homogeneous work; it constitutes a veritable treasure-house of Indian lore, both secular and religious. No other single work gives such insight into the innermost depths of the soul of the people. It is a "Song of Victory," commemorating the deeds of heroism in a war fought to avenge insults to womanhood and to maintain the just rights of a dynasty that

> extended the heritage of Bharata and knit together the North, East, West and South of India into one empire. It is a *purāṇa-saṃhitā* containing diverse stories of seers and sages, of beautiful maids and dutiful wives, of valiant warriors and saintly kings. It is also a magnificent poem describing in inimitable language the fury of the battle field, the stillness of the forest-hermitage, the majesty of the roaring sea dancing with billows and laughing with foam, the just indignation of a true daughter of a warrior line, and the lament of the aged mother of dead heroes. It is an authoritative book of law, morality, and social and political philosophy, laying down rules for the attainment of *dharma, artha* and *kāma,* called *trivarga,* and also showing the way of liberation expounding the highest religious philosophy of India.[5]

Since the sixth century C.E. the Mahābhārata has been called *śatasāhasrī saṃhitā,* the collection of 100,000 stanzas. In Western terms, this means that this huge work is four times as voluminous as the whole Bible, or eight times the text of the *Iliad* and the *Odyssey,* the greatest Greek epics, together. A work of this magnitude has its history. Generations of scholars have been busy trying to find the Ur-Mahābhārata within the huge mass of literature of the Great Epic. Attempts to strip away the various layers of narrative and arrive at the original saga have had as little success as the endeavor to explain the whole work as an invention designed to illustrate maxims of law.[6] The critical edition of the Mahābhārata, one of the greatest literary enterprises of any time in any language, did not even try to reconstruct the "original Mahābhārata," but aimed at constituting an "accepted text" by retaining all that was common to the numerous recensions, relegating to notes and appendices those portions that on account of their weaker textual evidence could be supposed to have been added after the final redaction around 400 C.E.[7] On the whole the traditional view has gained strength through the failure of the modern criticism regarding the origin and development of the Mahābhārata. Therefore many scholars today accept the view that the Mahābhārata underwent two major recensions: it began as *Jāya,* a poem about the victory of the Pāṇḍavas over the Kauravas, of about 7000 *ślokas.* This is supposed to have been the work of Vyāsa, also known as Kṛṣṇa Dvaipayana, the son of Parāśara and Satyavatī. It was augmented to about three times its former length in the *Bhārata* by Vaiśampayana, who recited it at the snake sacrifice of Janamejaya. The *Sūta,* who heard it there, related it as the Mahābhārata of 100,000 verses to the assembly of sages in the Naimiṣa forest during the sacrifice performed by Śaunaka.

The present edition of the Mahābhārata itself speaks of three beginnings:[8] *manvādi,* beginning from Manu, corresponding to the first twelve sub-*parvans* (sections) of the present work; *āstikādi,* beginning with Astika, comprising sub-*parvans* thirteen to fifty-three; *uparicarādi,* from sub-*parvan* fifty-four onward.

The text of the Mahābhārata that emerges in the critical edition is the form the work took after the Bhārgavas, a family of learned Brahmans, claiming descent from the Vedic sage Bhṛgu, who had specialized in dharma and *nīti,* rewrote it completely, making it primarily into a sourcebook of instruction on religious law. The new didactic materials were incorporated mainly in the *Śānti* and *Anuśāsana Parvans,* which now cover almost one-fourth of the whole Mahābhārata, raising the work to the rank of a *smṛti.* After this *Bhārgava-Mahābhārata* had become popular in India, the different regions developed their own recensions of it, incorporating material that seemed to be of local importance. The so-called northern and the southern recensions are the principal ones, differing by as much as a third of the full text. At some point, as yet unknown, the Mahābhārata was subdivided into 18 *parvans* (parts) of varying length: the smallest is the *Mahāprasthānika,* the seventeenth, with only 120 *ślokas*; the longest the *Śānti,* the twelfth, with 14,525 *ślokas.* Of greater importance is the subdivision into 98 sub-*parvans,* that topically subdivide the whole work into more congruous sections. As *khila-bhāga,* supplement to the Mahābhārata, the *Harivaṃśa,* a Kṛṣṇaite work is very often added in the editions; in itself it is a rather voluminous work of some 16,000 *ślokas.*[9]

The Mahābhārata consequently became a veritable encyclopedia, and it carries this verse about its own scope: Whatever is written here, may also be found elsewhere; but what is not found here, cannot be anywhere else either.[10]

Not content with the sheer mass of writing contained in it, which covers all possible aspects of secular and religious culture, traditional Hindu interpreters have widened the scope of its teaching exponentially, by explaining the Mahābhārata to have three different layers of meaning in each of its words. Thus Madhva, commenting on the aforementioned verse of the three beginnings, writes:

> The meaning of the *Bhārata,* in so far as it is a relation of the facts and events with which Śrī Kṛṣṇa and the Pāṇḍavas are connected, is *āstikādi,* or historical. That interpretation by which we find lessons on virtue, divine love, and the other ten qualities, on sacred duty and

> righteous practices, on character and training, on Brahmā and the other gods, is called *manvādi*, or religious and moral. Thirdly, the interpretation by which every sentence, word or syllable is shown to be the significant name, or to be the declaration of the glories, of the Almighty Ruler of the universe, is called *auparicara* or transcendental.[11]

A modern scholar, the initiator of the critical edition, took up this idea to explain the three planes on which the Mahābhārata must be understood in its complete meaning. On the mundane plane, the story deals with the realistic account of a fierce fratricidal war of annihilation with its interest centered on the epic characters. On the ethical plane the war is seen as a conflict between dharma and *adharma*, good and evil, justice and injustice, with the final victory of dharma. On the transcendental plane the war is fought between the higher and the lower self in man.

> Arjuna, the superman under the guidance of Kṛṣṇa, the Super-self, emerges successful in this conflict, after he has destroyed with the sword of knowledge the ignorance embodied in his illegitimate desires and passions symbolized by his relatives, teachers, elders and friends ranged on the other side. In this interpretation Śrī Kṛṣṇa is the *Paramātman*, and Arjuna the *Jīvātman*. Dhṛtarāṣṭra is a symbol of the vacillating ego-centric self, while his sons symbolize in their aggregate the brood of ego-centric desires and passions. Vidura stands for *Buddhi*, the one-pointed reason, and Bhīṣma is tradition, the time-bound element in human life and society.[12]

The main story of the Mahābhārata can be sketched out in a few lines.[13] Vicitravīrya, a king of the lunar dynasty, has two sons: Dhṛtarāṣṭra and Paṇḍu. According to custom Dhṛtarāṣṭra, the elder son is to succeed his father; but being born blind, his younger brother Paṇḍu is made king instead. Paṇḍu dies after a brief reign, leaving behind five minor sons from his two wives. Therefore the blind Dhṛtarāṣṭra assumes kingship. His hundred sons, the Kauravas, are growing up together with the five Pāṇḍavas, whom Dhṛtarāṣṭra appears to consider the rightful heirs. Duryodhana, the eldest among the Kauravas, however, claims the throne and attempts to eliminate the Pāṇḍavas through a series of criminal tricks. He refers to the fact that his father had been the eldest son and rightful heir to the throne and succeeds in exiling the Pāṇḍavas together with their common wife Draupadī. Duryodhana, thinking them to be dead, takes over the kingdom from his father.

During their sojourn in the forest the Pāṇḍavas, however, win allies and challenge Duryodhana to battle. To avoid a war, blind old Dhṛtarāṣṭra divides the kingdom into two parts, leaving one half to his own sons and giving the other half to the Pāṇḍavas. Yudhiṣṭhira, the eldest among the Pāṇḍavas, is installed as king of Indraprāsta, identified with the later Delhi; whereas Duryodhana remains king of Hastinapūra, the elephant fortress some 60 miles to the north. An uneasy peace prevails, riddled with quarrels and fights. During a visit to Indraprasṭha, Duryodhana falls into a pond. Draupadī finds the situation absurdly comical and breaks out in laughter. This loss of face has fatal consequences. Duryodhana challenges Yudhiṣṭhira to a game of dice where the winner takes all. Yudhiṣṭhira is carried away by his passion for gambling and loses everything to the Kauravas: his kingdom, his private possessions, his elephants, his brothers, himself, and finally Draupadī. Draupadī, on being called into the gambling den, refuses to come. The Kauravas rudely pull her in by the hair and tear off her clothes to humiliate her. Bhīma on seeing this takes a terrible oath: "May I never enter the resting place of my fathers unless I have torn open the breast of this stupid dog of a Bhārata in battle and drunk his blood!" Again, blind old Dhṛtarāṣṭra intervenes and prevails upon Duryodhana to return the kingdom to the Pāṇḍavas. This time Duryodhana does not give in: he demands that another round of dice be played with the imposition that the loser would have to go into the jungle for twelve years, remain incognito for one more year in the country, and only then be allowed to return openly. If during the thirteenth year they were found out, they would have to go back into exile for another twelve years. The Pāṇḍavas again lose the game and have to leave for the forest. The Mahābhārata fills the twelve years in the forest with beautiful stories through which the numerous hermits living there edify the refugees. They manage, in the thirteenth year, to get employment in the court of Virāṭa, without being recognized and appear at the beginning of the fourteenth year before the king to reclaim their kingdom. But Duryodhana is no longer willing to give up his empire. Hence both parties prepare for an all-out war.

The Great War, lasting for eighteen days, is described in 600 chapters. Using means both fair and foul, the Pāṇḍavas emerge as the victors. Very few, however, of those who entered the war on both sides, remain alive and the survivors' weeping and lamenting overshadows any joy that might accompany this hard-won victory. The Pāṇḍavas, although victorious, leave the kingdom in the hands of a younger relation and start towards the Himālayas to go to Indra's heaven. Four of the five brothers die on their way, only Yudhiṣṭhira reaches the goal. According to Indian tradition the Great War marks the beginning of the *Kaliyuga*, the Age of Strife, the age in which righteousness has given place to unrighteousness, where dharma is only one footed and humankind goes toward its inevitable doom. To give an example of one of the typical stories that abound in the Mahābhārata, one of the episodes from the *Āraṇyakaparvan*, the time when the Pāṇḍavas dwelt in the forest, may be related here.[14]

Toward the close of the Pāṇḍavas' exile, it happened that a deer carried away the firestone of a devout hermit. The man began to lament: "How shall I now offer my fire sacrifice, unable to light a fire?" He approached the Pāṇḍavas for help. They pursued the deer, but they could not catch it, because it was no ordinary deer. Exhausted and miserable they sat under a banyan tree and bewailed their fate: "So helpless and weak have we become; we cannot even render a small service to a Brahmin." Bhīma said: "Yes, it is true. We should have killed those scoundrels when they dragged Draupadī into the hall by her hair. Because we have not done it we have been reduced to such weakness!" Arjuna agreed with him: "I watched in silence while the vulgar creature insulted her. We have deserved our fate." Because Yudhiṣṭhira felt great thirst he asked Nakula to climb a tree to see whether there was a river or a pond close by. Nakula saw cranes and water plants in not too great a distance, so he went to fetch water. When he reached the pond he at once lay down to drink. No sooner had he dipped his hand into the water than he heard a voice: "Do not hurry! This pond is mine. Answer first my questions, then you may drink!" Nakula's thirst was too strong, he drank at once; immediately he dropped down lifeless. When Nakula did not return for a long time, Yudhiṣṭhira sent Sahadeva to fetch water. He met with the same fate as Nakula. Arjuna and Bhīma, too, sent after Sahadeva, did not return. Finally Yudhiṣṭhira had to go by himself. Seeing his four brothers dead beside the water, he began to lament: "Is this to be the end? You have been taken away just when our exile was coming to its end! The gods themselves have forsaken me in my unhappy state!" Still grieving he stepped into the pond to drink. The voice was heard again: "Your brothers died, because they would not listen to me. First give an answer to my questions, then drink, for this pond is mine!" Yudhiṣṭhira asked for the questions. The *yakṣa* said: "What makes the sun shine each day?" Yudhiṣṭhira replied: "The power of *brahman.*"—"What saves a man from every danger?" "Courage saves a man from all dangers!"—"Studying which science does a man become wise?" "Not through the study of any science but by living in the company of wise men does a man become wise!"—"Who is a more noble protector than the earth?" "The mother who brings up the children she has given birth to, she is a more noble protector than the earth."—"Who is higher than heaven?" "The father."—"Who is swifter than Wind?" "The mind!"—"Who is more miserable than a straw blown about the wind?" "A careworn heart!"—"Who is the traveler's friend?" "The willingness to learn!"—"Who is the husband's friend?" "The wife."—"Who is man's companion in death?" "Dharma alone accompanies a man on his lonely journey after death!"—"Which is the largest vessel?" "The earth, for it contains all other vessels!"—"What is happiness?" "Happiness is the result of proper conduct!"—"What makes a man popular by abandoning it?" "Pride! Because if a man renounces it, he will be loved by all!"—"Which loss brings joy and not mourning?" "Anger! If we give up anger we are no longer subject to suffering."—"What makes a person rich if he loses it?" "Desire! If we give it up we shall be rich!"—"What makes a man a Brahmin? Is it birth, good conduct, or erudition? Answer rightly!" "Birth and erudition do not make a man a Brahmin, only good conduct does. No matter how erudite a man may be, if he is the slave of bad habits he is no Brahmin. Even if he is well-versed in the four Vedas, if he has got bad habits he belongs to a low class!"—"Which is the most surprising thing in this world?" "Every day people see other creatures leave for the abode of Yama, yet those that remain behind behave as if they were going to live forever. This really is the most astonishing thing in this world." In this manner the *yakṣa* asked many questions and Yudhiṣṭhira replied to them. In the end the *yakṣa* addressed him thus: "O King! One of your brothers will return to life. Which one do you want?" Yudhiṣṭhira thought for a while and then said: "May Nakula, he who is of the colour of a dark cloud, lotus-eyed, broad-shouldered, long-armed, he who lies here like a felled oak tree, may he return to life!" The *yakṣa* was content and asked: "Why did you prefer Nakula to Bhīma, who has the strength of 16,000 elephants? I have heard that Bhīma is your favorite! And why not Arjuna, whose skill with weapons is your protection? Tell me, why did you chose Nakula and not these two?" Yudhiṣṭhira replied: "Dharma is the only protection of man, not Bhīma and not Arjuna. If dharma is violated, man will be annihilated. Kuntī and Mādrī were my father's two wives. I am a son of Kuntī, she is not entirely bereft of children. To fulfill the law of righteousness I pray that Mādrī's son Nakula be returned to life!" The *yakṣa* liked Yudhiṣṭhira's sense of justice and returned all his brothers to life. In fact, he was Yama in disguise, the lord of death who had adopted the form of the deer and the *yakṣa* to test his son Yudhiṣṭhira, whom he now embraced and blessed: "Only a few days and the twelve years will be over. The thirteenth year will also pass and your enemies will not find you out. Your undertaking will be brought to a happy end!"

The story ends with a familiar promise: "Those who listen to the story of Yudhiṣṭhira's meeting with his father Yama will never tread on evil paths. They will never seek discord with their friends nor envy others for their wealth. They will never be victims of lust and will never set their hearts on things that pass away."

THE HINDU'S FAVORITE BOOK

The Rāmāyaṇa, since ancient times considered to be the composition of Vālmīki,[15] is shorter, more unified, more appealing, and even more popular than the Mahābhārata. In its present form it constitutes about one-quarter of the volume of the Mahābhārata, about 24,000 *ślokas*. A good deal of textual criticism has been applied by Western scholars to this work. Some assumed that the original core of the book was identical with the Buddhist *Daśaratha Jātaka,*[16] a theory that was given up when it was proven that this *Jātaka* is a much later work. The traditional Indian view seems to emerge as historically substantially correct: before being reduced to writing, the story of Rāma, the Prince of Ayodhyā, was sung as a ballad by wandering bards in the assemblies of kings. The Rāmāyaṇa itself says that the first recitation took place in the forest before a gathering of sages, the second in the streets of Ayodhyā, and the third and final one in the palace of Rāma, after the horse sacrifice, through which Rāma confirmed his enthronement. It is not difficult to discern in the present Rāmāyaṇa text interpolations that often interrupt the flow of the narrative: Purāṇic stories, genealogical lists, imitations of motifs from the Mahābhārata, repetitions, and perhaps again under Bhārgava influence, additions of ethical, philosophical, and other didactic materials.[17]

In its numerous reworkings in the vernaculars the Rāmāyaṇa has become an inspiration for millions of Hindus. Mahātmā Gandhi praised the *Rāmacaritamānasa* of the sixteenth century poet Tulasīdāsa[18] as the greatest work in the entire religious literature of the world; countless Indian villagers know a large number of its *dohas*, summarizing not only the story of Rāma but also epigrammatically expressing the accumulated wisdom of India. Scholars have hailed it as "the perfect example of the perfect book."

The *Vālmīki Rāmāyaṇa*, also called *Ādikāvya*, or first epic poem, recently appeared in a critical edition. Work on this edition has brought to light a great number of recensions in various parts of the country, which can be grouped into a northern and a southern family of texts, with considerable differences. The southern text, which is less smooth and polished than the northern one, seems to be the older one.[19] The hypothesis of an Ur-Rāmāyaṇa, from which both recensions stem, has been considered quite valid. The present text is divided into seven *kāṇḍas* (parts) of fairly equal length.[20] Most scholars assume that the first and the last are later additions to the core of the story. As regards the interpretation of the Rāma story, most Western scholars consider the original tale as a ballad about a human hero, later made into an *avatāra* of Viṣṇu when the *avatāra* doctrine had become popular. Indians are inclined to consider Rāma a historical figure. They also assume that Vālmīki considered Rāma a divine being from the very beginning.[21]

The basic Rāma story as told by Vālmīki is quite brief.[22] In the *Bālakāṇḍa* we hear about the birth and childhood of Rāma, son of king Daśaratha and queen Kauśalyā, one of the three wives of the king, besides Kaikeyī, who bore Bhārata, and Sumitrā, the sons of whom were Lakṣmana and Śatrughna. The marriage of Rāma with Sītā, the lovely daughter of king Janaka of Videha is narrated at great length. The king had offered his daughter in marriage to any hero who would be able to bend the bow of Rudra, that was in his possession. The bow, which no previous suitor was even able to lift from the floor, becomes a willing instrument in Rama's hand.[23] Rāma and Sītā spend a brief happy time at Ayodhyā after their marriage. Daśaratha, feeling the burden of his age, intends to crown Rāma king and retire. Everything is prepared, and there is general rejoicing among the people of Ayodhyā, for Rāma has been a very popular prince. In the very night before the *abhiśeka*, however, Mantharā, the hunchbacked evil-minded servant of Kaikeyī, Daśaratha's favorite wife, succeeds in poisoning Kaikeyī's mind by suggesting that if Rāma became king, he would try to kill his potential rivals—the first of whom would be Bhārata, Kaikeyī's only son. Worried, Kaikeyī looks for means to prevent the coronation, and Mantharā comes up with some devilish advice: a long time ago Kaikeyī had carried the unconscious Daśaratha from the battlefield, thus saving his life. Daśaratha, recovered, promised to fulfill any two wishes Kaikeyī would utter. Kaikeyī had stored up this credit; now she wants to make use of it. Rāma should be banned for fourteen years into forest exile and her own son Bhārata should be crowned king. Daśaratha pleads and threatens, entreats and curses Kaikeyī, to no avail. He must keep his word. Bhārata is not in Ayodhyā at the time of this tragic happening, he has no hand in it. Rāma receives the bad news with a manly spirit; he consoles his father and expresses his willingness to go into the forest exile to help his father keep his promise. He even visits Kaikeyī to show that he does not bear a grudge against her. Sītā and Lakṣmana ask to be allowed to share Rama's exile. When the three of them leave, the whole town of Ayodhyā is plunged into grief and Daśaratha dies soon afterward of a broken heart. Bhārata on his return to Ayodhyā learns what has happened; he refuses to accept the kingship and proceeds with Śatrughna into the forest to persuade Rāma to return as king. Rāma refuses: his father's word is sacred to him. Bhārata then places Rama's sandals upon the throne, considering himself as his trustee till the time of Rama's return.

Rama's sojourn in the forest is filled with many incidents similar to those narrated in the Mahābhārata about the Pāṇḍava's exile. Fights against the *rakṣasas*, the hobgoblins and forest spirits of Indian folklore, interpreted by many Western scholars as the dark-skinned aboriginals, entertaining and edifying stories from forest hermits, and a variety of other adventures fill the *Āraṇya-kāṇḍa*. Vālmīki is a master of poetical painting in his descriptions of the beauty of the forests. Because Rāma kills many of the *rakṣasas*, making the forest a safe and peaceful place to live in for pious hermits, he befriends many Brahmins and becomes the enemy of the *rakṣasas*. One day Śurpaṇakhī, Ears-like-winnowing-fans, the sister of Rāvaṇa, the powerful king of the *rakṣasas*, comes to Rama's dwelling place. She is infatuated with Rāma and has turned herself into a beautiful woman. She asks Rāma to marry her. Rāma tells her that he is already married and counsels her to try her luck with his brother Lakṣmana. When he, too, refuses her, she returns to Rāma. That makes Sītā burst out laughing. Śurpaṇakhī is enraged, assumes a terrible form and threatens to devour Sītā. Lakṣmana cuts off her ears and nose and sends her home in disgrace. Rāvaṇa is infuriated and bent on vengeance. On his insistence the demon Marica transforms himself into a gold-spotted deer, appearing before Rama's hut, so beautiful and enticing that Sītā pleads and weeps, threatens and curses Rāma to get the deer for her. Rāma, suspecting an evil trick of a *rakṣasa*, prevails on Lakṣmana to guard Sītā and not to leave her alone under any circumstances. Rāma meanwhile pursues the elusive gold-spotted deer, killing it at last with an arrow. Dying, the demon cries out: "O Lakṣmana, O Sītā," sounding as if Rāma was in mortal danger. True to Rama's word Lakṣmana does not want to leave Sītā. But Sītā, quite mad with fear for Rāma, accuses Lakṣmana of evil intentions and threatens to kill herself. Lakṣmana now goes in search of Rāma, finds him quite unharmed, and returns with him to the hermitage only to find Sītā gone. Rāvaṇa, disguised as a pious hermit, had invaded the place in Lakṣmana's absence and had carried her off to Laṅka, his kingdom.[24] Rāma and Lakṣmana begin their search for Sītā. Many animals and trees give them clues. Jaṭayu, an aged vulture, who has been mortally wounded in his fight against Rāvaṇa, informs them about the identity of the abductor. They win numerous allies, the most important of them is Hanuman, the monkey-king, with his numerous troops. Hanuman's magic tricks are ultimately responsible for the success of the search. He can jump for miles and has the power to make himself as small as a mouse or as tall as a mountain. He finds out that Sītā is kept prisoner in Rāvaṇa's palace at Laṅka. Rāvaṇa, in a not ungentlemanly manner, tries to woo her with flatteries, promises, and threats; at one time he even produces a cutoff head that looks like Rama's. Sītā is unimpressed and remains faithful to Rāma. Hanuman visits Sītā, comforts her and carries messages between Rāma and his wife. At last Rāma prepares for war against Rāvaṇa. The monkeys build a bridge between Rameśvaran and Śrī Laṅka (the line of islands is even now called Hanumansetu, Hanuman bridge) across which the entire army invades Laṅka. A long and bloody battle ensues, in which both sides suffer heavy losses. Rāvaṇa has many powerful magic weapons at his disposal, and if it were not for Hanuman who fetches healing herbs from the Himālayas, Rāma and his friends would all be dead. Finally the monkey army storms Rāvaṇa's fortress city: Laṅka goes up in flames, and Sītā is reunited with Rāma. When the fourteen years of exile are over, Rāma triumphantly reenters Ayodhyā as king. But the happy end of the story, at which every reader rejoices is not the real end, after all. Because people entertain gossipy suspicions about Sita's fidelity, having spent a long time in another man's house, Rāma had asked Sītā to undergo a fire ordeal to prove her innocence. Sītā submits to it, passes the test, but despite her proven fidelity, nevertheless is sent off to the forest. After a long time she returns from the forest with her two sons and takes a final oath of purification: "I have never thought of another man but Rāma; may the earth receive me to confirm this! I have always worshipped only him in words, thoughts, and deeds; may mother earth receive me to confirm this! I have never known any man but Rāma; may the goddess earth accept me!" After these words the earth opens up and Sītā disappears in her.

The last chapters of the Rāmāyaṇa relate how Rāma, Bhārata, Śatrughna, and all the citizens of Ayodhyā leave the city and go to the River Sarayu. There Rāma and his brothers physically enter the body of Viṣṇu, thus proving their divine origin.

The beautiful language and the poetry of the Rāmāyaṇa would suffice to make it a favorite of the Indians; as well as this, they also admire Rama's obedience towards his father, his generosity toward Kaikeyī, Sita's fidelity in following Rāma into the jungle and during her captivity, Bhārata's and Lakṣmana's brotherly loyalty and the greatness and strength of Rāma. If ever there was an ancient literary work that is alive in our time, it is the Rāmāyaṇa! It is read and sung every day by numberless Hindus, humble and high; it is worshipped and held sacred and performed in *Rāma-Līlās* every year in small and big towns. After the monsoon rains are over, at the time of the Dasserah festival, people in villages and cities gather to re-enact the drama of Rāma and Sītā. The killing of Rāvaṇa and his retinue is the main attraction for small and big children. Depending on their means, each community erects tall figures on bamboo sticks, fills them with straw and covers them with colored paper, stuffing the limbs with firecrackers. At nightfall these demons are lit and explode to the delight of all; the forces of good, embodied in Rāma, have again proved victorious over the forces of evil, symbolized in Rāvaṇa.

"The Rāmāyaṇa will be read in this country of Bhārata as long as its rivers continue to flow and its mountains remain in their place" reads one verse, and the Hindu, who cherishes the Rāmāyaṇa, does so also to gain the award promised in one of its concluding *ślokas*: "Whoever reads this noble work that tells of Rama's deeds, he will be free from all his faults and sins; with all his kin and relatives he will go to heaven."[25]

The Mahābhārata and the Rāmāyaṇa have much in common; as well as having certain sections which have been borrowed from the Rāmāyaṇa and transposed into the Mahābhārata or vice versa, they reveal a common fund of mythology and a common mentality.[26]

THE PURĀṆAS: THE BIBLES OF HINDUISM

The Purāṇas, neglected and rejected by the rationalistic nineteenth century as representing a corruption of Vedic religion and childish fabulation[27] have regained, in Indological scholarship, too, the central place they have always occupied in living Hinduism.[28] According to Purāṇic tradition Brahma uttered the Purāṇas as the first of all the scriptures; only after this did he communicate the Vedas. As we have seen, some major schools of Hinduism accord the status of *śruti* to several of the Purāṇas, attributing equal age and authority to both Purāṇas and Vedas. According to the greatest authority in the field, R. C. Hazra, "it is difficult to say definitely how and when the Purāṇas first came into being, though their claim to great antiquity next only to that of the Vedas cannot be denied."[29] The word *purāṇa*, perhaps not yet in the precise sense of later time, occurs already in the *Atharva Veda*, the *Śatapatha Brāhmana*, the *Bṛhadāraṇyaka Upaniṣad*, and other early works.[30] According to Hazra,

> The way in which the *Purāṇa* has been connected with sacrifice as well as with the *yajus* in the *Atharvaveda*, the theory of the origin of the universe from sacrifice as expounded in the *Puruṣa-sūkta* of the *Ṛg-Veda* and the topics constituting the *pāriplava ākhyānas* or recurring narrations in the *aśvamedha* sacrifice, tend to indicate that the *Purāṇa*, as a branch of learning, had its beginning in the Vedic period and originated in the narrative portion (*ākhyāna bhāga*) of the Vedic sacrifice, which, in the *Brāhmaṇas*, is repeatedly identified with the god Prajāpati, the precursor of the later Brahmā, the creator.[31]

All the extant *Mahāpurāṇas*, eighteen in number, with, as tradition has it, altogether 400,000 *ślokas*, are said to have Vyāsa as their author. Textual criticism of the Purāṇas is even more complicated than in the case of the great epics; the sheer mass of material, the sectarian claims connected with quite a few of them and the great liberty taken by writers of all ages of interpolating passages into the Purāṇas, make any serious study of the Purāṇas at the present stage seem an almost hopeless undertaking.

The Purāṇas, representing the popular religious traditions, were never subjected to the process of codification through which the Vedic *sūktas* went, who were the official text at the official functions of state and had to be uniform. Having existed for centuries in oral versions, with many local variants at the same time, reduced to writing at very different times without following any strict rules, they probably cannot be brought out in any meaningful critical edition. Written Purāṇa texts, with many variants, have been around for many centuries and some sort of received text has developed that is often available in several printed editions. Motilal Banarsidass has recently reprinted all *Mahā-Purāṇas,* parallel to its projected fifty volume series of English translations. The undertaking of the Kashiraj Trust to bring out critical editions of the Purāṇas must be understood as an attempt to collate existing manuscripts and editions and establish some sort of accepted version, embodying what most text witnesses have in common. L. Rocher's argument against the possibility of critical editions is quite convincing: the Purāṇas were not meant to be books. There is a widely shared opinion among Indian scholars that centuries before the beginning of the Christian era, there was an "original Purāṇa Saṃhitā." According to V. S. Agrawala, Lomaharṣana, the original teacher of the Purāṇa taught the *Mūla-saṃhitā* to six pupils, the authors of the *Para-saṃhitās* of 4000 to 6000 *ślokas* each, dealing with essentially the same four topics, each constituting a *pāda*: *sarga* or creation of the world, *pratisarga* or dissolution, *manvantara* or world ages, and *vaṁśa* or genealogies. This original *catur-pāda* form is preserved in the extant *Vāyu Purāṇa* and the *Brahmanda Purāṇa.* The *Vāyu* is usually considered to come closest to the Ur-Purāṇa, and Agrawala thought he could recover from the present text of the *Vāyu Purāṇa* the *Mūlasaṃhitā* by eliminating some eighty spurious, interpolated chapters.

The *Amarakośa,* an ancient Sanskrit lexicon[32] defines *purāṇa* as *pañca-lakṣana,* having five characteristic topics; namely, the preceding four plus *vaṃśānucarita* or stories about the deeds of the descendants of the dynasties glorified in it.

The *Viṣṇu Purāṇa,* one of the oldest, conforms best to this pattern; but even here quite a number of additional topics are dealt with. In many other Purāṇas the "five topics" are barely touched; altogether the material illustrating *pañca-lakṣana* constitutes only about one-fortieth of the present texts. Important topics in addition to those already mentioned are the *puruṣārthas,* the four aims of life, namely, *artha* or wealth, *kāma* or enjoyment, dharma or rules for life, and *mokṣa* or spirituality; the *vratas* or religious observances; *śrāddha* or rites for departed ancestors; *tīrtha* or description of places of pilgrimage; *dāna* or gifts; *vṛtti* or means of subsistence; *rakṣa* or manifestations of higher beings; *mukti* or release; *hetu* or the potential *jīva;* and *apāśraya* or Brahman as the refuge.

R. C. Hazra thinks that from the third to the fifth century those matters have been added to the Ur-Purāṇa that formed the subject matter of the early *smṛtis*, whereas from the sixth century onward new topics were added dealing with holy places, image worship, astrology, and so forth which now form the bulk of the puranic lore. The oldest and most original part of the Purāṇas seems to be their mythology and history. Quite a few scholars are inclined to consider the puranic lists of dynasties as of considerable historical value. F. E. Pargiter spent the better part of his life in a reconstruction of the ancient Indian historical tradition[33] according to puranic records and has come up with some very interesting suggestions as regards the expansion of the Āryans in India, which would go a long way in explaining many puzzles of the Āryan origins but which also overthrows almost the whole of established Vedic historical scholarship.[34] According to one theory, the various Purāṇas came into existence as a consequence of the attempt to provide each of the Vedic *śākhas* with a Purāṇa of its own; another theory, no less plausible—especially in view of the numerous *Sthāla Purāṇas* or local chronicles—connects the various Purāṇas with different parts of India: "The *Brahmā Purāṇa* may represent the Orissan version of the original work, just as the *Padma Purāṇa* may give that of Puṣkara, the *Agni* that of Gāyā, the *Varāha* that of Mathurā, the *Vāmana* that of Thaneśvar, the *Kūrma* that of Benares and the *Matsya* that of the Brahmans on the Narmadā."[35] A Vaiṣṇava schema divides the 18 *Mahāpurāṇas* according to the three *guṇas* into *sāttvika* or Viṣṇu, comprising the *Viṣṇu, Bhāgavata, Nāradīya, Garuḍa, Padma,* and *Varāha*; *rājasa* or Brahmā, comprising the *Brahmā, Brahmāṇḍa, Brahmavaivarta, Mārkaṇḍeya, Bhaviśya,* and *Vāmana*; and *tāmasa* or Śiva, comprising the *Śiva, Liṅga, Skanda, Agni, Matsya,* and *Kūrma*. That this schema is entirely inadequate becomes apparent when one considers the fact, quite evident in the present texts, that several Purāṇas have been reworked more than once from different sectarian standpoints, combining Vaiṣṇava, Śaiva, and Śākta features. The *Upapurāṇas* lend themselves even less than the *Mahāpurāṇas* to a satisfactory classification. Not even their number can be determined exactly. A few of them claim to be, and have the status of, *Mahāpurāṇas*; that is, they are *śruti* for the followers of the particular group in question.[36]

In a general way one can state that the texts of the *Mahāpurāṇas*, as they have been printed, have been fixed between the time of 400 C.E. and 1000 C.E., the *Viṣṇu Purāṇa* being closest to the earlier date, the *Bhāgavata Purāṇa* nearer to the latter; but it is not possible to assign any specific date to any one of these works, containing as they do materials from hoary antiquity together with quite recent chapters, dealing among other things with Akbar's court and the British in India.[37] Most of the Purāṇas have been translated into English several times by different scholars, and it is quite easy for anyone interested in this literature to get acquainted with the contents and style of this class of writings, "whose importance for the development of Hinduism can never be overrated."[38]

The Purāṇas, like all Hindu scriptures, give at the end the succession of sages and saints through which they have been transmitted concluding with a *phala-śloka,* the promise of reward for reading them:

> Whoever hears this great mystery which removes the contamination of the Kali age, shall be freed from all his sins. He who hears it every day redeems his obligations towards *devas, pitṛs* and men. The great and rarely attainable merit that a man acquires by the gift of a brown cow, he derives from hearing ten chapters of this *Purāṇa*. He who hears the entire *Purāṇa* obtains assuredly the reward that attends the uninterrupted celebration of the *Aśvamedha*. He who reads and retains with faith this *Purāṇa* acquires such purity as exists not in the world, the eternal state of perfection.[39]

Apart from the texts in the Purāṇas that extol the merits of reading them there are *Māhātmyas,* Praises of the Greatness of each Purāṇa, very often printed together with the texts in the available editions. They pour lavish praise on the texts themselves and promise untold happiness and reward to all who even recite as little as a fraction of a verse or keep a part of the book in their dwellings. As the *Bhāgavata Māhātmya* says:

> It is better to preserve in one's house one half or even one quarter verse copies from *Śrīmad Bhāgavata* than a collection of hundred and thousands of other scriptures. There is no deliverance at any time from the noose of Yama for him whose house does not contain a copy of the *Śrīmad Bhāgavata* in the Kali age. I, the Lord take up my abode in the house of a person, that contains a verse, one half of a verse or even a quarter verse of the *Śrīmad Bhāgavata* written by hand. I never forsake the person who daily narrates my stories and is intent on hearing them and whose mind delights in them.[40]

Itihāsa-Purāṇa is great literature and with more adequate translations becoming available these books may become quite popular as well in Western countries. They contain fantastic stories that delight Western as well as Indian children, and they offer entertainment also to the more sophisticated lover of literature. Dealing as they do with timeless human experiences, the joys and tragedies of humankind anywhere, they speak to a Western audience as well as an Indian one.[41]

Students of myths and symbols will find them an inexhaustible source not only of materials but also of interpretations and theories, students of comparative law and ethics will find some of the most interesting resources in them.

Their vastness and their overall lack of a specific ideology make them very adaptable to changing circumstances and provide them with great strength and resilience, which is the sign of vigorous life.

6 The Bhagavadgītā

> He who reads this sacred dialogue of ours, by him I consider myself worshipped through the sacrifice of knowledge, And the man who listens to it with faith and without scoffing, liberated, he shall attain to the happy realm of the righteous.
>
> —*Bhagavadgītā* XVIII, 70f

Throughout the past thousand years of the history of Hinduism, the popularity and authority of the Bhagavadgītā, the Song of the Lord, has been, and still is, unrivaled.[1] It was accepted by Vedāntins as the third of the *prasthānas*, and it has been received by the masses as a book of spiritual guidance and comfort. Whoever reads it for the first time will be struck by its beauty and depth; countless Hindus know it by heart and quote it at many occasions as an expression of their faith and their own insights. All over India, and also in many places of the Western hemisphere, Gītā lectures attract large numbers of people. Many are convinced that the Bhagavadgītā is the key book for the respiritualization of humankind in our age. A careful study of the Gītā, however, will very soon reveal the need for a key to this key book. Simple as the tale may seem and popular as the work has become, it is by no means an easy book and some of the greatest Indianists have grappled with the historical and philosophical problems it presents.

The Bhagavadgītā in its present form constitutes Chapters 23 to 40 in the *Bhīṣmaparvan* of the Mahābhārata, one of the numerous philosophico-theological interpolations in the great epic.[2] Because we possess Śaṅkarācārya's commentary on the Bhagavadgītā, and this presupposes the same text that we possess,[3] we know with certainty that the Gītā has not been changed in the last 1200 or more years. The very fact that Śaṅkara commented upon it, despite its obvious theistic and kṛṣṇaitic bias would permit the conclusion that at the time it already enjoyed a very high standing among philosophers and ordinary people alike. Little is known about the text before that date and this is the reason why we find the most extraordinary range of views among scholars, both as regards the age and the original form of this poem.

R. D. Ranade, one of India's greatest religious scholars of the recent past, in a study entitled *The Bhagavadgītā as a Philosophy of God-Realization, Being a Clue Through the Labyrinth of Modern Interpretations,*[4] offered a critique of dozens of different opinions on the date and message of the Bhagavadgītā. Numerous Western scholars have tried to explain the obvious inconsistencies of the present text by stripping the Ur-Gītā from later additions and interpolations. According to Holtzmann, the original Gītā was Vedāntic in character, and the unorthodox *bhakti* doctrines have been grafted upon it; according to Garbe the original Gītā was a devotional and sectarian (Kṛṣṇaite) tract, to which the Vedāntic portions were tacked on under the influence of Brāhmanism. Hopkins thought that our Gītā was a Kṛṣṇaite version of an older Viṣṇuite poem, and this in turn was at first a nonsectarian work, perhaps a late Upaniṣad.[5] W. Garbe proceeded, on philological grounds, to sift out what he considered the additions and kept of the 700 *ślokas* only 530 as genuine, all of them non-Vedāntic.[6] H. Oldenberg, a reputable Sanskritist in his time, thought that the original Gītā comprised only the first 12 of the present 18 chapters, the last 6 being a later addition. R. Otto came to the conclusion that the original Gītā consisted of only 133 stanzas; the rest was added and interpolated later. The original text did not contain any doctrinal matter, whereas the eight tracts that were added brought in sectarian dogma. Several Western scholars—bitterly opposed by Indians—maintained that the Gītā betrayed a Christian influence.[7] The most articulate of these was probably F. Lorinser, who in 1869 prepared a metrical version of the Bhagavadgītā. He tried to prove that the author of the Gītā had used the New Testament, especially the Pauline epistles, weaving Christian ideas and conceptions into his system. A. Weber, a good Sanskrit scholar, saw in the *Nārāyaṇīya* section of the Mahābhārata a report of an Indian's visit to a Western, Christian country and attributed the Gītā to the authorship of such Brahmins that had familiarized themselves with Christianity at Alexandria. Necessarily these authors had to give to the Bhagavadgītā a fairly recent date, usually around 200 C.E. In the opinion of most scholars today, the Bhagavadgītā in its major portions antedates the Christian era. Some decades ago a

Kashmiri Buddhist reported on a study in which he tried to prove that the Gītā was a Buddhist work or at least that it borrowed heavily from Buddhism.[8] In our own day numerous practical interpretations of the Bhagavadgītā have been given. The one that attracted most attention and criticism may have been B. G. Tilak's *Gītā-Rahasya,* in which the Gītā is interpreted as "a Gospel of action."[9] Mahātmā Gandhi spoke quite frequently on the Bhagavadgītā, which he called his mother; and his secretary prepared a Gītā translation-cum-interpretation that reflects Gandhi's own thoughts.[10] Mahātmā Gandhi sees in the Bhagavadgītā an allegory of human life, which has to fight out the dilemma between divinely ordained duty and personal preference. Aurobindo Ghose finds in the Bhagavadgītā all the major points of his own philosophy: the ascending grades of consciousness, the gnostic ideal, the superman, and the transformation of matter into spirit.[11] S. Radhakrishnan, finally, whose edition tries to synthesize all the great classical interpretations of the Bhagavadgītā into a modern philosophy of life, eventually comes up with a modernized version of Advaita Vedānta as the original purport of the Bhagavadgītā.[12]

Without claiming to be able to solve all the questions raised by the many scholars who have written the most contradictory comments on the Bhagavadgītā, we may briefly summarize the views of S. K. Belvalkar, the editor of the *Bhīṣmaparvan* in the *Mahābhārata Critical Edition,* who also on other occasions has demonstrated his thorough knowledge of the problems related to the Gītā. Belvalkar assumes that, as the Mahābhārata underwent at least two recensions before it was fixed in the "modern" form, thus the Gītā also underwent a certain degree of rewriting. On the other hand, he maintains that the Gītā in its main contents has always been what it is today, that is, there has never been any original Gītā to which foreign and substantially different elements were added. He explains, quite plausibly, that the Gītā is a pre-Buddhistic work, representing a heroic brahmanical effort to reunite people, exposed to the most radical and most diverse religious ideas.[13] This reunion had to include all the still acceptable streams of religiosity of the time—brahmanic ritual, upanishadic knowledge, and devotional forms of cult and worship—with the firm frame of *varṇāśrama dharma* as the unifying bond, a concept also found in modern times, when everyone could call oneself a Hindu, regardless of the particular religious beliefs or rituals one followed, as long as one remained within the caste structure. Belvalkar calls the Bhagavadgītā the "Swan-song of the centuries of Śrauta religion" and thinks that

> the peculiar achievement of the *Bhagavadgītā* as a philosophical poem consisted precisely in having successfully gathered together under one banner the Brahmanic ritualists and the Upanishadic Vedāntists, the Sāṁkhya pacifists and the Yoga activists, the devotees of Kṛṣṇa and the free-thinking recluses, as also the majority of the average adherents of established institutions—not excluding women and the depressed classes, whom Brahmanism had denied the right of Vedic sacraments—requiring each of its constituents to give up or modify a part of his dogma in the interest of a compromise on a common platform with the other constituents. The ultimate position reached was philosophically quite self-consistent, special efforts being made to modulate the current opposition between *jñāna* and *bhakti*, between *karma* and *samnyāsa*, and between Ritualism and the Ātmanism.[14]

It may be easier for an Indian scholar, who has grown up in the thought-patterns of his or her own tradition, to see harmony where the Westerner, trained in analytical thinking, sees contradiction. Because the Bhagavadgītā is very much an Indian book, we should respect the traditional Indian attitude toward it and read it as a scripture rather than dissect it as a philosophical treatise.

Notwithstanding the critical approach of many Western Indologists, the Bhagavadgītā has become a favorite book of many Westerners as well. C. Wilkins made the Gītā known in Europe through his English translation which appeared in 1785. August von Schlegel produced a critical text edition and a Latin translation in 1823. Wilhelm von Humboldt who read this Latin version was so enthusiastic that he declared that "this episode of the *Mahābhārata* is the most beautiful, nay perhaps even the only true philosophical poem which we can find in all the literatures know to us."[15] Several good English translations have appeared in the last few decades and one can say, without exaggeration, that the Bhagavadgītā should be read by everyone who claims to have more than just a provincial education. W. Callewaert and Shilanand Hemraj in their *Bhagavadgītānuvāda*[16] not only try to trace the original text of the Bhagavadgītā, they also mention scores of commentaries and hundreds of translations into virtually all the major—and some minor—languages of the world. The Bhagavadgītā was one of the texts that every Vedāntācārya had to comment upon. In addition many others wrote commentaries both in Sanskrit and Indian vernaculars as well as in European languages. New translations into English keep appearing almost every year, apparently none of the existing versions is found satisfactory to all of those who use it and study it.

In the narrative of the Mahābhārata the Bhagavadgītā is inserted just before the outbreak of the actual battle between the Kauravas and the Pāṇḍavas. The two related clans are fighting for the kingdom: the Kauravas, who have usurped the reign, are defending their claim against the Pāṇḍavas, the rightful heirs, who have been cheated out of their possession. Arjuna, the hero of the Bhagavadgītā, is the leader of the rightful claimants. With him is Kṛṣṇa as his charioteer, a befriended king of Dwāraka, whose divine character is to become manifest only during the narration of the Gītā itself. Kṛṣṇa has sent his army to help the Kauravas, who are also his friends. Just when both armies are fully arrayed against each other, Arjuna realizes what he is going to do: he is about to fight and kill his relations, teachers, friends—and realizing that, he is ready to give up the war altogether, telling Kṛṣṇa: "I would not kill these, though killed myself, not for the rule over the three worlds—how much less for the sake of this earthly kingdom? What pleasure should we have after having slain the sons of Dhṛtarāṣṭra, our brothers? Only sin will we reap if we kill them!" He repeats the tenets of the traditional dharma that teaches that killing members of one's own family leads to the destruction of the whole family and punishments in hell. "Far better would it be for me if the sons of Dhṛtarāṣṭra, with weapons in hand, should slay me in battle, while I remain unresisting and unarmed." Arjuna then throws away his bow and arrow, depressed and overwhelmed by grief. In the second chapter, Kṛṣṇa begins to speak. The message itself is quite brief: "You have to fight, Arjuna!" Kṛṣṇa, however, persuades Arjuna with arguments taken from the various established viewpoints, appearing in the process not only as the charioteer of Arjuna but as the great teacher of wisdom, nay, as the Supreme revealing himself and his plans. He begins by telling Arjuna that his attitude is *anārya,* not noble, that it is not conducive to *svarga,* the old Vedic heaven, and that it leads to dishonor; it is unmanly not to fight here and now! Because Arjuna is familiar with these thoughts they do not impress him as a solution to his problem; he plainly admits his confusion and asks Kṛṣṇa to teach him as a guru teaches his disciple, and he again declares: "I will not fight!" Slowly Kṛṣṇa comes out with the New Philosophy that is able not to solve the moral dilemma, but to leave behind the Old Morality. Wisdom, he says, consists in realizing that the *ātman* is permanent, while the body by its very nature is doomed to die: there is no reason to grieve for either the dead or the living.

Never was there a time when I was not, nor you, nor these lords of men, nor will there ever be a time hereafter when we shall cease to be. . . .

He who thinks that this slays and he who thinks that this is slain, both of them fail to perceive the truth; this one neither slays nor is slain.

He is never born nor does he die at any time, nor having once come to be does he again cease to be.

He is unborn, eternal, permanent and primeaval. He is not slain when the body is slain.

Just as a person casts off worn-out garments and puts on others that are new, even so does the embodied soul cast off worn-out bodies and take on others that are new.

This philosophical argument by itself would not be sufficient to justify fighting a war; it just helps eventually to get rid of feelings of guilt over the action itself by suggesting that it does not involve the *ātman,* neither actively nor passively, but remains on the periphery of reality, in the sphere of change and inevitable death. The motivation to fight is supposed to come from the appeal to the *kṣatriya-dharma,* the iron rule that tells every one what is right and wrong. As Kṛṣṇa puts it: "There exists no greater good for a *kṣatriya* than a war enjoined by *dharma;* happy the *kṣatriyas,* for whom such a war comes of itself as an open door to heaven." A violation of this duty would be sinful and would bring shame, because it would make people think he is a coward—the worst that could happen to a professional warrior! Both the possibilities that the risk of war entails are preferable to the abstention from war: "If you are killed you will go to heaven; if you win, you will enjoy the earth; treating alike pleasure and pain, gain and loss, victory and defeat, get ready for battle; thus you will not incur any sin!"

Kṛṣṇa calls the teaching that he has given so far *Sāṁkhya,* and he is now ready to teach also the wisdom of Yoga, which, if accepted, frees from the bondage that karma imposes. And here he now speaks words that are really the gist of the whole Bhagavadgītā and that have influenced practical ethics in India throughout the centuries: "Your rightful claim extends to actions only, not to the results; the fruits of action should not be your motive but also do not cling to inaction. Established in Yoga, do your work after abandoning attachment, unmoved by success or failure." To drive away the idea of renouncing that has fascinated Arjuna so far and appeared to him as a solution of the dilemma,

Kṛṣṇa tells Arjuna that Yoga is neither inaction nor mere action but skill in action, action with understanding. He then describes the "wise man," the true yogi, as one who has given up all desires and whose *ātman* is content in the *ātman*. Untroubled in the midst of sorrows and free from lust amidst pleasures, free from passion, fear and anger, without attachment of any kind, neither rejoicing in the good nor dejected by evil, drawing away the senses from the objects of sense as a tortoise draws in his limbs under the shell, acting free from self-interest—this is the "divine state" that brings supreme happiness.

The basic message is thus given in the second chapter; most of the rest is a further explanation of the main points. Arjuna asks for a motivation of action, when Kṛṣṇa explains the insight of Yoga as the highest way of life. Kṛṣṇa clarifies the matter by pointing out that he had been of yore the teacher of two different ways of salvation: a way of knowledge for the contemplatives and a way of works for the actives. Nature, so he says, depends on continued work: "Do your alloted work, for action is better than inaction; even bodily life cannot go on without action. All work, except sacrificial action, causes bondage: therefore do your work as a *yajña*, free from all attachment." The work of the perfect man is not done with a view to further his own interests but in the interest of *loka-saṅgraha*, the good of the world. Kṛṣṇa points to his own example: he has no desire unfulfilled and yet he continually engages in action to give an example to humankind: "If I should cease to work, these worlds would fall in ruin and I should be the creator of disordered life and destroy these peoples."

Kṛṣṇa's teaching is not absolutely new at the time of the discourse with Arjuna; he refers back to Īkṣvāku, who taught it and who had received it from Manu via Vivasvān—Kṛṣṇa had taught it to him! Arjuna does not quite understand how Kṛṣṇa, who is about his own age, could possibly have been the teacher of mythical ancestors! Kṛṣṇa now explains his repeated coming into the world:

> Many are my lives that are past. . . . Though I am unborn and my Self is imperishable, the Lord of all creatures, establishing myself in my own nature I become embodied through my *māyā*.
>
> Whenever *dharma* declines and *adharma* rises up, I create myself (a body); for the protection of the good, for the destruction of the wicked and for the establishment of *dharma* I come into being in every age.

Kṛṣṇa is the creator of the *caturvarṇāśramadharma*: though himself unchangeable, he has ordained action to men, an action, however, that is not what ordinary people usually understand by that word. "He who in action sees inaction and in inaction action, he is the wise, the *yogi*, the one who has fulfilled his duty." Doing one's duty because of duty, *niṣkāma karma*, desireless action, is the ideal; and this activity does not entangle man in further karma but is in itself liberating: because it is centerd on Kṛṣṇa, who is free from karma and who destroys it.

The Bhagavadgītā explains Yoga in several chapters in very much the same way, often with the same words, as Patañjali in his *Yogasūtra*, and it also describes the origin of the world in the Sāṁkhya style, repeating the traditional two-way theory of the soul's course after death. It reaches its religious peak, however, in Chapters 9 to 11 where Kṛṣṇa pronounces his divine self-revelation, the *rāja-vidyā*, the regal wisdom, *rāja-guhya*, the royal secret, this most holy subject, open to realization and, within the traditional religion, the only way to escape from rebirth.[18] Kṛṣṇa says:

> By me this whole universe is permeated through my unmanifested form (*avyakta mūrti*). All beings are established in me but I am not established in them. My *ātman* sustains all things but is not established in them. As the air moves everywhere in space, thus are all things established in me because I support them. At the end of each *kalpa* all beings return into my *prakṛti*, from where I send them forth again at the beginning of the *kalpa*. Under my instructions *prakṛti* gives birth to all things and thus the world revolves.[19]

It is foolishness to despise God in a human body and wisdom to recognize him in all things:

> I am the ritual action, I am the sacrifice, I am the ancestral oblation, I am the medicinal herb, I am the sacred hymn, I am the *ghī*, the fire and the offering. I am the father of this world, the mother and the support. I am the object of knowledge, the sanctifier. I am the Om, the *ṛk*, the *sāma* and the *yajus*. I am the goal, the support, the lord, the inner witness, the secret abode, the refuge, the friend. I am the origin and the dissolution, the ground, the resting place and the imperishable seed. I give heat, I withhold and I send forth the rain. I am immortality and also death, I am *sat* and *asat*.[20]

Because Kṛṣṇa is the all-pervading and omnipresent Supreme, he is also the recipient of all devotion and offering. It is in the instructions for worship that the *bhakti* character of the Gītā appears clearest:

> Whosoever offers me with *bhakti* (devotion), a leaf, a flower, a fruit or water, that offering of *bhakti*, of the pure-hearted I accept. Whatever you do, eat, offer, give, suffer -dedicate it as a *tarpaṇa* (libation, offering) to me. Thus you will be freed from the good and evil results that accompany actions. I am alike to all beings, none is hateful to me, none a favorite. But those who worship me with *bhakti* are in me and I in them. Those who take refuge in me, be they low-born, women, *vaiṣyas* or *śūdras*, attain the highest abode. On me fix your mind, be devoted to me, worship me and revere me; having yoked yourself to my self you will attain me.[21]

The entire tenth chapter deals with the *vibhutivistara-yoga,*[22] the description of the manifestations of God in things—important for the time in which it was written because here Kṛṣṇa is explaining himself as the core and essence of Vedic religion and life. The eleventh chapter, called *viśva-rūpa-darśana,* the vision of the cosmic form of God, is the most powerful and quite overwhelming.

Arjuna, impressed by the oral revelation of God's greatness has one great desire: *draṣṭum-icchāmi te rūpam-aiśvaram puruṣottama,* I wish to see your divine body, o greatest of all beings![23] Kṛṣṇa is willing to fulfill this wish, but Arjuna is unable to see God with his natural vision; Kṛṣṇa has to endow him with divine eyes to see the divinity. What Arjuna then sees, terrifies him: "In your body, o Lord, I see all the *devas* and the hosts of beings, Brahmā seated on the lotus-throne and the *ṛṣis* and *nāgas*. I behold you, infinite in form on all sides, with numberless arms, bellies, faces and eyes, but I do not see your end or your middle or your beginning." More relevant for the concrete situation of the war into which Arjuna is about to enter, he sees how all the warriors whom he knows "are rushing into your flaming mouths as torrents rushing into the ocean. As moths rush swiftly into a blazing fire to perish there, so do these men rush into your mouths with great speed to their own destruction. Devouring all the worlds on every side with your flaming mouths you lick them up. Your fiery rays fill this whole universe and scorch it with their fierce radiance, O Viṣṇu!"

Kṛṣṇa responds with a profound revelation of the relativity of time: "*Kālo'smi,* time am I, world-destroying, come to the end to subdue the world. Even without you all the warriors arrayed in the opposing armies shall not live on. Therefore arise and fight and win glory. Conquering your enemies enjoy a prosperous kingdom. They have been slain by me already, you be the instrument alone. Slay Drona, Bhīṣma, Jayadratha, Karṇa and the other heroes who are doomed by me. Be not afraid. Fight! You will conquer your enemies in battle!"

Arjuna then falls prostrate and praises Viṣṇu under many titles, asking him at the end of his prayer to assume his familiar form again, because he is terrified by the *viśva-rūpa*, the All-form.

The twelfth chapter contains a brief discourse on the superiority of *bhakti* to *jñāna* and a description of the true *bhakta*, which repeats what had been said before. The thirteenth chapter, entitled *kṣetra-kṣetrajña-vibhāga-yoga*, the discrimination between the "field" and the "knower of the field" develops a *puruṣa-prakṛti* theory that agrees in many points with Sāṁkhya, assuming however that there is only one *puruṣa*, Viṣṇu-Kṛṣṇa. All the following chapters are occupied with demonstrating the applicability of the *triguṇa* scheme to various spheres of life and describing consequently three kinds of faith, of food, of sacrifice, of austerities, of gifts, of knowledge, of work, of doers, of understanding, of steadiness, and of happiness—implying always that the follower of Kṛṣṇa partakes of the *sattva-guṇa*, the nature of Viṣṇu. This, incidentally, is good āgamic-pauranic Vaiṣṇavism. From these chapters emerges the picture of the true Kṛṣṇaite as being fearless, pure of mind, steadfast in knowledge and concentration, charitable, devoted to the study of scriptures, dedicated to austerities, upright, nonviolent, truthful, free from anger, peaceful, forgiving, compassionate, gentle, modest, and humble. There is a touch of Advaita in the last passages where Kṛṣṇa describes the blessed state of the perfect sage:

> Endowed with a pure understanding, firmly restraining oneself, turning away from sound and other objects of sense and casting aside affection and aversion, dwelling in solitude, eating but little, controlling speech, body and mind and ever engaged in meditation and concentration and taking refuge in renunciation, casting aside egoism, violence, arrogance, desire, anger, avarice, tranquil in mind he becomes worthy to become one with *brahman*. Having become one with *brahman*, tranquil in spirit, he neither grieves nor desires. Regarding all beings as alike, he attains supreme *bhakti* to me. Through *bhakti* he gains knowledge of me, having gained knowledge of me in truth he enters into me.[24]

The Bhagavadgītā ends with a renewed injunction of Kṛṣṇa for Arjuna to fight, promising him final liberation: "You are dear to me,

I shall tell you what is good for you: Fix your mind on me, be devoted to me, sacrifice to me, prostrate yourself before me, thus you will come to me. I promise you truly, for you are dear to me. Abandon all reliance on (traditional) dharma and take your refuge (*sarana*) alone in me. Do not worry, I shall release you from all sins!"[25]

The Gītā attaches the customary blessings for all those who read it—an untold number of Hindus over twenty-five centuries. Many Indians, and increasingly many non-Indians, too, have considered the Gītā not only as a book to be read and studied but as a guide in their lives. A need for such guidance is felt especially in times of crises and confusion like ours, when the institutions are no longer able to provide orientation and when there are no longer commonly accepted values and standards. The Gītā is a book of crisis. Without referring to the Gītā, a modern writer describes the symptoms of the manifestation of crisis—and he clearly means our own time—in terms that could be taken straight from the Gītā: "loss of meaning, withdrawal of legitimation, confusion of orientations, anomie, destabilisation of collective identities, alienation, psychopathologies, breakdowns in tradition, withdrawal of motivation."[26] A direct modern Western reference to the Bhagavadgītā occurred in a context that to call *historical* is almost an understatement—it may better be called *apocalyptic*. In the course of his trial J. Robert Oppenheimer, who was accused of having passed on atomic secrets to the USSR, described the thoughts that passed through his mind when he witnessed the first atomic test explosion in the desert of New Mexico.

In the stage version by Heiner Kipphart, which closely follows the official protocol, the conversation between State Prosecutor Evans and defendant Oppenheimer reads like this:[27]

> *Evans*: I am addressing myself to the moral scruples, the contradiction that on the one hand you were prepared to go ahead with the matter of which you were, on the other hand, afraid of. When did you experience this contradiction for the first time?
>
> *Oppenheimer*: When we ignited the first atomic bomb in the desert of Alamogordo.
>
> *Evans*: Could you be more precise?
>
> *Oppenheimer*: On the sight of the fire-ball two ancient verses came to my mind. The one: "Of a thousand suns in in the sky if suddenly should burst forth the light, it would be like unto the light of that Exalted

One" (*BG* XI, 12). The other: "Death am I, cause of destruction of the worlds, matured and set out to gather in the worlds there" (*BG* XI, 32).

Evans: How do you know that a new idea is really important?

Oppenheimer: By the sense of a deep horror gripping me.

While the prophetic dimension of the *BG* can be clearly perceived as applicable to our own time—a time of crisis, a time of disorientation, a time of foreboding of universal doom—it is not so easy to establish the universal applicability of the ethics of the *BG*. Everybody can understand and even, up to a degree, practice desirelessness and selfless action. However, the promised effect can only be had within the *varṇāśrama-dharma*: only by selflessly following one's *svadharma* can one be united with the creator of dharma and the rewarder of self surrender. Dharma, as the Gītā understands it, is irrevocably tied up with *varṇāśrama-dharma*. *Varṇāśrama-dharma* as the eternal world order has ontological, built-in sanctions that simply do not apply to those who have no birthplace in it. The mutuality of *ethos* and *polis*, of ethics and society, demands that there first be an embodiment of an *ethos* before there can be an articulation of ethics.

India, too, has built its atom bomb, and the prospect of another fratricidal war of infinitely larger proportions than that described by the *Gītā* looms large not only over India but over the whole world. The modern world is not following *varṇāśrama-dharma*—its major decisions are not preceded by dialogues between the main actors and their God. Questions of ethics, of religious right and moral wrong, do not enter into the power calculus of today's mighty. Rewriting the Gītā from such a perspective, Rikhi Jaipaul, an Indian diplomat and poet, composed a kind of *Upagītā* that no longer offers transcendental hope in the face of a universal cataclysm. The new late twentieth century apocalypse is short:[28]

Kurukshetra Revisited

Clear-eyed Arjuna scanning the ruin ahead
his heart overcome with sorrow asked
which will be worse—to win or lose,
will the few with limitless power
condemn the many to karmas not their own,
will the mind that moves the soul prevail?
Pondering deep into the darkening night

of the long journey of man to his doom,
the silent Krishna had reason to lament
and washed his hands in innocence divine.
Soldiers and airmen will not fall with glory
like autumn leaves to sprout again in spring,
souls of sailors will not return as sea gulls,
warmongers will no longer sit on moonbeams
reaching to the stars for their profits;
no more the chivalries and virtues of war
nor hopes of living to fight another day,
foes and friends and neutrals alike
will perish together in the white nuclear night,
their fathers' souls will rise to die again.
Nevermore the ways of our fathers, nevermore,
for in one mad act man can outwit his God
and attain the nirvan of his own oblivion;
in his final fling of self defence there lies
the destruction of his world to make a legal point
of supervening sovereignty in pursuit of security;
helpless in the iron grip of cause and effect
his means shape his end, baring the moral flaw
and epic pride that feed the fires of his pyre;
alas that which may save him will die with him.

7 The World of the Hindu

> I wish to hear from you how this world was, and how in future it will be. What is its substance, and whence proceeded animate and inanimate things? Into what has it been resolved and into what will its dissolution again occur? How were the elements manifested?
>
> —Maitreya in *Viṣṇu Purāṇa* I, 1

Hinduism, like all traditional religions, offers a comprehensive world-view in which everything has its place and where all individual parts contribute to a meaningful total picture. All astronomical, geographical, historical, cultural information available at a given time is overarched by a philosophy that anchored its ethics, its anthropology and its socio-political laws ultimately in a creator and ruler of the universe. Throughout its long history, under the influence of expanding horizons and growing detail knowledge, the world-view of the Hindus has changed and developed. After the formation of sectarian Hinduism, differing notions of the identity of the Supreme Being and varying sets of sectarian mythologies brought about sectarian world-views laid out in the sectarian Purāṇas. In all their forms, however, Hindu world-views maintained their influence on the daily life and thought of Hindus, and numerous efforts to integrate contemporary scientific knowledge into the traditional framework, often backed by Indian scientists of repute, prove how important it has always been for Hindus to possess a workable and viable world-view.

VEDIC CREATION MYTHS

In the Ṛgveda, *pṛthvī-dyaus*, Earth-and-Heaven, are divinities.[1] India shares this 'heaven-earth' division and religion with a good many other peoples, who similarly explain the whole world as having originated from a pair of world parents. "Which was the former, which of them the later? How born? O sages, who discerns? They bear of themselves all that has existence. Day and Night revolve as on a wheel."[2] But this simple scheme could not accommodate the numerous new developments in Vedic religion, which uses a basic partition of the universe into *tri-loka*, "three worlds," the combination of the places for gods, ancestors and men. To each of the worlds eleven *devas* were assigned, with various functions. As S. Kramrisch explains:

> Heaven and earth, as dyadic monad, are a closed unit. It must be violated, split into its components, and these must be separated, lest they fall together and the world-to-be collapses. The act of creative violation and the power of keeping apart the pair so that they become Father Heaven and Mother Earth between whom all life is engendered is the test by which a creator god establishes his supremacy. He makes the Dyad into Two. He is the One and at the same time the Third, who plays the leading part in the cosmic drama. He is hero and artist in one.[3]

Speculation about the origin of the world is one of the staples of almost all religions, and quite frequently much of the rest of their philosophy is derived from this starting point. The earlier Vedic hymns have many scattered references to the origin of the world, involving a variety of gods; only in the later hymns does anything like a definite doctrine emerge. One hymn is addressed to *Viśvakarma*, The One-who-makes-all.[4] He is called mighty in mind and power, maker, disposer and most lofty presence, the Father who made us, the One beyond the seven *ṛṣis*. He is described as not to be found, "another thing has risen up among you."[5]

The two best-known Vedic descriptions of creation, however, are the so-called *puruṣa sūkta* and the *nāsadīya sūkta*. The former, true to the basic Vedic philosophy, derives everything from a ritual sacrifice. Thus it goes: "Thousand-headed was the *puruṣa*, thousand-eyed, thousand-footed. He embraced the earth on all sides, and stood beyond the breadth of ten fingers. The *puruṣa* is this all, that which was and which shall be. He is Lord of immortality, which he outgrows through (sacrificial) food. One fourth of him is all beings. The three fourths of him is the immortal in heaven." This *puruṣa* begets *virāj*, the "widespread", and both together bring forth *puruṣa*, the son, who becomes the sacrificial victim of the great sacrifice of the gods. From this great sacrifice originate the verses of the Vedas, horses, cattle, goats, and sheep. The four castes, also, have their origin in him, the sacrificial victim. The *Brahmin* was his mouth, out of his two arms were made the *kṣatriyas,* his two thighs became the *vaiśyas,* and from his feet the *śūdras* were born.[6] From his mind was born the moon, from his eye the sun, from his mouth Indra and Agni, from his breath Vāyu, from his navel the sky, from his head the heaven, from his feet the earth, from his ears the quarters.

Yajñena yajñam ayajanta devāḥ[7]—the gods offered the sacrifice through the sacrifice. The *yajña* is the great creative force. We find here the germ of the later *Pañcarātra* system, the idea that Viṣṇu is also the material cause of the universe, out of which everything is fashioned.

A more speculative treatment of the topic of creation is found in the *nāsadīya sūkta,* in the last book of the Veda:

> Neither being, nor non-being existed: there was no air, no sky that is beyond it. What was concealed? Wherein? In whose protection? And was there deep unfathomable water? Death then existed not, nor life immortal, of neither night nor day was there any token. By its inherent force the One breathed windless: no other thing existed beyond that. There was at first darkness, by darkness hidden; without distinctive marks, this all was water. That which, becoming, was covered by the void, that One by force of heat came into being. Desire entered the One in the beginning: it was the earliest seed, the product of thought. The sages searching in their hearts with wisdom, found the kin of being in non-being. . . . Who knows for certain? Who shall declare it? Whence was it born, and whence came this creation? The gods were born after this world's creation: then who can know from whence it has arisen? None can know from whence creation has arisen and whether he has or has not produced it: he who surveys it in the highest heaven, he only knows, or, perhaps.[8]

Several key words of Vedic religion are employed here: *tapas,* heat, the power of the yogi, is said to be responsible for the first stirring of creation; *kāma,* desire or lust, the cause of both the multiplicity and the inherent impermanence of things. The terms *asat,* "nonbeing," and *sat,* "being," do not have the Greek meaning we connect with them, but the Indian one, which differs considerably: *asat* is an entity without determination, akin to chaos, unstructured matter in the modern sense. The asymmetry of *sat* and *asat,* which is, as it were, complementary, is of a similarly fundamental nature as that between chaos and order, as understood by modern science, expressed in terms of entropy and negentropy. *Sat* and *asat* are the positive and the negative poles, complementary, whose tension produces and maintains the many things. As will become still clearer from later accounts, the Hindu idea of creation presupposes some kind of uncreated substratum, and the account is concerned more with the molding and ordering of this basic material than with its absolute beginning. As S. Kramrisch sees it:

> The three ontological moments in the relation of *sat* and *asat* correspond to different levels in the structure of creation. The dark Un-create on high has for its lower limit the first streak of the dawn of creation in the highest heaven. . . . Sunk below creation, the non-existent is negativity; the existent is the cosmos, the ordered world, the world of *ṛta*, a work of art. The non-existent is chaos, decomposition, the absence of *ṛta*, the domain of *nirriti*. It is the counterpart, *apud principium*, by the act of creation and separation, of the Darkness that was—and is—before the beginning of things.[9]

The Upaniṣads offer a great variety of theories to explain both the beginning of the universe and its structure. According to the *Bṛhadāraṇyaka Upaniṣad*, in the beginning the *ātman*, the Self, was alone, in the form of a *puruṣa*, a male being. He looked around and saw nothing except himself. He said: "I am." He was afraid and he had no joy; he longed for another being. He was as large as a man and woman embracing. He divided himself into two: husband and wife. Thus human beings were created. She turned into a cow, he became a bull. She turned into a mare, he became a stallion. And thus the various kinds of animals came into existence.[10] The account given here reveals the first traces of the Sāṁkhya system, in which everything owes its origin to the interaction between *puruṣa* and *prakṛti*, the uncreated principles, one male, the other female, spirit and matter, passivity and activity.

Another ancient motif is that of the world egg, which floats on the primordial ocean and from which spring the many creatures on earth.[11] According to some texts, the first being to come forth from the primeval egg was Viśvakarma, the Vedic creator-god. The world egg, and the origination of the universe from it, is a favorite theme of many later Hindu works, notably the Purāṇas.

Manu's account of creation is informed by his endeavor to derive the socio-ethical law of dharma from the nature and structure of the universe itself. In the beginning the world was in chaos, without distinguishable forms and attributes, as if in sleep. Then appeared the *svayambhu bhagavān,* the Lord-who-is-of-Himself, invisible and without distinguishing characteristics; he removed the darkness. This *paramātman* was filled with a desire to create beings. He created water and put the seed *śakti-rūpī,* power-form, into it. This seed shone with the splendor of a thousand suns. It then became an egg, as bright as gold, and from it issued Brahma, who shaped all the worlds. He, who is the origin of everything, eternal, of the form of *sat* and *asat, puruṣa* who issued from it, he is called Brahma. For a whole year he remained in the form of an egg, and then, through concentrated thought (*dhyāna*), he divided himself into two. From the two halves were created heaven and earth and space in between them: the eight points of the compass, the place of water and the sea. From the Self he produced mind (*manas*), containing in him both *sat* and *asat;* from this came individuality (*ahaṁkāra*),[13] with pride and dominion. The following chapters in *Manusmṛti* enumerate the successive creation of the 24 principles from which, according to the Sāṁkhya system, everything is made: *mahat,* the Great Principle, all that contain the three *guṇas* in themselves, the five sense organs, and so on. The various celestial beings are then created, along with *yajña,* the sacrifice. For it *Ṛk, Yajur,* and *Sāmaveda* were produced out of Agni, Vāyu, and Sūrya. *Tapas,* heat-power, as well as *rati,* erotic pleasure, *icchhā,* desire, and *krodha,* anger, are created. Dharma and *adharma* and all other pairs of opposites like *hiṁsā* and *ahiṁsā,* cruelty and kindness, are apportioned to the various beings by Brahmā himself. The origin of the four castes is explained in the same terms as the account in the *puruṣa-sūkta.* Brahma divides his body into two parts. Out of their union springs up the first human being, *Virāj. Virāj* practices *tapas* to create Prajāpati, who brings forth ten *maharṣis* as well as seven Manus, Devas, and the various kinds of good and evil spirits: the *yakṣas* and *piśācas, gandharvas* and *āpsaras, nāgas* and *garuḍas.*

In the *Mānusmṛti* we find already the idea of a periodical creation and destruction of the world, as well as all the divisions of time from the winking of an eye to the world ages.[15] One day and night are made up of thirty *muhūrtas,* each *muhūrtas* of thirty *kalās,* each *kalā* of thirty *kāṣṭās,* and each *kāṣṭā* of eighteen *nimeṣās.* "The sun divides days and nights, both human and divine; the night is for the repose and the day for work. A month is a day and night of the departed ancestors; the dark fortnight is their day of work, the bright fortnight their time of sleep. A year is the day and night of the *devas*; the half year during which the sun progresses to the north will be their day, that during which the sun goes southward, the night." There follows a description of the day and night of Brahmā and of the world ages: the *Kṛta-yuga* consists of 4000 years of the *devas*; the twilight preceding it consists of as many hundreds and the twilight following it of the same number. In the other three *yugas* with their twilights preceding and following, the thousands and hundreds are diminished by one each. "These 12,000 years are called one age of the *devas*. One thousand ages of the gods make one day of Brahman, and his night has the same length. . . . At the end of that day and night he who was asleep awakes and, after awaking, creates."[16]

The *Mānusmṛti* as well as the Purāṇas make use of the term *manvantara*, an age of Manu or an age of humankind, calculated as seventy-one ages of the *devas*. "The *manvantaras*, the creations and destructions of the world, are numberless; sporting as it were, Brahman repeats this again and again." Throughout we find what we might term *historical pessimism*: the world is in constant moral decline. "In the *Kṛta* age *dharma* is four-footed and complete; and so is truth, nor does any gain accrue to men by unrighteousness. In the other three ages *dharma* is successively deprived of one foot, and through theft, falsehood and fraud the merit is diminished by one fourth. Men are free from disease, accomplish all their aims, and live four hundred years in the *Kṛta* age, but in the *Treta* and the succeeding ages their life is lessened by one quarter."

Dharma too is different according to the ages: in the Kṛta age austerity is the chief virtue, in the Treta age wisdom, in the Dvāpara the performance of sacrifices, and in the Kali age, in which we now live, *dāna* or liberality.[17]

In all the Purāṇas our present age is described as being close to universal chaos and final destruction. The laws that governed and upheld humankind in former ages have broken down, humankind has become weak, oppressed by numerous calamities, and short lived.

PURĀṆIC COSMOGRAPHY

Before dealing with details of traditional history, which concerns almost exclusively the Kali age, it may be worthwhile to mention some features of the traditional world description offered mainly in the Purāṇas and presupposed in all historical or mythical narrations. The Hindus certainly had a quite accurate knowledge of those parts of India in which they lived, and at certain times they also ventured forth across the seas. Not content with their experiences, they constructed a complete world model in which everything found its exact place. Though these models as described in various texts differ in a number of substantial details, all of them begin with Mount Meru as the center of the world, around which *Jambu-dvīpa,* the known world (mainly India) is situated. The Mahābhārata has preserved an older version of the world model in which four *dvīpas* or continents were arranged around *Mount Meru,* with the Ocean of Salt as the southern border of the world, and the Ocean of Milk as the northern. The fully developed puranic model is much more complex: it knows of seven *dvīpas* surrounded by and surrounding seven concentric oceans. In the center of this world stands Mount Meru, forming with *Jambu-dvīpa* the innermost circle. Its boundary is formed by a vast ring of saltwater, the *lavana-sāgara,* followed by another concentric ring of land, and so on, according to the following scheme in Figure 7.1.[20]

The middle column indicates the width of each ring of sea or land, using the diameter of *Jambu-dvīpa* (given as 100,000 *yojanas*)[21] as the basic unit. The whole map has to be imagined as consisting of concentric circles, whose center is Mount Meru, the pivot of *Jambu-dvīpa. Jambu- dvipa* consists in detail of the following parts shown in Figure 7.2.[22]

Bhārata-varṣa (India) again is divided into nine parts, ruled over by kings from the dynasties descended from Satajit,[23] going back through various illustrious rulers to Pṛthu, from whom the earth (*prthvi*) took her name, because he "subdued the earth," leveling it and beginning to cultivate it. Whereas the other eight parts of *Jambu-dvīpa* are described as "places of perfect enjoyment, where happiness is spontaneous and uninterrupted, without vicissitude, without age and death, without distinction of virtue or vice, without any change brought about by the cycle of sages," *Bhārata-varṣa* is subject to the deterioration brought about by the succession of the four *yugas;* it knows suffering and death. But it is praised nevertheless as "the best of the divisions of *Jambu-dvīpa,* because it is the land of works" which enable people to gain heaven or even final emancipation. The gods themselves praise the good fortune of those born in *Bhārata-varṣa.*[24] We leave out the details of the description of the several parts of *Jambu-dvīpa,* which contain much valuable information about the geography and ethnology of ancient India. A few words about Mount Meru, the Golden Mountain in the center of *Jambu-dvīpa,* however, may be of value for an understanding of

Aṇḍakaṭaha Tamas	128	Shell of the World Egg Darkness
Lokālokaśaila Kañcanībhūmī	128	World–No-World Mountains Land of Gold
Jalasāgara Puṣkaradvīpa	64 64	Sea of Sweet Water Blue-Lotus Land
Kṣirasāgara Śākadvīpa	32 32	Milk Ocean Teak Tree Land
Dadhisamudra Krauñcadvīpa	16 16	Buttermilk Ocean Heron Land
Sarpisamudra Kuśadvīpa	8 7	Melted-Butter Ocean Kuśa Land
Surāsamudra Śālmadvīpa	4 4	Wine Ocean Silk-Cotton-Tree Land
Ikṣurasasamudra Plakṣadvīpa	2 2	Sugar-Cane-Juice Ocean Fig-Tree Land
Lāvaṇasamudra Jambudvīpa	1 1	Saltwater Ocean Roseapple-Tree Land
	510	Mount Meru

Figure 7.1 Purāṇic world model

The middle column of Figure 7.1 indicates the width of each ring of sea or land, using the diameter of *jambudvīpa* (given as 100,000 *yojanas*)[21] as the basic unit. The whole map has to be imagined as consisting of concentric circles, whose center is Mount Meru, the pivot of *Jambudvīpa*.[22] The parts of *Jambudvīpa* are illustrated in detail in Figure 7.2.

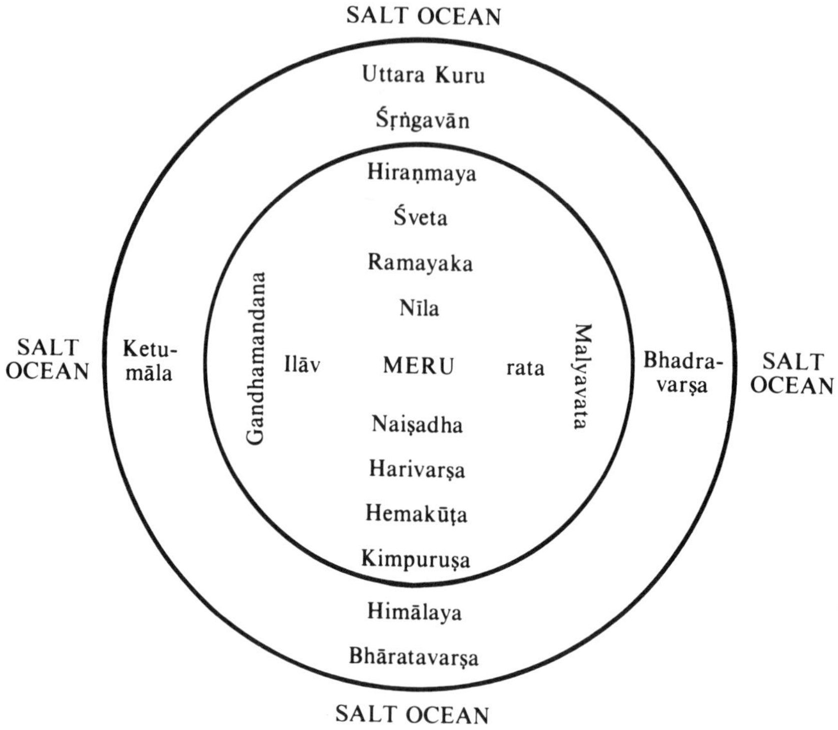

Figure 7.2 The map of the Purāṇic world model

Indian mythology. Its height is given as 84,000 *yojanas,* its depth below the surface of the earth as 16,000. Its diameter at the summit is 32,000 *yojanas* and at its base 16,000 *yojanas,* "so that this mountain is like the seed-cup of the lotus of the earth." From the base of Meru extend mighty mountain ridges; on its summit is the vast city of Brahmā, extending 14,000 *yojanas.* And around it, at the cardinal points and in the intermediate quarters, is situated the stately city of Indra and the cities of the other regents of the spheres. The capital of Brahmā is enclosed by the River Ganges, which, issuing from the foot of Viṣṇu[25] and washing the lunar orb, falls here from the skies, and, after encircling the city, divides into four mighty rivers.

The Purāṇas describe in detail not only *Jambu-dvīpa* but also the other continents with their geography and history. In the five continents outside *Jambu-dvīpa* the lives of people last for 5000 years; they are happy, sinless, and enjoy uninterrupted bliss. They have their own system of classes, corresponding to the four castes in *Bhārata-varṣa,* but this division does not result in any friction or any deprivation of one group of people compared with the other. In *Puṣkara-dvīpa* people live a thousand years, free from sickness and sorrow and unruffled by anger and affection. There is neither virtue nor vice, neither killer nor slain; there is no jealousy, envy, fear, hatred; neither is there truth or falsehood. Food is spontaneously produced there. There is no distinction of caste and order, there are no fixed institutes, nor are rites performed for the sake of merit. The three Vedas, the Purāṇas, ethics, policy, and the laws of service are unknown. It is, in fact, a terrestrial paradise where time yields happiness to all its inhabitants, who are exempt from sickness and decay. A *Nyāgrodha*-tree grows on this land, which is the special abode of Brahmā, and he resides in it, adored by *devas* and *asuras.*[26]

> Beyond the sea of fresh water is a region of twice its extent, where the land is of gold and where no living beings reside. Thence extends the *Lokāloka* mountain, which is 10,000 *yojanas* in breadth and as many in height; and beyond it perpetual darkness invests the mountain all around; which darkness is again encompassed by the shell of the world-egg. Thus the universe with its exterior shell is 500 million *yojanas* in extent. It is the mother and nurse of all creatures, the foundation of all worlds, and the principal element.[27]

The universe as described in Hindu cosmology is geocentric: the earth is the center of the entire universe, though not its best part as regards enjoyment. It is, however, best suited for "work," for the possibilities that it opens to gain the supreme end, liberation. The Hindu world is, however, less ethnocentric than the world-view of, for instance, the ancient Near Eastern peoples, in particular, of ancient Israel. Mount Meru, the center of the Hindu world, is far away from *Bhārata-varṣa.* Only later Hindu sects identify the center of the world with their centers of worship. Thus the Śaivites consider Cidāmbaram as the world center, the Vaiṣṇavas identify Vrindābana with the pivot of the world. The puranic accounts are also quite modest when comparing their own country with other countries; the people in other countries are described as materially much better off, they are free from most of the hazards that beset the people of *Bharat.*

A vertical section produces the following 'layers' or sheaths of the world egg, the *brahmāṇḍa:*[28]

Satyaloka	
Tapoloka	
Janaloka	
Maharloka	
Svarloka (planets)	
Bhuvarloka (sky)	Regions of the consequences of work
Bhurloka (earth)	
Atala (white)	
Vitala (black)	
Nitala (purple)	
Gabhastimat (yellow)	
Mahātala (sandy)	Netherworlds
Sutala (stony)	
Pātāla (golden)	
Śeṣa (the world snake)	
Raurava, etc.	28 *nārakas* or hells

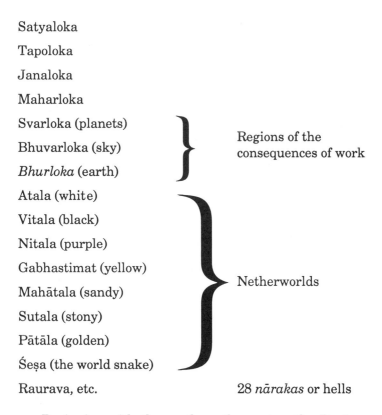

Beginning with the earth as the center, the Purāṇa explains the netherworlds, which are not to be confused with 'hells' or with the idea of netherworlds in the West. Each of the seven netherworlds extends 10,000 *yojanas* below the surface of the one preceding. "They are embellished with magnificent palaces in which dwell numerous *dānavas, daityas, yakṣas* and great *nāgas*. The Muni Nārada after his return from those regions to the skies declared amongst the celestials that *pātāla* was much more delightful than Indra's heaven."[29] Below these is *śeṣa,* the "form of Viṣṇu proceeding from the quality of darkness," also called *ananta,* the endless one, with a thousand heads, embellished with the *svāstika. Śeṣa* bears the entire world like a diadem upon his head. When *ananta,* his eyes rolling with intoxication, yawns, the earth, with all her woods and mountains, seas, and rivers, trembles. The hells "beneath the earth and beneath the waters" are the place of punishment for sinners—specified according to their crimes.[30] The sphere of the earth (moving upwards) "extends as far as it is illuminated by the rays of the sun and moon; and to the same extent the sphere of the sky extends upwards, till the beginning of the sphere of the planets." The solar orb is situated 100,000 *yojanas* from the earth and that of the moon an equal distance from the sun. At the same interval above the moon occurs the orbit of all lunar constellations. *Budha* (Mercury) is 200,000 *yojanas* above the lunar mansions. *Śukra* (Venus) is at the same distance from *Budha*. *Aṅgāraka* (Mars) is as far above *Śukra*; *Bṛhaspati* (Jupiter) as far from *Aṅgāraka*, whereas *Śani* (Saturn) is 250,000 leagues beyond *Bṛhaspati*. The sphere of the *Seven Ṛṣis* is 100,000 *yojanas* above *Śani*, and at a similar height above these is the *Dhruva* (Pole Star), the pivot of the whole planetary circle. *Bhur, Bhuvar,* and *Svar* form "the region of the consequence of works"—the region of the works that bring merit is *Bhārata-varṣa* alone.[31]

Above *Dhruva*, at the distance of 10 million *yojanas*, lies *Mahar-loka*, whose inhabitants dwell in it for a *kalpa* or a day or Brahmā. At twice that distance is *Jana-loka*, where *Sanāndana* and other pure-minded sons of Brahmā reside. At four times the distance, between the last two, lies the *Tapo-loka* inhabited by the *devas* called *Vaibhrajas*, whom fire cannot harm. At six times the distance is situated *Satya-loka*, the sphere of truth, whose inhabitants will never know death again. *Satya-loka* is also called *Brahmā-loka*. Some of the sectarian texts add above *Brahmā-loka*, *Viṣṇu-loka* (or *Vaikuṇṭha*) and *Śiva-loka* (or *Kailāsa*), assigning the supreme place to the deity of their own choice.[32]

The world egg (with its seven *dvīpas* and *samudras*, its seven *lokas* and its seven netherworlds, *Śeṣa*, and the hells beneath—all within the shell of *brahmāṇḍa*) is but the center of a greater universe which is stratified according to the following scheme:

Pradhāna-Puruṣa	(primaeval matter and spirit)
mahat	(the first principle)
bhutādi	(the gross elements)
nabhas	(ether)
vāyu	(wind)
vahni	(fire)
ambu	(water)
The World Egg	(earth)

The *Viṣṇu Purāṇa* explains in detail.[33] The world is encompassed on every side and above and below by the shell of the egg of Brahman, in the same manner as the seed of the wood-apple is encircled by its rind. Around the outer surface of the shell flows water, for a space equal to ten times the diameter of the world. The waters are encompassed by fire, fire by air, air by ether, ether by the gross elements, these by the first principle. Each of these extends in breadth ten times that layer which it encloses, and the last is enveloped by *pradhāna,* which is infinite and its extent cannot be enumerated: it is therefore called the boundless, the illimitable cause of all existing things, supreme nature or *prakṛti;* the cause of all world eggs of which there are thousands and tens of thousands, and millions and thousands of millions. Within *pradhāna* resides *puman,* diffusive, conscious, and self-irradiating, as fire is inherent in flint. Both are encompassed by the energy of Viṣṇu (*viṣṇu-śakti*), which is the cause of the separation of the two at the period of dissolution and the casue of their continuance in existence, as well as of their recombination at the time of creation.

PAST AND FUTURE WORLD RULERS

The universe of the Hindu is peopled by all possible degrees of being: inanimate objects, plants, animals, demons, *devas,* semidivine beings, humans, and so forth. The Purāṇas contain poetic genealogies of all of them. For our purpose it will be of interest to outline briefly the history of the human race, as reported in traditional Hindu literature. Several scholars have tried to reconstruct ancient Indian history with the names and dates supplied in Epics and Purāṇas; so far they have not come to an agreement as regards the most important dates, especially with regard to the Bhārata War, which is considered the central landmark in ancient Indian history.[34] Because here we are not directly concerned with history in the modern Western sense, we may content ourselves with a summary of the opinion of one authority in this area.[35] Without necessarily accepting his chronology, we nevertheless get an idea of a historically probable calculation and also gain some familiarity with the more prominent names in Indian history and mythology.

From Brahmā, the creator, was born Manu Svayambhuva,[36] who divided into a male and a female and produced two sons, Priyavrata and Uttānapāda, and two daughters, Prasūti and Ākūti. From these were born Dharma and Adharma and their progeny, Śraddhā (faith), Lakṣmī (good fortune), Krīya (action), Buddhi (intelligence), Śānti (peacefulness) as well as Hiṃsā (violence), Anṛta (falsehood), Nikṛti (immorality), Bhaya (fear), Māyā (deceit), Mṛtyu (death), Duhkḥa (pain), Śoka (sorrow), Tṛsna (greed), Krodha (anger), and so on.

We move into the realm of proto-history with the story of Vena, the grandson of Cakṣusa, in the line of the sixth Manu.[37] Apparently Vena offended the religious feelings of his subjects by proclaiming himself to be God and forbidding all other cults. The *ṛṣis* who were worshippers of Hari did not accept his claim to divine kingship and killed Vena, who left no heir. In the period following the death of the king, anarchy spread terror among the people, who clamored for a ruler. The *ṛṣis* drilled the left thigh of the dead king; out of it came a dwarfish black being, whom they called Niṣāda and who became the ancestor of the Nisadas in the Vindhya Mountains. They drilled the right arm of the dead king and produced Pṛthu, at whose birth heaven and earth rejoiced. His consecration is described at great length; he is celebrated as the initiator of agriculture, of road construction and city building. From his line sprang Manuy Vaivasvata, the savior of humanity at the time of the Great Flood. We have several accounts of the deluge, which also plays a great role in the popular traditions of other cultures.[38] Pusalker accepts the flood as an historical event that took place around 3100 B.C.E. In Hindu mythology it is connected with the *Matsya-avatāra* of Viṣṇu. A small fish swam into Manu's hands when he was taking his morning bath, asking for protection. Manu put it first into a jar, then into a pond, and, when it was fully grown, back into the sea. The fish gave Manu a warning about the coming flood and advised him to prepare a ship and enter it at an appointed time. Manu did so and when the flood finally came, the fish appeared again and pulled Manu's boat to the Northern Mountains. After the water had subsided, Manu was ordered to disembark and descend from the mountain, whose slope is therefore called *Manoravatāraṇam,* Manu's descent. He was the only human being saved—and with him humankind took a new beginning. He was also the first lawgiver and first tax collector. His eldest offspring had a double personality as the male Ila and the female Ilā. From Ilā, who married Budha, was born Pururavas, the originator of the Aila or Lunar dynasty. From Ila's eldest son, Īksvāku, who had his capital at Ayodhyā, sprang the Aikṣvāka or Solar dynasty. The other eight sons of Manu also became founders of peoples and dynasties, whose lines are recorded.

According to the most famous kings in the lists, Pusalker divides the history after Manu into a Yayāti period (3000–2750 B.C.E.), a Māndhātṛ period (2750–2550 B.C.E.), a Paraśurāma period

(2550–2350 B.C.E.), a Rāmacandra period (2350–1950 B.C.E.), a Kṛṣṇa period (1950–1400 B.C.E.). The end of this era coincides with the great Bhārata War, which according to Indian tradition marks the beginning of the Kali-yuga, the last and most evil of all the ages of humankind.[39]

The Purāṇas have lists of dynasties of kingdoms that flourished at the end of the Bhārata War and continued until they were absorbed by the great Nanda empire of Magadha in the fourth century B.C.E.[40] One of the prominent figures in the Purāṇas is Parīkṣit, a Paurava king who lived after the great war. Largely from Buddhist accounts we are informed about the kingdoms of Kośala and Kāśī. The kings ruling over Magadha gradually extended their influence till they were the only great power in Northern India.

Between Manu, the savior of humankind, and the Bhārata War, the Purāṇas list ninety-five generations of kings, on whom they report in the past tense. From Parīkṣit onward, "the ruling king,"[41] they use the future tense, thus giving these geneologies the character of prophecies and enhancing their authority. They offer quite precise information regarding names and important details of their lives and deaths up to the time of the Guptas in the fourth century C.E. Then again the names and stories are fanciful, further developing the idea of a constant deterioration of the quality of life during the Kali-yuga, which lasts for 360,000 years from the death of Kṛṣṇa.[42] After enumerating a large number of names the Purāṇa states:

> These will all be contemporary monarchs, reigning over the earth; kings of churlish spirit, violent temper, and ever addicted to falsehood and wickedness. They will inflict death on women, children and cows; they will seize upon the property of their subjects; they will be of limited power, and will, for the most part, rise and fall rapidly. Their lives will be short, their desires insatiable, and they will display but little piety. The people of the various countries will follow their example. . . . Wealth and piety will decrease day by day, until the world will be wholly depraved. Then property alone will confer rank; wealth will be the only source of devotion; passion will be the sole bond of union between the sexes; falsehood will be the only means of success in litigation; and women will be objects merely of sensual gratification. Earth will be venerated but for its mineral treasures, dishonesty will be a universal means of subsistence, presumption will be substituted for learning. No man's life will exceed three and twenty years. Thus in the Kali age shall decay constantly proceed, until the human race approaches its annihilation.

At the end of times *Kalki*, a divine incarnation, will arise, who "will destroy all the *mlecchas* and thieves, and all whose minds are devoted to iniquity. He will then re-establish *dharma* on earth, and the minds of those who live at the end of the *Kali* age shall be awakened. . . . The men who are thus changed by virtue of that peculiar time shall be as the seeds of human beings and shall give birth to a race who shall follow the laws of the *Kṛta* age." The Purāṇa adds some astronomical information from which the end of the times can be foretold; also included is the prophecy that Devapī of the race of Puru and Maru of the family of Īkṣvāku, will outlive all others and constitute the germ of the renewal of the Kṛta age, after 1200 years of Brahmā's night have elapsed.[43]

Hindus in more recent times have also become acquainted with geography and history in the modern sense, which in many details is in conflict with traditional teaching. There are some who tenaciously cling to the literal truth of their scriptures and reject modern scholarship as biased and ignorant. In a number of cases recent scholarship has vindicated the ancient traditions over against the rash assumptions of former generations of historians. There are also some who try to harmonize the scriptural accounts with modern scientific ideas in geology or biology, often in a somewhat forced way.[44] Others have compromised between tradition and modernity, sometimes demythologizing and allegorizing the scriptures so as to uphold their truth and to sound modern at the same time.

In a manner typical of modern enlightened Hinduism S. Radhakrishnan demythologized Hinduism in a speech before the *Viśva Hindū Sammelan* in New Delhi[45] stating that there was nothing sectarian or dogmatic about Hinduism, which was but the reconciliation of all paths to God. The Hindu myth of the creation of the world, he continues, implies that life came out of matter, animal life out of plant life, and gave rise in time to human reason. The famous myth of the churning of the milk ocean out of which the gods derived *amṛta*, the nectar of immortality, he interprets as the "churning of the spirit" out of which comes purity of heart.

Hinduism has shown throughout its long history an ambivalent relationship to the physical universe. This ambivalence is probably most clearly articulated in the positions assumed by Śaṅkara and Rāmānuja, authors from the Indian Middle Ages, but holding opinions which connect with Upaniṣadic texts. For Śaṅkara as well as Rāmānuja the visible world has its origin in *Brahman*, the Absolute. But while for Śaṅkara the world is *māyā*,[46] a kind of illusion or appearance and an alienation of the Self, for Rāmānuja it is the body of God, sharing some of the qualities ascribed to the Supreme, real and sacramentally necessary.

Over against the One Supreme the world is characterized by duality: the opposites of dharma and *adharma*, of good and evil, of hot and cold, of gods and demons are possible only in the world, and the world is constituted by them. This fundamental structure is articulated in the seemingly naive creation stories of the Purāṇas as well as in the sophisticated cosmological speculation of the *darśanas*. It appears in the self-partition of *brahman* in the Upaniṣads and in the *sura-asura* contest of the Churning of the Milk Ocean (Figure 7.3), in the *puruṣa-prakṛti* dualism of Sāṁkhya and in the *vyavahāra-paramārtha* distinction of Śaṅkara. Within the dualism a tripartite schema supplies the dynamics of development: the Pṛthvī-Dyaus polarity of the Veda becomes sacrificially relevant as *tri-loka*—three worlds. The *puruṣa-prakṛti* polarity is actualized toward liberation through the *tri-guṇa* dynamics. The *vyavahāra-paramārtha* dichotomy includes the active pursuit of the triad of the *puruṣārthas*. Behind the colorful and seemingly naive stories in which the traditional Hindu world-view is often described there are profound ideas and structural insights that could well be

Figure 7.3 *Amṛtā Manthana*: The churning of the Milk Ocean

expressed in modern abstract mathematical terms—as has been done. Subhash Kak, with his "decoding of the *Ṛgveda*" has opened up an entirely new approach to the study of Vedic cosmology from an empirical astronomical/mathematical viewpoint.[47] Vedic mathematics has been proven to be both ingenious and quite advanced.[48] With regard to the scientific accomplishments based on a Hindu world-view, much work has still to be done, in spite of the valuable contributions of such authors as B. N. Seal[49] and D. P. Singhal.[50] An interesting attempt has recently been made by B. A. Armadio to connect Vedic mantras with Whitehead and Pythagoras.[51]

8 The Many Gods and the One God of Hinduism

"Yes, said he, "but just how many gods are there Yajñavalkya?" "Thirty-three." . . . "Yes," said he, "but just how many gods are there, Yajñavalkya?" "One . . . "

—*Bṛhadāraṇyaka Upaniṣad* III, IX, 1

About a score of different Sanskrit words are rendered by the one English word *god.* We have to look at some of them in order to find out how Hindus can at one and the same time have many gods and believe in One God.

VEDIC *DEVAS*

When English publications on Vedic religion speak about gods, they use this term as translation for the Vedic word *deva* or *devata.*[1] Thus they enumerate faithfully the eleven celestial gods, the eleven atmospheric gods and the eleven terrestrial gods. F. Max Müller was struck by the evident fact that in a number of hymns the god to whom the song was addressed was praised as the only one, the supreme, the greatest, and that praise was not restricted to one god, but given to various gods in various hymns. This did not conform to the classical notion of polytheism, so Müller coined the new term *henotheism* (from the Greek term *hen(os)* = one) to distinguish this religion from *monotheism,* the revealed biblical religion. The Hindu *deva* is not God—at the most *deva* could be loosely translated as a "divine being." Etymologically it means "shiny," "exalted"; and thus we find that the term *deva* covers everything that has to do with the supernatural: all figures, forms, processes, and emotions, melodies, books, and verse meters—whatever needs the explanation of a superior origin or status—are called *devas* or *devata* in one place or another.[2] The functions of different parts of the body, symbols, and syllables are explained as *deva*. In Vedic religion we find the term used in a relatively restricted way; however, even there we are not entitled to equate it with "god," but rather with "supernatural powers" in a general sense.

Anthropologists have become aware of the importance of the idea of "power" in tribal religions. R. N. Dandekar has quite convincingly shown that behind the Vedic *deva* worship lies such an idea of an all-pervading ultimate power, of which the *devas* partake without being quite identical with it. According to him most of the Ṛgvedic *devas* are created for the myths and not the myths for the *devas*. Mythology is thus primary and the *devas* are secondary. The Vedic *ṛṣis* had a message that they conveyed in images for which they created the concretized figures of the *devas*. Thus we can see that Vedic mythology is evolutionary, implying a change of the character of a *deva* according to changed circumstances. Much more important than the variable figure of the *deva* was the basic underlying potency of which the individual *devas* were only expressions and manifestations; the Vedic counterpart to the *mana* power is the *asura* power, which is shared by all beings, especially the *devas*. That is also the explanation of the highly variable and flexible anthropomorphism of the Vedic *devas*. There is, strictly speaking, no Vedic pantheon in the sense in which there is a Greek or a Roman one.[3] The Vedic seer did not share the outlook of moderns. Though *agni* is the term for "fire" in the most general sense, to the Vedic religious mind the reality of *agni* is not simply the chemical process of carbonization of organic matter that a modern scientist would associate with the term fire. In fire the Vedic mind sees a *deva*, a transcendent aspect that makes *agni* fit to be used as an expression that hints at a something beyond the material reality investigated by modern chemistry. *Agni* is a *deva*, not a "personification of a natural phenomenon," as nineteenth-century Western scholarship would describe it, but the manifestation of a transcendent power. The physical reality of fire is so obvious and so necessary that the Hindu does not think of spiritualizing it away, but there is more to it than meets the senses—the *ṛṣi* is inspired to "see" and express the mystery behind all visible reality. Objective natural science never found *devas* nor will it find God in the physical universe; it requires the sensibilities of a *kavi*, the poet and the prophet to discover divine reality.

Granting that the hymns of the Ṛgveda in their present form are an ancient revision of a still more ancient text[4] and keeping in mind what has already been said about the evolutionary character of Vedic mythology, we find it quite acceptable that at different stages different *devas* were at the center of Vedic religion. In our present Veda text Indra dominates, a rather late arrival in Vedic religion, who is difficult to circumscribe because he assumes at least three different roles: Indra the cosmic power, Indra the war-like leader of the Āryans, and Indra the ancient mythical dragon-killing hero.[5] Popular books on Indian religion still carry the nineteenth century cliché of Indra as "personification of the rain storm" or "weather god." Quite apart from the misunderstanding of the nature of a *deva* we must also reject this idea, because "most of the descriptions of Indra are centered round the war with, and subsequent victory over, Vṛtra. A proper understanding of this point, would, therefore, serve as an adequate starting point for a critical study of Indra's personality and character."[6] What a study of this myth reveals is that Indra, contradictory as many of his single features may be, is the manifestation of the saving divine power defeating the opposing demonic power.[7]

Of the more than 1000 hymns of the Ṛgveda[8] about a quarter are addressed to Indra alone. Although not exhaustively dealing with all the questions surrounding the nature of the God Indra, we can get an impression of the nature of Vedic devotion to Indra by quoting one of them, expressing Indra's greatness. The titles given to Indra in this hymn—*maghavān, mahāvīra, deva eka, rāja,* and so on—are essential attributes of the High God, titles given to the Savior God in later developments of Indian religion. The hymns do indeed allude to historical events and historic person when describing the personality of Indra, but the sum total of attributes given to him is more than just the apotheosis of a warrior hero. That the Vṛtra slaying by Indra is more than the victory of a warrior over his enemy seems to suggest itself to us, when we read that the effect was that Indra "raised the Sun for all to see." It is the work of the High God to "chase away the humbled brood of demons," to "encompass the worlds from all sides," and to "divide day and night." It is the High God alone "before whom even the Heaven and Earth bow down," "without whose help our people never conquer," who is "the bestower of food and wealth," "man's helper from old, not disappointing hope, friend of our friends, rich in mighty deeds." His authority as High God is finally established through his victory over the demon, whom no human being would be able to defeat. Only if Indra is understood as a symbol for, and a manifestation of, the High God do the attributes given to him make sense, especially because the same attributes are given to other *devas,* the same deeds are ascribed to Agni, Soma, Varuṇa, and others. "They call him Indra, Mitra, Varuṇa, Agni and he is heavenly-winged Garutman. To what is One, sages give many a title."[9] Indra is only one of the names given to the Savior God. The Supreme was first, and only under specific circumstances did he receive the name of Indra. The Supreme is nameless—human beings give names to him, variously describing him in categories taken from cosmic events, from history, or from their own experience.

> He, who as soon as he was born became the first among the high-souled *devas*, their protector on account of his power and might, he who made the worlds tremble before his breath on account of his valour, he, O men, is Indra!
>
> He who fixed fast and firm the earth that staggered, and set at rest the agitated mountains, who measured out the air's wide middle region and gave the heaven support, he, O men, is Indra!
>
> Who slew the dragon, freed the seven rivers and drove the cattle forth from Vala's cave, who generated fire between two stones, the spoiler in warriors' battle, he, O men, is Indra!
>
> By whom the universe was made to tremble, who chased away the defeated host of dark-skins, and like a gambler gathering his winnings, seized the foe's riches, he, O men, is Indra!
>
> Of him the terrible, they ask: Where is he? They also say: He is not. He sweeps away like birds, the enemies' possessions. Have faith in him, for he, O men, is Indra.
>
> Inciter to action of the poor and humble, of the priest and the suppliant singer, fair-faced he gives his favours to the one who pressed Soma between two stones, he, O men, is Indra!
>
> He under whose supreme control are horses, all chariots, the villages and cattle, he who gave being to sun and dawn, who leads the water, he, O men, is Indra!
>
> To whom two armies cry in close encounter, both enemies, the stronger and the weaker, whom two invoke upon one chariot mounted, each for himself, he, O men, is Indra.
>
> Without whose help our people never conquer, whom, battling, they invoke to give them succour, who became the universe's likeness, who shook the unmovable (mountains), he, O men, is Indra.
>
> He who struck before they knew the danger, with his weapon many a sinner, who does not give pardon to one who provokes him, who slays the *dasyu*, he, O men, is Indra.
>
> Even the Heaven and the Earth bow down before him, before his breath the mountains tremble. Known as the Soma-drinker, armed with thunder, who wields the bolt, he, O men, is Indra![10]

Indra emerges as the power, which increases even more through the sacrifice and the mantras. The *devas* themselves depend on the mortals, religion is a two-way street to power![11]

Next to Indra, Agni is the *deva* most often addressed in the Vedic hymns; he is indispensable in the all-important business of sacrifice! The very first hymn of the Ṛgveda Saṁhitā and some 200 more are addressed to him. "I praise Agni, the *purohit* (priest), the divine *ṛtvik* (another class of Vedic priests), the *hotar* (a third class of Vedic priests), lavisher of wealth. Worthy is Agni to be praised by the living as by the ancient *ṛṣis*. He shall conduct the *devas* to this place. Through Agni one obtains wealth."[12]

Agni-fire is the medium through which the material gift of the sacrifice is transformed into the spiritual substance of which the gods can partake and from which they draw their strength!

One of the most impressive and beautiful hymns is addressed to Savitṛ, the "inspirer," sun, light, intelligence, the luster of beauty.

> Agni I first invoke for prosperity, I call on Mitra and Varuṇa to come to help, I call on night who gives rest to all moving life, I call on Savitṛ, the divine helper. Throughout the dusky firmament advancing, laying to rest the mortal and the immortal, borne in his golden chariot he cometh, the divine Savitṛ who looks upon every creature. The *deva* moves by the upward path, the downward, with two bright bays, adorable he journeys. Savitṛ comes, the helper from afar, and chases away all distress and sorrow.[13]

Heaven and Earth are hymned as *devas*; Aditi, "Mother Earth," is also mentioned separately; the Maruts, the storm winds, are a group of *devas* frequently mentioned; rivers and waters appear as divinities; the *soma* juice and the *kuśa* grass, both indispensable for the sacrifice, are variously referred to as *deva*.

The *devas* are not the moral ideals for people to follow, nor are they considered lawgivers. The hymns speak of *ṛta*, "the law," as independent of the *devas*, standing apart and above them as an impersonal and infallibly effective power. The word *ṛta* is connected with *ṛtu*, the seasons, the regular round of spring, summer, rain, autumn and winter. Beyond that we can understand *rta* as the principle of order behind all things and events. In a way *ṛta* foreshadows both the later karma and brahman. Several *devas*, especially Mitra and Varuṇa, are invoked as the guardians of *ṛta*, never as its creators. Both are also thought to reward good and punish evil.[14] The central role of Varuṇa in Vedic religion became the focus

4 Agni, Khajurāho twelfth century

5 Kubera, Khajurāho twelfth century

of H. Lüders's life work. In 1910 he gave a presentation to the Berlin Academy of Sciences in which the said that he intended to show that Varuṇa was originally the ocean surrounding the world by whom oaths were taken already in prehistoric times. During the Indo-Iranian period the notion of *ṛta* developed: "truth" as ruling power. Its seat was placed in the ocean and Varuṇa became its protector. Over the next three decades Lüders developed his thoughts in a monumental work comprising over 1800 pages of manuscript. At the end of the war it was looted and scattered. From the pages that could be salvaged, L. Alsdorf edited, after H. Lüders's death, the massive two volume work *Varuṇa*.[15] In addition to Varuṇa, Lüders also deals with various other important Vedic deities and some central notions of Vedic religion.

Kubera, the Vedic god of riches and treasure and the presiding deity of the North, was, and still is, a most popular deity. Vedic mythology makes him also the king of the *yakṣas* and *kinnāras*. He is often represented as deformed, with three legs, eight teeth and only one eye.

The fact that our Western culture has lost the ability to appreciate nature as a symbol of the divine makes many of us unable to appreciate Vedic *deva* worship without using categories drawn from a mechanized world. It is not just a superstitious remnant if today Hindus offer praises and prayers to the rising sun at the time of their morning prayer. There may be many a modern Indian among those sun worshippers who knows about the physical properties of the sun, its surface temperature and its chemical composition. Worship is not addressed to the astronomical body, not to a symbolized idea, but to the *sūrya-deva*, the metaphysical reality through which an aspect of the supreme reality becomes relevant for humans. Quite frequently one may observe a pious person worshipfully saluting the electric light after switching it on in the evening. The Indian peasant regards the cow as the seat of many *devas* and worships her; factory workers offer worship to their machines on certain days, to the *deva* of technology by whose operations they live. They all may grasp in their own way what many of us have not yet quite understood—that all things, whether made by humans or not, manifest a power that is beyond us.

UPANIṢADIC BRAHMAN AND PURĀṆIC ISVARA

In the *Bṛhadāraṇyaka Upaniṣad* we read a dialogue in which Yajñavalkya is asked the crucial question: *Kati devāḥ,* how many are the *devas*? His first answer is a quotation from a Vedic text: "Three hundred and three and three thousand and three." Pressed on, he reduces the number first to thirty-three, then to six, then to three, to two, to one-and-a-half and finally to One. "Which is the one *deva*?" And he answers: "The *prāṇa* (breath, life). The Brahman. He is called *tyat* (that)."[16] Though the *devas* still figure in sacrificial practice and religious debate, the question "Who is God?" is here answered in terms that has remained the Hindu answer ever since. *Brahman*, untranslatable, identified with the revealed word uttered by the Brahmins, with the soul of everything, with the creator and maintainer of the world, with the inner principle of the universe—*Brahman* becomes the term around which the loftiest religious speculation has revolved for thousands of years and it is still the term used to designate the supreme being. *Brahman* has always retained an aura of the not quite concrete, the spiritual, that escaped the grasp of the ordinary worshipper. The terms used to express the supreme in its concreteness are equally old: *Īśa* or *īśvara*, the lord, or *bhagavān*, the Exalted One, are titles given to the Supreme Being by Hindus even now. The name associated with this title now becomes rather crucial. Whereas the Vedic *ṛṣi* was casual in associating names with the title *deva*, because a plurality of *devas* seemed quite natural and even necessary to grasp different facets of the nameless one, to the new theologians a plurality of Lords seems intrinsically impossible and they insist that the One, with whom they associate the title *īśvara* or *bhagavān*, is the only One—as Brahman is by necessity one only, ultimately identical with the Lord.

The exclusive association of the title *Lord* with one particular name has led to the development of mutually exclusive religions whose worship and mythology centered around the One God, dismissing in this process the gods of the others as minor beings. Later attempts to unify different traditions (at least theoretically) and to consider their rival Lords as equal sharers of one divine power in the *trimūrti* have sometimes led to wrong conclusions among Western students of Hinduism. Hindu texts do indeed speak of the triad of Brahmā as creator, Viṣṇu as preserver, and Śiva as destroyer, fulfilling the functions of the One God, but all those texts belong to one of the traditions in which the Supreme is identical with one of those names and the three separate names are but different aspects of the same being.[17] Some of the famous *trimūrtis* are quite clearly recognizable as artistic expressions of different modalities of one and the same *īśvara*.[18]

Brahmā, the first of the three, has no following worth mentioning today; only a few temples in India are known to offer worship to him. Several sectarian accounts try to explain why he has receded into obscurity. According to an ancient Śaivite myth he was born with five heads. When he became interested in Pārvatī, the wife of Śiva, the latter chopped off one of Brahmā's heads. Since that time he has been shown with four heads only. In his four hands he carries the Vedas, a water-vessel, a ladle, and a *mālā*. In the Mahābhārata he is addressed as *pitāmahā*, the grandfather, who instructs the *ṛṣis* on religious matters. In Vaiṣṇava mythology he has the role of the demiurge: enthroned on the lotus that grows out from Viṣṇu's navel, he shapes the world. The Śaivite tale that Brahmā was deprived of worship because of a lie may be understood as a blackmail of the Brahmins, whose special Lord he must have been and who did not recognize the Śaivites as orthodox.[19]

Within the present-day practice of the *pañcāyata-pūjā* among nonsectarian Hindus the worship of Sūrya, Śiva, Viṣṇu, Devī, and Gaṇeśa takes place.

Sūrya is possibly the most vedic of the five; we find his worship already in the Ṛgveda, under the title of Savitṛ. As the source of life, light and warmth he is the natural "Lord of creation." He is also the source of inner enlightenment as the famous *Gāyatrī mantra* suggests. Purāṇic accounts associate Manu, the ancestor of mankind, and Yama and Yamī, the god and goddess of the netherworlds and of death, with *Sūrya* as his children. The same Purāṇa has given him four wives: *samjñā* (knowledge), *rājñī* (splendour), *prabhā* (light) and *chāyā* (shade). At certain times there had been a strong movement of worshippers of Sūrya as Lord, as evidenced by Sūrya temples and *Saura Purāṇas.*

Śiva figures as the One God and the Lord for many millions of Hindus today. Śaivism may indeed be the most ancient of India's religions. Several soapstone seals found in excavated sites of the Indus civilization have been interpreted as part of the Śaivite tradition, depicting *Śiva Paśupati,* the Lord of the Animals, *Śiva Trimukha,* the three-faced Śiva and *Śiva Mahāyogi,* Śiva the ascetic.[23] Numerous *liṅgas* have been found in these sites too—a further link with present-day Śaivism in which the *liṅga* is the main object of worship.[24] A second important source for the development of Śaivism is the ancient Draviḍa culture. The name *Śiva,* the benevolent or gracious one, may be but a Sanskritisation of an old Tamil name *Śivan,* the red one.[25] The mythology and basic philosophy of Śaivism seems to have grown in the Draviḍa country; Tamilnādu is still the center of Śaivism. Tribal religions may also have had their share in the development of Śaivism. According to various scholars the Śibi in northwest Punjab show in their very name an association with Śaivism.[26] Some of the Austric and Proto-Australoid tribes in Northeastern India are thought to have been responsible for the development of *liṅga* worship; the very word *liṅga* is thought to derive from Mon-Khmer languages.[27] Vedic religion, in which the numerous fearsome Rudras played a great role, may have added another dimension to Śiva worship. Despite his name his prominent feature is wrath, and terror and destruction are much more prominently associated with him than grace. One of the most interesting texts, the *Śatarudrīya* of the *Yajurveda* uses titles and epithets for Śiva that are still in common use; he is called *Nīlakaṇṭha*, the blue-throated,[28] *Paśupati*, the lord of the animals, *Śārva*, *Bhava*, and *Śobhya*. His divinity is affirmed when he is described as the one who stretched out the earth, as the one who is immanent in places and objects, in stones, plants, and animals. Also the paradoxical ascription of contradictory attributes is used: after being praised as the great Lord of all beings, he is called *cheat* and *Lord of thieves*, a dwarf and a giant, fierce and terrible and the source of happiness and delight.

The main sources of Śaivism, however, are found in later texts which are considered as revelations by the followers of Śiva. The *Śvetāśvatara Upaniṣad* has for Śaivas the same importance as the better known Bhagavadgītā has for the Vaiṣṇavas. Then there are several *Śaiva Purāṇas*, and *Śaiva Āgamas*, as well as Śaivite sections in the Mahābhārata. The *Śvetāśvatara Upaniṣad* quite openly identifies Brahman with Śiva when it says: "The immortal and imperishable Hara exercises complete control over the perishable *prakṛti* and the powerless *jīva*: this radiant Hara is the One Alone."[29]

The Rāmāyaṇa contains some very old versions of Śiva myths. The *Mahābhārata* has a catalogue of 1000 names of Śiva, a litany that still occupies a central place in Śaivite devotion. It mentions all the salvific deeds of Śiva, from whom most of his popular names are derived; he is identified with the sun; he is called the artificer of the universe, the Master and Lord of all creatures. He gives boons, he destroys and creates again, he smites and heals. He is the *Maheśvara*, the Great Lord.[30] Some of the great myths of Śiva that are found in the Purāṇas still stand in the center of Śaivite liturgy and theology.

The worshippers of *Bhairava*, the fearsome form of Śiva, who are quite numerous in Mahārāṣṭra, derive their motivation from the myth of Dakṣa, who, from being an enemy of Śiva, was converted by Śiva's forceful intervention in the form of *Bhairava* into a devotee, reciting with his goathead the thousand names in praise of Śiva.[31]

Śaiva-siddhāntins, a large group of sophisticated Śiva worshippers in South India, see in *Śiva Nīlakaṇṭha* the most convincing [illegible] of God's love for humankind. According to the myth Śiva was [illegible] the poison that threatened to destroy all life, [illegible] e Ocean of Milk to obtain *amṛta*, [illegible] son was so powerful that it left a [illegible] pious it is the sign of Siva's self- [illegible] ering.[32]

[illegible] if is that of the *Naṭarāja*, the King [illegible] tion a *taṇḍava*, a dance of world [illegible] ce of the enamored Śiva. A South [illegible] g details of the myth: Followers of [illegible] Mīmāṁsā tried to destroy Śiva by [illegible] tiger, a serpent, and an elephant, [illegible] sent the embodiment of evil in the [illegible] o overthrow Śiva, but Śiva began his [illegible] warf and thereby liberating the world. [illegible] a *Naṭarāja* has been immortalized in [illegible] es, especially in South India. Śaivite theology [illegible] detail of this image with meaning. Therefore it symbolize [illegible] ay for the pious the divine activities of God: "Creation arises from the drum, protection proceeds from the hand of hope, from fire proceeds destruction, from the foot that is planted upon *muyalahan* proceeds the destruction of evil, the foot held aloft gives deliverance."[33] His smile shows his uninvolved transcendence, the three eyes are interpreted either as sun, moon, and fire, or as the three powers of Śiva: will, knowledge, and action. The garland of skulls around his neck identifies him as time, and the death of all beings. The single skull on his chest is that of Brahmā, the creator of the world—all beings are mortal, only Śiva is eternal.[34] Śiva also appears in 28 *avatāras*, said to be the revealers of the 28 *Śaiva Āgamas*, the scriptures held sacred by the Śaivites. Quite often one finds representations of Śiva with five heads. The famous *Śivāṣṭamūrti* combines eight forms of Śiva. Those combinations may be the reflection of amalgamations of individual local or tribal cults that were unified into Śaivism in historical times. A frequent representation shows *Śiva ardhanārī*, half man–half woman in one figure, symbolizing the inseparable unity of Śiva and Śakti.[35]

6 Śiva Sadāśiva, Mahārāṣṭra, Heras Institute Bombay

Siva's abode and paradise is Kailāsa, open to all who worship Śiva, irrespective of caste or sex.[36] *Śaiva Purāṇas* abound in descriptions of hells and in means to escape from them. The famous *mṛtyuñjaya-kavaca*[37] is believed to have been given by Śiva himself to his devotees so that they might overcome the fear of death.

The most important manifestation of Śiva, his presence and the object of worship for his devotees, is the *liṅga*. This is the only "image" of Śiva, the formless absolute Being, to be found in the innermost sanctuary of a Śiva temple. The most ancient sculpture of a *liṅga* that still receives public worship is found in Guḍimally, South India, and dates from the second century B.C.E. Its phallic origin is established beyond doubt, but it also can be safely said that it does not evoke any phallic associations int he minds of the worshippers. Many local myths describe the *Śiva liṅgodbhava,* Śiva's appearance from within an icon of this kind. The twelve famous *jyotir-liṅgas,* each the center of a pilgrimage, are said to have come into existence by themselves, without human hand, and therefore manifest special potency. Many miraculous events are reported from those places.[38] An ancient custom associated with Śaivism is the wearing of a garland of *rudrākṣa* beads, used for *Śiva-japa,* the repetition of the bliss-giving name of Śiva and a sign of belonging to Śiva. Also numerous Śaivites smear their bodies with white ashes—Śiva is said to have a white body!

One of the great Śiva centers is Cidāmbaram, a town not far from modern Madras. For the devotees it is the very center of the world. In its thousand-pillared hall daily festivals are arranged for the worship of Śiva, splendid and awesome spectacles. Here in Cidāmbaram Śiva is said to dance his cosmic drama, but as the Śiva mystics say: Cidāmbaram is everywhere! Thus speaks Tirunāvukkaraśu Swāmi: "He is difficult to find, but he lives in the heart of the good. He is the innermost secret of the scriptures, inscrutable and unrecognized. He is honey and milk and the bright light. He is the king of the gods, within Viṣṇu and Brahmā, in flame and wind, in the roaring seas and in the towering mountains."[39]

In front of Śiva temples one usually finds the image of *nandi,* a bull, quite often of huge proportions. The bull is Śiva's mount, associated with Śiva from time immemorial. This again may be one of the remnants of a formerly independent animal worship that became part of Śaivism.

Numerically, Viṣṇu commands the largest following. Vaiṣṇavas are split into numerous sects and schools of thought, *saṃpradāyas,* and *matas.*

7 Viṭhobhā (Viṣṇu), Mahārāṣṭra, Heras Institute Bombay

Viṣṇu is one of the *devas* of the Ṛgveda; certain passages in the Brāhmaṇas suggest that Viṣṇu is of solar origin.[40] But here too the name Viṣṇu, translated as the "all-pervading one," may be only a Sanskritization of an older Dravidian name (*viñ*, "the blue sky"), an opinion that receives confirmation from the fact that Viṣṇu even now is always painted a dark-blue color.[41] The totemism of tribal cults may have led to the development of the doctrine of the *avatāras*, the descents of Viṣṇu, as may also the Buddhist teaching of the *bodhisattvas*, appearing at different ages. The Nārāyana and the Vāsudeva Kṛṣṇa cults merged into Vaiṣṇavism in pre-Christian times and gave it perhaps the most powerful stimulus for further development. It seems fairly certain that the basis for the latter was a historical Kṛṣṇa, a hero from the Vṛṣṇi clan of the Yādava tribe residing in and around Mathurā, one of the oldest cities of India.[42] Pāṇini mentions "*bhakti* to Vasudeva" and we have the testimony of Megasthenes that Kṛṣṇa worship was established already in the fourth century B.C.E. in the region. Possibly this Kṛṣṇa is also the founder of Bhāgavatism, which found its literary expression in some of the favorite scriptures of the Hindus, especially the *Bhāgavata Purāṇa*. The Viṣṇu tradition is perhaps the most typical of all the forms of Hinduism, and the greatest books of Indian literature reflect it strongly. The Mahābhārata is mainly a Vaiṣṇava book; the Rāmāyaṇa treats of Rāma, the *avatāra* of Viṣṇu. One of the most ancient of the Purāṇas is the *Viṣṇu Purāṇa* and the numerous *Vaiṣṇava Saṁhitās* have been the models on which the sectarian works of other religions have been based. The most popular book of the entire Hindu literature, the Bhagavadgītā, is a Kṛṣṇa scripture. Countless inspired devotees of Viṣṇu have composed throughout the ages an incomparable store of *bhakti* hymns that live in the literally incessant *bhajans* and *kīrtans* throughout India even today.[43] *Viṣṇu-bhakti* knows all shades of love, from the respectful devotion of the servant to his masters, through the affectionate relationship between parent and child, to the passionate eroticism of Kṛṣṇa and Rādhā.

The most important Viṣṇu myth is that of *Viṣṇu trivikrama*. Viṣṇu, appearing as a dwarf at the feet of Bali, the ruler of the earth, asks for as much land as he can cover with three strides. His first stride conquers the earth, his second the sky, and for the third step Bali offers his own head as support. In this way he establishes himself as the ruler of the world.

In Vaiṣṇava mythology the myths connected with the *avatāras* occupy the foremost place both in the imagination of the people and in the scriptures.[44] In addition to the ten most common ones—Matsya, Kūrma, Varāha, Vāmana, Narasinha, Paraśurāma, Rāmacandra, Kṛṣṇa, Balarāma, and Kalki who will come at the end of the Kali-yuga—some scriptures list a score of others, including, for example, Buddha and Kapila. Rāma and Kṛṣṇa enjoy particular favor, and an immense literature has grown around them; Ayodhyā and Mathurā-Vṛndāvana are *the* centers of pilgrimage where their presence is still alive in many ways. The images of Viṣṇu are of particular importance; they are the real and physical presence of the god, who has the earth and the individual souls as his body. Viṣṇu, too, is praised by his devotees in a litany of thousand names, which glorify his mythical exploits and enumerate his divine qualities.[45] *Hari* is the most common name under which he is invoked. *Nārāyana, Keśava, Puruṣottama* are other favorite names that are not only signs of identification but also powerful spells in themselves.

Ekanāṭha, a sixteenth century Mahratta poet, sings:

> How sweet is the curdling of liquid *ghī*. So blissful is the seeker, when the hidden one reveals his form. Dark is he, dark is the totally unknown and locked is the way to thoughts and words: the scriptures are silent, the Vedas do not utter a word. Not so the revealed one. How bright! How near! Our thirst is quenched if only he appears, who is so dear to our heart. The ever perfect one, eternal bliss, being and thought—see, it is Govinda, source of ecstasy and rapture. Strength, courage, honour and exalted spirit—see, we witness our God sharing all this. If I but catch a glimpse of God, my eye-sight is restored. I have escaped the net of life, the guilt of my senses is cancelled. In the light of the lamp all hidden things are made apparent—so it is when I think of my God: the God from faraway is here![46]

Viṣṇu's heaven is called Vaikuṇṭha; but the various subdivisions of Vaiṣṇavism have also introduced new heavens such as Kṛṣṇa's celestial Vṛndābana or Goloka and Rāma's heavenly Ayodhyā. Viṣṇu's *vahana* is the winged Garuḍa; a special landing post is available for him in South Indian temples.

Usually Śiva and Viṣṇu are represented together with their wives, Pārvatī and Śrī, around whom the Purāṇas have also woven a rich mythology. In Śāktism, however, the Goddess assumes the role of the Supreme Being, whether depicted without a male consort or as superior to him.

Śakti means "power" personified in the Goddess, the Divine Mother to whom are ascribed all the functions Viṣṇu has for the

Vaiṣṇavas or Śiva for the Śaivas: creation, maintenance, and destruction of the world, illusion and liberation. The female terra-cotta figures found in many sites of the Indus civilization so much resemble the *devī*-images kept in the homes of today's Indian villages that one may safely infer that they bear witness to a cult of the Goddess. The Indus civilization again may be considered part of a larger culture, spreading from the Mediterranean in the West to Central India in the East, in which the Great Mother was the creator, the Lady of humans, beasts, and plants, the liberator and the symbol of transcendent spiritual transformation.[47] The very name *Umā*, as well as her association with a mountain and the lion, seems to connect her with Babylonia, Accad, and the Dravidian culture.[48] Another important current of Devī religion comes from indigenous village cults, "the most ancient form of Indian religion."[49] The Goddess is implored to drive away the evil spirits that cause diseases and is asked to help grow vegetables.

Many ancient Indian (non-Āryan) tribes also had goddesses, whose worship coalesced in the course of time with that of the Great Mother. The forms of worship practiced by the tribes—bloody, including human, sacrifices—are still associated with Devī worship. Very often the worship of deceased women of a village merges with the worship of the Great Mother, a process of "making religion" that can still be observed in Indian villages. Many of the names of the Goddess, found in the litany of thousand names, are probably the names of these local village goddesses. Also many of her functions are taken unmistakably from village religion. Generally the Āryans must have been hostile toward the cult of the Mother, but already in the Mahābhārata we find Durgā established as war goddess, superseding Indra in this function.[50] The goddess of war also played a major role in Tamilnādu.[51] There are, no doubt, Vedic elements also in Devī religion—the worship of the earth (*pṛthvi*) as a goddess for instance, or the worship of *vāk*, the Word, as pointed out. But in the Purāṇas and Tantras, which perhaps already show influences from Inner Asia, Śāktism becomes fully developed in its mythology and cult. In Śāktism *prakṛti* or *māyā* becomes the active principle of the universe, both as a metaphysical principle and a concrete personality. The most important center of Śakti worship was, and still is, Kāmarūpa in today's Assam. Also the great rivers of India, principally the Gaṅgā and the Yamunā, have been worshipped as Goddesses since ancient times.[52] The most important Devī myth, her killing of *mahiṣāsura*, the embodiment of evil in a buffalo form, is the focus of the immensely popular

8 Durgā, Khajurāho twelfth century

Durga-pūjā celebrations still held in Bengal. Devī is represented figuratively in many forms, particular depictions usually alluding to one of her mythological exploits. A peculiar feature of Tantricism, however, are the *yantras*, symbolic diagrams considered by Śāktas to be representations of Devī.[53]

Śiva mythology associated Gaṇeśa, another popular deity, with Śiva's family.[54] But it seems that the elephant-headed, pot-bellied patron-god of business persons and scholars comes from an older stratum of religion, in which animal worship was predominant. This may also be the case with Hanuman, the monkey god, who in the Rāmāyaṇa is made the chief ally of Rāma and thus comes to be associated with Viṣṇu worship. The genealogies and family trees of the main deities that we meet so frequently in the Purāṇas are attempts, not always successful, to coordinate the various popular deities and make them appear, if not as manifestations of the one God, then at least as his children or servants.[55]

God is not dead in India and not a mere memory of the past. Numerous "living Gods" and "Incarnations" are everywhere in India today; some of them claim to continue the ancient line of Viṣṇu or Śiva or Devī *avatāras,* whereas others simply assume that they are the Supreme in a human body. It is not uncommon in India to get an invitation "to meet God the Father in person," to listen to the latest revelation through an *avatāra* of God, or to be confronted by someone who utters the word of God in the first person singular.

Many Hindu homes are lavishly decorated with color prints of a great many Hindu gods and goddesses, often joined by the gods and goddesses of other religions and the pictures of contemporary heroes. Thus side by side with Śiva and Viṣṇu and Devī one can see Jesus and Zoroaster, Gautama Buddha and Jīna Mahāvīra, Mahātmā Gandhi and Jawaharlal Nehru, and many others. But if questioned about the many gods even the illiterate villager will answer: *bhagvān ek hai*—the Lord is One. He may not be able to figure out in theological terms how the many gods and the one god hang together and he may not be sure about the hierarchy obtaining among the many manifestations, but he does know that ultimately there is only One and that the many somehow merge into the One.

Hindu theology has many ways of explaining the unity of Brahman in the diversity of *iṣṭa-devatās*: different psychological needs of people must be satisfied differently, local traditions and specific revelations must be accommodated, the ineffable can only be predicated in—quite literally—thousands of forms. Among the *sahasranāmas*—the litanies of thousand names, which are recited in honour of each of the great gods—the overlap is considerable: each one would be named creator, preserver, destroyer of the universe, each one would be called Truth[56] and Grace and Deliverance. Each one, in the end, is the same: One.[57]

Part 2

TRIMĀRGA: THE THREE HINDU PATHS TO LIBERATION

One of the oldest, most popular, and most important divisions of Hinduism is that into the three paths: *karmamārga,* the path of works, *jñānamārga,* the path of knowledge, and *bhaktimārga,* the path of loving devotion. Some conceive of these as representing a kind of evolution of Hinduism—depending on which path one considers the highest, the sequence would be altered accordingly.

Although it is a historically established fact that the prevalence and full recognition of *bhaktimārga* took place after that of *jñānamārga* and that Vedic religion placed a major emphasis on *karma* or sacrificial ritual, the three paths coexisted for a long time, and they mix and merge at many points. The practice of the average Hindu contains elements of all of them with particular emphasis given to one according to personal preference.

The idea of "religion" as a "path" is found in other cultures, too; the idea of a plurality of equivalent paths is fairly unique to Hinduism. True, there is also rivalry between adherents of different Hindu paths and some suggest that only one of them is the true path, the others being lower or incomplete—but the general understanding is that of equally valid options. Within each *mārga* the latitude varies. *Karmamārga* is a discipline that has to be followed fairly uniformly allowing only for minor local variants. *Jñānamārga* comes in various shapes, already the Upanisads specify 32 different *vidyās.* However, the need to have a teacher and the requirement of absolute loyalty toward the guru restrict individual choices once the guru has been selected. *Bhaktimārga* leaves personal choices widely open. Not only can one choose one's *iṣṭadevatā* and call oneself a devotee of Viṣṇu, Śiva, Devī or another *deva,* one can also choose within each sect a variety of interpretations and practices. It is especially the *bhaktimārga* that constantly brings forth new developments and movements.

In spite of what has been said about the options between and within the different paths, Hindu religion is highly structured and tends to embrace a person's entire life with its regulations.

Hinduism is basically very conservative and many of the regulations going back to Vedic times are still effective in shaping the daily routine of millions of Hindus. Some of this routine is described in the chapter "*Karmamārga*: The Path of Works." Hinduism, like all traditional religions, was always aware of the ethical dimension of life and of the fact that the moral universe is fragile and in need not only of being preserved but also of being constantly restored. Notions of guilt and sin play a great role in Hinduism, and devices for righting wrongs and the atonement of sins occupy a large place in the life of many Hindus. Rites of passage are fairly universal—Hinduism has designed elaborate rituals in its *saṁskāras* not only to accompany its members into the next stage of life but also to augment their spiritual powers and to ensure personal fulfillment.

More than anything else the *jñānamārga,* the path of knowledge, was found attractive by non-Hindus, who admired the deep wisdom and spiritual insights of the Hindu sages. The Upaniṣads and the literature based on them deal with human universals, the discovery of one's true self and the soul of the world, liberating knowledge and the final emancipation.

Although the *karmamārga* presupposes high-caste standing and the *jñānamārga* is largely for an intellectual elite, the *bhaktimārga,* the path of loving devotion, has universal appeal: it promises salvation and heaven also to low-caste people, women and children, and even animals. Great waves of God love have swept over India periodically and left behind large congregations of devotees, an enormous treasure of inspired poetry, thousands of beautiful temples, and millions of images in which the deities are physically present to their worshippers. Only some moments of this history of God intoxication can be recalled in the chapters on Viṣṇu, Śiva, and Devī—only a small amount of literature can be referred to and only very inadequately can the fervor be described that animates Hindus who celebrate the great feasts in honor of their deities in the major centres of devotion. All of India has in the course of the last 3000 or more years come under the influence of, first, Vedic and then, Purāṇic and Tāntric Hinduism, and all regions of India have preserved some of their own local traditions in temple architecture, festivals, and songs, but one region stands out in India for its distinct culture and its independent tradition: Tamilnādu, the Land of the Tamils in South India. Tamil belongs to a family of languages totally different from Sanskrit and the rest of the North Indian languages. Tamilians claim that both their language and their culture are older than that of the North. There is no doubt that in spite of the extensive Sanskritization that took place and resulted in most of the Tamils today being Śaivites or Vaiṣṇavas recognizing the same sacred books and traditions as the rest of India, Dravidian elements are strong and distinctive enough to warrant a special chapter on the gods of the Tamils. This, too, of course, is an incomplete sketch of a rich and colorful tradition within Hinduism. It may serve as a first introduction to a large subject and as a further reminder that traditional Hinduism has, in addition to its Vedic and Sanskritic heritage, important non-Vedic and non-Sanskritic components.

9 The Path of Works: *Karmamārga*

> In ancient days the Lord of creatures created men along with sacrifice and said: "By this shall you bring forth and this shall be unto you that which will yield the milk of your desires."
>
> —*Bhagavadgītā III,* 10

In February 1962 Indian newspapers were carrying numerous articles describing measures to meet a predicted *aṣṭāgraha,* a particular astronomical conjunction of earth, sun, moon, and five planets. The astrologers were unanimous in considering it an extremely evil omen, possibly the harbinger of the end of the world. Some journalists were serious; others tried to joke a little; none dared to call the whole thing a humbug. Quite apart from the fact that astronomically speaking the *aṣṭāgraha* was not quite accurate, millions of Hindus were frankly worried, expecting a ghastly catastrophe. Many sold all their belongings and went to Prayāga or Kāśī or to some other holy place from where one goes directly heaven at the time of death or one can attain *mokṣa.* The rich engaged thousands of pandits and Brahmins to organize Vedic *yajñas* that would go on for weeks and weeks on end, reciting millions of Vedic mantras. The dreaded event passed without a major disaster. What had happened? The world had been saved through the creation of the auspicious karma produced in the ritual appropriate for the occasion.

Ritual is one of the most prominent and most important features of Hinduism, and it has two main sources: the Vedic and the Āgamic traditions.[1] For the sake of a more methodical presentation a separate treatment of Vedic ritual, as it emerges from the classical texts, will be given here before describing other forms, which are more popular today. The rationale of both of these forms of ritual, as expressed in the Pūrva-Mīmāṁsā system and the Āgamic treatises is quite different, too, as shall be seen.

THE VEDIC WAY TO HEAVEN

Quite early in the Veda the distinction was drawn between the *karma-kāṇḍa* and the *jñāna-kāṇḍa*, the part dealing with "works" and the part dealing with "knowledge," different not only in their contents but also in their ultimate aims. The aim of the *karma-kāṇḍa* lies within *tri-loka*, the tripartite universe of heaven, earth, and netherworlds. It promises bliss and wealth, and a sojourn in *svarga*, a heaven with earthly pleasure, as the highest goal after death. *Jñāna-kāṇḍa* is not interested in things of this earth nor in heaven; it wants insight into, and communion with, a reality that is nonsensual and not transient: Brahman. It was meant for those who had given up all worldly liabilities, with interests that went beyond wife and children, house and property, business and entertainment. The householder living within his family circle had to choose *karma-mārga* to secure for himself what he needed and wished for and also to conform to the social pattern established upon a firm basis of ritual. Later theorists try to demonstrate that the two elements, the life of the householder and the life of the houseless, constituted the even balance of an ideal social order. In reality there was and is considerable friction and competition between the two. There are texts in which the householder is praised as the one who provides nourishment for all, and there are other texts that speak of the spiritual merit that the whole society derives from the *samnyāsis'* efforts; but there is also ample evidence of householders' polemics against *samnyāsa*, which was considered by many an exaggeration, said to go against the *śāstras* and to be a violation of the basic duties ordered by the Vedas.[2]

The householder knew that everything depended on his work; what was true for food and drink and shelter was assumed to be true of sunshine and rain, of happiness and ill luck, too. Religion for him was work, which, when properly done, produced its fruits. From that basic consideration developed an intricate system and a theology of sacrifice that explained everything as being the result of ritual, *yajña*, including the creation of the universe.[3] As the importance of the proper performance of religious work rose, so did the importance of the Brahmins, the professionals of ritual sacrifice. An explanation may be required to prevent a possible misunderstanding of the term *sacrifice*. In the fully developed Vedic system it had little to do with the devotion with which Hindus today offer their *pūjā*. *Yajña* in Vedic tradition is an act that has its own intrinsic power and "exercises compulsion not only over the gods but also over natural phenomena without requiring the co-operation of the gods."[4] When we understand the nature of the *devas* as manifestations of a power greater than themselves and not wholly identical with any of them, we may also appreciate the Vedic analysis of the *yajña* as requiring four components: *dravya* or sacrificial matter, *tyāga* or the relinquishing of the object sacrificed, a *devatā* to be addressed as the recipient, and a mantra, or effective word, none of which may be omitted. As a reality the *yajña* is more comprehensive than a *deva*: it has power over the *deva*.[5] A businesslike atmosphere prevails in Vedic sacrificial religion: every desired object has its specified sacrifice, every sacrifice has its price. Because the *devas* are believed to depend on the *yajña*, the Vedic sacrificer can tell them quite openly: "If you give me what I want, I shall give to you. If you don't give me, I shall not give to you. If you take something away from me, I shall take away from you."[6]

Offering sacrifices (Figure 9.1) was part of dharma, of the established world order and the particular social order. Kings had to arrange for public *yajñas* for the welfare of their people; householders had to maintain domestic sacrifices for the well-being of their families. The expense involved in performing *śrauta* sacrifices, especially the elaborate ones, like the *aśvamedha*, was so high that it could strain the resources of an entire kingdom, and this ultimately was the major cause for their discontinuance.[7] However, even in ancient times the possibility of substitution existed. Material substitution was regulated through specific texts—supplements to ritual texts such as the *Mūlādhyaya-pariśiṣṭa* of Kātyāyana[8]—that gave precise monetary equivalents for cows and bulls mentioned as *dakṣina* in the texts themselves, usually fixed at a nominal level, such as Rs. 1 for one cow or bull. Spiritual substitution mentioned especially in *bhakti* texts of later times went so far as to equal the spiritual worth of reciting the name of God, or of a *pūjā* to a *mūrti*, to a great many of the most expensive *śrautas*, such as the *aśvamedha*.

Public sacrifices were splendid and costly events in former ages; they have become relatively rare but they are still performed occasionally. At the occasion of the aforementioned *aṣṭāgraha* quite a number of such public vedic sacrifices were performed by thousands of Brahmins, paid by rich business people and industrialists who alone were able to afford the hundreds of thousands of rupees required. On November 27, 1957, the *Times of India*, under the headline "Sādhus Perform *Mahā Yajña* to Fight Menace of H-Bombs," reported a public sacrifice arranged by a former governor

Figure 9.1 Vedic fire sacrifice

of Bombay. More than 500 *sādhus* and paṇḍits gathered in Bombay for a *Mahā Yajña* to reconcile the *devas* and increase the spiritual strength of humankind, "to purify the evil, morbid and dangerous atmosphere pervading the world because of atom bombs and H-bombs."[9] The Indian weekly *Blitz* carried a report about a Vedic sacrifice ordered by Jana Sangh politicians with the intent of killing Indira Gandhi through spells.[10]

In 1975, the Dutch-American Indologist Frits Staal had Kerala Brahmins perform an ancient Vedic sacrifice, the *agnicayana*. The whole procedure, the preparations including burning and laying the bricks for the fire altar, putting up the *paṇḍal*, performing the *yajña* itself, and demolishing the fire altar after its use are shown on the hour-long film that was made by the experts who also set down their observations and reflections in an impressive two-tome study under the name of *Agni*.[11] The subsequent controversy arising around the performance—the challenge to the claim that what we see in the film is exactly what Vedic Brahmins did 3000 years ago—need not be dealt with here. The point Staal has proven is that Vedic traditions are preserved in some parts of India and that the detail laid down in ancient ritual works is observed on occasions like this—and also how enormously expensive such grand sacrifices are.[12]

According to an Upaniṣadic teaching man owes his existence to the "five fire sacrifices,"[13] and the classical *śāstras* circumscribe with the term *pañca mahāyajña,* five great sacrifices, the routine of daily duties of the Brahmin. When the Brahmin had no other obligations, the execution of these occupied all of his time; under the pressure of changing circumstances the five sacrifices were reduced to mere symbolic gestures. Thus *deva-yajña,* the sacrifice to the gods, could be performed by throwing a stick of wood into the fire; *pitṛ-yajña,* the sacrifice to the ancestors, could be fulfilled by pouring a glass of water onto the floor; *bhūta-yajña,* sacrifice to all creatures, can be reduced to throwing out a small ball of rice; *manuṣya-yajña,* the sacrifice to men or hospitality in the widest sense, is fulfilled by giving a mouthful of rice to a Brahmin; *brahma-yajña,* the mantra sacrifice or study of the Veda, may consist in the recitation of one single line of scripture. Those, however, who can afford the time, frequently perform the elaborate ceremonies detailed in the *śāstras* and fill their days with holy ritual and sacred chant. The ideal daily routine of the Brahmin as outlined in the law books may be followed in its entirety by very few people in India today, but surprisingly many practice part of it quite regularly.

THE VEDIC WAY OF LIFE

Vedic tradition endows also the biological facts and necessities of hygiene with a religious meaning and provides for a detailed regulation of everyday life.[14] The Hindu householder is enjoined by his *śāstras* to rise at dawn. The first word he speaks should be the name of his *iṣṭa-devatā,* the chosen deity. He should direct his eyes toward the palms of his hands, to behold an auspicious object as the first thing every morning. Then he is to touch the floor to perform as the first work of the day an auspicious action, and then to bow before the images of gods in his room. The mantras and prayers vary according to denomination and family tradition. Various scriptures enjoin the householder to begin the day by thinking what he is going to do today to increase dharma and *artha,* righteousness and wealth, and about the efforts he will take toward this end.

The scriptures provide very detailed rules for daily hygiene. In an age concerned about environmental pollution we can appreciate the great subtlety of the ancient Hindus in promoting physical cleanliness, when we see how they surrounded the vital functions with many religious thoughts and rules. The daily bath is a necessity in India as well as a religious precept. While pouring water with the *loṭha* (brass vessel) over himself the pious Hindu is supposed to recite a mantra, such as the following: "O you waters, in the manner that makes you the source of our fortune, pour strength into us so that our vision may be wide and beautiful. This your essence, which is so auspicious, let us enjoy here, you who are like loving mothers. Be our refuge for the removal of evil, wherewith you delight us. O waters, truly you have created us."

Tarpaṇa as part of the morning ablutions must be specially mentioned. The bather folds his hands to hold some water and lets it flow back into the river while reciting mantras to *devas* and *pitṛs*. Each day after the bath clean clothes are put on. The sacred thread, called *yajñopavita* or *janëu,* is never removed at bath but according to the different occasions worn differently. After sipping some water from the hollow of his hand the Hindu, if he belongs to one of the more recent *saṃpradāyas,* applies the specific marks of his denomination to his body. This spiritual makeup is done very lovingly and carefully: vertical lines on the forehead for the Vaiṣṇavas, horizontal lines for the Śaivas, with many variations according to the particular subsect. Many write the name of their God or short mantras with white paste on their skins. According to many religious books all ceremonies and prayers are fruitless if the devotee does not carry the signs of his God on his body.

The Śaivite *Bhasmajābala Upaniṣad* is concerned exclusively with the preparation and significance of the *tripuṇḍra,* the three lines in honor of Śiva. It describes how the sacred ashes are to be prepared from the dung of a brown cow and how the markings are to be applied.

> For Brahmins the wearing of *bhasma* (ashes) alone is the right conduct. Without wearing the sign one should not drink nor do anything else. He who has given up the sign out of negligence should neither recite the *gāyatri-mantra* nor put offerings into the sacred fire, nor worship the gods, the *ṛṣis* or the *pitṛs.* That alone is the right path to destroy all sin and attain the means of salvation. . . . He who makes use of this sign of ashes in the early morning is delivered of the sin he may have committed during the night and of the sin that originates in the stealing of gold. He who resorts to this at midday and looks, meditating, into the sun, is freed from the sin of drinking intoxicating beverages, the stealing of gold, the killing of Brahmins, the killing of a cow, the slaying of a horse, the murder of his *guru,* his mother and his father. By taking his refuge to the sign of ashes three times a day, he attains the fruit of vedic studies, he attains the merits of ablutions in all the three and a half crores of sacred waters; he attains the fullness of life.[15]

The morning prayer that follows, called *saṃdhyā,* is still observed by millions of Hindus every day. It is to take place before sunrise and to end when the sun's disk is fully above the horizon. The main text is the *gāyatri mantra,* which is to be repeated several times; the scriptures recommend to the faithful to prolong it as much as possible because the ancestors had attained long life, understanding, honor, and glory by this means. One of the strangest rites still practiced today is the daily "driving out of evil." The Brahmin takes water into the hollow of his right hand, brings it close to his nose, blows onto the water through the right and the left nostrils, repeats the mantra three times and pours the water out. The *saṃdhyā* rites have been lengthened in later schools by the inclusion of many texts from Purāṇas; very few people use those long versions.

The orthodox *smārta* is enjoined to proceed to *agniṣṭoma* after his *saṃdhyā* is completed, to redeem the first of his debts, with which every man is born. Most ordinary Hindus will perform *japa* instead, the repetition of a brief mantra or of one of the names of God. These vary according to the religious affiliation; but all believe that the name of their own God, if recited often, would confer blessing and ultimate redemption. If *japa* is to be effective, the recitation has to be done with the help of a *mālā,* a string of beads, different again according to the different sects. Vaiṣṇavas use a *mālā* made up of beads from the wood of the *tulasī* tree; Śaivites are obliged to put their faith in the *Rudrākṣa-mālā* made from the seeds of a shrub. Usually the *mālās* have 16, 32, 64, or 108 beads. Numerous treatises explain the merits of the *mālās* and recommend their use through an account of their divine origin. Thus the Śaivite *Rudrākṣajabala Upaniṣad* writes: "Thus spoke the Lord Kālāgnirudra: 'To bring about the destruction of Tripura, I had to close my eyes. From my eyes fell waterdrops. These drops turned into *rudrākṣas.* For the sake of the deliverance of all living beings I have disposed that by the mere uttering of their names as much merit is gathered as by the gift of ten cows, and by looking at them and touching them twice as much. . . . If worn by the pious the *rudrākṣas* absolve of all sins committed by day or by night . . ." Precise instructions follow, how many of these beads to wear, what kind of beads to choose, and so on.[16]

Every morning All India Radio broadcasts *śahnai* music; not necessarily because the oboe-like instrument is a favorite with the program director but because it sounds are traditionally considered auspicious and the Hindu is enjoined to listen to such to ensure a happy day for himself. The radio morning program also includes recitations from the Mahābhārata or the Rāmāyaṇa. Hindus devote much care to the separation of auspicious from inauspicious objects, sights, sounds, and times. Hind newspapers contain a daily extract from the *pañcāṅga,* with an indication of the astrological data, lists of auspicious and inauspicious colors and directions. There are differences of opinion on many of these, but some are universally recognized typifications. A Brahmin, a cow, fire, gold, *ghī,* the sun, water, and a courtesan, for instance, are considered to be auspicious objects to behold, and one may look forward to a good day if any of them is seen first thing in the morning. Quite serious people delay a long-planned journey or postpone an important decision if they happen to meet a cripple, a madman, a drunkard, a bald-headed man, or a *samnyāsin,* considered to be inauspicious sights.

A BRAHMIN'S DUTIES

The orthodox Brahmin is supposed to fill the first part of his day with these religious exercises. After that he is to study or to read his Veda, do his *svādhyāya,* to gather firewood, flowers, and grass for worship. The third part of the day should be devoted to earning money. In the olden days there were strict rules for it, a distinction between permitted and forbidden occupations. Formerly the nonobservance of such rules entailed punishment like expulsion from the caste; today, especially in big cities, much of this has been forgotten. Since ancient times the teaching of the Veda had been the Brahmin's privilege; he was not allowed to ask for payment but the student was bound regularly to give his guru presents according to the wealth of his family. "Receiving gifts" is the Brahmins' privilege even today, and many insist on it. The common expression "to honor a Brahmin" means to make a gift to him. Today Brahmins are found in a great many different professions. They are farmers, government officials, lawyers, teachers, but also cooks, soldiers, and employees are found among them. Because by tradition Brahmins had an educational privilege, they have been able even in modern times to occupy relatively more influential posts and to some extent today's India is still Brahmin dominated.[17]

After midday the orthodox Brahmin was instructed to take another bath and to offer an elaborate *tarpaṇa* to the *devas,* the *pitṛs,* and *ṛṣis*: "May the *devas, ṛṣis, pitṛs,* the human beings, all beings from Brahmā right down to the blade of grass be satiated, likewise all ancestors, the mother, the maternal grandfather and the rest, may this water do good to the millions of families of bygone days who live in the seven *dvīpas*."[18] The longer formula takes up a great deal of time, enumerates 31 *devatās* singly, mentions a long list of *ṛṣis* and relations. At the mention of each single name water is sprinkled, with the invocation "may he be pleased with it."

The *deva-yajña* used to be an elaborate ritual. As regards the domestic rites, it has been largely replaced by *pūjā*, the worship of an image according to Āgamic scriptures. Official Vedic worship did not make use of images, as far as we know, but popular religion was certainly not totally identical with Vedic orthodoxy, as already the Artharva Veda shows. Purāṇas, saṃhitās, Āgamas, and tantras have taken over a good deal of Vedic terminology and regulations and combined these with material from other traditions. Thus we find countless chapters detailing the obligatory daily domestic rites that are followed by many households. The average Hindu family has its *mūrti* before which daily worship is offered quite formally several times a day. The particulars—vessels to be used, materials to be employed, color of flowers, and so forth—vary from sect to sect. In its elaborate form *pūjā* consists of sixty-four individual ceremonies; in daily ceremonies at home usually only part of them are performed. These are *āvāhana*, invitation of the *iṣṭadevatā*; *āsana*, offering a seat to the deity; *pādya*, offering water to wash the feet; *arghya*, offering water for washing the hands; *ācamanīya*, offering water to rinse the mouth; *snāniya*, water for a bath; *vastra*, leaves for clothing the deity; *yajñopavita*, offering a sacred thread; *candana*, sandalwood paste; *puṣpa*, flowers; *dhūpa*, incense; *dīpa*, a lighted lamp; *naivedya*, offering cooked food; *tāmbūla*, a betel nut; *dakṣina*, some money; *nāmaskāra*, a solemn greeting; *pradakṣiṇā*, circumambulation; and mantrapuṣpa, scattering a handful of blossoms before the image, reciting some honorific mantras. Each individual gesture is accompanied by appropriate mantras, varying from sect to sect. Many of the ancient *śāstras* give explicit order to distribute food to different deities in various parts of the house, to gods and *caṇḍālas*, the outcastes,[19] to lepers and cripples, to crows and insects. Eating is considered to be a "sacrifice to the gods who dwell in the body."

Almost all nations consider hospitality a virtue. *Manuṣya-yajña*, one of the basic duties of the Brahmin, is interpreted by Manu as "honoring guests." There is a possibility of understanding it in an allegorical sense, too. *Agni*, the fire, is the "guest of the householder" and whatever is thrown into the fire is considered to be an offering of food "to the guest." On the other hand, there are also Hindus who retain the literal meaning of the precept and make it a point to invite at least one guest to every major meal. The interpretation of *atithi*, guest, given in the *śāstras* says that only a Brahmin can be, properly speaking, a guest, that hospitality is restricted to one meal and one overnight stay if he arrives late in the evening and cannot return to his village. A guest who has been disappointed or turned away can unload all his sins upon the householder and can take away from him his *punya*, his merit.[20] If a samnyāsi turns up as a guest, the host has, according to Hindu theory, to consider himself lucky; it is not the guest who should be grateful for hospitality but the host must thank the samnyāsi for the opportunity to earn merit. The practice, at least today, is less than ideal though, and few samnyāsis would approach an unknown family for hospitality. However, the invited guest, especially if he is a swāmī, is showered with effusive attention. India still has a tradition of hospitality that has no parallel in the contemporary West. Wealthy pious Hindus of the past and the present have established numerous guest houses in places of pilgrimage; those *dharmaśālas* offer usually free shelter and quite frequently also free food to travelers and pilgrims, irrespective of their creed or color.

"He who goes to a meal without having performed the various sacrifices consumes only sin, he does not really eat," says an old proverb. Only one who fulfills the rules of dharma gains strength from his food. "All beings live by food. The Veda explains: 'Food is life; therefore one should give food!, eating is the supreme sacrifice!'" thus the Upaniṣads.[21] *Anna*, food, and *bhojana*, eating, occupy the first place among the topics of conversation of the average Hindu. Mahatma Gandhi's writings convey some impression of the solicitude and anxiety the Hindu bestows on daily meals, diet, and their preparation. There is good reason behind it, of course. India has known famines and times of scarcity throughout recorded history and the Indian climate makes it necessary to take care of one's health far more than in moderate zones. Many a Hindu knows hundreds of health rules from home, and it is common for religious books to give instruction also with regard to food and meals. The traditional Indian housewife spends most of her time in the kitchen preparing the meals. Indian cuisine has a not undeserved reputation, although the majority of the population has to be satisfied with a somewhat monotonous routine. The Upaniṣads even offer a theology of food: "If food is pure, the mind becomes pure. When understanding is pure it allows strong concentration (on the Self).

If this is safeguarded, all the knots (which fetter the Self to the world) are loosened."[22]

Next to the treatment of marriage, food in all its aspects takes up the most space in the *dharma-śāstras*. Caste rules concern primarily intermarrying and interdining, specifying who may receive food from whom and who may not, thereby drawing very close social borderlines between different groups of people. Whereas the ancient Vedic Indians seem to have had but few food taboos—according to available documents they were meat eaters, not excluding beef—under Buddhist and Jain influence meat eating became considered irreligious. Several Hindu rulers (and even some Muslims) forbade the slaughter of animals. Animal sacrifices were replaced by flower *pūjās*, meat dishes by vegetarian food. The majority of Hindus today are vegetarians for religious reasons, which are frequently fortified by hygienic arguments. The religious books specify the kinds of food that may be taken by particular groups of people. The rules also have regional variations. The Brahmins of Uttar Pradesh avoid all meat, fish, eggs and many other things; the Brahmins of Bengal must have a piece of fish with their rice and they also eat eggs. The strictest rules have been devised by the Vaiṣṇavas, who classify all foods into *rājasik*, exciting, *tāmasik*, foul, and *sāttvik*, pure: only the last category is permitted, excluding thereby not only all meat and fish but also onions, garlic, red fruit like tomatoes, and many other things. Special rules obtain for the frequent days of fast observed by different groups at different times.[23]

THE THEORY OF VEDIC *YAJÑA*

The understanding of Hinduism as a whole calls for a somewhat more thorough study of the public Vedic sacrifices, though most of them belong irrevocably to the past. Indological scholarship has done an enormous amount of work in this area, editing and translating virtually all the preserved texts and making detailed studies of many historical problems.[23] The Vedic saṃhitās were meant exclusively for use at the public sacrifices and official rituals; the highly technical *śrauta-sūtras* lay down with great precision the details of the public sacrifices. We read in Hindu literature of *yajñas* to which thousands of Brahmins were invited and at which hundreds of sacrificial animals were slaughtered, *yajñas* lasting for months, even years, that cost so much that they could impoverish the richest man.[25] Because the effect of the Vedic sacrifice depended on the correct pronunciation of the mantra, the precision of the ritual and the observance of hundreds of minute circumstances, it very soon became the exclusive domain of sacrificial specialists, the Brahmin priests. The significance of brahmanical priesthood increased in proportion as the sacrifice became more complicated. Even for the humblest of Vedic sacrifices four to five Brahmin specialists were required, hundreds for the major ones.

The efficacy of the Vedic sacrifice was supposed to depend on the offering: several remarks in Vedic works give some reason to assume that the most noble and most efficacious sacrifice was the *puruṣa-medha*, the human sacrifice.[26] It made the sacrificer equal to Prajāpati, the creator. The accounts we have give the impression that this was a real sacrifice according to an elaborate ritual, not just a symbolic ceremony.[27]

Animal sacrifices were very common; one proof of this is the opposition of early religious reformers like Buddha and Mahāvīra against them. The greatest was the *aśva-medha*, the horse sacrifice, to be performed by kings as part of their assuming "universal power."[28] So highly was it regarded, even in later times when its performance had become extremely rare,[29] that the *Bhāgavata Purāṇa* can declare that the extermination of the whole of humankind could be atoned for by one single *aśva-medha*. It was also taken as the highest unit for religious merit in describing the *puṇya* accruing from pilgrimage to certain holy places. The Daśāśvamedha Ghāt in Vāraṇasī has been so named because a bath in the Ganges at this particular spot is supposed to bring as much merit as the performance of ten horse sacrifices. The animal most often sacrificed, however, was the goat. The *Brāhmaṇas* give the following explanation for it: "When the *devas* had killed a man for their sacrifice, that part of him which was fit to be made an offering went out and entered a horse. Thence the horse became an animal fit to be sacrificed. From the horse it went into the ox, from there into the goat. In the goat it remained for the longest time, therefore the goat is best fitted to be sacrificed."[30] The goat contains the most *medha*, "sacrificial substance," which is required for ensuring the proper result in sacrifice. The common daily oblation consisted of rice, barley cakes, butter, curds, and milk, in short the *devas* were supposed to have the same taste as humans. A very important ingredient of most sacrifices was *soma*, the intoxicating sap of a plant.[31] It is often called *amṛta*, nectar of immortality; an entire hymn collection of the Ṛgveda consists of nothing but *soma* hymns. According to tradition an eagle brought it to Indra; by partaking of it the *devas* gained immortality. *Soma* is called "child of heaven" and is supposed to have healing powers, to drive away blindness and lameness. In one hymn we read: "We have drunk *soma,* we have become immortal; we have gone to the light, we have found the *devas.* What can hostility now do to us, and what the malice of mortal men, O immortal one!"[32]

The Vedic sacrifices are intimately connected with the course of time and with the movement of the heavenly bodies. They are an expression of an awareness that human existence is precarious and time bound. Over and over the sacrifice is equated with the year, the month, the day or the various seasons and the sacrifice itself is considered essential for maintaining the flow of time. The full-moon and new-moon sacrifices have always been, and still are, of fundamental importance; their ritual became the model for all the other *iṣṭis.* If the new-moon sacrifice was not offered, there would be no more moon. Even today, the religious calendar of the Hindus is a united lunar-solar calendar, with all the complications and difficulties that result from such a combination. The lunar month is divided into 30 *tithis,* 15 *tithis* of the dark half and 15 *tithis* of the bright half, which do not coincide at all with the 'days' of our calendar and have to be learned from the indispensable *pañcāṅga.* Because the "auspicious time" in which important events must take place—marriage ceremonies, the opening of great buildings, the beginning of the parliamentary sessions, and so on—is calculated according to *muhūrtas,* subdivisions of the lunar *tithis* (there are 30 *muhūrtas* in each *tithi* of approximately 45 minutes duration), the specialists acquainted with the *pañcāṅga* who sit on the pavements of small and big cities are never without a clientele in need of their services.

NEW MEANINGS OF SACRIFICE

Whereas the Vedic sacrifice gives the impression of a transaction in which little or no emotion is invested—the *devas* do not have to be won over through any sign of affection or love—in later times the emotional content of the sacrifice becomes predominant. The value of the gift offered may be insignificant, the sacrificer may be ignorant of Vedic mantras and ceremonial, what counts is devotion to the God, whose grace is sought and who considers only the heart. As Kṛṣṇa tells Arjuna in the Bhagavadgītā: "Whosoever offers to me with devotion (*bhakti*) a leaf, a fruit, a flower, a cup of water—that offering of love, of the pure of heart, I accept."[33] The Purāṇas compete with each other in telling the masses, who could never hope to participate in a Vedic public ceremony, that devotion alone counts. This devotion may be expressed in a symbolic gesture, perhaps the repetition of the name of God or the offering of an incense stick or a flower. But inevitably the formalism at work in the Vedic religion also entered the Āgamas: they abound in detailed regulations for worship, ordering and forbidding certain acts and words as firmly as the Vedic sūtras did.[34] Worship at the major temples follows a very strict ritual that according to tradition has been usually instituted by the God himself through a revelation to a leading *ācārya* who codified it.[35] The basic pattern of worship follows the pattern of personal attention devoted to an honored guest or a king.[36] Whereas the *deva* in the Veda is but a transitory symbolic fixation of the ultimate power, the *īśvara* of the Purāṇas is the Ultimate in person, present in his image, ready to give his personal grace to the one who worships him. The rationalization of karma, the ritual act, in this "new devotion" is quite different from that of the Vedic sacrificial religion.

According to the *Pūrva Mīmāṁsā*, the school of orthodox Vedic interpretation, each Vedic sacrifice, duly performed, produced an incorruptible substance called *apūrva*, independent of *devas*, which was at the sacrificer's disposal after his death. Whatever else the sacrificer might have done, if he had the *apūrva* from a sacrifice that ensured a sojourn in heaven, he would come to heaven, whether or not the *devas* were willing. In the "new religion" the devotee had to be constantly on the alert to remain in his or her God's favor; eternal salvation could be gained or lost even in the last moment of life. Popular stories tell of great sinners, who according to all the Vedic rules would be condemned to the lowest hells, winning immediate eternal bliss through an even inadvertent utterance of the name of Hari or Śiva.[37] The Purāṇas insist on regular worship of God as means to win God's grace and a good deal of the activity of the pious is directed toward gaining *puṇya* by performing actions that are described in the holy books as ordained by God for this end: *japa*, the repetition of the name of God, singing the praises of God, reading holy books, attending temple services, worshipping the image, going on pilgrimages and so on. Though there are constant reminders of the affection and emotion with which a devotee has to do the daily worship to "fulfill the law," quite frequently these actions are performed mechanically, as if they could become effective automatically and magically.

Comparative studies of ritual have pointed out a great many parallels between the Vedic Indian and other peoples' notions of sacrifice and cult.[38] Anthropologists and ethologists speak of "ritual behavior" even in animals, assuming that not only human societies but also animals feel an urge to perform acts that among humans are called *ritual*. The implications are farreaching. For one, the beginnings of ritual would not lay in rational deliberation and conscious reflection but in the subconscious psyche, perhaps even in the biological sphere. The other conclusion to be drawn would be that rituals are likely to continue, in spite of periodic major enlightenments that belittle and ridicule them as meaningless and unable to achieve their purpose. Meaningless they may be, as F. Staal has tried to prove,[39] but not purposeless. Cārvākas and Buddhists derided Vedic ritual and succeeded to some extent in interrupting Vedic sacrificial tradition. New forms of ritual developed, also among the Buddhists. Nineteenth century reformers debunked old as well as new forms of ritual and sacrifice. And again, other forms developed and have found acceptance among contemporary Hindus.

10 Purity and Merit: The Twin Concerns of *Karmamārga*

> Pure, Maruts, pure yourselves, are your oblations; to you, the pure, pure sacrifice I offer. By Law they came to truth, the Law's observers, bright by their birth, and pure, and sanctifying.
>
> —*Ṛgveda* VI, 56, 12

Although certain aspects of purity in Hinduism certainly have to do with bodily fluids and their discharge—menstruating women are considered ritually impure, to mention the most obvious of such instances—it would be wrong to identify the issue of purity in Hinduism totally with this aspect, as some Indologists, under the influence of a certain school of anthropology, seem to do. In addition to the materially conditioned purity there is a very sophisticated notion of a higher purity, partly ethical, partly spiritual. Therefore the central theme of the teaching of the present Śaṅkarācāryas, the *jagad-gurus*, or "world teachers," who are listened to with great seriousness by a great many of Hindus and whose words carry authority—is purity of mind.[1] "Purity of mind is thought to bring the mind to greater understanding. Purity of mind, requisite for devotion and meditation, leads on to religious knowledge. Two classic qualifications for self-knowledge are freedom from desires and purity of mind." To some extent the notion of auspicious-inauspicious central to Hinduism runs parallel to that of purity-impurity. Here, as in most other cases, Hindu practice and belief does not follow simply from a logical extension of one basic idea but there is a plurality of basic notions from which, quite logically, but not always in mutually compatible fashion specific beliefs and practices flow. The Hindu notion of merit is also multidimensional. In addition to the Vedic idea of *apūrva*, the merit accruing from a sacrifice that can be stored up for later use in heaven, we find Purāṇic ideas of gaining merit by either reciting the names of a deity or by performing *pūjā*. Quite different, but not unrelated, is the idea, very widespread too among Hindus, that tapas, self-mortification, self-imposed and voluntary, both purifies and confers merit. Equally, the idea of gaining purity and merit not only for oneself, but also for ancestors and others, by going on pilgrimage and bathing in a *tīrtha*, is fairly universally acceptable to Hindus.[2] It is not really a Vedic idea but it combines with Vedic ideas in the practical life of Hindus. More on this will be said in a later chapter, which explains how gaining of purity and merit is tied to specific times and places.

The inextricable conjunction of the rather impersonal vedic and the highly personal Purāṇic traditions make it impossible to clearly differentiate in the activities of traditional Hindus between acts done to obtain ritual purity, to gain merit, or to win the grace of God, which, in a certain sense, obviates everything else.

Hinduism is not a primitive magico-ritualistic tribal cult (if such exist) in which purely externalized and quite mechanical criteria would be used to decide who was to participate in the tribal rites, but a very complex and a very sophisticated tradition. It certainly did preserve archaic and magical elements, but it integrated those with ethical reflection and theological thought. It will be good if in addition to observing what can be observed by way of ritual action one also reads, or listens to, reflections on ethical issues by learned and thoughtful Hindus, past and present. The Upaniṣads already throw doubt on the efficacy of Vedic ritual: they recommend asceticism and introspection as means to gain purity and earn merit.

Throughout the history of Hinduism there is, on the one hand, an insistence of performing the prescribed ritual for achieving and maintaining one's status within the *varṇāśrama-dharma* and there is, on the other hand, the clearly expressed conviction that rituals alone are not sufficient and that the purity which they effect is not enough to reach the ultimate aim of life, *mokṣa*. Numerous Hindu saints and singers denounced ritualism and ridiculed the belief that ritual purity would win a person entry to the realm of God. Personal virtues as well as social engagement, genuine devotion and service of God are stressed as means to reach purity and gain merit.

The majority of today's Hindus would agree. The equivocal nature of the Hindu notions of purity and merit is underscored by the fact that most Hindus make use of all available means offered to earn merit and to purify themselves, regardless from which source they come. Devout Hindus will accept the blessing of a

Christian priest as well as the *aśīrvādas* of Hindu *pūjāris,* they will visit places of pilgrimage regardless of which religion they belong to and they will participate in all forms of worship that appeal to them. They will, however, follow their own traditional, Vedic practices where religion intersects with their standing in society and will undergo the prescribed *saṃskāras.*

ETHICAL STANDARDS OF HINDUISM

Hindu tradition has devoted a great deal of intellectual work to the clarification of moral and ethical issues; in this context it is impossible even to mention all the important authors and views.[3] As the brief discussion of dharma has shown, religion and the morality connected with it are defined within the framework of the *varṇāśrama* scheme as *svadharma,* morality appropriate to each class and each stage in life. Certain moral precepts, however, are supposed to be common to all humankind. The so-called *sādhāraṇa-dharma* has a number of features in common with the Ten Commandments of the Bible or the Natural Law of the Western classical philosophical tradition. Hindu ethics as a whole, however, shows so many peculiar features that it would be misleading to represent it in Western terminology. Nor is the Hindu tradition united in the articulation of its ethical thought. Numerous schools have produced sometimes radically different views on important matters. Only some of these will be described here; for others more specialized works will have to be consulted.[4]

Hindu ethics, generally speaking, is strongly "scriptural"; that is, orienting itself on the mandates given in recognized *ṣruti.* The Vedic tradition was largely replaced and absorbed by the Purāṇic-Āgamic tradition, which, in addition to general rules and precepts, has numerous special provisions for the followers of each individual sect and group. Combined with what we would call moral and ethical principles we find rules relating to forms of worship, ritual purity, and also items of practical wisdom and hygiene.

The supreme ideal of most branches of Hinduism is the sage, who is imperturbed, free from affection and hatred, not influenced by good or bad luck. For him there is, strictly speaking, no more morality. He is "beyond good and evil" in a literal sense, because *pravṛtti,* volition, the spring of action has dried up. This is the situation of the fully realized person, as the Vedānta describes it. Not too well-informed people derive from such statements the impression that Hinduism as a whole does not care for ethics. Good and evil are relative according to the teaching of the Upaniṣads; relative to the whole world of karma. As long as someone participates in it through actions one is bound by it as by an absolute rule!

A discussion has been going on in India for many centuries whether righteousness affects the innermost self or whether it is just accidental to it. Many Indians consider morality a quality of the *ātman* and a subjective category to depend also on the intentions of the doer.[5] In order that a moral rule may qualify as a precept apart from its scriptural basis, its inherent goodness must usually also be proven. Because scriptural precepts, which also include rituals, are of such great importance, Hindu thinkers have devoted much thought to finding out the reasons for their validity. According to the orthodox *Mīmāṃsā* school, the scriptural laws express something like a Universal Moral Imperative, which produces *ātmākūta*, an impulse in the self to do what has been prescribed, together with an insight into the rightness of the precept.[6]

According to the Naiyāyikās, the professional logicians,

> whatever the Lord commands is good and is good *because* the Lord commands it. Similarly, whatever the Lord forbids is evil and is evil because the Lord forbids it. The authority of the scriptural prescriptions on the will of the agent is such a *vyāpāra* or process in the agent himself: it is the desire for the good and aversion toward the evil involved in the injunctions and prohibitions of scripture as the Lord's commands. It is these desires and aversions in the agent that are the real operative forces, and moral authority is the operation of good and evil through the agent's subjective desires and aversions.[7]

Many authors operate with a basic distinction of *sukha* (agreeable)—*duhkha* (painful) or *hita* (wholesome)–*ahita* (unwholesome), which may be considered a rule of thumb for moral decisions in concrete situations. Thus for instance the precept of truthfulness has to be realized within this situational ethics, as expressed by a leading contemporary Indian thinker: "The final standard of truth is the amount of good that is rendered to people by one's words. Even a mistatement or a false statement, if beneficial to all beings, should be regarded as preferable to a rigorous truthful statement."[8] That this is not just the isolated opinion of an avant-garde thinker is proven by numerous sayings and proverbs in popular scriptures.

A different, absolute, standard is introduced by the Bhagavadgītā with *niṣkāma karma*, the disinterested pursuit of the Lord's command as duty for duty's sake.[9]

VICE AND VIRTUE IN HINDUISM

Both popular and scholarly books describe *moha, lobha, krodha*—delusion, greed, and anger—as the roots of all vices, "the gates to hell," as the Bhagavadgītā says.[10] Some authors try to reduce the first two into one, but all are unanimous in considering the deeds performed under the influence of these passions as sinful.

Jayanta specifies the three roots further[11] and identifies with their help the most common vices. *Moha* is given the title *pāpatama,* "head sin," because without delusion, he says, there cannot be greed and anger. The direct consequences of delusion are misjudgment, perplexity, conceit, and heedlessness. The consequences of desire are sexual craving, extreme niggardliness, worldliness, thirst for life enjoyment, and greed. Aversion produces anger, envy, jealousy, malevolence, and malice.

Before proceeding with a detailed description of the system of vices in the classical *śāstras* it may help to quote some popular scriptures, the source of the common Hindu's ethical education, to see what a Hindu considers to be the life a good person should live. Because a great deal of traditional Hinduism is quite patently patriarchal, it is no use to apply inclusive language: many of the texts speak of men only and highlight male ideas and ideals, virtues and vices of men rather than of all humans. The *Viṣṇu Purāṇa* enjoins the respectable man to worship gods, cows, brahmans, *sādhus,* elders, and teachers. He should dress in neat garments, use delicate herbs and flowers, wear emeralds and other precious stones, keep his hair smooth and neat, scent his person with agreeable perfumes and always go handsomely attired, decorated with garlands of white flowers. He should never appropriate another's belongings nor address anyone in an unkindly way. He should speak amiably and truthfully and never make public another's faults. He should not mount a dangerous vehicle, nor seek shade under the bank of a river. He should not associate with ill-famed people, with sinners or drunkards, with one who has many enemies, with a harlot or her gallant, with a pauper or a liar, with a slanderer or a knave. He should not swim against the current of a rapid stream, not enter a house on fire, nor climb to the top of a tree. When together with others he should not grind his teeth or blow his nose or yawn with uncovered mouth, he should not clear his throat noisily nor cough or laugh loudly nor break wind noisily; he should not bite his nails nor scratch the ground, nor put his beard into his mouth. He should avoid going by night to a place where four roads meet, to the village tree, to the cemetery or an ill-famed woman's house. He should not cross the shadow of a venerable person, of the image of a deity, of a flag, or of a heavenly body. He should not travel alone through the forest nor sleep by himself in an empty house. He should stay away from hair, bones, thorns, filth, remnants of offerings, ashes, chaff, and the bathing place of someone else. He should not go near a beast of prey and should rise from his bed as soon as he awakens. He should avoid exposure to frost, wind, sunshine. He should not bathe, sleep, or rinse his mouth when naked. He should not offer any oblations or greetings with only one garment on. He should not engage in a dispute with superiors or inferiors because, the text says "controversy and marriage are to be permitted only between equals." He must never circumambulate the temple on his left hand,[12] nor spit in front of the moon, fire, the sun, water, wind, or any respectable person; he must not urinate while standing, nor upon a highway. He must not treat women with disrespect, but he also should not trust them completely. He is to be generous toward the poor. He should carry an umbrella for protection against sun and rain, a staff when walking by night, and also wear shoes. He should speak wisely, moderately, and kindly. "The earth is upheld by the truthfulness of those who have subdued their passions and are never contaminated by desire, delusion and anger. Let therefore a wise man ever speak the truth when it is agreeable, and when the truth would inflict pain let him hold his peace. Let him not utter that which, though acceptable, would be detrimental; for it would be better to speak that which would be salutary. A considerate man will always cultivate, in act, thought and speech, that which is good for living beings, both in this world and the next."[13]

Detailed instructions are given for each activity and situation in life, giving guidance in a very practical form, interspersed with religious precepts. A very similar list is provided in the *Cāraka Saṃhitā*, a classical text on medicine, which as well as dealing with technical medical matters provides general rules for a good and healthy life.[14] That health and religion go hand in hand is a commonly accepted truism among the Hindus. There attaches, therefore, also a moral stigma to people afflicted with leprosy or other deforming diseases, which makes their lot still more miserable. But, generally, the traditional Hindu has a quite sound moral sense—old-fashioned, perhaps, and tinged with sectarian overemphasis on ritual, in some cases, but practical and sure in the essentials. To introduce also sources in languages other than Sanskrit, a few verses from the *Tirukkuṛaḷ*, the sacred book of the Tamils, which the Hindus in South India treasure as the "Tamiḷveda," may be quoted here.

> People without love think only of themselves; people who have love free themselves of the self for the sake of others.
> Heaven and earth are not enough reward for a friendly service that is given without any thought of gain.
> The joy of the revengeful lasts but a single day, but the peace-lover's joy lasts forever.
> Those who fast and mortify themselves are great, but greater are they who forgive wrongdoing.
> This is wisdom supreme: do not repay with evil, evil done to you.[15]

GREAT SINS AND LESSER SINS

The classical dharma-śāstra developed a fairly comprehensive casuistry, classifying and cataloging sins and their appropriate penances. Sins have their special consequences and therefore social sanctions as well as religious ones. It is worth noting that the digests of Hindu law treat *prayaścittas,* penances and atonement for sins, after dealing with purity and impurity.[16] The principal division of sin that obtains in the *śāstras* is that between *mahā-pātakas,* great sins, and *upa-pātakas,* minor sins. The former are generally given as five, interpreted differently by various authors.

Brāhmaṇa-hatyā, the killing of a Brahmin, was considered the most grievous of all offences, unforgivable and expiated only by death. Some paṇḍits hold that it includes all members of the upper three castes who have studies the Vedas. The killing of an unborn child and a pregnant woman was considered equally vile. The killing of a man of a lower caste or an outcaste is treated by some lawbooks only as a minor offence, a far lesser crime than the killing of a cow. The *śāstras* provide also for non-Brahmins by saying that it would be a *mahā-pātaka* for a *kṣatriya* to flee from the battlefield or to mete out, as a rule, unjust punishment; for a *vaiśya* to use false scales and false weights; for a *śūdra* to sell meat, to injure a Brahmin, to have sexual intercourse with a Brahmin woman, and to drink milk from a *kapila* (brownish) cow, reserved for the Brahmins. There is no dharma proper for the casteless. From the orthodox point of view they are on a level with the animals as far as religious merit is concerned. Accordingly, offenses committed by them against caste people were punished with disproportionate harshness and crimes against them by people from higher castes were absolved very easily with a merely formal penance.

The second *mahā-pātaka* is *sūra-pāna*, drinking intoxicating beverages. It is the object of long treatises, classifications, restrictions, and excuses, to find out what exactly was meant by *sūra*. Strict interpreters forbid all alcoholic drinks and all drugs. Most paṇḍits allow the *śūdras* to drink their toddy and liquor without incurring sin. Among *sādhus*, especially the uneducated ones, it was common practice to improve their capacity for meditating by using drugs.

Steya, stealing, is the third grave sin; but this is a qualified theft defined as "stealing a large amount of gold from a Brahmin." Long treatises specify quantity, persons, and circumstances. Generally speaking, traditional India did not know the capitalist idolization of personal property and even the *śāstras* formally allow theft of food for cows, materials for sacrifice, or modest quantities of food for one's personal use. Again, almost daily occurrences of brutal punishment meted out to Harijans for minor theft show that the law was written by, and for the benefit of, the higher castes.

The fourth *mahā-pātaka* is *guru-vaṅganā-gama*, relations with the preceptor's wife. Some authorities interpret guru in this context as father and not as religious master and the prohibition would relate to incest, applicable also to the spiritual father.

The last of the great sins is *mahā-pātaka-saṃsārga*, association with a great sinner. The law forbids one to eat with him, live with him, ride with him, or accept him as friend or a pupil.

Some of the later texts broaden the concept of "great sin" and add a series of offenses that they consider equivalent: kidnapping, horse stealing, theft of diamonds or land, sexual relations with members of the lowest castes, relatives, or a holy person.

All the *mahā-pātakas* are technically unpardonable, and no penance would make a person, who has incurred one of these sins, acceptable again in his caste. From the religious point of view some *śāstras* say that such sinners could expiate through their death the offenses they have committed. The sectarian texts of the Purāṇas, however, handle such cases quite easily by recommending some religious practice associated with the Lord, who, if worshipped, forgives and condones everything.

As regards the *upa-pātakas*, the minor offences, there is wide discrepancy and a lack of an accepted classification. One authority mentions five: relinquishing the sacred fire, offending the guru, atheism (*nāstikya*, disregard for the traditional religion) gaining one's livelihood from an unbeliever, and sale of the *soma* plant. Others add forgetting the Veda, neglecting the Veda study, violation of *brahmacarya,* the vow of celibacy. Longer lists enumerate more than fifty minor sins, many of them quite serious offenses that can, however, be made good by performing the prescribed penance. Thus offenses like the preparation of salt (breaking a state monopoly), accepting money for teaching the Veda, the study of false *śāstras*, killing a woman, marrying off a younger son before the elder brother, installation of devices that kill living organisms or cause injury, like an oil press, and the sale of one's wife are mentioned together with common theft, adultery, cruelty toward parents, unrestrained pleasure seeking, and the usurpation of the priestly office.[17]

PENANCE AND ATONEMENT

Manu decrees that he who causes pain to a Brahmin, steals, cheats and commits unnatural venery loses caste. One who kills a donkey, a horse, a deer, an elephant, a snake, or a buffalo is transferred to a mixed caste.

The *śāstras* underline the importance of undergoing the prescribed penances by pointing out the evil consequences a sin may have in another rebirth, if it has not been washed away through *prayaścitta.* Thus, according to Manu, gold stealing shows in diseased nails and spirit drinking in black teeth; Brahman murder in consumption; violation of the guru's wife in skin disease; calumny in stinking breath; stealing of cloth in leprosy: "Thus, in consequence of a remnant of the guilt are born idiots, dumb, blind, deaf and deformed men, despised by the virtuous."[18]

In addition to possible consequences in rebirth, Hindu scriptures quite frequently give detailed descriptions of the hells in which individual sinners are punished for their sins: people who have injured living beings have to suffer being cut with sharp blades for ages, people who have committed adultery are punished by being tied to a red-hot image that they have to embrace for many years, liars are hung with their mouth in pools of foul matter.[19] The ancient *śāstras*, which belong to a period in which religious and secular authority were one, have, however, quite precise rules in their criminal code; for the sake of preserving society they could not be as extravagant or as lenient as the Purāṇas. They distinguish between unintentional and intentional acts; the former are usually expiated by reciting Vedic texts, the latter demand special penances.[20]

Those special penances constitute in fact the criminal code of ancient India and are still of great importance in traditional jurisprudence. Some of the modes of atonement have gone out of practice, other still apply.

Manu, for instance, prescribes for unintentional murder of a Brahmin "to make a hut in the forest and dwell in it for twelve years, subsisting on alms and making the skull of a dead man one's flag," or to try to expose oneself in a battle to archers or to surrender one's whole property to a Brahmin or to sacrifice one's life for the sake of Brahmins or cows—or verbal absolution from three Brahmins.[21] Austerities, recitation of Vedic texts, performance of special sacrifices, breath control, gifts, pilgrimages, ablutions, and rituals are among the means imposed by religious authorities even now for offenses; if performed properly they are supposed to take away the sins and their consequences in this and future births. Thus Manu says: "By confession, by repentance, by austerity and by reciting the Veda a sinner is freed from guilt, as also by liberality. . . . In so far as his heart loathes his evil deed, so far is his body freed from that guilt. He who has committed a sin and has repented is freed from that sin, but only by ceasing with the promise: 'I will do so no more'."[22]

Normally, in addition to repentance, an actual atonement is demanded. One of the most widely practiced penances is *prāṇayama,* breath control. The "man of sin" is "burnt" by regular controlled inhalation and exhalation and retention of air.

Tapas, literally heat, designating all sorts of austerities, is the general means for making reparation for wrong doing. It may include sexual continence, truthfulness, frequent bathing, wearing wet clothes, sleeping on the floor, and fasting for a specific length of time. "*Tapas* quickly consumes all sins" goes the proverbial saying. Under certain circumstances *tapas* can also be won by proxy: devout widows perform penances meant to profit their deceased husbands. The rich pay the poor to perform *tapas* on their behalf. Merit bestowed upon another is lost to oneself; therefore one can read in popular books moving stories of the ultimate penance somebody performs by giving away as a gift the whole store of *tapas* acquired in many years of hard work.

Agniṣṭoma, a gift consumed by fire, is one of the traditionally accepted means of atonement. It is to be accompanied by shaving the head and beard, bathing in holy water, muttering mantras, pouring *ghī* into the fire, abstinence, and truthfulness in speech. The sin is thrown into the fire and burned along with the offering.

Japa may be the most common and most widespread means of atonement for Hindus today. It can be of three kinds: *vācika,* an audible murmuring, is the lowest; *upāmṣu,* inaudible lisping, confers ten times more merit; *mānasa,* a mental recitation, is worth a hundred times as much. For the purpose of atonement the books prescribe a high number of recitations of certain formulae or names. In ancient times *japa* was accessible only to the upper castes, who had the right to recite the Veda. It was forbidden to the *śūdras* and outcastes; if they practiced it nevertheless, it remained without effect. Later a special kind of *japa* was created for *śūdras* and women. The Purāṇas again are full of mantras and *stotras* that carry with them the promise of expiating all sins if recited even once by anyone; the mere utterance of the revealed name of God frees many generations from hells and punishments.

Dāna, the offering of gifts to Brahmins, is among the acts most often recommended in the *śāstras* to atone for crimes. The gift of gold is especially effective, and so is the gift of a cow, a horse, land; gifts are even potent enough to annihilate the accumulated guilt of former lives. Numerous copperplates are preserved that document the gift of land to religious merit for the donor and his ancestors. Even today industrialists build temples and resthouses for pilgrims for the same purpose; hundreds of beggars and cripples give to the pious Hindus who visit a temple ample opportunity to rid themselves of their sins by distributing money, food, and cloth.

Upavāsa, fasting, is another popular form of penance. In its strict sense it entails total abstinence from food and drink and even at present numerous Indians keep up a total fast on a good number of days in a year. For the more sophisticated and theologically astute Hindus *upavāsa* often means nothing more than observing certain restrictions in the kind of food they take, with the same religious merit attached to it. Thus the Vaiṣṇavas, who are strict vegetarians, keep *ekādaśī,* every eleventh day in each half of the lunar month, as a fasting day. On those days they are not supposed to eat cereals grown above the ground: rice, wheat, barley, *dāl.* Whatever grows below the ground, all roots and tubers, as well as milk and dairy products may be eaten.

Tīrtha-yātra, pilgrimage to holy places, is another popular penance. The Mahābhārata mentions already the "seven holy cities"—Kāśī, Prayāga, Mathurā, Ujjainī, Haridvāra, Ayodhyā, and Gāyā—each of them is the goal of millions of Hindu pilgrims seeking to make atonement for their own sins and the sins of their ancestors. The Purāṇas carry numerous *māhātmyas,* praises of those holy places, in which the merits of visiting the sacred spots are described in detail. Even in the modern India of steel combines, jet travel, and political parties millions of people are constantly on the move to wash away their sins: many people retire to one of the holy cities in their old age, and quite a few arrange to be brought to Banaras to die there, because then one need not fear punishment or rebirth.

Many Hindus undertake these penances of their own accord; others are told to do so, often by the caste *pañcāyat*, which oversees the affairs of its members and interferes, if necessary. Crimes that were of social relevance were also punished by the secular authority. According to Manu, the Brahmins could, however, take the law into their own hands, because they were superior to the *kṣatriya*. But that they, too, had in reality to abide by the decisions of the ruler, becomes clear when we hear that they may "punish through their own weapon, which is the word of the Veda" and use the spells of the Atharvaveda against those who have offended them.[23]

THE IDEAL OF HOLINESS

It is only natural that the sin consciousness of a person is the more acute, the more aware one is of the holiness of the Lord. Thus we find in texts that were meant for the more exclusive circles of religious professionals a far more scrupulous determination of sins and a greater urgency for acts of atonement. The Vaiṣṇavas, considering seva or service of the Lord Viṣṇu the sole aim of life, have special lists of "sins against service." These include entering the temple on a car or with shoes on, neglecting to celebrate the feasts of Viṣṇu, greeting the image of Viṣṇu with one hand only, turning one's back toward it, stretching one's feet toward the image, lying down or eating before the image, gossiping before the image, eating one's food without first having offered it to Viṣṇu, and so forth. All signs of disrespect or negligence before the bodily presence of the Lord in his image are therefore considered sins, to be atoned for through the repetition of the name of Viṣṇu. The "sins against the name," however, cannot be atoned for. They are ten according to the authorities: offending a Vaiṣṇava by scolding him; thinking that both Viṣṇu and Śiva are Lord; thinking that the guru is a mere human being; reproaching the Vedas, Purāṇas, and other scriptures; interpreting the name; speaking or thinking ill of the name; committing sins on the strength of the name; considering other good works as equal to the recitation of the name; teaching the name to people who have no faith, and disliking the name even after having heard about its greatness.[24]

NEW DEPARTURES ON THE PATH OF WORKS

A new understanding of the "path of works" developed from the late eighteenth century onward—possibly under the influence of contact with the British and a socially conscious Christianity. The eagerness with which Ram Mohan Roy responded to New Testament ethics and with which he successfully fought against cruel traditions like *satī* and infanticide did not lead to a large-scale Hindu conversion to Christianity but to a "Hindu Renaissance" with clearly social and ethical overtones. The call to action of Kṛṣṇa in the Bhagavadgītā was interpreted as a call to remedy the social ills of Hindu society, and eventually as a call to liberate the homeland of the Hindus from foreign domination. B. G. Tilak's commentary on the Gītā—"the Gospel of Action"—gives an explicitly socio-political slant to the old notion of *karma-mārga*. So did Mahātmā Gandhi and many others in his footsteps.

Age-old notions of purity still are of importance to groups of traditional high-caste Hindus and the idea of holiness, as the *bhakti* prophets of the late Middle Ages preached it, is still meaningful to large numbers of devotees. But increasingly Hinduism understands its mission as a secular, cultural, political one—the mission to form a strong modern nation-state on the basis of Hindutva, a distinct tradition grown out from older forms of Hinduism and capable of sustaining a modern society.

11 The Hindu Sacraments: The *Saṃskāras*

With holy rites, prescribed by the Veda, must the ceremony of conception and other sacraments be performed for twice-born men, which sanctify the body and purify in this life and after death.

—*Manusmṛti* II, 26

The *saṃskāras,* usually described as the sacraments of Hinduism, are rites by means of which a Hindu becomes a full member of the socio-religious community.[1] They begin with conception and end with cremation, "sanctifying the body and purifying it in this life and after death."[2] The classical *śāstras* list a great number of *saṃskāras* that apparently were in use in former times; nowadays only a few are practiced but an immense importance attaches to these in the practical life of Hindus.

Manu explains the effect of the different *saṃskāras* (see Figure 11.1) thus:

> In the case of the twice-born[3] the sins that come from seed and womb are redeemed through *homas* during pregnancy, through *jātakarma,* the ritual performed at birth, through *cauḍa,* the tonsure of the whole head leaving only one lock at the crown of the head, and the girdling with *muñja*-grass. This body is made fit for the attainment of Brahmā through *svādhyāya,* the study of scripture, by observance of *vratas,* holy vows, through the so-called *traividyā,* by worshipping the *devas, pitṛs* and *ṛṣis,* by begetting a son and through the daily performance of the *pañca mahāyajñas* as well as public *yajñas.*[4]

Hindus associate great significance with the ceremonies surrounding the birth of a child and the name giving. Popular works like the *Viṣṇu Purāṇa* offer instructions like these:

1. *Annaprāśana:*
First Feeding of Solid Food

2. *Cuḍākarma:* Tonsure Before
Receiving Sacred Thread

3. *Vivāha:* Marriage

4. *Nāmakāraṇa:* Name Giving

5. *Saṁnyāsa:* Renouncing

Figure 11.1 Some *saṃskāras*

> When a son is born, let his father perform the ceremonies proper on the birth of a child. . . . Let him feed a couple of Brahmans and according to his means offer sacrifices to the *devas* and *pitṛs*. . . . On the tenth day after birth[5] let the father give a name to his child; the first term of which shall be the appellation of a god, the second of a man as Śarma for a *brahmin*, Varma for a *ksatriya*, Gupta for a *vaiśya* and Dāsa for a *śūdra*. A name should not be void of meaning: it should not be indecent, nor absurd, nor ill-omened, nor fearful, it should consist of an even number of syllables, it should not be too long or too short, nor too full of long vowels, but contain a due proportion of short vowels and be easily articulated.[6]

Manu adds that the names of women should be easy to pronounce, not imply anything dreadful, possess a plain meaning and be auspicious, ending in long vowels and containing a word of blessing (*aśīrvāda*).[7] In the fourth month the "leaving-of-the-house" ceremony should be celebrated; in the sixth the first feeding with rice and other family customs. In the first or third year all boys of the three upper castes are supposed to get *cauḍa* or tonsure.

THE SECOND BIRTH

Upanayana, the initiation, is among the most important *saṃskāras* still in fairly universal use, even in liberal Hindu families. According to the *śāstras* it is to take place in the eighth year for a Brahmin boy, in the eleventh for a *Kṣatriya* boy and in the twelfth for a *Vaiśya* boy.[8] The investiture with the *yajñopavīta* or *janëu*, the sacred thread, marks the end of the young twice-born's childhood and innocence, as he enters the first of the four *āśramas* or stages of his life: studentship. From now onward he is held responsible for his actions. As a child he had no duties and could incur no guilt; he did not have to observe restrictions regarding permitted and prohibited food, he was free in his speech and his lies were not punished. In ancient time the young *brahmacari* took up residence with his guru to be taught in the Vedas; nowadays the boys normally remain with their families and continue attending the same school as before. Nevertheless it marks an important occasion in the life of a Hindu boy, because it is often the first personal and conscious encounter with his religion as part of his own life. Most families keep contact with their traditional paṇḍit who instructs the boys in their dharma.

The exact time for the ceremony of *upanayana* is determined by the family astrologer. The occasion still retains something of an initiation ceremony; a crucial rite of passage that in olden times could result in the death of the candidate. The boy is given a wooden staff and dressed with a belt of *muñja* grass. The head is shaved, except for the *śikha*. The Brahmin who performs the ceremony recites mantras to Sāvitṛī, asking him not to let the boy die. Then the sacred thread is put on for the first time, to be worn henceforth day and night. It consists of three times three single threads about two yards long, and normally is worn over the left shoulder (during the last rites it is worn over the right). The origin of the *janëu* has not been explained as yet; many believe it to be the remnant of a garment. Neglect of the *janëu* can lead to expulsion from the caste, and good works without the *janëu* bring no fruit. Traditionally also the *gāyatrī-mantra* was imparted to the young Brahmin at this occasion; its repetition was meant to be the common means of expiation for sins. The ancient *śāstras* contain a complete *brahmacari-dharma* for the boys, to be observed from the time of initiation till marriage. The reformist Ārya Samāj attempts to revive it in its *gurukulas*, where young boys and girls are kept under strict discipline from the age of 4 to 20. There are also still a few Vedic schools in India where young boys spend several years in the manner prescribed by the *śāstras*: mornings and evenings the boys chant Vedic hymns in chorus, the daytime is devoted to memorizing the Veda, studying the *Vedāṅgas*, and collecting firewood. Quite strict rules must be observed with regard to food. The boys have to be very respectful toward the guru, never addressing him without certain honorific titles. Complete sexual continence was of the essence; the very name of this mode of life was synonymous with chastity. A *brahmacari* who failed in this respect had to submit to very humiliating, painful, and lengthy penances. Manu says he must go around clad in the skin of a donkey for a whole year, beg food in seven houses while confessing his sin, eating only once a day and bathing three times daily. Usually this stage of life ended with marriage at the age of around 20. But there had always been *naiṣṭhika brahmacarins* who continued to live as *brahmacaris* without ever marrying.[9]

THE SACRAMENT FOR MEN AND WOMEN

The most important *saṃskāra* had always been, and still is, *vivāha*, marriage. Hindu law knew eight forms of marriage of which it recognized four as legal, though not all of them equally worthy.[10] In addition to the normal case of arrangement through the parents,

Hinduism knows also legalized forms of love marriage. Monogamy is the rule today, though traditional Hindu law permitted a man to marry up to four wives. After many years of work, and against the opposition of many traditional Hindus, the government of India in 1955 passed the Hindu Marriage Act, which, with several amendments, in 1976 became the official marriage law for Hindus, replacing earlier legislation. It unified Hindu marriage law, which had existed in a number of regional variants, and it also brought such law closer to modern Western law by recognizing civil marriage and allowing divorce, also at the request of the wife. Its enactment was not universally welcomed, not even among Western experts in Hindu law.[11]

The Mahābhārata describes a society in which polyandry was practiced; Draupadī is the wife of the five Pāṇḍava brothers. A few tribes in the hills around Tehri Garhwal practice it even now.

Popular books and *śāstras* alike give advice about the "auspicious" and "inauspicious" signs to look for in one's marriage partner. Thus we read that a man should select a maiden "who has neither too much nor too little hair, is neither black nor yellow complexioned, neither a cripple, nor deformed." He must not marry a girl who is vicious or unhealthy, of low origin, ill-educated, with a disease inherited from father or mother, of a masculine appearance, with a croaky voice, a harsh skin, with white nails, red eyes, fat hands, too short or too tall. She also should be "in kin at least five degrees removed from his mother and seven from his father."[12]

The actual ceremonies of the marriage culminate in a feast very often so sumptuous that poor families take up ruinous loans to meet the expenses and provide food for all those who expect to be invited. Depending on status, a richly decorated horse or an elephant must be hired, dancers and musicians must entertain the numerous guests, paṇḍits and Brahmins must be paid their *dakṣinas*. The ceremonies differ from one region to the other, but everywhere they follow a certain pattern that is meaningful and rests on ancient traditions.[13]

One of the texts details the following ritual. To the west of the fire on the altar, there is to be placed a grinding stone, to the northeast a water jug. The bridegroom sacrifices while the bride holds his hand. He faces west, the woman looks toward the east, while he says: "I take thy hand in mine for happy fortune."[14] He takes her thumb only, if he wishes only for sons, the other fingers only, if he wishes only for daughters, the whole hand, if he wants both boys and girls. Three times the bridegroom leads the bride around the fire, murmuring: "I am *amā* (this), you are *sā* (she); I am heaven, you are earth; I am *sāma*, you are *ṛk*. Let us marry each other, let us beget sons and daughters. Kind to each other, friendly, with well-meaning mind may we live a hundred years." Each time he makes her step onto a stone with the words: "Step on this stone, be firm as stone, overcome the enemies, trample down the adversary." Then the bridegroom pours *ghī* over the bride's hands, the bride's brother sprinkles grains of rice over their hands, three times. The bridegroom loosens the hairband of the bride with the words: "I deliver you from the bonds of Varuṇa." He asks her to take seven steps toward the north, saying: "May you take a step for power, a step for strength, one for wealth, one for fortune, one for descendants, one for good times. May you be my friend with the seventh step. May you be faithful to me. Let us have many sons. May they reach a ripe old age." The officiating paṇḍit brings the heads of bride and bridegroom close together and sprinkles them with water. The bride is supposed to spend the three nights following the wedding ceremony in the house of an older Brahmin woman, whose husband and children are still living. When the bride has seen the pole star, the star *arundhatī*, and the *Seven ṛṣis,*[15] she must break her silence by saying: "May my husband live long and may I bear him children." When entering her own house she is to say: "May your happiness increase here through your sons and daughters." The bridegroom then kindles their own sacred fire. The bride sits on a bull's hide and is first given curds to eat with the mantra: "May all gods unite our hearts."

There are countless variations and additions to the ceremony just described. Some prescribe that the couple should look into the sun, that the bridegroom should carry the bride over the threshold, that he should touch her heart with mantras, that he should offer silver and gold before the statues of Śiva and Gaurī. Depending also on the patriarchal or matriarchal tradition prevailing in the area the relative importance of bride or bridegroom is expressed in the wedding ceremonies and the home bringing, too.

According to the Ṛgveda the goal of marriage is to enable a man to sacrifice to the *devas* and beget a son who will ensure the continuity of the sacrifice. Woman was called *half of man* and the domestic sacrifice could be performed only by husband and wife jointly. The son, *putra*, is so called, the scriptures say, because he pulls his parents out (*tra*) from hell (*pu*). He is necessary not only for the pride of the family to continue its line but also for its spiritual welfare in the next world. *Śrāddha*, the last rites, could be properly performed only by a male descendent. Without *śrāddha* the deceased remains forever a *preta,* a ghost.[16]

There are special sections in traditional Hindu law, called *strīdharma,* that regulate the rights and obligations also of married women, who even in patriarchal Hindu India were not simply the slaves of men. Manu has some flattering remarks about the mother being the goddess of the house, and the gods showering happiness on the house where woman is honored.[17] To underline this he says: "The house, in which female relations, not being duly honored, pronounce a curse, perishes completely as if destroyed by magic. Hence men who seek happiness should always honor women on holidays and festivals with gifts of jewelry, clothes and good food. In that family where the husband is pleased with his wife and the wife with her husband happiness will assuredly be lasting."[18]

On the other hand, Manu also warns men against woman, the perpetual temptress,[19] and decrees that she should never be independent: "In childhood a female must be subject to her father, in youth to her husband, when her lord is dead to her sons. She is not to separate from her husband. Though destitute of virtue, seeking pleasure or devoid of good qualities, a husband must be constantly worshipped as a god by a faithful wife."[20] She must always be cheerful, clever in her household affairs, careful in cleaning her utensils, economical in expenditure, and faithful to her husband not only as long as he lives but until her own death.[21] In former times the highest test of fidelity was the voluntary self-immolation on the husband's funeral pyre; occasionally it is said that this is still performed, though it has long been forbidden by law. In places of pilgrimage numerous widows spend the rest of their lives attached to temples and religios establishments, singing *bhajans* for some wealthy donor, who provides them with food and shelter.

PROVIDING FOR THE BEYOND

Antyeṣṭi, the last rites, also called *mṛtyu-saṃskāra,* the sacrament of death, is still performed today by practically all Hindus, orthodox as well as liberal. Hindus usually burn their dead, except in times of great disasters. Some sects like the Vīraśaivas practice burial. Also small children and *saṁnyāsis* are buried; poor people for whom nobody is willing to pay the expenditure of cremation, are often unceremoniously thrown into the nearest river. But ordinarily a Hindu will provide already during his lifetime for a *śrāddha* to be performed according to the *śāstras.* Details of the rites vary greatly according to the status of the departed, but there is a basic pattern followed by most.

After the hair and nails of the dead person have been cut off, the body is washed, the *tilaka* applied to the forehead, and it is wrapped in a new piece of cloth and garlanded with flowers. The one who performs the rites, normally the eldest son, washes his feet, sips water, does *prāṇayama,* and prays to the earth. Then the litter is carried by some men or on a cart drawn by cows to the *smāsana,* the cremation grounds. The eldest son circumambulates the place prepared for cremation and sprinkles water over it. With an iron rod he draws three lines on the floor, saying: "I draw a line for Yama, the lord of cremation; I draw a line for *kāla,* time, the lord of cremation, I draw a line for *mṛtyu,* death, the lord of cremation." Some sesame seeds are put into the mouth of the deceased and the body is put upon the funeral pyre. After several minor rituals during which five little balls made of flour are placed on different parts of the dead body, the pyre is lit by the eldest son. Rich people burn their dead with sandalwood which spreads a powerful and pleasant scent, strong enough to cover up the smell that is so typical of the cremation grounds. While the pyre is burning, lengthy sections from the "hymns for the dead" are recited.[22] Yama is called upon to give the deceased a good place among the ancestors, the *pitṛs* are invoked as patrons of the living, Agni is invited not to harm the deceased but to carry him safely across with his body into the kingdom of the fathers. Pūṣan, the creator, the life of the universe is besought to keep the departed in safety. Finally, the earth is besought to be good to the dead. One of the mourners is appointed to lift a filled earthen water jug onto his left shoulder, make a hole into the back of the jug and walk three times around the burning corpse. The jug is knocked three times and then completely broken. The relatives (no other people are allowed to participate) then turn to the left and leave the cremation grounds without looking back, the youngest child in front.

Old taboos attach to the last rites; dealing with corpses causes ritual impurity and thus the relations first go to a place where there is a brook or river, immerse themselves three times, facing south (the direction of Yama, the god of the netherworlds), sip some water, and deposit the stone used for breaking the jug on the shore. They then sacrifice water mixed with sesame, saying: "O departed one, may this water, mixed with sesame, reach you." On the threshold of the house they sip water and touch auspicious objects like fire, cow dung, and water before entering. The burning place is cooled with a mixture of milk and water under recitation of Ṛgvedic verses. On one of the following days the skull is shattered and the remnants of the bones are gathered into an earthenware jar that after some time is either thrown into a holy river, preferably the Ganges or Yamunā, at some *tīrtha,* to ensure the felicity of the departed, or buried with some ritual, on a piece of land set apart for that purpose.

Samnyāsis, those who have received *dīksa* that anticipates cremation, are buried in a yoga posture. Frequently a chapellike memorial called *samādhī* is erected over the tombs of famous and popular *sādhus,* and people keep coming to those places, seeking advice and assistance from the heavenly master.

Cremation rites are only the first part of *antyeṣṭi*: for ten days after the burning, water mixed with sesame is offered every day together with the leaves of certain trees. On the tenth day the eldest son, who officiated at the cremation, goes to the cremation ground and offers a *piṇḍa,* a small ball of rice, saying: "May this *piṇḍa* benefit the *preta* of so-and-so of this family so that his ghost may not feel hunger and thirst." According to the belief of many Hindus it is important that crows should come and peck at the *piṇḍas*; if they do not come the relatives believe that the deceased has left the world with wishes unfulfilled. Often they try to attract the crows for hours, with promises to fulfill the wish of the departed. The stone upon which the sacrifice was offered is anointed and thrown into the water. A handful of water is then offered to the *preta.* There is a popular belief that a man for whom the proper *śrāddha* ceremonies have not been performed has to remain forever a *piśāca,* an evil ghost, even if numerous sacrifices are offered on his behalf at some later date. In the Purāṇas we read that immediately after cremation every person receives a *yatanīya-śarīra,* a body that will be subject to tortures and suffering in relation to the sins committed; the *bhaktas* of Viṣṇu, however, receive an incorruptible body like Viṣṇu's, with four arms, in which to enjoy forever the presence of Viṣṇu and serve him eternally. The subtle body of the deceased, so another story goes, in which they lives for some time before the next rebirth in another body, is built up by means of the funerary rites.

Present Hindu practice seems to rest on an imperfect synthesis of various strands of belief relating to the afterlife: on the one hand, the Purāṇas faithfully describe the Vedic cremation ritual without adding anything sectarian,[23] on the other hand, they abound in descriptions of rebirths, heavens and hells that are quite obviously irreconcilable with the Vedic conception,[24] which aims at transforming the dead soul into a venerated ancestor, without any hint at rebirth or sectarian heaven and hell.

According to the sūtras the admission of the *preta* into the circle of the *pitṛs* is obtained through the *sapiṇḍī-kāraṇa,* which normally takes place one year after death. On every new-moon day until then, a special *śrāddha* called *ekoddiṣṭa* is performed for the benefit of the deceased. Four earthen vessels are filled with a mixture of water, sesame seeds and scents, one for the *preta,* and one each for his father, grandfather, and great-grandfather. The contents of the pot for the *preta* is poured into the other three pots while mantras are recited. From now on the new *preta* ranks as the first of the *pitṛs;* his great-grandfather drops out from the list according to the Vedic rule: "There can be no fourth *piṇḍa.*" Now the "ghost" has become a "father," regularly mentioned in the numerous ancestor libations throughout the year. Hindu scriptures contain numerous chapters detailing the *śrāddha* ceremonies that form one of the most important parts of Hindu cult.

Thus, through the last sacrament, the meaning of the *saṃskāras* is fulfilled: the Brahmin, transformed into a twice-born being through *upanayana,* attaining the fullness of manhood in *vivāha,* becomes a "complete being," who is worthy of worship, through *śrāddha,* and is thus able to provide blessings for his descendants.

It is through the performance of *saṃskāras* that all Hindus practice the *karma-mārga,* the Path of Works, though as far as their beliefs and intellectual convictions are concerned they may choose to follow the *bhakti-mārga* or the *jñāna-mārga,* the ways of devotion and knowledge. We have to remember this before dealing with the Path of Devotion and the Path of Knowledge. Although theological polemics of representatives of either one path often may create the impression of an exclusivity and a rejection of "wrong paths," in actual life the average Hindu participates in all three ways and would not risk the condemnation associated with missing out on any of them.

12 The Path of Knowledge: *Jñānamārga*

He who knows Brahman as the real, as knowledge, as the infinite, Set down in the secret place (of the heart) and in the highest heaven, He obtains all desires, Together with the allknowing Brahman.

—*Taittirīya Upaniṣad* II, 1

The Upaniṣads, also called *Vedānta* or *the end of the Veda,* are the basis for the main stream of the Indian philosophical and mystical tradition, which refers to them as to its source and ultimate authority. The hymns from the Vedic saṃhitās today serve mainly a practical purpose as part of the ritual; very few draw there personal religion and beliefs from them. The Upaniṣads, however, are studied, quoted and used even now in arguments and in attempts to build up a contemporary spirituality.

Chronologically the Upaniṣads constitute the last part of *śruti,* connected via specific *brāhmaṇas* and *āraṇyakas* to the saṃhitās.[1] It has become customary, however, to consider them as a class of texts by themselves and to publish them independent of the rest of *śruti.*[2] By some authors they are treated as a kind of protestant countercurrent to the prevailing Vedic sacrificial religion, by others as a plain continuation of the same tradition. Both views have their merits and their evident shortcomings: the Upaniṣads quote the Vedas quite frequently and use Vedic ideas; they also contain anti-Vedic polemics and represent unorthodox viewpoints.[3] There is, however, a difference between the saṃhitās and the Upaniṣads, recognized since early times by the Hindu interpreters: the Vedas and *Brāhmaṇas* centre around the sacrificial ritual whose ultimate goal is *svarga* or heaven; the Upaniṣads proclaim an esoteric teaching, the dispensability of ritual and the attainment of freedom and immortality through a process of concentration and spiritual interiorization, a difference that prompted ancient writers to classify the religion of the Upaniṣads as *jñāna-mārga*, "the way of knowledge" over against the *karma-mārga*, "the way of works" propounded by saṃhitās and *brāhmaṇas*. The Upaniṣads vary considerably in length; among the thirteen Upaniṣads normally considered as the authentic or principal ones the longest amounts to about a hundred printed pages, the shortest to only about three pages.

THE PRINCIPAL UPANIṢADS: THEIR AUTHORS AND THEIR TEACHINGS

The following chronology has been fairly commonly accepted by scholars: *Bṛhadāraṇyaka* and *Chāndogya* form the oldest group, then come *Īśa* and *Kena*; the third group is made up of *Aitareya*, *Taittirīya*, and *Kauśītakī*, the fourth of *Kaṭha*, *Muṇḍaka*, and *Śvetāśvatara* with *Praśna*, *Maitrī*, and *Māṇḍūkya* concluding the "principal Upaniṣads."[4] This chronology does not take into account the different strata in each of the more lengthy texts, pertaining to different eras. The rest of the 108 Upaniṣads, which are commonly considered canonical in one way or other, belong partly to much later times and normally represent sectarian teachings of various groups which would preclude their universal acceptance.

Quite frequently the *Īśa (vāsya) Upaniṣad* is described as the most important one, the essence of all the Upaniṣadic teaching; this may be due partly to its brevity, partly to its concentrated contents, but the Upaniṣads mentioned before contain much that differs in content from the *Īśa* and much that adds to it.

The designation *Upaniṣad* is usually explained as derived from *upa* (close by) *ni* (down) *ṣad* (sit), implying a form of teaching from the teacher's mouth to the pupil's ear, a secret doctrine, or at least a teaching that was not common knowledge of the people. Because the date given to the principal *Upaniṣads* varies between 4000 B.C.E.[5] and 600 B.C.E.[6] no precise information about their authors' identities can be given. The Upaniṣads do mention a great number of names both in the texts and in the lists of *guru-paramparā* at the end of the texts, and we must assume that many of those names do refer to actual historical person who might be called Upaniṣadic philosophers.[7]

In certain parts of the Upaniṣads, intended to convey a teaching through hyperbole or metaphor, the names of *devas* and *ṛṣis* are mentioned as authors of certain doctrines or practices, an ascription that does not allow any historical verification. Other parts of the Upaniṣads have over the centuries been transmitted anonymously; numerous individual theories and exercises, however, are connected with definite names, most probably representing eminent historical persons. Maitrī, after whom one entire Upaniṣad is called, must have been a great mystic who lived and taught the things laid down in his Upaniṣad. Kauśītakī, another name connected with an entire Upaniṣad, could have been the author of the doctrine of the three meditations and the first to have identified *prāṇa,* life breath, with *Brahman.* Jaivali can well be considered the author of the *pañcāgni vidyā,* the understanding of the entire cosmic process as being a symbol of and model for sacrifice in the Vedic sense.[8] Uddalaka can be identified from the *Chāndogya Upaniṣad* as the author of a quite interesting cosmology, differing in his views from other early cosmologists whose names are mentioned as well.[9] Kauśala Aśvalāyana is an early psychologist whose teachings are recorded briefly in the *Praśna Upaniṣad.*[10] He is superseded by the psycho-metaphysician Pippalāda who developed the doctrine of *rayī* and *prāṇa,* the Indian equivalent of the Aristotelian *hyle* and *morphe* (matter and form) dualism. A Vāmadeva appears as a master theoretician of the doctrine of rebirth, who held that man is born three times: at the time of his conception, at the time of the birth of his own child, and at the time of rebirth after death.

The most important group of Upaniṣadic philosophers are those connected with spirituality, the real core of Upaniṣadic teaching. We have the teaching of Śaṇḍilya preserved in a section of the *Chāndogya,*[11] that of Dadyac in a section of the *Bṛhadāraṇyaka* expounding the *madhuvidyā,*[12] and the interdependence of all things. Another famous name is that of Sanatkumāra, introduced as the preceptor of Nārada in the *Chāndogya*: for him happiness, *ānanda,* is the centre of all human effort.[13] Aruṇi and Yajñavalkya, his pupil, emerge as the two most frequently mentioned and most important Upaniṣadic teachers. Both develop what might be called a *metaphysical psychology,* a rigorous method of realization and an appropriate theory of its working. Gārgī, one of the two wives of Yajñavalkya, plays a major role in a section of the *Bṛhadāraṇyaka Upaniṣad.* She is the first Indian woman philosopher we know of.[14]

Before reading any of the Upaniṣad texts it is necessary to familiarize oneself with the method of teaching used by them, which is often so different from our current philosophical or theological presentation as to bar any true understanding of it. The Upaniṣads are fond of riddles and enigmatic comparisons,[15] employing images and illustrations drawn from ancient Indian experiences and theories rather than from ours. Often one must familiarize oneself with a great deal of background before being able to follow the argument of the Upaniṣads. Sometimes the Upaniṣads also employ the aphoristic method, condensing an entire world-view into one sentence or even one syllable.[16] Closely connected is the apophatic method, the way in which Socrates preferred to teach: instead of a positive answer the student is given a question or a piece of purely negative information about what is *not* truth, thus compelling him to transcend the merely verbal and conceptual understanding and to see the proper answer to the truly important questions as consisting in silence rather than in talk.[17] Quite often the Upaniṣads derive certain teachings from an etymology of key words; those etymologies, too, do not always follow the paths of contemporary Sanskrit scholarship but employ certain models that demand some study of the historical background beyond mere linguistics. Myths are quite frequently employed, and these often constitute (in literary terms) the most beautiful portions of the Upaniṣads.[18] Analogies are utilized to lead the student gradually to the level of insight required to understand the teacher's perception of reality. Monologues are not absent, though they are much less frequent than in later philosophical and theological teaching. The most interesting and potentially most valuable method is the dialectics employed in some of the major *Upaniṣads*. The ancient Indians certainly were great debaters, as we know also from other sources. They sharpened their dialectical skills in protracted controversies with exponents of other views as the accounts in the Pali canon, for instance, show. Buddhists actually were largely responsible for the refinement in dialectical skills used by the Hindus to overthrow them. It was an ancient Indian practice to challenge an adversary to a public debate that had to end with the defeat of one of the two contestants; the one who lost the argument, at the same time usually lost all of his disciples, who went over to the conqueror. Thus the biographer of the great Śaṅkara entitles his work the *Digvijāya*, the conquest of the four quarters by his hero, who was successful in debate after debate against his rivals.

With regard to the contents of the Upaniṣads, a reader should not expect them to contain a systematic treatise of philosophy but a string of more or less developed insights, theories, and principles.

A *Vedāntasūtra* (also called *Brahmasūtra*), ascribed to Badarāyaṇa, attempts to summarize and systematize the basic philosophy of the Upaniṣads in four *adhyāyas* or treatises, containing altogether 550 aphorisms. It has become the basic text of all the schools of Vedānta philosophy, and the *bhāṣyas*, or commentaries, written upon it constitute the main works of the different systems, often offering diametrically opposed interpretations of the same brief sūtra. As research has shown quite convincingly, this *Vedānta-sūtra* represents largely the position taken by the *Chāndogya Upaniṣad*, with a few additions here and there; it leaves out much of the contents of the other *Upaniṣads*, which can hardly be brought together under one system.

MAJOR THEMES IN THE UPANIṢADS

The problems raised by the Upaniṣads do not coincide with the approaches developed by recent Western academic disciplines: they deal with physics, biology, psychology, religion, and philosophy as well as with mythology and astrology.

One of the threads that runs through much of the Upaniṣadic quest is the enquiry into the hidden ground of being and the root of one's existence, the essence of things, and the bond that keeps them together. This search concerns as much the physical structure of material things as the spiritual dimension of human existence. Like the philosophizing of the pre-Socratics of ancient Greece, the Upaniṣadic approach is neither purely physical nor purely metaphysical, neither purely psychological nor purely logical according to modern categories; we are able again to appreciate the holistic approach that allows us to put the elements of knowledge acquired through different methods into one mosaic of our world, rough in its details, but impressive in its totality.

We have mentioned before some of the Upaniṣadic ideas concerning the origin of the universe. The search for the substratum common to all beings and its source and origin is one of the main themes dealt with in different Upaniṣads. As well as the attempts to understand water, air, fire or *ākāśa*, ether or space as the Ur-element we have the interesting theory of the *Taittirīya*, which assumes five basic elements, fire, water, earth, wind, and space. The whole universe is structured in pentads, corresponding to the elementary pentad, resulting in an ontic interrelationship, a true cosmic harmony: "Fivefold verily, is this all, with the fivefold indeed does one win the fivefold."[19] This theory gains importance in connection with rebirth. At the time of death the faculties and organs of the body return to their respective places in the cosmos: the eye to the sun, the vital breath to the wind, the flesh to the earth, the fluids to the water, thought to space. We cannot overlook the relevance of the *pañcāgni vidyā* here, the doctrine of the five fires that explains the entire creation as an interlocking succession of five sacrifices. This connection again gains importance in Yoga philosophy, where an attempt is made to establish real connections between the corresponding parts of the microcosm and the macrocosm, ideas that, incidentally, are not foreign to the Western tradition either.[20]

Imagined contests between the individual organs of the body and the various functions, concerning their relative importance for the others, look like entertaining children's stories; in fact they are quite serious philosophy, attempting as they do to reduce the fivefold reality of the microcosm to the One, which in its turn must be the principal element of the universe itself, sustaining all being. The conclusion that *prāṇa*, the breath of life, which supports the life of all the other functions, brings us very close indeed to the central *ātman-brahman* speculation, which we shall examine more closely in the next chapter.[21]

A different Upaniṣadic seer derives the existence of all being from hunger, the equivalent of death.[22] Knowing means controlling; thus the Upaniṣads set out to teach the conquest of death. It cannot take place in the sphere of phenomena, where rebirth and redeath are necessarily part of nature; it must reach beyond. The conquest of the inner space, the opening of the seemingly closed world of nature, constitutes the most precious portion of the Upaniṣads for us today. The "ultimate," the "point of rest," the "immutable," the Upaniṣads find, is the inner core of all things, the reason for their existence. Though invisible, it is more powerful than the visible. It is delicate and subtle, impervious to the senses but "self-evident." It cannot be made into the object of objective reasoning, but exists only as the identity found in introspection. The ultimate, to be sure, is unborn, unchanging, and immortal. Its abode is "the abode of the heart"—seemingly manifold, but in fact one. It is not identical with any thing, it is no-thing; it is neither the object seen nor the faculty of seeing: it is the seeing of the seeing, the hearing of the hearing, the thinking of thinking. As such it is inscrutable, and yet it is present in everything and realizable in all situations. It is the truth and the reality of things, not only *satya*, but *satyasya satya*.[23]

THE QUEST FOR REALITY BEYOND APPEARANCE

Reality is the term that stands at the centre of all the endeavor of Indian philosophy; the differentiation between the obvious and the real, the conditional and the essential, the apparent and the true. The quest for Reality finally leads to the discovery that Reality cannot be found outside but only inside. Thus the *jñāna-mārga,* the path of knowledge, does not constitute a system of objective conceptual statements but a way toward self-discovery. The ground of the universe and the ground of our own existence are identical.

This self-discovery takes place in stages, of which the Upaniṣads usually enumerate four. The most systematic exposition of this four-step process of cognition is given in the *Māṇḍūkya.*[24]

The first and lowest stage of awareness is *jāgarita-sthāna,* the normal state of being awake and hence open to sense perception and rational thought. The spirit of man is poured out into a multitude of objective things, bound to space and time and to the laws of the physical universe.

Svapna-sthāna, the dreaming state, "in which one cognizes internal objects" is already higher, because the spirit of man is no longer subject to the laws of the physical world or bound to space and time. Man himself now creates the world in which he moves, he steps out of the limitations of physical nature by creating whatever the mind conceives.

Suṣupti, profound and dreamless sleep, is the third state, higher again than dream. It is a "blissful state," a state of unification in which the spirit is no longer scattered over a profusion of objective and subjective things, but there is no consciousness of this unification and bliss.

Turīya, the fourth state, is beyond all that: it is neither perception of external nor internal objects, neither knowledge nor ignorance, it is without describable qualities, it is supreme consciousness of consciousness, a cessation of all movement and all multiplicity, complete freedom. It is the self. And it is the knowledge of the self. Which is the same, because the self, as the Upaniṣad understands it, is pure knowledge being bliss. The knowledge that we ordinarily possess is a knowledge of something. The knowledge of *turīya* is a knowledge of nothing in particular, but of the ground of all things and all knowing. It is the self knowing itself as the self, not the function of an isolated capacity of the mind, but an awareness, a lighting up of the subject itself as pure perception. Thus *jñāna* is not a conceptual synthesis of a subject-object polarity but the experience of the subject as reality as such. The *aporia* of the coexistence of the finite and the infinite, the real and the unreal, the temporal and the eternal, the subjective and the objective is not resolved but seen as nonexistent. *Jñāna* is the self-enlightenment of reality as such, the self-consciousness of reality. In *jñāna* consciousness rests in itself, knowing nothing beyond this self-consciousness that has no objective content. The difficulty lies in interpreting and communicating this knowledge through concepts whose validity is negated in this very knowledge. The concepts are all taken from the sphere of objective knowledge, in which *jñāna* cannot happen. On the level of the perception of the ultimate as reality there cannot be any concepts, because there is no more multiplicity, no thing with which this knowledge could be identified. It is not possible to have some of this knowledge; either one has it fully or one does not have it at all. Perception of *ātman* is indivisible. There is, however, scope for growth: the knowledge may be dimly perceived first before becoming overwhelmingly clear. The *Muṇḍaka Upaniṣad* distinguishes between a *para*, a higher, and an *apara*, a lower knowledge. The lower is the knowledge of the *Vedas* and *Vedāṅgas*, or traditional knowledge. The higher is that "wherewith the imperishable is grasped." Therefore it says: "That which is invisible, incomprehensible, without family or caste, without eye and ear, without hand or foot, eternal, all-permeating, omnipresent, extremely subtle: that is the imperishable recognized by the wise as the source of all beings. Just as the spider emits a thread and absorbs it again, or as grass sprouts from the earth or as hair grows on a living body, thus everything has its roots in the imperishable."[25]

THE PECULIARITY OF VEDĀNTIC KNOWLEDGE

It is very difficult to express Vedāntic knowledge, or the way leading to it, in Western terminology, which is heavily dependent on Greek thought.[26] Knowledge and way in the Indian understanding have stages, not set side by side, but within each other, in depth, within consciousness itself. Its aim is to reach reality itself, not to abstract a concept from it. This means a training not only of the mind but the development of a life-style of inwardness, from within which life then develops in a new way, whose knowledge is simply incommensurable with the knowledge achieved through sense perception and abstraction from it. The closer this knowledge comes to reality, the less can concepts express it adequately. It is possible to make statements about this knowledge—as well as about the *ātman* and about *turīya*, all ultimately identical!—statements that are to be understood as dialectical approximations only: it is immanent and transcendent at the same time, and neither immanent nor transcendent nor a combination of both. Every concept employed must at once be negated. Affirmation and negation at the same time, the *neti neti,* not this, not this, leads to a higher level of consciousness, where there is neither affirmation nor negation.

Human existence has not only a horizontal, historical dimension, but a vertical, non-historical as well. To cope with actual human existence this movement toward the centre, the attainment of a level of consciousness of the self, is indispensable. In our age of popularized technology all problems seem to be understood as questions concerning quantifiable material entities. Our "soul science" declares all ultimate questioning as sickness because it presupposes the negation of a transcendent reality. Upaniṣadic thinking "rests" and is static as far as the outward movement and change in topic is concerned; for people unused to probing the depths this vertical movement does not "lead further" and is considered uninteresting. There is no visible progress, and one needs time and patience. There are signs that some of our contemporaries have realized that technological toys cannot serve as substitutes for the soul and that technical progress does not simply spell happiness. They have taken up ideas developed 3000 years ago in a materially far less developed culture in which nevertheless dissatisfaction with things could be strong enough to come to understand the nothing as supreme bliss and fulfillment of man. In the Upaniṣads the specific knowledge is always emphasized as being new and different, *brahma-vidyā* as compared to sacrificial knowledge is considered to be much higher and incomparably better. Vedic ritual religion is in the light of *jñānamārga,* ignorance and darkness, a shaky raft unable to cross the ocean of existence. But the Upaniṣads know well that a knowledge boasted of becomes an expression of ignorance, worse even than plain and naive not knowing. Thus the *Īśa Upaniṣad* says: "Into blind darkness enter they that worship ignorance; into darkness greater than that, as it were, they that delight in knowledge."[27]

Compared to the way of work and its solid factual knowledge of the mechanism of sacrifices, the way of knowledge means a turning toward the subject and the correct realization that the subject can never be understood as part of something else, but only as a self-contained totality; it cannot be grasped in a concept but only in a realization. The realization is not *of* the ultimate, but it *is* itself the ultimate. He who knows himself knows Reality. The *method* of knowing reality is what the Upaniṣads can teach. They cannot teach reality. Everyone has to find it for himself or herself, using the method taught.

There are outward conditions to be fulfilled; according to some Upaniṣads the membership in the Brahmin caste is absolutely required and the disciple must have gone through the Vedic *saṁskāras,* especially the *upanayana,* before taking up the *jñānamārga* with a reputed teacher. Then the student has to undergo a long process of physical, mental, and moral preparation before being led to the formulae of knowledge. The preparation seems to be the more impressive part—the realization may be imparted in a sentence, a word, even in silence at the very end of the period of training. It is not the acquisition of some outward knowledge but an awareness of actual reality, the removal of so many layers of nonreality. Basically it is nothing new that is made known in realization; it is a subjective change to see everyday things and happenings as manifestations of the absolute; to see the self not as the individual "I" with physical needs and demands but as reality in the ultimate sense. The imparting of *jñāna* does not have the characteristics of an instruction but of a revelation. Therefore it is important not only to approach a scholar of all the traditional sciences but someone who has received revelation through a chain of bearers of this same light, a guru standing in the *guru paraṁparā.* The teacher does not choose his students, the students come and ask the teacher to be admitted. The students must serve their master faithfully and submit to strict discipline; little of the long time is spent in oral instruction, most of it is *tapasya,* ascetical training, which sharpens the energies of the intellect, especially the power of discrimination, which is most essential. A person must learn to distinguish the self from what is not the self, reality from appearance; one must be strong enough to reject all that is nonessential and nonreal. Through this the students gain access to new depth and new horizons that enable them to understand the true meaning of the words used to express the higher knowledge. Self-realization can be neither gained nor taught vicariously; everyone has to gain it personally. The guru points the way, supervises the training, clarifies doubts.

The discussions between master and pupil as recorded in the Upaniṣads are very often a Socratic kind of maieutic questioning, to bring to light truth from within the disciple. Words are imperfect instruments through which to discover the unspeakable. They can be understood only when realization has already taken place; and by then they are redundant. They serve to repudiate wrong conceptions and prevent false identifications. The common instruments of logic—to arrive at conclusions from certain premises by way of syllogisms—are considered to be inadequate: they can provide only particular and finite object knowledge, never an all-encompassing subject realization. The means, therefore, for finding truth is not discursive reasoning but meditation. The Upaniṣads differ in their methods of meditation; some begin with gradually widening cosmic contemplations, others utilize the Vedic religious symbolism, others employ mantras like the *Om*; from the audible sound the aspirant reaches out to the soundless until he can finally say: "*Om* is Brahman, *Om* is the universe."

The Upaniṣads are not only records of ancient India, they are part of the living Hindu tradition. Quite often they are recited as other scriptures are, memorized and quoted by people who do not spend all of their time as disciples of a guru. The recitations are quite frequently begun by the following *sloka*, which in itself sums up the essential teaching of the Upaniṣads:

> *pūrṇam adaḥ pūrṇam idam pūrṇāt pūrṇam udacyate*
> *pūrṇasya pūrṇam ādāya pūrṇam evāvaśiṣyate*
>
> "Fullness is this, fullness is that. Fullness proceeds from fullness. Having taken fullness from fullness, fullness itself remains."

The conclusion of the Upaniṣad, again recited, is often a promise of liberation as the following:

> This Brahmā told to Prajāpati, Prajāpati to Manu, Manu to mankind. He who has learned the Veda from the family of a teacher according to rule, in the time left over from serving his teacher, he who after having returned to his family settled down in a home of his own, continued to study what he has learned and has virtuous sons, he who concentrates all his senses in the self, who practices kindness toward all creatures, he who behaves thus throughout his life reaches the Brahmā-world, does not return hither again, verily he does not return hither again."[28]

The Upaniṣads are the great book of principles, India's *protē gnósis*, its basic philosophy, from which branch out the many systems of Vedānta of all later centuries.

13 *Ātman* and *Brahman*: Self and All

Verily, this body is mortal. It has been appropriated by Death. But it is the standing ground of the deathless, bodiless Self.

—*Chāndogya Upaniṣad* VIII, XII, 1

Despite the great number of interesting topics dealt with in the Upaniṣads their central concern is undoubtedly the knowledge of, and path to, *ātman* and *brahman*. It is, however, impossible to synthesize all the statements of even the principal Upaniṣads and expound the *ātman-brahman* philosophy of the Upaniṣads; what can be done is to indicate certain main trends of thought. One of these very obvious tendencies is the attempt, made repeatedly in the Upaniṣads, to arrange the seemingly infinite plurality of things in a limited number of categories, coordinating macrocosm and microcosm, and to understand manifold reality as a combination of relatively few primordial elements. By means of a progressive reduction one can finally arrive at the One, which is further reduced to an immaterial essence pervading everything without being identical with any one object. One could initially express it thus: the sages of the Upaniṣads seek to grasp the real as the ultimate support of all phenomena. They follow, in the main, two distinct paths. One begins with the outside world and the manifold objects and reduces them to five elements, to three, and finally to one. The other begins with a person's subjective consciousness and discovers in its depths the real that proves to be the source of everything. Finally the realization dawns that the immanent *ātman* is identical with the transcendent *brahman*: *ātman* is *brahman*. We have simplified things to establish a pattern; from the texts themselves we shall see that Upaniṣadic thought is much more complex and subtle.

We have a record of a lively discussion between the great philosopher Yājñavalkya and his wife Gārgī Vacaknavī, in which the first of those two ways is demonstrated.

"Yājñavalkya," said Gārgī, "since all this world is woven, warp and woof, on water, on what, pray, is the water woven, warp and woof?" "On wind, O Gārgī!" "On what is the wind woven?" "On the sky, O Gārgī." The questioning goes on, and Yājñavalkya explains the "warp and woof" of each world within the cosmology of the time, which we saw before: the sky is "woven" on the world of the *gandharvas*, this on the sphere of the sun, this on the sphere of the moon, this on the world of the planets, this on the world of the *devas*, this on the realm of *Indra*, this again on the *prajāpati-loka*, the world of the creator of all beings. "On what then is the world of the Lord of Creation woven?" "On the world of *brahman* says Yājñavalkya. Gārgī tries to press on, wanting to know what comes after *brahman* as its substratum, but Yājñavalkya rejects the question: "Gārgī, do not question too much lest your head fall off. Verily you are asking too much about the divine being, about which we are not to question too much. Do not, Gārgī, question too much." Thereupon Gārgī Vācaknavī kept silent.[1]

Before proceeding with texts it may be of some help to give a brief etymological explanation of *ātman* and *brahman*, though an understanding of both terms emerges, better perhaps, from the texts themselves, because there we can appreciate their deep ambiguity, the impossibility of really defining them.

Ātman is the grammatical form of the reflexive pronoun in Sanskrit; according to the context it can mean the body, anything that one considers as mine or myself, a meaning that leads to the probing question of what this "my self," the subject of all feelings, thought, and wishes, really consists.

Brahman has many meanings. It is derived from the verbal root *bṛh-*, to grow, to become great. In the Vedas, *brahman* means sacred utterance; that through which the *devas* become great. Later it came to be used as a term denoting ritual and also those who were in charge of it, the brāhmaṇas. The Upaniṣads, finally, use it as a designation for the ultimate reality, to be understood as the life breath of the universe and everything in it.[2] But it is also used more loosely, in an analogous way; the word, the eye, the ear, the heart, the sun, space are all called *brahman*. Elsewhere every identification with any concrete object is denied, and *brahman* became a synonym for the unfathomable, the unthinkable, the mysterious that has no name. The popular Hindu sects equate *brah-*

man with Viṣṇu, Śiva, or Devī respectively, giving it the qualities and attributes of the creator, the preserver, and the destroyer, seeing in it a "supreme person" with qualities that are described in detail. Advaita Vedānta has refused to identify *brahman* with any activity or quality and rather prefered to draw a distinction within *brahman* to express the conviction that the ultimate ground of all being is without any qualities or activities, since that would denote change; it is therefore *nirguṇa*.

A word of caution may be appropriate here: it would be misleading to translate *ātman* as "soul" and *brahman* as "supreme being," as we find quite frequently in popular books. Both words have a Western background and already reveal a specific solution of a problem that is left open in the Upaniṣads; namely, the question of the oneness and the plurality of reality. We shall avoid a wrong identification of *ātman* and *brahman* with foreign concepts if we consider in detail how the Upaniṣads arrive at their *ātman-brahman* realization.

> Om. The brahman-knower obtains the supreme. As has been said: he who knows *brahman* as the real (*satya*, which also means truth), as knowledge (*jñāna*) and then as the infinite (*ananta*), placed in the secret cave of the heart and in the highest heaven realizes all desires along with *brahman*. From this *ātman*, verily arose *ākāśa*, which means space or ether, a fine and subtle substance permeating the universe; from this came air, from air fire, from fire water, from water the earth, from the earth herbs, from herbs food, from food *puruṣa*, the 'person'. . . . From food (*anna*) verily are produced whatsoever creatures dwell on the earth. By food alone they live. And at the end they pass into it. Food is verily the first-born of the being. . . . Verily those who worship *brahman* as food obtain all food.
>
> Different from, and within that sphere that consists of food (*annarasamaya*) is the self that consists of life-breath (*ātma prāṇamaya*) by which it is filled. This has the form of a *puruṣa*. . . . The *devas* breathe this life-breath (*prāṇa*), as also do men and beasts; *prāṇa* is the life (*ayus*) of all. They who worship *brahman* as *prāṇa* attain a full life . . . this is the *ātman* of the former. Different from it and within the *prāṇa*-sphere is the self made of mind (*atma manomaya*), by which it is filled. This (again) has the form of a *puruṣa* . . . Different from and within it, is the self that consists of understanding (*ātma vijñānamaya*), by which it is filled. This too has the form of a *puruṣa*. Faith (*śraddhā*) is his head, order (*ṛta*) its southern side, truth (*satya*) its northern side, yoga its soul (*ātma*) and the great one (*mahā*) its foundation. Understanding directs the sacrifice and the actions. All *devas* worship the *brahman* which is understand-

ing as the foremost. . . . Different from and within that which consists of understanding is the self consisting of bliss (*ātma ānanda-maya*), by which it is filled. This too has the form of a *puruṣa* . . . his body is the bliss (*ānanda ātma*), *brahman* the foundation. . . . He who is here in the *puruṣa* and yonder in the sun, he is one. He who knows this, on departing from this world, reaches the *ātman* consisting of food, of life-breath, of mind, of understanding, of bliss. Where words do not reach and the mind cannot grasp, there is the *brahman* full of bliss; who knows it does not fear anything.[3]

We can learn from this one text, among other things, the rather complex meaning of the term *ātman*; a meaning that would not allow us to equate it with the term *soul* as normally used in the West.

The distinction of the five strata of *ātman*, corresponding to five different *brahman* realities is quite instructive: each reality is the inner core of the one preceding it till we reach the very heart of being, which is *ānanda*, bliss, that cannot be further qualified as having an "exterior" and an "interior." The self of a person needs nourishment, which builds up a material self; it requires life breath, which builds up a subtle material self; it requires mind, which develops the intellectual self; further on, it requires understanding, developing the sphere of deep insight. The core and the heart of reality, finally, is the sphere of bliss, where *ātman* is seen as consisting of, and resting on, *brahman*. For each sphere of the self there is a corresponding ultimate, to be realized as relative, step by step, till the true ultimate is reached.

What is *brahman*? We have seen one answer to the question. Another approach is given in the *Chāndogya Upaniṣad*. A father, whose son has just returned form his guru full of pride in his knowledge, questions him about the *brahman*. The son has to admit his ignorance and has to hear from his father that unless he knows *brahman*, he knows nothing at all. The father tries to teach him by way of practical experiments: "Bring a fig," says the father. Śvetaketu, the son, brings it. "Divide it. What do you see?" "Tiny seeds," is the answer. "Divide one of the seeds. What do you see?" "Nothing." Now follows the essential teaching: "My dear, that subtle essence which you do not perceive, that is the source of this mighty Nyagrodha tree. That which is so tiny (*aṇimā*) is the *ātman* of all. This is the true, the self, that you are, *Śvetaketu*!"[4]

The teaching drawn from the next experiment is the same: Śvetaketu is asked to throw a handful of salt into a vessel filled with water, to taste it in different places, and then to try to separate salt again from water. The salt is one with the water, it cannot be separated, though Śvetaketu knows that it is different from it. This is the *ātman*, all-pervading, inseparable from objects, not identical with them. And his father concludes this lesson with the same formula: *Tat tvam asi*, that you are! The invisible substance that makes the Nyagrodha tree grow is the life of humans, too, even more—the one who knows it, is it!

The same Upaniṣad has another well-known instruction on *brahman*: Prajāpati, the Father of all that is born, announces: "The *ātman* who is free from all evil, free from old age, free from death, free from worry, free from hunger and thirst, whose desire is *satya*, truth and reality, whose purpose is *satya*, he should be sought, him one must strive to understand. He who has found this *ātman* and understands him, he attains all worlds and the fulfillment of all desires." The *devas* and *asuras* hear this; they too are without this ultimate fulfillment, they too have everything to learn. Indra, the king of the *devas*, and Virocana, the chief of the *asuras*, approach Prajāpati for instruction. For thirty-two years they live as *brahmacaris*; they serve their guru without hearing a word about *ātman*. After the time is up, Prajāpati asks them for what purpose they had originally come. They repeat the words Prajāpati had used and state that they were seeking the sorrowless, deathless *ātman*. Now Prajāpati instructs them. They are told to look at themselves in the mirror of a sheet of water and report their impressions. They find that they see themselves, "a picture even to the very hairs and nails." Prajāpati asks them to put on their best clothes, adorn themselves and look again in the mirror, and to report about it. The two say that they see themselves well-dressed and neat. And Prajāpati concludes: "That is the immortal, fearless *brahman*." The two leave, satisfied that they have got what they wanted. Prajāpati looked after them and said to himself: "They go away, without having perceived, without having known the self. All who follow such a doctrine will perish." Virocana declared to the *asuras* that bodily happiness is the one and all there is. Indra, however, before returning to the *devas* realized an objection: if the *ātman* is identical with the bodily reality, it will suffer as the body suffers, become blind, lame, crippled as the body, perish together within the body. "I see no good in this," he concludes and returns to Prajāpati. He serves him another thirty-two years and is asked at the end of this long term the same question, but gets a different answer: "He who happily moves about in a dream he is the *ātman*, the immortal fearless *brahman*." At first Indra is satisfied and takes leave; before reaching his heaven he discovers the fault in this answer, too: someone who dreams of being chased and tortured, of mourning and dying, suffers sorrow and cannot be called happy. And back he goes to serve again for thirty-two years. Now Prajāpati comes up with a new secret: "He who dwells in deep, dreamless sleep is the *ātman*, the immortal fearless *brahman*." Indra, after a brief satisfaction with this answer, becomes skeptical again. One who sleeps is not aware of himself and his bliss. It is as if he did not exist at all. Prajāpati commends Indra's sharp mind and tells him to serve him for only another five years, after which time he will really impart the ultimate secret to him. When the time has come he instructs him as follows:

> Mortal, indeed, is this body. It is held by death; but it is the support of his deathless bodiless *ātman*. Verily with a body one cannot have freedom from pleasure and pain. But pleasure and pain do not touch the bodiless. Bodiless are air, clouds, lightning, thunder. . . . Even so that serene one, when rising up from this body and reaching the highest light, appears in his own form. Such is the Supreme Person. . . . He who finds this *ātman* obtains all worlds and the fulfillment of his wishes.[5]

Indra, the king of heaven, had to wait for 101 years before he was given the full insight; a human should not desist, therefore, from his effort, even if realization is not reached at the first attempt.

A fairly systematic treatment of the *ātman-brahman* theme is provided by the *Muṇḍaka Upaniṣad*. After demonstrating the social and secular necessity of Vedic rites and sacrifices and their intrinsic inadequacy to save from repeated old age and death, it develops the exigencies and methods of *brahman* knowledge. Realization of *brahman*, the imperishable, the *puruṣa*, the true, the real, can only be attained through a guru.

> That is the truth: as from a fire, blazing, sparks like fire issue forth by the thousands, so many kinds of beings issue forth from the imperishable and they return to it. Splendid and without a bodily form is this *puruṣa*, without and within, unborn, without life breath and without mind, higher than the supreme element. From him are born life-breath and mind, all the sense-organs, also space, air, light, water and earth, the support of all. Fire is his head, his eyes are the sun and the moon, the regions are his ears, the revealed *Vedas* are his speech, air is

> his life-breath and his heart is the universe. Out of his feet the earth is born, indeed he is the soul of all beings.

One by one, the text explains how everything issues out of this *brahman*. He must be known both as being (*sat*) and nonbeing (*asat*), as the support of everything, upon whom the sky, the earth and space is woven.

In the highest sphere, made of gold, is *brahman* without stain, without parts, pure, the light of lights. The sun shines not there, nor the moon nor the stars, nor the lightning either, whence then this fire? Everything has its shine from this shining one, his shine illumines the world. *Brahman,* indeed is immortal, in front, behind, to the right and left is *brahman*. It spreads forth below and above. *Brahman,* indeed is this all, the greatest . . . When a seer sees the creator of golden color, the Lord, the *puruṣa*, the womb of *brahman,* then he becomes a knower, freed from good and evil.[6]

The *Bṛhadāraṇyaka Upaniṣad* explains the immanence of *brahman* in all things as the result of its entering into them after creating them. "He entered into them even to the tips of the nails, as a razor is hidden in the razor case. They do not see him. When breathing, he is called *prāṇa,* breath, when speaking he is called *vāk,* speech, when seeing he is called *cakṣus,* eye, when hearing he is called *śrotra,* ear, when thinking he is called *manas,* mind."

The Upaniṣad instructs us also that by meditating on the *ātman* one realizes all things to be one, and oneself to be one with it: "Whosoever knows thus, *aham brahmāsmi,* I am Brahman, becomes this all. Even the *devas* cannot prevent him from becoming thus, for he becomes their *ātman*."[7]

Here we have one of the four *mahā-vākyas,* the Great Sayings, which are supposed to express the gist of the Upaniṣadic teaching in one word. Earlier, we have seen another one, *tat tvam asi,* the that-you-are teaching of Uddālaka.[8] Elsewhere we read: *ayam ātma brahman,* this self is the *brahman,*[9] and *prajñānam brahman,* wisdom is *brahman.*[10] The *mahā-vākyas* cannot be applied to the three lower stages of consciousness, they are true only of *turīya*.

If one were to attempt an understanding of the *ātman-brahman* from a Western perspective it would be difficult to find the right categories of interpretation. Some have chosen an easy way by just calling the Upaniṣads *pantheistic* and thus having done with them. This is, however, no longer possible. The Upaniṣads never state that objects, as they are and as they are normally perceived, are simply identical with the absolute. The Upaniṣads demand first of all a transcendence into another level of being and consciousness. It would be wrong to compare the Upaniṣads with rationalist theology; comparisons, if any are legitimate, can be valid only on the level of what is commonly and vaguely called *mysticism*. The Upaniṣads do not present us with a fully developed theological system, they offer experiences and visions.

The upanisadic *ātman* is not simply and unequivocally identical with *brahman* under all circumstances, only in *turīya*, the real consciousness of the Upaniṣads, which is not easily accessible. Only persistent effort opens up the depths of the self. Reality, once discovered, appears as "self-evident," but before we come to this conclusion we have to go through a long and time-consuming process of *neti, neti,* of physical and spiritual discipline. We recognize our self and the absolute, *ātman* and *brahman,* as the same reality only after having penetrated to the state of being wherein we are stripped of all qualities. If we follow the steps outlined in the *Kena* and *Bṛhadāraṇyaka,* to realize the *satyasa satya,* the reality of reality, we will be led into an *aporia,* a perfect darkness, a last portal that we find ourselves unable to pass, unless it be opened from within.

14 Karma, *Vidyā*, *Mokṣa*: Liberation from Rebirth

> From the unreal lead me to the Real, From darkness lead me to light, From ignorance lead me to knowledge, From death lead me to immortality.
>
> —*Aitareya Brāhmaṇa* II, 1

Thus does the *Bṛhadāraṇyaka Upaniṣad* describe the death of a man:

> Just as a heavily loaded cart moves creaking, so the *ātman* of the body with the *ātman* of wisdom on it moves creaking, when breathing becomes small through old age or disease then just as a mango or some other fruit loosens itself so this *puruṣa* frees himself from these limbs and returns again to the womb. . . . When this *ātman* becomes weak and confused, as it were, all the *prāṇas*, the life-breaths gather round him. He takes into himself those sparks of light and recedes into the heart. When the eye-*puruṣa* departs, he cannot recognize forms any more. "He is becoming one, he does not see' so they say; 'he is becoming one, he cannot small', they say; 'he is becoming one, he does not taste', they say; 'he is becoming one, he does not speak', they say; 'he is becoming one, he does not hear', they say; 'he is becoming one, he does not think', they say; 'he is becoming one, he does not feel', they say; 'he is becoming one, he does not know', they say. The point of his heart becomes lighted up and by that light the *ātman* departs either through the eye or through the head or through other apertures of the body. And when he thus departs, the *prāṇas* depart after him. He becomes understanding, he follows after understanding. His knowledge and his deeds follow him as does also his previous wisdom. Just as a caterpillar, when it has come to the end of one blade of grass, and after having made its approach to another one, draws itself together towards it, so this *ātman*, after having thrown away this body and after having dispelled ignorance, draws itself together. And as the goldsmith, taking a

piece of gold, turns it into another, newer and more beautiful shape, even so does this *ātman*, after having thrown away this body, make unto himself newer and more beautiful shapes like that of the *pitṛs*, the *gandharvas*, the *devas*, of *prajapati*, of *brahmā* or some other being. This *ātman* indeed is *brahman* consisting of understanding, mind, life, sight, hearing, earth, water, air, space, light and darkness, desire and desirelessness, anger and freedom from anger, righteousness and unrighteousness and all things. This is what is meant by saying: 'It consists of this and consists of that'. As one acts and as one behaves so one becomes. The one who does good becomes good; the one who does evil becomes evil. One becomes righteous by righteous action, unrighteous by unrighteous action. Others, however, say: a *puruṣa* consists of desire (*kāma*). As his desire is, so is his determination, as his determination is, such deed he commits; whatever deed he commits, that he attains.

On this there is the following verse: The object to which the mind (*manas*) is attached, the subtle self (*liṅga*) goes together with the deed, being attached to it alone. Exhausting the results of whatever works he did in this world he comes again from that world to this world for work. This is true for the mind with desires. The mind who is free from desire, whose desire is satisfied, whose desire is the *ātman*, his *prāṇas* do not depart. Since he is *brahman*, he goes into *brahman*.

On this there is the following verse: 'When all the desires that dwell in the heart are cast away, then does the mortal become immortal, the he attains *brahman* here.'[1]

Death is a theme that looms large in the Upaniṣads. Death is the creator and the destroyer of all that is. Death, especially in the form of redeath (*punar-mṛtyu*)[2] is the greatest evil that threatens the existence of man. Faith in rebirth seems to be accepted in the Upaniṣads without further argument. Scholars generally assume that it forms part of the religion of the indigenous peoples of India, which influenced Vedic religion quite heavily. According to the Upaniṣads the Vedic *yajña* cannot save from repeated death, to which even the *devas* are subjected in one way or another. At the root of the Upaniṣadic search for the liberation that goes beyond the attainment of the status of *devas*, there is already a certain skepticism with regard to the nature of the *devas*: for the Upaniṣads, they are in the sphere of sense experience and therefore in the lower ranges of consciousness and reality. The process of liberation does not, therefore, depend on any intervention from the side of the *devas*. The Upaniṣads do not deny a Supreme God; certain texts quite clearly speak of the *puruṣottama*, of grace and election as essential for liberation;[3] but their concern is the immanent process of liberation in the subjective consciousness. Death is a happening on the periphery of external consciousness, as are all physical and psychical ills, and so one is affected by these only so long as one is caught up in the lower stages of consciousness. Reality and consciousness are identical, a unity of bliss and immortality, freedom from change, freedom from rebirth and redeath.[4]

The most important synonym for death in the Upaniṣads is *kāla*, time. Everything that is created by time must also find its end in time: *manas, apas, arka, prithvī, tejas,* the body and the senses, sun, earth, and water, everything must die. Only that which is not born from death-time, the *ātman,* is not liable to die. The dialogue between Naciketas and death in the *Kaṭha Upaniṣad,* a most beautiful and profound passage, makes it quite evident that the basic aim of the Upaniṣads is to show a way of escape from repeated death.[5]

Fundamental to the Upaniṣadic understanding of death and liberation is the metaphysical anthropology presupposed in it, which differs substantially from both the popular and the academic philosophical understanding in the West. We have seen before the five different *ātman* corresponding to five different components or "sheaths" of human existence. Barring more detailed subdivisions, Vedāntic anthropology considers the human person to be composed of *sthūla śarīra, sūkṣma śarīra,* and *ātman-brahman.* The gross body is destined to disintegrate at the time of death. The subtle body with all the imprints of deeds and thoughts of the previous life, is preserved and clings to its *ātman;* this results in intermediate existences in heavens or hells, depending on the quality of the deeds, and finally in an earthly rebirth. Karma keeps in motion the vicious circle of action, desire, reward, and new action. The karma of former births is worked out in the present birth; and karma acquired in this birth, good or bad, works toward a future birth. The Upaniṣads have several similar accounts of the route that the dead take before they are reborn as human beings; these texts, often elaborated, have found a place also in the Purāṇas and other popular Hindu scriptures. The Upaniṣads generally describe a *devayāna* and a *pitṛ-yāna,* the former leading to no return, the latter leading to relatively enjoyable rebirths on earth; those who go neither way are reborn as animals or demons, before slowly ascending the ladder of being again.

Thus says the *Bṛhadāraṇyaka Upaniṣad:*

> Those who meditate on the truth in the forest with faith, pass into the light, from the light into the day, from the day into the half-month of

> the waxing moon, from the half-month of the waxing moon into the six months which the sun travels northward, from these months into the world of the *devas*, from the world of the *devas* into the sun, from the sun into the lightning. Then one of the mind-born goes to the sphere of lightning and leads them to the *brahma-loka*. In the *brahma-loka* they live for a long time. For these there is no return. Those who, through *yajñas*, gifts and austerities, conquer the worlds, pass into the smoke, from the smoke into the night, from the night into the half-month of the waning moon, from the half-month of the waning moon into the six months during which the sun travels southward, from these months in the world of the fathers, from the world of the fathers into the moon. Reaching the moon they become food. There the *devas*, as they say to king Soma, increase, decrease even to feed upon them there. When that is over, they pass into space, from space into wind, from wind into rain, from rain into the earth. Reaching the earth they become food. Again they are offered in the fire of man.[6] Thence they are born in the fire of woman with a view to going to other worlds. Thus do they go round. But those who do not know these two ways, become insects, moths and whatever there is here that bites.[7]

Other texts describe rebirth as the search for a womb of the *puruṣa*, the thumb-sized homunculus made up of subtle body and *ātman*.

The cause of rebirth is karma, inherent in the subtle body; the cause of liberation from rebirth is the cutting of the bond that ties *ātman* to the subtle body and with it to karma.

Though it is easy to give a correct etymology of karma from the root *kṛ-* to do, to act, and although the word has become one of the favorite terms of the present generation, its meaning is difficult to explain.[8] Literally, it is simply the deed done, work performed. But the deed is not terminated when a certain action comes to an end; the accomplished deed itself is a new entity that as such continues to exert its own influence, even without the will and activity of the doer. The whole *karmamārga* is based on this teaching of the objective efficacy of the accomplished deed; the *apūrva* of the Mīmāṃsākas, the suspended latent causality of ritual actions is quite an ingenious invention in this direction; it allows substantiated causality to accumulate like a bank account for later use in heaven. Karma is neither material nor spiritual in the usual sense of those terms. It can be produced and annihilated, it can lead to good and to evil consequences, but it is always finite, however powerful its influence may be. It is, in a sense, the law of nature; universal, because it applies to all of nature, but finite, because nature itself is finite. Karma is often understood as fate, especially by Westerners;[9] they might then also relate it to the Greek *moîra*. But we must take note of a very important difference: the *moîra* of the Greeks cannot be influenced; karma can! To the Greek mind, this helplessness makes tragedy possible, tragedy being the ultimate and inevitably fatal clash of human will with fate. Indian literature does not know tragedy; karma can be influenced or even totally neutralized through religion! The aspect of life, so prominent in Western thought, that decisions once made cannot be revoked, that the "laws of being" cannot even be changed by the Supreme, himself a being—this aspect is absent from Indian thought; the possibility of rebirths, of world creations and destructions in an endless series, offers the possibility of ever new changes in decisions made, of ever new developments, so that no being's downfall is final and irredeemable. Karma does not cancel free will and genuinely free decisions; nor do free will and one's own decisions neutralize karma. Karma has been called *scientific* by many modern Indians, and serous psychologists are investigating experimentally the memories of former birth in such people who claim to have them.

The Upaniṣads maintain that they have found a way to deal with karma that is better than that of the Vedas: not to produce good karma as counterbalance for bad karma, but to eliminate karma altogether!

> Unsteady, verily, are these boats of the eighteen sacrificial formulas, which are said to be the lower *karma*. The deluded, who delight in these as leading to good, fall again into old age and death. Abiding in the midst of ignorance, wise in their own esteem, thinking themselves to be learned, fools, afflicted with troubles, they go about like blind men led by one who is himself blind. The immature, living variously in ignorance, think 'we have accomplished our aim'. Since those who perform sacrifices do not understand because of their attachment, they sink down, wretched, when their *lokas* are exhausted. These deluded men, regarding sacrifices and works of merit as most important, do not know any other good. Having enjoyed heaven won by good karma they enter this world again, or a lower one. But those who practise *tapas* and *śrāddha* in the forest, the *śānta,* the tranquil and peaceful ones, knowers, who live the life of a mendicant, depart free from sin, through the door of the sun to the place where dwells the immortal, imperishable *ātman.*[10]

The Upaniṣads contain a sacred teaching that does what Vedic work could not do. The Vedas give to the Ārya the means to influence karma, and he is far above the *mleccha* who is excluded from it; but the knowledge contained in the Upaniṣads grants a degree of happiness and freedom and light that makes the Vedas look like a fetter, like night and unhappiness. Far from providing only a temporary relief from the ills of the world, the knowledge of the Upaniṣads uproots the weed called karma and deprives it of its soil, the body. The body is where karma operates and from whence it comes: at the level of the *dvandvas*, the pairs of opposites, that make up the world—heat and cold, pleasure and suffering, birth and death—it is impossible to obtain pure and eternal bliss and life. The body cannot be redeemed, because it is part of the world of the *dvandvas* itself. Freedom implies freedom from the pairs of opposites, from the body. The one who is completely free is "beyond good and evil" in an ontological sense. "As water does not cling to the lotus leaf, so evil deeds do not cling to one who knows *brahman*."[11] There is not a transformation of the finite into the infinite, of the mortal into the immortal; there is only the separation of the finite and the infinite, of the mortal from immortal, of the subtle body with its karma from the *ātman* that is by nature free, infinite, immortal. "The knot of the heart is cut, all the doubts are dispelled and karma comes to an end when He is seen."[12]

The path of the Upaniṣads was and is that of an elite which could afford to cut all ties with society and devote itself to the spirit. For the majority of Hindus, in ancient as well as in contemporary India, the path of works is what religion is understood to be: pilgrimages, almsgiving, recitation of prayers, and other good works are supposed to create *puṇya*, which allows one to dwell for some time in heaven and attain a good rebirth. The Purāṇas, however, in an attempt to assimilate Vedāntic teaching as well as popular practices, promise "enlightenment" as the result of the uttering of the name of God or of devotional worship of the image, and assure the devotee that the Supreme God will take upon himself all the karma of his devotees. The *bhakta* is freed from rebirth, not so much through the process of gradual sublimation, as through an act of grace of God.[13]

There is no longer any meaning in ritual actions if one has wholly transcended the sphere of karma. But the *Brahma-sūtras* enjoin the one who has knowledge to continue performing the usual rituals, lest he be considered an irreligious man. *Nitya karma*, the daily obligatory ritual does not result in karma for one who performs it with wisdom, but augments *vidyā*. Work done in a disinterested way, as *niṣkāma karma*, does not entangle in this world, but is a symbol of freedom to act without considering the results of one's actions. The Upaniṣads have the notion of a *jīvan-mukta,* the one who is completely free while still living in a body: like a potter's wheel that turns for some time after the pot has been shaped, due to the impetus given to it by the potter, so the physical life of the free person is carried on without any connection to the *ātman* that has found its meaning in itself.

Mokṣa or *mukti,* liberation, the key term of Vedāntic philosophy, is hardly ever used by the Upaniṣads to describe the ultimate condition; they prefer expressions like *immortality, bliss, becoming brahman.*[14] This freedom is "not a new acquisition, a product, an effect or result of any action, but it always existed as the Truth of our nature; we are always emancipated and always free."[15] In the Upaniṣadic doctrines a person is given the means to remove the obstacles, the wrong notions; liberation itself is an event that comes from the *ātman*'s own interiority. This is the deeper truth beneath apparently paradoxical statements. The Upaniṣads say that release from old age and death, bliss and immortality consists in "knowing the unknowable *brahman.*"[16] It entails both a separation of consciousness from sense-object knowledge and an extension of consciousness until finally it includes everything. The Upaniṣads say "the liberated becomes everything."[17] The statement "*ātman* is *brahman*" is the liberating truth itself and as such it *is* immortality. From the standpoint of objective knowledge the ultimate knowledge is a negation of knowledge: *brahman* is not to be seen, not be heard, not to be thought, but those who understand the seeing of the seeing, the hearing of the hearing, the innermost principle underlying all, know *brahman* also in a positive way. The very differentiation between the Self and the not-Self is enlightenment about the Self; there is no further need to prove the nonexistence of not being. The supreme condition of man, his true freedom, is identical with Truth-Reality-Being-Bliss: it is "self-awareness" that has no object-subject polarity but is everything as pure consciousness.[18] There is no further need to cleanse the *ātman* from sin and make it perfect: being free from sin, incapable of sin, incapable of being perfected, is a result of the fact that it *is.* "Deathlessness," then, consists in becoming conscious of the innermost support of the personality, in gaining unity with the Ultimate.[19] Whatever has been created goes back to its source, the body with all its parts and faculties is dissolved into the elements from which it was derived. The *ātman* withdraws its support to these its creations and thus they fall back into their nonexistence, into their difference from *ātman* that proves them to be nothing by themselves. By leaving everything it gains the whole, and by reducing its consciousness to the barest subject awareness it becomes all-consciousness.[20]

Mokṣa is but the recognition of a situation that always existed as such; it is a psychological breakthrough, not an ontological change. It is not a quickening of the dead, not a resurrection and transfiguration of the body, but is its rejection. It is not heaven but the overcoming of heaven, making all objective bliss redundant.

Liberation is beyond happiness and unhappiness, beyond heaven and hell. He who wants something must take its opposite into the bargain; he who seeks redemption as a positive reality must accept bondage with it. For the Upaniṣads the way out from the tragic hopelessness, which sees human life as a constant frustration, is given by the insight that sorrow and death do not touch the innermost core. The way of knowledge is, therefore, strictly speaking, not a path to salvation but a method of discrimination; the *jīvan-mukta* is not a saint, but a wise person. As the Upaniṣad says: "Such a one, verily, the thought does not torment: Why have I not done the right? Why have I committed sin? One who knows this, saves oneself from these. Truly, from both of these one saves oneself—one who knows this."[21]

However, it would be a mistake to conclude that the Upaniṣads are amoral. On the contrary, they contain many passages with rigorous ethical commands. Thus the *Taittirīya Upaniṣad* contains the following instruction to a pupil: "Speak the truth! Practise dharma! Do not neglect the study of the Veda! Be one to whom mother, father, teacher and guest are like *devas*! Do not do what others find reproachable!"[22] The very prerequisite for being accepted as a student was a high moral standard, and the life of the student itself demanded a more rigorous self-discipline than would normally be considered necessary. But morality is only a prerequisite; it is a matter of course for the one whose interests are no longer in sense gratification and possession of material goods. There comes a point when a person realizes that real goodness is not to be found in the accidental quality of a finite act, but in the heart of being itself, at one with the ultimate reality. Although several other ideas are at work in the *karmamārga*, as we have seen earlier, and in the *bhaktimārga*, which will be described in the following chapters, the Upaniṣads as the basis of the *jñānamārga* had, and have, a tremendous impact on Hinduism as such and are representative of one of the major themes of eastern religion: the acceptance of the aloneness of human existence not only as inevitable but as fulfilling, the overcoming of suffering and sorrow by realizing their nonreality, liberation through insight into one's true nature, the negation of redemption because of a profound recognition of its intrinsic impossibility. It is useless to try to save a human—all are saved, if they would only see it! "Just as the flowing rivers disappear in the ocean casting off shape and name, even so the knower, freed from name and shape, attains to the divine *puruṣa,* higher than the high. One, indeed, who knows the Supreme *brahman* becomes *brahman* himself."[23]

15 The Path of Loving Devotion: *Bhaktimārga*

> Fix thy mind on Me; be devoted to Me, sacrifice to Me; prostrate thyself before Me; so shalt thou come to Me. I promise thee truly, for thou art dear to Me.
>
> —*Bhagavadgītā* XIII, 65

The majority of Hindus today are followers of the *bhaktimārga,* whose exterior manifestation in temples, images, processions, feasts, and popular gurus characterize so much of present-day India. The term *bhakti,* used so frequently as the key word in this form of religion, defies an exact and adequate translation.[1] In addition to the general difficulty of translating crucial words from Sanskrit into English, the problem is compounded by two quite peculiar handicaps. First, the etymology of the word is not clear. Grammatically, *bhakti* is an abstract noun formed from a past participle. It can be derived from two different roots: if derived from the root *bhañj,* to separate, *bhakti* would have to be translated as separation. That makes sense insofar as *bhakti* systems presuppose the supreme, absolute Being to be nonidentical with and separated from the being of the individual. In this view, inner longing for reunion is the characteristic of human life, and the *bhakta* is one who is aware of the painful separation between himself or herself and God and tries to overcome it. The majority of Indian scholars, however, derive *bhakti* from the root *bhaj-,* to worship, to be devoted to. This, too, makes sense, because *bhakti* religion consists of acts of worship and loving devotion toward God. According to Vallabha *bhakti* is derived from the root *bhaj* and the suffix *kti;* the suffix means "love" and the root, "service." *Bhakti* thus means the action of service (*seva*). *Seva* is a bodily affair; in order that it may be complete it implies love, and without love the service would be troublesome, but not desirable; love also for its completion requires service.[2] The second problem in trying to find an English equivalent for *bhakti* is the diversity of definitions given to *bhakti* by the numerous schools of thought and groups of worshippers, providing many subtle specifications and subdivisions of *bhakti*, which are considered by the respective believers to be of the very essence of *bhakti*. We shall examine a few of them.

Two classical texts call themselves *Bhakti-sūtras*, purporting to present the authoritative definition of *bhakti* and quite openly imitating the style of the *Vedānta-sūtras* to impress those for whom these were the supreme authority.[3] Thus Sandilya begins: *athato-bhakti-jijñāsa*—"now, then, an enquiry into *bhakti*." He continues defining it as, "passionate longing for the Lord from one's whole heart," and he says that in it a person finds immortality. In it is contained the knowledge of God; but because haters of God also have this knowledge, only loving devotion combined with knowledge can save person.[4]

Nārada, the author of the other *Bhakti-sūtra*, defines *bhakti* as *parama premā*, highest affection for the Lord, possessing immortality in itself "gaining which a person becomes perfect, immortal and satisfied, attaining which a person does not desire anything, does not hate, does not exult, does not exert himself of herself (in furtherance of self-interest). Having known that, a person becomes intoxicated, becomes motionless, becomes one who enjoys the self."[5]

The Bhagavadgītā, probably the best known *bhakti* scripture, sees the essence of *bhakti* in fixing one's mind on Kṛṣṇa and worshipping him; this description probably would cover most of the general features of the different kinds of *bhakti*.[6]

DEVELOPMENT OF *BHAKTI*

In its full development and almost complete domination of the Indian religious scene, historically the *bhaktimārga* comes as the last path for the attainment of salvation, after *karmamārga* and *jñānamārga*. However, it would be wrong to set the three paths into some sort of evolutionary sequence; in all probability all three *mārgas* were present throughout Indian religious history, though their official recognition and preference varied. P. V. Kane sees in many hymns of the Ṛgveda evidence of *Indra-bhakti* or *Varuṇa-bhakti*. The fact that Varuṇa is in many respects the Vedic equivalent of the Puraṇic Viṣṇu may be understood as a first stage of *Viṣṇu-bhakti*, which later became so prominent.[7] We do not find the word *bhakti* in the principal Upaniṣads, but the *Kaṭha Upaniṣad* and the *Muṇḍaka Upaniṣad* have a doctrine of grace, which is typical for *bhakti*: "This *ātman* cannot be reached through insight or much learning nor through explanation. It can only be comprehended by him who is chosen by the supreme *ātman*—to him He reveals His form."[8] Similarly the frequent use of the word *puruṣa uttama*, the supreme person, to describe the Brahman in the Upaniṣads, a term that became a proper name of Viṣṇu in *bhakti* religion, would indicate the presence of *bhakti* ideas in Vedic times.[9]

The *Śvetāśvatara Upaniṣad*, which is a fairly early text, expounds a fully developed *Śiva-bhakti*; certainly this attitude took time to mature into such a systematic treatise. The later Upaniṣads are in fact mostly *bhakti* treatises, quite close in terminology to the *Saṁhitās* and Āgamas, the recognized scriptures of Vaiṣṇavism and Śaivism. The most popular class of literature in India, the Mahābhārata, the Rāmāyaṇa, and the Purāṇas are the sources from which *bhakti* religions have drawn their inspiration for centuries. These books frequently constitute encyclopedic summaries of the entire religious heritage of India, seen from the viewpoint of a *bhakta*.

Bhakti movements have produced inner-Indian missionary thrusts and are now also reaching for Western converts. The best known and most numerous (but not only) bhakti movement in the West is the Hare Krishna movement (International Society for Kṛṣṇa Consciousness), which has done much to translate and distribute classical *bhakti* literature and especially the literature of the Caitanya school of Bengal Vaiṣṇavism, to which it is affiliated. *Bhakti* has inspired thousands of Indian poets and singer-saints, whose hymns are still popular with large masses of Hindus. Even illiterate Indian villagers are familiar with the songs of the Āḻvārs and Nāyanmārs in South India, or with couplets from Tulsīdās, Kabīr, Sūrdās, Tukārām, Rāmprasād, and many others from the North, whose stanzas they chant and quote as summaries of their own religious wisdom.[10]

A number of Western scholars have taken up the study of what is termed the *Sant* tradition,[11] which is held to be "the universal path to sanctity,"[12] including not only Vaiṣṇavas like Tulsīdās and nonsectarian poet-saints like Kabīr, but also most of the Sikh gurus and several Muslims. "Who were the Sants?" C. Vaudeville asks and answers:

> Socially, they belonged to the lower strata of Hindu and Muslim society: nearly all were Śūdras, some of them even Atiśūdras, i.e.

Untouchables. They were poor, mostly uneducated or even illiterate; quite a few were women. They had no access or right to Brahmanical knowledge, were not acquainted with Sanskrit and could only express themselves in the local languages of the people, the archaic Indo-Āryan vernaculars of Hindustan and central India. With the possible exception of Marathī, these languages were still in a state of infancy, apparently not suited to the expression of metaphysical or mystical truth. The poetry of the Sants largely contributed to the development of the northern vernaculars into 'literary' languages. It was especially the case with Hindī, which was to become the national language of India in modern times.

Bhakti had a wide appeal from the very beginning, not only because it recognized the emotional approach to God as fully valid, but also because it broke down all the barriers of privilege, which had kept large groups of the population from *karmamārga* and *jñānamārga*. *Bhakti* became the way of salvation for everyone: women and children, low-castes and outcastes, could become fully recognized members of the bhakti movement. Some of the great *bhaktas* are saints for Hindus, Muslims, and Sikhs alike. Even Christians in India are beginning to accept them as theirs and are finding the religiosity of these *bhaktas* to be deep and genuine. Some of the universally revered *bhaktas* were outcastes, like Nanda and Cokamela, some were women like Mīrabāī and Āṇṭāl, others were great sinners for whom orthodoxy could not find means of salvation. Kabīr, one of the finest Hindī poets of mediaeval India, reputedly belonged to a Muslim weaver caste. His songs are a favorite with countless Hindus in Northern India even today. He says in one of them: "It is foolish to ask a saint as to his caste. The *brahman*, the *kṣatriya*, the *vaiśya* and the *śūdra*, all seek but God. The barber has looked for God too, and so has the washerman and the carpenter; even Rāīdās was a seeker after God. Ṛṣi Svapaca was a tanner. Hindus and Muslims have equally realized God, there is no scope of distinction in the ultimate aim." Saints like Kabīr may be considered as even transcending *bhakti* in its more specific sense when he sings:

> My true *guru* has shown me the way: I have given up all rites and ceremonies, I bathe no more in holy rivers. I then became aware that I alone was mad, the whole world sane. I had been disturbing those intelligent people! No longer could I live in the dust of subservience; no longer do I ring the temple-bells, nor do I enthrone a divine image. I no longer offer flowers. Mortification does not please the Lord; we do not reach Him by going about naked and torturing ourselves. They who

are kind and righteous, who do not get entangled in this world's dealings, who consider all creatures on earth as their own self, they attain to the Immortal, the true God is with them forever. Kabīr says: Those attain the true name[13] whose words are pure, who are devoid of pride and self-deceit.

C. Vaudeville would consider Kabīr an exponent or *nirguṇa bhakti,* seeker of the Absolute, closer to the Upaniṣadic tradition than to the popular Purāṇic religion of *avatāras* and a plurality of *Īṣṭa devatās.* Nevertheless, they are *bhaktas* insofar as they conceive of the Absolute in terms of a person, and of life as an ethical challenge to be met in a spirit of devotion to God and service to fellow men. "Whether they be born Śaiva, Vaiṣṇava or Muslim, all the Sant poets stress the necessity of devotion to and practice of the divine Name (*nāma*), devotion to the Divine guru (*satguru*) and the great importance of the 'company of the Sants' (*satsaṅg*). The Name, the Divine Guru and the *satsaṅg* are the three pillars of the Sant *sādhana.*"[14]

THE PRACTICE OF THE *BHAKTIMĀRGA*

Most of what Kabīr rejects constitutes the routine of the average *bhakta* and we will have to deal with it in some detail to draw a sketch of a follower of the path of devotion. *Bhaktas* are organized into a large number of *saṃpradāyas,* sects or denominations. Certain features are common to them and thus the most popular *Stotra-ratnas,* the prayerbooks, contain hymns to all the main deities, who form the object of loving devotion and adoration of many groups of *bhaktas;* included are prayers to Gaṇeśa, Viṣṇu, Śiva, Sūrya, Devī, Datta, Rāma, Kṛṣṇa, in addition to hymns to Gaṅgā and Yamunā, the planets, and various less popular *avatāras* of the main deities.[15] Numerically the Viṣṇu *bhaktas* with their many subdivisions are the most important group. Śiva *bhaktas* come second, and Devī *bhaktas* or *Śāktas* rank third, followed by the rest. Though there are enough differences between the various groups to make mutual vilification, or even persecution, far from uncommon in Indian religious history, they all have so much in common with regard to practices and beliefs that it is possible to describe *bhakti* in general without specifying in each instance to which particular *saṃpradāya* one is referring.

The promise of salvation for all resulted in a tendency to simplify the requirements for it, so that all might be able to fulfill the essence of righteousness, however poor and unlearned they might be. This has led practically all the *bhakti* schools to teaching that the name of God is sufficient to bring salvation to everyone who utters it. The story of saint Ajamila, very popular with Viṣṇu *bhaktas,* is typical. Ajamila was a Brahmin who had married a wife of his own caste according to the proper rites. After some time, he fell in love with a low-caste woman, repudiated his rightful wife and had ten sons with the concubine. He wasted his whole life in gambling and thieving. When he reached the age of 80 he felt that he was going to die. Before his death he wanted to see his youngest son and called out with a loud voice: Nārāyaṇa! Nārāyaṇa also happens to be one of the name of Lord Viṣṇu, and though Ajamila had not thought of Him, the utterance of the Name wiped out all his sins and he was given a place of honor in Viṣṇu's heaven.[16]

In several places the *Bhāgavata Purāṇa* underlines this belief when it teaches: "The utterance of the Lord's name completely destroys all sin, even when it is due to the name being associated with something else, or is done jocularly, or as a result of involuntary sound or in derision."[17]

A contemporary "Appeal for *Japa* of the Divine Name" exhorts its readers to recite the "*mantra* of the sixteen names," which is the "Great Mantra" for the *japa* of Kṛṣṇa *bhaktas*:

Hare Rām Hare Rām Rām Rām Hare Hare
Hare Kṛṣṇa Hare Kṛṣṇa Kṛṣṇa Kṛṣṇa Hare Hare.

It carries the following message:

> The whole world is groaning inwardly at present. Tyranny, persecution, immorality, disputes, sin, war and destruction are on the increase everywhere. The mounting irreverence toward religion and God is turning humanity into a race of cannibals. As a result natural calamities have also multiplied. Earthquakes, floods, drought, famine, food scarcity and epidemics have become alarmingly frequent. None knows where they will lead us to. Under such circumstances, resorting to God is the only way out of this inferno of calamities. Taking to the repetition of the Divine Name is essential for complete self-surrender to God. There is no calamity which will not yield to the Divine Name and there is nothing which cannot be achieved by the Divine Name. Powerful counter-forces might delay the achievement, but the Divine Name is infallible in bringing its reward. In this dark age of Kali the Divine Name is our only resort. Therefore for the good of India and the world at large, everybody should repeat and sing the Divine Name

> both for worldly gains and otherworldly peace and happiness, nay even for reaching the ultimate goal of our existence, viz. God-Realization.

There follows an appeal to the readers of the magazine to make a vow to perform *japa* and to send in an account of the number of times the complete mantra has been recited, aiming at twenty crores of repetitions.[18] "Persons of all castes and communities and of every age and sex can undertake this *japa*. Everyone should repeat the mantra at least 108 times every day. Intimation of the *japa* should be sent to the *nāma-japa* section of *Kalyāṇ* office, Gorakhpur, U.P."[19]

Equal power is attributed to the name of Śiva or Devī by the Śaivites and Śāktas, though usually the wearing of certain marks and signs also is considered essential to benefit from *japa*. The great devotion to the "name" has led to the composition of litanies of the thousand names of God, the *sahasra-nāmas*; a large number of the names given in these to Viṣṇu, Śiva, and Devī by their followers are identical. Apart from the great popularity of the practice among the masses of Hindus, the theologians of the *bhaktimārga* have developed theological arguments for it, too. To be effective, the *nāma-japa* must be undertaken with a name that God himself has revealed in the scriptures; with such a self-revealed name, God's *śabda*, God himself is identical and that lends power to the sound of the name itself. Repetition of the name is the most powerful remedy against all sins and faults; the sins against the name itself, however, are unpardonable and exclude a person from the community of *bhaktas* as a heretic.[20]

However generous the *bhaktimārga* might be toward the traditionally unorthodox, it has created its own divisions between orthodox and heretics. The *Varāha Purāṇa*, a Vaiṣṇava scripture, declares that at Viṣṇu's instance Śiva proclaimed the *Śaiva-siddhānta* to lead astray those who should not be saved.[21] The *Padma Purāṇa*, another Vaiṣṇava scripture, declares all non-Vaisnavite doctrines to be paths leading to hell. It says:

> Hear, O goddess, I declare now the *tamāsa-śāstras*, the scriptures of darkness, through which a wise man becomes a sinner even if he only thinks of them. At first I declared through my *moha-māyā*, my deluding form, the Śaiva teachings such as the *Paśupata* system. The following doctrines were laid down by Brahmins who were deluded by my illusionary power: Kaṇāda proclaimed the great *Vaiśeṣika* system; the *Nyāya* and *Sāṁkhya* systems were taught by Gautama and Kapila;

> the much maligned Cārvāka system was explained by Bṛhaspati, while Viṣṇu took on the form of Buddha to destroy the *daityas* who proclaim the false teachings of the Buddhists and go about naked or in blue garments. I myself, O goddess, took on the body of a Brahmin and in *Kaliyuga* proclaimed the wrong *śāstras* of the *māyā*-doctrine (i.e., Śaṅkara's *Advaita Vedānta*), which is but Buddhism in disguise. The Brahmin Jaimini composed the great system of *Pūrva Mīmāṁsā* which is worthless because it advocates atheistic doctrines.[22]

Bhakti means not only love for God, but also enmity toward those who do not love him in the same way. Even a saint like Tulsīdās, whose verses generally exude a very humane form of religiosity, teaches the Rāma *bhaktas*: "Avoid those who do not love Rāma and Sītā, as your most bitter enemies, no matter how near of kin they may be. Prahlāda resisted his father, Vibhiṣāna left his brother and Bharata his mother. Bali dispossessed his *guru* and the *gopīs* left their husbands in order to come to the Lord and their mode of conduct became a source of joy and happiness for the whole world. Only insofar as they are related to God are children and relations worthy of one's love."

So too the Bhagavadgītā, often quoted as a document of Hindu tolerance, condemns the people, who are not Kṛṣṇa *bhaktas*, as evildoers and bewildered fools.[23]

THE THEORY OF DEVOTION

The extreme conclusions drawn from a dogmatic understanding of *bhaktimārga* should not make us blind to the very great contribution *bhaktas* have made to religious thought and practice. They represent a Way that has recently been gaining great popularity in the West: the activation of emotions as a genuine path to God and to personal fulfillment. The teachers of *bhakti* have developed systems that reveal a good deal of psychological insight. They usually distinguish different degrees in *bhakti*; perfect love has to grow and to mature over the years and to permeate gradually the whole life of the *bhakta*.

Thus Nārada in his *Bhakti-sūtras* enumerates eleven degrees of *bhakti*: *bhakti* begins with the glorification of Kṛṣṇa's greatness; then the *bhakta* proceeds to the love of Kṛṣṇa's beauty, to worship him according to the rules of his religion, he remembers him constantly, considers himself first as the Lord's slave, then as his companion, as his parent; finally he evokes the love that a wife has toward her husband, surrenders completely to him, feels completely absorbed in him—and feels nothing else but the pain of separation from the Lord! It is quite remarkable that Nārada considers the pain lovers experience when they are separated from each other as the highest form of love.[24]

The *Bhāgavata Purāṇa* has a more popular enumeration of nine steps of *bhakti* (see Figure 15.1), which begins with listening to talks about Viṣṇu, continues with the recitation of his name, remembrance and veneration of his feet, offering *pūjā* before his image, prostrating oneself before him, considering oneself a slave of Viṣṇu, a friend, and finally to surrender completely to him.[25]

Rāmānuja, the greatest *bhakti* theologian so far, enumerates six prerequisites for someone embarking on the *bhaktimārga*: a *bhakta* has to observe certain dietary rules, has to show complete disregard for worldly objects, continue faithfully all religious activities, must perform *pūjā*, has to behave virtuously, and to be free from depression.[26]

The central act of *bhakti* is *prapatti*, self-surrender, which consists of five individual components: the intention of submitting to the Lord, the giving up of resistance to the Lord, the belief in the protection of the Lord, the prayer that the Lord may save his devotees, and the consciousness of utter helplessness.

Taking refuge in the Lord, the *śaraṇā-gatī* of both popular and theological *bhakti* writings, is considered the act that makes the person a *bhakta*. Some, like Madhva wish the devotees to proclaim their surrender to God outwardly, too, by branding themselves with the *cakra*, the sign of Viṣṇu, or by stamping their bodies with his name.[27]

Bengal has produced in Gauḍīya-Vaiṣṇavism the most emotional and also the most subtle form of *bhakti* teaching.[28] It makes use of the concept of *rasa*, a key term in literary criticism in which a scale of emotions and their conditions have been developed.[29] Nine basic *rasas* are usually given, corresponding to as many fundamental "feelings." The most intense of these is *śṛṅgāra*, erotic love. Then come *hāsya*, laughter, derision, followed by *karuṇa*, compassion and pain. *Krodha*, anger, and *bibhatsā*, vexation, are important as well as firmness and steadfastness (*vīrya*). *Bhayānaka*, fearfulness, *adbhuta*, admiration, and *śānta*, tranquillity, conclude the classical scheme. For the Caitanyites, Kṛṣṇa is the *akhila-rasāmṛta-mūrti*, the embodiment of the essence of all sentiments. Their method of realization is a gradual development of feeling to such a high pitch, that Kṛṣṇa alone can be its object. Even more, the devotee realizes

1. Śravaṇa: Listening

2. Kīrtana: Singing

3. Smaraṇa: Remembering

4. Arcana: Worshipping

5. Pādasevana: Serving

Figure 15.1 The nine degrees of devotion

6. Vandana: Praising

7. Dāsya: Servitude

8. Sakhya: Companionship

9. Ātmanivedana: Self-Surrender

Figure 15.1 (cont.)

that ultimately the love he has for Kṛṣṇa is just a sharing of Kṛṣṇa's own *hlādinī-śakti,* Kṛṣṇa's power of joyful love.

The fully developed teaching of this school distinguishes among three grades of *bhakti,* each again subdivided several times. *Sādhana-bhakti,* the first stage, contains *vaidhi-bhakti,* ritualistic devotion, and *rāgānugā,* or passionate following. It begins with having faith in Kṛṣṇa, enjoins association with good people, participation in worship, avoidance of the worthless, steadfast devotion, and a real liking of the Lord, which results in attachment and love. The next major stage is *bhāvana-bhakti,* emotional devotion, in which the theory of *rasas* finds a masterful application. Beginning with the sentiment of peacefulness, continuing through servitude, companionship, parental love, and culminating in *madhu-rasa,* sweet love, the authors expound a complex system of religious psychology, at the center of which is Kṛṣṇa's divine bodily presence.

When emotional devotion has fully matured it develops into the third stage of *bhakti, premā,* which is simply love at its highest level. This is considered to be permanent and cannot be taken away from the devotee under any circumstances.[30] One who has reached this stage may be called an ideal *bhakta* according to the description in the *Caitanya-caritāmṛta:*

> In pure love the devotee renounces all desire, all ritual, all knowledge and all actions and is attached to Kṛṣṇa with all powers. The true *bhakta* wants nothing from the Lord, but is content with loving him. A Kṛṣṇabhakta is kind and truthful, treats all people alike, hurts no one and is generous, tactful, pure, unselfish, at peace with himself and others. A *bhakta* does good to others and clings to Kṛṣṇa as only support. A *bhakta* has no wishes, makes no efforts except to honor Kṛṣṇa, is constant and controls all passions. A *bhakta* is always ready to give honor to others, humble, and willing to bear grief without a complaint. A *bhakta* seeks the company of the truly pious and gives up association with those who do not adhere to Kṛṣṇa.[31]

The same text describes the true Vaiṣṇava as "more humble than a blade of grass, more patient than a tree, honoring others without seeking honor" and says "such a one is worthy of uttering Kṛṣṇa's name."

The ethical overflow of the loving devotion to God is stressed by Puruṣottamācārya, a teacher of the Śrī Vaiṣṇava school of South India, who considers the six constituents of *bhakti* to be treating everyone with good will and friendliness and discarding what is

9 Playing Kṛṣṇa's flute in Sevākuñj

contrary to it; refraining from all malice, backbiting, falsehood and violence; having strong faith in the protection of the Lord; praying to the Lord; discarding all false pride and egotism; completely entrusting oneself and whatever belongs to oneself to the Lord, being convinced that such complete resignation earns God's grace and mercy.[32]

Śaiva and Śākta schools have developed systems of Śiva and Devī *bhakti*. These are often quite similar to the Vaiṣṇava *bhakti* which we have briefly discussed. Thus the *Paśupatas* prescribe certain activities designed to express and augment a person's love for Śiva. One is told to repeat the name of Śiva, to meditate on Siva's nature, to bathe in ashes, to behave like a madman, to sing, to laugh, and to shake.[33]

The most sophisticated system of Śiva *bhakti*, however, is known as *Śaiva-siddhānta*; a living faith for millions of Hindus in Tamilnādu to this very day. According to its main texts *bhakti* to Śiva develops in four stages: *dāsamārga*, the slave's way, consists of practices such as cleaning a Śiva temple, smearing its floor with cowdung, weaving garlands of different kinds of flowers for the decoration of the image of Śiva, uttering the praises of the Lord, lighting the temple lamps, maintaining flower gardens, and offering one's services to any devotee of Śiva. This is the beginner's form of Śiva *bhakti*. The next stage, *satputramārga*, the true son's way, prescribes the preparation of the articles necessary for Śiva *pūjā* (Figure 15.2) and meditation on Śiva as of the form of light. The third stage is called *sahamārga*, the associate's way and consists of *yoga*: withdrawal of the senses from their objects, breath control, suspension of mind activity, recitation of mantras and directing the vital breaths through the six body centers. The last and highest stage is called *sanmārga*, the way of truth and reality: *bhakti* in the form of Śiva knowledge has now been fully developed and is identical with liberation and bliss.[34]

As just one example of devotion to the Goddess, a hymn by the famous Bengali Śākta poet Rāmprasād may be given here:

> Mind, worship her who saves on the other side of the Ocean of the World. Know once and for all what worth is in the trash of wealth. Vain is hope in men or money, this was said of old. Where wast thou, whence has thou come, and whither, O whither wilt thou go? The world is glass, and ever amid its snares delusion makes men dance. Thou art in the lap of an enchantress, held fast in thy prison. Pride, malice, anger, attachment to thy lovers, by what wisdom of judgment

Figure 15.2 Implements used for daily *pūjā*

> was it that thou didst divide the kingdom of thy body among these? The day is nearly done: think therefore in thy heart, the resting place of Kālī, that island filled with jewels, think upon the things that day has brought thee. Prasād says: the name of Dūrgā is my promised Land of Salvation, fields flowing with nectar. Tell thy tongue evermore to utter her name.[35]

THE IMPORTANCE OF GOD'S NAME

"Taking the Name" is perhaps the most essential step in the process of becoming a *bhakta.* Because *bhakti* teachers do not stress traditional scholarship or ascetical practices, which require long training and above average strength of will and intellect, they have developed an entire *sādhana* around the name, and individual *japa* as well as congregational *saṃkīrtan* have become the most typical expressions of *bhakti.* At the centers of *bhakti* religion hundreds of people, often paid, chant day and night, in special *Bhajanāśramas* the names that spell merit and salvation. One of the better known saints of our time, Swami Rama Tirtha says:

> As creation owes its origin to the 'word' (OM) so the sacred names of Rāma, Kṛṣṇa, Hari are the vehicle that brings the individual back to him. Keep to them and you can obtain *sākṣāt-kāra,* or vision, of the *iṣṭa-devatā,* your chosen deity, whose name or mantra you have chosen, as well as his *dhāma,* his sphere. The chanting of OM goes on in all eternity in the tiniest atom of creation and it acts instrumentally in *pravṛtti,* the expansion and in *nivṛtti,* the contraction of the worlds. If we would trace back the steps and catch the sound and precede *nivṛtti* on its return, we would arrive at the eternal *Vaikuṇṭha,* Viṣṇu's heaven. It is our aim to reach this world of divine bliss where all rebirth ends, and this we hope to attain through *saṃkīrtan.*[36]

Bhaktas attribute to *saṁkīrtan* an infallible effect: the great saints Caitanya, Mīrābāī, Kabīr, and Tukārāma entered Viṣṇu's body without leaving behind their physical bodies on earth. They find effusive praise for the practice of the singing of the name: "The name of the Lord is truly a drop of nectar, a heavenly taste in my mouth. My *guru* has taught me the greatness of the name; today I have experienced its power."[37]

Traditionally five rules have to be followed in the recitation of the name. The name must express the supreme divinity, it must be given by a guru at the time of initiation, it must be practiced in a spirit of devotion and it must be accompanied by a saintly life. The name must also be sung melodiously with a heart full of love and longing. The various tunes correspond to various spheres and it is necessary to choose the appropriate melody.

The guru has been mentioned repeatedly in connection with the name—for the *bhakti* schools he or she is of the utmost importance. *Bhaktas* see in the guru the personal representative of the Supreme Lord himself; contrary to the *samnyāsis* they keep a lifelong connection with, and dependence upon, the guru. Quite often the guru is considered an incarnation of God, already during lifetime receiving formal worship. More frequently still, he or she is worshipped after death in a sanctuary built over the tomb. One school of thought is inclined to put the guru even above the transcendent God. A text says: "The *guru* must always be worshipped, the guru is exalted because the *guru*is one with the mantra. Hari is pleased if the *guru*is pleased. Millions of acts of worship are otherwise rejected. If Hari is angry, the *guru*is our defence; but from the *guru*'s wrath there is no protection."

Gurus in the *bhakti* schools are usually surrounded by a group of devotees who serve and worship them as their guides and gods. Often this is quite beautiful and one can meet really religious families around spiritual fathers or mothers, but quite frequently, if the guru is an unbalanced, moody, and capricious person, the resulting forms of religious life are grotesque and little edifying. Devotees then are told that they have to consider the whims and temper tantrums of their gurus as Kṛṣṇa's own *līlā*, His play that cannot be rationalized but has to be accepted as divine manifestation. Because according to the *bhaktas*' understanding serving God, *sevā* is the essence of religion, the service offered to the gurus—cooking, sweeping, obeying their orders—forms the exercise of religion in an immediate sense.

True and genuine religion, beginning with a fascination for God, who is Truth, Goodness and Beauty, results in genuine humility, joy, and contentment. In the words of Nārada: "Attaining love of God a person has no more desire for anything, is free from grief and hatred, does not get excited over anything; does not make exertions in the furtherance of self-interest; becomes intoxicated and fascinated, as it were, and completely immersed in the enjoyment of the bliss of *ātman*."[38]

10 Platform for *rasa-līlā* dance in Sevākuñj, Vṛindāban

16 Lord Viṣṇu and His Devotees

> Viṣṇu is the instructor of the whole world: what else should anyone learn or teach, save Him, the Supreme Spirit?
>
> —*Viṣṇu Purāṇa* I, 17

Worshipping and praising God is the most prominent activity of Viṣṇu *bhaktas*. They place themselves, as the following well-known hymn shows, in the company of all beings in the universe, which owes its very existence to him.

> Praise be to you, O lotus-eyed, praise to you, O Supreme Being! Praise to you, the soul of all worlds, praise to you, armed with the sharp discus. Praise be to him, who created the universe as Brahmā, supports it as Viṣṇu and destroys it as Rudra at the end of times. Praise to the Trinity, the one who exists in three forms. Devas, Yakṣas, Asuras, Siddhas, Nāgas, Gandharvas, Kinnaras, Piśācas, Rakṣasas, men and beasts, birds, immovable things, ants and reptiles; earth, water, fire, ether and air, sound, touch and taste, sight, smell, mind, intellect, ego, time and the qualities of primaeval matter—of all these you are the underlying reality; you are the universe, changeless one! Knowledge and ignorance, truth and untruth, poison as well as nectar, are you. You are action leading to bondage and also action leading to freedom taught by the Vedas. The enjoyer, the means and the fruits of all actions are you, O Viṣṇu. The Yogis meditate on you and to you the sacrificers sacrifice. You accept the sacrificial oblations to *devas* and the food offered to the *pitṛs*, assuming the form of *devas* and *pitṛs*. The universe before us is your all-form, a smaller form of yours is this world of ours. Still smaller forms of are the different kinds of beings and what is called their inner self is an exceedingly subtle form of yours. Praise without end to the Lord Vasudeva, whom no one transcends but who transcend all![1]

In those and similar words countless pious Hindus praise Viṣṇu, whom they have accepted as their only and supreme Lord.

The prayer mentions a few of the fundamental tenets of Vaiṣṇava faith—especially the immanence of Viṣṇu in all beings and his transcendence—and we shall consider a few more, without claiming to be able to exhaust the wealth of imagery and speculation produced in the long history of the various schools of Vaiṣṇavism.

Contemporary Vaiṣṇavism, the largest among the Hindu traditions, has its sources not only in Vedic religion but also in Dravidian traditions and in tribal and local cults, the earliest of which were the worship of Nārāyaṇa and of Vāsudeva Kṛṣṇa, as described in some portions of the Mahābhārata and the Pañcarātra cults of Bhāgavatism, records of which still exist in the early Viṣṇu-Purāṇas and the Vaiṣṇava Saṃhitās.[2]

Vaiṣṇavism has developed the most variegated and richest mythology of all the schools of Hinduism. The core of Vaiṣṇavism, however, is Lord Viṣṇu as savior, a belief that, again, has found expression in countless myths. The oldest, and perhaps most basic, myth of this kind is that of Viṣṇu *trivikrama,* Viṣṇu who took the three steps, later combined with a myth of one of the *avatāras, vāmana,* the dwarf. Allusions to it are found in the Ṛgveda,[3] establishing a connection of a Viṣṇu cult with the worship of the sun in the morning, at noon, and in the evening. It is embellished in the Epics and Purāṇas and is designed to give a basis to the claim that Viṣṇu's is the whole universe! Bali, the ruler of the earth, invited the *devas* and princes to a great sacrifice. As was the custom, each guest could express a wish that the king was eager to fulfill. Viṣṇu in the form of a dwarf appeared and asked for nothing more than as much ground as he could cover with three steps. Bali wanted him to demand more, half of his kingdom, if he liked, but no, *vāmana* wanted just that and nothing else. Bali resigned himself to the guest's wish; it was his own fault, after all, if he did not receive more. Before Bali's eyes, however, the dwarf began to grow: his first step covered the whole earth, the second reached out to the sun and there was no more room for the third. Humbly Bali offered his head for Viṣṇu to step on, thereby acknowledging Viṣṇu's rule and supremacy.

Another Vedic hymn[4] has become the basis of all later Vaiṣṇava speculation about Viṣṇu as the material cause of all beings. The very important, and most probably very old, *Nārayāṇīya* section of the Mahābhārata[5] tells about a revelation of a religion of salvation given to two sages, Nāra and Nārada in *Śveta-dvīpa,* the White Island, situated to the north and inhabited by a race of white wise beings, all of them worshippers of Nārāyaṇa. This interesting text, around the turn of the century, prompted some scholars to suspect Christian influence in Vaiṣṇavism.[6]

VIṢṆU *AVATĀRAS*

The most popular, and consequently the most important part of Viṣṇu mythology centers around the *avatāras*, the bodily descents of Viṣṇu exercising his function as savior of the world.[7] The Bhagavadgītā explains that the Supreme One comes down to earth whenever dharma is in danger, to save the good and to destroy the wicked.[8] Generally one speaks nowadays of the *daśāvatāras*, ten embodiments of Viṣṇu, though some texts mention a large number, including a good many historical figures like Buddha and Kapila, the founder of the Sāṁkhya system. In all probability the systematization of the *avatāras* belongs to a relatively late period: the animal forms such as *matsya*, the fish, *kūrma*, the tortoise, and *varāha*, the boar, are possibly Vedic Prajāpati transformations and reminiscence of old tribal totems; the human forms like Rāma and Kṛṣṇa could represent deifications of historical persons, tribal heroes, and founders of sects, although other forms may go back to local gods and tribal deities.[9] Vaiṣṇavism, taken as a more or less unified religion, represents the constant effort to bring the growing mass of mythology together under one principle and harmonize the heterogeneous elements from various local traditions. The ten most widely recognized *avatāras* are described in so many texts that it will suffice to merely mention them and some features of the myths connected with them without going into details.[10]

Matsya, the fish, defeated the *asuras*, who had stolen the Vedas, and returned the Vedas to the Brahmins. *Ekasṛṅga*, the unicorn, saved Manu from the flood in which the whole of humankind perished. *Kūrma*, the tortoise, supported the mountain Maṇḍara, which was used by the gods to churn *amṛta*, nectar, from the Milk Ocean. *Varāha*, the boar, lifted the earth from the waters into which she had sunk and thus saved her. *Nṛsinha*, the man-lion, saved the *bhakta* Prahlāda from his father and persecutor Hiraṇyakaśipu and in doing so he saved the whole world. *Vāmana*, the dwarf, defeated Bali, the king of the earth, and regained the three worlds for the *devas*, who had been exiled form it. From his feet arose the Ganges. *Paraśurāma*, Rāma with the battle axe, saved the Brahmins by annihilating the Ksatriyas. The Rāma and Kṛṣṇa *avatāras* (Figure 16.1) are the most popular ones and occupy a category by themselves. They are the universal saviors, not lim-

11 Varāha *avatāra,* Khajurāho twelfth century

Figure 16.1 Viṣṇu in human form

ited to a particular epoch as the others are; they save all who surrender to them. Balarāma, the brother of Kṛṣṇa, is remembered as the killer of Pralamba and a host of other demons. *Kalki avatāra* is the only one to come in the future: as the eschatological manifestation of Viṣṇu on a white horse, he is to be the final liberator of the world from *kali,* the embodiment of strife, and all his evil influences. Apart from these, a number of other *avatāras* play a certain role in some of the Vaiṣṇava scriptures and cult centers.[11]

The *Bhāgavata Purāṇa* teaches the famous *Nārāyaṇa-kāvaca,* the prayer called the *protective shield of Viṣṇu* in which all the *avatāras* of Viṣṇu are invoked, remembering their salvific deeds in the past as a guarantee for present and future salvation.[12]

Rāma was worshipped locally as a hero and a divine king probably long before he came to be considered as an *avatāra* of Viṣṇu,[13] and he is certainly older than the *Vālmīki Rāmāyaṇa,* the celebrated epic narrating his adventures. But his worship as a Viṣṇu *avatāra* must be comparatively late; certainly later than that of Vāsudeva Kṛṣṇa. Even now the human features of Rāma and Sītā, his consort, seem to be more in the foreground of popular religious consciousness than his divinity. There is a late work, the so-called *Adhyātma Rāmāyaṇa,* which explains Rāma and his exploits as manifestations of the supreme Viṣṇu in the following manner: "The Lord of Jānakī, who is intelligence itself and, though immutable, being requested by the *devas* to remove the afflictions of the world, took the illusory form of a man and was apparently born in the solar dynasty. After attaining to fame eternal, capable of destroying sins by killing the foremost of the demons, he again took up his real nature as *brahman.*"[14] Ayodhyā, the city of Rāma, has become the center of the Rāma *bhaktas,* with millions of devotees flocking to the sacred sites each year. Ayodhyā, the "city without war" has also become the focus of worldwide attention through the agitation of the Hindu political parties that clamoured for years for a restoration of the legendary birthplace of Rāma, which since Babur's time was partly occupied by a mosque. Plans for a new Rāma temple were drawn up and made public through the media and millions were mobilized in the Rām-śilā movement, which encouraged people to contribute one brick inscribed with the name Rāma toward the future temple. The agitation reached its apex when, on December 6, 1992, a group of *kārsevaks* (R.S.S. workers) demolished the Bābri-Masjīd and reclaimed the area for the Rāma temple. The widespread outbreak of Hindu-Muslin rioting that followed all over India, leaving thousands dead and hundreds of thousands homeless, has tarnished the name of Rāma, whose rule was always extolled as *dharma-rājya,* the kingdom of justice and peace.[15]

The most popular among the Viṣṇu *avatāras* is, undoubtedly, Kṛṣṇa, the black one, also called Śyāma.[16] Many of his worshippers consider him not only an *avatāra* in the usual sense, namely Viṣṇu accepting a human disguise in which he appears, but as *svayam bhagavān,* the Lord Himself in His eternal body. The many scriptures inspired by the Kṛṣṇa cult do not tire of emphasising that Kṛṣṇa is the savior, the ultimate and definite manifestation of Viṣṇu, for the benefit of all who choose to become his devotees.

Present-day Kṛṣṇa worship is an amalgam of various elements.[17] According to historical testimonies, Kṛṣṇa-Vāsudeva worship already flourished in and around Mathurā several centuries before Christ. A second important element is the cult of Kṛṣṇa Govinda, perhaps the tribal deity of the Ahirs. Still later is the worship of the Divine Child Kṛṣṇa, a quite prominent feature of modern Kṛṣṇaism[18]. The last element seems to have been Kṛṣṇa, the lover of the *gopīs,* among whom Rādhā occupies a special position[19]. It is possible that this latter element developed under Tāntric influence. In some books Kṛṣṇa is considered to be the founder and first teacher of the Bhāgavata religion. The question of Kṛṣṇa's historicity is being studied quite seriously.[20]

The numerous myths reveal a faith in Kṛṣṇa as a manifestation of God, capable of liberating mankind. His birth is surrounded by miracles. As a little baby he already gave proof of his divine power. As a young man he lifted up Govardhana and defied Indra. He is the object of passionate love that inspired some of India's greatest poets to unrivaled masterpieces, like Jayadeva, who wrote the immortal *Gītāgovinda.* He also is the teacher of the way of salvation in the Bhagavadgītā and the *Bhāgavata Purāṇa,* certainly the most popular religious books in the whole of India.[21]

Not only was Kṛṣṇaism influenced by the identification of Kṛṣṇa with Viṣṇu, but also Vaiṣṇavism as a whole was partly transformed and reinterpreted in the light of the popular and powerful Kṛṣṇa religion. Bhāgavatism may have brought an element of cosmic religion into Kṛṣṇa worship; Kṛṣṇa mythology has certainly brought a strongly human element into Bhāgavatism. Kṛṣṇa is not a God enthroned in majesty, inaccessible to man, but a sweet child, a naughty boy, a comrade in youthful adventures, an ardent lover—and thus a savior! The center of Kṛṣṇa-worship was always *Brājbhūmi,* the district of Mathurā, with Vrindāvan, Govardhana, and Gokula, associated with Kṛṣṇa from time immemorial. Millions of

Kṛṣṇa *bhaktas* visit these places every year and participate in the numerous festivities that reenact scenes from Kṛṣṇa's life on earth.[22]

Though there is no mention of Śrī, the consort of Viṣṇu, in the earlier sources, in later Vaiṣṇavism Śrī becomes part of Viṣṇu religion. Apparently also Śrī was worshipped independently before her cult was integrated into Vaiṣṇavism. Now she is considered inseparable from Viṣṇu: Viṣṇu has on his body a mark called *śrī-vatsa*, representing his consort. In later Vaiṣṇavism she is identified with Rādhā, and Caitanya, the sixteenth century Bengali Kṛṣṇa mystic, is held by his followers to be an *avatāra* of Kṛṣṇa and Rādhā together. The most prominent form of South Indian Vaiṣṇavism is called Śrī-Vaiṣṇavism because of its strong emphasis on the role of Śrī. It draws heavily on the popular *bhakti* religion of the Ālvārs, so that we can see in Śrī worship an element of popular Indian religion, in which worship of goddesses always occupied a prominent place.[23]

VIṢṆU THEOLOGY

Vaiṣṇavism is intimately connected with image worship. Its rationale is provided in the Pañcarātra[24] theology which has been fairly commonly accepted by all groups of Vaiṣṇavas. Following the description in a widely acknowledged handbook, we may give a short sketch of it. Īśvara, the Lord Viṣṇu, is the ruler of all, the giver of all gifts, the preserver of all, the cause of all effects, and he has everything, except himself and his own consciousness, as his body. Īśvara is thus the material cause of the universe, becoming through the act of creation the efficient cause, as well as the concomitant cause of all things, insofar as he is immanent in time. Īśvara, who animates the whole world, is not touched by its imperfections. He is omnipresent through his form, through his knowledge of all things and events, and through his body. He is free from the limitations of space, time and objects. He is *sat-cit-ānanda*, being, consciousness, and bliss, and he is free from sin. He is the refuge and the protector of all beings, having the qualities of gentleness and mercy.

Īśvara exists in five different forms: as *para, vyūha, vibhava, antaryāmin,* and *ārcāvatāra*. Viṣṇu in his own supreme and transcendent form is called *para*: expressed in names like *Parabrahman, Paravasudeva*. He is endowed with a divine body having four arms and adorned by the insignia of his supreme Lordship, seated on *śeṣa*, the infinite world snake, residing in *Vaikuṇṭha*.

12 Keśighāṭ in Vrindāban, where Kṛṣṇa subdued the demon Keśi

He manifests his powers severally in four *vyūhas,* whose names are Vāsudeva, Saṁkarṣana, Pradhyumna, and Aniruddha and who exist for creation and worship. Vāsudeva is filled with the six divine qualities; the others have two each, namely, *jñāna* and *bala,* knowledge and strength; *aiśvarya* and *vīrya,* lordship and heroism; *śakti* and *tejas,* power and splendor. Each of them descends into three sub-*vyūhas,* such as Keśava, and so on, who are the presiding deities of the twelve months, each having his special insignia and powers. Keśava shines like gold, and he carries four *cakras* or discuses. The dark-skinned Nārāyaṇa carries four *śaṇkhas,* conches. Madhva, who is bright like sapphire, holds four *gaḍas* or clubs; Govinda who shines as the moon, carries four *śārṅgas* or bows; Viṣṇu, of the color of the blue lotus, has four *halas,* or ploughs; Madhusūdana, who is like a bright-hued lotus, carries four *muśalas,* or hammers; the fire-colored Trivikrama bears four *khadgas* or swords; Vāmana, radiant like the dawn, holds four *vajras,* or thunderbolts; Śrīdhāra, like a white lotus, bears four *paṭṭīsas,* or spears; Hṛṣikeśa, brilliant as the lightning, carries four *mudgaras,* or axes; Padmanābha, effulgent as the midday sun, bears five *audhas,* or shields. Damodāra, red-white like an Indragopa beetle, holds four *pāśas,* or nooses.

Under the category *vibhava* come the *avatāras,* which were mentioned before. The text distinguishes between full and partial *avatāras.* It also teaches: "The cause for the descent of an *avatāra* is only the free will of Īśvara and not karma. Its fruit is the protection of the good people and the destruction of the wicked."

Antaryāmin is the form of Īśvara that resides in the human heart. He stays with the *jīvātman* as friend in the experiences of heaven and hell and is recognizable by the Yogi. For practical religious purposes the *ārcāvatāra,* the visible image of God, is the most important. The text describes it as follows:

> The *ārcāvatāra* is that special form which accepts as body, without intervention of spatial or temporal distance, any kind of matter which the *bhakta* might wish to choose, descending into it with an *aprākṛtaśarīra,* a non-material body; he then depends on the devotee concerning bathing, eating, sitting, sleeping, etc. He is filled with divine qualities and tolerates everything, being present thus in houses, villages, towns, holy places, hills and so forth. He is fourfold on the basis of the difference as *svayamvyakta,* self-manifest, *daiva,* manifest through *devas, saiddha* manifest through saints and *mānuṣa* manifest through ordinary human beings.[25]

Images, understood as a physical presence of Viṣṇu, are a very important part of Vaiṣṇavism. The fame of a temple depends on the power of its *mūrti,* and each devout Vaiṣṇava family maintains at least one figure of Viṣṇu or of one of the *avatāras* in the house, which receives regular worship. Apart from the anthropomorphic images also the *tulasī* plant, usually kept in a pot in the yard of the house, and the *śālagrāma,* an ammonite from the Gandak River (in Nepal), are worshipped as embodiments of Viṣṇu.

Vaiṣṇavism has also a highly developed temple architecture. Some of the most impressive buildings in the world, such as the Śrīraṅgam temple near Tiruchirapalli, are consecrated to Viṣṇu. In most images Viṣṇu is represented either standing upright or lying on his couch, the world snake *śeṣa,* and usually accompanied by Śrī. The *avatāras* have been represented, quite frequently, in the poses described in the myths. Feasts observed in honor of Viṣṇu are so numerous that it is impossible to mention them all; a few will be described in a later chapter. Today, the feasts of the *avatāras* are in the foreground, especially Kṛṣṇa's and Rāma's birthdays.

Despite the prevalence of a highly emotional *bhakti* and often quite unstructured forms of worship we must not overlook the very rich systematic theological heritage of Vaiṣṇavism and its compendious, minutely ordered liturgies.

Vaiṣṇavas generally insist that *their* interpretation of the great classics, which are universally accepted by Hindus, is the only correct one, rejecting for instance Śaṅkara's Advaitic interpretation of the Upaniṣads as heretical. There is good reason to assume that the first commentary on the *Brahma-sūtras,* the lost gloss by Bodhāyana, had indeed been theistic. Vaiṣṇavas, then, interpret many passages in the Vedas and the Upaniṣads in a Vaiṣṇava way. According to Rāmānuja, for instance, all words in the Veda like *power, form, splendor, body,* and similar expressions mean Viṣṇu, and similarly Viṣṇu is intended by the Upaniṣads when they mention *the soul of all, the highest brahman,* the *supreme reality,* and so on. The earliest attempts to systematize Vaiṣṇavism seem to rely upon the Sāṁkhya system, as testified to by the *Pañcarātra Āgamas.* The difference of Vaiṣṇava Sāṁkhya lies in its attributing to Viṣṇu the authorship of *prakṛti* and of liberation. The *Bhāgavata Purāṇa,* which considers Kapila an *avatāra* of Viṣṇu, contains the fullest account of Vaiṣṇava Sāṃkhya, concluding with the exhortation: "Therefore through devotion, dispassion and spiritual wisdom acquired through a concentrated mind one should contemplate the Inner Controller as present in this very body, though apart from it."[26]

13 Viṣṇu Upendra, Khajurāho twelfth century

VAIṢṆAVA VEDĀNTA

More prominent today in Vaiṣṇava theology are the systems deriving from Vedānta and developing from the tenth century onward. They begin with the *ācāryas* of Śrīraṅgam who combined the fervor of the popular religious literature of the Āḷvārs with Upaniṣadic *jñāna*. Nāṭha Muni, the first of them, was the son of the great Pañcarātra master Īśvara Muni. He gave to the Tamil *Prabandham* of the Āḷvārs the status of *śruti* in Śrīraṅgam and established himself as the supreme teaching authority. His successor, Yamunācārya, was a great Vedāntin who left several systematic works. According to a legend he kept three fingers bent on his deathbed, interpreted by Rāmānuja, his successor, as three unfulfilled wishes that he was going to redeem; namely, to give to the Vaiṣṇavas a commentary on the *Brahma-sūtra*, to perpetuate the memory of Parāśara, the author of the *Viṣṇu Purāṇa*, and to spread the glory of Nammāḷvār (Figure 16.2), considered to be the greatest among the Āḷvārs.[27] He proved to be a great organizer and a great writer. He made the most successful attempt to establish a theistic Vedānta interpretation over against Śaṅkara's Advaita. In addition to the commentary on the *Brahma-sūtra*, called *Śrī-bhāṣya*, Rāmānuja wrote a commentary on the Bhagavadgītā, as well as several minor independent and valuable works. Perhaps the best known of these is the *Vedārtha-saṁgraha*, a veritable compendium of Vaiṣṇava Vedānta, written in beautiful language.[28] In Ramanuja's theology *Brahman* is identical with Viṣṇu, who is described as *rakṣaka*, the Redeemer. Viṣṇu comes down from his heavenly throne to enter *saṁsāra* for the sake of assisting the struggling *jīvas* to attain salvation; he suffers and endures pain with them and leads them by the hand like a friend. This guidance is given through the medium of the *avatāras* and the guru, the "fully trustworthy person" who tells the lost *jīvas* about their real identity and returns them to their father.[29] Though in his original nature the *jīvas* are particles of the divine nature, due to certain limitations, described as "heedlessness," they become entangled in *saṁsāra* and thereby unhappy. The Lord remains with the *jīvas* as *antaryāmin* to guide them, without taking away the *jīvas'* freedom to follow their own ways. "The Lord then, recognizing those who perform good actions as devotees who obey His commands, blesses them with piety, riches, worldly pleasures and final release, while those who transgress His commands He causes to experience the opposite of all this."[30] Viṣṇu himself is the *muktidātā*, the giver of salvation, and the role of humans is to prepare the way for God to meet them, to dispose themselves for God's grace. The central act is *prapatti*, self-surrender.

The following text, in Rāmānuja's words, gives in a nutshell the way to salvation:

> The pathway through which the supreme brahman is to be attained is as follows: By an accumulation of great merit the sins of the past lives are destroyed. Thus liberated a person will seek refuge at the feet of the Puruṣottama. Such self-surrender begets an inclination toward Him. Then the aspirant acquires knowledge of reality from the scriptures aided by the instruction of holy teachers. Then by a steady effort the *bhakta* develops in an ever increasing measure the qualities of soul like the control of mind, sense-control, austerity, purity, forgiveness, sincerity, fearlessness, mercy and non-violence. The *bhaktas* continue with the ritual duties and offer their very own self at the lotus-like feet of the Puruṣottama. They ceaselessly worship Him with dedication. The Puruṣottama, who is overflowing with compassion, being pleased with such love, showers His grace on the aspirant, which destroys all inner darkness. In such a devotee there develops *bhakti*, which is valued for its own sake, which is uninterrupted, an absolute delight in itself, and which is meditation that has taken on the character of the most vivid and immediate vision. Through such *bhakti* is the Supreme attained.[31]

Rāmānuja underscores the importance of the guru with the beautiful parable of a young prince, who in the course of a boyish play loses his way in the forest. He is reared by a good Brahmin, who knows nothing about the boy's background. When the boy has reached his sixteenth year, a "fully trustworthy person" tells him who his father is, and that he longs to see him. The boy is exceedingly happy and starts on his way to his real home; his father has gone out from his palace to meet him halfway. Rāmānuja sees in the "fully trustworthy person" a model of the true guru. The first among the gurus is Śrī, mediating between God and *bhakta*. She is the embodiment of divine grace and mercy whose entreaties win the forgiveness of Viṣṇu for the *jīva*. The human guru should be like her: entirely free from egotism, always desirous of the welfare of others, not swayed by the love of fame or profit.[32]

Shortly after Ramanuja's death the unity of Śrīvaiṣṇavism was disrupted and two major schools developed, based on dogmatic as well as linguistic tenets. The Vaḍagalais, or Northerners, whose main teacher was Vedāntadeśika, maintained that Sanskrit scriptures were the only true ones, whereas the Teṅgalais, or Southern-

Figure 16.2 Nammālvār

ers, whose principal master was Lokācārya Pillai, preferred the Tamil scriptures. They are also known as the *monkey school* and the *cat school*, respectively, because the Northerners likened the process of salvation to the activity of a young monkey, who must cling to his mother if he is to be carried away from a fire, whereas the Southerners saw the best illustration of the process of salvation in a young kitten, which its mother picks up and carries out.[33]

One of the most colorful of all Vaiṣṇava *ācāryas* was Madhva, the exponent of Dvaita Vedānta, who became known as "hammer of the Jains." He demanded stigmatization of the Viṣṇu *bhakta* with a *cakra* as a prerequisite for salvation. Madhva considered himself as the third *avatāra* of Vāyu, a mediator between Viṣṇu and humankind. According to him the *jīva* is an image of Viṣṇu, like a reflection in a mirror; and the relationship between God and person is described as *biṃba-pratibiṃba,* splendor and reflection. His doctrine of predestination is quite unique in Indian religion. According to his understanding there are certain persons who are destined never to become liberated and remain in eternal bondage. He also assumed that there would be differences in the bliss experienced by those who have reached heaven. He described the oneness of the perfect *bhakta* with Viṣṇu in a beautiful image: "The released takes everything with the hand of Hari, sees through the eye of Hari only, walks with the feet of Hari." The perfectly free ones even enter into Viṣṇu at will and issue out from him.[34]

Another great master of the Vaiṣṇava tradition is Nimbārka; with him the role of the guru becomes all-important. "Surrender to the guru" is the central act of saving faith, and the disciple makes a statement to the effect that the guru is considered the only savior from mundane existence.[35]

VALLABHA'S WAY OF GRACE

Vallabha (1481–1533), a Telugū Brahmin belonging originally to the Viṣṇuswāmi school,[36] became the founder of a distinct *saṃpradāya* with a specific doctrine of salvation that became known as *puṣṭimārga,* the way of grace.[37] It counts several million followers especially in Northern India and maintains hundreds of vibrant centers of worship. It became first known in the West through the unsavory "Mahārāja-case"[38] and became tainted through unfavorable early nineteenth century reports.[39] Recently, both Indian and Western scholars, as well as adherents of the Vallabha *saṃpradāya,* have come out with text translations and studies of various aspects of Vallabha's teachings.[40] Both the size of the membership of the Vallabha *saṃpradāya,* and the weight of the writings of Vallabha and his followers warrant a more extensive treatment of this branch of Vaiṣṇavism.[41]

Vallabha elevates the *Bhāgavata Purāṇa* to the position of most authoritative scripture; his school considers it to be the only authentic commentary on the *Brahma-sūtras.*[42] Vallabha discredits all attempts, especially those made by Advaitins, to use reason for probing the nature of *brahman.*[43] His is a "revelation-only" theology, a teaching that prefers to put up with what appear as inconsistencies and contradictions in scriptural statements rather than to judge these by reason and fit them into a logically coherent system.

It is also a "family religion," both in the sense that Vallabha himself was a family man, and in the sense that his teaching emphasizes the virtues of family life as means to earn God's grace. "The worship of the Lord requires the services of all members of the family, and they are promised the highest bliss that always results from worship, or *sevā.* This mode of worship makes the whole family free from worldy ties even when leading a householder's life, and their whole life becomes divine."[44]

Vallabha was convinced that in his time and age the duties of the *varṇāśrama-dharma* could no longer be properly fulfilled and that formal *saṃnyāsa,* far from being of spiritual help, could be spiritually harmful if not undertaken in response to the love of the Lord. What was important, however, and what was demanded of each and every member of the *saṃpradāya,* was *ātma-nivedana,* self-surrender and surrender of all of one's own to the guru. There is no doubt that this teaching lead not only to misunderstandings but also to malpractice.

Vallabha understands his *puṣṭimārga* not only as different from *karmamārga* and *jñānamārga,* but also as superior to the *bhaktimārga* of all other schools. *Puṣṭi* is the uncaused grace of God, for which the devotee prepares but cannot direct or influence: "It is impossible to say for what reason God is pleased to extend his grace; it cannot be for the relief of suffering, for there are many sufferers to whom God does not do so."[45]

On the human side, *puṣṭi* means doing things out of pure love and not because an action is enjoined by the Vedā, and also not because the intellect recognizes the majesty and exalted nature of God. The *puṣṭimārga* is open to all, also to women and low-caste people, even to the *patita,* the "fallen," for whom other schools of Hinduism hold out no hope of salvation. It is free from Vedic command and is interested in establishing only a relationship between the soul and its Lord—even if this relationship is one of anger and resentment.[46]

Vallabha distinguishes between *mokṣa* and *nitya līlā* as ultimate aims. Without denying the possibility of Vedantic *mokṣa,* he holds that *nitya līlā,* eternal enjoyment of the company of God, is much preferable.

> When the Lord desires to favor a particular soul—and be it remembered that in showing His favor He is not guided by any other consideration but His own will—He brings out the soul from Himself, gives him a divine body like His own, and plays with him for all time. In this play, which is called *nitya līlā,* the Lord, remaining subordinate to the devotee, gives him the pleasure of His company, which is generally known as *bhajānanda* (bliss of devotion) and *svarūpānanda* (the bliss of the Lord Himself), which is referred to in the *Taittirīya Upaniṣad,* the *Bhāgavata,* and other *Purāṇas.*[47]

The uncaused grace of God and the enjoyment of His company are best exemplified by the *gopīs* of Vrindāban, who are the models for the followers of the *puṣṭimārga.* The highest title of God is *Gopījana-vallabha,* the Darling of the Milkmaids. Becoming such a devotee is the highest aim of a follower of Vallabha:

> He who thinks of God as all and of himself as emanating from Him, and who serves him with love, is a devotee . . . the highest devotee leaves everything, his mind is filled with Kṛṣṇa alone . . . he is wholly absorbed in the love of God. No one, however, can take the path of *bhakti,* except through the grace of God. Karma itself, being of the nature of God's will, manifests itself as His mercy or anger to the devotee . . . the law of *karma* is mysterious . . . we do not know the manner in which God's will manifests itself; sometimes, by His grace He may even save a sinner who may not have to take the punishment due to him.[48]

Vallabha seems to assume that the seed of *bhakti* exists as *premā,* through the grace of God, in all human beings. It has to be nurtured and increased by self-surrender, by listening to the scriptures, and by chanting His name. It becomes strong if, while leading a householder's life, one remains absorbed in Kṛṣṇa and performs one's duties with a mind fixed on God. This love of God may develop into such a passion (*vyasana*) that one feels unable to do anything else but sing His praises. *Vyasana* is the "inability to remain without God"; under its influence a householder my leave his home and become a *saṃnyāsi*.[49] "The firm seed of *bhakti* can never be destroyed; it is through affection for God that other attachments are destroyed, and by the development of this affection, that one renounces the home. It is only when this affection for God grows into a passion that one attains one's end easily."[50]

Sevā, "service," is very central to the *puṣṭimārga*. It is a distinctive feature of Vallabha's *saṃpradāya* in so far as it denotes the worship of *Śrī Govardhana-nāthajī* alone. All worship rendered to other manifestations of the Lord is called *pūjā* and is directed to the Lord's *vibhutis* only, not to his embodiment as Śrī Nāṭhajī. The original image, supposedly revealed to Vallabha on the hill of Girirāja, is the only full presence of the Lord. Vallabha's *puṣṭimārga* emphasizes the sovereignty of the Lord as no other religion does: those whom He has chosen may attain a state almost like His own; those whom He does not choose, may remain in bondage and *saṃsāra* forever.

VAIṢṆAVA SAINTS AND SINGERS

Caitanya is one of the most renowned figures in modern Vaiṣṇavism and he has become known to many Westerners as the Mahāprabhu, the Great Lord of the Hare Kṛṣṇa movement.[51] Though he is not really the author of the emotionally refined Gauḍīa Vaiṣṇavism, he and his learned disciples made it into an important religious movement, influential far beyond the boundaries of Bengal. He knew the *Bhāgavata Purāṇa*; he had read the Kṛṣṇa poetry of Caṇḍīdāsa and Vidyāpati; he was familiar with Bilvamaṅgala's *Kṛṣṇakarṇāmṛta* and Jayadeva's *Gītāgovinda*; and the practice of *kīrtaṇa* was already widespread in his time. Caitanya never wrote a book,[52] but among his disciples were very able men who formulated the theology of the movement that Caitanya initiated. Rūpa Goswāmi's *Hari-bhakti-rasāmṛta-sindhu* is the authentic *summa theologica* of the Caitanyites, and Gopala Bhaṭṭa's *Hari-bhakti-vilasa* codifies the accepted form of their ritual.[52]

Caitanya's is a pure Kṛṣṇa religion. At its center stands Kṛṣṇa as the full manifestation of God and the continued presence of Kṛṣṇa in Brāja, more specifically the Kṛṣṇa of Vṛndāvan, the great lover of the *gopīs*, the perfect partners in this love. According to the Caitanyites the *Bhāgavata Purāṇa* is *śruti* as well as the only authentic commentary on the *Brahma-sūtra*. Nevertheless another

Caitanyite, Baladeva Vidyābhuṣaṇa, felt impelled to write a formal *bhāṣya* on the *Brahma-sūtra* as well, called *Govinda Bhāṣya*.[54]

The real source of the continued vitality and popularity of Vaiṣṇavism seems to lie in its poets and singers, who for centuries traveled up and down the subcontinent to kindle *bhakti* to Viṣṇu in the hearts of their compatriots.[55] Their concern is not theology or liturgy, but *bhakti* for the sake of liberation. Their main topic is the misery of this life and the glory of the life of God. A very striking feature is their insistence on the cultivation of a high moral standard: purity, truthfulness, patience, forbearance, love, renunciation, giving up all selfishness, contentment with one's state of life, self-control, pity, freedom from greed and from hypocrisy, sincerity, and humility—all this is taught in simple language as prerequisite and sign of true *bhakti*. They recommend the traditional Vaiṣṇava practices of *nāma-japa, saṁkīrtan, mūrti-pūjā,* submission under a guru, and so on.[56]

Simple as their words may be, understood by each and everyone, their thoughts are reaching great depth and their devotion is grounded in philosophical insight. Some samples must suffice. For those who know Indian vernacular, there are literally hundreds of books to draw from; for English-reading students of *bhakti* also an increasingly rich amount of translations and scholarly studies are becoming available.[57]

Sūrdās (1478–1560 ?), according to tradition, was blind from birth.[58] Yet his poetry, aflame with the love of Kṛṣṇa, was so famous all over North India, that the Muslim Emperor Akbar invited him to his court to converse with him and listen to his recitation. In addition to a massive work, still widely read, the *Sūrsāgar*, "Sur's Ocean," which recreates in contemporary *brāj-bhāṣā* the tenth canto of the *Bhāgavata Purāṇa*, Sur wrote many couplets that are sung at popular *bhajan* sessions. An English translation cannot bring out the musicality of the original, its clever use of double meanings of words or closely related sound images, its rhythm, and its color. It will, however, convey some of the content and give an impression of the down-to-earth metaphors used to deliver the transcendental message. For the reader not familiar with this type of poetry it may be worth mentioning that, as a sort of copyright, the Indian authors of poems usually inserted their own names in the last verse.[59]

Misguided by illusion after illusion
Stuck [like a fly] in the juice of sense objects,

[and yet] far from understanding [things]
You have lost the jewel Hari inside your own house.
[You are] like a deer that sees mirages, [which are]
Unable to quench thirst even if approached from ten different directions
Having produced in one life after another
Much karma in which you have entangled yourself
[You] resemble the parrot who pinned his hope on the
fruit of the silk-cotton tree.
Having set his mind on it day and night,
He took it in its beak [and found] its shell empty—
The cotton had flown up and away.
[You are] like a monkey that is kept tied on a rope
By the juggler who makes him dance for a few grains at every crossroads.
Sūrdās says: without devotion to God you will make yourself
into a morsel [to be eaten] by the tiger Time.[60]

In spite of its use of Vaiṣṇava history and scriptures, this kind of *bhakti* is quite transsectarian. At the *bhajan* gatherings one may hear poems by Rāma *bhaktas* and Kṛṣṇa *bhaktas*, recited side by side with those of Kabīr, who did not follow any particular Vaiṣṇava affiliation at all.

What those *bhaktas* search for is true experience.[61] Their basic experience is that God is reality. For Kabīr the religious experience is a "penetrating to the heart of reality"; for Mīrābāī Viṣṇu is "the invaluable jewel of reality." Quite often they report about suprasensuous phenomena that accompany realization, the most prominent being the hearing of the *anahaṭ-śabda,* the transcendent sound. Kabīr speaks of the "sky-reaching sound" that breaks forth from the full lake of mellifluous nectar, the means of illumination. Many also describe a taste of sweetness perceived in ecstasy: it is called *Rāmras* or *Hariras* and partaking of it equals immortality. Most *bhaktas* firmly believe that one can have *sākṣāt-kāra,* a bodily vision of God in this life, that would seal one's love to God with the assurance of final deliverance.

Vaiṣṇavism had and has a deep appeal to women. One of the woman-saint Mīrābāī's songs may help to appreciate the depth of feeling that is Viṣṇu *bhakti*:

The Name is gone deep into my mind.
Day and night do I chant it.

O Lord, I am humble and low, can I sing thy praises?
I am encaged in the agony of separation.
I gain solace only by repeating thy name!
Guided by the grace of the *guru* I have turned out
evil thoughts from my mind.
I stretch the arrow of the Name on the bow of Love,
I arm myself with the shield of wisdom
and sing my Lord's praises cheerfully all the time.
Making my body a sound-box
I play on it many notes with the mind
in order to wake up my slumbering soul.
I dance before my Lord
to gain a place in his divine abode. O Giridhāra, confer
thy blessing on me,
Who sing of thy sports,
and let me place the dust of thy lotus-feet on my head,
for that boon I cherish the most.
So sings Mīrābāī.[62]

Vaiṣṇavism has not lost its attraction in our time. Not only do the centuries-old *saṃpradāyas* continue and intensify their activities, new movements have also arisen to reactivate *saṁkīrtan* and regular *pūjā*. Swami Rāma Tīrtha has carried the message of Lord Viṣṇu to the West, and Swāmi Viṣṇupāda Bhakti Vedānta founded in ISKCON, a mission to propagate Gauḍīa-Vaiṣṇavism, not only in India but throughout the whole world. An Englishman, who under his Indian name Kṛṣṇa Prem became the guru of Indian as well as Western *bhaktas*, may still be rather exceptional, but there is no denying the fact that Vaiṣṇavism, in its many forms, with its basic message of love, has universal appeal to religiously minded persons. In late 1992 the first issue of a quarterly *Journal of Vaiṣṇava Studies* under the general editorship of S. J. Rosen began to appear from Brooklyn, New York. Its booklength issues carry important scholarly as well as devotional articles and the new journal is likely to stimulate research and disseminate knowledge on this major religion associated with the name of Viṣṇu.

17 Śiva: The Grace and the Terror of God

Śiva, you have no mercy. Śiva you have no heart. Why did you bring me to birth wretch in this world, exile from the other?

—Basavanna[1]

Among the many hymns recited by Śiva worshippers all over India, the following summarizes best the various motives that make him dear to his devotees:

Praise Viśvanatha, the Lord of the City of Benares,
whose locks are the charming ripples of the Ganges,
adorned on his left by Gaurī, the beloved of Nārāyaṇa,
the destroyer of the god of love.

Praise Viśvanātha, the Lord of the City of Benares,
beyond speech, the repository of different qualities,
whose feet are worshipped by Brahmā, Viṣṇu and the
other *devas*, with his wife to the left.

Praise Viśvanātha, the Lord of the City of Benares,
the wielder of the trident, adorned by a snake, wearing
a tiger skin and matted locks, the Three-eyed one, who
keeps in two of his hands the noose and the goad and
offers blessing and grace with the two others.

Praise Viśvanātha, the Lord of the City of Benares,
Wearing a crown with the moon, who burnt the Five-Arrowed
One to ashes with the fire emerging from his third eye on
the forehead, whose ears are adorned with the shining
rings of *śeṣa*, the king of the snakes.

Praise Viśvanātha, the Lord of the City of Benares,
the Five-faced-one, the lion destroying the mad elephant
of sin, the Garuḍa destroying the vicious demons, the
world fire that burns to ashes the jungle of birth, death
and old age.

Praise Viśvanātha, the Lord of the City of Benares,
who is effulgent, who is with and without qualities, the One
without a second, bliss itself, the unconquerable one,
the unknowable one, who is dark and bright and the form
of the soul.

Praise Viśvanātha, the Lord of the City of Benares,
after you have given up all desires, all reviling of
others and all attachment to sinful conduct, enter into
samādhi and meditate on the Lord, seated in the lotus of
the heart.

Praise Viśvanātha, the Lord of the City of Benares,
who is free from all emotion such as attachment and others,
who is fond of his devotees, the abode of austerities
and bliss, the companion of Girija endowed with his throat
stained with the poison.

The person who recites this hymn to Śiva, the Lord
of the City of Benares, attains in this life learning,
prosperity, immense happiness and eternal fame and
after death liberation.[2]

To *Viśva-nātha*, Śiva, the Lord of the Universe, the most sacred of all the temples of the holy city of Banaras is consecrated; only Hindus are allowed to enter it.

SOURCES OF ŚAIVISM

Śiva worship has been traced back to the Indus civilization in which it appears to have been an established tradition. *Liṅgas* have been found there, the main object of Śiva worship to this day, as well as figures on seals interpreted as Śiva Mahāyogi and Śiva Paśupati.[3]

The historical homeland of Śiva religion in more recent times, however, has been the Tamil country. Both Siva's name and his main mythology seem to come from there; the "Red God" was only later given a Sanskrit name, phonetically close to the Tamil one, which is translated as "the graceful one." Tribal religions of Northwest India have contributed other features. The ambivalence of this Great God (Figure 17.1), however, owes a great deal to the fusion of Śiva with Rudra, the howler—a deity well known from the Vedas. In the Vedas, Rudra is regarded as "an apotropaic god of aversion, to be feared, but not adored."[4]

He may have been one of the tribal gods as well, too powerful to be suppressed by the official Vedic religion, too alien to be accepted among the *devas*. This opinion appears to be supported by the arguably oldest and most popular Śiva myth: Śiva coming uninvited to Dakṣa's sacrifice, who had prepared offerings to all the other *devas*, destroying the sacrifice and, after killing Dakṣa, bringing him back to life, converting him into a Śiva worshipper, and ensuring for himself a permanent portion of the sacrifice.[5] The myth relating to the destruction of Dakṣa's sacrifice by Śiva, according to all sources the first of Siva's exploits, may in fact have a historical core: the conquest of Kanakhala, a *tīrtha* close to modern Hardwār, which was of great importance to Śaivites, Vaiṣṇavas, and Śāktas alike and which was linked to an important Vedic settlement associated with the famous patriarch Dakṣa. As a story of the occupation of a holy place beyond the range of the high Himalayas, the region where Śaivism was at home before it entered the plains of India, it provided legitimacy to the Śaivas, who were originally shunned by the Vedic Āryans.[6]

Śiva *bhagats* are mentioned by Pāṇini, and the Indian worshippers of Dionysos, referred to by Megasthenes, may possibly have been Śiva devotees. The oldest Śaivite sect about which we know anything with certainty is that of the *Pāśu-patas*, whose teachings are largely identical with the even now flourishing *Śaiva Siddhānta*. Their founder was, according to legend, Śiva himself in the form of Lakuliṣa. Modern research is inclined to see in Lakuliṣa a historical person of the second century C.E.[7] The epics are full of references to Śiva; the Rāmāyaṇa usually contains the oldest versions of Śiva myths. In the Mahābhārata we find several hymns to Śiva and the mention, even at this early stage, of four different Śiva sects.

The Śiva Purāṇas and Āgamas, the main sources of "modern" Śaivism, seem to be comparatively late compositions, though they contain much ancient material. A good deal of Śiva mythology and theology seems to be an imitation of earlier Vaiṣṇava material.[8]

Figure 17.1 Śiva *trimūrti* from Elephanta

Several powerful kings in the Indian Middle Ages were Śaivas who sometimes forced Śaivism on their subjects and built magnificent sanctuaries in honor of Śiva.[9] Between 700 and 1000 C.E. Śaivism appears to have been the dominant religion of India, due largely to the influence of the sixty-three Nāyanmārs who flourished during this time and propagated Śaivism among the masses in the form of Śiva *bhakti*. The greatest among India's theological philosophers, Śaṇkarācārya, according to an ancient tradition, was "an incarnation of Śiva, born for the purpose of consolidating Hindu *dharma* in answer to the implorings of Śaivaguru and Āryanda."[10] In the twelfth century a powerful reformist Śaiva movement arose in Kaṇṇaḍa, the Liṅgāyats, who still exercise great influence.

The Ṛgveda contains but a few hymns to Rudra, mainly imploring him to stay away and not to do harm,[11] occasionally beseeching him as "the great physician who possesses a thousand medicines" to give health and remove sorrow. In a significant study[12] Doris N. Srinivasan states that Rudra belongs to the Vedic *asuras*, "a primordial group which includes both gods and demons possessing the potential to create the truly wondrous, including life itself." Rudra is associated with the North, and he is given offerings that are defective. Omniscience is acribed to him, the possessor of a thousand eyes. Rudra has a special relationship to Soma, even forming a dual deity Soma-Rudra. Soma-Rudra is implored in Ṛgveda 6.74 to provide medicines and drive away all sins. Soma-Rudra shows the ambivalence of the later Śiva: on the one hand, he is gracious and helpful; on the other, he is vengeful and possesses deadly weapons. Rudra is called a "promoter of the sacrifice"[13] and "priest of two worlds"[14]. In some predominantly agricultural rituals Rudra is prominent, too.[15]

The *Yajurveda* offers one of the most interesting texts concerning Rudra, the so-called *Śatarudriya*.[16] It displays many features of classical Śaivism: Śiva is described as both terrifying and as gracious. The hymn constantly switches from one Rudra to many Rudras, from praise to earnest prayer not to do any harm. "Innumerable Rudras are on the face of the earth," the text says, but names given to them are quite often identical with titles given in later Śaivism to Śiva, the only Lord. Apart from names like Nīlakaṇṭha, Śārva, Paśupati, Nīlagrīva, Bhava, and so on, Rudra is described as the one who stretched out the earth, who is immanent in places and objects, in stones, plants and animals. There is also the paradoxical ascription of contradictory attributes: after being praised as the Great Lord of all beings he is called *cheat* and *Lord of thieves*, he is fierce and terrible and also the source of happiness and delight. The singer asks Śiva-Rudra to turn away his fearful form and approach the worshipper in his auspicious, friendly form. The *Vrātya* section of the *Atharvaveda*, again perhaps a remnant of pre-Āryan religion,[17] contains hymns that use the well-known Śiva titles *Bhava, Bharva, Paśupati, Rudra, Mahādeva,* and *Iśāna.*[18] In Vedic ritual, as described in the *Śatapatha Brāhmaṇa,* Rudra is treated differently from the other *devas*. At the end of the sacrifice a handful of straw is offered to him for propitiation, at the end of a meal the leftovers are placed to the north for Rudra. The *Aitareya Brāhmaṇa* states that "Rudra is an embodiment of all the dread forms of whom *devas* are afraid."[19] The bull that is to be sacrificed to him must be killed outside the village.

We find a fully developed Śiva-Vedānta system in the *Śvetāśvatara Upaniṣad,* a text that plays a part in Śaivism comparable to that of the Bhagavadgītā in Vaiṣṇavism.[20] It rejects at length a large number of different theological opinions, surely a sign of its rather late date. Śiva is identified with *brahman*. Thus it teaches: "The immortal and imperishable Hara exercises complete control over the perishable *prakṛti* and the powerless *jīva*: the radiant Hara is one alone." Śiva manifests himself in many forms: as *viśva-rūpa* or the universe, as *liṅga-śarīra* in the hearts of all beings, as omnipresent on account of his all-pervasiveness, as *antar-ātman* of the size of a thumb, to be realized by the Yogis. It also says that in reality all beings are Śiva and it is due to an illusion that people perceive a difference. "One attains peace on realizing that self-effulgent, adorable Lord, the bestower of blessings, who, though one, presides over all the various aspects of *prakṛti* and into whom this universe dissolves, and in whom it appears in manifold forms."[21]

Here we already notice the trend in Śaivism to develop a monistic world-view, in contrast to the Vaiṣṇavas, who always maintain an essential difference between Viṣṇu and all other beings.

The Rāmāyaṇa of Vālmīki, though pertaining to the Vaiṣṇava tradition, mentions several Śiva myths: Śiva destroying Dakṣa's sacrifice, Siva's marriage with Umā, Śiva drinking the poison, Śiva killing the demon Andhaka, Śiva destroying Tripura, and Śiva cursing Kaṇḍarpa. All of them have remained vital within Śaivism, and some of them also became the focus of Śaiva theology.

The Mahābhārata tells the strange story that Kṛṣṇa was initiated by Śiva, remaining his whole life a Śiva *bhakta*. It also explains that *Hari* (Viṣṇu) and *Hara* (Śiva) are the same and that among the thousand names of Viṣṇu there also are Śiva, Śārva, Sthānu, Iśāna, and Rudra.[22]

In the Purāṇas, Śiva mythology reaches its fullest development and also its exclusivity: Śiva is the Only Lord, Viṣṇu and Brahmā are inferior to him.[23] Śiva is even described as the killer of Yama, the god of death, and the mantra that celebrates him as the *mṛtyuñjaya,* the victor over death, is used by his devotees to gain [illegible]

[illegible] Śiva Naṭarāja, the lord of dance, is [illegible]lptures and bronzes.[25] The Śiva [illegible]em, the legendary authors of the [illegible]ly conceived after the Vaiṣṇava model [illegible]e.[26]

[illegible] images of Śiva are very numerous [illegible]c quality, the object of veneration in [illegible]*ga,* an image of Siva's formlessness. [illegible]festivity of the Śaivas, commemorat- [illegible] Śiva to a hunter, who inadvertently [illegible]*ṅga.*[27]

[illegible]he mode of worship that has to be fol- [illegible]homes; largely the ritual resembles [illegible], except for the fact that Śaivas still [illegible]ally human) sacrifices.[28] From very [illegible] connected with rigorous asceticism. Yogis are traditionally Śaivas, seeing in Śiva himself the Mahāyogi. Madhava describes a group called the Raseśvaris who had the peculiar habit of consuming mercury to build up an immortal and incorruptible body.

ŚAIVA SECTS AND SYSTEMS

The *Pāśu-pata* sect subdivided into numerous sub-sects, possessing a common philosophy. They consider Lakulin, an *avatāra* of Śiva their founder and have in their *Pāśu-pata-sūtra* a scripture of their own, dealing mainly with ritual. According to this text Śiva taught five subjects, the knowledge of which is essential for the total annihilation of sorrow: *kārya,* the condition of bondage, *kāraṇa,* the lord and liberator; *yoga,* the means to liberation, *vidhi,* the ritual, and *duḥkhānta,* the final liberation. The person in bondage is also called *paśu,* an ox, whose Lord is Śiva, kept in bondage through *pāśa,* a noose, formed through illusion, unrighteousness, attachment and ignorance. To free oneself practices like *japa* and meditation are recommended as well as bathing in ashes, laughing and dancing like a madman, singing, muttering hum, hum, "like the bellowing of a bull,"[29] snoring, trembling, limping, in general behaving not quite normally. This theology insists on the complementarity between one's own efforts and Śiva's gracious help.

The most important of all the Śaiva systems up to the present time is Śaiva Siddhānta, "the final truth of Śiva." It is based upon the recognized twenty-eight Āgamas and the teachings of the sixty-three Nāyanmārs, the most famous among whom are Appar, Jñānasambhandar, Sundaramūrti, and Manikkavācakar. Meykaṇḍa's *Śiva-jñāna-bodha* has acquired high authority and has often been commented upon.[30]

Śaiva Siddhānta acknowledges three principles: *pati, paśu* and *pāśa*, the Lord, the person, and bondage. To gain freedom, four elements are necessary: *vidyā*, knowledge; *kriyā*, ritual actions; *yoga*, austerities; and *cārya*, a virtuous way of life. Śiva is the supreme reality: he is greater than the *tri-mūrti* of Viṣṇu-Brahmā-Rudra and the only eternal being. He has eight qualities, namely independence, purity, self-knowledge, omniscience, freedom from sin, benevolence, omnipotence, and blissfulness. The most comprehensive terms to circumscribe the essence of Śiva are *sat* and *cit*, being and consciousness. Śiva is immanent in the five elements, in the sun, the moon and in sentient beings as *aṣṭa-mūrti*. He is male and female and neuter. According to *Śaiva Siddhānta*, Śiva cannot have any *avatāras*, because this would involve him in both life and death, which contradicts the very nature of Śiva. He appears in a bodily form as the guru out of his great love for humans to save them from *saṁsāra*. "Śiva is Love" is the most precise description, and Śaiva Siddhānta has only one great theme: the grace of Śiva. Śiva exercises his fivefold activities, *anugraha*, attraction; *tirobhava*, concealment; *ādāna*, taking away; *sthiti*, preservation; *sṛṣṭi*, creation; and *udbhava*, appearance, through his form of *Sada-siva*, often represented in art.

Bondage is of three kinds: "*Karma, māyā*, and *aṇava*, like sprout, bran and husk hide the real nature of the soul and delude it. They cause enjoyment, embodiment and the state of being the enjoyer."[31] *Māyā* comprises the whole process of evolution and involution. Karma leads to the fruition of heaven and hell, as ordained by Śiva. "Pleasures and pains are the medicines administered by Śiva, the physician, to cure the diseases and delusions caused by *mālā*."[32] *Aṇava*, beginningless and eternal, is the primary bondage of the souls: if *aṇava* is removed, the souls will be restored to their essential nature as pure spirits. In the *kevala* state the soul's cognitive, conative, and affective functions are entirely thwarted by *aṇava*; in the *sakala* state, humans do exert their powers, but only under the influence of *moha*, delusion, *mada*, intoxication, *rāga*, passion, *viṣāda*, depression, *śoṣa*, dryness, *vaicitriya*, distraction, and *harṣa*, improper merriness.

The process of liberation itself is a chain of interlinking conditions. *Dīkṣa*, initiation, is the direct cause of liberation; but *dīkṣa* is not possible without knowledge. Knowledge presupposes *yoga*; *yoga* requires ritual acts; and ritual acts are not possible without proper life. There are three different kinds of knowledge: *paśu-jñāna* and *pāśa-jñāna* give only the knowledge of the soul, of words and things. Only *pati-jñāna* gives liberation. The way to it leads through the guru's teaching; it is Śiva who appears in the form of a guru, opens the eyes of the devotee, performs the purificatory rites, and removes the obstacles.

Śaiva Siddhāntins emphasize that only in a human birth and only as a Śaiva has one the possibility of putting an end to the cycle of births and deaths. Only a human being can worship Śiva in the five modes essential to liberation: contemplating him with the mind, praising him with the mouth, exerting the body in different ways in his worship. If a human being does not realize liberation in this life, it might be hard to get another chance. The Siddhantins claim that only *their* faith is *siddhānta*, that is, final truth. All other beliefs and philosophies lead their followers to one of the thirty-six *tattvas*, below Śiva. Ignoring the *siddhānta* would be a great sin and foolishness, and those despising it have to suffer in hell.

Liberation is but the appearance of the hidden *sīvatva* in the soul through *jñāna*: in their free state humans realize their true and original Śiva nature that was hidden and curtailed through sin. There can also be *jīvan-mukti*, full Śiva realization, while still in this physical body. *Jīvan-muktas* are one with Śiva in their innermost being while *prārabdha* of different kinds still works itself out in their bodies: "*Śiva-jñānis* may do any good or bad deed—they remain unaffected by the changes and never leave the feet of the Lord. It is difficult to determine the nature of the *jīvan-muktas*: some of them may be short-tempered, some sweet-tempered, some free from desires, some lustful." One of the more famous examples is offered by Saint Sundaramūrti, "who was free from attachment, though outwardly he seemed to live a life of sensual pleasures." Those who have achieved *jñāna niṣṭha*, "knowledge establishment," are beyond good and evil. Engaging in activities, they do not care for the results. They need not practice austerities nor observe any religious duties, nor do they have to engage in meditation or wear external signs of their religion. "Coming to have the qualities of children, of mad people, and people possessed by evil spirits, they may even give themselves up to singing and dancing by reason of their ecstasy."[33]

Śiva resides in the soul always, but only the enlightened will consciously live a Śiva life according to this grace. Whatever the enlightened one does is Śiva's deed, be it good or evil. Śaiva Siddhānta knows of seven different degrees of *jīvan-mukti,* liberation while still in a body, likening them in their bliss to the sweetness of sugar cane, fruit, milk, honey, candy, sugar, and nectar. It also knows of a complementarity between the love of God and love of one's neighbor. A person's love for the devotees of Śiva is a sign of love for Śiva. Because Śiva is in all souls, those who love him truly, will also love all beings. All the activities of God are ordered toward the liberation of humans. God's essence is it to be "full of grace."

Śrīkaṇṭha's *Śaiva-Vedānta,* classified with the Vedānta systems as *bhedābheda,* difference and no difference, may be considered as a special form of Śaiva Siddhānta. Śrīkaṇṭha aims at reconciling the Upaniṣads with the Āgamas, quoting extensively from both sources. For him Śiva Nīlakaṇṭha is the symbol for God showing care. He differs slightly from classical Śaiva Siddhānta in his assertion that the liberated ones are completely free and enjoy the same bliss and freedom which Śiva himself enjoys. Thus he says:

> The place of the husband of Umā is like millions of suns, the first, full of all objects of desires, pure, eternal, indestructible. Having attained that celestial place they become free from all miseries, omniscient, capable of going everywhere, pure, full. Further they come to have pure sense-organs and become endowed with supreme Lordship. Then again they assume bodies or discard these at will. Those engaged in the pursuit of knowledge and *yoga* concentration who attain this supreme place, do not return to the frightful earthly existence. The liberated ones have Śiva as their souls and shine forth with Śiva in all places at all times.[34]

Despite the similarity in conception to the Vaiṣṇava Vedāntists, Śrīkaṇṭha proves to be a staunch sectarian Śaiva: liberation begins only after the souls have crossed the river *virajā,* the boundary between *Viṣṇu-loka* and *Śiva-loka.* Viṣṇu's heaven is still within *saṃsāra.* Beyond *Viṣṇu-loka* is *Śiva-loka,* where the souls find final liberation and fulfillment.

Kāśmīr Śaivism, the most important North-Indian school of Śaivism, also called *Śaiva-Advaita, Trika,* and so forth, is represented today by only a few living masters.[35] The earliest writings belong to the eighth or ninth centuries, but the roots of the system may be several centuries older. Its two main branches, *Spaṇḍa-śāstra* and *Pratyābhijña,* have much in common. Some of the most respected names in Indian philosophy, like Abhinavagupta, are associated with Kāsmīr Śaivism, which must have been quite popular in former centuries, if the extensive treatment accorded to it in the *Śiva Purāṇa* is any indication.[36] Whereas in most other systems *adhikāra,* the fulfillment of certain qualifications, is important, here it is stated explicitly that no prerequisites are asked for from students wanting to enter this school. Because all reality, Śiva and Śakti and their union, is mirrored in one's own *ātman,* liberation is an introspection and a recognition of this mirrored image, an idea that is expressed in the very name of the system. Because one of the qualities of Śiva is *ānanda,* bliss, one also acquires Śiva's blissfulness by recognizing one's own Śiva nature. The follower of this system aims at becoming a slave of Śiva, "one who is being given everything according to the pleasure of the Lord."[37] The reason for human unhappiness lies in the five hindrances through which Śiva nature is restricted: the All becomes an atom; the universal, omniscient, eternal, blissful Śiva becomes a finite, ignorant, limited and unhappy *puruṣa.* One is bound by karma, *māyā,* and *aṇava*—terms that we encountered before. Bondage is a work of *śakti*—*śakti* also helps to liberate a person. In individuals *śakti* is present as *Kuṇḍalinī,* represented as a coiled, dormant snake. The innermost core of human being is *caitanya,* consciousness, identical with Śiva. *Śakti-patā,* descent of *śakti,* is the advent of grace. Though under the influence of bondage, the five essential activities of Śiva are at work, developing a person toward "becoming Śiva." The state of awakening while still in the body is called *samaveśa,* a "contemplative experience of unity consciousness, in which the entire universe is experienced as identical with the self." As Abhinavagupta says: "It is Śiva himself of unimpeded will and pellucid consciousness who is ever sparkling in my heart. It is his highest *Śakti* herself that is ever playing at the edge of my senses. The entire world gleams as the wondrous delight of pure I-consciousness. Indeed I know not what the sound 'world' is supposed to refer to."[38]

The stage of consciousness that the Pratyābhijñā system claims

14 Śiva Taṇḍava, Khajurāho twelfth century

to achieve is beyond the *turīya* of the Upaniṣads and therefore called *turyātīta,* divided into "broken" and "unbroken" consciousness. The means to reach this stage is the specific *yoga* of the school that has much in common with later Kuṇḍalinī yoga.

The youngest among the major Śaiva schools is Vīra-śaivism, "heroic Śiva religion," which is closely connected with the name of Basava.[39] The sect itself seems to go back to a more remote time about which, however, we have no reliable information. Under Basava's inspiration Vīra-śaivism developed into a vigorous missionary movement. Vira-śaivas are recognizable by the *liṅga* around their neck, which they always wear and which for them is the real presence of Śiva. It is worn to make the body a temple of Śiva. As the sources of their religion they recognize the twenty-eight Āgamas and the Tamil Nāyanmārs, as well as later writers. They have a *Vedānta-sūtra* commentary of their own in Śrīpati's *Śrīkara Bhāsya.*[40] The system is also called *Śakti-vīsiṣṭādvaita,* the essence of which is "There is no duality between the soul and the Lord, each qualified by *Śakti.*" The *jīva* is the body of Śiva; *Paraśiva* is both the material and the instrumental cause of the universe. *Śakti* resides eternally in *Parama-śiva:* it is the creative principle, also called *māyā.* At creation all things issue forth from *śakti;* at the time of the destruction of the world all return into it and remain there in a seminal form. *Jīva* is in fact a part of Śiva; on account of his ignorance he imagines himself to be different from him. *Bhakti,* which is a part of Śiva's own *śakti,* is the means of final deliverance, subdivided into many stages and steps. Vīra-śaivas lay great stress on rituals, which are considered indispensable.

Pañcācāra, fivefold worship, comprises daily worship of the *liṅga,* moral and decent life and work, amity toward all Liṅgāyats, humility, and active struggle against those who despise Śiva or ill-treat his devotees.[41]

Aṣṭāvaraṇa, the eightfold armor, comprises obedience toward the guru, wearing a *liṅga,* worship of Śiva ascetics as incarnation of Śiva, sipping water in which the feet of a guru have been bathed, offering food to a guru, smearing ashes on one's body, wearing a string of *rudrākṣa* beads and reciting the mantra: *Śivāya nāmah.*[42] Whereas for the ordinary Vīra-śaiva release is the result of the faithful observance of all these commandments, Śrīpati introduces a Vedāntic element into the faith, teaching that in the end, through worship and meditation, full oneness with Śiva is attained.

Vīra-śaivas are social reformers and constitute a vigorous community today around Mysore. They have abolished caste differences and are generally quite progressive in economic and social matters. Also instead of burning their dead, as do most other Hindus, they bury them.

Almost from the beginning of Indian history severe austerities and self-mortification have been connected with Śiva and Śaivism. Yoga itself, as expounded by Patañjali, is traced back to the teaching of Śiva, the *mahāyogi*.

ŚAIVA SAINTS AND SINGERS

Śaivism has produced a large number of popular saints, of which the historical sixty-three Nāyanmārs of South India are probably the best known.[43] Māṇikkavācakar is the author of the celebrated *Tiru-vācakam*. He suffered persecution for his faith, and Śiva appeared in person to him, an event he celebrates in a song: "O highest Truth, you came to the earth and revealed your feet to me and became the embodiment of grace." His poetry is an ardent appeal for Śiva's grace. Therefore he sings: "Madman clad in elephant's skin, Madman with a hide for his garb. Madman that ate the poison, Madman on the burning-ground fire, Madman that chose even me for his own. Whether I adore you or revile you, I crave your forgiveness for my evil deeds which I rue. Leave me not, O you who took mercy on the gods and drank the poison in order to save them. How much more do I stand in need of your loving mercy!"[44] In a beautiful stanza Mānikkavācakar describes the perfection he is hoping for: "I shall raise my hands in prayer to you; I shall clasp your holy feet and call on your name. I shall melt like wax before the flame, incessantly calling out 'My Beloved Father'. I shall cast off this body and enter the celestial city of Sivapura. I shall behold your effulgent glory. In joyful bliss shall I join the society of the true devotees. Then I shall look up to hear you say with your beauteous lips: 'Fear not!' The assurance of your all-embracing love alone can set my soul at ease and peace."[45]
Appar became a martyr for Śiva's sake. Sambandhar vehemently fought the Jainas and Buddhists as enemies of Śiva. Tirumular wanted to reconcile in his songs the Vedas and the Āgamas.[46]
Sundaramūrti Swami is a favorite with the Tamils even today. The metrical translation of one of his hymns[47] may convey something of the emotional appeal of this Śaiva to us:

> I roamed, a cur, for many days, without a single thought of thee.

Roamed and grew weary, then such grace as none could win,
Thou gavest me Vennai-nallur, in 'Grace's shrine',
Where bamboos fringe the Pennai.
There, my shepherd, I became all thine; how could I now myself foreswear?
Henceforth for me no birth, no death, no creeping age, bull-rider mine.
Sinful and full of lying breath am I, but do Thou mark me Thine.

From relatively early times there had also been certain rather unsavory Śaiva sects with "horrible, almost demoniacal practices, which form a ghastly picture of the wild aberrations of the human intellect and spirit."[48] They took their origin from the worship of the Rudra nature of Śiva; though not completely extinct, they play a minor part in today's Śaivism. The most notorious are the Kapālikas and the Kālamukhas. Kapālikas worship Bhairava, the terrible form of Śiva, and eat disgusting stuff; they drink wine and are known to have performed human sacrifices. Kālamukhas believe that they may attain salvation by eating their food from a human skull, smearing their bodies with the ashes of the dead, and also eating those ashes. But those extremists should not unduly darken the image of Śaivism, which is generally characterized by serious asceticism and genuine devotion, combined with a high degree of sophisticated speculation.

Although the popularity of Śaivism in India was never seriously in doubt since it found acceptance by Vedic orthodoxy and although Śaivism provided the background to much of India's speculative theology—from the *Śvetāśvatara Upaniṣad* to Kāśmīr Śaivism, from Śaṅkara to Śaiva Siddhānta—the intense interest for Śaivism among Western scholars is something new. Śaivism used to be the form of Hinduism upon which most abuse was heaped by early Western observers: imagine the worship of the phallus, the ritual slaughtering of animals, the frenzied dancing! Something must have happened to have made contemporary Western scholars look with so much more sympathy and understanding upon this expression of Hinduism. Stella Kramrisch, whose *The Presence of Śiva*[49] is the undisputed masterwork of its genre, a veritable summa of Śaivite mythology and theology, was reputedly initiated into a Śaiva community.[50]

Also A. Daniélou, whose *Hindu Polytheism*[51] is a monument of insight, became a member of a Śaivite *saṃpradāya* while in

15 Śiva Bhairava, Mahārāṣṭra, Heras Institute Bombay

Banaras. Another one of the most widely known scholars of Hinduism in the United States, Wendy O'Flaherty, has devoted much of her life's work to a study of Śiva.[52] Recently a Śaiva Siddhānta Mission has begun operating in the West; it seems to be quite successful in Australia. Kāśmīr Śaivism has attracted the attention of Western scholars after its more popular teachings were introduced to the West by Gopi Krishna who aroused the interest also of the philosopher-scientist C. F. von Weizsäcker.[53] All this new sympathy for Śiva may have to do with the more liberal attitude toward sexuality that developed in the West in the past thirty years, as well as the experience of terror, and the dark attraction to horror, so evident in contemporary films and TV plays. We can hope only that in addition to Śiva the Terrible also Śiva the Graceful will exert his influence on the present world.

18 Devī: The Divine Mother

> The Mother is the consciousness and force of the Divine, or, it may be said, she is the Divine in its consciousness-force. The *Īśwara* as Lord of the cosmos does come out of the Mother who takes her place beside him as the cosmic *Śakti*—the cosmic *Īśwara* is one aspect of the Divine.
>
> —*Śrī Aurobindo on the Mother* (p. 447)

It is in the very nature of *bhakti* to elevate the deity to whom one renders worship to the highest position in the universe, to identify the object of one's praise with the principle of creation and salvation. Followers of the Goddess, the Śāktas, adore Devī and give to her all the attributes of divinity, as the following hymn shows. This *stotra* is recited every year at the time of *Durgā-pūjā* by millions of Hindus. Brahmā addresses the Goddess in these words:

> By you this universe is borne, by you this world has been created. By you it is protected and you, O Devī, shall consume it at the end. You are the Great Knowledge and the Great Illusion, you are Great Power and Great Memory, Great Delusion, the Great Devī and the Great Asurī. You are Primordial Matter, you are the ground of the three *guṇas*, you are the Great Night of the end of the world and you are the Great Darkness of delusion. You are the goddess of good fortune, the ruler, modesty, intelligence with knowledge, bashfulness, nourishment, contentment, tranquillity and forbearance. Armed with the sword, the spear, the club, the discus, the conch, the bow, with arrows, slings and iron mace you are terrible and also more pleasing than everything else and exceedingly beautiful. You are above all, the supreme Mistress. You are the *śakti*, the power of all things, sentient and others, you are the soul of everything. Who is capable if praising you, who has given form to all of us, to Viṣṇu, Śiva and myself?[1]

We have encountered the Goddess before as the consort of Viṣṇu or Śiva; for the Śāktas she is the real Ultimate Power; the other great gods are merely her instruments and servants. This chapter intends to sketch some of the more important myths concerning Devī and to give some idea of the highly technical literature known as *Tantras,* which are considered by the Śāktas as scriptures in addition to the universally accepted *śruti.*[2]

DEVĪ MYTHS AND FEASTS

Devī mythology appears fully developed in the Purāṇas associated with Śāktism—all of them *Upapurāṇas,* which indicates their comparatively late origin. The most important one is the *Devī Bhāgavata Purāṇa,* a treasury of Devī lore and speculation.[3] Some of the *Mahāpurāṇas* contain important sections concerning Devī that may be later interpolations, as for example the famous *Devīmāhātmya,* which forms part of the Śaivite *Mārkaṇḍeya Purāṇa.* The Devī Purāṇas themselves very often restructure otherwise popular Viṣṇu or Śiva myths in such a way as to show the supremacy of the Goddess.[4]

The most prominent and most popular myth connected with Devī is her killing of the buffalo demon. It is narrated in several Purāṇas, with significant differences, and even in village religion it seems to figure quite prominently.[5] It may in fact constitute an ancient myth connected with an ancient ritual.[6]

The *Mārkaṇḍeya Purāṇa* reports how for a hundred years *devas* and *asuras* fought against each other. The *devas* were defeated and Mahiṣāsura, the buffalo demon, became the Lord of heaven. The defeated *devas* approached Śiva and Viṣṇu for help, who had to concede that they were powerless against the Great Demon.

> On hearing the voices of the *devas* Viṣṇu's anger knew no bounds, nor did Śiva's, and their faces became distorted. A great light sprang from Viṣṇu's countenance, full of anger, and also from the faces of Śiva and Brahmā. This light merged into one, bright as a burning mountain, filling the whole universe with flames. This powerful blast piercing the three worlds took the shape of a woman: Siva's splendor became her face, Yama's her hair, Viṣṇu's her arms, Candra's her breasts, Indra's her body, Varuṇa's her thighs, the Earth's her hips, Brahmā's her feet, Sūrya's her toes, Vasu's her fingers, Kubera's her nose, Prajāpati's her teeth; through Agni's light her three eyes took form.

ॐ जयन्ती मंगला काली भद्रकाली कपालिनी । दुर्गा क्षमा शिवा धात्री स्वाहा स्वधा नमोऽस्तुते ।।
महिषासुरनिर्णाशिनि भक्तानां सुखदे नमः । रूपं देहि जयं देहि यशो देहि द्विषो जहि ।।

Figure 18.1 *Devī Mahiṣāsuramārdiṇī:* The Goddess slaying the buffalo demon

Śiva drew out a trident from his own weapon, Viṣṇu a discus from his, Varuṇa gave her a conch-shell, Agni gave her a spear, Maruta gave her a bow and quivers filled with arrows, Indra gave her a thunderbolt and a bell, Yama gave her the staff of death, Varuṇa gave her a rope, Brahmā gave her a string of beads and a water vessel, Sūrya gave her the rays of the sun, Kāla gave her a sword and a shield. "The heavens were filled and trembled with her incredibly powerful and terrible roar, all the world was in an upheaval, the sea was in turmoil."

Devi's "loud roar with a defying laugh" is the sign for the beginning of the battle between Devī and Mahiṣāsura. With the numerous weapons she carries she kills thousands of demons. Before Mahiṣāsura falls, all the demon generals are killed.

> *Mahiṣāsura* terrified the troops of the Goddess with his own buffalo-form: some he killed by a blow of his muzzle, some by stamping with his hooves, some by the lashes of his tail and others by the thrusts of his horns, some by his speed, some by his bellowing and wheeling movement, some by the blast of his breath. Having laid low her army *Mahiṣāsura* rushed to slay the lion of Mahadevī. This enraged Aṁbikā. *Mahiṣāsura,* great in valour, pounded the surface of the earth with his hooves in rage, tossed up high mountains with his horns and bellowed terribly. Crushed by his wheeling the earth distintegrated, and lashed by his tail, the sea overflowed all around. Pierced by his swaying horns the clouds broke into fragments. Cast up by the blast of his breath, mountains fell down from the sky in hundreds.

This description of the evil embodied in Mahiṣa provides the backdrop for the appreciation of the greatness of Devi's deed who saved the universe from destruction. First the Goddess uses the noose to capture Mahiṣāsura. He sheds his buffalo form. The Devī uses her sword to cut down the lion form he assumes. Then the demon appears as a human being. Devī assails him with bow and arrows. The demon assumes an elephant form which the Goddess attacks with her mace. Finally the demon assumes again his original buffalo form. Now the final battle takes place. "Enraged, Caṇḍika, the Mother of the Universe, quaffed a divine drink again and again and laughed so that her eyes became red." She now kills the buffalo demon, pressing down his neck with her foot and striking him with her spear, finally cutting off his head with her sword. Thus the salvation of *devas* and humans has been accomplished and Devī receives due praise as the resort of all, as Durgā, the boat that carries men across the ocean of worldly existence; as Vidyā, the cause of liberation; as Śrī, who has taken her abode in the heart of Viṣṇu, and as Gaurī, who has established herself with Śiva. The *devas* ask her to grant delivery from all evil whenever necessary. Devī fulfills her promise by appearing again and again to slay demons who are too powerful to be overcome by Viṣṇu or Śiva. The result of Devi's victory is cosmic relief: "When that evil-natured one was slain the universe became happy and regained perfect peace and the sky grew clear. Flaming portent clouds that were in evidence before became tranquil and the rivers kept within courses. Favourable winds began to blow ad the sun became very brilliant." In the final hymn the *devas* praise Devī as the Mother of the Universe, the cause of final emancipation, the bestower of enjoyment and liberation, the one who removes all sufferings, who frees from all fear and from all evils.

Devī then prophesies her repeated incarnations in different ages as Vindhyavāsinī, as Raktadantā, as Śatākṣī, as Śakambharī, Durgādevī, Bhīmadevī, and *Bhramaradevī*. All these names are titles under which the Goddess is still worshipped in India. To those who keep her feasts and praise her, Devī promises protection, riches and victory.

> The chanting and hearing of the story of my manifestations removes sin and grants perfect health and protection from evil spirits. One who is in a lonely spot in a forest or is surrounded by forest fire, or who is encircled by robbers in a desolate spot, or who is captured by enemies, or who under the orders of a wrathful king is sentenced to death, or has been imprisoned, or who is tossed about in a boat by a tempest in the vast sea, or is in the most terrible battle under showers of weapons, or who is amidst all kinds of dreadful troubles, or who is afflicted with pain—such a person, on remembering this story of mine, will be saved from all straits.[7]

This hymn of the greatness of the Goddess is recited every year by countless Hindus at the time of the great *Dūrgā-pūjā*, the major feast of Bengal.[8] It also carries reminiscences of a time in which the structure of society was matriarchal: all the girls who have married away from home, gather at their homes and celebrate *Dūrgā-pūjā* with their parents. Statues of papier-mâché and plaster, representing Devī in the act of killing Mahiṣāsura are placed in public places and in homes; special local committees are formed for the consecration and worship of these images. Processions and a series of individual feasts are celebrated for eight days; on the ninth day *Durgā-pūjā* proper commences. It ends with interminable processions to the sea, the Ganges or another river nearby: the figures of Devī are thrown into the water, after Devī has departed from them.

It is quite impossible to bring all the different names and forms, under which the Goddess appears in the Purāṇas, into one system. By and large the various names are local varieties of Devī. One text in the *Devī Purāṇa* clearly states the Devī is worshipped as Maṅgalā in the region between the Vindhyas and the Mālayās, as Jayantī in the coastal area between Vindhyas and Kurukṣetra, as Nandā between Kurukṣetra and the Himālayas, as Kālikā, Tārā and Umā in the mountains, as Kālaratrī in the Sākya mountains, as Aṁbā in Candhamadanā, as Ujjainī in Ujjain, and as Bhadrakālī in Vaideha.[9] Similar to Viṣṇu and Śiva *avatāras*, Śāktism has also developed the notion of Devī *avatāras* for different ages.[10]

The Mātrikās, the divine Mothers, are usually a class apart, worshipped as a group, especially in the villages, as protectresses against all kinds of ills, and particularly those that befall children. The worship of Manasā, the snake-goddess, and Śītalā, the goddess of smallpox, is very widespread in India. The *Kālikā Purāṇa* has a peculiar system of differentiating the Goddess according to the different parts of her body. It describes how Satī, without having been invited, attends Dakṣa's, (her father's) sacrifice, how she is hurt by Dakṣa's insult of her husband Śiva, and how she voluntarily gives up her life. Śiva then takes Satī's body on his shoulders. Brahmā, Viṣṇu, and Sanaiścara enter into it, cut it into pieces, and let these fall to earth. Wherever one of the fifty-one parts of her body touched the earth a sanctuary of Devī would be founded, called *Śākta-Pītha*, named after the particular limb of her body.[11]

DEVĪ IN THE *TANTRAS*

In the *Tantras* the Goddess comes to occupy the supreme place: according to the *Tantras*, Brahman, being neuter and incapable of creation, produced Śiva and Śakti. Śiva is the cause of bondage, Śakti the cause of liberation. She is the life power of the universe; without her, who is symbolized in the letter *i*, Śiva is *Śava*, a dead body.[12] A large number of texts bear the title *Tantras*; numerous Purāṇas also contain sections (probably added after the eighth century C.E.) that are unmistakably Tāntric. Tāntricism is not restricted to Hinduism. Possibly Hindu *Tantras* owe their development to Buddhist Mahāyāṇa cults connected with the goddess Tārā.

16 Lakṣmī, Khajurāho, twelfth century

Tārā, the "one who saves," is the personification of Buddha's kindness. According to the *Tantras*, people in our Kali age have become too weak to practice any other kind of religion than the worship of the Goddess who offers salvation without demanding austerity.

Tāntrikas distinguish three *mārgas*, subdivided into seven stages altogether. The first three are identical with practices found among all Hindus: common worship, devotion to Viṣṇu, and meditation on Śiva. From the fourth onwards we have the peculiar Śākta-Tantra forms of worship. *Dakṣinācāra*, "right-handed worship," consists of worshipping Devī as the Supreme Goddess with Vedic rites including a *japa* with the name of the Goddess on the *Mahaśaṇkha-mālā*. *Vāmācāra*, "left-handed worship," consists of the "worship with *cakras*" in which the "five *m*'s" play a great role.[13] As one author says, "it requires proper training at the hands of a *guru* and the acquisition of the necessary courage to disregard social conventions about sexual purity, to defy taboos about food and drink and to look upon all women as manifestations of Śakti and all males representatives of Śiva."[14]

The next stage is *Siddhāntācāra*, "perfect worship," in which the aforementioned practices are no longer kept a secret, because for the realized one there is no longer any distinction between pure and impure, good or bad. The highest stage is reached with *Kulācāra*, the "divine way of life," when

> the aspirant transcends the likes and dislikes of earthly life like God himself to whom all things are equal. Pity and cruelty are equally meaningless in an ultimate reference and so too are approved and unapproved conduct. Just as one of the Upaniṣads has said that to one who has attained the knowledge of Brahman no sin attaches for any kind of antinomian act, so also the Tantras place the *Kaula* above every moral judgement and put no prohibitions and restraints in his way as being unnecessary for one who has pierced the veil of space and time, process and differentiation. A *Kaula* roams in all *ācāras* at will—being at heart a Śākta, outwardly a Śaiva and in social gatherings a Vaiṣṇava. He sees himself in all things and all things in himself.[15]

Dīkṣā becomes of utmost importance in Tāntricism: a special initiation is necessary for anyone who wishes to enter the Tāntric way. It is open to all without distinction of caste or sex, but even a Brahmin has to apply for it, otherwise he is not entitled to take part in the Tāntric mysteries. Terrible punishment is in store for those who invite anyone not initiated. The purification of the *pañca mā-*

kāras plays a great role. The Tantrikas are aware that the enjoyment of the five *m*'s involves the violation of all moral laws. They are the great temptations of ordinary men. Tāntricism is designed as a spiritual homoeopathy: by the very poison of the snake the snakebite is cured. But the administering of this antidote must take place in a controlled way under an expert physician. The *pañca mā-kāras* have to be purified and are to be taken only under the guidance of a guru, lest they devour the unthinking.[16] The purification takes place by means of mantras whose meaning is clear only to the initiated. Before partaking of any of the *m*, the *sādhaka* has to recite the mantra; only then is the *mā-kāra* a sacrament and not a sin.

One of the most conspicuous elements of tantricism is the use of the *yantra* (shown in Figure 18.2). The *yantra* is the symbol of the goddess and upon it are inscribed the letters of the alphabet, or short monosyllabic mantras, which constitute the mantra- or *śabda*-body of the Goddess.[17] The design as such is intended to focus on the center point, which is formed by the very essence of the Goddess, usually symbolized with a dot and the sign *śrī*. It is situated in a system of interlocking triangles, forming a polygonal (six to fourteen) pattern. The Δ triangle stands for Śiva, identified with *puruṣa*, the ∇ triangle for Śakti, or *prakṛti*. They are encircled by time. On lotus petals within the rims of concentric wheels are inscribed the letters of the alphabet and *bīja-mantras*, "seed spells," identical with certain aspects of the divinity. The whole system is surrounded by two walls with four gates; one at each cardinal point. Again, the gates are connected with major manifestations of the Goddess, with seed mantras and *mudrās*, that is, gestures accompanying the recitation of mantras. The gates, as well as the corners of the walls, are fortified with the *siddhis*, miraculous yogic powers. The idea behind it all is that the devotee is supposed to choose one aspect of the Goddess as *iṣṭā*: through this "door" one enters the wall that separates the profane world from the realm of worship, using as vehicle the appropriate *mudrā* and mantra and acquiring the supersensory power through the signs on the lotus petals, as an expression of the deity, until one finally realizes the Goddess in her own nature as the inmost core of all beings. There one's attention remains fixed, because one's whole search has found its goal.[18]

The identification of Śakti with *prakṛti*, with "matter" rather than "spirit," has one further implication: the body is the seat of the divinity and that, too, expresses itself in the form of worship and

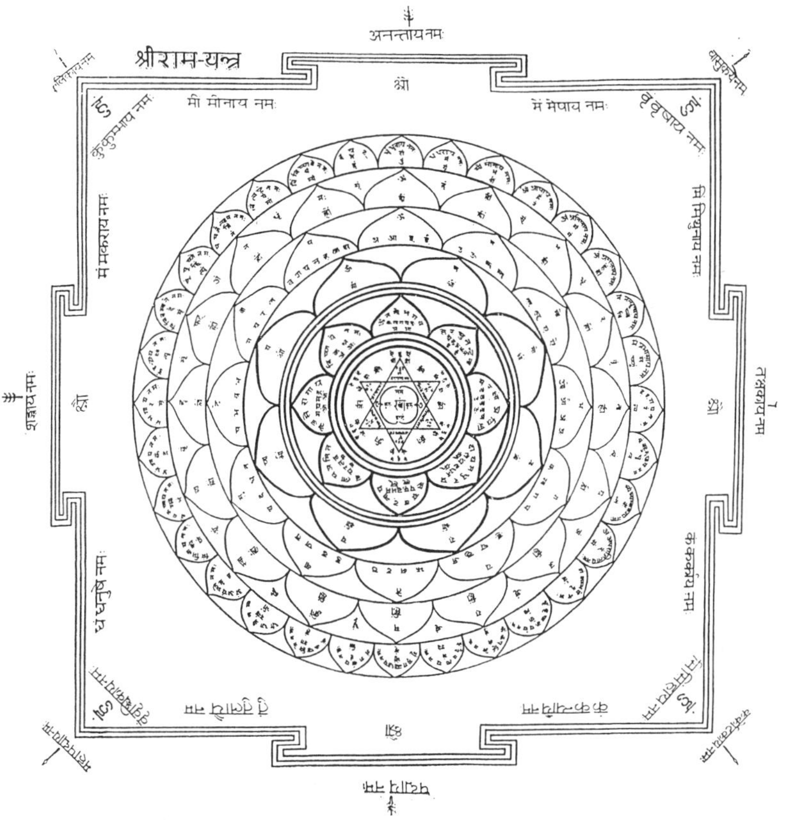

Figure 18.2 Śrī Rāma *yantra*

meditation. The fifty letters of the alphabet constitute the body of the goddess as well as that of the worshipper. Through *nyāsa* the worshipper places the letters upon different parts of the body, transforming it, limb by limb, into a divine one. In most forms of tantric worship the awakening of the *Kuṇḍalinī śakti* plays a great role—again demonstrating the close connection between physiology and metaphysics in Śāktism. Śakti is supposed to lie dormant, coiled up like a snake at the base of the spine: through *yoga* in the Tāntric sense she is awakened and sent through the six *cakras* or nerve centers[19] up through the spinal cord into the thousand-petalled lotus, situated above the base of the nose, where Śakti meets with Śiva. Their blissful union there is at the same time liberation and supreme joy for the devotee.

According to Tāntric physiology the human body contains 35 million *nāḍīs,* conceived as fine tubular canals through which Śakti is moving. Of these, fourteen are of primary importance. Three of these, *Iḍā, Piṅgalā,* and *Suṣumnā* constitute the central complex. *Suṣumnā* runs through the hollow of the spinal cord. Fire, sun, and moon are associated with it as its *guṇas.* On its sides lie *Iḍā* and *Piṅgalā. Iḍā* encircles *Suṣumnā* on the left and ends in the left nostril; *Piṅgalā* forms its right counterpart. *Iḍā* is of a bright hue and contains "the liquid of immortality"; *Piṅgalā* is red and contains "the liquid of death." The three main *nāḍīs* are also identified with the Ganges, the Yamunā, and the Sarasvatī, the three principal holy rivers of India, identified with forms of Devī.

The *cakras* correspond to *yantras* in all their details. Thus *mūladhāra,* the first of the *cakras,* lying at the base of the spine, the root of *suṣumnā* and the resting place of *Kuṇḍalinī,* is depicted as a triangle encircled by an orb with four lotus petals, on which the syllables *vaṃ, śaṃ, ṣaṃ, saṃ* are written. In the center of the lotus lies the *śyaṃbhu liṅga* of a rust-brown color. There is *citra nāḍī,* a tube through which Devī descends and closes the *brahman* door. Inside the fiery red triangle that encloses the *liṅga* is *kandarpa-vāyu,* the "wind of the love-god," and outside a yellow spot, called *pṛthvī maṇḍala,* the place of the *bīja-mantra laṁ.*

The next *cakra* is *svādhiṣṭhāna,* a six-petalled lotus at the base of the sexual organ; above it is *maṇi-pura,* the jewel-city, a ten-petalled golden lotus in the navel. In the region of the heart is *anāhata cakra,* a deep-red lotus with twelve petals; above it, at the base of the throat, is *viśuddha cakra,* the dwelling-place of the goddess of speech, a lotus with sixteen petals. Between the eyebrows we have *ājñā-cakra,* a two-petalled lotus, also called *paramakula* or *mukta-triveni,* because here the three main *nāḍīs* separate. This is the place of the *bīja-mantra* Om and the dwelling place of the three main *guṇas.* Here dwell Para-Śiva in the form of a swan and Kālī-Śakti. Brahmā, Viṣṇu, and Śiva are in the three corners of the triangle within the lotus. Above this is *manas-cakra* and *soma-cakra,* with sixteen petals. These are *kṛpā,* grace; *mṛdutā,* sweetness; *dhairya,* firmness; *vairāgya,* renunciation; *dhṛti,* constancy; *sampat,* wealth; *hasyā,* gaiety; *romāñcā,* enthusiasm; *vinaya,* discipline; *dhyāna,* meditation; *susthiratā,* relaxation; *gambhīrya,* seriousness; *udyamā,* effort; *akṣobhya,* imperturbability; *audārya,* generosity; and *ekāgratā,* onepointedness. Above this *cakra* is the *nirālaṁbanā purī,* the city without support, wherein the yogis behold the radiant Īśvara. Above it is *praṇava,* luminous as a flame; above this is the white crescent of *nāda,* and above this the dot *biṇḍu,* forming the altar for the *parama-haṁsa,* who in turn provides the cushion for the guru's feet. The body of the swan is *jñāna-māyā,* knowledge and illusion, the wings are *āgama* and *nigama,* the scriptures, its feet are Śiva and Śakti, the beak is *praṇava,* the eyes and the throat are *kāma-kāla.* The supreme *cakra* is the thousand-petalled lotus, which is the dwelling place of the First Cause, *Śiva-sthāna* for the Śaivas, *Devī-sthāna* for the Śāktas. Here shine the sun of illumination and the sun of darkness; each petal of the lotus contains all the letters of the alphabet and whatever appears in the world is represented here in its *avyakta bhava* or unmanifested form.

While the *Kuṇḍalinī śakti* moves upward it assumes all the deities and qualities inherent in the different *cakras,* thus becoming "everything." Devī is ultimately identical with *brahman—brahman* not conceived as supreme spirit but as supreme matter or, better, as life force. Most of the Tāntric literature, including the hymns, is written in *saṁdhyā-bhāṣā,* "twilight style," which has a double meaning. Only the initiated are able to grasp the true, spiritual meaning.

DEVĪ WORSHIP AND DEVĪ PHILOSOPHY

Devī worship differs sharply in its two main branches, left-handed and right-handed Śāktism. The latter could be described as *Devībhakti,* differing little from other forms of *bhakti,* except that instead of Viṣṇu or Śiva the name of the Goddess is invoked. Left-hand practices are even today surrounded by secrecy: sexual mysteries and human sacrifices are associated with it, a combination that was not restricted to the barbaric gangs of *thag,* but also found its way into the holy books of Śāktism. The *Kālikā Purāṇa* describes in great detail the ritual of a human sacrifice followed in some temples of Devī as a regular weekly rite.[20] Even now, the Indian dailies report from time to time cases of both human sacrifice and self-immolation in honor of the Goddess.

In former times, the Śāktas did not attribute any importance to pilgrimages, because the union of Śiva and Śakti was found in one's own body. But later, the fifty-one *Śakti-piṭhas* came to be recognized as centers of pilgrimage; each has its own legends and promises of gain and merit in this world and the next.[21] Assam, whose old name is Kāmarūpa, has been the center of Śāktism as far back as our knowledge of it goes. The most famous of the Assamese

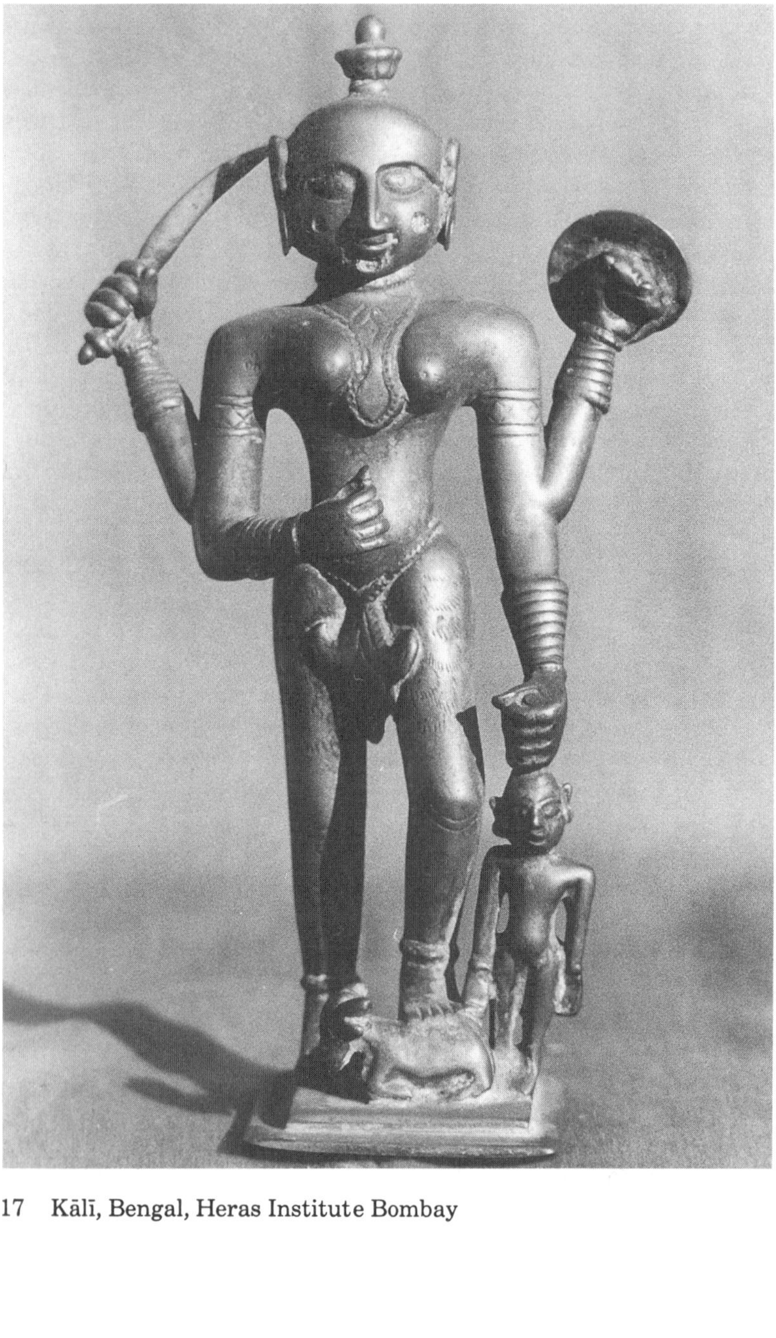

17 Kālī, Bengal, Heras Institute Bombay

temples, Kāmākhyā near Gauhatī, is the most important of the *Śakti-pīṭhas,* being the place where the *yoni* of Devī fell; which is worshipped in the form of a cleft rock under the title Kāmeśvarī. Reportedly, even now, both right-hand and left-hand rituals are performed in this temple, and animals are slaughtered at its altars.

Devī worship intensifies in times of epidemics, which are seen as signs of her wrath for being neglected. She is then appeased by the sacrifice of buffaloes, pigeons and goats. Devī is also invoked if someone has been bitten by a snake or otherwise shows signs of poisoning.[22]

A good deal of the philosophy of Śāktism forms an integral part of certain schools of Śaivism. Śiva and Pārvatī are considered to be "world parents": their mutual dependence is so great that one cannot be without the other. In the figure of *Śiva ardha-nārī,* Śiva and his consort are combined into one being manifesting a dual aspect. It is often only a matter of emphasis whether a certain philosophy is called Śaiva or Śākta. The roots of this thinking may be traced back to the sources of Vedic religion.[23] Fully developed Tāntric philosophy is characterized by its acceptance of the material world as the basic reality and its emphasis on the real existence of *māyā.* Śakti is often called *ādya*—or *mūla-prakṛti,* primaeval matter (associating *matter,* as the Latin word does, with "mother"!) and *mahā-māyā,* the great illusion. An important Tāntric text, the *Tripurā Rahasya,* explicitly says: "Do not conclude that there is no such thing as the world. Such thinking is imperfect and defective. Such a belief is impossible. One who tries to negate the whole world by the mere act of thought brings it into existence by that very act of negation. Just as a city reflected in a mirror is not a reality but exists as a reflection, so also this world is not a reality in itself but is consciousness all the same. This is self-evident. This is perfect knowledge."[24]

At the same time it is not possible to classify Śāktism proper under any of the other Vedāntic systems. The *Mahānirvāṇa Tantra* calls it *dvaitādvaita vivarjita,* freed from both dualism and monism. For Śāktism, the fetters that bind humans are neither illusory, as the Advaitins claim, nor are they pure evil to be removed from the *ātman,* as the Dvaitins attempt to do. The imperfections are the very means to perfect freedom. The oneness of *bhukti* and *mukti,* of the enjoyment that binds to the world and the renunciation that frees, of *māyā* and *vidyā,* of illusion and knowledge, are characteristics of Śākta thought. Thus the *Tripurā Rahasya* declares: "There is no such thing as bondage of liberation. There is no such thing as the seeker and the means for seeking anything. Partless, non-dual conscious energy, *Tripurā* alone pervades everything. She is both knowledge and ignorance, bondage and liberation too. She is also the means for liberation. This is all one has to know."[25]

The metaphysical principle behind this teaching is the realization that the body is not evil, but the incarnation and manifestation of Śiva-Śakti, taking part in this divine play. In poison there are healing qualities, if rightly applied by a wise physician. In the body, seemingly the prison of the spirit, lies the coiled-up energy that enables a person to reach absolute freedom. The awakening of the *Kuṇḍalinī-śakti,* as described before, is only partly understandable through theory: it is primarily a practice, requiring the supervision of those already enlightened in order that no harm should come to the *sādhaka.* Certain stages are critical and more than once novices have developed serious physical and psychic or mental illnesses as a result of practising Kuṇḍalinī Yoga without proper guidance. This is not due to any superstitious belief in a magical intervention of the Goddess, but simply and truly based on experience: the system of Kuṇḍalinī Yoga as a psychophysical realization undoubtedly has repercussions on the nervous system that can also be observed clinically.

NEW DEVELOPMENTS IN ŚĀKTISM

Historically, the development of Śāktism as an organized form of religion with a theology of its own came after the development of Śaivism and Vaiṣṇavism. Today, almost all schools of Hinduism have strong elements of Śāktism blended with their teaching. Rāmakṛṣṇa Paramahaṁsa, the great Bengali saint whose name is connected with one of the most vigorous neo-Hindu movements, was the priest of Kālī at the Dakṣiṇeśvara temple near Calcutta. He had frequent visions of the Divine Mother and spent countless hours in trance before her image. Yet he did not accept the *vāmācāra* as a reputable way. Asked about certain groups of Śāktas he answered: "Why should we hate them? Theirs is also a way to God, though it is unclean. A house may have many entrances—the main entrance, the back door and the gate for the *bhaṅgi* who comes to sweep the unclean places of the house. These cults are like this door. It does not really matter by which door one enters; once inside the house, all reach the same place. Should one imitate these people or mix with them? Certainly not!"[26]

Today among the numerous *śāktas* there are still followers of the left-hand way, who worship the cruel and horrible aspect of the

Goddess. But there are also philosophers like Aurobindo Ghose who find in Śāktism the basis of a religion for our age, in which life and matter are accepted as reality and not shunned as illusion. As V. S. Agrawala writes:

> Mother Earth is the deity of the new age. The *kalpa* of Indra-Agni and Śiva-Viṣṇu are no more. The modern age offers its salutations to Mother Earth whom it adores as the super-goddess. The physical boundaries of the Mother Land stretch before our eyes but her real self is her cultural being which has taken shape in the course of centuries through the efforts of her people. Mother Earth is born of contemplation. Let the people devote themselves truthfully to the Mother Land whose legacy they have received from the ancients. Each one of us has to seek refuge with her. Mother Earth is the presiding deity of the age, let us worship her. Mother Earth lives by the achievements of her distinguished sons.[27]

Lately Western scholars have shown great interest in the various forms of Devī and her worship.[28] This is partly due to the development of feminist perspectives also in religion. It is no longer uncommon for Westerners to speak of God as Mother rather than as Father and address Her in terms not unlike the prayers Hindus have uttered for centuries to Devī. In addition, the importance of Devī in the practical political sphere of India has been highlighted. The universal name *śakti* given to each and every form of the Goddess had not only cosmological and theological overtones but also pragmatic political implications. The king required the sanction of the local temple of the Goddess that embodied power. As Gupta and Gombrich express it: " . . . while (*Śakti*) *has* no authority, she *is* authority, concretised or personified as god's *ajñā* . . . the sign of royal authority is the *mudrā* or seal which the king gives to his officers. *Śakti* is called *mudrā*. To have god's *mudrā* is thus to have his authority, to be empowered to act on his behalf. A person thus empowered is called *ajñadhāra* 'bearer of authority', 'wielder of the mandate'; the term is common to (Tāntric) religion and politics."[29] The relation between Śakti and political power does not belong to the past alone. Several śāktas like Yogi Dhirendra Brahmacari were associated with top-ranking politicians of post-independence India, and at one point a Tantrika priest was hired by members of an opposition party to perform a Tāntric ritual with a view to killing Prime Minister Indira Gandhi.[30]

19 Mudalvan, Murugan, Māl: The Great Gods of the Tamils

A, as its first of letters, every speech maintains; The Primal Deity is First through all the world's domains.

—*Tirukkural* I, 1, 1

The Sanskritization of India that took place gradually with the spread of Vedic religion brought about a certain measure of uniformity and universality of ritual and belief. As the Vedic *catur-varṇa* organization of society took hold of the entire country, so the celebration of Vedic *yajñas* became a status symbol all over India from North to South. The systematic expansion of *Ārya-vārta* through missionaries like Agastya resulted in the all-India acceptance and use of Sanskrit for religious purposes.[1]

Legend associates Ṛṣi Agastya with Śiva. The people from the South, who had gone in great numbers to witness Siva's marriage to Pārvatī, asked for a sage. Śiva chose Agastya. He was very short but immensely powerful: in a fit of rage he once drank the whole ocean. Agastya, keen on familiarizing himself with his mission country asked Śiva to initiate him into Tamil language and literature. He settled in the Podhukai Hills, in today's Tinnelvelly District, with his family and a group of Northern farmers. Agastya is supposed to have written the *Āgastyam*, a large grammatical work on Tamil, which is lost except for a few fragments. Some, if not most, of the greatest works on Hindu philosophy and religion (such as Śaṅkara's, Rāmānuja's and Madhva's numerous treatises on Vedānta, the *Bhāgavata Purāṇa* and many others) originated in the South. Since Śaṅkara established the four strategic *maṭhas* in the four corners of India, South Indian priests serve in several of the temples of the Kedarnāth complex in the Himalayas. As F. W. Clothey observed, "At its apex between the eighth and fifteenth centuries, the Tamil region was the major center of Hindu civilization, and indeed, one of the major centers of civilization in the world."[2]

It was assumed by scholars for long that in the religion of the epics and Purāṇas the indigenous traditions and religions mingled and mixed with the Vedic-Āryan and that, in the major heroes and heroines of these works, non-Āryan deities, often with Sanskritized names, found entry into Hindu orthodoxy.

In the Northern and Central parts of India, where people speak Sanskrit-derived languages, it is difficult to identify pre-Sanskritic traditions and cults, except on a local level. In the South, however, where Dravidian languages prevail, and with the renewed pride especially of Tamils in their distinct cultural heritage, an impressive case can be stated for the non-Āryan and pre-Sanskritic religions of the area.

Some Tamilians have gone so far as to claim for Tamil culture, superiority in age and sophistication over Sanskrit culture. Some of the literary documents connected with the so-called Saṅgam period have been assigned dates that would place them into pre-history.[3] Although much research is still necessary to fix dates and establish a chronology of South Indian literary documents, it does seem certain that there was not only an Āryanization and Sanskritization of South India, but also a penetration of Āryan Vedic religion and culture by Dravidian elements. N. Chaudhuri's claims that "the south Indian languages are Dravidian only in syntax and the workaday part of the vocabulary," that "all the words which embody cultural notions are Sanskritic," and that "there is not a single element in the culture of any civilized group in South India which is not Āryan Brahmanic"[4] has been refuted by the work of a serious scholars like T. Burrow, who points out that the Ṛgveda already contains twenty words of Dravidian origin and that later classical Sanskrit, too, borrowed a great many words from Tamil sources.[5]

Tamiḻnādu, the country of the Tamils, comprised in former times a much larger area than it does today and included roughly the areas where today Dravidian languages are prevalent, that is, as well as the present state of Tamiḻnādu also the states of Andhra Pradeś, Karnāṭaka, and Kerala.[6]

The country was inhabited for at least 300,000 years and possesses some of the earliest remnants of late stone-age flint industries, rock paintings, neolithic sites, and megalithic monuments.[7] It is also dotted with a great number of temples and sanctuaries—some of them of all-India importance, but with roots in the pre-Āryan past of the country. Even the original (and still widely used) names of all-

Indian deities like Śiva and Viṣṇu are different in the South and the legends associated with them are either quite peculiarly Dravidian or have significant variations compared to the North Indian versions. In addition, many local deities and customs have no equivalents in other parts of the country. The feasts, too, which are celebrated there, have their own distinctive trappings and rituals.[8]

Several lessons can be learned from a brief survey of the major deities of South India. First, they represent a local tradition within Hinduism that is largely intact and quite strong and thus exemplifies a situation that in other parts of India is no longer as clearly discernible, suggesting the composition of Hinduism from a mosaic of local cults and traditions. Second, they demonstrate the transformation ("Sanskritization") of a formerly independent tradition, the adaptation of a distinct mythological lore to the wider context of Hinduism. Third, they still exhibit elements of indigenous religious traditions, which have resisted absorption into an all-India Hinduism. Major South Indian temple complexes like the Mīnākṣī temple of Madurai or the Viṣṇu-temple of Śrīraṅgam, the temple complex of Tanjore, or the expansive site of Cidāmbaram, have nothing comparable in North India, or anywhere in the world, for that matter. Some of these magnificent places were developed after the North had come under Muslim rule; when Islam came to South India it had spent most of its iconoclastic fervor and left most of the Hindu tradition untouched. Nothing surpasses or even matches the splendor of the temple feasts of Kerala, Tamiḷnādu, or Andhra, as they are still celebrated today by millions of Hindus.

THE ĀRYANIZATION OF THE TAMIL GODS

Śiva is so powerfully present in Tamiḷnādu's artistic heritage and literature that one thinks of Tamiḷnādu predominantly as Śiva country and Śaivism as a South Indian religion. In fact, the name Śiva occurs rather late in Tamil documents, and by then, as a matter of fact, he is considered to be the same as the indigenous Mudalvan, who had a Tamilian background and a history of his own.[9] A tradition peculiar to the Tamil country, in evidence to this day, is that of ritual dance in connection with the worship of Śiva. The Śiva Naṭarāja image is a creation of the South, admired all over the world especially in the masterful bronzes from the Chola age.[10] While the *liṅga* is associated with Śiva worship throughout India, it seems to have been a tradition in the South long before the emergence of Śaivism as an organized religion. A South Indian representation of a *liṅga* with a bull crouching in front of it has been ascribed to the Neolithic age,[11] and up to the Saṅgam age, stumps of trees known as *kaṇḍu* were worshipped as *liṅgas*.[12] Many of the Śiva myths found for example, in the *Śiva Purāṇa* have been incorporated into Śiva lore also in South India. It is significant, however, that major changes took place in the process of adaptation.[13]

Thus in the Tamil version of the Dakṣa saga, originally a North Indian Śiva myth, dealing with the Śaivite conquest of the famous sub-Himalayan *tīrtha* of Kanakhala, Dakṣa, who in the original myth was a Vedic patriarch with Vaisnavite leanings, is represented as a devotee of Śiva whose mind was temporarily clouded.[14] The association of Śiva with burning *ghaṭs* and death in general seem to represent a "Sivaization" of the pre-Dravidian *Suḍalai māḍan.*

Viṣṇu is known in South India as Māl, meaning great.[15] Kṛṣṇa worship seems also to have been prominent among the shepherds and cowherds of Tamiḷnādu and many references to it are found in ancient Tamil literature. It is highly probable, that the *Bhāgavata Purāṇa*, the major text of the Kṛṣṇa worshippers, received its final form in Tamiḷnādu. Viṣṇu is also known as Māyon, Māyan, or Māyavan[16]—references to the dark complexion of the God: also the Sanskrit form Kṛṣṇa means black. It is hard to say how many of the myths now associated with Viṣṇu in the all-India context of Vaiṣṇavism originated in Tamiḷnādu. There certainly are also peculiar local variants of otherwise commonly known Viṣṇu myths.

Bālarāma or Bāladeva, in North Indian mythology, considered the younger brother of Kṛṣṇa, figures in Tamiḷnādu as the elder brother of Viṣṇu under the name of Valiyon.[17] Tirumāl and Valiyon together are "the two great Gods." Valiyon's features are entirely South Indian (in spite of his later association with Bālarāma). He was described as of white complexion, resembling the combination of the conch and milk. He had one earring and used a ploughshare as a weapon. His emblem was the palmyra tree.[18]

It is interesting to note that, in South India, Indra retained and even gained prominence at a time when he was supplanted in North India by other deities. Lavish Indra festivals were celebrated by the Chola kings, the so-called Indravīḷa lasting a full moon-month with royal participation.[19]

NON-ĀRYANIZED TAMIL GODS

Whereas the amalgamation of Mudalvan with Śiva, and of Tirumāl with Viṣṇu became fairly complete in the course of time, the Tamilians adopting the Sanskrit names also in their own texts, wholly Tamilian deity Murugan largely resisted this process.[20] Attempts were made in later times to associate him with Śiva and his son and equate him with Skanda, the North Indian god of war, but these were neither fully successful nor did they dislocate Murugan from the prominence he always had. K. K. Pillai states that "Murugan has been doubtless the pre-eminent God of the Tamils through the ages."[21] The name Murugan evokes associations with beauty, youth, and divine freedom. According to ancient Tamil texts, Murugan was the lord of all Seven Worlds. He was the war god of the Tamils, the spear was his favorite weapon. Known also as Śey, Vel, and Neduvel (his priests were known as Velān) he is associated with both the blue-feathered peacock and the elephant. A frenzied form of sacred dance is associated with his cult, the so-called Veriyadāl: "It was the dance of the priest in a frenzy, when he was supposed to be under divine inspiration. It took place when the parents of a love-sick girl wanted to know the cause of, and remedy for, her indisposition. After offering prayers and sacrificing a goat, the priest danced, as if possessed. Invariably under the influence of intoxicating liquor and consequently in a state of delirium, he used to proclaim his diagnosis, prescriptions and predictions."[22]

The Tamils of old also knew a variety of war dances, which were performed by men and women at the beginning of an expedition. War, obviously, played a major role in the life and thought of Tamilians.[23]

The common worship of Murugan consists of offering flowers, paddy, millet, and honey and usually ends with the sacrifice of a goat. During the Saṅgam era Murugan became Āryanized into Subrahmania and several North Indian legends became associated with him. Murugan's sanctuaries were primarily on hilltops. In Saṅgam works his name and place of worship is associated with six military camps, which have been largely identified with modern settlements. Two of these sites, now the places of Viṣṇu temples, may have seen transformation from Murugan to Viṣṇu worship.[24] Palani, the second most frequented pilgrimage site in Tamiḷnādu, is associated with Murugan. So are several other popular temples.[25] In addition to Murugan, the god of war, the Tamilians also worshipped Koṭṛavai, the goddess of war.[26] Being of early Dravidian (and possibly pre-Dravidian) origin, she was later associated with the Hindu deity Mahiṣāsura-mārdiṇī. She is also called the younger sister of Māl. The all-Indian Lakṣmī, venerated in Tamiḷnādu under the name of Ilakkumi, is also known as Tiru, the exact equivalent of the Sanskrit *Śrī*, and used today as *Śrī* in the rest of India, as honorific.

Nature worship as a dimension of Hinduism is much more in evidence in Tamiḷnādu than in most other parts of India. Thus sun and moon had—and have—a special place in Tamil worship. Also the worship of trees and of animals, especially the snake, is very prevalent.[27]

The local association of Hindu deities goes beyond the specific Tamilian traditions associated with pan-Indian religions like Vaiṣṇavism, Śaivism, and Śāktism. Within the Tamil country itself separate regions were assigned to the major Tamilian deities; hence Śeyon (or Murugan) was the favorite deity of Kuriñchi, Māyon (or Māl, Viṣṇu) of Mullai, Vendan (or Indra) of Maridan, and Varuṇa of Neydal.[28]

As has happened in other countries and in the context of other religions as well, the Tamilians, after being converted to Vedism, became the staunchest and most conservative defenders of Vedic religion. The Tamil kings of the Saṅgam age performed enormously expensive Vedic sacrifices.[29] One of the Chola monarchs, Rājasuyam Vetta Perunarkilli, obtained his title through the performance of the extensive Vedic *rājasuya* sacrifice.[30] Also, the Chera kings were renowned for their orthodox Vedic performances.[31] Today South Indian Brahmins are renowned for their tenacious traditionalism; and again, not uncharacteristically, Tamiḷnādu has also brought forth the most articulate organised anti-Brahmin movement.

The Madras government's Hindu Religious and Charitable Endowments Administration Department, which goes back to the 1920s, oversees the administration of Tamiḷnādu's ca. 32,000 public temples, which together own about half a million acres of land and have a yearly income of hundreds of millions of rupies. Temples are administered by largely government appointed trustees; in the most important pilgrimage temples, a resident executive officer controls the books and prepares the budget. Several changes enacted recently have met with resistance from the priesthood.[32]

ANTI-BRAHMIN, ANTI-HINDU, ANTI-CASTE

From the beginning of the twentieth century movements arose in South India that attempted to promote, simultaneously, the creation of an independent Dravidian state, the cultivation of a pure, de-Sanskritized Tamil, the abolition of caste and the demotion of

Brahmins from their leading positions. By 1912, the Brahmins, who formed about 3 percent of the population of the then Madras presidency, occupied about 60 percent of the government positions, and they dominated also the politics of the state. That same year a Dravidian association was formed that aimed at forming a separate state under British supremacy with a government for and by non-Brahmins. In 1917 the famous "Non-Brahmin Manifesto" was issued, which called on the non-Brahmins of South India to unite against the Brahmins. In its wake the Justice Party arose which published a paper by the name *Justice*. In 1925 E. V. Ramaswāmī Naickker, later called "Periyar" (great man), founded the Self-Respect movement. He wanted to get rid of caste altogether and thereby break the influence of the Brahmins and the Hindu religion. He denounced the epics and Purāṇas and called for burning the *Manusmṛti*. An early member of the movement was C. N. Annadurai, who was later to found the Draviḍa Munnetra Kazhagam (Dravidian Progress Movement). Several vernacular newspapers were founded to spread the anti-Brahmin and anti-Hindu sentiment. The Justice party started an anti-Hindī agitation in 1938 and pressed for the creation of a federal republic of Draviḍanāḍu, comprising the states of Tamiḷ Nādu, Kerala, Andhra Pradeś, and Karṇāṭaka. Annadurai asked his followers to drop all caste suffixes and proper names, so as to transform Tamiḷnādu into a de facto casteless society. Although the DMK succeeded in taking over the government of Tamiḷnādu it was not able to realize all its declared socio-political aims.

Constant splits in the Tamil movements and shifting alliances with outside parties have considerably toned down the radicalism of the erstwhile Draviḍa Kazhagam. The All India Anna DMK, which formed a government in Madras in 1977, showed little of the former movement's anti-Hindu and anti-Brahmin stance. Its representatives visited temples and Anna himself, widely popular and revered by high and low, was buried in a *samādhi* on the shore of the Arabian Sea, which has become like a place of pilgrimage for thousands of devotees, who lay down flowers and fruit for him.[33]

THE FOLK RELIGION OF TAMIḶNĀDU[34]

The typical religiosity of Tamiḷnādu also manifests itself on the level of folk beliefs and superstitions. As in all such traditions fate, called *Ūḷ* or *Ūḷ Vinai*, plays a major role. The Tamil classic *Tirukkural* devotes an entire chapter to it: "What powers so great as those of Destiny? Man's skill some other thing contrives; but fate's beforehand still."[35] Also in line with other folk traditions, ghosts and demons play a major role in Tamiḻnādu. Ghosts were formerly associated especially with the battlefield—they were supposed to feed on corpses. It is still believed that mustard seed spread around a house and the burning of camphor and incense would keep them away at night from homes.[36] To protect children from the malicious actions of goblins mothers carry a twig of margosa leaves with them when leaving the house.[37] Margosa leaves are also tied to the entrances of houses during epidemics of smallpox. Infectious diseases, especially of children, and in particular smallpox, which ravaged India's countryside in previous times, brought on the cult of specific goddesses: Mariamma, associated with smallpox, received many offerings designed to placate her.[38] Belief in auspicious and inauspicious times and places is prevalent throughout Hindu India. Tamils follow a calender of their own, according to which Rahukālam, inauspicious time, is indicated during which all major new ventures and business transactions are avoided.[39]

At some time, roughly from the second century B.C.E. to the eighth century C.E., Buddhism and Jainism were very strong in South India, dominating the cultural life of the country. Major literary and scientific works were created by Jains and Buddhists and several of the influential rulers are said to have been active in promoting Jainism and Buddhism and persecuting Śaivas and Vaiṣṇavas.[40] The tables were turned during the time of the Āḷvārs and Nāyanmārs, roughly from the sixth century onwards, when some quite sensational conversions of royalty to Śaivism took place and when Vaiṣṇavas gained majority status in some districts. Śaivite kings supposedly persecuted Jains.[41] There is a series of gruesome murals in the temple of Madurai, illustrating the killing of Jains by impaling and boiling in kettles. Śaivites also purportedly persecuted Vaiṣṇavas: Rāmānuja had to flee from his see in Śrīraṅgam because he refused to accept Śiva as his Lord and one of his faithful servants who pretended to be Rāmānuja had his eyes put out. The faithful Viṣṇu devotee got his eyesight miraculously restored through the grace of Viṣṇu when Rāmānuja wept over him.

THE SAINTS OF TAMIḺNĀDU

Tamiḻnādu is the birthplace of a great many saints and religious scholars of all-India repute. In a volume entitled *Ten Saints of*

India, T. M. P. Mahadevan,[42] formerly Professor of Philosophy at the University of Madras, includes nine saints from Tamiḷnādu, the only "foreigner" is the Bengali Ramakrishna. Besides the Vedānta *ācāryas* Śaṅkara and Rāmānuja there are the Śaivite Saints Tirujñāna Sambandhar, Tirunāvukkaraśu, Sundaramūrti, and Māṇikkavācakar, the author of the famous *Tiru-vācakam*, the Vaiṣṇava saints Nammālvār and Āṇṭāl, and the twentieth century saint Ramaṇa Maharṣi, who inspired a great many Western seekers through his presence and his insistent questioning: "Who are you?" Śaṅkara and Rāmānuja wrote in Sanskrit and had already during their lifetime a large following outside Tamiḷnādu. Ramaṇa Maharṣi knew some English and composed his simple didactic verses in both Sanskrit and English (as well as in Tamil) and obtained international stature. The others knew only Tamil and are little known outside Tamiḷnādu (except by interested scholars). Their expressions of Śaivism and Vaiṣṇavism are quite peculiarly Tamilian and are apt, even in translation, to convey something of the specific religiosity of Tamiḷnādu. To underscore their importance within the major Hindu communities in Tamiḷnādu, it must be mentioned that their Tamil devotional hymns did attain canonical status and form part of the officially sanctioned temple worship throughout Tamiḷnādu.

The legend and poetry of Tiru Jñāna Saṁbandamūrti Swāmi, who flourished in the seventh century C.E. is both typical and instructive.[43] It was a time when Buddhism and Jainism had all but eliminated Śaivism from the Tamil country. One of the few Śiva devotees remaining prayed to Śiva in the temple of his hometown, Sīrkāḷi, that a son be born to him who would win his people back to Śiva. The child of such a prayer uttered his first hymn in praise of Śiva at the age of 3, after he was fed milk by Śiva's spouse, from which event his name "the man connected with divine wisdom" derives. When he grew up he went on pilgrimage to all the Śiva sanctuaries of South India. He was deeply worried by the conversion of the king of Madurai to Jainism. The queen-consort and her prime minister, however, had remained Śaivites, and with their help Sambandar not only reconverted the king but had him also impale 8,000 Jains. In another part of Tamiḷnādu he converted a great number of Buddhists to Śaivism. Saṁbandar is an example of the formation of sectarian Hinduism in opposition to non-Hindu religions, a process that made Śaivism much more of a dogmatically defined "religion" than it had been through its earlier history. Still, Saṁbandar does articulate something of the *bhakti* that knows no

18 Sundaramūrti, South India, Heras Institute Bombay

boundaries, the generosity of heart and mind that makes Hinduism overall so attractive a faith. Thus does he sing:

For the Father in Ārur
    Sprinkle ye the blooms of love;
In your heart will dawn true light,
    Every bondage will remove.
Him the holy in Ārur
    Ne'er forget to laud and praise;
Bonds of birth will severed by,
    Left behind all worldly ways.
In Ārur, our loved one's gem,
    Scatter golden blossoms fair.
Sorrow ye shall wipe away
    Yours be bliss without compare.[44]

The Vaiṣṇavas were no less fervent in preaching devotion to Viṣṇu, whose sanctuary at Tirupati draws hundreds of thousands of pilgrims every year. Among the Āḷvārs, the Viṣṇu-intoxicated singers who were responsible for kindling an all-India Viṣṇu *bhakti*, there was a woman, Āṇṭāl, whose fame has spread far and wide. Her birth was preceded and surrounded by a great many miraculous events and prophecies. She was believed by her father to be the incarnation of Bhū Devī, one of the two consorts of Viṣṇu. Āṇṭāl considered herself the bride of Viṣṇu as he is worshipped in Śrīraṅgam. It is interesting that she began to imitate the ways of the *gopīs* of faraway Vrindāvan and desired to marry the Kṛṣṇa of the *Bhāgavata Purāṇa*.[45]

The lyrics of these God-filled souls not only captured the hearts of the simple people in Tamiḻnādu but they also shaped the theology of the major centers of Vaiṣṇavism and Śaivism and became part of the ornate worship that is continued up to this day. Statues of Āḷvārs and Nāyanmārs decorate homes and temples in Tamiḻnādu and receive homage.

Towards the end of the Indian Middle Ages, in the twelfth century, when large parts of India were already under Muslim rule, the goad of another major religion hurting the flank of Hinduism and making it react in a specific way, the Liṅgāyat movement arose in Karṇāṭaka.[46] In a certain sense the Liṅgāyat movement represents a monotheistic radicalization of Śaivism, as a parallel to the radical monotheism of Islam. The Liṅgāyats, after initiation, have to wear a *liṅga* at all times and consider themselves the property of

Śiva. On the other hand the Liṅgāyats are reformist. They abolished caste differences, they engaged in public works for the benefit of the community, they no longer cremated their dead but buried them—again, perhaps under the influence of Islam. Basavanna, the reputed twelfth century reformer of Liṅgāyatism sings

> The rich will make temples for Śiva
> What shall I, a poor man do?
> My legs are pillars, the body the shrine,
> The head a cupola of gold.
> Listen, O lord of the meeting rivers,
> things standing shall fall,
> but the moving shall ever stay.[47]

SCHOLARSHIP AND FOLK-TRADITION

Tamiḻnādu has brought forth its share of philosophers and theologians in the past and in the present; such luminaries of modern India as S. Radhakrishnan, T. R. V. Murti, T. M. P. Mahadevan, and many well-known living representatives of Indian philosophy originated from Tamiḻnādu. On the other hand, the religion of Tamiḻnādu has always had, and still has, a quality of earthiness and joie de vivre. Nothing is better suited to prove this point than the celebration of Pongāl, the great national feast of Tamiḻnādu,[48] a feast in which cattle are honored. Cows and oxen, water buffaloes, and goats are decorated, garlanded, and led in processions. Large amounts of rich and varied food is consumed in day-long celebrations, punctuated with the singing of hymns, the exploding of fireworks, and joyous noises day and night. All the gods receive worship and are invoked for blessings—but the central focus of all is life and that which sustains it: the food grown in the fields and the faithful bovines, without whose help humans could not subsist.

Part III

The Structural Supports of Hinduism

Throughout this book it was emphasized how much Hinduism is a way of life for all Hindus and not only a religious or intellectual concern in the more narrow sense of these words. Hinduism is what it is because of the reality of India: the land and its people.

To an incredible degree Hinduism is identified with the physical landscape of India. It centers around the mountains, the rivers and the oceans of India: holy mountains, sacred rivers, and mysterious oceans. It has brought forth and requires for its functioning images: the Divine is present in India in stone and wood, in metal and on paper. Hinduism has created and was in turn profoundly shaped by its holy cities, and attracts millions each year to the famous temples in North and South, East and West. Hinduism, finally, has an acute awareness of the qualitative differences in time, of holy and profane days, of auspicious and inauspicious occasions. A great many professionals are employed to interpret the signs of time: an essential ingredient of Hinduism because all the necessary rites have to be performed in time and not all times are the same.

Although sacred spaces, places, and times are connected with the physical reality of India and provide a sacred structure in its nature, the age-old *caturvarṇāśramadharma* provides a sacred structure to society and history. By divine fiat society was divided into functional sections, and the life of the individual was structured so as to give room to the realization of all essential values. The caste structure provided Hinduism with a social and political basis strong enough to not only accommodate change and development but also to withstand attacks from outside.

The assignment of a specific function in society provided individuals with a purpose in their lives, ensured on the whole a noncompetitive kind of society, and created a social security net for all its members. Its major failing was not toward those who belonged to it but toward those who did not: the outcastes. Either by expelling from its folds such members who did not conform to the caste regulations or by not accepting outsiders into it, Hindu society created a vast pool of *Untermenschen,* a parallel society of people without social standing and without rights, considered good for doing only the most degrading work and treated worse than cattle. Twenty percent of the total population of India belong to this category—the way they were treated by the majority of caste Hindus is not something Hinduism can take pride in.

Hinduism has always reserved the highest respect for those who made religion their profession. It expected the members of the upper castes toward the end of their lives to cut off all attachment to the world and concentrate all efforts on *mokṣa,* spiritual liberation. Hinduism accepted also the renunciation of desire and the entering into the stage of *samnyāsa* at an early time in life. *Samnyāsis* have been the backbone of Hinduism for many centuries, and they are so today as well. There are millions of them, distributed over hundreds of orders and associations. They include all types of men and women: attractive and repulsive, old and young, learned and illiterate, pious and fanatical, serene and excitable. In more than one way they provide the ultimate support to Hinduism. They are the living example to the rest of the Hindus of a life dedicated to the activities and ideals that they only casually partake in or aspire to. As an ideal *samnyāsa* has enormous attraction also for many a modern educated Hindu, not to mention Westerners, who have joined modern Hindu movements in fair numbers. One can safely predict that Hinduism will flourish as long as *samnyāsa* is followed by a significant number of Hindus. There can be no doubt that this is the case today.

A reviewer of this book's first edition pointed out the absence of a systematic treatment of the position of women in Hinduism. In light of both the timeliness as well as the importance of the issue, an importance that was always seen by Hindus, although from a different perspective, I have added a chapter on *strīdharma,* which will make up for the deficiency.

As important as the physical support and the social structure Hinduism gave itself is the structure of thought that holds the symbolic world of Hinduism together. Philosophical speculation and systematic enquiry were characteristic for Hinduism throughout its long history. The Hindu mind excels in both analytic and systematic thinking and the controversies that periodically erupted, leading to the formation of new schools of thought—the best known and most long lived being Jainism and Buddhism—sharpened concepts and logic to a degree probably not reached anywhere else. The assumption made by some of the greatest exponents of Hinduism, that eternal felicity and release from rebirth depended on a specific kind of knowledge and that wrong notions about the nature of Self and Reality could cause misery and suffering not only in this life but in many lives to come, gave to philosophical debates an urgency that has hardly any parallel in history.

Hindu orthodoxy had repeatedly to define itself over against opponents from within and without. It early on insisted on membership in one of the four *varṇas* and the observation of the rules governing them, it prescribed public and domestic rituals and it drew boundaries between the *ārya* insiders and the *mleccha* outsiders. It evolved a set of beliefs that included karma and rebirth, the existence of gods and demons, the possibility of either going to heaven or to hell after death, and many others. As the Upaniṣads show, the latitude with regard to the interpretation of the Vedic utterances was considerable and so was the freedom to devise ways of liberation from rebirth.

The *ṣaḍdarśanas* are often called the *six orthodox philosophical systems* of Hinduism. To avoid a misunderstanding of the term, a few explanations may be given before dealing with each one in some detail. *Darśana* literally means "seeing" and provides a fairly exact equivalent to the original meaning of the Greek *theoría*. It is a "viewpoint," a seeing together of all that is of importance. Each of the six *darśanas* has sufficiently different interests and methods to distinguish it from the others. Within certain *darśanas*, for example, those of *Mīmāṃsā* and *Vedānta*, further controversies lead to the emergence of more schools of thought that, while sharing many more presuppositions, also entered into sharp exchanges and mutual strife.

20 The Divine Presence in Space and Time: *Mūrti, Tīrtha, Kāla*

> A Hindu is he . . . who above all addresses this land, this Sindhusthan, as his *puṇyabhū*, as his Holyland—the land of his prophets and seers, of his godmen and gurus, the land of piety and pilgrimage. . . .
>
> —Vir Savarkar, *Hindutva*[1]

That space and time are permeated and filled with the presence of the Supreme is not a mere theological idea with the Hindus, it is a tangible reality in India. Countless temples, many of impressive dimensions, many also of very recent origin, manifest the presence and power of Hinduism in all towns and villages. Numberless images, artistic creations in stone, metal, and wood and cheap prints on colored paper, reveal the intensity of devotion of the Hindus. A great many centers of pilgrimage attract a continuous stream of pilgrims, and an unbroken string of festivals impress the foreign visitor as much as the indigenous worshipper with a sense of the sacredness of time.

The Vedic Indians did not know temples and images; the object of worship was the *vedi*, the sacrificial altar, to be built according to certain specifications on a preselected site, which for the time of the sacrifice became the place where *devas* and *pitṛs* shared with humans the gifts offered for sacrifice. The constantly maintained fire in each home, too, was considered to be a divine presence, as were the more striking natural phenomena like thunderstorms and the heavenly bodies. We do not know whether a deeper conviction that the divine could not be captured in finite forms or inability of artistic expression made the Āryans in the early texts pour contempt on the image worshippers and temple builders, who must have been present in India since time immemorial. The Indus civilization may have known both temples and cult images.[2]

In and around Mathurā, an ancient center of trade and religion, as well as in many other places, terracotta figurines of mother goddesses have been found, dated around 500 B.C.E. Figurative representation reached a first peak in the Indo-Greek art of the golden time of Buddhism.[3] Individual specimens of Hindu sculpture can be traced to the second century B.C.[4] The great theoretical development according to which temples and figures had to be fashioned belongs to the fifth century C.E. In all probability there was an early Hindu art and architecture that used wood as the basic material.[5] Even now a number of temples and statues are fashioned of wood and several famous temples give the impression that they are copies in stone of more ancient wooden models.[6] With regard to the size and number of temples and images, Hindu India has no equal in the world; compared with temple cities like Śrīraṅgam, Madurai, Khajurāho, or Bhuvaneśvara, Western religious centers and even cathedrals look modest and poor. And we must not forget that what we admire in India today is largely what the Muslim invaders either did not destroy (an account of the extent of their devastations can be had from Muslim historians themselves) or allowed to be built.[7] A great many temples also of considerable proportions are being constructed in our time, temples associated with modern Hindu movements as well as temples funded by pious individuals and families. Indeed, during the last forty years, since India's independence, more temples have been built than in the previous 500 years!

MŪRTI: THE EMBODIED GOD

For the Hindu, the most important of all the spatio-temporal manifestations of the Divine is the *mūrti* or image.[8] *Mūrti* means literally "embodiment"; technically it designates the images of the divinities, made of metal, stone, or wood but sometimes also of some perishable material for special purposes. Though the first impression is that of an infinite variety of figures and poses, a more thorough acquaintance with the subject reveals that each artist has to follow very definite rules with regard to proportions, positions, gestures[9]. The Purāṇas, the Āgamas, Saṁhitās and Tantras contain many chapters detailing the way in which images to be used in worship have to be made; these rules are supposed to go back to divine revelation and therefore must not be violated if the image is to become an abode of the divine. These works do not constitute the source for the canons they prescribe: we have old Buddhist texts that specify the proportions of the Buddha images and also other Indian texts, not yet sectarian in their character, that provide guidelines for architects and sculptors.[10] One of the most important works is the *Viśvakarma Vāstuśāstra,* ascribed to Viśvakarma, the architect and director of all arts of the *devas,* the patron of all the artists and artisans in India.[11] The various *vāstu-śāstras* in existence manifest the variety of different artistic traditions in India. Though one can say that all images that are to be used as cult objects in temples and homes have to conform to definite rules, one cannot reduce these rules to one single canon. We have, in different centers, different canons of art.[12]

The *mūrti,* produced by the sculptor according to the prescribed canons, is not yet an object of worship: it has to be consecrated in a formal ceremony of *pratiṣṭhāpana,* the solemn installation. Rituals vary according to the religious affiliation and locality, but the consecration of the *mūrti* is an essential requirement and usually marks the formal opening of a new temple. In older temples one finds quite often so-called *svayam-vyaktā mūrtis,* images not fashioned by human hands but miraculously sent by God himself: washed up on the sea shore, carried to a place by a river, or found by someone instructed in a dream. Local tradition often tells that a *ṛṣi* received the image of the temple directly from the deity. Depending on the material used and the rite employed the consecration is limited to a certain time. The clay-and-paper images used, for instance, for *Durgā-pūjā* by the Śāktas at the time of the Dassera festival, are consecrated only for the duration of the festivities; when the celebrations are over, the images, after the Goddess has left them, are thrown into the sea or a river.

A worshipper who has no other image may even use a paper image or an image drawn in sand and invoke the divine presence upon it for the time of his worship. Images made of stone or metal are usually given a *nitya-abhiṣeka,* a consecration forever, which is terminated only when the image suffers a major injury.[13]

The *Bṛhatsaṃhitā* of Viramitrodaya, one of the most important and interesting texts of early Hindu literature, describes this ceremony in the following way:

> To the south or east (of the new temple) a pavillion, furnished with four *toraṇas,* arches, should be erected, decorated with garlands and banners. Inside, an earthen altar should be raised, sprinkled with

sand and covered with *kuśa*-grass upon which the image should be placed. The image should be bathed successively with various kinds of water; first a decoction of *plakṣa, aśvatha, uḍuṃbara, śirīṣa* and *vaṭa* should be used; then the auspicious *sarvauṣadhi* water and next the water from *tīrthas*, in which earth raised by elephants and bulls, earth from mountains, anthills, confluences of rivers, lotus ponds and *pañca-gavya*, the five products of the cow[14] are mixed, should be poured. When the image has received this bath and is sprinkled with scented water in which gold and precious gems are put, it should be placed with its head toward the east; during this ceremony the *turya* trumpet should be blown and Vedic mantras should be uttered. The most respected of the Brahmins should then chant mantras connected with Indra in the eastern and mantras connected with Agni in the south-eastern quarter; these Brahmins should be honored with handsome fees. The Brahmin then should offer *homa* to the fire with the mantra peculiar to the enshrined deity. If during the performance of the *homa* the fire becomes full of smoke, or the flames turn from right to left or the burning faggots emit frequent sparks, then it is not auspicious; it is also inauspicious, if the priest forgets his mantras or the flames turn backward. After having bathed the image and decked it with new cloth and ornaments and worshipped it with flowers and sandal paste, the priest should lay it down on a well-spread bed. When the image has rested for its full time it should be aroused from sleep with songs and dances and should be installed at a time fixed by the astrologers. Then, after worshipping the image with flowers, garments, sandal-paste, and the sounds of the conch shell and trumpet, it should be carefully taken inside the sanctum from the pavilion, keeping the temple to the right. After making profuse offerings, and honoring the Brahmins and the assembly, a piece of gold should be put into the mortise hole of the base and the image fixed on it. The one who installs the image, honoring specifically the astrologer, the Brahmins, the assembly, the image maker, and the architect, enjoys bliss in this world and heaven hereafter. The installation should take place in the bright fortnight in the period of the summer solstice and during certain particular positions of the planets and asterisms, on days other than *maṅgalvāra* (literally, "auspicious day," our Tuesday) and in a time particularly auspicious to the donor of the image.[15]

Later texts have much more elaborate ceremonies; the interested reader must consult special works that provide all the details.[16] Whereas the main image of a Vaiṣṇava and Śākta temple is always a figurative image, the object of worship in the *garbha-gṛha*, the central shrine of a Śaiva temple is the aniconic *liṅga*. The older centers boast of *svayambhu liṅgas, liṅgas* that have been revealed by Śiva himself and not fashioned by human hands;

indeed quite many of them are natural objects and not artifacts. Some of them are oblong stones; the *liṅga* at Amarnāth in the Himalayas is formed by water dropping from the ceiling of the cave and congealing into a cone of ice. The *svayambhu liṅgas* are surrounded by legends, contained in the *sthāla-purāṇas,* the local chronicles of the temples. The legend connected with Kālahasti in Andhra Prades̀ may serve as a typical example: the main *mūrti* of the temple consists of a natural oblong slab of stone, with some imagination one can find that it resembles the head of a two-tusked elephant on one side and the head of a five-hooded cobra on the other side, with a small marking that is reminiscent of a spider. Legend has it that these devout animals offered daily *pūjā* to the *liṅga*: the spider would weave a net to protect it from the sun's rays, the elephant sprayed it with water, and the snake shielded it with its hood. One day the snake, ignorant of the elephant's devotion, noticed that some leaves had fallen on the *liṅga* and this aroused her anger. When the elephant returned, the snake thought him to be the culprit and got hold of his trunk. The elephant, mad with pain, smashed his trunk against the stone, killing both snake and spider and also dying himself. Śiva, pleased with the devotion that those animals had shown, granted *mukti* to all of them. This *liṅga* is also one of the *pañcabhūta liṅga,* connected with *vāyu,* the wind, because an oil lamp kept burning in front of the *liṅga* flickers continuously, although there is no visible opening anywhere.[17]

Though there is no uniformity as regards the theology of images in Hinduism and though one can hear Hindus nowadays, in a liberal way, explain the images as only symbolizing God, the average Hindu still sees in the images a real and physical presence of God and not only a symbolic one. Vaiṣṇavas connect the worship of the *mūrti* with their theories of the five different manifestations of Viṣṇu: the *ārcāvatāra* is the Lord himself present in an image. Thus the *Arthapañcaka* says: "Although omniscient, [Viṣṇu in his image] appears unknowing; although pure spirit, he appears as a body; although himself the Lord he appears to be at the mercy of men; although all-powerful he appears to be without power; though perfectly free from wants, he seems to be in need; although the protector of all he seems helpless; although invisible, he becomes visibly manifest; although unfathomable, he seems tangible."

Other Vaiṣṇava scriptures speak of the suffering that the supreme takes upon himself, making himself present in an image because of his love for men.

Mūrti-pūjā, worship of God who is present in the image, is one of the prominent features of contemporary Hinduism both in temples and homes. The rules for it vary greatly from place to place and from sect to sect; manuals are available that, in thousands of details, set out the form of worship obligatory in a temple or a *saṃpradāya*[18].

The *Bhāgavata Purāṇa* offers the following instructions:

> Having purified oneself and having gathered the materials of worship, the devotee should sit on his seat of *darbha* grass facing east or north and conduct the worship with the image in front of him. He should then utter the mantras with proper *mudrās* which render his different limbs duly charged with spiritual power.[19] He should then invoke with mantras and proper *mudrās* my presence in the image. He should keep in front a vessel of sanctified water and with that water sprinkle thrice the image, the materials of worship, himself and the vessels. When the devotee's whole being has become pervaded by my form, which is the inner soul of all beings, the devotee shall, having become completely immersed in myself, make my presence overflow into the image established in front of him and then, with all the paraphernalia, conduct my worship. He must first offer me a seat; my seat is made of nine elements: virtue, knowledge, dispassion and mastery as the four feet, and the opposite of these as the enclosed plank upon which I sit, the other parts of my seat are the three sheets spread over it representing the three *guṇas* of which my *māyā* is composed; there are also to be established on the seat my nine *śaktis*. With clothes, sacred thread, jewels, garlands and fragrant paste my devotee should decorate my form suitably and with love. With faith my worshipper should then offer me water to wash, sandal, flower, unbroken rice, incense, light and food of different kinds; also attentions like anointing, massage, showing of mirror etc. and entertainments like song and dance; these special entertainments may be done on festive days and even daily. One should engage in singing of me, praising me, dancing with my themes, imitating my exploits and acts, narrating my stories or listening to them. With manifold hymns of praise of me, taken from the *Purāṇas*, or from vernacular collections, the devotee should praise me and pray to me that I bless him and he should prostrate before me. With his hands and head at my feet, he should say: "My Lord, from the clutches of death save me who have taken refuge under you!" Having consecrated an image of me one should build a firm temple for me and have beautiful flower gardens around for conducting daily worship and festivals. For the maintenance of my worship in special seasons as well as every day, one should bestow fields, bazaars, townships and villages.[20]

THE HINDU TEMPLE

True to the suggestion given in the text just quoted, Hindus have over the centuries built "firm temples" for the God, embodied in the *mūrti*. The Hindu temple is not primarily the assembly room of the congregation, like the synagogues and churches of the biblical religions, but the palace of the *mūrta bhagavān*, the embodied Lord. The more powerful is the *mūrti* of a temple, the larger are the crowds that come for *darśana*, and the richer and bigger, usually, also the temple. Most temples are the hereditary property of individual families; quite a number of the larger temples are nowadays administered by temple trusts under the control of a government department.[21]

Indian temple architecture has lately attracted the interest of many Western scholars who have studied the ancient *vāstu-śāstra* texts and gained an understanding of the symbolism expressed in it.[22] "[The] structure [of the Hindu Temple] is rooted in Vedic tradition, and primeval modes of building have contributed their shapes. The principles are given in the sacred books of India and the structural rules in the treatises an architecture. They are carried out in the shrines which still stand throughout the country and which were built in many varieties and styles over 1500 years from the fifth century."[23] The Indian architect worked under the supposition that his creation had to conform to, and be expressive of, the cosmic laws. The cosmos, as he saw it, was the combination of the perfect and the imperfect, the absolute *brahman* and the contingent *jīva*, of the eternal and of time. The eternal is symbolized in the square, the circle is the symbol of time. As the symbol model of the *vāstu-puruṣa* (Figure 20.1) reveals,[24] also in India "the person is the measure of all things": the figure of a person enclosed by a square is the basic pattern from which all temple architecture develops. "The gods are settled on the *vāstu-puruṣa*. The fight between the demons and the gods is over, for it is won conjointly. Every building activity means a renewed conquest of disintegration and at the same time a restitution of integrity so that the gods once more are the limbs of a single 'being', of Existence, at peace with itself."[25]

The center square (equal to 3 x 3 small squares) is occupied by Brahmā who gave shape to the world (see Figure 20.2). The inner ring is occupied by the main gods, the outer ring by the thirty-two minor gods, representing at the same time the lunar mansions so that the *vāstu-puruṣa maṇḍala* becomes the instrument to determine both the spatial and temporal components of temple construc-

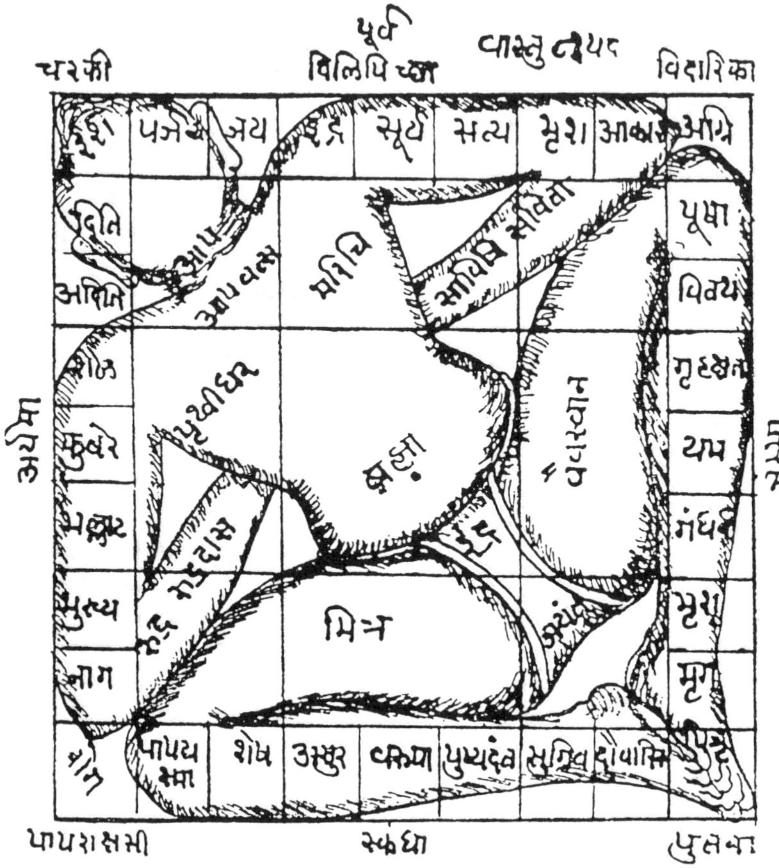

Figure 20.1 *Vāstu-puruṣa maṇḍala*

tion. The gods in the corners and in the middle of each side of the square are the *dig-pāla,* the guardians of the cardinal points, determining the spatial orientation of the *maṇḍala.*[26]

The *vāstu-puruṣa maṇḍala* serves the town planner as well as the temple builder: the whole town is ideally structured according to this cosmic model; within the town a certain area is reserved for the temple, which again is patterned according to the laws of the cosmos.[27] The dimensions and proportions of the temple to be built depend on an intricate system of calculations designed to bring the edifice within the framework determined by six prerequisites. Apart from achieving an aesthetically pleasing harmony of propor-

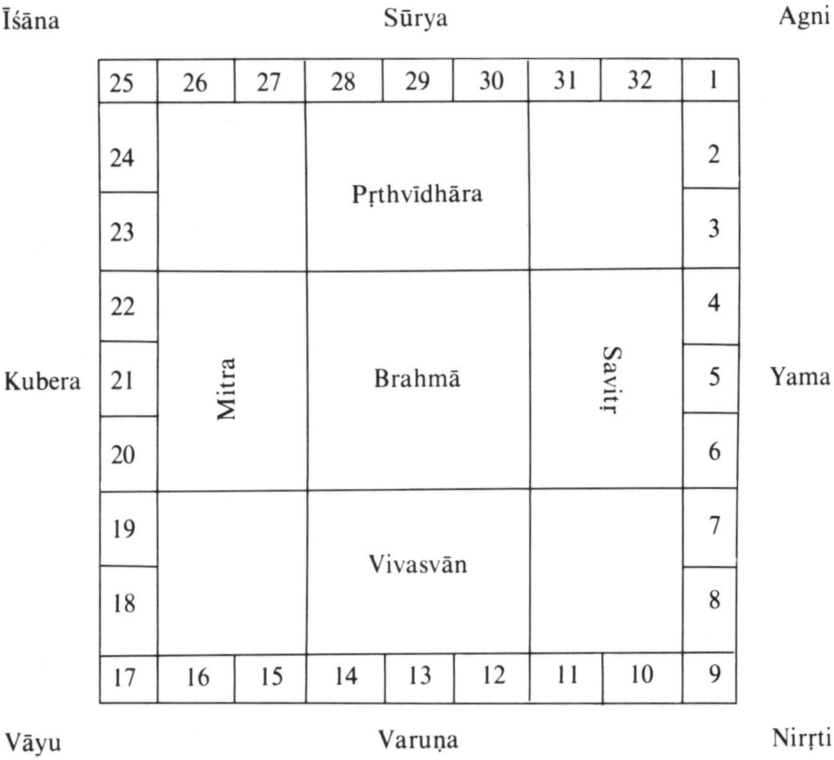

Figure 20.2 The pattern of a *Vāstu-puruṣa maṇḍala*

tions between height, length, and width of the building, the actual dimensions must also express the caste of the builder and the calculations must also determine the spatio-temporal position of the temple.[28] A good example of the application of this scheme is offered by the *Brahmeśvara* temple in Bhuvaneśvara.[29]

In South India a slightly different ground plan is followed. The *padmagarbha maṇḍala* of the *Bṛhadeśvara* temple at Tanjore (Figure 20.3) will illustrate these differences. Note the following in the figure:

1. Brahmā — Sanctuary (*garbha-gṛha*) with interior *pradakṣina-patha*
2. Spheres of the gods — Circumambulatory path (exterior *pradakṣiṇā-patha*)

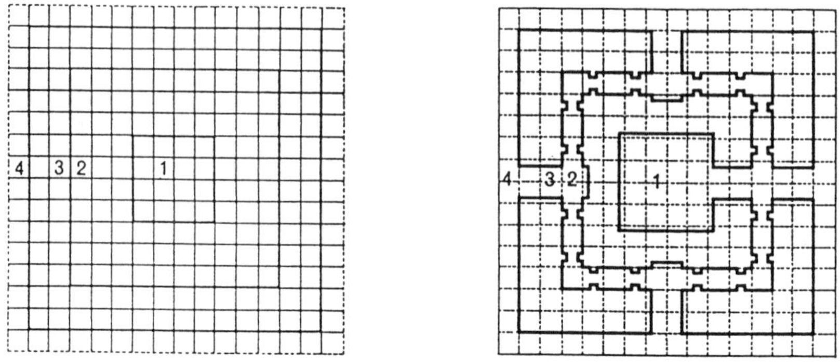

Figure 20.3 Diagram of *Padmagarbha* maṇḍala of the Bṛhadeśvara Temple

3. Sphere of humans Circuit wall
4. Sphere of demons Terrace

The center and essence of the cosmos is Brahmā: it is surrounded by an inner ring, the world of the *devas*. Around these, another ring is formed by the world of humans. Still further removed, but within the realm of *jīvas*, and therefore of importance for all the other living beings, are the *asuras*. The *sthaṇḍila maṇḍala* that forms the model for the temple at Tanjore consists of 16 x 16 fields: 16 are occupied by the *Brahmā-sthāna*, identical with the *garbha-gṛha*; 84 by the world of the *devas*, identical with the *pradakṣiṇā patha*; 96 for the world of the humans, identical with the *prakāra*, the outer wall of the sanctuary. The ring of the *asuras*, occupying sixty fields, is situated outside the wall on the terrace that surround the temple. Later the *maṇḍapas* and other shrines within the temple compound have been added.

In a grandiose way the original South Indian *sthaṇḍila maṇḍala* has been realized in the temple city of Śrīraṅgam.[30] The central sanctuary of Viṣṇu is surrounded by seven concentric walls, representing the outer spheres. Each wall is broken through at the four quarters: the pilgrims on their way to seeing the Supreme have to pass through seven gates, topped by mighty *gopuras*, before reaching the goal of their endeavors. Within the outer enclosures normal city life goes on: shops and coffee bars run along the huge walls. In the inner enclosures are *maṇḍapas*, places where the pilgrims can rest without being disturbed by worldly traffic. When passing through the last gate they first encounter the *garuḍa-stambha*, the roosting place of Viṣṇu's *vahana*. Then only do they enter the sanctuary where Viṣṇu's image, representing the Lord of the World resting on Śeṣa, is offering itself for worship.

Students of Indian temple architecture have developed a number of classifications for describing the various styles that have developed over the centuries in various parts of India. For details the reader is referred to specialized works mentioned in the notes and bibliography.

Whereas the oldest extant temples show a basic pattern that is taken from profane or Buddhist models, from the seventh century onward the development of two definite Hindu styles set in (modified later in various regions), the so-called *nāgara* or North Indian style and the so-called *drāviḍa* or South Indian style.

One of the most interesting sights in India are the five *rathas* or monolithic temples at Māhabalipuram, not far from Madras on the sea coast. King Narasimhavarman apparently founded a school for the architects and sculptors of his kingdom to develop models for temples that would then be built in full size in different parts of the kingdom.[31] As well as imitations of Buddhist Caitya halls and existing wooden structures, the spatial realization of the *yantra*, as shown in the Dharmarāja *ratha* became the most successful model for the further development of the *drāviḍa* style.[32] It can be seen in the famous *Virūpākṣa* temple at Paṭṭadakal, which in turn served as the model of the *Kailāsa* temple at Ellora, carved out from the mountain on a previously unheard of scale. The most magnificent specimen of the *drāviḍa* model is, however, the aforementioned *Bṛhadeśvara* temple at Tanjore: its tower is more than 200 feet tall, topped by a block of granite weighing 80 tons.[33] Situated in flat country, it can be seen from miles away. The *garbhagṛha* houses the largest *liṅgam* in any Indian temple.

The *nāgara* style seems to have developed from bamboo buildings, which gave way to the towerlike *śikhara*, the most typical element of this style, its characteristic form. Originally the *garbha gṛha*, in the base of the *śikhara*, was the only structure of the North Indian temple; later a place was added for the worshippers to assemble, the so-called *jaga-mohan* or *mukha-śāla*, also topped by a towerlike structure. In several instances also a *naṭa-maṇḍira*, a dancing hall, and an *artha-maṇḍapa*, a place for the sacrificial offerings, were added.[34] Some of the best known examples of this style are the Brahmeśvara temple at Bhuvaneśvar,[35] the Khandārīya Mahādeva temple at Khajurāho,[36] and the Sun temple

19 Outer hall in a South Indian temple

at Konārka,[37] all built between the ninth and the twelfth centuries C.E. An interesting fusion of the *nāgara* and the *drāviḍa* styles, called *vesara*-style, can be seen in the temples built in the thirteenth century by the later Cālukya rulers of Hoysala in Belur, Halebid, and Somnāthpur.[38] Under Tāntric influences circular temples, imitating the *cakra*, were constructed in several parts of India.[38]

It goes without saying that these models neither exhaust the basic types of temples found in Hindu India nor do they reflect, even in a minor way, the extraordinary richness of Indian temple architecture in every detail of the temple structure.[40]

Although Hindus are quite often also truly appreciative of the beauty of the temple, the most important reason for going to the temple is the *darśana* of the *mūrti*: an audience with God.[41]

In addition to the chief image, installed in the *garbha gṛha* of the main temple, the temples usually have a large number of minor images. The second most important is the processional image, the *utsava bera*, often a replica of the *mūla bera* or fixed image. Though the ritual books prescribe the details of *mūrti pūjā* very strictly, the impression an observer of Hindus worshipping the image gets is that of a rather informal and very personal style of cult: some people throw money into the small enclosure where the image is kept, hoping to get a wish fulfilled, others prostrate before it, uttering prayers in a murmur or quite audibly, still others practice meditation with *yoga-āsanas*, people ring the bell before the image to rouse its attention, they get *tilakas* painted on their forehead by the *pūjāris*, receive small morsels of sweets or fruit as *prasāda*, sip holy water; children play hide and seek, women chatter and giggle, letting their children touch the image; sick people lie around waiting for a cure, others again sit in a corner and read holy books. At least three times a day the priests offer worship according to the prescribed ritual, usually with a large crowd participating. Waving lights, ringing bells, and reciting hymns and mantras are common ingredients of this worship. There is no formal obligation for Hindus to visit the temple, but there will hardly be any Hindu who would not go to the temple once in a while, and many make it a point to honor the Lord through a daily visit and receive *prasāda* as a kind of communion and a talisman against misfortune. Many of the larger temples have a fixed order of services, the timing of which can be learned from their notice boards. Temples built in our own time often resemble Christian churches in their attempts to create a large hall where people congregate for common worship and regular religious instruction. In large cities, where the Sunday is kept as public holiday, those temples have begun to conduct regular Sunday services with sermons. The Birla temples, built by one of the members of perhaps the richest Hindu industrial family, possess besides the *maṇḍira* and also *dharmaśālas* or hostels for pilgrims, parks for recreation, and many other facilities. The number and size of temples recently built or under construction is very considerable—another sign of the vitality of Hinduism.

HINDU FESTIVALS

All temples have feasts that attract huge crowds. It may be as impossible to describe a Hindu temple festival to someone who has not seen it as it is to describe a surrealist painting to a blind person. The basic structure of the festival is quite simple. Usually it is a procession in which the *mūrti* is taken through town. But what makes it such an interesting experience is *how* this is done. When the feast of a famous *mūrti* is coming near, many thousands of people gather days ahead; they camp on the roadside, squat together in picturesque groups, cook their curries and bake their *capāttīs* on cow-dung fires, roam the streets loudly singing their religious songs—and wait for the great occasion. Usually, too, *sādhus* in their thousands and of all denominations flock together. Yogis demonstrate their tricks; all sorts of crippled and deformed human beings and animals are exhibited; lepers come from far away, sitting in a row on the roads leading to the temple. The streets are lines with hawkers of devotional articles and with kitchen carts. Finally the great day has come. If the temple is large and the festival a big one, the procession will be repeated several times to allow participation by all who want to do so. Often a *ratha*, a processional chariot, is used, several stories high. It is a temple on wheels with the *mūrti* as its center. Pulled with thick ropes, often by hundreds of men, it moves along, swaying and creaking, quite often stopped by means of wooden blocks, thrown under its wheels, by those whose task it is to keep it on its track. Richly caparisoned elephants, horses, and groups of *sādhus* in festive robes walk in front. Huge crowds move with the procession, throwing flowers, coins, and fruits into the chariot. A silver trumpet gives the sign to stop and to move on again. The *mūrti* is taken to a cooler place at the beginning of summer or returned to its temple until the heat abates, or it is simply shown its realms: even legally, the *mūrtis* of the big temples are the owners of the temple land, amounting very often to thousands of acres, as well as possessing jewels and other valuables. It is difficult to tell someone following the Western Gregorian calendar the dates of the great Hindu feasts. Apart from the various eras in which Hindus count their years—Vikram, Śaka, Gupta, Harsa, etc.[42]—their year is slightly longer than the true solar year and the months are moon-months, not coinciding with the Western divisions. Each lunar month is divided into a *kṛṣṇa-pakṣa* and a *śukla-pakṣa,* a dark and a bright half of fifteen *tithis* each; on these are based the dates of the feasts, which always coincide with certain phases of the moon. Usually new moon and full moon are holidays and several days in between as well. Even a hired worker will not work on a holiday because that would bring ill luck. The seven days of the week are connected with the planets and special *devatās: Ravi-vāra* is the day of the sun, an auspicious day for beginning Vedic studies and journeys. *Soma-vāra,* the moon day, is consecrated to Śiva. It is auspicious for weddings and births, inauspicious for the purchase of clothing, and for a journey eastward. *Maṅgala-vāra,* the day of Mars, is not auspicious for sowing, shaving, entering a new house, or for journeys northwards. Whatever is done on *Budha-vāra,* Mercury day, brings double fruit; it is a good day for purchases and court cases. *Bṛhaspati-vāra* is named after the teacher of the *devas,* auspicious for the opening of schools, inauspicious for a journey southward. *Śukra-vāra* is sacred to Venus and a good day for buying land; inauspicious, however, for journeys westward. *Śani-vāra,* the day of Saturn, is inauspicious for practically everything.

The right time is important for every undertaking; its determination is in the hands of the *jyotiṣi,* the astrologer. In India astrology is closely linked with scientific mathematics and calendarmaking. *Jyotiṣa* was cultivated as one of the *Vedāṅgas* from earliest times to determine the right time for sacrifices; time, *kāla,* also formed one of the most important topics of speculation in the Upaniṣads. As the *Maitrī Upaniṣad* says:

> From time are all creatures produced. Through time they grow, through time they fade. There are indeed two kinds of *brahman:* time and timelessness. That which is prior to the sun is timeless, that which begins with the sun is time having parts; the year is the form of time with parts. All beings are produced by the year, they grow by the year and fade by the year. Therefore the year is *Prajāpati,* time, nourishment, *brahmā's* dwelling and *ātman.* It is said: "Time cooks all things in *paramātman.* He who knows in what time is cooked, he is the knower of the *Veda.*"[43]

The need to find the right *kairós* is theologically supported by the Vaiṣṇava theory that Viṣṇu's grace waxes and wanes like the moon: he has times of *anugraha* or attraction and of *nigraha* or rejection. One must seek him when he is "full of grace."[44]

As the divine becomes spatially available in the *mūrti*, according to its own will and decision, so it determines its temporal availability in the *utsava*, the feast celebrated at the auspicious and revealed time. Because Hinduism is still very much a cosmic religion, despite its superstructure of mytho-history, the essence of time must be found in the interaction of all the cosmic bodies. The fixing of the right time for a religious action depends as little on human will as does the time for the ripening of a fruit or the course of the year. Grace and merit are insolubly and divinely linked with time. Therefore, it is essential to know about the auspicious time; the astrologer, conversant with the movement of the celestial bodies and their various influences, is indispensable for the average Hindu in all important situations. In many families the competent paṇḍit will draw a child's horoscope immediately after birth; and all the important occasions in the child's life will be determined according to it. There will be very few Hindu weddings for which the astrologer has not selected the *muhūrta*, the auspicious hour, when the marriage is being solemnized.

The public festivals are also determined by the "right time," celebrated at such junctures as to ensure the full benefit of grace to those who participate in it. It is meaningless to try to enumerate all the Hindu festivals.[45] Apart from the more or less universal ones there are countless local feasts; catalogues count more than a thousand, enough to demonstrate that no Hindu can practice all of Hinduism.

Kṛṣṇa-jayānti, celebrated all over India, falls on the eighth *kṛṣṇa-pakṣa* of *Śrāvaṇa*: Kṛṣṇa's birth is celebrated at midnight, after a day of fasting, midnight being the exact hour in which he was born in the *bandha-gṛha*, the prison house, at Mathurā. Through his birth he manifested this hour to be the most auspicious—and so it is.[46]

Rakhi bandhan, on the full-moon day of the same month, has a more social character: girls tie colored threads round their brothers' wrists and make them their protectors, receiving a small gift in return. According to a legend Indra was saved from the demon Bali through the magical armlet that his wife had tied for him. On this day Brahmins also usually renew their *janëus*.

Gaṇeśa catūrthi is celebrated on the fourth *śukla-pakṣa* of

Bhadra; business people and students place their books before the image, artisans implore Ganeśa's blessing upon their tools.

Dassera, in the first half of *Aśvina* is celebrated all over India as a holiday season. It is a string of festivals during the most beautiful time of the year after the monsoon. The great heat of summer is broken by then, and the sun sparkles in a radiantly blue sky. The first nine days, *nava-rātri* are also the time for *Durgā-pūjā*, the greatest festival of Bengal. The *pūjā* is not only limited to the Great Mother: taxi drivers decorate their cars, farmers their cows, and factory workers their machines and perform *pūjā* before them; all worship that by which they live. On the tenth day the victory of Rāma and his monkey allies over Rāvaṇa is celebrated.

Another series of festivals is connected with *Divālī*, also called *Dipāvalī*, the feast of the lamps, in the second half of *Aśvina*. Countless little oil lamps on houses and temples and along the rivers and roads softly illuminate the darkness of the star-studded tropical sky—a sight no one who has seen it could ever forget and every Hindu living abroad remembers nostalgically every year.

Feasts like the commemoration of Prahlāda's rescue by Nṛsinha or *Vāmana Dvādāśī* are celebrated by small groups only.

Nāga-pañcamī is still quite popular especially in the South, where many people regularly feed the cobras in the house with milk, worshipping them as guardians.

At the time of the winter solstice, a kind of harvest festival is celebrated in the North Indian countryside. In February *vasant*, spring, is greeted by women and children wearing bright yellow dresses, the color of the *dāl* that flowers at this time.

Śiva-rātri, on the thirteenth *kṛṣṇa-pakṣa* in *Magha*, is about as widespread as Kṛṣṇa's birthday. It is the principal feast of the Śaivas and also celebrated by Vaiṣṇavas for whom Śiva is Viṣṇu's first devotee and servant. The *liṅga* is decorated and painted for the occasion, bathed in honey and milk.[47]

Holi, in *śukla-pakṣa* of *Phālguṇa*, has much in common with the Western carnival. It is New Year's day for many Hindus, celebrated with gaiety and abandon. According to temperament and upbringing the festivities are funny to rough. In better circles people are content to sprinkle each other with colored water and red powder; less civil big and small boys shout indecent words after people and throw dirt from the gutters on everyone. One legend explains the feast thus: Once upon a time there lived a demoness named Holikā who ate a child every day; the place where she had her dwelling had developed a system so that the burden was distributed evenly. One day the lot fell on a poor widow's only son. A good *sādhu*, seeing the woman's sorrow and despair gave her the advice to gather all the children of the place and receive Holikā with a cannonnade of filthy abuse. The advice was followed and Holikā was sensitive enough to die of shame and anger.

These are just a few examples of Hindu festivals that occupy a prominent place in the life of the ordinary Hindu even today.

THE IMPORTANCE OF PILGRIMAGE: *TĪRTHA*

As the Supreme becomes concretized in space and time through images and festivals, so his grace becomes localized at the *tīrthas* forever, intensified at certain times but always available to the pilgrim.[48] There are thousands of recognized *tīrthas* in India, and millions of Hindus are constantly on pilgrimage. Numerous *samnyāsis* spend their whole life wandering from one *tīrtha* to another—the most meritorious way of utilizing one's time. Just as worldly globetrotters boast of the many countries and cities they have visited, so one can find *sādhus* competing with each other in enumerating the *tīrthas* visited by each. Places of pilgrimage are not made; they are found. They are, what they are, by divine manifestation, not by human arrangement. A complex set of rules surrounds the important undertaking of the pilgrimage: fasting, worship of Ganeśa, and continence are required before departure: for the pilgrimage itself a certain mode of clothing is prescribed, a copper ring and a brass vessel. Tonsure before or after pilgrimage is still quite common. Ideally the pilgrim should walk the whole distance; today most Hindus take public transport or private cars to come to the places of grace. Of importance is the *saṁkalpa*, the explicit declaration of intention to undertake a pilgrimage to a certain place. Pilgrimage by proxy is also possible; the *śāstras* lay down in detail what percentage of the merit accrues to the donor, to his parents, or his guru. The rivers are the great streams of grace in India; most of the famous *tīrthas*, literally fords, are situated on the banks of the rivers. All the *tīrthas* have *māhātmyas*, praises of their greatness, sometimes of book length, enumerating all the sacred spots and the merits attached to visits.[49]

Mother Gaṅgā is the first among India's holy rivers, sacred from where she flows through such famous *tīrthas* as Haridvāra, Prayāga, and Kāśī till she reaches the estuary in the Bay of Bengal. The Ganges is considered the supreme *tīrtha* in this *Kaliyuga*. Already the utterance of her name is supposed to cleanse the sinner and a bath in the Ganges or the drinking of her water, said not to putrefy, purifies the families seven generations back. As long as even a fraction of the bones of a person are lying in the Ganges or touching Ganges water, can they remain in heaven. Pilgrims carry small bottles of Ganges water home to use it on many occasions; even after years it is supposed to be fresh and unspoiled[50].

The three main *tīrthas* on the Ganges, called *tristhalī,* are considered to be superior to any other place in the world. They are Prayāga, renamed Allahābad by the Muslims, on the confluence of Ganges, Yamunā, and the invisible Sarasvatī; Gāyā, sacred also to the Buddhists as Bodhgāyā, the place of enlightenment of Gautama; and Kāśī, also called Vārāṇasī (anglicized into Banaras) for some time renamed Mohammadābad by the Muslim rulers. One of the maxims of pilgrims goes: "One should shave one's head in Prayāga, offer *pindas* in Gāyā, give presents in Kurukṣetra, and end one's life at Kāśī"—continuing: "Why offer *pindas* in Gāyā, why die in Kāśī, when one has shaved one's head at Prayāga?"

A question much discussed in the ancient *śāstras* and among Hindu *sādhus* even today is that of religious suicide.[51] Quite a few famous *tīrthas* were for hundreds of years the final goal of many pilgrims who took their lives there in order to break out from the cycle of rebirths. Generally Hinduism considers suicide a crime leading to miserable rebirths. But at certain places it can become the supreme act of liberation. The *śāstras* mention several famous precedents and the Purāṇas are definite that whosoever dies in Prayāga, be it naturally or through one's own hand, is sure to obtain *mokṣa.* Four kinds of ending one's life were considered legitimate: burying oneself in a fire fed with dried cowdung; drowning oneself by hanging head downward in the Ganges; disappearing in the waters where Ganges and Yamunā meet; and cutting off one's flesh to feed the birds. Only a few years ago a popular Hindu magazine, in an appeal for the ban of cow slaughter wrote: "Starving oneself to death in a religious cause like the protection of cows is a sort of penance. In the *sanātana dharma* such fasts are recommended."[52]

The most famous of all holy cities in India is Kāśī. Although it is first and foremost Śiva's holy place, who as Lord of Kāśī resides in the Golden Temple, all sects, including the Buddhists, consider it a place of pilgrimage. The city must be extremely old; archeological excavations should reveal much more than has been known so far about this interesting place.[53] The praise showered upon Banaras surpasses everything that has been said about other Eternal Cities of the world. In the *Matsya Purāṇa* Śiva is saying: "Vāraṇasī is always my most secret place; the cause of liberation for all creatures. All sins which a man may have accumulated in thousands of previous lives disappear as soon as he enters Avimukta. Brahmins, Kṣatriyas, Vaiṣyas and Śūdras, people of mixed castes, worms, *mlecchas* and other casteless people, insects, ants, birds, all mortal beings find bliss in my auspicious city." Even today, many old people settle down in Banaras toward the end of their lives, others are taken there when dying. One funeral procession after another treks through the narrow lanes of this holy place, funeral pyres burn constantly at the Maṇikarṇikā *ghaṭ*, which may mark the oldest site of an ancient Āryan settlement. Banaras is filled with a peculiar atmosphere: death and life, piety and cynicism, asceticism and abandon, learning and superstition side by side; an illustration of the Lord of Kāśī who dispenses grace and terror.[54] Banaras suffered greatly under Muslim rule; its temples were destroyed repeatedly and what we see today has been rebuilt only after the eighteenth century. Before the Muslim invasion Banaras must have been a splendid city with thousands of temples and sanctuaries. The *liṅga* of the Viśvanātha temple is said to have been saved from the invader's fury and reinstalled in its old place, which is now partly occupied by a mosque. Many miraculous cures are said to have happened to people who touched this embodiment of the Lord of the Universe. For many centuries Banaras has also been the seat of Hindu scholarship and even today almost every school and sect has an establishment at Banaras. Banaras was chosen as the seat of the Hindu University, toward whose foundation the theosophist Madame Besant also contributed her own college. It is also the seat of the Sanskrit University, founded in 1791 by the British resident Jonathan Duncan "primarily with a view to appease the restive citizens of Vāraṇasī after the siege of Chet Singh's fort and secondarily to collect ancient texts and carry out research on them and to produce *paṇḍits* who could be readily available to assist the English judges for the correct interpretations of the Hindu personal law."[55] A number of famous Indian and Western scholars taught at this institution which even now conducts most of its classes in Sanskrit.

Banaras is not the only holy city, nor the only center of Hindu learning; there are thousands of *tīrthas* and dozens of places famous for scholarship. All of them convey the unique atmosphere of Hinduism, of the Supreme being present in different ways and forms in places, images and temples, approachable at certain times and distributing his grace to those who are watchful enough not to miss the occasion of its appearance and to recognize it under its manifold guises.[56]

When the Vedic dharma was carried into the South of India, attempts were made ot duplicate the most sacred features of the *Āryavārta*, the Holy Land of the North, in the South and local rivers such as Kṛṣṇa and Kauverī were termed the "Ganges" or "Yamunā" of the South, Kāñcipuram, the "Banaras of the South," to create local *tīrthas* providing as much merit to pilgrims as a visit to the more distant places in the North. In the course of time the South overtook the North in wealth and splendor, and both the size of the holy cities and the number of people attending temple festivals are greater now in the South than anywhere else in India. Veritable temple-cities are associated with either Śiva or Viṣṇu, which have a large permanent population, where almost incessantly some festivity or the other is in progress. At particular occasions hundreds of thousands of pilgrims arrive to join in the celebrations and to augment the treasures of the temple. The arguably richest temple in the world is the Tirupati complex in Andhra Pradesh.[57] Situated in picturesque hill country, formerly reached only after days of arduous climbing, it consists of a great number of different temples to various manifestations of Viṣṇu, crowned by a chapel on the hill top, surrounded by small dwellings, where pilgrims can stay. Tens of thousands of pilgrims arrive every day by bus, car, and train, receive blessings from the temple priest, and leave some token of appreciation.

Largely unknown outside India, the former Kacheri Nammāḷvār Temple within the Tirupati compound has been transformed into the S.V. Museum on Temple Art, the most complete of its kind, with a number of well-described exhibits explaining all aspects of temple worship, from the planning stage to the completion of the building, from the daily routine of *pūjās* to the musical instruments used.

The most famous Śaivite centres in Tamiḷnādu are Cidāmbaram, where Śiva according to legend first danced his cosmic *taṇḍava*, and Kāñcīpuram, the "Golden City," which boasts 124 temples.[58] The former capital of the Pallava rulers, it attracts hundreds of thousands of pilgrims each year. The most famous of its temples, Kailāsanāthadevaram, was built in the eighth century and is famous for its ancient paintings. Towering *gopuras* give the whole city the impression of a fortress of God.

The Mīnākṣī temple in Madurai,[59] another city of God in Tamil country, although administered by Śaivite priests, propagates the glory of the Goddess, called *fisheyed* here. The major celebrations at the Mīnākṣī temple are famous all the world over and can even be viewed on various films and videocassettes.

The largest temple-complex anywhere may be Śrīraṅgam, situated on an island in the Kauverī River, not far from Tiruchirapalli. Śrīraṅgam, the seat of the Śrī-Vaiṣṇava pontiff, is the goal of hundreds of thousands of Vaiṣṇava pilgrims from all over India.[60]

Murugan, the old Tamilian war god, has several popular centers of pilgrimage in Tamiḷnādu which continue to attract large crowds, of which Tiruttanī, the birthplace of the former president-philosopher Sarvepalli Radhakrishnan may be the best known.[61]

The most famous Hindu place of pilgrimage in religiously mixed Kerala is Guruvayūr, a Kṛṣṇa sanctuary that may be unique among major temples because of its wooden construction. It burned down some years ago and was reconstructed in an identical fashion. Many miracles such as healing incurably sick persons have been reported by pilgrims.[62] Guruvayūr is also famous for the recitation of the *Nārāyanīyam*, a very artful short rendering of the *Bhāgavata Purāṇa*, composed by the sixteenth century Meppattur Nārāyaṇa Bhaṭṭatiripad, which is regularly recited at the temple.

In all those places there is constant routine worship going on and thousands of *pūjāris* are busy performing rituals on behalf of and for the benefit of those who pay the sums specified for each particular form of worship. This uninterrupted, and often quite noisy, worship in thousands of sacred places all over India, the flow of millions of Hindus on pilgrimage across the country and the mass celebration of countless local and regional feasts lends to India, also in this age of secularization and westernization, of motor cars and airplanes, an air of timeless religiosity and widespread concern for another kind of reality.

21 The Hindu Social Order: *Caturvarṇāśramadharma*

> In order to protect this universe He, the most resplendent One, assigned different occupations and duties to those who originated from his mouth, arms, thighs and feet.
>
> —*Manusmṛti* I, 87

Caste[1] has been seen as an essential institution of Hinduism from the very beginning, both by Hindus and outsiders. A great many studies have been devoted to this phenomenon, either in its entirety or to particular aspects of it. As L. Dumont observed:[2] "It has often been said that membership in Hinduism is essentially defined as the observance of caste rules and respect for the Brahman. T. Parsons, following Max Weber, is categoric: 'Hinduism as a religion is but an aspect of this social system, with no independent status apart from it' (*The Structure of Social Action,* 557). More subtle is the following judgement: 'In some regards, it (Hinduism) is inseparable from philosophic speculation; in others, it is inseparable from social life' (L. Renou, *L'Hindouism,* 28)."

The historic development and the theory of caste has been expertly described and analyzed in such classics as H. Hutton's *Caste in India*[3] and more recently in L. Dumont's *Homo Hierarchicus.*[4] It has been both defended as the best and most natural functional division of society, a model for the whole world, and also attacked as the root cause of all evil and socio-economic backwardness.

Whatever one's judgment may be, there is no doubt that caste has shaped Indian society throughout the last several thousands of years and that it is still of large practical significance. R. Inden rightly warns against isolating caste from the context of Indian civilization, "substantializing" it and in general conceiving it as

"India's essential institution . . . both the cause and effect of India's low level of political and economic 'development' and of its repeated failure to prevent its conquest by outsiders."[5] Caste in India has lost much of its economic importance but it has gained immensely in political significance during the past few decades. In contrast to a process of fission, which produced more and more subcastes, who for one reason or another had separated from the major body, a process of fusion has recently been noticed: clusters of castes unite behind a political candidate, who in turn becomes their spokesperson and representative.

These developments have enormous practical consequences that we cannot fully explore in the context of this book. However, it should be clearly understood that the caste structure of Hinduism is much more flexible in many more ways than previously assumed and that the meaning of caste in India has changed but its importance is not diminished.

THE FOUR ORIGINAL CASTES: *CATURVARṆA*

The origin of the caste structure is associated already in the most ancient works with the very act of creation. The *puruṣa-sūkta* of the Ṛgveda[6] dramatically explains the origin of humankind out of the sacrifice of the primaeval puruṣa and his dismemberment: out of his mouth originated the Brahmins, from his chest came the *kṣatriyas*, from his belly issued the *vaiśyas*, and from his feet the *śūdras*. From as far back as we know the division of *varṇas*, and later the division of *jātis*, as based upon this, had multiple aspects. The name *varṇa*, "color," was for a long time understood to refer to skin color, a differentiation between the supposedly fairer skinned immigrant Āryans and the darker-skinned earlier inhabitants of India. D. Bernstorff, based on convincing evidence, suggests that *varṇa* originally did not refer to skin color but designed the four directions identified by white, black, red, yellow according to which the participants were arranged during the Vedic *yajña*[7].

As the ordinances of Manu imply, the division was also occupational. The *Brahmins* as custodians of ritual and sacred word were to be the teachers and advisors of society. The *kṣatriyas* as defenders and warriors were to be the kings and administrators. The *vaiśyas* comprised farmers and merchants, the backbone of the economy, the middle class to introduce a modern term. The *śūdras* were to be the large mass of virtually unpropertied laborers, a class of servants and menials.

The *caturvarṇa* system also embodied a religious hierarchy; combined with the universally accepted dogma of karma it implied meritoriousness. Brahmins were born into the highest caste on account of karma accumulated over past lives. Lesser karma resulted in lesser births. The birth as a *śūdra* was designed to atone for sins past. The three upper castes were eligible for initiation and the other *saṁskāras*. They had a degree of purity not to be attained by the *śūdras*. Within the *dvi-jātis*, the twiceborn, again a hierarchy obtained that was important in the regulation of intermarriage and commensality: on principle, the higher caste was the purer, and the lower caste member could accept food from a higher without incurring pollution.[8]

In practice the system is much more complicated and beset with, what appears, like contradictory regulations. The mere fact that in the end there were more than 3,000 *jātis*, arranged hierarchically within the four *varnas*, regionally not always following the same ranking and observing traditions not always in line with what would logically follow from the *caturvarṇa* scheme, should caution any observer not to draw conclusions too hastily from a superficial knowledge of the principle of how caste works. A number of detailed studies of caste ranking in specific villages or studies of *jātis* (subcastes) over a region are available to gain some understanding of the intricacies of caste in India.[9]

Every observer of Indian life will attest to the immense importance of caste and caste rules also in the present, post-Independence India. It is not true, as many outsiders believe, that the constitution of the republic of India abolished caste or intended to. It abolished the notion of "outcaste" and made it a punishable offence to disadvantage a person because of such a status.[10] Within political parties, professional groups, municipalities, in social and economic life, in education, and in government service, caste has remained an important fact of life.

Though theoretically the position of one's caste is determined by birth (otherwise it would be meaningless of speak of *svadharma*), a certain upward mobility (as well as downgrading as a result of certain offences) is found throughout history. Quite a number of *ādivāsis*, the aboriginals of India, have been made Hindus by being associated with one of the three lower castes. According to Indian tradition Candragupta, the founder of the Maurya dynasty, was a *śūdra* who rose to the rank of a *kṣatriya*.

Many Mahratta princes came from low castes and were helped by Brahmin experts to reconstruct their family tree in such a way as to show *kṣatriya* ancestry, often claiming Rāma as their ancestor. In our own time quite a number of people from the lower castes have risen to prominence in administration and education. But the Brahmins defend their exclusivity: only those who are born Brahmins, are Brahmins; nobody can become a Brahmin. There is a curious ancient tale about king Viśvamitra, a *kṣatriya* who underwent extremely hard *tapasya* to compel Brahmā, the creator, to make him a Brahmin.[11] Brahmins however contended that not even Brahmā can change someone born a non-Brahmin into a Brahmin.

L. Dumont, attempting a structuralist interpretation of the institution of caste comes to the following conclusion:[12]

> First Hocart, and still more precisely than Hocart, Dumézil have shown that the hierarchical enumeration of the four *varṇas* was based on a series of oppositions, the principle of which was religious[13]. The first three classes, respectively priests, princes and herdsmen-husbandmen, are taken together as twiceborn or as those bestowing gifts, offering sacrifices and studying (the Veda) as opposed to the fourth class, the *śūdra*, who are devoid of any direct relation to religion, and whose sole task is to serve the former without envy. (*Manu* I, 88–91) Among the three kinds of twice-born, the first two are opposed to the third, for to the latter the lord of creatures has made over only the cattle, to the former all creatures. It is worth noting that this particular opposition is the least frequent of all in the texts. On the contrary, the solidarity of the first two categories, priests and princes, vis-à-vis the rest, and at the same time their distinction and their relative hierarchy are abundantly documented from the *Brāhmaṇas* onward.

THE FOUR STAGES IN LIFE: *CATURĀŚRAMA*

Hindus possess an irresistible urge to classify and to organize everything into neat and logical patterns. The number 4 serves not only to classify the Veda (into four *saṃhitās* and into four classes of books considered Veda in the wider sense) and to divide humanity into basic sections, but also to structure the life of individuals themselves. The successive stages of life of a high-caste person was correlated to another tetrad, the *caturvarga* or the "four aims of life" (*puruṣārtha*): dharma (moral law), *artha* (material goods), *kāma* (enjoyment), and *mokṣa* (liberation).[14] During studenthood (*brahmacarya*), the first stage in the life of (mostly) Brahmins, which would normally make up about twelve years and begin after initiation (*upanayana*), the young Brahmin would, in the family of his preceptor, learn the sacred texts, acquire the necessary skills for the ritual function, get grounded in discipline, and receive his preparation for his future life. The classical writings from the Upaniṣads onward are full of descriptions of *āśramas,* training schools for Brahmins, and the routine followed there. The young novice was supposed to serve his teacher in many practical ways in return for what he was taught. Normally the stage of *brahmacarya* would terminate with the marriage of the student, with which he entered the second stage of his life: *gṛhastya,* the life of a householder, devoted to the enjoyment of life and the duties associated with the care for a family, the acquisition of *artha,* material wealth. When his own children had become adults or, as one text describes it, when his temples started graying, the householder was supposed to hand over his worldly business to his sons and lead a retired life, devoted to spiritual pursuits.

The term used is *vānaprasthya*—life in the forest. Older literature describes how the now elderly couple should set up house outside the village and its bustle and devote itself to *mokṣa,* liberation in preparation for the end of life. Ideally, this stage should be followed by an even more radical renunciation: *samnyāsa,* the life of a homeless ascetic who possessed nothing and desired nothing but liberation from the body.[15]

Although not all Hindus would follow this sequence of stages in their lives the structure that the *caturāśrama* scheme suggests and the interests to be pursued according to the *caturvarga* scheme certainly have deeply influenced the personal and social history of Hindus and Hinduism.

Its structure apparently so well reflects what Hindus understand to be the essence of Hinduism that R. N. Dandekar chose it as the schema for his representation of Hinduism in the influential *Sources of Indian Tradition.*[16]

It also appeals to contemporary Hindus, who believe it to have great practical value to provide orientation to today's India. As Dindayal Upadhyaya, the then general secretary of the Bharatīya Jana Sangh wrote in 1961: "The ideal of the Hindu life on the basis of the four-fold *puruṣārthas*—*dharma, artha, kāma* and *mokṣa*—can take us out of the morass. Hinduism and not socialism is the answer to the world's problems. It alone looks at life as a whole and not in bits."[17]

THE CONTEST BETWEEN BRAHMINS AND KṢATRIYAS

In many civilizations we have the phenomenon that the holders of intellectual and spiritual power and those who wield economic and political power vie with each other for supremacy and that this contest, supported by historical and legal arguments on both sides, often breaks out in open rivalry. Hinduism is no exception.

Throughout the history of Hindu India there has been a contest of supremacy between Brahmins and *kṣatriyas,* the religious and the secular powers.[18] Depending on the viewpoint, therefore, Hindu theories of society and state emphasize the one or the other as the sovereign power, arriving at quite different schemes of the ideal society.

In a somewhat simplified manner we may say that the *dharma-śāstra* tradition in classical Hindu literature represents the typical Brahmin view of society, whereas the *kṣatriya* views are expressed in the *artha-śāstra* literature; the very terms express the direction of thought.

The *Manusmṛti,* again a Brahminical text, takes for granted the division of society into the four *varṇas* and elevates the Brahmin to the position of the preserver and protector of the universe by means of the sacrifice:

> The very birth of a *brahmin* is an eternal embodiment of *dharma;* for he is born to fulfill *dharma* and worthy to become *Brahman.* He is born as the highest on earth, the lord of all created beings, for the protection of the treasure of *dharma.* Whatever exists in this world is the property of the *brahmin;* on account of the excellence of his origin the *brahmin* is entitled to it all. The *brahmin* eats but his own food, wears but his own apparel, bestows but his own in alms; other mortals subsist through the benevolence of the *brahmana.*[19]

The duties of all the *varṇas* are spelled out in such a way as to strengthen the authority of the Brahmin. The Brahmins are to study and teach the Veda, to sacrifice for themselves and others, to give and accept alms. The *kṣatriyas* are to protect the people by means of their alms and offer gifts to Brahmins. The *vaiśyas* must tend cattle and devote themselves to agriculture and make gifts to the Brahmins, as well as engaging in trade and money lending. The *śūdras* are to serve the three upper classes. This Brahmin's view of society is also repeated in other works. In the Mahābhārata and the Purāṇas we find contemporary reflections and a contemplation of the evils of the present age, the Kali-yuga, whose corruption consists mainly in the abandonment of the duties of castes, as contained in the Brahminical codes. The need to fulfill *svadharma,* to stick to one's caste duties irrespective of the immediate consequences, for the sake of the world order is also the central message of the Bhagavadgītā.[20]

From the time of Gautama Buddha to the contemporary *Draviḍa Kazḥagam* there have been anti-Brahmin movements, trying to undermine the claim of the Brahmins to leadership by exposing their theories of superiority as fallacious. Despite all these efforts the Brahmins have continued to enjoy the most respected positions in society, not only because people in India believe the Brahmin's version of religion, but also because of their overall intellectual and educational superiority.

Evidently, quite a number of the ruling *kṣatriyas* in ancient times considered themselves to be superior to the Brahmins; not only did they possess the actual political power but they also had a theoretical framework that founded this superiority on the divine institution of kingship.[21] All the ancient accounts agree in describing the original political constitution of humankind as close to what we would call today democratic or republican. As the Mahābhārata has it:

> Neither kingship nor king was there in the beginning, neither scepter[22] nor the bearer of a scepter. All people protected each other by means of *dharma*. After some time they became lax in it[23] and were overcome by *moha*, a state of mind in which they lost their sense of righteousness. As a consequence of this, *lobha*, greed, developed and desire for each other's property. Then *kāma*, lust, overcame them, along with attachment to things that should be avoided and general moral decay set in. The *devas* in their distress approached Viṣṇu who brought forth from his mind Virajas who became the first king.[24]

According to this *kṣatriya* version of the origin of kingship, the king does not need Brahmin sanction but is divinely appointed. According to the Brahmins' account he becomes king effectively only through the Brahmins' consecration. That Brahmins did exert considerable influence over the appointment of kings and also their eventual removal, if necessary by violent means, is amply born out by the facts of Indian history as known to us. The Purāṇas contain an account of a regicide perpetrated by Brahmins that must have a historical core: Vena, a mythical king, proclaimed himself supreme Lord and forbade sacrifices and donations to Brahmins.[25] The *ṛṣis* sent a delegation to him, which politely but strongly urged him to rescind his edict and restore the rights of the Brahmins "for the preservation of your kingdom and your life and for the benefit of all your subjects." Vena refused to acknowledge anyone superior to himself and maintained the thesis that the king, a *kṣatriya,* is the embodiment of all divinities and therefore the supreme being. The first duty also of the Brahmins, he explained, is to obey the king. The text proceeds: "Then those pious men were filled with wrath and cried out to each other: 'Let this wicked wretch be slain. This impious man who has reviled the Lord of sacrifice is not fit to reign over the earth'. And they fell upon the king, and beat him with blades of holy grass, consecrated by *mantras* and slew him, who had first been destroyed by his impiety toward God." Down with the "wicked king" went also the firm hand needed to deal with the unruly, and universal chaos broke out, leaving the people at the mercy of large bands of marauders and robbers. Thus the Brahmins were forced to find another king. Apparently there were two contenders: according to the story they arose through the activity of the Brahmins who rubbed or drilled the right thigh and the right arm of the dead king; thus alluding perhaps to their castes.[26] They rejected Niṣāda and accepted Pṛthu, on whom they conferred universal dominion and who accepted and confirmed the Brahmins' demands and superiority. For the writers of this story the beginning of true kingship dates from Pṛthu, the Brahmin-appointed ruler, "a speaker of truth, bounteous, an observer of his promises, wise, benevolent, patient, valiant and a terror to the wicked, knowing his duties, compassionate and with a kind voice, respecting the worthy, performing sacrifices and worshipping *brahmins.*"[27] The prosperity of his rule is ascribed to his orthodoxy and his submission under the Brahmin's dharma. To drive the point of their story home to all, the very name of the earth, *pṛthvi,* is associated with this king, the first to be appointed by Brahmins and in their eyes the first who really and rightfully bore the title *raja.*

In a different, and perhaps more historical context, the name of India, Bhārata, is associated with King Bharata, the son of Ṛṣabha, who is praised as virtuous and who in recognition of his merits was later reborn as a Brahmin, revealing again the Brahmin claim to superiority over the *kṣatriyas.*

Throughout Indian history, state and religion lived in a symbiotic alliance, more or less happy according to the circumstances and persons involved. The Brahmins served as counsellors and advisors, developing a complex *rāja-dharma,* designed to combine the exigencies of statecraft with brahmanical ideology.[28] In the Brahmins' view dharma was the central point and the source of political power and economic prosperity; in the *kṣatriyas'* opinion *artha,* statecraft, political power and economic strength were the basis of dharma.

The *arthaśāstra* works, therefore, are treatises recommending Realpolitik, utilizing, if necessary, religious beliefs and customs to strengthen the king's position. Most of these manuals are lost and we know about them only from quotations. The *Kauṭilīya Arthaśāstra,* however, whose full text was recovered and published in 1905 by R. Shamasastry, and translated into English ten years later, and which is, according to its testimony, a compendium of all its predecessors, gives a fairly typical picture of the style and contents of this type of literature. Ancient Indian tradition identifies Kauṭilya with Cānakya or Viṣṇugupta, the minister of Candragupta Maurya.[29] Some Western scholars have expressed doubts about this dating and would place the work around the fourth century C.E. Historically, Kauṭilya's work is of great interest, as it gives us a fairly realistic idea of the life in ancient India, of the working of the Mauryan administration, and the economic and social conditions before Aśoka. Not content with wise maxims and theological principles, as are the authors of *dharma-śāstra,* Kauṭilya offers precise instructions of a very concrete nature concerning all aspects of government. The lip service which he pays to dharma in the introductory pages is completely overwhelmed by Machiavellian schemes designed to make the king an absolute monarch and the state he serves the most powerful one around. *Vārtā* and *daṇḍa,* economy and law enforcement, constitute the two pillars of the king's power.

However powerful the king's position may be in Kauṭilya's scheme, he is but one of the elements of the state; the real theme of *artha-śāstra* is the absolutism of the empire—the actual emperor can be exchanged as any other functionary. "The king, the ministers, the country, the fort, the treasury, the army, the friend and the enemy are the elements of sovereignty." These depend so much on each other that they can only stand or fall together and the king should never make the fatal mistake of thinking of himself as being the state! Kauṭilya's ideal ruler is equally far removed from any type of altruistic dedication and world-saving fanaticism of a religious autocrat as he is far from the cynicism and power play of a modern self-made dictator.[30] Kauṭilya demands that the ruler be educated and really competent in the art of ruling a country. In many ways the *Artha-śāstra's* approach may shock a modern democrat, but we must not forget that this book was not supposed to be read by the common man who is told to follow his traditional dharma. It is a royal art—the art of being master. Success in power politics, as history teaches us, does not depend on sensitivity and piety but on determined ruthlessness to acquire power, to keep it, and to increase it. That is *artha*.[31]

In a broader classification Kauṭilya describes his work as belonging to *rāja-nīti*. *Nīti* is often translated as "ethics"; the associations that most of us have with the term *ethics* would not necessarily coincide with what we have just described. *Nīti* is the art of surviving in a world of enemies, thriving on the folly of others, making the best of a given situation.

TRADITION VS. MODERNITY

The Muslim invasion and occupation, the British rule and modernity in general have made their inroads into Hindu society for better and for worse. The basic caste structure of the four *varṇas*, subdivided into some 3,000 *jātis*,[32] is still remarkably strong in many areas of life. Though social reformers have attacked it for almost two centuries as the major cause of all social and economic ills in India, it has provided not only large sections of the population with a minimum of social security and status in society, but it also has deep emotional roots that cannot be severed easily without doing great harm.

Much has been written on "tradition and modernity in India" from the sociological viewpoint, and for everyone with even a cursory acquaintance with India it is clear that Indian society has enormous problems to contend with, problems arising largely out of India's history and not amenable to modern Western solutions (if there are such!). A. D. Moddie, himself a modern Indian, has written a thoughtful book, *The Brahmanical Culture and Modernity*,[33] in which he analyzes the situation in quite an original way. Thus he writes: "If any country had the problem of two cultures in a bad way, with the leaden weight of dead history and an archaic society behind it, it is India. But here the split is not between anything as simple, as purely intellectual as the literary and the scientific. It is deep and sociological and historical: it is more than an intellectual gap between two quite different types of minds." He goes on to define the attributes of the brahminical culture as traditional, caste dominated, hierarchical, authoritarian, village and land based, status oriented, inherently averse to change, essentially undemocratic, accepting as law, life and reality what is written in the *patra*, the authoritative book.

In contrast to this the modern, industrial culture is essentially international, not village or caste based in its social motivations, scientific, rational, achievement oriented, with a mobile elite of intellect, skills, and wealth, making material advancement its major objective. Whereas Moddie quite frankly sides with modernity,[34] others, seeing the same dilemma facing Hindu society, try to return to pure Hinduism as the only hope for India's future. Mahātmā Gandhi's aversion to modern technology and scientific progress had at its source a concern for the masses, who would be left without work and without a frame of moral rules if industrialization and the impersonal, exclusively profit-oriented mentality that goes with it, were to take over in India. Deeper down, however, Gandhi also felt a concern for Hinduism as a way of life and a religion, which he saw threatened and which he treasured and wanted to see preserved.

THE SHADOW OF THE *CATURVARṆĀŚRAMA* IDEAL: THE OUTCASTES

Theoretical and theological the *caturvarṇāśrama* scheme may have been. But it also translated into Indian reality so that socially, and quite often also economically and physically, nobody could survive outside his or her caste. Basically, the Brahmins did not develop "human rights" but "caste rights," which had the side effect that in the course of time about one-fifth of the total population, as "outcastes," had virtually no rights. They were treated worse than cattle, which even in legal theory ranked above them.[35] People became casteless by violating the rules of their castes, either by marring contrary to the caste regulations, by following professions not allowed by to caste rules, or by committing other acts punished by expulsion from the caste. Some books give them the appellation *fifth caste,* but that may leave a wrong impression: they were cut off from all the rights and privileges that caste society extended to its members, ritually impure and ostensibly the product of bad karma coming to fruition.

A notorious example of the distance that Brahmins put between themselves and the outcastes was offered by the Nambudiris of Kerala. Whenever a Nambudiri left his house, a Nayar had to precede him to proclaim that the great Lord was about to come. All outcastes had to hide, the mere sight of them would make a Nambudiri unclean. If by any accident the shadow of a *paria* fell upon a Nambudiri, he had to undergo lengthy purificatory ceremonies. Though the Indian constitution has abolished untouchability, it is still an unpleasant reality in the lives and minds of many Hindus even today. In the villages the former untouchables still usually live in secluded quarters, do the dirtiest work, and are not allowed to use the village well and other common facilities.[36] The government tries to help them through privileges in schools and offices; but these are often eyed with jealousy and suspicion by the caste Hindus. Mahātmā Gandhi fought for their rights, especially the right to enter Hindu temples (quite often they are still refused admission!) calling them *Harijan*, God's people. But even he wanted to maintain the caste structure and was extremely angry with Dr. Ambedkar, the leader of the outcastes, who severed all ties with caste society by turning Buddhist and drawing some 3 million of his followers with him.[37] The casteism of the outcastes, however, is highlighted by the fact that, despised and humiliated as they are, they have established among themselves a caste structure analogous to the *caturvarṇa* system and jealously observe their own ranking within it. They have begun organizing recently under the banner of a number of *Dalit* (oppressed) movements and have made modest progress, at least economically. Few people in leading positions even dare to speculate how a casteless Indian society could function, because they usually depend on support from fellow caste members. Given the historic identification of Hindu society with the caste system, it is hard to imagine that a revivalist political Hinduism would not in some way or other strengthen caste structure, or even end up with a new caste system, based on a new concept of *varṇa* according to the political spectrum.

22 The Professional Religious: *Saṃnyāsa*

> He, who having cut off all desires with the sword of knowledge, boards this boat of Knowledge Supreme and crosses this ocean of relative existence, thereby attaining the Supreme Abode—he indeed is blessed.
>
> —Śaṅkarācārya, *Vijñāna-nauka* 10

The Vedic system of the *caturvarṇāśrama* singled out one of the four great sections of society for professionally practising religion: studying and teaching the Veda, performing sacrifices for themselves and others was defined as the foremost social duty of Brahmins.[1] In the course of their individual lives, too, a progressive spiritualization was provided for. After the period of *brahmacarya,* youth spent in studying with a guru, and after the period of *gṛhastya,* family life devoted to fulfilling the duties enjoined by scriptures and offering sacrifices for the benefit of *devas, pitṛs,* and humans, the Brahmin was supposed to become a *vānaprastha,* a forest hermit practicing meditation of the Upaniṣadic type, and finally a *samnyāsi,* a renouncer, without a fixed abode and without any possession or attachment, solely devoted to the realization of the absolute.

This ideal schema never corresponded in its entirety to the reality of Hindu life, but it institutionalizes a very strong current within Hinduism: the desire to make religion one's whole life rather than just one of the many things in life. Whereas the oldest law books explicitly state that *samnyāsa* is only for Brahmins who have passed through the other three stages of life,[2] Hindu practice, for as long as we know it, has been less strict. Many Brahmins chose *samnyāsa* right after *brahmacarya,* as its continuance and perfection and many non-Brahmins took up this mode of life as well.

VARIETIES OF HOLY MEN AND WOMEN

The terms used to identify the "religious" vary, and despite the quite precise definition of some of them, they are used very loosely by the average Hindu. *Sādhu,* holy man or its feminine form, *sadhvī,* or *sant,* saint, are common designations applied by most people to all categories of religious. *Samnyāsi* (female, *samnyāsinī*), "renouncer," is a fairly common term, too, though sometimes it is restricted to the members of the order founded by Śaṇkarācārya, the *Daśanāmis* (who do not accept women ascetics). In contrast to these the Vaiṣṇava religious are called *vairāgis* (feminine, *vairāginī*), a word that has the same meaning but is used in a more exclusive way. *Yogi* (*yoginī*) as a professional designation can also mean holy men or women in general or it can designate members of particular groups. Quite often the designation of the *saṃpradāya,* or specific order, is used as a name particularly in those places where either one *saṃpradāya* is especially prominent or where so many *sādhus* and *sādhvīs* live that people are familiar with the more subtle distinctions among them. Not all the estimated 8 to 15 million religious, male and female, of today are formally members of a particular order; many are *svatantra sādhus,* people who, without going through the formalities of initiation through a guru and membership in an order, don the religious garb and follow a way of life within the general frame of Hindu religious life. Quite often English books speak of the *sādhus* as "ascetics" or "monks," terms with associations within the Western Christian religion that do not really apply to Hinduism. The etymology of *sādhu* goes a long way toward clarifying its meaning. It is derived from the root *sadh-,* to accomplish, and describes someone who follows a certain *sādhana,* a definite way of life designed to accomplish realization of one's ultimate ideal, be it the vision of a personal God or the merging with the impersonal *brahman.* As long as one has not yet reached the goal one is a *sādhaka;* the perfect one is called *siddha,* having achieved *sādhya,* the end to be reached.

The various groups of religious differ in their *sādhana;* differences that sometimes concern doctrinal and dogmatic issues, sometimes ways of life and behavior, sometimes rituals and practices. It is hardly possible even to list all the *saṃpradāyas,* numbering 300 or more. Though there have been efforts on many occasions in the past to organize and classify them, all these attempts have been overtaken by the development of ever new groups and orders.[3] Especially in modern times there has been a proliferation of new religious orders, often with a reformist or activist character; almost every popular swāmī becomes the founder of a new *saṃpradāya.*

A very impressive demonstration of the variety and strength of Hindu religious orders is offered by the *Kuṃbha melās.* Not only do the many thousands of *sādhus* and *sādhvinīs* assembled form an ordered procession, in which a place is assigned to each group according to a strict canon of precedence, but they also hold their own *saṃpradāya* conferences there and settle disputes concerning teachings and practices.

The forerunners, and quite often still the ideals, of the *samnyāsis* of today are the Vedic *ṛṣis,* the sages of the Upaniṣads, the ancient *kavīs* and saints. The history of Hindu *samnyāsa* thus goes back into the mythical past and appears to have been a well-established institution of long standing by the time of Jīna Mahāvīra and Gautama Buddha. Jain and Buddhist sources offer us a detailed account of many different orders.

The Mahābhārata enumerates what may have been the four original and oldest *saṃpradāyas*: *kuṭicakas,* who practiced religious life while living with their families; *bahūdakas,* who lived near settlements and begged their food from Brahmin families only; *haṃsas,* literally "swans," wandering ascetics, still enjoying a minimum of comfort; *paramahaṃsas,* homeless and divested of everything, including their begging bowl, their staff, and their clothes, "a condition that is divested of sorrow and happiness, auspicious and free from decrepitude and death, knowing no change."[4]

The Mahābhārata also described various *vratas* practiced by these people; they very often constitute what was later called *sādhana.* The *Paramahaṃsa Upaniṣad* describes the highest ideal as follows:

> The way of the *paramahaṃsa* is very difficult to find; truly such a one ever rests in pure *brahman,* he is *brahman* as proclaimed in the Vedas, for his spirit always rests in me and I in him. Having left his sons and friends, his wife and relatives behind and having cut off the *śikhā,*[5] put away the sacred thread, given up Vedic studies, all karma and the entire world, he may possess only the *kaupina,* the staff and food enough to keep his body alive. He does not need anything beyond that. He experiences neither heat nor cold, neither joy nor sorrow, neither honor nor disdain. Having given up all deceit, untruth, jealousy, arrogance, pride, affection and disdain, lust and anger, selfishness and conceit, envy and avarice, he considers his own body like a corpse, getting altogether rid of the body-idea. Forever liberated from the root of doubt, from false and unfounded knowledge, realizing *brahman,* he

lives in the self and knows: 'I myself am He, I am That which is ever calm, immutable, undivided, conscious of itself and blissful; this alone is my true nature!' This knowledge alone is his *śikhā*, his sacred thread, his *saṃdhyā*. He who has renounced all desire and finds his supreme peace in the One, he who holds the staff of knowledge, he is the true *ekadaṇḍi*. The four quarters of heaven are his clothing, he prostrates before none, he no longer offers sacrifices, he scolds none and praises none. The *samnyāsi* is always independent. For him there is no invocation, no ceremony, no *mantra*, no meditation, no worship; this phenomenal world does not exist for him, nor the world beyond. He neither sees duality nor unity; he neither sees I nor Thou nor all this. The *samnyāsi* has no home. He will not accept gold or disciples, nor any other gift. If asked, why not, he will reply: 'Yes, it is harmful!'[6]

THE *SAṂNYASI'S* PROGRESS

Very few at any given time have reached this ultimate freedom of the *paramahaṃsa*; for the rest there have been rules that regulate their lives and offer a certain framework within which they can develop. All *smṛtis* have special sections on the rights and duties of *samnyāsis* and later writers have brought these together into the *yati-dharma*, which leaves a certain freedom in quite a few matters, but also regulates the basic structure of the life of the religious.[7]

It begins by stating the *adhikāra*, the prerequisite qualification in aspirant and master: normally the birth as a Brahmin and the performance of the prescribed *saṃskāras* are insisted upon, together with certain physical qualities: a pleasing appearance, certain auspicious marks on hand and feet, unimpeded speech and absence of physical defects in the limbs. As the *Yati-dharma* says: "A *brahmin* after examining those worlds which are reached through Vedic rituals should become indifferent after seeing that these actions do not result in anything that is eternal. The learned teacher should correctly explain to the disciple, endowed with self-control and a tranquil mind, the knowledge of *brahman*, revealing to him the imperishable and eternal Being."[8]

Moral purity, sincere thirst for ultimate reality, and trust in the guru are the basic requirements in practically all schools. Rāmānuja demands, in addition, a real calling from the side of Viṣṇu.[9] Śrīpati requires the *sādhaka* to wear a *liṅga* on his body as prerequisite for *sādhana* proper.

The surest sign of a religious vocation for the Hindu is the formal acceptance of the novice by the guru whom he approaches. Also the qualification of the spiritual master must be established. Very often the guru is well known as an authority and there is no need for further tests. An important factor is the *guru paraṃparā*, the succession of spiritual masters.[10] It is one of the first things each disciple learns and recites. According to Śaṅkara only a Brahmin can be a proper guru. The guru must be "endowed with the power of furnishing arguments pro and con, of understanding questions and remembering them; he must possess tranquillity, self-control, compassion; he must have a desire to help others, must be versed in the scriptures, be unattached to enjoyments, a knower of *brahman* and firmly established in *brahman*. He must never transgress the rules of good behaviour, must be free from pride, deceit, cunning, jugglery, jealousy, falsehood, egotism. He must have as his sole aim the wish to help others and the desire to impart *brahma-vidyā*."[11]

To some extent the guru must be perfect; this is the more true in Vaiṣṇava *saṃpradāyas*, where the role of the guru becomes all-important as the representative of God on earth and the association of guru and disciple lasts for a lifetime.

After the disciple has been accepted by his guru, there follows a period of training and probation, differing in length and depth from one group to the other. Conscientious gurus will see to it that the disciple has made genuine spiritual progress before *dīkṣā*, the official ordination is imparted. Others, who pride themselves in having a large number of disciples, will undertake it almost without any instruction. Though they vary from one *saṃpradāya* to the other, some elements of initiation are common enough to be mentioned: the body of the novice is completely shaved, including the *śikhā*, nails on hands and feet are cut. The novice prepares a pyre and lays down on it for a short while. Then he gets up and lights it, thus performing his own cremation; from now on he is considered dead to the world. When he dies, he will be buried and not cremated. The candidate then immerses himself in the water of a nearby river or tank. He strips completely and takes a few steps naked, like a newborn, before his guru binds the *kaupina*, a piece of cloth, around his waist, and invests him with staff and water bowl. One of the common features is the imparting of the mantra, which is whispered into the ear, not to be revealed to anyone, except to one's own disciple. Śaṅkara *Daśanāmis* normally get a *śloka* from the Upaniṣads, and Vaiṣṇavas a *śloka* from the *Bhāgavata Purāṇa* as their mantra.

Usually a final *upadeśa*, a lesson of religious instruction, is given. According to the classic tradition, maintained by the

Daśanāmis, the newly ordained religious sets out for a year-long pilgrimage, traversing the length and breadth of India and visiting as many *tīrthas* as possible. Vaiṣṇavas continue to stay with their guru, quite frequently also in a *maṭha*, a kind of monastery, where a large number of monks may live together. Nowadays many Hindu religious change from one order to another or return to family life, although in former times quite heavy penalties had been instituted for such practices.[12] The *saṃpradāya* may also expel members who are found to hold unorthodox views or commit offences against the rules. Without attempting to offer anything like a complete list of Hindu *saṃpradāyas*, we may give a few details, following the classification in an authoritative Hindu work.[13]

SAṂNYASI ORDERS

Vedānta is basically nonsectarian and the main tradition built upon it calls itself *smārta*, claiming to represent the mainstream Vedic religion rather than particular later churches. Its *paraṃparā* includes all the great Vedāntins mentioned in the *Vedānta-sūtra*, beginning with Bādarī, Kārṣṇa, Atreya, Audulomi, and so on to Śaṅkara,[14] who reputedly founded the order of the Daśa-nāmi Samnyāsis, so called because they are divided into ten groups, each of which attaches one of the following names to its accepted religious name: Āraṇya, Āśrama, Bhāratī, Giri, Pārvata, Pūrī, Sarasvatī, Sāgara, Tīrtha, and Vāna.[15] The religious names proper usually end with *-ānanda*, bliss: Yogānanda finds his bliss in Yoga, Vivekānanda in discriminatory knowledge, Dāyānanda in mildness, and so forth.

Śaṅkara wanted his orders to become the vanguard of orthodoxy, the scourge of Buddhism, and the protagonists of reform of Hinduism. In contrast to the Buddhists, who were somewhat decadent at this time, Śaṅkara insisted on rigorous discipline and intellectual activity. He founded bulwarks of Advaita in the four corners of India:[16] Vimalā Pīṭha at Jagannatha/Puri on the East Coast, with which the Āraṇyas and Vānas are associated, having as their mantra: "*prajñānam brahman*"; Jyoti Maṭha near Badrināth in the Himalayas, the center of the Giri, Pārvata, and Sāgara, with the mantra: "*ayam ātman brahman*"; Kalikā Pīṭha in Dvāraka on the West Coast, with the Tīrthas and Āśramas, having as their mantra: "*tat tvam asi*"; and Śāradā Pīṭha in Śṛṅgerī in Kārṇāṭaka, the home base of the Bhāratis, Pūrīs, and Sarasvatīs, with the mantra: "*aham brahmāsmi.*" The *ācārya* of the latter is considered to be the actual head of the entire order, addressed as *jagadguru*, spiritual master of the whole world.

The *Daśa-nāmis* are the most respected group of religious in India, usually well versed in Sanskrit learning and Vedānta philosophy and often possessing a modern education. In former times they had to suffer the attacks of the Bauddhas and Vaiṣṇavas; being bound to *ahiṃsā* they recruited armies of *Daśa-nāmi nāgas*, equipped with a heavy iron trident, who defended the *samnyāsis*. As late as the nineteenth century there were regular battles between these and the Vaiṣṇava *nāgas*, in which hundreds were killed.[17] At present there are six *ākhāḍas*, as the centers of *Daśa-nāmi nāgas* are called, with several hundred members each. They are often illiterate, and their religious program is limited to *haṭha yoga*, physical exercises, which are meant to make them insensitive to pain and endow them with supernatural powers.

The Śaṇkarācāryas of the four *maṭhas* trace their *guru paraṃparā* back through a number of illustrious Vedāntins like Padmapada, Maṇḍanamiśra, Vācaspatimiśra, Vidyāraṇya, Ānandagiri, Appaya Dīkṣita, Sadānanda, and others to Ādiśaṅkarācārya, the founder.

The living Śaṇkarācāryas "represent an institution and are themselves an institution in India's religious life."[18] They are not only fairly universally respected in India as successors to the great Śaṅkara, the restorer of Hinduism in the eighth century, but they exert a major influence through their educational institutions they maintain. Each of the Śaṅkara *maṭhas* has a number of schools attached to it in which Sanskrit and the traditional subjects of Hindu learning are cultivated. These schools are a major employer of India's traditional paṇḍits and they produce most of todays traditionally trained Hindus. These schools employ Sanskrit as a medium of instruction and the Śaṇkarācāryas propagate Sanskrit as not only the sacred language of India but also the lifeblood of Indian culture. These eminent leaders of Hinduism are wholly committed to their tradition, but most are not fanatics. They have their parallel in the institutionalized *samnyāsa* of other Hindu denominations, the heads of the Śrīraṅgam *maṭha*, of Uḍipī and other places. There is no doubt at all that in and through them *samnyāsa* proves to be an institutional support of Hinduism—perhaps the most important one. Their position has gained in strength in the past decades and is likely to increase more so in the future.

Śaṅkara, the great reformer of Hinduism in the eighth century, also redefined the idea and ideal of *samnyāsa*. Whatever its conception may have been before his time and whatever forms of religious life prevailed after him, the description of *samnyāsa* in terms of study and self-consciousness rather than Yoga, devotional practices, or self-mortification is due to him and his ideas of self-realization. In its intellectuality and its outward moderation, its emphasis on introspection and unperturbed serenity of mind it has created a prototype of universal appeal, free from sectarian fervor and masochistic self-torture.

Vaiṣṇava religious are usually known as *vairāgis*. A conference in the eighteenth century affiliated the numerous groups to four *saṃpradāyas* in a rather artificial way; the system has been broken up through many new developments.

The *Śrī-vaiṣṇavas* are organized in the *Rāmānuja-saṃpradāya*, whose head is the ruling *mahant* of the temple *maṭha* of Śrīraṅgam, endowed since Rāmānuja's time with infallibility in matters of doctrine and ritual. The second is the *Brahmā-saṃpradāya*, founded by Madhva, also called Ānanda Tīrtha or Pūrṇa Prajña. Beginning as a *Daśa-nāmi*, Madhva became Advaita's bitterest enemy. Madhvites are largely restricted to the South, where they keep custody over the *maṭhas* established by the founder. In former times they must have been quite numerous. Among their peculiar customs is the adoption of a name of Viṣṇu and branding the body with a red-hot iron to imprint upon it forever the *cakra* of Viṣṇu.

The third *saṃpradāya* is associated with Nimbarka, a twelfth century Vaiṣṇava. The *Nīmavats*, however, claim to owe their foundation to Viṣṇu himself in the form of the Haṃsa *avatāra*; they have several centers in the district of Mathurā, in Bengal and Rājasthān.

Vallabha, the founder of the *Rudra-saṃpradāya*, was a married man; in his order the feasts honoring his two sons and seven grandsons are still celebrated as major events. As mentioned earlier, he taught the *puṣṭi-mārga*, which promises salvation to those who unconditionally follow the guru.

Caitanya's followers belong technically to the Madhva *saṃpradāya*, but they are in fact a quite distinct branch by themselves, quite numerous in Bengal and Northern India, augmented recently by numerous Westerners in the Hare Kṛṣṇa movement.

One of the largest *saṃpradāyas* today is that founded by Rāmānanda, called *Śrī-saṃpradāya*; its members worship Sītā and Rāma as their divine patrons. Rāmānanda, born around 1300 in Prayāga, accepted people from all castes, including women, into his order. His twelve best known disciples founded subsects, known as *dvāras*. Their main center, called *bara sthāna* is in Ayodhyā, the home town of Rāma. They have several hundred centers today in India, peopled by thousands of fervent, if uneducated, people. They are said to indulge quite frequently in kidnapping to provide new members for their order. As part of their initiation rites they burn the name of Rāma into their skins and usually suffix the word *dāsa*, slave to their accepted names. Their formula of greeting is "*jay sītārāma*."

As some Kṛṣṇa worshippers take on the role of *gopīs*, thus there are also Rāmānandis who imagine themselves to be Sītā, dressing in women's clothing and walking around laden with jewelry. It is not unusual for Rāmānandis to run *Gośālās*, old-age homes for cows.

The counterpart to the *Daśa-nāmi nāgas* are the so-called *catur-saṃpradāya nāgas*, militant Vaiṣṇavas organized into *ākhāḍas*. They are subdivided into two groups: one carries a banner with the image of Rādhā-Kṛṣṇa, the other one with Sītā-Rāma. Of one Vaiṣṇava *nāga* it is reliably told that he had taken a vow not to eat one mouthful before he had killed at least one Śaiva monk. A Śaiva in his turn had sworn never to eat his daily meal, unless he had first slain at least one Vaiṣṇava. Bloody clashes, frequent in former centuries, have become rare nowadays, but they are not unknown.[19]

Śiva is the *samnyāsi* par excellence; he is described as the great *tyāgi*, the one who renounced to such an extent that he even cut off his member with his own hand, living on burning *ghaṭs* and in mountain recesses. Śaiva *samnyāsis* claim to have the oldest tradition of all, and in fact they predate the writing of the Mahābhārata. Śaṅkara knew of several distinct Śaiva schools in his time; one can classify the numerous sects into those that follow the benevolent, or Śiva, aspect of the deity and those that follow the terrible, or Rudra, aspect. Among the former figure prominently the Vīra-śaivas, mentioned before, and the Pāśu-patas, reputedly a foundation of Lakuliṣa, a Śiva *avatāra*. Among the latter, the most prominent are the Kālamukhas and the Kapālikas, practicing rites and a mode of life that few people in the West would associate with religion.[20] The Aghoris are closely associated with them and are quite numerous even today, especially in Banaras. According to their rules, they are not allowed to beg nor are they allowed to refuse anything that is offered to them. All their rites are performed on cremation grounds from which they also get all their belongings. They are reputed to even eat meat from human corpses and spend entire nights dancing around them. They smear their bodies with the ashes from the cremation grounds and are also considered to be masters of the occult arts. They claim to owe their supernatural powers to the *pretas*, the spirits of the departed, whom they worship.

The *samādhī* of their founder, Bābā Kinarām,[21] is a famous place in Banaras; he is said to have worked many miracles during his life time, to have called dead animals back to life and to have restored the sight of the blind. In a contemporary report about Banaras the following information was offered:

> The Aghori leader who now presides over the Baba Kinaram Ashram is Baba Avadhut Bhagvan Ram. He is, no doubt, a true representative of the Aghori Panth in all its *raudra* and *tamasa* aspects. But he is—what a paradox!—essentially a humanitarian. He has dedicated himself completely to the cause of providing relief for the lepers. He is the moving spirit of the Leper Asylum at Rajghat on the east bank of the Ganges. Indeed, the *Aghoris* are as fond of the living as they are of the dead. Avadhut Bhagvan Ram is a big burly man, full of cleverly concealed contempt for the so-called normal human being. "He bores me," he says with a sinister smile and lapses into silence. Suddenly, after a prolonged pause, he bursts out good-humouredly: "You see, I can't even eat him till he is dead."[22]

Yogis, the next major section, are also divided into numerous subsections, the largest and best known of which are the Nāṭhapanthis, followers of Gorakhnātha.[23] They have a male branch and a female branch and are subdivided into Aughara and Kānphata. They wear red and yellow garments and use a vessel without handle for eating and drinking. This vessel used to be a human skull; nowadays it is usually the blackened half of a coconut shell. Around their neck they wear a thread made of black sheep's wool with a single *rudrākṣa* bead and a goat's horn on a cotton string. The goat's horn is blown before the meals. Often they carry a long pair of iron tongs with a ring. The name of the Kānphaṭis, "hole in the ear," derives from their initiation ceremony: the guru pierces the ear of the novice with a double-edged knife and inserts an iron ring. Though they also have their centers, most of them are constantly on the move. One of their peculiarities is the circumambulation of the River Narbadā. They begin their pilgrimage in Broach, on the Arabian Sea, go up to the source at Amarakanṭaka, and return on the other bank. In their *maṭhas* they always keep a fire burning and a bunch of peacock feathers near it.

20 Śiva Kānphaṭa, Mahārāṣṭra, Heras Institute Bombay

A more recent foundation are the Caraṇadāsis, originating with Śukadeva (1760–1838), who wrote a number of books, dealing with different aspects of Yoga. In former times the worshippers of Gaṇapati and Sūrya formed separate orders; little of these movements remain.[24] A considerable number of *saṁpradāyas,* however, have developed within Śāktism, divided mainly into right-hand Tāntrikas and left-hand Tāntrikas. Of the twelve *saṃpradāyas* (with subsections) the most important today are the *Lopāmudrā* and the *Manmathā.*[25]

Numerous orders cannot be classified under these groups, and Rāmdās Gaur characterizes them as *sudhāraka,* reformist. Taking their inspiration from the *Bhāgavata Purāṇa,* many saints like Jñāneśvara, Nāmadeva, and Nabhajī, founded movements that can be loosely put together under the name of Bhāgavata Saṃpradāya. Tukaram, born 1665, one of the most popular saints of Mahārāṣṭra, did not really found a new *saṃpradāya,* but out of the groups he led to the sanctuary of Vittal in Pandharpur developed the order of the *Vārkarīs,* consisting mostly of householders who follow a certain mode of life.[26] Rāmadāsa Swāmi, born 1865, became the founder of another popular order, which attracted mainly low-caste people.[27] A somewhat less reputable order is the Dattā saṃpradāya, also called Mānabhāū,, a Vaiṣṇava sect founded in the fourteenth century and proscribed by several rulers. There is also a Narasinha saṃpradāya, of unknown origin and date, a Rāmavata saṃpradāya quite close to the *Rāmadāsis* mentioned previously. Kabīr, the Muslim weaver who became a Hindu saint, and some of whose hymns have become part of the *Adi Granth,* the holy book of Sikhs, became the founder of the Kabīr Panth, which comes close to a nonsectarian religious brotherhood, if that is possible.[28] Popular are also the Dadu Panth and the Lāldāsī Panth. An interesting group are the Satya-nāmis: claiming a very ancient history, they suffered persecution and near extinction at the hands of Aurangzeb. They were revived in the late eighteenth century by Jagjīvandās and today are found mainly in Western India. The Vaiṣṇava suborders of the Śrī-rādhā-vallabhis, the Śrī-haridāsī saṃpradāya, the Śrī-svāmi nārāyanī saṃpradāya, the Śrī-satani saṃpradāya, and the Parai-nāmi saṃpradāya are popular and quite numerous in certain localities.[29]

In our own time numerous new religious movements sprang up around famous living saints like Ānandamāyī or Śrī Satya Sāī Bābā. The disciples of recently departed gurus like Śrī Aurobindo and Śivānanda, as well as numerous others, have begun to develop into independent quasi-saṃpradāyas.

SĀDHUS AND THE MODERN AGE

Gulzarilal Nanda, a former Home Affairs minister of the central government in Delhi and a devout Hindu, in 1962 established the Akhil Bhāratīya Sādhu Samāj, the All-India Society for the *sādhus*, with the aim of organizing and controlling the rather confusing variety of movements and utilizing the moral authority of the *sādhus* for the general uplift of Indian society. A considerable number of criminals try to escape from the clutches of the police by donning a "holy robe" and numerous vagrants misuse the respect people still have for the *sādhus* to live a relatively easy life without having to work. Generally speaking the reputation of the *bābājīs*, as many people call them (not very respectfully), is rather low. The Home Affairs minister wanted to enforce registration and issue identity cards for the genuine *sādhus*. He also tried to employ them in the anticorruption campaign started by the government. Only a few thousand enlisted with the *sārkarī sādhus*, the government monks, as they were sarcastically called by the independent *sādhus*. The attempt to establish centers of training for the *sādhus*, with something like a standard theological education, has not produced many results to far.

Nowadays a number of *sādhus* are also politically active. In the eighteenth century they led the famous *samnyāsi* revolt in Bengal, aimed at overthrowing the British and reestablishing Hindu rule. The widespread discontent of the populace with the secular government, which has been unable to perform miracles, economic or otherwise, is utilized by many *sādhus* to promise utopia for all, if only they would work for the Kingdom of God by faithfully reverting to the observance of the *smṛtis*. Karpātrijī Mahārāj, a Vaiṣṇava *sādhu*, founded the Rāma-Rājya-Pariṣad, the Kingdom of God party, which advocated reactionary right-wing Hinduism. In this Kingdom of God there is no room for Christians or Muslims, Marxists or Democrats.[30] Another *sādhu*, Swāmi Dvijayanātha, was for many years general secretary of the Hindū Mahāsabhā, a radically fascist Hindu party, out of whose ranks came the murderer of Mahātmā Gandhi. Swāmi Rameśvarānanda, a member of Parliament on a Jana Sangh ticket, was the instigator of the "black Monday" November 7, 1965, in Delhi, leading a "*sādhus* war for cow-protection" that came dangerously close to a coup d'état on behalf of the right-wing fascists.[31] Swāmi Cinmayānanda, who established a huge enterprise in Bombay to train Hindu missionaries, acted as the first president of the Hindū Viśva Pariṣad, the Hindu World

Fellowship, which was designed to actively propagate Hinduism in India and abroad and which was founded in 1964 to counteract the Eucharistic Congress in Bombay.[32] In 1986 Swāmi Vāmadeva, a Daśanāmi *samnyāsi*, founded the Akhil Bhāratīya Sant Samiti (All India Saint's Association) designed to agitate for a restoration of Hindu political power in India. They had been in the forefront of the Ayodhyā agitation and in the fight against secularism.[33] Among other things they demand that the name India be substituted by Bhārat also in English language documents and that the present national anthem, which "carries the foul smell of slavery" (because it was sung at a ceremony welcoming King George V to India), be replaced by the "Bande Mātaram."[34]

Many Westerners have joined Hindu *saṃpradāyas* of all varieties: an Englishman, under the name Kṛṣṇa Prem, became a recognized guru of Vaiṣṇavas; the Ramakrishna Movement has a number of Western disciples, and people like Mahesh Yogi Maharishi, the founder of the Transcendental Meditation Society, or Swāmi Bhaktivedānta, the founder of the International Society for Kṛṣṇa Consciousness, have emerged as major figures of the Western counterculture, initiating thousands of young Americans and Europeans. There may be a good deal of faddism in it, which will rub off after a few years, but for many it is more than a fad: it is the discovery of a life-style that is rooted in the ultimate by way of inner experience.

The frustrations of life, its disappointments and sorrows, which thousands of years ago prompted people in India to look for the unchanging and never disappointing Reality, are still with us, and that makes it possible to understand someone like Bhartṛhari, who in his *Vairāgya-śatakam* explains the deeper meaning of *samnyāsa* in poetical language:

> I have travelled to inaccessible and perilous places without becoming rich; I have sacrificed self-respect and dignity of birth and position to cater to the wealthy, in vain; like the crows have I fed myself in others' houses hoping for gain—but, you, desire, you prompter of evil deeds, you are not satisfied and keep growing. I have dug into the earth in quest of precious minerals, I have smelted metals from rocks, I crossed the ocean and I sought the favors of Kings, I have spent nights on cremation grounds with my mind occupied with *mantras* and *pūjās*—nothing have I got for it, oh desire! In our servile attendance on the filthy rich, their shabby manners and their silly talk we did not mind; suppressing the tears that welled up from our hearts we have smiled

> out of vacant minds; we have paid homage to idiots spoiled by too much wealth! What more folly would you have me suffer, you desire, never satisfied? We have forgiven, but not out of forgiveness; we have renounced the comforts of the home but not because we were content; we have suffered heat and cold, but not because we wanted to undergo austerities; we have brooded day and night on money, and not on Śiva—we have done what the *munis* do, but we have deprived ourselves of their rewards! We have not enjoyed pleasures, they have eaten us up; we have not practiced asceticism but we have been chastised; time is not gone, but we have lost it. Desire is not reduced, but we are now senile. With the hand as a cup, with food begged on pilgrimages, with the quarters of the sky as the garment and the earth as the bed—blessed are they, who have given up all connections with desire and self-contented with a heart fully matured through their acceptance of *samnyāsa* root out all karma. O earth, my mother; O wind, my father, O fire, my friend, O water, my good relation, O sky, my brother! Here is my last salutation to you! I have cast away illusion with its wonderful power through pure knowledge gained from my association with you, and now I merge into the *parabrahman*![35]

Not all of the many millions who are generically called *sādhus* by the populace are ideal persons—in fact the complaints against them are numerous: some of them commit criminal acts, others irritate their fellow men through their aggressive begging and their uncivilized behavior. However, even Hindus critical of some of practices of presentday *sādhus* would defend *samnyāsa* as something essential to Indian culture. Thus a writer in *SEMINAR*, a decidedly progressive and unquestionably secular monthly, after highlighting some of the more common complaints against *sādhus* goes on defending them against government regulations and public condemnations alike by stating that "the *sādhu* is in our blood and cannot be excised from the total Indian community. . . . So long as the Indian people wish to maintain their *sādhus* the *sādhu* will survive. And so long as India is an India with heart, *sādhus* will be maintained."[36]

More specifically he protects the *sādhus* from accusations as being useless and unproductive members of society by pointing out that "if he pays no taxes, he costs the government nothing. If he is not gainfully employed, he neither competes for employment nor seeks poor relief. In an overpopulated country he practices and preaches sexual abstinence. Where greed and corruption are rife the true *sādhu* demonstrates a life based on honesty, truthfulness, and self-restraint." All this and in addition the engagement of modern *sādhus* in works of charity and education seems, however, to be a rather superficial excuse for the radical challenge which *saṃnyāsa* is to the Hindu. Thus the writer concludes: "Above all, the people look to the man of the spirit to provide them with a meaningful interpretation of existence and from him draw courage to face the tribulations of their lives."

23 *Strīdharma*: The Position of Women in Hinduism

> We will have to produce women, pure, firm and self-controlled as Sītā, Damayantī and Draupadī. If we do produce them, such modern sisters will receive the same homage from Hindu society as is being paid to their prototype of yore. Their words will have the same authority as the *śāstras*.
>
> —M. K. Gandhi[1]

Recent incidents of *satī* and a rash of "dowry murders" have made headlines not only in India, but all around the world, and have focused attention to women's issues in India, evoking all kinds of responses: from spokesmen for Hindu orthodoxy, from representatives of political parties, from vocal Indian women's movements, and from social scientists and observers of contemporary India. In the wake of the discussion it emerged that Indian women's problems are not only problems of Hindu women or problems caused by traditional Hinduism. It also became clear that within the long history of Hinduism itself, the story has many plots and subplots, and the narrative takes us down many different avenues.

WOMEN AS EQUALS OF MEN IN EARLY VEDIC RELIGION?

Minoti Bhattacharyya, herself a Hindu woman, argues that in Vedic times women and men were equal as far as education and religion were concerned.[2] Women participated in the public sacrifices alongside men. One text[3] mentions a female *ṛṣi* Viśvara. Some Vedic hymns[4] are attributed to women such as Apalā, the daughter of Atri, Ghoṣā, the daughter of Kakṣīvant, or Indrāṇī, the wife of

Indra. Apparently in early Vedic times women also received the sacred thread and could study the Veda. The *Haritāsmṛti* mentions a class of women called *brahmavādinīs* who remained unmarried and spent their lives in study and ritual. Pāṇini's distinction between *ācaryā* (a lady teacher) and *ācaryāṇī* (a teacher's wife), and *upādhyayā* (a woman preceptor) and *upādhyayīṇī* (a preceptor's wife) indicates that women at that time could not only be students but also teachers of sacred lore. He mentions the names of several noteworthy women scholars of the past such as Kathī, Kālapī, and Bahvici. The Upaniṣads refer to several women philosophers, who disputed with their male colleagues such as Vācaknavī, who challenged Yājñavalkya.[5]

The Ṛgveda also refers to women engaged in warfare. One queen Biṣpalā[6] is mentioned, and even as late a witness as Megasthenes (fifth century B.C.E.) mentions heavily armed women guards protecting Candragupta's palace.

The Vedic pantheon includes a substantial number of female goddesses. There are beautiful hymns to Uṣas, the dawn, imagined as an alluring young woman:

> Dawn on us with prosperity, O Uṣas, daughter of the sky,
> Dawn with great glory, goddess, lady of the light, dawn thou with riches, bounteous one. . . .
> O Uṣas, graciously answer our songs of praise with bounty and with brilliant light . . . grant us a dwelling wide and free from foes . . . [7]

One of the most important of all Vedic hymns, the so-called *Devīsūkta*, is addressed to Vāk (speech, revelation), the goddess who is described as the companion of all the other gods, as the instrument that makes ritual efficacious: "I am the queen, the gatherer-up of treasures . . . through me alone all eat the food that feeds them. . . . I make the man I love exceedingly mighty, make him a sage, a *ṛṣi* and a *brahmin* . . . "[8] It is not unimportant, that Earth (*pṛthivī*) is considered female, the goddess who bears the mountains and who brings forth vegetation.[9]

Some Vedic goddess worship may be an echo of goddess-worship indigenous to India before the spread of Vedic religion; the Vedic hymns to the Goddess certainly made it easier in later centuries to legitimize Goddess worship as orthodox in the context of *bhakti* and *śākta* traditions, where Vedic and non-Vedic elements were blended.

A GROWING NET OF RESTRICTIONS FOR WOMEN

With the expansion of Vedic religion in Northern India and the growing specialization of Brahmanic ritual, possibly also under the impact of threats from the outside, a definition of the place of women in Āryan society took place, which amounted to increasing restriction of their independence and a clear preponderance of patriarchal rule. Hindu lawbooks contain specific and detailed sections on *strīdharma*,[10] the socio-religious law as applicable to women. Much of this law, which was considered binding till very recently (and would still be considered normative by orthodox Hindus today), restricts the rights of women considerably. It is based largely on the notion that the husband is "god" for the wife, the source of her salvation, the purpose of her life, in whom she realizes her *puruṣārthas*.[11] Manu holds that marriage is the sum total of a woman's *saṃskāras*, including the *upanayana*, *gurusevā*, and *agnihotra* for males.[12] He also admonishes women to serve their husbands like a god and not to take a vow, religious orders, or any other religious obligation without the husband's permission.[13]

Manu reflects popular opinion, when describing women as fickle and unstable, and he voices what must have been already practice all along, namely, never to give independence to a woman.[14] Hindu tradition did not normally impose the death penalty for adultery by women, but it did consider it a criminal act which had to be atoned for by lengthy and arduous *prayaścittas*.[15] A woman would not get much of a chance to commit such a crime, because her life was regulated and supervised from many sides. The Hindu family functioned as a joint family, where not only the husband, but also the in-laws and other relations would keep an eye on a young wife. Public opinion would connect a woman's independent going outside the house, association with strangers, and her drinking liquor with adulterous behavior.[16] A woman's duty would be so exhausting and time filling that she would have hardly any inclination to seek for adventure outside the home. As one text[17] details:

> The housewife is to be the first to get up in the morning; she then has to clean the house, light the fire, prepare the early morning meal. She has to work throughout the day to provide food for the family, serve everybody's needs. She was not to indulge in games and plays. At mealtime she had to serve everyone first and had to eat what was left over, all by herself. The metaphors which Vyāsa employs are telling: a

wife has to follow her husband everywhere like a shadow, she has to support him like a companion, has to execute his orders like a servant or slave. Such good behaviour, the *śāstras* say, will be rewarded in this life by well-being, and after this life by heaven; contrary behaviour will be punished by lengthy sojourns in hell and a bad rebirth.

All lawbooks devote sections to the "impurity caused by the menses." Women were supposed to completely withdraw from the family for three days to an outhouse, to keep silent, not wear any ornaments, to sleep on the floor, not to show themselves to anyone. According to one *smṛti* text[18] the menstruating woman is on the first day impure like *caṇḍāla* (outcaste; the traditional sweepers and removers of refuse), on the second like a brahman murderess, on the third like a washerwoman. After a bath on the fourth day she is considered "pure" again.[19]

Although from a modern perspective traditional Hindu law certainly severely restricted the freedom of women in many ways, it also created for them "a room of their own," an area of competence and a sphere of authority, which guaranteed her considerable power in domestic concerns. Somehow reversing what Vyāsa had said, the *Dakṣasmṛti* calls the wife and mother of the house the "pillar of domestic well-being" and considers her the source of *artha*, dharma, and *kāma* for her husband. Through her friendliness and good disposition she can transform the home into a heaven; she can also turn it into a hell for all, if she is disagreeable and badly treated.[20]

What has been described so far as "Vedic law for women" was largely the tradition followed in North India, the Ārya-vārta, the Hindu heartland. South India, and to some extent also Bengal and Assam, preserved elements of pre-Vedic matriarchy. In certain South Indian castes the line of inheritance is from mother to (eldest) daughter, and marriage is a "visiting" relationship. Naturally, the role of a wife and mother in such a context will be quite different compared to the "servant of the god-husband" described previously, and women were much more independent and free in every respect.

THE LIBERATION OF WOMEN IN THE PURĀṆAS

If originally the Purāṇas were meant to entertain the nonactive participants at the great public Vedic sacrifices through the long stretches of brahmanical Veda recitation, they became, from the fifth century C.E. onward, the main source of popular Hindu religion and were considered scriptures containing everything required for finding salvation. One of their major innovations consisted in granting to women equal access to the means of grace and promising them liberation independent of their role as wives and mothers. On the whole conservative in social matters, religiously the Purāṇas were progressive by describing practices accessible to everyone, irrespective of gender or caste.

In all Purāṇas goddesses play a major role as consorts of gods like Viṣṇu and Śiva; they often persuade their spouses to reward the offerings of the faithful, and they serve as channels of their grace. There are also Purāṇas in which the Goddess herself is equated with the Supreme Being, and where the whole religion centers around Goddess worship. One such is the famous *Devī-bhāgavata Purāṇa,* a huge work with many goddess myths and long litanies and prayers to the Goddess. In the Goddess tradition to which the *Devī-bhāgavata* belongs, women not only had an equal chance of salvation, but even became the preferred gurus to initiate also male devotees to religion. Throughout the past several centuries there were women heads of *āśramas,* who provided guidance to a mixed following of women and men. Some were considered already during their lifetime *avatāras* of the goddess, and were themselves elevated to the rank of a goddess themselves after death. Śāktism and Tantrism are fairly integral elements of today's popular religion in India, regardless of sectarian affiliation. In some parts of the country, like Bengal and Assam, the worship of Devī, especially in the form of Durgā, is hugely popular. Bengal's most famous modern saint, Paramahaṃsa Ramakrishna was a devotee of the Goddess, often falling in trance before her image, and seeing her in visions. Admittedly, not all of Tantricism is a religion for and by women; but it certainly shows the importance attributed to the female aspect of the deity, and the power associated with the goddess.

DRAUPADĪ AND SĪTĀ: HEROIC WOMEN OF THE EPIC TRADITION

The Mahābhārata is certainly dominated by male characters on both sides of the warring factions, but some women stand out, playing a not insignificant role. The most important of these is Draupadī, the wife of the five Pāṇḍava brothers. Polyandry was practiced in some parts of India in ancient times and is still in existence in some areas of the Tehri-Gharwal region in the Himalayas. Draupadī accompanied the Pāṇḍavas on their journeys during their long years of exile. She became the focus of contention, when, after a lost game of dice, with nothing else to lose, the Pāṇḍavas gambled away Draupadī, and the Kauravas humiliated her publicly. The hatred this action evoked in the hearts of the Pāṇḍavas, together with their feeling of shame because of their helplessness and ignominy, was one of the leading causes for the subsequent Great War.

More than Draupadī, who remained a more remote figure in Indian popular imagination—both because of the age of the epic and the rather unusual polyandric situation—Sītā, the heroine of the Rāmāyaṇa, has captured the minds and hearts of the Indian population. The Rāmāyaṇa, through re-creations in several Indian vernaculars and frequent theatrical performances, remained alive throughout the centuries and today is better known in the whole of India than any other tale. In its reworkings in regional languages the figure of Sītā has undergone quite typical transformations as well. Because of her fame and frequent references to her as a role model, the figure of Sītā has become the focus of feminist resentment against traditional Indian notions of womanhood.

Sītā in the Vālmīki Rāmāyaṇa is not exactly representative for Vedic *strīdharma*. To begin with, she chooses her own husband in a competitive *svayamvara*, only the strongest and the smartest prince will do.[21] Again, after Kaikeyī's intervention, when Rāma goes into forest exile, she insists on accompanying him. She is not an obedient servant to a godlike husband; she has a will of her own and her relationship to Rāma is governed by love for him, rather than by obedience to his orders. She shows her determination and independence throughout the years in the forest; her insistence that Rāma get the gold-spotted deer and her command that Lakṣmaṇa come to his rescue, eventually leads to her abduction by Rāvaṇa. It is in the context of this "dwelling in another man's house" that Vedic regulations for women are invoked and popular sentiment demands an ordeal to prove her purity.

The "romantic" elements in Vālmīki's Rāmāyaṇa are heightened in Tulasīdāsa's *Rāmacaritamānasa,* the late medieval Hindī re-creation of the epic, and Sītā appears both more contradictory and more goddesslike. The very fact that Rāma and Sītā are always mentioned in one breath endows Sītā with equality: whatever status Rāma occupies, this will also be Sītā's. If he is king, she will be queen; if he is god, she will become goddess. However, she is queen and goddess out of her own merit, not because of Rāma's grace.

Tulasīdāsa's Sītā shows many features of the ideal of a wife of which the Hindu man was dreaming: submission to elders and persons of respect, loyalty in adversity, and courage in the face of danger, beauty and sweetness, total devotion to husband and children. Those old-fashioned virtues have made her the target of modern Indian feminists. It could be argued that, although Tulasīdāsa draws a quite differentiated picture of Sītā, endowing her with life-like, often contradictory, qualities, in the present day polemics the figure of Sītā becomes stereotyped into something quite artificial. Also, the perspective is skewed in the process. Tulasīdāsa, following the Hindu tradition of epic writing, depicted a religious ideal, giving a transcendental rationalisation of the characters, but the contemporary debate proceeds as if Sītā and Rāma were an all-India middle-class couple. The average modern Indian woman, emancipated or not, is certainly not expected to accompany her husband on a twelve-year jungle tour, nor is the average Indian man likely to become king of Ayodhyā and one of Viṣṇu's *avatāras*.

The "down-to-earth" interpretation adopted by many contemporaries does a disservice also to another one of India's great female characters and goddess representations: Rādhā. Admittedly, the Rādhā-Kṛṣṇa dalliance, as described in some of the more colorful Vaiṣṇava writings, such as Jayadeva's *Gītagovinda* or Rūpa Gosvāmi's *Ujjvala Nilāmanī*, was found offensive even by some Hindu contemporaries, who felt that their authors had gone too far in their transcendental realism. However, when the figures of Kṛṣṇa and Rādhā are completely divested of their divine character and the love they demonstrate becomes reduced to mere sexuality, the figure of Rādhā turns into something rather bizarre, and her relationship with Kṛṣṇa becomes rather perverse.

Rādhā, as visualized by the fervent followers of Caitanya in the sixteenth century, was not a historical but an emotional reality. As A. K. Majumdar has observed:

> It is not possible, nor indeed is it necessary, to establish her identity on an empirical basis. She is the idealized form of an ontological conception, nevertheless real, because she is ethereal. The pious Goswāmis of Vrindābana have gone into great details in describing her, it is in their language that Rādhā takes a definite form, a human form, and the *līlā* of Rādhā-Kṛṣṇa adds a human dimension to subtle theological and philosophical discussions. The vivid description of Rādhā and of her union with Kṛṣṇa are related in everyday human terms, but still, it is a *līlā*, a sport, but a divine sport, for no ordinary human being can take part in it or perceive it. . . . Rādhā is the realization of the principal emotion . . . the dance of duality ends in ultimate unity.[22]

To reduce Rādhā to a commonplace adulteress and to speak of the Rādhā-Kṛṣṇa *līlā* as expressing "coitus fantasies," as Nirad Chaudhuri does,[23] is certainly doing an injustice to the Vaiṣṇava poets and completely misses their point.

Figures like Sītā or Rādhā live in a multidimensional universe. It is the contemporary fashion to reduce all reality to one dimension, that of the grossly material and pragmatic. In that kind of "realism" there is no category to deal with figures like Sītā and Rādhā. Their "ideal" character is not held up for imitation but for contemplation and worship. The imagination that concretized such ideas into humanlike figures does not agree with a one-to-one translation of its religious vocabulary into present-day sociological or feminist notions. The "divine couple" Sītā-Rāma cannot be used as a model for working out budget problems in a modern family, be it in India or anywhere else. And the Rādhā-Kṛṣṇa *līlā* is not a valid subject for Freudian psychoanalysis, whether performed by professionals or amateurs.

WOMEN POET-SAINTS IN SOUTH AND NORTH

The *bhakti* movement that initiated the religious liberation of women was largely promoted and supported by women devotees. Among the many popular poet-saints whose compositions are heard throughout India (and beyond), were a fair number of women. Only two of these, Āṇṭāl from South India and Mīrābāī from the North, will be highlighted here, recognizing that numerous others deserve to be known and written about.

In the Tamil country the name of Āṇṭāl is as fresh today as it had been for the past 1,000 or more years, and her songs, too, are sung every day in temples during worship.[24] According to traditional accounts, Kōtai (Āṇṭāl's original name) grew up in the shadow of the temple of Śrīvilliputtūr—now boasting the tallest *gopuram* of the whole of India, built in honor of Āṇṭāl—where her father Viṣṇucitta served as priest. Without her father's knowledge Kōtai would take up the garland of flowers prepared for the evening *pūjā*, put it around her neck, and admire herself in a mirror, playing God's bride. Ordinarily this would be considered sacrilegious; one cannot offer a garland to the deity that has been worn by anyone else. When Viṣṇucitta discovered Kōtai's playful secret one day, he was very disturbed and conducted the evening service without offering the already used garland to the image. That night Viṣṇu appeared to him in a dream and told him that a garland, which

Āṇṭāl had worn before, was even dearer to him than any other and so Viṣṇucitta realized that his daughter Kōtai was a very special person in the eyes of the Lord.

Confirmed in her devotion to Viṣṇu, Āṇṭāl spent her days in contemplation, composing a series of hymns in praise of Viṣṇu and refusing all suggestions of marrying: she would not accept any man but Viṣṇu as her husband. Viṣṇucitta, worried about Āṇṭāl's state of mind, was comforted again by Viṣṇu in a dream, telling him that Āṇṭāl would indeed be his bride. Legend has it that Viṣṇu miraculously organized a marriage party with musicians and dancers, to accompany Āṇṭāl from Śrīvilliputtūr to Śrī Raṅgam. When Āṇṭāl left the palanquin and stepped up to the reclining Viṣṇu image, she mysteriously vanished into the image. Viṣṇu appeared again to Viṣṇucitta, accepting him as his father-in-law, and requested him to continue serving him at Śrīvilliputtūr. There, a shrine was built in honor of Āṇṭāl within the compound of the Viṣṇu temple containing her richly adorned bronze statue and a long inscription, phrased as a love letter from Viṣṇu to Āṇṭāl. Her hymns are sung daily in Śrīvilliputtūr and other Viṣṇu shrines in the Tamil country.[25]

Mīrābāī is a household name all over Northern India; her songs are still sung at countless gatherings and people look up to her as one of the perfect devotees, who was granted the privilege of not dying but being absorbed into one of the *murtīs* of Viṣṇu in Vrindāban.[26] She was born in Mārwāḍ in 1547, and from early childhood on loved and worshipped an image of Kṛṣṇa as her future bridegroom. She used to adorn it, bathe it, sleep with it, sing to it, dance around it, and she imagined herself to be wedded to it. When she grew up, she was betrothed to Bhojrāj, the prince of Chitor, a fiercely independent Rājput ruler, who would never accept Muslim rule, whatever the cost. The ruling family of Chitor worshipped Śakti, the Goddess. Mīrā, invited by her mother-in-law to join in the worship of the Goddess, refused, saying that she had given her heart and her head to Kṛṣṇa. She used to spend entire nights in a small Kṛṣṇa temple, conversing with the idol, singing her own songs to him, and dancing in front of it. According to tradition, some of her sisters-in-law reported her to her husband, accusing her of secretly meeting at night with a paramour, while refusing to join her husband. Enraged, Bhojrāj threatened to kill her. But when he burst into the room, from which Mīrā's love songs and whispered conversations had come, he found her alone, sitting in raptures before a Kṛṣṇa image. Declaring her crazed, he left her alone, till another incident infuriated him even more. Having heard about

Mīrā's beautiful *bhajans,* and unable to invite her to the court, Emperor Akbar and his court musician Tansen traveled incognito to Chitor to listen to the famous *bhaktā.* They were overwhelmed by the fervor and ardor of Mīrā's devotion and the emperor pressured her into accepting a necklace on behalf of Kṛṣṇa. When the news came out about the identity of the mysterious visitors, Bhojrāj, for whom the Mughal rulers were archenemies, forced Mīrā to leave his kingdom. He advised her to drown herself in atonement for the shame she had brought upon him. When about to do so she was rescued by Kṛṣṇa himself and admonished to turn toward Vrindāban and serve him in his holy city.

Everybody in Vrindāban treated her as someone special; her fame spread throughout Northern India, and she began to believe that in a previous incarnation she had been Rādhā herself. One day the unexpected happened. Her husband, going to Vrindāban disguised as a pilgrim, asked for her forgiveness and requested her to come back with him to Chitor, free to pursue her Kṛṣṇa worship as she liked. She did so, but after the death of her husband she had to suffer much under the persecution by the new rānā. Several miracles reportedly saved her life: under her touch a snake, meant to kill her with her deadly bite, turned into an image of Kṛṣṇa; a cup of poison became a draught of nectar; a board full of nails was transformed into a bed of roses. She eventually returned to Vrindāban completely immersed in her love for Kṛṣṇa, who eventually absorbed her into his image.

Mīrābāī and Āṇṭāl, although thousands of miles and more than half a millennium apart, share many features: both were devotees of Viṣṇu/Kṛṣṇa, whose brides they considered themselves. Both were gifted poet-singers, totally devoted to the praise of their Lord. Both were accorded the ultimate honor of not dying but being bodily united with the object of their devotion, an event reported of only a few other devotees throughout the centuries. Both are honored by women and men alike as embodiments of the purest *bhakti* and the most ardent emotion. The memory of both is alive in today's India and their songs inspire contemporary devotees as much as they did those of past centuries.

THE "MOTHERS"

An interesting phenomenon of twentieth century Hinduism is the emergence of "*Mās,*" "Mothers," with a large following of male and female devotees, who act as gurus and spiritual advisers on a large scale. Aurobindo Ghose, after fleeing to Pondicherry to escape possible British retribution, dedicated himself completely to the task of preparing for the *śakti-nipāta*, the divine empowerment, that would turn him into the *avatāra* of the twentieth century. He was soon joined by M. and Mme. Richards, who increasingly took over the burden of looking after the worldly needs of the sage. After her husband's departure, Mira Richards, of mixed Egyptian-French descent, became the key organizer of the growing *āśram* and, sharing Aurobindo's spiritual aspirations, she also became the channel for his teaching and ministrations. For the twenty or so years before Aurobindo's *samādhī*, "The Mother" guided the outer and inner affairs of the Aurobindo Ashram. Ordinarily she would convey visitors' requests to Aurobindo, and he would respond through her, insisting that her mind was the same as his and that she fully participated in his consciousness. After her death in 1982 a group of devotees started to worship her as the embodiment of the Goddess. Her memory is kept alive in Auroville, and her devotees claim to receive evidence of her continued presence and power.

Ānandamāyī Mā, like many other god-intoxicated individuals, was considered mentally unstable, until someone recognized and appreciated her quite unique status. Without the aid of a male guru, she acquired a reputation for spiritual power and insight and began attracting a varied congregation. Over the decades her fame spread in India and abroad and she established a number of ashrams in major places of pilgrimage, which in addition to maintaining temples, also began to produce literature by and about her.[27]

Mahātmā Gandhi throughout his life not only defended the dignity and rights of women but found them valuable fellow fighters in his struggle for India's freedom. In his autobiography he described his own maturing process starting out as a 13-year-old husband with a child wife. Although much of his experimenting with different lifestyles at home was done at the expense of his wife's freedom and self-determination, he eventually arrived at a stage where he could acknowledge the strength and wisdom not only of his wife but of womanhood in general. He was aware of the injustices that the Hindu and other legal systems had done to women, and he believed that a reform could be effected without abandoning the Hindu tradition in toto. As he said: "Of all the evils for which man had made himself responsible, none is so degrading, so shocking, or so brutal as his abuse of the better half of humanity to me, the female sex, not the weaker sex. It is the nobler of the two, for it is even today the embodiment of sacrifice, silent suffering, humility, faith and knowledge."[28]

Gandhi early on insisted on equality of women, on women's education, and on women taking their rightful place also in public life. He also argued for an abolition of the dowry system, of purdah and for remarriage of widows. Time and again he came back to the classical ideals of woman as depicted in the great epics and he rejected the criticism of those who believed that Sītā represented a wrong idea of womanhood. At several occasions he stated: "My ideal of wife is Sītā and of a husband Rāma. But Sītā was no slave to Rāma; or each was slave to the other. Rāma is ever considerate to Sītā."[29] Gandhi believed that women were by nature more predisposed toward practicing *ahiṁsā* and that they had a special role to fulfill in India's Independence struggle. Some of his fellow workers like Sarojinī Naidū rose to prominence in post-Independence India and made major contributions to the country's progress.

FROM *SATĪ* TO DOWRY MURDERS

Even small local papers in North America found the report about an 18-year-old, otherwise unknown woman, who on September 4, 1987, became a *satī* in Deorala, a small village in Rājasthān, "newsworthy." A large audience, notified in advance, watched the young widow, married for only eight months, mount the pyre of her 24-year-old deceased husband and die in the flames. Police, which were alerted, were kept off by armed relations of the bridegroom. The bride's parents honored the voluntary self-immolation of their daughter by participating thirteen days later in a *satī* ceremony. Soon afterwards a shrine was built at the site, a *satī* shrine as so many others, which have become the centers of popular pilgrimages and fairs.

Satī, the ritual burning alive of a widow together with her deceased husband, has a long history in India.[30] Although not restricted to India in antiquity, the custom has attracted much attention from people visiting or describing India. The word *satī* means a wife who is faithful, true to her vows, loyal, joining her deceased husband in death as the supreme proof of such faithfulness. *Satī* is also the name of one of the daughters of Dakṣa, the Vedic patriarch. Satī married Śiva against the will of her father. When Dakṣa arranged a great Vedic *yajña* and failed to invite Śiva, Satī, humiliated and despairing, took her own life. Thus in the worship of a *satī*, and *satī* memorials can be found all over India, the memory of a heroic faithful woman and Satī, the wife of Śiva, are combined. It is interesting to see also emancipated Indian women,

21 Memorial for a *satī*

who abhor such a practice, point with pride to *satī* memorials in their villages.[31]

The eighteenth century British traveler and painter William Hodges was one of the few Westerners to actually observe and describe a *satī*. Normally, foreigners would be kept away. The ceremony of *satī* resembled the marriage rites. The widow had to indicate her willingness to become a *satī*. Dressed like a bride, she was taken in procession to the cremation site. Before mounting the pyre she distributed her ornaments and was believed to possess at that moment supernatural powers. The pyre itself was compared to the marriage bed on which she joined her husband for their wedding in heaven.[32]

The rationalization of *satī* was complex. A wife, whose husband died young, was supposed to have been guilty of husband murder in one of her previous incarnations. She could atone for that crime by self-immolation. Also, widows were not allowed to remarry. Because after marriage they belonged to the family of their husbands, they often were seen as an economic burden by that family. Rules governing the lives of widows were so severe, that many may have considered voluntary death preferable to the miserable life they could look forward to. Especially so, because all kinds of celestial blessings were promised to those who became *satīs*.

The practice of *satī* was common throughout Northern India, but the actual numbers apparently were not very large. They were certainly much smaller than the numbers of dowry murders in today's India. Whereas economic motives were probably part of the background to *satī*, they are unquestioningly the *only* reason for dowry murders. Like *satī*, the giving of dowry was originally only a high-class practice, first introduced by *kṣatriyas*, and associated with high status. In the course of time it seeped down into lower strata of society and was believed to confer status on those who practice it, until it became the thing to do for everyone.

Initially, dowry was meant to provide some kind of security to a daughter who married into a stranger's household. If things went wrong, if her husband deserted or divorced her, she could fall back on what was her own property, given to her by her father. Today a dowry is a gift from the bride's family to the bridegroom's family, often specified exactly in rupee figures and never quite finalized. The bridegroom's family, after the first and initial payment, often tries to extort more and more, by threatening or even abusing the young wife, to intimidate her and her family to provide more dowry. If the young wife does not relay the messages to her father or if the father is unwilling or unable to pay up, attempts are made on her life. Dorothy Stein in "Burning Widows, Burning Brides"[33] mentions that in Delhi alone, between 1979 and 1988, 2,055 young wives, aged 18 to 25, died in presumably prearranged kerosene-stove burning accidents, victims of "dowry murder." A large number of such deaths are also reported from all over the country. The veritable epidemic of such deaths has provoked protest marches from women's groups demanding that no dowry should be given or taken.[34] Ironically, since 1961, India has a Dowry Prohibition Act, passed by Parliament subsequent to a number of Dowry Restraining Acts. The act intends to suppress a custom that, even when not leading to dowry murders, often ruins the brides' families financially, especially if they have more daughters than sons.

INDIAN FEMINISM AND HINDU TRADITION

Modern feminism everywhere had to struggle against political and religious establishments, which generally tended to be conservative, male dominated, and patriarchal. The story is no different in India. In spite of the worship of Śakti and the important role the "mother" plays in the extended family, the struggle for more adequate legal protection of women generally, and for their acceptance in public life, had to be waged against traditional religious prejudice, which stereotyped women as submissive wives and devoted mothers, with no rights to a development of their own. The large number of successful Indian businesswomen, women politicians, lawyers, professors, and other high-profile professionals is certainly proof of some success of feminism in India. Indian feminists are not satisfied with what has been accomplished so far; overall, Indian women are still disadvantaged, undereducated, overworked, and exploited. Like other patriarchal religions, Hinduism has a blind spot when it comes to questions of social justice, equality, and women's rights. Not surprisingly, prominent orthodox representatives of Hinduism have resisted every improvement of the lot of women, be it the abolition of *satī*, the ability to file for divorce, the freedom to choose their own careers, or the right to receive an education equal to that of men. As the examples of recent *satī* and dowry deaths demonstrate, there is a great risk in keeping the outer shell of a tradition that has lost its social substance. Traditional *satī* may have been a barbaric custom, but it was part of a functioning social system, with safeguards of its own. Contemporary *satī* lacks these. Reportedly most of the post-Independence *satīs* were pregnant women, who would have been forbidden under the traditional rules from electing *satī*. Hindu tradition would unqualifiedly forbid the killing of a wife for the sake of material profit, as is done in the dowry murder. Although one might respect someone who, out of a sense of honor or motivated by a strong transcendent faith, sacrifices his or her life in the hope of winning a better existence, one feels nothing but horror and contempt for those who drive others into death for filthy lucre and have no regard even for elementary rights of their fellow humans.

Traditional Hinduism is still strongly supported by women; women form the largest portion of temple goers and festival attendants, and women keep traditional domestic rituals alive and pass on the familiar stories of gods and goddesses to their children. One can only hope that the representatives of traditional Hinduism reciprocate this faithfulness by developing within Hinduism regard for contemporary women's concerns and support the endeavors of those who are working toward full equality. There is much in the various strands of the Hindu tradition that would lend itself to a timely defense of women's rights and to the development of a contemporary *strīdharma* anchored in genuine spirituality and flexible to accommodate the changing concerns of today's society. The well-being of women should not be the concern only of feminists but of the whole society. Violence against Indian women and deprivation of their rights is a cause for shame for all. Population increase and the diminishing of resources will, in the next few decades, put great pressure on Indian society and it is to be feared that women and children, as the traditionally most vulnerable sections, will bear the brunt of it.

24 Hindu Structures of Thought: The *Ṣaḍdarśanas*

> Thus there are many different opinions, partly based on sound arguments and scripture, partly based on fallacious arguments and scriptural texts misunderstood. If a man would embrace some of these opinions without previous examination, he would bar himself from the highest beatitude and incur grievous loss.
>
> —Śaṅkara, *Brahma-sūtra-bhāṣya* I, 1

All cultures, as the languages associated with them reveal, have attempted to transform their life experiences into thoughts and coherent mental world pictures. Indian culture has done so more than most others: coining words, translating reality into concepts, elaborating systems of explanation on the basis of universal principles are some of the most prominent features of Indian civilization. The sheer mass of writing we possess, probably only a fraction of what once existed, is eloquent testimony to this.

In the enormous Indian religious literature one cluster of words and ideas stands out: words and ideas designing mind, consciousness, thought, *cit, caitanya, caitta.* Indian religions have been consciousness conscious from very early on. Not that all are going as far as the "consciousness only" school of *Vijñāna-vāda* Buddhism or the "absolute consciousness alone" school of *Advaita Vedānta,* but the awareness of mind as irreducible reality, a reality different from nature and society, was a very important factor in the history of Hinduism as a whole.

To consider the physical realities of the Hindus' holy land as a support of Hinduism will be quite easily acceptable. After all, Hindus live in this sacred geography. To see in the specific societal arrangements Hinduism created a structural support of Hinduism will equally appear quite plausible. All Hindus are, in very important ways, affected by *varṇāśrama-dharma*. It may need some arguing, however, to prove that the *ṣaḍdarśana* are structural supports of Hinduism of equal importance.

HINDUISM: A TRADITION OF LEARNING

Hindu tradition has always shown great respect for scholarship. It rested upon a book, the *Veda*, that was memorized, studied, surrounded by other books, which were designed to protect it, explain it, and apply it. Not only had a Brahmin, according to traditional Hindu law, to devote the first part of his life to study, *svādhyāya*, study on his own, was one of the duties imposed upon him for his whole life. Although the injunction to devote the first part of his day to study may not always have been literally followed by all Brahmins, study as a habit certainly characterized them throughout and formed the whole class. Study, according to Manu, was enjoined by the creator himself "in order to protect the universe" and it was also the most effective means to subdue sensual desires and obtain self control. Manu quotes an ancient verse: "Sacred Learning approached a *Brāhmaṇa* and said to him: 'I am thy treasure, preserve me, deliver me not to a scorner; so preserved I shall become extremely strong'."[1] The learning that a Brahmin acquires is his only claim to eminence: "A man is not considered venerable because his head is grey; him who, though young, has learned the Vedas, the gods consider to be verenable."[2] Veda study, Manu says, has been declared the highest form of *tapas* (austerity, self-mortification) of a Brahmin.

Correspondingly, the role of the teacher has always been important. "They call the teacher 'father' because he gives the *Veda*: for nobody can perform a sacred rite before the investiture with the girdle of *muñja* grass."[3]

The teacher was compared to a God, even placed above God: because he could not only convey the sacred knowledge but could also intercede on behalf of his pupils in case of their wrongdoing. The king, according to Kauṭilya, had the duty to see to it that no student and no teacher in his realm would be wanting the needful.

The prominence of the Brahmins, whose "natural" function was to learn and to teach, is a further indicator of the central place study occupied in Vedic society. The true centers of Hinduism were always centers of study: be it the *āśramas* of classical India, or the *patha-śālas* of later times, the private libraries of individual scholars, or the large universitylike centers of major denominations.[4]

To the extent to which Brahmanic ideas shaped the outlook of Hindu society—and they did so with great effectiveness—scholarship and study occupied a prominent place in it.[5] Although much of Brahmanic learning consisted in memorizing the sacred texts and acquiring the skills to perform the rituals, reflection and critical examination of the content of the tradition is also in evidence from very early times. The Upaniṣads contain accounts of debates between learned sages and indicate that certain lines of thought had already crystallized into schools associated with prominent names.[6]

The emergence of Buddhism and Jainism, and a host of other movements within Hinduism, critical of certain aspects of it, shows that by the fifth century B.C.E. complete systems of thought had formed, challenged by rival systems, and that the notion had arisen that it was important to have a clear and correct idea of the intellectual supports of practical life.[7] The fierce polemics carried on between representatives of different schools of thought—polemics not restricted to books and academic retreats, but carried out in public with the participation of large numbers of people—is a further fact that corroborates the importance given to thinking and system building. The fully developed Hindu systems of early mediaeval India leave no doubt that they consider it of the highest importance to have correct notions of the key concepts of religion: a person's ultimate felicity depends on it, as Śaṅkara explains.[8]

Contrary to the West, were philosophical and theological discussion, with very few exceptions, was a concern for professional philosophers and theologians only, in India this debate interested all levels of the population. Although not everybody in India is capable of arguing the finer points of śāstraic controversies, nearly everyone even today knows about the controversy between the followers of Śaṅkara and Rāmānuja, can discuss the points where Buddhism differs from Hinduism, or is able to marshall arguments for or against *saguṇa* and *nirguṇa brahman* and so on. Many of the most popular *bhajans,* religious lyrics sung at popular gatherings, contain an amazing amount of such highly philosophical thought.[9]

Intellectual penetration of reality, enlightenment, knowledge, and insight are absolutely central in Hinduism. The classical systems are part of the structure of Hinduism as much as anything else. As in other supports, there is a reality that corresponds to it. The Hindu *darśanas* have provided real insight, have helped people to acquire real knowledge, and have been found reliable guides in the search for Truth. It is that element of truth realized, that freedom gained, and that transcendence experienced which has prevented Hinduism from becoming an ideology for a power structure, an escape for dreamers, or a merely romantic view of nature.

The close proximity of religious theory and social practice in India through the ages brought with it strong repercussions in "real" life of changes in philosophico-theological orientation. Therefore acceptance of Buddhism or Jainism brought about a loss of caste, with enormous consequences for those concerned. It also, of course, deprived a person of felicity after death. In the context of the practice of *śrāddha,* which was supposed to secure the bliss of the ancestors, this had repercussions not only with regard to one's own fate but with regard to one's entire lineage as well. Although Hinduism throughout its history has shown a great fondness for speculation and system building, the need to remain within the socio-cultic context of the Ārya tradition brought up the question of how far one could go with critical thinking. Vedic tradition did not consider itself the result of human thought: it related its content to a revelation received by seers and sages in meditation and trance, it aimed at maintaining and duplicating these states of mind through Yogic practices, it exempted Vedic teaching from criticism by declaring its origin *apauruṣeya,* not human-made, but eternally present. Thus the Veda was taken to be the foundation of all thinking, and not its object, to be analyzed or discussed. No tradition is founded on analytical and critical thought alone; a society needs more than speculative philosophy to flourish and provide for the needs of its members.

Wide ranging and deep searching as Indian philosophy may be, it had to respect the boundaries practical life had set. If one wanted to get beyond these boundaries one placed oneself outside society. The *nāstikas,* those who did not accept the Veda as authority did just that.[10] The *āstikas,* those who wished to remain inside tradition, had to stay inside the framework of questions permitted by the Veda. That this was not easy to ascertain appears from the polemics carried on between the *āstika* systems from the seventh century onward. Kumārila Bhaṭṭa, a great authority in *Mīmāṃsā* and a staunch defender of *sanātana* dharma against Buddhism, considers *Sāṁkhya, Yoga, Pāñcarātra,* and *Pāśupata* philosophies as *nāstika.*[11] Some of the followers of Madhva would classify Śaṅkara's *Advaita Vedānta* as *pracanna-bauddha,* crypto-Buddhist, and thus unorthodox. This is a position taken even at the present, not only by the Caitanyites and their modern Western exponents but also by some scholarly philosophers.[12] Śaṅkara himself condemns Sāṁkhya as non-Vedic and the teaching of *pradhāna* as heretical.[13] S. Radhakrishnan, quite clearly placing himself within the orthodox tradition, explains the rationale for this attitude thus: "If the unassisted reason of man cannot attain any hold on reality by means of mere speculation, help may be sought from the great writings of the seers who claim to have attained spiritual certainty. Thus strenuous attempts were made to justify by reason what faith implicitly accepts. This is not an irrational attitude, since philosophy is only an endeavour to interpret the widening experience of humanity. . . . If we cannot establish through logic the truth of anything, so much the worse for logic."[14] And "The acceptance of the *Veda* is a practical admission that spiritual experience is a greater light in these matters than intellectual reason. . . . The philosophical character of the systems is not much compromised by the acceptance of the *Veda*."[15] The options that the Veda leaves are indeed quite liberal. It did not demand a creed nor a declaration of faith in this or that God.

Vedic tradition embodied the principle of pluralism insofar as a number of family traditions (*śakhas*) were considered as equally authoritative, and it also recognized a variety of valid local traditions. Even the *nāstikas* developed the pluralistic spirit in orthodoxy: it was faced with alternative viewpoints and had to engage in rational argumentation, admitting in the process that many questions had to remain open, questions that permitted a plurality of answers.

Hindu intellectual tradition has dealt in various ways with this pluralistic situation. Some have accepted it as a matter of fact and simply pursued their own path without looking left or right. Others have taken a defensive stance and polemicized to vindicate the truth—often absolute, final, *siddhānta*—of their own school of thought. Still others again have made a scholarly study of the whole of it, seeing a kind of complementarity of viewpoints. Among the classical writers Vācaspati Miśra deserves mentioning: he wrote scholarly commentaries on most of the *darśanas*, entering, as it were into the spirit of each and clarifying its teachings. Among the modern writers S. Radhakrishnan comes to mind, whose catholicity of thought was able to see the essential unity of Hindu thought behind the diversity of systems.[16]

HINDU PHILOSOPHY OR HINDU THEOLOGY?

Neither "philosophy" nor "theology" (whatever these terms may mean today) is an adequate translation for the Indian term *darśana.*[17] *Darśanas* contain psychology and physics, exegesis of Vedic texts and speculation about language, psycho-physical practices as well as meditation, and much more. They demonstrate another type of intellectual approach to the world, alternatives not only to the answers given, but to the very questions asked by the Western tradition. We are only slowly beginning to appreciate and to understand them. The reason for dealing with them here in this book is that without exception they identify their raison d'être as leading to an ultimate existential ("religious") aim and that they represent the cumulative reflection of Hinduism through the ages.

A common characteristic of all *darśanas* is that at some time their basic teachings were condensed into sūtras, "leading threads," which helped to express precisely the content of the systems in a technical terminology and also served as texts for students to memorize. Instruction would largely consist of commenting upon the pithy sūtras and expanding on the meaning of the terms used in them, pointing out differences between one's own system and others and providing proof for the truth of the sūtra. Because many of the sūtras are (almost) unintelligible without a commentary and explanation, often the commentary (*bhāṣya*) has become the most important exposition of a system. These *bhāṣyas* in turn have become the object of subcommentaries (*vṛttis* and *ṭīkas*) and further glosses (*ṭippaṇīs*), which constitute the material an expert in that particular branch of learning has to study. Hindu scholars have invented most peculiar names for their subcommentaries and glosses.[18] The sūtras we possess today are not always the oldest texts of the schools and they are not always the work of the authors to whom they are ascribed. But they can be relied upon as containing the gist of the teaching of the systems and providing the technical terminology for each.

And here we encounter another peculiarity. The basic vocabulary is shared by virtually all six *darśanas*. But the meaning given to the terms and the place value accorded to each is very different. This situation has lead to the necessity of specializing in one specific *darśana* rather than calling oneself a philosopher or a theologian of Hinduism. Each *darśana* possesses a highly technical terminology; often new terms are coined or very specific meanings are given to terms used otherwise, a terminology that one does not pick up by learning classical Sanskrit and reading courtly Sanskrit literature. Traditional Indian scholars who specialize in a *darśana* indicate in their academic title their specialization,[19] and they would not consider themselves competent to instruct in other fields.

Reading into a text of a specific *darśana* resembles in many ways the learning of a new language: familiar as the sounds of the words may be, their meaning has to be learned anew and must not be confused with that of other systems.

Representations of "Indian philosophy" in English often restrict themselves to describing those elements from the Hindu *darśanas* that have a parallel in contemporary Western philosophy and leave out the rest.[20] This not only gives a slanted impression of Hindu thought, it often deprives the student of the most valuable lessons to be learned from such a study, the really original and specific contributions to human thought India has made. Although restrictions of space and considerations of accessibility do not allow us to go into much technical detail of the Hindu *darśanas* in the following chapters, the description attempts to convey the idea that Hindu *darśanas* offer not only parallels to Western thought but contain also novel elements for which there are no parallels. Translations of many of the major texts as well as specialized studies are available for a more detailed investigation.[21]

The enumeration and combination of the *darśanas* follows the traditional schema, which has been accepted for at least the past 1,000 years. In works like Mādhava's *Sarva-darśana-saṁgraha* many other *darśanas* are mentioned that do not find place among the six described here.[22] Also the designation of the classical *darśanas* has not always been the same in Indian history. Thus *Nyāya* was used in former times to designate the system today called *Mīmāṁsā, Yoga* was used as a name for *Vaiśeṣika, Anvīkṣikī* designated our *Nyāya,* and so on.[23] Information like this may not appear of great significance for a reader who is looking for basic information on the Hindu systems, but it will be of importance for those who consult sources and wish to learn more about the history of each *darśana.* Doing so they will discover that the description offered here focuses on what might be called the "classical phase" of each *darśana.* Much of the origin and early development has yet to be uncovered, conflicting views found in older sources have to be reconciled. More recent developments often go off in many different directions and have become much too intricate to permit a nontechnical summary.

This enumeration does not represent an evaluation. Each of the following systems considers itself the best suited to achieving its aim. India's intellectual history over the past millennium (and before) consists of sustained debates between the *āstika* and *nāstika darśanas* as well as between the adherents of the *ṣaḍdarśanas,* and between rival schools of one and the same *darśana.* Even texts that are not explicitly polemical—and many are!—contain innumerable references to and attacks against other systems. Precision in expression and incisiveness of thought were qualities aimed at by all professional Hindu thinkers. The English translation of texts does not do full justice to this aspect of Indian systematics because it has to fill in many words and circumscribe many terms to provide an intelligible text for readers not steeped in the subtleties of an intellectual tradition that enjoyed prestige and renown already at a time when Greek thought was only beginning to form and crystallize. It is not without significance that in our age Western scientists of repute like H. Weyl, E. Schrödinger, C. F. van Weizsäcker, D. Bohm, and many others discover parallels between modern scientific thinking and some of the Hindu *darśanas.* Some contemporary Western logicians and linguistic philosophers avidly dig into the intricacies of *Mīmāṃsā* and *Nyāya. Yoga,* too, is now widely studied and practiced all the world over. If we can learn from India it is certainly from the *śaḍdarśanas,* which can teach us some valuable lessons both in areas in which we feel competent and in areas unknown to us and so far unmapped.

The very notion of philosophy, which has acquired in the West the meaning of independent systematic and critical thought, of coherent reflection and sustained argumentation has to be used with qualifications when applied to "Indian philosophy." As the student of the major histories of Indian philosophy, such as S. N. Dasgupta's, S. Radhakrishnan's or M. Hiriyanna's scholarly accounts, will discover soon, Indian philosophy as a whole is not separate from Indian theology: systematic thought in India has been pursued throughout with the aim of finding salvation. The specializations within Indian philosophy—physics and logic, anthropology and metaphysics, and so on—again do not correspond to the Western notions employed.

Using technical terms coined by the Western cultural tradition to describe the thinking and systematizing of Indian traditions is at one time unavoidable and misleading. Unavoidable, because these are the terms we know and understand. Risky, because they have connotations not wholly appropriate. Thus, writing on "logic in the West and in India" Kuppuswāmī Sastri remarks: "Those who are familiar with Western logic and desirous of studying Indian logic from a historical and comparative point of view will do well to bear in mind the fact that, while one may find striking parallels in the Indian and Western systems of logic, one would not be misled by such parallels and lose sight of the fundamental differences in respect of scope and method, which Indian logic discloses in its rise and development, as compared with Western logic."[24]

The six "orthodox" systems have been grouped in three pairs from early times. The reason for doing this is in most cases quite clear: they complement each other in various ways. However, it should not be overlooked that each of them was developed as a quite independent system, capable of achieving its aims by its own methods.

THE *ṢAḌDARŚANAS* AND MODERN WESTERN PHILOSOPHY

A large number of traditional Indian scholars, usually called *paṇḍits* or *śāstris*, mainly through the medium of Sanskrit, still keep the knowledge of the *ṣaḍdarśanas* alive. Their contributions to the translation and interpretation of Sanskrit texts is indispensable, as most Indologists would readily admit. Usually they are attached to vernacular schools of traditional learning, *āśramas* and *pathaśālas*, but also modern Indian universities usually employ some in their departments of philosophy or Sanskrit. Their knowledge of detail of the particular specialty in which they hold their degrees is unsurpassed. They usually begin their training at age 4 and by the time they get their degrees they have memorized hundreds of substantial philosophical texts, which they can recall instantly. They are able to identify implicit references in texts without referring to any written source and can reproduce quotes with incredible speed and accuracy. They have their own gatherings, the *śāstrārthas*, to debate problems that arise in the understanding of certain points of traditional doctrine. Until recently, however, most of them kept away from contact with exponents of non-Indian systems of thought.

In this context M. P. Rege from the University of Poona took a bold and innovative step by arranging in 1983 a *saṃvāda*, a dialogue between Western trained Indian professors of philosophy and traditional Indian paṇḍits of *Nyāya*, followed by similar conferences in subsequent years in Tirupati on *Mīmāṃsā*, and in Śrīnagar on Kāśmīr Śaivism.[25] To everybody's surprise and delight the paṇḍits not only agreed to participate in such ventures but made original and meaningful contributions to this philosophical dialogue. While for the past several centuries the major preoccupation of Indian traditional scholars had been to preserve the tradition and to appropriate the past, there is now an endeavor to take up the challenge and further develop the tradition for the future. India's philosophical tradition has developed over the centuries such a richness of approaches and has dealt with so many issues that time and again one discovers not only uncanny parallels to modern Western thought but also a great many novel ideas and insights that lead to fruitful new areas of enquiry.

25 Hindu Logic and Physics: *Nyāya-Vaiśeṣika*

> The Supreme Good results from the knowledge, produced by a particular *dharma*, of the essence of the predicables: substance, attribute, action, genus, species, and combination, by means of their resemblances and differences.
>
> —*Vaiśeṣika Sūtra* I,1,4

The *Vaiśeṣika Sūtras*, ascribed to Kaṇāda, are, in the words of Dasgupta, "probably the oldest that we have and in all probability are pre-Buddhistic."[1] That does not entitle us, however, to make any statement about the age of the system itself, which is known particularly for its interesting early atomistic theory and its classification of categories. *Vaiśeṣika* may initially have been a school of Vedic thought, as its emphasis on dharma and its traditional opinion on *adṛṣṭa* as its fruit would suggest.[2] The book that, in addition to the sūtras, contains the most complete representation of the system, the *Daśapadārtha Śāstra,* is no older than the sixth century C.E.[3]

Several recent works deal with *Nyāya-Vaiśeṣika* as if it were one single system.[4] Though they have much in common and supplement each other in many areas, they began as separate systems with quite different aims. Kuppuswāmi Sastri has this to say on the conjunction of *Nyāya-Vaiśeṣika*: "That Indian logic is usually described as the *Nyāya-Vaiśeṣika* system is not because it is the result of the syncretism of the two opposing systems—*Nyāya* realism and Atomistic pluralism; rather it is so described because at a very early stage in the history of Indian logic, the *Vaiśeṣika* stress on the inductive phase of inference came to be synthesised with its deductive phase in the *Nyāya* theory of syllogistic reasoning."[5]

The recent Western philosophical preoccupation with logic, especially under the influence of the Anglo-American school of linguistic analysis, brought about an extensive and intensive study of *Nyāya* texts during the last few decades. Much of it is far too technical and too difficult to summarize as to find a place in this survey. The interested reader is asked to consult the more specialized books available.[6]

The beginnings of the *Nyāya* systems may go back to the disputations of Vedic scholars; already in the times of the Upaniṣads debating was cultivated as an art, following certain rules in which the basic elements of logical proofs were contained.[7] The *Nyāya Sūtras,* ascribed to Gautama, the main text of the school, have received very important commentaries. They cannot be assigned to a definite date. All scholars agree that a considerable part of the sūtras consists of additions to an original work, additions that suggest early Buddhist interpolations and later Hindu insertions to invalidate the Buddhist arguments. From the probable identification of *nyāya* with the *anvīkṣikī* in Kauṭilīya's *Artha-śāstra*[8] we may assume that the *Nyāya* system already existed in some form in the fourth century B.C.E. Kuppuswami Sastri mentions some more references that prove that "these two schools should have appeared in a fairly definite form with their characteristic methods of reasoning and metaphysics by the middle of the fourth century B.C.E. though the chief doctrines of these schools came to be systematized and redacted in their basic sūtras at a relatively later date."[9] Followers of the *Nyāya* system have produced a large body of important works, and of all the Hindu systems, *Nyāya* enjoys the greatest respect on the part of Western philosophers, who are coming to discover the enormous subtleties and intricacies of Indian logic.

A BRIEF SUMMARY OF *VAIŚEṢIKA*

"Now an explanation of *dharma*" begins the Kaṇāda Sūtra. "The means to prosperity and salvation is *dharma.*" The attainment of salvation is the result of the cognition of the six categories of substance, quality, action, class concept, particularity, and inherence.[10] The substances are earth, water, fire, air, ether, time, space, *ātman,* and mind. The qualities are taste, color, odor, touch, number, measure, separation, contact, disjoining, prior and posterior, understanding, pleasure and pain, desire and aversion, and volitions.

Action (karma) is explained as upward movement, downward movement, contraction, expansion, horizontal movement. The feature common to substance, quality, and action is that they are existent, noneternal, and substantive; they effect, cause, and possess generality and particularity. A major part of the sūtra consists in a further elucidation of the various terms just mentioned, much in the same way in which the early Greek philosophers of nature analyzed and described the elements, their qualities, and the interrelations. In the third book the sūtra deals with the inference of the existence of the *ātman*, which is impervious to sense perception, from the fact that there must be some substance in which knowledge, produced by the contact of the senses and their objects, inheres. Therefore the *ātman*'s existence may be inferred from inhalation and exhalation, from the twinkling of the eyes, from life, from movements of the mind, from sense affections, from pleasure and pain, will, antipathy and effort. It can be proven that it is a substance and eternal. Eternal (*nitya*) is that which exists but has no cause for its existence. The noneternal is *avidyā*, ignorance.

In the seventh book we are told that *dṛṣṭa*, insight based on observation and rationality, is able to explain even natural phenomena only up to a certain point. All the special phenomena of nature are caused by *adṛṣṭa*, an unknown invisible cause. *Adṛṣṭa* is also said to be the cause of the union of body and soul, of rebirth and of liberation. This "invisible fruit," which is the cause of ultimate happiness, is produced by ablutions, fasting, continence, life in the guru's family, life in the forest, sacrifice, gifts and alms, observation of the cosmic cycle, and following the rules of dharma. Thus *Vaiśeṣika* places itself quite explicitly in the tradition of Vedic orthodoxy. The sūtra also discusses at some length the means and instruments of valid knowledge, topics dealt with more thoroughly in the sister system of *Nyāya*. The *Vaiśeṣika Sūtras* contain no polemics against the Buddhists, although these are opposed to some of their quite fundamental tenets: Buddhism denies the "thing in itself" and explains all phenomena merely as a chain of conditions that ultimately can be reduced to nonexistence; the Vaiśeṣikas, on the contrary, hold fast to the real existence of things.

Later works of the school, the commentaries on the sūtra by Śaṅkara Miśra and Candrakānta, the *Padārtha-dharma-saṅgraha* by Praśastapāda, and the *Daśa-padārthī* by Maticandra (preserved only in a Chinese version) also give a more detailed explanation of Indian atomism. What we hear, feel, see, and so forth are not continua but discreta (quanta we would say today), and these again are not units but compounds of infinitely small indivisible parts (*aṇu*) that clearly differ from one another. Things are products, therefore, and not eternal.

The primordial elements, earth, water, fire, and air, are partly eternal, partly temporal. Only ether is completely eternal. The first four elements have mass, number, weight, fluidity, viscosity, velocity, characteristic potential color, taste, smell, or touch. *Ākāśa,* space or ether, is absolutely inert and structureless, being only the substratum of *śabda* or sound, which is thought to travel like a wave in the medium of air. Atomic combinations are possible only with the four basic elements. Both in dissolution and before creation, the atoms exist singly; in creation they are always present in combination. Two atoms combine to form a *dvyaṇuka,* a molecule. Also *tryaṇukas, caturaṇukas,* and so on, that is, aggregates consisting of three or more molecules, are possible. Atoms are possessed of an inherent incessant vibratory motion; but they are also under the influence of the *adṛṣṭa,* the will of Īśvara, who arranges them into a harmonic universe. Changes in substances, which are limited within the frame of possible atom combinations, are brought about by heat. Under the impact of heat corpuscles, a molecule may disintegrate and the characters of the atoms composing it may change. The heat particles that continue to impinge on the individually changed atoms also cause them to reunite in different forms so that definite changes are effected through heat. In many details the *Vaiśeṣikas* reveal a keen observation of nature and describe in their books a great number of phenomena, which they try to explain with the help of their atom theory. Similar to modern physicists, the ancient *Vaiśeṣikas* explained heat and light rays as consisting of indefinitely small particles that dart forth or radiate in all directions rectilineally with inconceivable velocity. Heat also penetrates the interatomic space or impinges on the atoms and rebounds, thus explaining the conducting and reflecting of heat. All the *paramāṇus* are thought to be spherical. Attempts have been made to link the atomism of the Vaiśeṣika *darśana* with Democritus—so far without any positive evidence.

Leaving out most of the technicalities of the system, a brief explanation of *viśeṣa*—the term that gave the name to the whole system—may give an idea of the specific approach taken by this school of classical Indian philosophy.[11]

Praśastapāda writes:

> *Viśeṣas* are the ultimate specificatives or differentiatives of their substrates. They reside in such beginningless and indestructible eternal

> substances as the atoms, *ākāśa*, time, space, *ātman*, and *manas*—inhering in their entirety in each of these, and serving as the basis of absolute differentiation of specification. Just as we have with regard to the bull as distinguished from the horse, certain distinct cognitions—such, for instance as (a) that is a 'bull', which is a cognition based upon its having the shape of other bulls, (b) that it is 'white', which is based upon a quality, (c) that it is 'running swiftly', which is based upon action, (d) that it has a 'fat hump', which is based upon 'constituent parts' and (e) that it carries a 'large bell', which is based upon conjunction; so have the Yogis, who are possessed of powers that we do not possess, distinct cognitions based upon similar shapes, similar qualities and similar actions—with regard to the eternal atoms, the liberated selves and minds; and as in this case no other cause is possible, those causes by reason whereof they have such distinct cognitions—as that 'this is a peculiar substance', 'that a peculiar self' and so forth—and which also lead to the recognition of one atom as being the same that was perceived at a different time and place—are what we call the *visesas*.[12]

According to the teaching of the Vaiśeṣikas, there are many different *ātmans* distinguished by their relative and specific *viśeṣas*. The common person, however, is able to recognize their diversity only on account of externally perceptible actions, qualities and so on. Only the Yogi has the "insight into the essence of the soul itself and thus into the real cause of their diversity." The *ātman* is eternal and not bound to space and time. But the actions of *ātman*,—thought, will, emotions—are limited to the physical organism with which it is united at a given time. *Jñāna*, knowledge, is according to the Vaiśeṣikas only an accident of *ātman*, not one's nature as such, because in dreamless sleep there is no cognition. Emotions and will are, likewise, mere accidents. The "spiritual" is not substantial but accidental. *Manas*, the mind given to every *ātman*, is merely its instrument and does not produce anything of itself. On the other hand, the cooperation of *manas* is necessary.

The state of *mokṣa* or freedom "is neither a state of pure knowledge nor of bliss, but a state of perfect qualitylessness, in which the self remains in itself in its own purity. It is the negative state of absolute painlessness."[13] Concerning the way to reach it we read in the *Daśa-padārtha Śāstra*:

> One who seeks eternal emancipation ought to devote himself to *śīla*, or morality, *dāna* or liberality, *tapas* or austerities, and *yoga*. From these comes supreme merit which leads to the attainment of emancipation

> and *tattva-jñāna*, or knowledge of ultimate truth. 'Prosperity' is enjoyment of pleasure in *svarga* or heaven. Knowledge of ultimate truth brings *mokṣa*, or permanent liberation, when merit and demerit have been completely destroyed and *ātman* and *manas* no longer come in contact with each other, that is when the nine things are no longer produced.[14]

Dharma and *adharma* together form *adṛṣṭa* which supports the cycle of *saṃsāra*, of attraction and aversion, and continuously drives the *ātman* back into bodily existence. The activity guided by the feeling of the particular existence depends on *avidyā*; when a person realizes that things as such are only varying combinations of atoms of the particular elements, all affection and aversion ceases. If the right knowledge of the self is achieved, egotism and all selfish activity ceases. When *adṛṣṭa* is no longer produced, the transmigratory cycle comes to an end. On the other hand, *ātman* is never completely without *adṛṣṭa*, because the series of births is beginningless. When the soul has rid itself of its gross body it still is and remains attached to the subtle body, even in *pralaya*, the dissolution of the universe. Time, place, and circumstances of birth, family, and duration of life are all determined by *adṛṣṭa*, and it is not possible ever to destroy it completely.

Kaṇāda's sūtras do not require the idea of an *īśvara*. The substances are eternal; movement is due to the impersonal, eternal principle of *adṛṣṭa*. Later authors introduce an eternal, omniscient and omnipresent Īśvara who is responsible for the universal order of atoms and their movements. This *Vaiśeṣika* God, however, resembles very much the *deus otiosus* of deism. *Ātman* and the *aṇu* do not owe their existence to a creator, they are eternal and independent. Īśvara differs from the *ātman* only insofar as he is never entangled in *saṃsāra*. He gives laws to the world but never interferes with it subsequently. He winds the clock and lets it run its course.

NYĀYA AND *NAVYA-NYĀYA*:

Nyāya was, even in ancient times, composed of two parts: *adhyātma-vidyā*, or metaphysics, and *tarka-śāstra*, or rules of debate, often simply called *logic*. Thus the *Nyāya Sūtra*, famous for its acute analysis of discursive thought as such, also has substantial sections on suffering, soul, and salvation. It begins with the following aphorism: "It is the knowledge of the true character of the following sixteen categories that leads to the attainment of the highest good: (1) The Means of Right Cognition; (2) The Objects of Right Cognition; (3) Doubt; (4) Motive; (5) Example; (6) Theory; (7) Factors of Inference; (8) Cogitation; (9) Demonstrated Truth; (10) Discussion; (11) Disputation; (12) Wrangling; (13) Fallacious Reason; (14) Casuistry; (15) Futile Rejoinder and (16) Clinchers."

Logic here is practiced for the sake of salvation. That gives greater weight to the *Nyāya Sūtra* within Hinduism than a book on logic would normally have within a religious tradition. Logic as a way to truth is a means of liberation: "Suffering, birth, activity, mistaken notions, folly—if these factors are cancelled out in reverse order, there will be *mokṣa*."[15]

S. K. Sarma makes an important point when he states: "*Nyāya* is not logic in the strict sense of the word. It is a system of philosophy. It is true that it lays stress on inference or reasoning as a means to correct knowledge, but it is not formal. It is not a mere device for correct thinking, but a well-thought-out and complete metaphysical thesis."[16]

A definite break in the development of *Nyāya* took place in the twelfth century, which marks the rise of *Navya-Nyāya* or the new logic. Whereas the earlier works had been concentrating on the elucidation of the categories, as enumerated in the *Nyāya Sūtra*, the *Tattva-cintāmaṇi* by Gaṅgeśa, the major work of the new school emphasized the *pramāṇas*, the means of valid cognition, devoting one chapter each to perception (*pratyakṣa*), inference (*anumāna*), analogy (*upamāna*), and verbal testimony (*śabda*).

In spite of the intention to keep the description nontechnical it may be remarked that *Navya-Nyāya* not only developed a highly complex epistemology but also created a technical language with the help of newly coined terms and thus initiated a quite peculiar style of philosophical writing in India that stands out for its brevity and precision. The development of *Navya-Nyāya* and the focus upon *pramāṇas* instead on the categories of the *Nyāya Sūtra* did not prevent the continued production of works of the "old school" alongside the flourishing "new logic." Works in both branches keep appearing, even in our day.

The special field of *Navya-Nyāya* is epistemology. It acknowledges four legitimate means of finding truth: *pratyakṣa*, or sense perception; *anumāna*, or inference; *upamāna*, or analogy; and *śabda*, or scriptural authority. *Pratyakṣa* is the perception that results from the contact of one of the senses with its proper object: it is definite, uncontradicted, and unassociated with names. *Anumāna* is of three kinds: *pūrvavat,* or from cause to effect; *śeṣavat,* or from effect to cause; and *sāmānyato dṛṣṭa,* or from common characteristics. *Upamāna* is the knowing of anything by similarity with any well-known thing. *Śabda* is defined as the testimony of reliable authority, which may also transcend one's own experience.

The objects of knowledge are *ātman,* the body, senses, sense objects, *buddhi* or understanding; *manas,* or mind; *pravṛtti,* or endeavour; rebirths, enjoying pleasure and suffering pain, sorrow and liberation. Desire, aversion, effort, pleasure and pain, as well as knowledge, indicate the existence of the *ātman.* Whereas the classical Aristotelian syllogism has three members—major, minor and conclusion—the Nyāya syllogism has five:

1. *pratijñā,* or the stating of the point to be proved;
2. *hetu,* or the reason that establishes the proof;
3. *udahāraṇa,* or illustrative example;
4. *upanaya,* or corroboration by the instance;
5. *nigamana,* or inference, identical with the initial assertion.

The standard example of Indian logic for many centuries has been the following:

The mountain there in the distance is ablaze (1);
Because it is wreathed in smoke (2);
Whatever is wreathed in smoke is on fire, as for example a stove (3);
The mountain there is wreathed in smoke in such a manner (4);
Therefore, the mountain there in the distance is ablaze (5).

The discussion of fallacies and doubt demonstrates the lucidity and sharpness of the Naiyāyikas' intellects. All kinds of fallacies are analyzed and the causes of doubt are explained, but the general skepticism of the Buddhists, who maintained that nothing can be known with certainty, is refuted. The polemics against Buddhism, especially the *Śūṇya-vādins,* plays a large part in *Nyāya* literature. Naiyāyikas dissolve the extreme skepticism of the Buddhists with their critical realism and take the wind out of the Buddhists' sails by disproving their teaching of emptiness and the impossibility of true cognition with the very arguments the Buddhists have used. The Naiyāyikas seek to demonstrate that real liberation is possible through true cognition of reality. They largely agree with the Vaiśeṣika metaphysics when they define *mokṣa* only in negative terms as "absolute freedom from pain."[17] It is a "condition of immortality, free from fear, imperishable," to be attained only after bodily death—there can be no *jīvan-mukta*.[18]

Quite unique in Indian philosophy are the arguments for the existence of Īśvara, which we find in Nyāya works.[19] The *Nyāya Kusumañjalī* states that the experience of contingency, eternity, diversity, activity and individual existence requires an *adṛṣṭa*, an unseen cause, responsible ultimately for the joys and sorrows of human life. Above the *adṛṣṭa* of the Vaiśeṣikas, the Naiyāyikas postulate a Lord as the cause of right knowledge, of creation and destruction. "From effects, combination, support, etc. and traditional arts, authority, *śruti*, and so on, an everlasting omniscient being must be assumed." The commentary on this text explains:

> The earth etc. must have had a maker, because they have the nature of effects like a jar; by a thing's having a maker we mean that it is produced by some agent who possesses the wish to make, and has also a perceptive knowledge of the material cause out of which it is to be made. 'Combination' is an action, and therefore the action which produced the conjunction of two atoms, initiating the *dvyaṇuka* at the beginning of a creation, must have been accompanied by the volition of an intelligent being, because it has the nature of an action like the actions of bodies such as ours. 'Support' etc.: the world depends upon some being who possesses a volition which hinders it from falling, because it has the nature of being supported. . . . By traditional arts etc.: The traditional arts now current, such as that of making cloth, must have been originated by an independent being, from the very fact that they are traditional usages like the tradition of modern modes of writing. 'From authority': The knowledge produced by the Vedas is produced by a virtue residing in its cause, because it is right knowledge, just as in the case in the right knowledge produced by perception. 'From *śruti*': The *Veda* must have been produced by a person, from its having the nature of a *Veda* like the *Ayur Veda*. . . . At the beginning of creation there must be the number of duality abiding in the atoms, which is the cause of the measure of the *dvyaṇuka* but this number cannot be produced at that time by the distinguishing perception of beings like ourselves. Therefore we can only assume this distinguishing faculty as then existing in Īśvara.[20]

The Lord is qualified by absence of *adharma*, of *mithyā-jñāna*, or false knowledge, and of *pramāda*, or error, and the positive presence of dharma, right knowledge and equanimity. He is omnipotent, though influenced in his actions by the acts of his creatures.

He acts only for the good of his creatures and acts toward them like a father toward his children.[21] The Naiyāyikas also develop a theory of grace:"Īśvara indeed supports the efforts of people, i.e. if a person tries to attain something special, it is Īśvara who attains it; if Īśvara does not act, the activity of people is fruitless."

A good deal of *Nyāya* is so technical that it taxes the understanding of even a specialist in Western logic, not to speak of the general reader. Much of it is of interest mainly against the background of inner-Indian disputes, especially with the Buddhist logicians. It is, however, important to note that India, too, has its schools of critical logicians and that, despite the popular opinion of Indian philosophy being merely opaque mysticism, there is also the disciplined reasoning of logic.

Tarka-śāstra, the study of formal logic, is a difficult business and no more popular in India than anywhere else. Keśava Miśra of the fourteenth century, the author of a concise textbook that is still widely used, starts off his course in the following gruff manner: "I am writing this 'Exposition of Reasoning' consisting, as it does, of short and easy explanations of arguments, for the sake of the dull youth who wishes to have to learn as little as possible for the purpose of entering the portals of the Nyāya *darśana.*"[22]

Nyāya-vaiśeṣika has remained a living philosophical tradition even in our age. The more it is studied, the more respect it commands for its incisiveness and brilliance of definition. It could also possibly make a substantial contribution to the contemporary philosophy of science, anticipating, often by many centuries, problems that we are only now discovering.

26 Hindu Psychology and Metaphysics: *Sāṁkhya-Yoga*

Absolute freedom comes when the *guṇas,* becoming devoid of the object of the *puruṣa,* become latent; or the power or consciousness becomes established in its own nature.

—*Pātañjala Yoga Sūtra* IV, 34

Yoga is one of the most popular and most ambiguous words in Indian literature, a word with which every Westerner seems to be familiar, as the advertisements of numerous Yoga schools suggest. Etymologically the word is derived from the root *yuj-,* to join, to unite. Pāniṇi, the grammarian, explains the meaning of *yoga* as virtually identical with that of our word *religion,* union with the Supreme. Patañjali, in his *Yoga Sūtra,* defines *yoga* as "cessation of all changes in consciousness." According to the Vedāntins *yoga* means the return of the *jīvātman,* the individual being, to its union with the *paramātman,* the Supreme Self. In a more general sense Hindu scriptures use the word *yoga* as a synonym to *mārga,* denoting any system of religion or philosophy, speaking of *karma-yoga, bhakti-yoga, jñāna-yoga.*

We propose here only to deal with *yoga* in its technical and classical sense; with the Yoga system as explained by Patañjali. The system is called *Rāja Yoga,* the "royal way" in contrast to *Haṭha Yoga,* the "tour de force"[1] of most Western Yoga schools, or the *Kuṇḍalinī Yoga* of the Śāktas, mentioned before. It is also called *Sāṁkhya-Yoga,* because of its intimate connection with the *darśana* known as *Sāṁkhya*[2]

HISTORICAL SURVEY

Sāṁkhya-Yoga is possibly the oldest among the Indian systems. It has become, in one form of another, part and parcel of most major religions of India: hence we find *Sāṁkhya-Yoga* combined with Vaiṣṇavism, Śaivism, and Śāktism, and most of the Purāṇas contain numerous chapters on *Sāṁkhya-Yoga* as a path to salvation.[3] It fell into disfavor at a later time when *Vedānta* in one of its denominational schools became the predominant theology of Hinduism. The reasons for this development are twofold. First, *Sāṁkhya* does not base its statements on scripture; it even explicitly rates *śruti* no higher than reasoning. Second, it did not recognize a Lord above *puruṣa* and *prakṛti*, an idea that was crucial to the theistic systems of mediaeval Hinduism.

The interpretation of some Mohenjo-daro seals showing figures in what has been interpreted as yoga posture would suggest a prehistoric root of practices later brought together in the *Yoga* system. The basis of the *Sāṁkhya*, the male-female polarity as the source of all development, does not need a specific 'inventor', it can easily be considered a "natural system." In some of the earlier Upaniṣads we find allusions to doctrines that could be termed *Sāṁkhya*, leaving open the question whether the Upaniṣads used an already developed philosophical system or whether the system developed out of the elements provided in the Upaniṣads. To explain the name *Sāṁkhya*—in modern Indian languages the word for "number"—some scholars have resorted to the hypothesis of an original *Sāṁkhya* that, like the school of Pythagoras, was concerned with numbers and conceived of the world as being constructed from harmonious proportions.[4] S. N. Dasgupta sees, moreover, a close inner relationship between *Sāṁkhya-Yoga* and Buddhism. He writes: "*Sāṁkhya* and the *Yoga*, like the Buddhists, hold that experience is sorrowful. *Tamas* represents the pain-substance. As *tamas* must be present in some degree in all combinations, all intellectual operations are fraught with some degree of painful feeling."[5] The original meaning of *Sāṁkhya* must have been very general: understanding, reflection, discussion, so that the name simply came to connote philosophy or system. Kapila, its mythical founder, figures in the Indian tradition quite often as the father of philosophy as such. Later *Vedānta*, which assumes a different position on many basic issues, polemizes quite frequently against the *Sāṁkhya* system, but there is hardly a book that does not deal with it or that would not betray its influence.

Sāṁkhya ideas may be found already in the cosmogonic hymns of the Ṛgveda, in sections of the Atharvaveda, in the idea of the evolution of all things from one principle, dividing itself, in the

Upaniṣads and also in the Upaniṣadic attempts to arrange all phenomena under a limited number of categories. The Mahābhārata has sections explaining the full *Sāṁkhya* system, though with significant differences as compared to the classical *Sāṁkhya*. The Great Epic makes Kapila the son of Brahmā; according to the *Bhāgavata Purāṇa* he is an *avatāra* of Viṣṇu who teaches *Sāṁkhya* as a system of liberation through which his mother reaches instant release.[6] There is not much historical evidence for the opinion, found in some works on Indian philosophy, that as a historical person Kapila belongs to the sixth century B.C.E. The oldest traditional textbook of the school is the *Sāṁkhya-karikā* of Īśvara Kṛṣṇa, dating probably from the third century C.E. This work, which has received numerous important commentaries in later centuries, claims to be the complete summary of the entire *Ṣaṣṭi-tantra*, perhaps an older work. The *Sāṁkhyakarikā* are a short treatise, containing only seventy aphorisms.[7] The *Sāṁkhya-sūtra*, ascribed to Kapila himself, is a later work, much longer than the *Karikā* and going into more detail.[8]

Yoga as a system is already dealt with quite extensively in some of the later Upaniṣads, which in fact are sometimes brief compendia of Yoga.[9] The *Tejobindu Upaniṣad* gives a rather detailed description of *raja-yoga*. Many of the teachings found in it can be discovered word for word in Patañjali's *Yoga Sūtra*, which has become the classical textbook, commented upon by great scholars like Vyāsa and Bhoja.[10] This Upaniṣad suggests to the Yogi, who is intent on realization, to repeat constantly: "I am Brahman." He is advised sometimes to affirm and sometimes to negate the identity of all things with *brahman*. "Renouncing all the various activities think thus: 'I am Brahman—I am of the nature of *sac-cid-ānanda*.' And then renounce even this!"[11]

Most Indian schools, be they followers of the *Sāṁkhya* or of the *Vedānta* philosophy, accept *Patañjali-yoga* as a practical and indispensable means for purification and concentration. In 1952 a commentary to the Patañjali *Yoga Sūtra*, ascribed to Sankara, has been published from a manuscript in Madras. Many scholars assume it to be genuine, in spite of the polemic against *Sāṁkhya-Yoga* in the *Brahmasūtrabhāyṣa*.[12]

THE BASIC PHILOSOPHY OF *SĀṀKHYA*

The Sāṁkhya Karikās begin with the aphorism: "From torment by three-fold misery the inquiry into the means of terminating it."[13]

Our frustrations and pains, caused by *devas* and *asuras,* fellow people, beasts and inanimate objects as well as by oneself[14] are the stimulus for the quest for freedom from misery: *Sāṁkhya* offers the solution. *Sāṁkhya* denies neither the reality of experience nor the reality of pain accompanying every experience, but it offers a possibility of terminating this pain of experience. Rejecting all other means, the *Karikās* establish the thesis that "the discriminative knowledge of the evolved, the unevolved and the knower is the means of surpassing all sorrow."[15]

Basically *Sāṁkhya* defends, or rather presupposes, a dualistic realism. There are two beginningless realities: *prakṛti* and *puruṣa,* the female and the male principle, matter and spirit. Ideally, before the development of concrete existences, they exist separately in polarity. In actual existence they are combined and interacting. *Puruṣa,* in itself pure consciousness, experiences the changes that *prakṛti,* on account of its three *guṇas,* is undergoing, as if these were its own. *Puruṣas* are originally many—*prakṛti* is originally one. The association with a *puruṣa* makes *prakṛti,* as the evolved being, manifold and makes *puruṣa* interact with it. Under the influence of *puruṣa,* out of the unevolved primordial *prakṛti,* develop macrocosm and microcosm according to a fixed pattern. Each part of it is characterized in a different measure by the presence of the three *guṇas.* Originally the three *guṇas*—*sattva* or lightness, *rajas* or passion and *tamas* or darkness—had been in equilibrium in *prakṛti.* Under *puruṣa*'s influence the equilibrium is disturbed and evolution begins. The first product of this evolutionary process, which simply takes its course without needing a creator or a world soul, is *mahat,* the Great One, also called *buddhi,* the intellect. From *mahat* issues *ahaṁkāra,* the principle of individuation. Having the *tri-guṇa* structure, *mahat* communicates it to the further evolutes: the senses and the elements that form their object. The enumeration of the twenty-four basic elements is intended also to provide a physically correct description of the universe and prepare the ground for the way back to the source. Against those who assume that there is only one spirit in the universe, the *Karikās* establish the following argument: "The plurality of *puruṣas* follows from the fact of individual death and individual birth, and from the fact that the organs of cognition and action are individual; moreover not all people are active at the same time and the relationship of the three *guṇas* varies from person to person."[16] In *devas* and saintly people *sattva* dominates; in ordinary people, *rajas;* and in animals, *tamas.* To dispel the objection that *prakṛti* is mere fiction because it cannot be seen, heard, touched and so forth, the *Karikās* state: "The non-perception is due to its subtlety, not to its non-existence, since it is cognized from its effects."[17] Knowing *prakṛti* as *prakṛti* is becoming free from it; for *prakṛti* is not only the means to bind *puruṣa* but also the means to free it. A person who is able to analyze experience in such a way as to differentiate *puruṣa* from *prakṛti* in consciousness, seeing in *prakṛti* the reason for the contingence of all things and the basis for all change and multiplicity, is free. Though *puruṣa* is free by nature, one is incapable of acting and thus unable to free oneself when united with *prakṛti*. "Certainly no *puruṣa* is in bondage and none is liberated nor has he to undergo any changes; it is *prakṛti*, dwelling in many forms, which is bound, freed and subject to change. *Prakṛti* binds herself sevenfold and through one form she causes liberation for the benefit of *puruṣa*."[18] The *Karikās* compare *puruṣa* and *prakṛti* with a lame man being carried by a blind man: it is the seeing lame one that directs the blind walking one and realizes his own purpose. In another simile the *puruṣa* is compared to a spectator, observing a dancer. After the dancer has shown all her skills, she cannot but repeat her performance over and over again. The onlooker, becoming aware of the repeat performance, loses interest. And the dancer, seeing that the spectator pays no more attention to her, ceases to dance. Although the union still persists, nothing more is produced from it. "*Puruṣa*, because of former impressions, remains united with the body, just like the potter's wheel continues to rotate for a while without being impelled again, due to the impulse received before."[19]

When the separation from the body finally takes place and the aim has been fulfilled, *prakṛti* ceases to be active and *puruṣa* reaches *kaivalya*, aloneness, perfect freedom. By doing away with objective sense perception, by tracing back egoism and discursive reasoning to *prakṛti*, by coming to know the true nature of *prakṛti*, *puruṣa* becomes emancipated. Spirit, having been restless in connection with matter, realizes matter to be the cause of its restlessness. By realizing the nature of *prakṛti* as contrary to its own nature and recognizing all objective reality as but evolutes of *prakṛti* the spirit becomes self-satisfied and self-reliant. The very dissociation of *puruṣa* from *prakṛti* is its liberation.

THE THEORY AND PRACTICE OF YOGA

The practical process of discriminative knowledge leading to the actual achievement of the "isolation" of the puruṣa is proposed in

Patañjali's *Yoga Sūtras*. Yoga is not mere theoretical knowledge. It also implies physical training, exertion of will power and acts of decision, because it wants to deal with the complete human situation and provide real freedom, not just a theory of liberation.

The sūtra itself, a short work of but 194 aphorisms, is clearly structured into four *pādas*, with the subject-titles *samādhi, sādhana, vibhuti,* and *kaivalya*. The first sūtra, defining the aim and meaning of Yoga as *citta-vṛtti-nirodha*, goes to the very core of *Sāṁkhya* metaphysics. *Citta* is the same as the *mahat* of the *Sāṁkhya*, the first evolved, whose changes ultimately cause all suffering. For *citta* the cessation of all changes means merging into *prakṛti*. *Prakṛti* then becomes again undifferentiated and dissociated from *puruṣa*: the *puruṣa* achieves *ekagratā*, one-pointedness, *kaivalya*, aloneness, being with oneself only, being nothing but consciousness. The changes that may affect *citta* are enumerated as fivefold: perception, delusion, imagination, deep sleep and memory.[20] The means to do away with them is *abhyāsa* and *vairāgya*, the dialectic interaction of positive effort and renunciation. The *Yoga Sūtras* introduce Īśvara, the Lord, as one of the supports of concentration. Īśvara is defined as a *puruṣa*, untouched by suffering, activity, and karma. He is the teacher of the ancients and is denoted by the sign Om, whose constant repetition is recommended to the Yogi to attain *kaivalya*.[21] The Lord is also a help in removing the obstacles that hinder self-realization—sickness, suffering, indecision, carelessness, sloth, sensuality, false views, and inconstancy—that cause distraction. In the company of these distractions come pain, despair, tremor, hard and irregular breathing. For the purification of the mind the *Yoga Sūtra* recommends truthfulness, friendliness, compassion, and contentment together with indifference toward happiness and unhappiness, virtue and vice. Breath control, too, is recommended.

The second part of the *Yoga Sūtra*, dealing with *sādhana*, the means to liberation, begins with the aphorism: "The *yoga* of action is constituted by *tapas*, austerities, *svādhyāya*, or scriptural study, and *īśvara praṇi-dhāna*, meditation with the Lord as object." Its goal is to attain *samādhi*, which may be translated as blissful inner peace, and to terminate the *kleśas*, the frustrations and afflictions. The cause and source of all suffering is identified as *avidyā*, lack of insight and wisdom. It manifests itself in four principal forms, namely, as *āsmita*, egoism, *rāga*, attachment, *dveṣa*, aversion, and *abhiniveṣa*, love of physical life. *Avidyā* is further explained as mistaking the non-eternal for the eternal, the impure for the pure, the painful for the pleasurable, and the not-self for the Self.[22] To combat these afflictions the *Yoga Sūtras* commend *dhyāna* or meditation. The actual vehicle of liberation is *viveka*, discrimination, implying understanding of the Self as the only true and worthwhile being and the rest as illusory. This knowledge arises only after the impurities of the mind have been destroyed by the practice of the eight *yogāṇgas*, limbs of Yoga. These are *yama* and *niyama*, ethical commands and prohibitions, *āsana*, certain bodily postures, *prāṇayama*, breath control, *pratyāhāra*, withdrawal of the senses, *dhāraṇa*, concentration exercises, *dhyāna*, meditation, and *samādhi*, inner composure.

The *Yoga Sūtras* find that the cause of all sin lies in *lobha*, *moha*, and *krodha*, greed, delusion, and anger, whereas the practice of the virtues produce many side effects that are helpful either for the Yogi's own realization or for his fellows. Thus when *ahiṃsā*, nonviolence, is firmly established, others, too, will give up their enmity and violence in the presence of the Yogi; not only people but also animals will live peacefully with each other. When *satya*, the love of truth, is perfected, it enables a person to perform great deeds. When *asteya*, abstention from misappropriation is practiced, the treasures from which the Yogi runs away will run after him. When *brahmacarya*, perfect continence, is practiced, great strength will come to the Yogi. The practice of *aparigraha*, of generosity in the widest sense, brings with it a knowledge of the round of births. *Śauca*, or disgust with one's own body, is accompanied by the end of the desire to have bodily contact with others. Purity also helps to attain physical wellbeing, control over one's senses and concentration. *Santoṣa*, or contentment, brings inner peace and happiness to the Yogi. *Tapasya*, practice of austerities, purifies from sins and makes the Yogi acquire *siddhis* or supernatural faculties. Through *svādhyāya*, scriptural study, one can reach the *Īṣṭadevatā*. *Īśvara praṇidhāna*, surrender to the Lord, brings about *samādhi*, inner illumination.

Āsana, posture, is defined as a way of sitting that is agreeable and enables the practicant to sit motionless for a long while without falling asleep or straining. It is intended to overcome the distraction caused by the *dvandvas*, the pairs of opposites like heat and cold, hunger and thirst, comfort and discomfort. Although *Haṭha Yoga* manuals develop a veritable science of the *āsanas*, enumerating altogether eighty-four frequently extremely difficult bodily postures for curing or preventing diseases or attaining certain other results, Patañjali is of the opinion that any position will serve, provided that it allows a person to practice continued concentration and meditation: his aim is neither self-mortification for it own sake, nor the cure of bodily ailments, but spiritual realization.[23]

In the third *pāda* Patañjali speaks about the extraordinary or miraculous faculties of the Yogi, *siddhis* or *vibhutis* that appear as side effects of Yoga. Despite Patañjali's warning that they should not be cultivated, because they detract from the principal aim of Yoga as spiritual realization, a number of Yogis at all times have practiced Yoga for the sake of those *siddhis*: becoming invisible, reducing one's size to that of a grain of sand or increasing it to the volume of a mountain, adopting a radiant body or leaving the body and re-entering it at will.

Patañjali stresses the moral aspects of the preparation for *kaivalya*. If evil desires and intentions are not completely purged, there is the danger that the increased power a Yogi wins through concentration may be used for evil purposes, rather than for realization of the highest aim.

Dietetic rules are rather prominent in many books on Yoga; whatever is sour, salty, or pungent should be avoided. Non-stimulating food will allow the body to come to rest; milk alone is the ideal food for *Yogis*.

THE CORE OF YOGA

In the Yoga Sūtras one of the most important topics is *prāṇayama*. The great significance of *prāṇa*, or life breath, in philosophical speculation was mentioned earlier. *Prāṇayama* is one of the most widely practiced disciplines and one of the most ancient methods of purification. Perfect breath control can be carried so far that, to all appearances, a person does not breathe any more and the heartbeat becomes imperceptible. Hence we hear quite frequently about Yogis who are buried for days or weeks and let themselves be admired on coming out from their graves. According to all indications neither fraud nor miracle is involved. The secret lies in the consciously controlled reduction of metabolism to the minimum required for keeping the life processes going and in overcoming fear through concentration; for fear would increase the need for oxygen. The *Yoga Sūtra* end the explanations on *prāṇayama* with the statement: "The mind's ability for concentration." Breath control is the basis of body control and of mental realization.

Pratyāhāra, withdrawal of the senses, is dealt with immediately afterward: "When the senses do not have any contact with their objects and follow, as it were, the nature of the mind."[24] The senses, in this condition, not only no longer hinder the intellect, but the power invested in them actively helps it.

The next section is probably the most crucial one: it deals with three stages of realization. They are briefly explained as follows: "*Dhāraṇa* is the fixation of the intellect on one topic. *Dhyāna* is the one-pointedness in this effort. *Samādhi* is the same (concentration) when the object itself alone appears devoid of form, as it were."[25] The commentaries explain the first stage as a concentration of the mind on certain areas in the body: the navel, the heart, the forehead, the tip of the nose, or the tip of the tongue. In the second stage all objects are consciously eliminated and the union with the absolute is contemplated. In its perfection it glides over into the third and last stage. Here the identification has gone so far that there is no longer a process of contemplation of an object by a subject, but an absolute identity between the knower, that which is known and the process of knowing. Subject-object polarity disappears in a pure "isness," a cessation of the particular in an absolute self-awareness.

The three stages together are called *saṃyama*. They are understood not as something that incidentally happens to someone but as a practice that can be learned and acquired and then exercised at will. The specific schooling of the Yogi is to acquire those tools with which one masters the world. Though we must omit the details here, suffice it to say that as with the mastery of any science, Yoga requires a certain talent, hard work, and progress through many small steps, avoiding numerous pitfalls on the way, before one can competently use the instruments. If the training is applied to the various objects and the various levels of reality, the Yogi can win knowledge of the future and the past, obtain a knowledge of all languages and the sounds of all living beings, understand the language of the animals, know about former births, read other people's thought, become invisible, foresee the exact time of death, become full of goodwill toward all creatures, gain the strength of an elephant, have knowledge of what is subtle, distant, and hidden, know the regions of the firmament, the stars, and their orbits, and the whole anatomy of the human body, suppress completely hunger and thirst, see the *devas*, have foreknowledge of all that is going to happen, receive extrasensory sight, hearing, and taste, acquire the ability to enter other bodies mentally at will, walk freely on water without even touching it, walk across thorny and muddy ground without getting hurt or dirty; acquire a body that is bright and weightless; leave the body and act without it, become master of all material elements; obtain a body that is beautiful, strong, and as hard as a diamond, have direct knowledge of the *pradhāna*, the ground from which all beings come, and mastery over all conditions of being as well as omniscience.[26]

More than anything else those *vibhutis* have been described and dreamed about in literature about Indian Yogis. Biographies and autobiographies of Yogis are full of reports about achievements following the line of the *Yoga Sūtras*. In actual Indian life one hardly ever encounters any miracles of this sort. Living for two years in a place where thousands of holy men and women dwelled and where countless rumours about such things circulated, the author never witnessed a single incident corresponding to this idea of the miraculous. Not too many years ago, a Yogi called a press conference in Bombay and announced that he would demonstrate walking on water without wetting even his feet, against a reward of 1 million rupees. The bargain was agreed upon and a tank was built and filled with water. The Yogi could choose the auspicious time for his performance. When the hour had come, scores of journalists and hundreds of curious onlookers were present to watch the Yogi win his million. He lost it, being unable even to swim like an ordinary mortal. Later "unfavorable circumstances" were blamed for the Yogi's failure, and another attempt was announced for an undisclosed future date.

According to Patañjali the purpose of many of these *vibhutis* is fulfilled if the Yogi experiences in trance those miraculous happenings as if they were real. In the overall context of *rāja-yoga*, the *siddhis* are an obstacle on the way to *samādhi*.

The fourth and last *pāda* of the *Yoga Sūtras* deals with *kaivalya*, the goal of Yoga. The introductory aphorism states that the aforementioned *siddhis* are brought about either by imprints left in the psyche from previous births, by drugs, by mantras, or by *samādhi*. The proper thrust of *samādhi*, however, is not backward into the world of objects, from which it is freeing the spirit, but forward into the discrimination of *puruṣa* from the *guṇas* that belong to *prakṛti*. *Viveka*, discriminatory knowledge, means freedom from the influence of the *guṇas*: they return to their source as soon as their task is fulfilled. *Prakṛti* withdraws as soon as *puruṣa* has seen it as *prakṛti*. When the *guṇas* cease to be effective, activity and passivity, action and suffering also cease. "*Kaivalya* is realized when the *guṇas*, annihilated in the objectives of a person, cease to exert influence, or when *citta-śakti*, the power of consciousness, is established in her own proper nature."[27]

Yoga is the reversal of the evolutionary process demonstrated in the *Sāṁkhya* system, it is the entering into the origins. It is not, however, simply an annihilation of creation. *Sāṁkhya* does not think in terms of the model of the genetic method of modern science, but phenomenologically. *Prakṛti*, "matter," is not an object of physics but of metaphysics. Its eternity is not the nondestructibility of a concrete object but of potentiality.[28] When *puruṣa* combines with it, there is no need for any additional cause from outside to set evolution going. It is an unfolding of primeval matter that until then had existed as mere potency, but that is always there. Yoga, comes close to what we today would call psycho-science, that is, a detailed observation of human nature, but with a deep conviction of an ultimate that is missing in modern psychology.

27 Hindu Theology, Old and New: *Pūrva Mīmāṃsā* and *Vedānta*

Dharma is that which is indicated by means of the *Veda* as conducive to the highest good.

—*Mīmāṃsā Sūtra* I, 1, 2

Brahman is that from which the origin, subsistence and dissolution of this world proceeds.

—*Brahma Sūtra* I, 1, 2

Mīmāṃsā, enquiry, is the name of two very different systems of Hindu theology that have, however one thing in common: out of the statements of *śruti* they develop a complete theology.

Pūrva-Mīmāṃsā (often simply called *Mīmāṃsā*), the "earlier enquiry," has dharma as its proper subject and the *karma-kāṇḍa* of the Vedas as its scriptural source. *Uttara Mīmāṃsā*, the "latter enquiry," better known as *Vedānta*, has *brahman* knowledge as its subject and the *jñāna-kāṇḍa* of the Veda as its scriptural basis. Though historically there was a considerable amount of friction between the two systems, they are also in many ways complementary and considered to be the two most orthodox of the six systems. Certainly they are the two *darśanas* that come closest to the idea of theology as developed in the West.

THE OLD THEOLOGY

Mīmāṃsā, the "old theology," uses as its basic textbook the *Mīmāṃsā Sūtras* ascribed to Jaimini, dated around 200 B.C.E. The terse sūtras have received ample commentaries by various writers; the most extensive and famous of these is the *Śabara-bhāṣya*, written probably in the first century B.C.E.[1] The "old theology" has also produced brilliant philosophers like Prabhākara and Kumārila Bhaṭṭa; the latter is supposed to have been an older contemporary of the great "new theologian," Śaṅkara.[2] Though a good deal of the specific theology of *Mīmāṃsā*, dealing with the Vedic sacrificial ritual, has ceased to command the leading role and has been replaced by the more speculative approach of the Vedāntins, the old theology is still of unquestionably great importance. As Dasgupta writes: "Not only are all Vedic duties to be performed according to its maxims, but even the *smṛti* literatures which regulate the daily duties, ceremonials and rituals of the Hindus even to the present day are all guided and explained by them. The legal side of the *smṛtis* which guide Hindu civil life, . . . is explained according to Mīmāṃsā maxims."[3] The principles of Vedic exegesis developed by the Mīmāṃsākas, as well as their epistemology, are accepted by the Vedāntins, too, who otherwise disagree with some of their fundamental tenets.[4]

Athāto dharma-jijñāsa, "Now, then, a enquiry into *dharma*," is the first sentence of the *Jaimini Sūtras*. It goes on to explain: "*Dharma* is that which is indicated by Vedic injunctions for the attainment of the good."[5] The Mīmāṃsakas took it for granted that the performance of sacrifices was the means to attain everything and that the Veda was meant to serve this end alone. Despite their insistence that the Veda was *a-pauruṣeya*, not human-made, and infallible revelation, they were prepared to drop all those parts of the Veda as nonessential that had nothing directly to do with sacrificial ritual. "The purpose of the Veda lying in the enjoining of actions, those parts of the Veda which do not serve that purpose are useless; in these therefore the Veda is declared to be non-eternal."[6]

Classical Mīmāṃsā does not admit the existence of any *īśvara* as the creator and destroyer of the universe. Mīmāṃsakas even formulate arguments that positively disprove the existence of God.[7] The world, in their view, has always been in existence and the only real agent of a permanent nature was the sacrifice, or rather its unseen essence, the *a-pūrva*. Sacrifice, therefore, is the only topic that really interests the Mīmāṃsakas. The texts treat of the eternity of the Veda, of the means to its correct understanding, and of the validity of human knowledge as preliminaries to this question.[8]

Many times we read in the Brāhmaṇas; "Desiring heaven one should perform sacrifice." Consequently, the Mīmāṃsakas emphasize that "desire for heaven" is the basic presupposition for performing a sacrifice. In addition to animals, *devas*, and the Vedic *ṛṣis*, women and *sūdras* are categorically excluded from the performance of sacrifices. So are those who lack sufficient wealth or suffer from a physical disability.[9] The theory of *a-pūrva* is intended to explain the infallible effect of a sacrifice. The Mīmāṃsakas say that the *a-pūrva* is related to the verb of the Vedic injunction because this expresses something as yet to be accomplished. More subtly Mīmāṃsā distinguishes between principal and secondary *a-pūrva*.[10]

The *Mīmāṃsā Sūtra* is very brief in its description of the state to be achieved through sacrifice, namely, *svarga* or heaven. Mīmāṃsakas are probably convinced that one cannot know much about it. By the very principles that it establishes, it must come to the conclusion that those passages in the Vedas which describe heaven, not enjoining certain acts, cannot be taken as authoritative. One sūtra says: "That one result would be heaven, as that is equally desireable for all."[11] To which the commentator adds: "Why so? Because heaven is happiness and everyone seeks for happiness." The *Mīmāṃsā Sūtra* does not mention the term *mokṣa* at all. Śabara declared that the statements concerning heaven found in the Mahābhārata and the Purāṇas can be neglected because these books were composed by men; and also that Vedic descriptions of heaven were mere *arthavāda*, that is, without authority.[12] Later Mīmāṃsakas, perhaps influenced by Vedānta, introduce the term *mokṣa* into their vocabulary and describe it as not having to assume a body after death.[13] They also offer a description of the way to liberation: First of all a man becomes disgusted with the troubles that he has to undergo during his life on earth; finding the pleasures of the world to be invariably accompanied by some sort of pain, he comes to lose all interest in, and longing for, pleasures. He thereupon turns his attention toward liberation, ceases to perform such acts as are prohibited and lead to misfortune, as well as those that are prescribed only to lead to some sort of happiness here or hereafter; he attenuates all previously acquired merit and demerit by undergoing the experiences resulting from them; he destroys the sole receptacle or abode of his experiences by the knowledge of the soul, and is aided by such qualities as contentment, self-control and so forth, all of which are laid down in the scriptures as helping to prevent the further return of the soul into this world. Only when all this has come about does the soul becomes free, *mukta*.[14]

With their interest in language and analysis the Mīmāṃsakas are often close to the Grammarians, who developed a philosophical school of their own. Quite important epistemological observations are to be found already in the *Śābara-bhāṣya,* observations that have prompted contemporary scholars to undertake interesting investigations.[15]

The *Mahā-bhāṣya* by Patañjali (which is ascribed to the second century B.C.E.) contains questions concerning the nature and function of words. The unquestionably most famous name in Indian linguistic philosophy, however, is Bhartṛhari (ca. 500 C.E.), whose *Vākya-padīya* has been studied with great interest by Western scholars in recent years. His system is also called *sphota-vāda* after its most characteristic teaching which compares the sudden appearance of meaning at the enunciation of a word with the process of the sudden ejection of liquid from a boil.[16]

THE NEW THEOLOGY

Athāto brahma-jijñāsa, "Now, then, an enquiry into *brahman,*" begins the *Vedānta Sūtra,* also called *Brahma Sūtra,* which is ascribed to Bādarāyaṇa, and forms the basic text of Vedānta *darśana.* The 550 sūtras, purporting to summarize the teaching of the Upaniṣads, are usually so short—often consisting of not more than one or two words—that without a commentary they remain incomprehensible. In all probability there had been a living tradition of Vedāntins in which the meaning of the *Vedānta Sūtra* was passed on from one generation to the next. As the Upaniṣads themselves took great care to maintain the *guru paraṃparā,* the succession of authorized teachers of the *vidyā* contained in them, so also the systematized aphoristic sūtra text and its meaning was preserved in a carefully guarded tradition, the beginning of which we are unable to identify.

According to a very old Indian tradition there had been other *Brahma Sūtras* before the one composed by Bādarāyaṇa. The most famous of these predecessors must have been an Ācārya Bādarī, who is credited with having written both a *Mīmāṃsā Sūtra* and a *Vedānta Sūtra.*[17] Other *ācāryas,* whose names are found in ancient texts as forerunner to Bādarāyaṇa include Karṣṇajini, Atreya, Audulomi, Asmarāthya, Kasakṛtsna, Kaśyapa, Vedavyāsa—all mentioned in the extant *Brahma Sūtra*—whose works have not been preserved. In all probability Bādarāyaṇa's sūtra impressed his contemporaries as being superior so that in the course of time it completely replaced the others.[18] The *bhāṣyas,* or commentaries to the *Brahma Sūtra,* have gained authoritative position in the recognized ten branches of Vedānta, combining a textual exegesis with other living traditions, as we saw earlier when dealing with Vaiṣṇavism and Śaivism.[19] The oldest of the extant complete commentaries is that by Śaṅkarācārya, said to have lived from 788 to 820 C.E. We know that there had been earlier commentaries associated with names like Bhartṛprapañca, Bhartṛmitra, Bhartṛhari, Upavarṣa, Bodhāyana (whose authority is several times invoked by Rāmānuja against Śaṅkara), Brahmānaṇḍi, Ṭaṅka, Brahmadatta, Bhāruci, Sundarapāṇḍya, Gauḍapāda, and Govinda Bhagavatpāda, the guru of Śaṅkarācārya.[20]

As the commentators, expounding the most diverse theological views, demonstrate, the original *Brahma Sūtra* is merely a kind of general frame for a further development of ideas, which are left fairly vague and undetermined. Looking at the bare sūtras without a commentary one can only give a general idea of their structure without discussing their import.

The *Vedānta Sūtra* is divided into four *adhyāyas,* chapters, each subdivided into four *pādas,* literally "feet" or parts, which again are made up of a varying number of sūtras or aphorisms.

The entire first *adhyāya* is devoted to a discussion on *brahman*: *brahman* is the sole and supreme cause of all things. Systems that teach otherwise are rejected as heretical. The detailed polemics against the Sāṁkhya system is continued into the second *adhyāya,* which also refutes Vaisesika theories. Toward the end of the second *pāda* the *Bhāgavata* system is mentioned. The comments on this part of the text (II, 2, 42–48) are a classic example of the wide diversity that exists in the commentaries. Śaṅkara understands the sūtra to say that the *Bhāgavata* system is untenable; Rāmānuja sees in it a recognition and justification for the *Bhāgavata* system. The next two *pādas* show the origin of the various phenomena that go into the making of the universe. The third *adhyāya* discusses the *jīvātman,* the individual living being. The condition and circumstances of the soul after death and the various states of dream, dreamless sleep, and so on are inquired into. A long series of sūtras deals with meditation and the types of *brahman* knowledge. The fourth *adhyāya* takes up again the topic of meditation and ends with a description of the *brahman* knower's fate after death.

SCHOOLS OF VEDĀNTA

As it is not possible to expatiate on all the questions broached here and because complete texts and translations of the most important *bhāṣyas* are available to those who are interested in Vedānta, this exposition will limit itself to a few essential points and illustrate them with excerpts from the writings of Śaṅkara, the great *Advaitin*, from Rāmānuja, the famous exponent of *Viśiṣṭādvaita*, and from Madhva, the illustrious defender of *Dvaita*—thus covering the most important sections of the spectrum of the Vedānta *darśana*.

The specifying terms given to the different systems within Vedānta have as their point of reference the relationship between the absolute supreme *brahman* and the individual *ātman*: thus Advaita, literally, "nonduality," implies ultimate identity of *brahman* and *jīvātman*. Viśiṣṭādvaita, literally, "qualified nonduality," maintains a crucial differentiation as well as a fundamental identity. Dvaita, literally, "duality," opposes *advaita* on almost all points and maintains an ultimate diversity of *brahman* and *jīvātman*.[21] Translations which one can sometimes find in books explaining Advaita as Monism and Dvaita as Dualism are misleading, because the Western terms have quite different frames of reference and therefore quite different implications, which are inapplicable to the Indian systems.

The commentaries to the *Vedānta Sūtra* have become the main works of the *Vedāntācāryas*, whose very recognition as such depends on this as well as the commentaries on the Upaniṣads and the Bhagavadgītā, constituting the *prasthāna-trayī*. The last one to have done this is S. Radhakrishnan, a former President of India, and one of the foremost of twentieth century Indian thinkers.

ADVAITA-VEDĀNTA

Śaṅkarācārya, according to many the greatest Vedāntin and perhaps the greatest of India's philosophers, born, according to tradition, in 788 A.D. at Kālādi in today's Kerala, became a *saṁnyāsi* at the age of 18. He vanquished all his opponents in debate, established four headquarters in the South, East, North, and West of India for the missionaries of his doctrine, the *Daśanāmi Saṁnyāsin*, wrote numerous books and died at the age of 32.[22] He constructed his Advaita-Vedānta upon principles set forth by Gauḍapāda in his *Kārikā* to the *Māṇḍukya Upaniṣad*.[23] Gauḍapāda is thought to be Śaṅkara's *prācārya*, that is, his guru's guru. Śaṅkara's commentary on this *Kārikā* may be considered the earliest and most concise statement of his philosophy, which he then expands in his great *Śarīraka-bhāṣya*.

Like all Indian philosophical theologians, Śaṅkara clarifies his epistemological position in the introduction to his main work. He

Figure 27.1 Ādiśaṅkara

offers his own critique of human knowledge and states that all subject-object knowledge is distorted by *adhyāsa*, superimposition, which falsifies knowledge in such a way that the subject is unable to find objective truth. Quoting the familiar example of the traveler mistaking a piece of rope on the road for a snake (or vice versa) he proceeds to call all sense perception into question as possibly misleading due to preconceived, superimposed ideas. But though all object cognition can be doubted, the existence of the doubter remains a fact. Every perception, be it true, doubtful, or mistaken, presupposes a subject, a perceiver. Even if there were no objective perception at all, there would still be a subject. This cannot be proven, nor does it have to be, because it precedes every proof as its inherent condition. It is distinct from all objects and independent. *Ātman* is pure consciousness that remains even after *manas*, rational thought, has passed away. *Ātman* is ultimately *sac-cit-ānanda*. Śaṅkara does not regard the world of things as "pure illusion" (as is sometimes said of him): the world is neither *abhāva*, nonexistence, nor, as Buddhist idealism has it, *śūnyatā*, emptiness. For Śaṅkara the Buddhists are the archantagonists of *brahman* knowledge; using Buddhist patterns of thought (which later earned him the title *crypto-Buddhist* by zealous Vaiṣṇavas) he sets out to reestablish Brahmanism. Sense objects, in his view, are different from fiction, but they also differ from reality in the ultimate sense. To understand Śaṅkara's statements one must always see them in the frame of reference in which they are made: all his assertions are explicit or implicit comparisons with absolute reality, which alone is of interest to him. The "natural" person does not know how to distinguish between relative and absolute being, between "things" and "being," between *ātman* and non-*ātman*. This is congenital *avidyā*, the nescience that one is not even aware of. This ignorance keeps a person in *saṁsāra*. *Ātman* is *brahman*—that is good Upaniṣadic doctrine; the self of a person is identical with the ground of all being. *Brahman*, however, is invisible, impervious to any sense or mind perception: *brahman* is not identical with any one particular thing. Some Upaniṣadic passages speak of a "lower" and a "higher" brahman,[24] they speak of the immutable supreme *brahman* and also of the *īśvara* who is creator, Lord and ruler of the world. Śaṅkara takes those passages as the occasion to introduce his most controversial distinction between *brahman saguṇa* and *brahman nirguṇa*, the Supreme with attributes and the Supreme without attributes, the *isvara* of religious tradition and the absolute and unqualified reality, a no-thing. According to Śaṅkara *īśvara* is only a temporal manifestation of *brahman,* creator for as long as creation lasts. Śaṅkara is credited with numerous beautiful hymns to the traditional Lords of religion, to Viṣṇu, Siva, and Devī.[25] Devotion is one of the stages that one has to go through, but not a stage to remain at: the ultimate goal is deliverance also from God, a complete identification with the Reality, which neither develops nor acts, neither loves nor hates but just *is.* The process of achieving this complete liberation is a cleansing process that separates the *ātman* from all untruth, unreality, and temporality. The doing away with *avidyā,* obscuring ignorance, is in itself already *vidyā,* knowledge that is identical with being. In this *vidyā* the self experiences its identity with *brahman nirguṇa,* the pure and immutable reality.

Commenting on the first sūtra of the *Vedānta Sūtra,* Śaṅkara writes:

> The special question with regard to the enquiry into Brahman is whether it presupposes the understanding of dharma. To this question we reply: No! Because for a person who has read the Vedānta it is possible to begin the inquiry into the nature of *brahman* before having studied the dharma. The study of dharma results in transitory heaven and this depends on the performance of rituals. The inquiry into the nature of *brahman,* however, results in *mokṣa,* lasting liberation. It does not depend upon the performance of ceremonies. A few presuppositions preceding the inquiry into the nature of *brahman* will have to be mentioned. These are
>
> 1. Discrimination between the eternal and the noneternal reality;
> 2. Giving up the desire to enjoy the fruit of one's actions both here and hereafter;
> 3. The practice of the recognized virtues like peacefulness, self-restraint, and so on;
> 4. The strong desire for liberation.
>
> If these conditions are fulfilled, then a person may inquire into *brahman* whether before or after the dharma inquiry; but not if these conditions are not fulfilled. The object of desire is the knowledge of *brahman* and complete understanding of it. Knowledge is therefore the means to perfect *brahman* cognition. The complete knowledge of *brahman* is the supreme human goal, because it destroys the root of all evil, namely, *avidyā,* which is the seed of *saṃsāra.* One may now ask: is *brahman* known or unknown? If *brahman* is known then there is no need for further inquiry; if *brahman* is unknown we cannot begin an inquiry. We answer: *brahman* is known. *Brahman,* omniscient and

> omnipotent, whose essential nature is eternal purity, consciousness and freedom, exists. For if we contemplate the derivation of the word *brahman* from the root *bṛh-*, to be great, we understand at once that it is eternal purity, etc. More than that, the existence of *brahman* is known because it is the *ātman*, the self of everyone. For everyone is conscious of the 'self' and no one thinks: I am not. *Ātman* is *brahman*. If the existence of the self was not known each one would think: I am not. But if *ātman* is generally known as *brahman*, one does not have to start an inquiry. Our answer is: No. Because there is a diversity of opinions regarding its nature. Uneducated people and the Lokāyatas are of the opinion that the body itself, having *caitanya*, consciousness, as an attribute, is the *ātman*. Others believe that the sense organs, endowed with the potency to experience, are the *ātman*. Others again believe that *cetana*, reasoning, or *manas*, mind, is the *ātman*. Others again believe the self to be simply a momentary idea, or that it is *śūnya*, emptiness. Some others explain that there is besides the body some supernatural being, responsible for the transmigrations, acting and enjoying; others teach that this being enjoys only but does not act. Some believe that besides these there exists an omniscient, omnipotent *īśvara*, and others finally declare that the *ātman* is that enjoyer.—Thus there are various opinions, partly founded on reasonable arguments and texts from scripture. If these opinions were accepted without thorough prior investigation and inquiry, one would exclude oneself from liberation and suffer deplorable loss. The sūtra, therefore, presents a discussion of the Vedānta texts with the motto: "Inquiry into *brahman*," which proceeds with appropriate arguments and aims at supreme bliss.[26]

Already his direct disciples and successors considered Śaṅkara a superhuman teacher, the embodiment of divine wisdom, and his words were treated on a par with the words of revelation.[27] Extreme care was taken not only to preserve his written works but also to ensure the succession in the *maṭhas* founded by him.[28]

VIŚIṢṬĀDVAITA-VEDĀNTA

Rāmānuja (Figure 27.2), who, after an eventful life of ecclesiastical glory but also some persecution, died according to traditional accounts in 1137, aged 120, as the resident head of the great temple monastery of Śrīraṅgam in South India, is the greatest among the Vaiṣṇava Vedāntins, offering a theistic interpretation of the *Brahma Sūtra*.[29] For Rāmānuja, too, reality is ultimately one, but reality is tiered. It is composed of three components: the world of material things, the multiplicity of *jīvātmas*, individual living

Figure 27.2 Rāmānuja

beings, and *brahman*, who is identical with *īśvara*, who is none other than Viṣṇu. Creation is the body of *brahman* but not without qualification.[30]

At the time of Rāmānuja Hinduism was firmly established. Buddhism had all but disappeared from India, and Jainism was concentrated in relatively small areas of Western India. The inner-Hindu controversy was taken up again and Rāmānuja's main opponents were Śaivites, as far as religion was concerned and Advaitins in the area of philosophy. Rāmānuja's *Śrī-bhāṣya* contains many pages of polemics against Śaṅkara, finding fault with Śaṅkara's distinction between *nirguṇa* and *saguṇa brahman* and his presupposition of *adhyāsa*.[31] Īśvara, as the creator and lord of *prakṛti* and the *jīvas*, has an infinite number of supreme and auspicious qualities; this makes him, ipso facto, *brahman saguṇa*, above whom there is none. He has a most perfect body that is eternal and immutable. He is radiant, full of beauty and youth and strength. With his body full of *satva*, devoid of *rajas* and *tamas* he is omnipresent; he is the *antaryāmin*, the inner ruler of all. For Rāmānuja the process of salvation is not just a process of isolation, the elimination of *avidyā*, the disengagement of nonreality but it is the product of divine grace and human self-surrender. His *viśiṣṭa* theory enables him to incorporate into the philosophical system of Vedānta all the traditional Hindu notions of the *bhagavān* from the epic-Purāṇic-Āgamic tradition. Rāmānuja himself established a detailed code of ceremonial worship at the *maṭha* of Melkote, where he spent the twelve years of his exile and where, according to tradition, the *Draviḍa Prabandham* was recited at his deathbed together with the Vedas and the Upaniṣads. Those passages in the Upaniṣad that speak of a *nirguṇa brahman* are interpreted by Rāmānuja as meaning "absence of inauspicious qualities" rather than absolute qualitilessness. *Jīvas*, individual souls, are of three kinds: *nitya-muktas*, who are always free; *muktas*, who have become free in time; and *baddhas*, who are still bound. For these the "way" is essential. Despite the prevalent opinion, also held by Western scholars, that Śaṅkara represents Vedānta in its purest form, we must say that Rāmānuja probably can claim to have Hindu tradition on his side and his interpretation of the Upaniṣads may on the whole be fairer than Śaṅkara's. This is also the opinion of S. N. Dasgupta, who writes: "The theistic Vedānta is the dominant view of the *Purāṇas* in general and represents the general Hindu view of life and religion. Compared with this general current of Hindu thought, which flows through the *Purāṇas* and the *Smṛtis* and has been the main source from which the Hindu life has drawn its inspiration, the extreme Sāṁkhya, the extreme Vedānta of Śaṅkara, the extreme Nyāya, and the extreme dualism of Madhva may be regarded as metaphysical formalisms of conventional philosophy."[32]

In his commentary on the first aphorism of the *Brahma Sūtras*, Rāmānuja emphasizes his difference from Śaṅkara's position wherever possible. He adds to the explanation of the four words of the sūtra an exposé of his own theology, covering more than a hundred pages in print.

> The word *athā*, now, expresses direct sequence; the word *ata*, then, intimates that what has taken place before (namely the study of dharma), which forms the basis (for the *brahman* inquiry). For it is a fact that the desire to know *brahman*—the fruit of which is infinite and lasting—follows immediately when someone who has read the Veda and Vedāṅgas realizes that the fruit of rituals is limited and temporary and thus wishes for final release . . .
>
> The word *brahman* means *puruṣottama*, who is by his very essence free from imperfections and possesses an unlimited number of auspicious qualities of unsurpassable excellence. The term *brahman* applies to all things possessing greatness, but primarily it denotes that which possesses greatness essentially and in unlimited fullness; and such is only the Lord of all. Hence the word *brahman* primarily denotes him alone and in a secondary sense only those things that possess a small amount of the Lord's qualities. . . . The term is analoguous with the term *bhagavat*. It is the Lord alone who is sought for the sake of immortality by all those who are afflicted by the threefold misery. Hence the All-Lord (*sarveśvara*) is that *brahman* which according to the sūtra constitutes the object of enquiry. . . . The *Pūrva-Mīmāṃsā* and the *Uttara Mīmāṃsā* differ only in the material they teach as the two halves of the *Pūrvamīmāṃsā Sūtras* differ. The entire *Mīmāṃsā-śāstra*, beginning with the sūtra *Athāto dharma-jijñāsa* and ending with the sūtra *an-āvṛttis-śabdāt*[33] has, due to the special character of its contents, a definite order of internal succession.

At this juncture Rāmānuja takes to task the Advaitins, whose main arguments he summarizes in his own words as follows: "Eternal and absolutely immutable consciousness, whose nature is pure undifferentiated reason, shows itself—owing to an error—illusorily as divided into multifarious distinct beings: knower, object of knowledge and acts of knowledge. The discussion of the Vedānta texts aims at completely destroying *avidyā*, which is the cause of this error, to attain a firm knowledge of the unity of *brahman*, whose nature is pure consciousness—free, without stain and eternal."

Then Rāmānuja introduces his hundred-page counterargument, the *mahā-siddhānta* or great final statement, as follows:

> This entire theory [of the Advaitins] rests on a fictitious foundation of altogether hollow and vicious arguments, incapable of being stated in definite logical alternatives, and devised by men who are destitute of those particular qualities that cause individuals to be chosen by the *puruṣottama* revealed in the Upaniṣads, whose intellects are darkened by the impression of beginningless evil and who thus have no insight into the meaning of words and sentences, into the real purport conveyed by them and into the procedure of sound argumentation, with all its methods depending on perception and the other instruments of right knowledge. The theory therefore must be rejected by all those who, through texts, perception and the other means of knowledge, assisted by sound reasoning, have an insight into the true nature of things.

In a massive offensive, in the course of which countless passages from the Upaniṣads, the *Smṛtis*, and the Purāṇas are quoted, Rāmānuja then proceeds against the main views of Śaṅkara. There is, he says, no proof for the acceptance of undifferentiated being; on the contrary, all arguments speak for a differentiation: the use of language, sense perception, and inference. Sense perception does not show us a being in its undifferentiated absoluteness but a being endowed with attributes. The multiplicity of things is not unreal; being and consciousness without an object and consciousness can undergo changes. Consciousness is a quality of a conscious self and it is preposterous to assume that the conscious subject is something unreal. The subject exists even when there is no actual consciousness, as in dreamless sleep. And the conscious subject continues to exist also in the state of perfect liberation. Rāmānuja quite boldly states that no *śruti* text teaches an undifferentiated *brahman* and that also *Smṛtis* and Purāṇas were against it. The *avidyā* theory cannot be proved, because all knowledge relates to what is real. Again, no scripture teaches it. Nor does *śruti* support the teaching that *mokṣa* is realized by the cognition of an unqualified *brahman*. Moreover, ignorance does not simply cease if one understands *brahman* as the universal *ātman*. In this connection Rāmānuja explains the *mahā-vākya* "*tat tvam asi*," one of the core texts of the Advaitins, in his own way:

> In texts such as *tat tvam asi,* the coordination of the constituent parts is not meant to convey the idea of the absolute unity of a nondifferentiated substance: on the contrary, the words *tat* and *tvam* denote a *brahman* distinguished by difference. The word *tat* refers to the omniscient etc. *brahman*. . . . The word *tvam,* which stands in coordination to *tat* conveys the idea of *brahman,* which has for its body the *jīvātmas* connected with *prakṛti.* If such duality of form were given up there could be no difference of aspects giving rise to the application of different terms, and the entire principle of coordination would thus be given up. And it would further follow that the two words co-ordinated would have to be taken in an implied sense. There is, however no need to assume *lakṣaṇa* or implication in sentences such as "this person is Devadatta." . . . Moreover, if the text *tat tvam asi* were meant to express absolute oneness, it would conflict with a previous statement in the same section, namely, *tadaikṣata bahu syām*; that is, it thought, may I be many.[34]

We cannot decide here whether Rāmānuja has always been fair to Śaṅkara and whether he does justice to his rather subtle thinking, but it is very clear that he wished to distinguish his position as sharply as possible from that of the Advaitins.

DVAITA-VEDĀNTA

Madhva (Figure 27.3), the representative of the Dvaita Vedānta, lived from 1238 to 1317 A.D. The son of one of his disciples wrote a biography of him, considered authentic.[35] Madhva was born into a humble Brahmin family in a village not far from Uḍipī, now in Kannāḍa. When he was 16 he entered the Ekandaṇḍi order of the Ekānti Vaiṣṇavas and was given the name Pūrṇaprajñā, fullness of wisdom. He quite frequently disagreed with the Advaita interpretation of Vedānta given by his teacher, a fact that did not hinder the guru from installing Madhva under the name of *Ānandatīrtha* as the head of his own *maṭha.* He then went on a missionary tour, engaging Jains, Buddhists, and Advaitins in discussions and defeating them not only by the power of his words but also with the help of a king who, on Madhva's insistence, had thousands of Jains impaled and exiled other infidels. According to tradition he wrote his *Brahma Sūtra-bhāṣya* after a pilgrimage to Vyāsāśrama in the Himalayas. The image of Kṛṣṇa that Madhva installed at his Uḍipī *maṭha* is still an important focus of pilgrimage, and the rotation of the headship of the *maṭha,* taking place every twelve years, is also a major social occasion about which newspapers report. Madhva was the most prolific of all the great Vedāntins; he left more than thirty major works as well as a number of minor ones. In addition to the traditional commentaries on the Gītā, the Upaniṣads and the *Brahma Sūtra,* he wrote commentaries on the *Bhāgavata Purāṇa,* the Ṛgveda and portions of the Mahābhārata, along with several philosophical monographs and short summaries of his own commentaries, the most famous of which is the *Aṇuvyākhyāna,* a masterful exposition of the *Brahma Sūtra* in eighty-eight verses.[36]

In his arguments he uses not only traditional *śruti,* but also quotes from the *Viṣṇu-* and *Bhāgavata Purāṇa,* from *Pāñcarātra saṁhitās* and other sectarian writings. All Śaiva literature is taboo for him. He is closer to Rāmānuja than to Śaṅkara, but he goes a decisive step further toward uncompromising Dvaita. He develops his whole system upon the presupposition of the *pañca bheda,* the five differences between *īśvara* and *jīvātman,* between *prakṛti* and *īśvara,* between the individual *jīvas* and the various inanimate objects. Īśvara, who is Viṣṇu, is absolute: he has an infinite number of excellent qualities and a spiritual body with which he shows himself at will in the *vyūhas* and *avatāras.* The world is made through his *līlā,* the free play of his disinterested will; everything depends on his will: "All knowledge is to be ascribed to the action of Hari, the ties of the world and the release therefrom, rebirth and the unfolding of all things. Hari permeates everything, even the souls, and he lives there as the inner witness, the *sākṣi;* in nature he lives as the *antaryāmin,* the inner ruler. *Prakṛti* is the opposite of Hari, insofar as she is pure dependency, total contingency. It is true, she exists from eternity, but in the hand of Hari she is a mere instrument."[37]

The *jīvas* have, individually, a spiritual self-consciousness. They are of the nature of *sac-cit-ānanda,* even if for the duration of bodily life this is obscured. The *ātman,* therefore, is a mirror image of God. It is completely dependent on God in all its actions. The way to liberation is perfect self-surrender to Viṣṇu through an active love that centers on ritual worship of the image. Vāyu as mediator between Viṣṇu and the *jīvas* plays an important role. It is important to note that Madhva considered himself an *avatāra* of Vāyu. Madhva begins his commentary on the first sūtra of the text thus:

> The basis for the inquiry into *brahman* is the grace of the Lord Viṣṇu. Since greater grace can be gained from him only through appropriate cognition, *brahman* inquiry is indispensable as a source of *brahman* knowledge in order to gain his attention. Inquiry into *brahman* itself is to be ascribed to the grace of the Great Lord, for he alone is the

Figure 27.3 Madhva

mover of our minds. There are three grades of preparedness for the study of Vedānta: an eager person who is devoted to Lord Viṣṇu is in the third grade; a person who has the six-fold moral qualification of self-discipline etc. is in the second grade; and the person who is attached to none but the Lord, who considers the whole world as transitory and is therefore completely indifferent, is in the first grade. The following of the Vedic injunctions can merely give us a claim to the lower grace of the Lord; the listening to the texts of scripture provides us with a somewhat higher grace; but the supreme grace of the Lord, which leads to *mukti* can be secured only through knowledge. Right knowledge can be acquired only through *śravaṇa*, the listening to scripture, *manana*, meditation, *nidhi-dhyāsana*, contemplation, and *bhakti*, devotion; nobody can attain right *jñāna* without these. The term *brahman* designates primarily Viṣṇu, of which some vedic texts say: "He who dwells in the ocean and is known only to the sages, he who surpasses understanding, who is eternal, who rules all things, from whom issue the great mother of the universe and who brings the *jīvas* into the world, bound to life by their actions and prisoners of the five elements." And another passage: "He is the embodiment of pure wisdom, he is consciously active and is, according to the sages, the one Lord of the universe."[38] From the following sentence: "And may therefore Viṣṇu inspire us" it is clear that only Viṣṇu is meant in the preceding passages.—All the Vedas speak of him only; in the *Vedas*, in the *Rāmāyaṇa*, in the *Mahābhārata* and in the *Purāṇas*, in the beginning, in the middle and in the end—everywhere only Viṣṇu is sung of.[39]

TEXTS AND COMMENTARIES

These short extracts from the commentaries to the four first words of the *Vedānta Sūtra* may allow the reader to gauge the great amount of diversity within the one Vedānta *darśana* and also provide a glimpse into the very rich and subtle philosophical tradition drawn upon. Because these *bhāṣyas*, very often commented upon in *ṭīkās* (subcommentaries) and *ṭippaṇīs* (glosses) by the disciples and followers in later ages, are both difficult and lengthy, the great masters themselves wrote smaller manuals, *prakāraṇas*, for the laity in which they provided the gist of their teaching in an abbreviated form, without compromising the essentials. Two valuable little works expounding Advaita-Vedānta, ascribed to Śaṅkarācārya himself, are the *Ātma-bodha*, "The Self-Cognition," and *Upadeṣa-sahasrī*, "The Thousand Teachings."[40] The most widely used and easiest introduction, however, may be Sadananda's *Vedānta-sāra*, a small literary work offering a clear and full explanation of the major terms of Śaṅkara's thought.[41] The greatest among the post-

Śaṅkara Advaita treatises, however, is the celebrated *Pañcadaśī* of Vidyāraṇya, one of the greatest Hindu scholars of the fourteenth century.[42] The *Vedānta-paribhāṣa,* written by the seventeenth century Advaitin Dharmarāja, is a manual still used in Indian universities.[43]

The Viśiṣṭādvaitins have also their shorter compendia. The most famous and most beautifully written is Rāmānuja's *Vedārtha-saṅgraha,* with ample quotations from scriptures, despite its brevity.[44] For beginners the most suitable book may be Śrīnivāsadāsa's *Yatīndra-mata-dīpikā.*[45] Easy to understand and now easily accessible in an English translation, is also Bucci Venkatācārya's *Vedānta-kārikāvalī.*[46]

In addition to the minor works of Madhva himself, the manual by Jayatīrtha called *Vādā-valī,* written in the fourteenth century, may offer the most systematic introduction to the thought of Dvaita-Vedānta.[47]

Vedānta does not belong to the past only, but is also perhaps the most important contemporary expression of Indian philosophy and theology. An unbroken tradition of scholars and saints leads from the great *ācāryas* into our time; all their major institutions are still centers of living Vedānta. Vedānta is not only speculative, abstract thought, but also mysticism, realization and the way to ultimate freedom. The basic types of this spiritual life thought, as they are represented by the great *ācāryas* whom we have briefly dealt with, may be representative of basic types of mysticism, for which we also have parallels in the Western tradition. Alive in India are numerous gurus, who express their own experiences and convictions in the terminology of Śaṅkara, Rāmānuja and Madhva, thereby acknowledging the timeless greatness of these thinkers of the absolute.

Part 4

THE MEETING OF EAST AND WEST IN MODERN INDIA

The endeavor of this book had been throughout to provide a contemporary perspective to the description of the various dimensions of Hinduism in addition to outlining the origins and historic development. It seemed appropriate, however, to devote the last part to a discussion of the consequences that the irruption of the modern West had in nineteenth and twentieth century India. Although European powers already in the late fifteenth century began to establish trade posts and expand their influence in India, it was with the beginning hegemony of England and the simultaneous disintegration of the Mughal Empire that the impact of modern Europe made itself felt through large parts of the subcontinent. The British, determined to take upon themselves "the white man's burden," systematically transformed India in the image of their homeland: they established a European-style administration and judicial system, they built thousands of miles of railroad, dug irrigation canals, introduced an English-language higher education system, and generally made the Indians understand that England was the cultural standard by which their country's development was to be measured.

Pressure, as is universally known, induces counterpressure. Some Indians accepted Anglization as their own and their country's future, but others resisted it and attempted to renew their country from indigenous cultural and spiritual resources. "Reform movements," usually combining socio-ethical concerns with nationalist aspirations, grew in many parts of the country, especially in Bengal and Maharashtra. Some of them emphasized religious and spiritual issues, others advocated political radicalism and independence from England. The struggle for independence eventually amalgamated many of the reform movements and provided a cause for the majority of Hindus. Mohamdas Karamchand Gandhi, later called "Mahātmā," Great Soul, succeeded by virtue of his own personal integrity and his leadership abilities in mobilizing large section of the Hindu population in a movement that promised not only to bring about political independence of India but also transcendent salvation to its citizens. Gandhi's importance for twentieth century India and, indeed, for the whole world can hardly be exaggerated. He embodied the best of Hinduism and, notwithstanding his deep-seated antipathy to the soulless technology that characterized so much of "modernity," he was a thoroughly "modern" person. In spite of his archetypical Indian character, he also was a model world citizen. In the turmoil that has overtaken India and Hinduism lately, he may serve as a beacon to show the way also for the Hinduism of the twenty-first century. Much of organized Hinduism in our time is politically radicalized and confrontational. It seems to have forgotten its spiritual roots and its religious heritage. That, however, should not blind us to the enormous potential that Hinduism possesses, in virtue of its great past and its still present spiritual giants. Hinduism could become the religion of the future, a true and genuine world religion.

28 Hindu Reforms and Reformers

> Religion must establish itself as a rational way of living. If ever the spirit is to be at home in this world and not merely a prisoner or a fugitive, secular foundations must be laid deeply and preserved worthily. Religion must express itself in reasonable thought, fruitful actions and right social institutions.
>
> —S. Radhakrishnan[1]

The history of Hinduism consists of a series of challenges and responses to challenges, reforms and efforts to resist change, struggle between those who tenaciously cling to tradition and those who wish to go with the times. It took centuries before Hinduism responded as a body to the challenge which Buddhism and Jainism had posed—it needed a Maṇḍana Miśra and a Śaṅkara to consolidate and reform Hinduism and to return the initiative to it. Although much of this response was creative, advancing the theory and practice of Hindus over against the times of Buddha and Mahāvīra, the reaction to the challenge posed by Islam was totally negative and defensive. Except for a few movements, which became more or less independent from mainstream Hinduism,[2] the Hindu reaction to Islam was one of withdrawing, letting the shutters down, hardening customs and beliefs, not admitting any change.[3] That did not prevent Hinduism from decaying and corrupting. The picture eighteenth century visitors to India draw is not only one of a Mughal rule no longer really in control, but also of a Hinduism, still the majority religion, beset by cruel customs, superstition, and abysmal ignorance.

Foreign visitors considered Hinduism a hopeless case and expected it to die of degeneration within a century. To quote but one example, here is a page from a book that appeared in its second edition in Madras in 1900, published by the Christian Literature Society for India, entitled *India Hindu and India Christian or, What Hinduism Has Done for India and What Christianity Would Do for It. An Appeal to Thoughtful Hindus.*[4] It enumerates as the fruits of Hinduism: ill-health or shortness of life, poverty, national ignorance, intellectual weakness, despotism and religious intolerance, polytheism, animal worship, idolatry, pantheism, the sanction of robbery, murder, and human sacrifices; and it promises India under Christian rule better health and longer life, increase of wealth, diffusion of true knowledge, intellectual strength, national greatness, the brotherhood of man. There is for us, a century later, some irony in the following remark: "England is now one of the richest countries in the world. One great cause of this is her commerce. Every sea is traversed by her ships; her merchants are to be found in every land where wealth can be gained. The Parsis have copied their example and have similarly benefitted. Hinduism teaches the people of India to regard all foreigners as impure *mlecchas*. 'In their country the twice-born must not even temporarily dwell'. The folly of this is now acknowledged by enlightened men; but the above is the doctrine of Hinduism."[5] Hindus have changed. So has England. History has not been kinder to the following assertion made in the same book under the title "Hinduism Incapable of Reform."

> All intelligent Hindus admit that great reforms are needed to purify Hinduism. Many think that this is all that is necessary to render it worthy of retention. Some even affirm that it would then occupy one of the highest places among the religions of the world.
>
> Let the changes necessary to reform Hinduism up to the light of the nineteenth century be considered:
>
> 1. Reformed Hinduism should be neither polytheistic nor pantheistic, but monotheistic. All intelligent men now believe in the existence of only one true God. There are no such beings as Vishnu, Śiva, Sarasvati, Durgā, or the thirty-three crores of the Hindu Pantheon. The Vishnu *bhakti*, the Śiva *bhakti*, etc., would all come to an end. No sectarial marks would be worn. The blasphemous assertion *aham Brahmāsmi*, I am Brahma, would no longer be made.
> 2. All idols would be destroyed, and no longer worshipped as giving false and degrading ideas of God. The indecent images on some temples would be broken down. There would no longer be Vaishnava nor Śaiva temples.
> 3. The *Vedas*, the Code of Manu, the *Rāmāyana*, *Mahābhārata*, the

Purāṇas, etc., as teaching polytheism, pantheism, containing debasing representations of God, unjust laws, false history, false science, false morals, would no longer be considered sacred books.

4. Hindu worship in temples would cease. Festivals would no longer be celebrated. Pilgrimages to supposed holy places would come to an end. *Pūjā* to idols would not be observed in private families.
5. As Hindu temples contain only small shrines for idols, buildings like churches would require to be erected, in which people might assemble for public worship, and receive instruction in the duties of life.
6. Caste would no longer be recognised, and the brotherhood of man would be acknowledged; all caste distinctions would cease.

Every one of the above changes is necessary to meet the view of enlightened men.

Take away sweetness from sugar, and it is no longer sugar; deprive a man of reason, and he is no longer a human being. Hinduism without its gods, its sacred books, its temples, its worship, its caste, would be no longer Hinduism, but an entirely different religion, like the Sadhāraṇa Brahmo Samāj. It would be simply Theistic.[6]

Hinduism, as we well know now, has been capable of reform. It has not given up its belief in Viṣṇu, Śiva, or Durgā, it has not abandoned its images, has not ceased to worship in temples. Pilgrimages are as popular as ever, *pūjā* continues to be offered in homes.

Contrary to all predictions Hinduism not only survived but recovered and in many ways may be today stronger than ever. The revival and regeneration of Hinduism is largely the achievement of Hindu reformers, who for the past two centuries tirelessly worked for the betterment of their country on the basis of religion. There have been too many of them to mention individually. The issues they concerned themselves with and the institutions they founded to address these concerns are too numerous again to find place within such a short survey.[7] Briefly one can say that they tried first to rid Hinduism from practices perceived to be inhuman and cruel, like the burning of widows and female infanticide. Some felt that the strictures of caste should go, especially the disrespect shown to people considered to be outside the caste system altogether. Improving the social standing and the education of women became a major issue, too. Although it may be admitted that these reforms were effected under the impact of a new social consciousness sharpened by the contact with representatives of Christianity and often in response to accusations by Western missionaries, the religious reform, properly speaking, the intensification of devotion, the purification of ritual, and the new seriousness shown in the study of the religious classics were inner-Hindu phenomena that in the end turned out to be more important for Hinduism.

Reforms and reformers brought new tension to Hindu society: the tension between the secular and the religious, which in that form was unknown to traditional Hinduism. Western secular civilization became both a fascination and a terror to Hindus. Some found it so attractive that they were able to envision India as a secular society with Hinduism as the private mystical religion of those who had a taste for it, mere interiority and piety. Other considered the onrush of secularism to be a challenge to recapture the *dharmakṣetra,* to rehinduize the public life of India.

Swāmi Vivekānanda, himself one of the foremost of Hindu reformers, expressed it well when he said: "There are two great obstacles on our path in India: the Scylla of old orthodoxy and the Charybdis of modern European civilization. Of these two I vote for the old orthodoxy and not for the Europeanized system, for, the old orthodox man may be ignorant, he may be crude but he is a man, he has a faith, while the Europeanized man has no backbone, he is a mass of heterogeneous ideas picked up at random from every source—and these ideas are unassimilated, undigested, unharmonized . . . "[8] And, "This is my objection against the reformers. The orthodox have more faith and more strength in themselves, in spite of their crudeness. But the reformers simply play into the hands of the Europeans and pander to their vanity. Our masses are gods as compared with those of other countries. This is the only country where poverty is not a crime."[9]

A NINETEENTH-CENTURY HINDU RENAISSANCE

The momentum of Hindu reforms, especially in the area of social customs, gained considerable strength in the early nineteenth century, when several European powers had established themselves in India, welcomed by many Hindus as liberators from the corrupt Muslim rule and admired for their technical achievements. There is an extensive literature in English on these so-called Hindu Renaissance movements; because many of the modern Hindu reformers wrote and spoke English, it is the most easily accessible area of Hinduism for people without a knowledge of Indian languages. The sheer bulk of books available in this area and the captivating attribute "modern" has led many people in the West to believe that these modern Hindu reform movements are identical with contemporary Hinduism, except perhaps for a few remnants of "unreformed" Hinduism, which one needed not take seriously. Quite the contrary, these modern Hindu movements, despite their appeal to Westerners and Westernized Hindus, represent only a small fraction of actual Hinduism, which is still much more rooted in its ancient and mediaeval traditions than inclined toward the modern movements.

The real Hindu Renaissance took place in traditional Hinduism: the traditional *saṃpradāyas* consolidated their influence, generous donations made it possible to restore hundreds of old temples and build thousands of new ones, grassroots religious organizations gave new life to the religious observations and festivities. This cautionary remark seems necessary for gaining a correct perspective, when we now go on to consider a number of reformers and their work.

The first of the really significant modern Hindu reformers was Rām Mohan Roy (1772–1833) who was called *Father of Modern India* by his admirers; a genial and many-sided person.[10] His father was a Vaiṣṇava, his mother came from a Śākta family, and as a boy he was sent to Patna to study at the Muslim University, learning Arabic and Persian and becoming interested in Sufism. This turned him against image worship, an issue over which he fell out with his father. He left for Tibet. His father, however, gave in under the condition that he spend twelve years at Banaras, the center of Hindu learning, before returning to his home in Bengal. Rām Mohan Roy engaged in a study of Sanskrit and Hindu scriptures; but he also studied English and entered the service of the East India Company at Calcutta. In 1814, he left its service and devoted himself fully to religious propaganda and reform. He tried to purify Hinduism by returning to the Upaniṣads and translated several books. He sought connection with the English missionaries, who had opened a college at Serampore, not far from Calcutta; he studied Greek and Hebrew to translate the Bible into Bengali. The publication of a little pamphlet, *The Precepts of Jesus: The Guide to Peace and Happiness*, estranged him from both his Hindu friends and the missionaries. The former accused him of canvassing for Christianity, the latter objected to his Hinduizing of Christianity. In the course of quite bitter polemics Rām Mohan Roy accused the missionaries of having misinterpreted the words of Jesus; a reproach that has been leveled against the Christian missions ever since. Rām Mohan Roy won a triumph in his battle against the practice of *satī*, the (not always voluntary) burning of widows together with their deceased husbands. As a boy he had witnessed the forced *sāti* of a much-liked sister-in-law, which had stirred him so profoundly that he vowed to devote his life to the abolition of this cruel custom, allowed by the British officials as part of their policy of noninterference with local religions. Rām Mohan Roy succeeded in convincing the government that *satī* did not form part of original and pure Hindu dharma and thus, against violent opposition, the anti-*sāti* law was passed.[11] Interestingly a number of prominent Englishmen, among them the famous Indologist H. H. Wilson supported Hindu orthodoxy against Rām Mohan Roy, arguing that *sāti* was part of the Hindu religious tradition and that England's policy of not interfering with religious practices should also apply there.[12] It is an ominous sign of the times that more than a century after the abolition of *sāti* and the prohibition of infanticide by the British government of India, instances are dramatically on the rise where young women are burnt to death by their husbands or their husbands' relations to obtain dowry (which is officially abolished as well) and that thousands of cases of poisoning of baby girls have recently been reported among just one group in South India.[13]

Several times Rām Mohan Roy tried to organize a group of people to begin a new religious movement, embodying his ideas of religion. He finally succeeded five years before his death with the Brahmo Samāj, somehow combining Hinduism and Christianity. Rām Mohan Roy kept his sacred thread and wanted to remain a faithful Hindu. Hindu orthodoxy, however, excommunicated him. Rām Mohan Roy also became instrumental in establishing English schools in Calcutta, emphasizing the value of modern, scientific education. In its heyday many Europeans thought the Brahmo Samāj would become the future religion of India; subsequent history has proved the traditional streams of Hinduism stronger than this courageous new attempt.[14]

Rām Mohan Roy's successor was Debendranāth Tagore, called *Mahārṣi*, the father of the more famous Nobel Prize winner for literature, Rabindranāth Tagore. Mahārṣi founded a Bengali paper and a school for Brahmo missionaries with the explicit purpose of checking the spread of Christian missions. He also openly broke with orthodox Hinduism by declaring the Vedas as neither free from error nor inspired. His book *Brahmo Dharma*, an anthology from Upaniṣads and *Smṛtis*, became the official catechism of the movement.[15] With the entrance of Keshub Chandra Sen (1838–1884), some explosive issues were brought into the Brahmo Samāj.

Because Keshub was not a Brahmin, several members left in protest. The development of peculiar rituals to replace Hindu *saṃskāras* and his close connections with Christians led to a split within the Samāj: Debendranāth Tagore remained with the Ādi Samāj, whereas Keshub became the leader of the Brahmo Samāj of India, which due to his extravagance suffered another split in later years. Keshub developed tremendous social activity, collecting funds for victims of famines and floods, founding schools for boys and girls, a workers' association, agitating for literacy and civil marriage legislation against the widespread Indian custom of child marriage, pleading for intercaste marriage and widow remarriage. Ironically, he married off his own daughter while she was still a child, an incident that estranged quite many of his followers. In his youth he lectured enthusiastically on Christ; later he considered himself a superman and expected to be worshipped as such. He preached the New Dispensation, to replace the Old and the New Testaments. While he was becoming increasingly engrossed in ideas like these, the social activities of the Brahmo Samāj declined.[16]

Whereas the largely idealistic Brahmo Samāj is all but defunct as an organized movement, its more radical and often fanatical sister foundation, the Ārya Samāj, not only continues to attract members to its local centers but has also spawned a number of notable organizations exerting considerable influence on India's present-day politics.

Swāmi Dāyānanda Sarasvatī (1824–1883), from Morvi in Gujarat, describes how he lost faith in Śiva and image worship while keeping night vigil on Śivarātrī, compelled to do so by his father. He saw rats climbing onto the image, which was powerless to defend itself. Meanwhile his pious father was sound asleep. At the age of 24, just before he was to enter a marriage arranged by his parents, he fled from home in search of the means to overcome death. After twelve years of wandering from one guru to the other, dissatisfied with all, he met Swāmi Virājānanda Saraswatī of Mathurā. A temperamental man, the blind old swāmi succeeded in completely subduing the restless spirit of Dāyānanda and prophesized that he would become the restorer of Hinduism of his age. His was a strictly orthodox Vedic religion, rejecting the religion of the epics and the Purāṇas, the Saṁhitās and the Āgamas, as corrupt and untrue. In his *Satyārtha Prakāśa* he lays down the principles of his *sanātana dharma,* quoting Vedas, Upaniṣads, the *Manusmṛti,* and some *Dharmasūtras.* The last two chapters are devoted to a refutation of Islam and Christianity. A quotation from the Bible induces the *samīkṣaka*, literally, "inquisitor," to ask for its meaning. The Īsāī, representing Christianity, gives an unsatisfactory answer. A dialogue ensues in which the Ārya Samājist proves his superiority over the man of the Bible. He closes by saying that the Bible is a bunch of lies and that only the Vedas teach truth. In practice the Ārya Samāj, founded in 1875 in Bombay, went further, using persuasion or even moral and physical violence to reconvert Muslim and Christians. The Ārya Samāj has founded *gurukulas*, training institutions, in which children from the age of 4 are brought up strictly along Vedic lines.

After initial successes in Punjab, Dāyānanda Saraswatī shifted his headquarters to Lahore and plunged into numerous social and religious activities. After his death the Ārya Samāj split into a conservative branch that had its center in the Kaṅgrī Gurukula, now D.A.V. University, and the progressives who kept their headquarters in the D.A.V. College, Lahore. The Mahātmā party became more and more aggressive, and its leader Śraddhānanda was shot dead by a Muslim in 1925. They founded many schools all over India and started many activities with the aim of spreading Vedic culture. They tried to counteract Christian missions by means both fair and foul and performed the *śuddhi* ceremony on thousands of converts.[17]

In a very real sense one can also include Mahātmā Gandhi among the great Hindu reformers of the Indian Renaissance whose work had considerable impact on the West.[18] He never left any doubt about his Hindu identity. Thus he declared early on in his Indian career:[19]

> I call myself a *sanātani* Hindu because
>
> 1. I believe in the Vedas, the Upaniṣads, the Purāṇas and all that goes by the name of Hindu Scriptures, and therefore in *avatārs* and rebirth.
> 2. I believe in the *varnāśrama dharma* in a sense, in my opinion, strictly Vedic, but not in its present popular and crude sense.
> 3. I believe in the protection of the cow in its much larger sense than the popular.
> 4. I do not disbelieve in idol worship.

He qualified and explained all these points in a lengthy commentary: "I have purposely refrained from using the words 'divine origin' in reference to the Vedas or any other scriptures. For I do not believe in the exclusive divinity in the Vedas. I believe the Bible, the Koran and the Zend Avesta to be as much divinely inspired as the Vedas. My belief in the Hindu scriptures does not require me to accept every word and every verse as divinely inspired. . . . I do most emphatically repudiate the claim (if they advance any such) of the present Śaṅkarācāryas and Shastris to give a correct interpretation of the Hindu scriptures . . . "[20]

The great merit of Gandhi and of his disciples was their tolerance and a genuinely religious spirit that comprises both love of God and service to humanity. Many Gandhians were engaged in activities designed to overcome the hostility and exclusivity of the various religions, most notably the "Gandhian Patriarch" Kaka Kalelkar, who started a Viśva Samanvaya Saṅgha, working toward a "familyhood of religions."[21]

HINDUISM REACHING OUT FOR THE WORLD

The best known of all the Hindu reform movements is the Ramakrishna Mission, founded by Swāmi Vivekānanda (1863–1902), a disciple of Paramahamsa Ramakrishna (1836–1886). Ramakrishna (Figure 28.1), a temple priest at Dakṣineśvar and a mystical devotee of Kālī, became a source of religious renewal for a large number of Bengalis who met him during his lifetime.[22] Totally withdrawn and averse to any organization or reformist activity, after his death he nevertheless became the central figure in the world movement initiated by his favorite disciple after the later's appearance at the world Parliament of Religions in Chicago in 1893. Touring America and Europe, Swāmi Vivekānanda brought home to India a new self-consciousness of Hinduism and a sense of social mission, which induced him to work restlessly for the improvement of his compatriots through relief organizations, schools, hospitals, and innumerable other activities. Basically an Advaitin, he was open to the other *mārgas* and also to religions other than Hinduism, though he considered them inferior and spiritually underdeveloped. The *Ramakrishna Mission* is a well-organized community today, with some 700 permanent members and a large number of associated workers, maintaining several colleges, high schools, hostels, hospitals, and publishing an impressive amount of religious literature. It also established, with grants from the Indian government and the Ford Foundation, the well-known Institute of Culture in Calcutta. Swāmi Vivekānanda inspired HinduIndia with immense pride and a sense of mission. He articulated the rationale for the new Hindu religious movements in the West in the following manner: "We Hindus have now been placed, under God's providence, in a very critical and responsible position. The nations of the West are coming to us for spiritual help. A great moral obligation rests on the sons of India to fully equip themselves for the work of enlightening the world on the problems of human existence."[23]

And, "Once more the world must be conquered by India. This is the dream of my life. I am anxiously waiting for the day when mighty minds will arise, gigantic spiritual minds who will be ready to go forth from India to the ends of the world to teach spirituality and renunciation, those ideas which come from the forests of India and belong to Indian soil only. Up India, and conquer the world with your spirituality. . . . Ours is a religion of which Buddhism, with all its greatness is a rebel child and of which Christianity is a very patchy imitation."[24]

The Ramakrishna Mission, as is well known, not only promotes a nonsectarian (neo-) Hinduism but also a kind of religious universalism. Ramakrishna is the source of the widely accepted "all-religions-are-the-same" theory. Accordingly, the Ramakrishna Mission not only spreads Hinduism in the West but also invites representatives of other religions to its temples and centers in India to speak about their own traditions.

Swāmi Vivekānanda inspired many young people in India not only to join his mission and devote themselves to the causes of reform and uplift but also to continue his rearticulation of Hinduism and its application to the modern world as well as its reaching out to the West.

Aurobindo Ghose, beginning as a nationalist firebrand, became one of the leading spiritual leaders not only of India, but beyond, from his exile *āśram*, in Pondichery. His followers are not organized in an order, but their sense of mission is strong and active, as can be seen in the development of Auroville, a city that tries to realize and put into practice the principles of Aurobindo's spirituality.[25]

In the eyes of the educated Westerner the most impressive figure of twentieth century neo-Hinduism is surely Sarvepalli Radhakrishnan, a former president of India. Educated in Protestant mission schools in South India, well read in Eastern and Western philosophical and religious literature, a successful diplomat and politician, a prolific writer, and an excellent speaker, he seems to embody what all are looking for: purified, spiritualized, nonsectarian Hinduism, the "religion of the spirit" and "the world religion of

Figure 28.1 Rāmakrishna Paramahaṃsa

the future," a valid and final answer to all the great questions of our time. As head of state he served, in an eminent way, as the "conscience of the nation," and wherever he spoke he stressed the importance of spirituality, regardless of his audience. More than any other representative of the Indian intelligentsia Dr. Radhakrishnan has taken up the concrete problems of India, attempting to contribute a religious dimension to their solution.[26]

Universalism and worldwide validity of its principles is claimed by many exponents of Hinduism, both at home and abroad. Few however, would go as far as M. S. Golwalkar, the former leader of the R.S.S. who wrote: "The mission of reorganizing the Hindu people on the lines of their unique national genius which the Saṅgh has taken up is not only a process of true national regeneration of Bhārat but also the inevitable precondition to realize the dream of world-unity and human welfare . . . it is the grand world-unifying thought of Hindus alone that can supply the abiding basis for human brotherhood. This knowledge is in the safe custody of the Hindus alone. It is a divine trust, we may say, given to the charge of the Hindus by destiny . . . "[27]

A great many well-known and respected and popular representatives of Hinduism of the more charismatic type, who have their major audience in India, have attracted Western followers, who very often establish centers in their own countries, propagating the words and works of their masters.

Ramaṇa Maharṣi (1879–1950) has been among the greatest and deepest spiritual influences coming from India in recent years. He was not educated in the traditional sense but he intuited Advaita-Vedānta and became something like a Socrates among the Indian yogis. He relentlessly questioned his visitors: "Who Are You?" until they lapsed into silence, arriving finally at some intimation of their true self. Even after his death the place where he lives is said to be somehow charged with spiritual power, emanating from him.[28]

Swāmi Śivānanda (died 1964), the founder of the Divine Life Society, with headquarters at Śivānandāśram in Rishikesh, began as a physician before he turned *samnyasi*. His interest, however, continued to be devoted to body and soul. At Rishikesh his followers collect herbs to produce Ayurvedic medicines, and disciples from many countries are living a religious life that intends to synthetize the great world religions.[29]

J. Krishnamurti, groomed to be the *avatāra* of the twentieth century by Annie Besant, developed into quite an independent

22 Ramaṇa Maharṣi

man, denouncing his mother-in-God and theosophy. He became known in his own right as a lecturer and writer on spiritual topics.[30]

Among the better known women saints of our time was Mā Ānandamāyī, with establishments in Banaras, Vrindavan, and Bombay and quite a considerable following who consider her a living deity.[31]

Paramahaṁsa Yogānanda, author of the *Autobiography of a Yogi* and founder of the Yoga fellowship of California,[32] is far better known in the United States than in India. Mahesh Yogi Maharishi, became the founder guru of the International Transcendental Meditation Society.[33] Swāmi Bhaktivedānta, at a very advanced age established the Krishna-consciousness movement in the United States.[34] Swāmi Taposwāmi Mahārāj, quite well known in his own right,[35] has become more famous through his world-touring disciple Swāmi Cinmayānanda, who not only gives well-advertised Gītā lectures in large Indian cities but has also founded Sandeepany Sādhanālaya, a training institution for Hindu missionaries in Bombay.[36]

One of the most colorful of the contemporary saints is easily Śrī Sathya Sāī Bābā sporting a bright-red silk robe and an Afro hairdo. As a boy of fourteen he declared that he had no more time for such things as going to school, announcing that he was Sāī Bābā and that his devotees were calling for him. The Sāī Bābā he was referring to was a well-known saint, living in Śirdī (Mahārāṣṭra), who is credited with many miracles and who is even now supposed to appear to people and initiate them in their dreams.[37] The first miracle of the now living Sāī Bābā, who is going to be 70 in 1994, was to create sweets for his playmates and flowers for the villagers of Puttaparti in Andhra Pradeś. The sacred ashes that he now creates (following the lead of the old Sāī Bābā, on whose images often a curious ashlike substance forms) is said to have miraculous properties to effect cures in sickness and accord mental relief. Modern as he is, he also creates photographs of his own holy person out of nowhere and distributes them, still damp, to his followers. His healing powers are said to be phenomenal, and people come from far and wide so that he may help their bodies and their souls. He is said to be able to read thoughts and have the gift of prophecy and of multilocation. Thus he speaks: "Trust always in me and lay your burden upon me; I shall do the rest; It is my task to prepare you for the grace of Bhagvān, when you receive it, everything else will be simple." He does not demand any special exercises, only trust: "Sāī is mother and father. Come to him without fear, doubt or hesitation. I am in your heart."[38]

INDIAN SECULARIST CRITIQUE OF HINDUISM

The difference between orthodox and reformist, so pronounced in the nineteenth century, is no longer easy to make out. Some of the reformist movements have settled into orthodoxies of their own, and some of the staunchest defenders of orthodoxy advocate quite radical reform. K. M. Munshi, a great literary and political figure and the *spiritus rector* behind the establishment of the Bhāratīya Vidyā Bhavan, certainly as articulate a defender of Hinduism in our century as any, declared that the *varṇāśramadharma* was now obsolete and that "exercises in faith must be satisfying to the modern mind, ceremonies and rituals must be uplifting and religious symbols inspiring. Temples must be clean, set in a sanctified atmosphere, the music accompanying prayers must be soulful and the officiating priests must be men of learning and faith."[39]

The Śaṅkarācārya of Puri, Swāmi Niranjan Dev, considered the most conservative of the traditional defenders of *sanātana dharma,* is also quoted as having pleaded for the abolition of caste and class differences.

The difference between religious and secularists, however, has become more pronounced and is quite an issue in present-day India. Secularism in India emerged as an ideology with Hindu reform in the nineteenth century. Foreign-educated Indians, impressed by what they had seen in the "secular West" and impatient with the obscurantism of traditional religion, the interminable clashes between the religious communities and their obvious inability to agree on essentials of matters important for Indian society, pressed for a secular India. Thus, in spite of his close association with the devout Hindu Mahātmā Gandhi, the first premier of India, Jawaharlal Nehru, pushed through his concept of the Indian republic as a "secular democracy" in contrast to the simultaneous emerging of Pakistan as "Islamic theocracy." A whole generation of modern educated and highly placed Hindus distanced themselves from religion and went to work to transform India into a modern state with a secular outlook. Although antireligious movements as such were few, pro-secular statements by intellectuals are quite pronounced. M. N. Roy's "Radical Humanism" is perhaps the best known formulation of it.[40] Another Bengali philosopher, P. C. Chatterji more recently came out with a spirited defence of *Secular Values for Secular India.* He goes into the recent history of communal rioting in India, identifying the narrow factionalism of the representatives of religious communities and pleading for a science-based secularism as the basis of Indian society.[41]

The urban modern educated class, which is more interested in careers and living standards than in traditional loyalties and pieties, is often quite articulate in its critique of Hinduism. An important Indian weekly some years ago invited some prominent Indians to express their ideas on "the role of religion in our lives." One Hindu had the following to say:

> The influence of religion on our lives has been detrimental. The dependence on religion and religious gurus has reduced us to a state of helplessness and we are always tempted to look out for an invisible, higher power, which is supposed to solve all our problems. The common people are unable to understand the philosophy of religion and therefore they content themselves with ridiculous ceremonies, making a mockery of everything that is sublime and holy. The impossibility of practicing the lofty commands of religion, the lack of a synthesis between these high values and the daily demands of secular life and the endeavor of every Indian to pretend to live according to these ideals have made us the most hypocritical amongst all the peoples on earth. This hypocrisy pervades every aspect of our life. Also the false emphasis on the 'other world' while we are engaged in securing an existence for ourselves here on this earth has made us the most corrupt of all nations—a people which shirks work and is always hoping that something will come, making fate responsible for its misfortune. If our religion, instead of teaching us renunciation could give us guidance in our life and work, to make this world a better place to live in, then we Indians, with all our masses of men and our economic potential could be one of the leading nations of the world. In short—our religion has taught us, instead of 'elevating us to the state of spiritual ecstasy' to be hypocrites and like Triśaṅku we have lost touch with both heaven and earth. We have remained behind in the race for a higher living standard because of the queer belief, that we could live in the twentieth century according to ideals that had been proclaimed long, long ago. The result is a hopeless stagnation in our spiritual values.[42]

Another modern Hindu, writing on "Our Changing Values,"[43] called the present intellectual situation in India "A World of Make-Believe," deploring the aspects of hypocrisy and falseness that pervade everything.

> A half-hearted mysticism justifying India's failure to face life squarely leads the Indian intellectual to a sphere where the individual human being loses his significance in the mumbo-jumbo of a sham mysticism. A deep-rooted apathy toward change and development—born out of frustration and the certificates that the pseudo-intellectuals get from

> their fellow-travelers in the West have jointly created a world of make-believe. . . . To rub out the rugged edges of their spiritual bankruptcy many Indian intellectuals entertain some make-believe picture of India and use it as a short of spiritual sand-paper. . . . Power has become the cornerstone of goodness. . . . The ordinary Indian bestows respect on the powerful. Even a cursory survey of the causes for the reverence of the Bābās and Mās and astrologers will convince us that the average Indian does not respect them for any spiritual upliftment. He respects them for very mundane reasons—for getting promotions in his job, for being successful in business, for curing his diseases etc. Today he is finding that he can be more benefitted by the politically powerful and that is why he has developed reverence for them.[44]

A major source of friction between the Hindu reformers and the secularizers are laws that affect Indian society as a whole. A case in point is the Hindu Marriage Act of 1956, which, with amendments of 1978, recently became signed into law by the president of India. Although still basically respecting the rights of the religious communities to follow their own traditions the Indian government drastically secularized Hindu marriage laws and legislated changes that go quite manifestly against the letter and the spirit of the traditional Hindu law.[45] Other points of conflict are the Hindu demand to ban cow slaughter all over India,[46] to prohibit the consumption of alcohol, the government control of temple boards, and the support of schools maintained by various religious communities.

Modern India's intellectuals were supposed to be the principal support of secularism, believed to be the only ideology capable of promoting harmony among the followers of the great diversity of religions in India. According to V. K. Sinha, "the major responsibility of accelerating the secularization of Indian society will rest on non-governmental associations and groups. It is the press, the universities, the intellectuals and the artists who will have to take the initiative in promoting secularism in India."[47]

However, some leading intellectuals seem to have second thoughts. Thus T. N. Madan, the director of the Institute of Economic Growth in Delhi, an internationally known social scientist, declared secularism as "the dream of a minority, which wants to impose its will upon history but lacks the power to do so under a democratically organised polity."[48] The great majority of Indians, Madan holds, are still guided by their religious traditions. These traditions are "totalizing," that is, they encompass the whole of life and do not permit a distinction between a "secular state" and a "private religion," typical for Western countries.[49]

That Hinduism, after having been abandoned and shrugged off as a relic from the past by the progressive, Westernized, modern-educated Indians, is making a comeback is evident in all big cities in India. Among the more popular swāmis attracting large crowds also of young people are many with a modern scientific education, which they use to advantage in explaining the Vedas or the Bhagavadgītā. In many well-to-do modern neighborhoods new temples are being built, *bhajan* groups are forming, committees are established to support religious causes.

In the wake of the recent Ayodhyā agitation it became quite clear, that although the by now fairly large modern-educated Indian middle class may not be in favor of rioting and violence, it is sympathetic to the ideology of the Hindu movements.[50] Secularism as the West understood it, has no chance in today's India. The best one could hope for is tolerance on a religious basis, the kind of Hinduism advocated by S. Radhakrishnan or Mahātmā Gandhi.[51]

Hindus, as we have seen, can be very critical of Hinduism too—but that should not mislead us into thinking that they are waiting for Westerners to solve their problems. Self-righteous as many Westerners still are, the social, psychological, and spiritual problems of the West are of such a magnitude that we should think twice before offering our advice to India. Even the most critical Indians admit at the end of their devastating self-criticism that they believe in the self-regenerating power of their culture and people and, if they see any hope, expect the solution of their difficulties to come from within their own culture rather than from without. Two world wars, racial and political tensions, flagrant greed and materialism have disillusioned India about the West's savior role, which it assumed in the nineteenth century. The best we can do is to try to become partners in a worldwide economic and spiritual community.

29 Mahātmā Gandhi: A Twentieth-Century Karmayogi

> A leader of his people, unsupported by any outward authority: a politician whose success rests not upon craft nor the mastery of technical devices, but simply on the convincing power of his personality; a victorious fighter who has always scorned the use of force; a man of wisdom and humility, armed with resolve and inflexible consistency, who has devoted all his strength to the uplifting of his people and the betterment of their lot. . . . Generations to come, it may be, will scarce believe that such a one as this ever in flesh and blood walked upon this earth.
>
> —Albert Einstein[1]

Gandhi, the film, was, in many ways, a surprising success both outside India and inside. No doubt the acting of Ben Kingsley, the photography of Sir Richard Attenborough, and the dramatic mass scenes filmed in India did much to make it so attractive to so many. However, it surely also succeeded in getting something of Gandhi's own life and thought across, and Gandhi himself proved to be the main attraction.[2]

The fact that it was a Hindu who shot Gandhi, one of the extremists who believed that in the communal conflict Gandhi took the side of the Muslims, reveals the whole dilemma when highlighting Mahātmā Gandhi in a survey of Hinduism. Fully aware of the hostility against Gandhi from the politically right-wing Hindus, as well as of the disdain for him from many "secularists" and progressives, with all his contradictions, he may serve as a live example of a modern Hindu and, at the same time, offer the opportunity to discuss substantive issues that have become worldwide concerns, issues that Gandhi farsightedly addressed already in his life. Gandhi's secretary, Mahadev Desai, issued in 1936 what came to be known as Gandhi's *Autobiography*.[3] Urged on and helped by his close collaborator, Rev. Andrews, Gandhi reported under the title "My Experiments with Truth" his inner development up to the year 1924. Then, he believed, he had reached the point in his life, from which events could be interpreted on the basis of his by now mature convictions. The book has become a classic of twentieth century spirituality and provides insight into the growth of possibly the greatest human that the twentieth century has seen in the sphere of public life.

AN AVERAGE INDIAN CHILDHOOD

Mohandas Karamchand Gandhi was born on October 2, 1869, in Porbandhar, Gujarāt. The Gandhis belonged to the Bania caste, although both his father and his paternal grandfather were premiers in princely states in Kāthiāwār. Gandhi's mother was a devout Vaiṣṇava who used to pay daily visits to the temple and who kept many *vratas*. She imbued little Mohandas with her religious mind. Mohandas went to elementary school in Porbandar. Reports describe him as friendly, conscientious, and of average intelligence. His third engagement took place when he was 7 (two earlier brides had died by then), followed by marriage at age 13. By then Gandhi had moved to Rajkot High School. He was a good student, but he did not read anything besides his textbooks. He preferred to be by himself and did not join the school sports. A somewhat older fellow student attempted to draw the overly introverted Mohandas out from his shell. He induced him to eat meat, to drink liquor, to smoke cigarettes, even to visit a brothel, from which he ran away, frightened. The crisis was getting serious. Gandhi called himself an atheist and planned to commit suicide in a temple. The performance of a religious drama effected a kind of conversion in him. He confessed all his wrongdoings to his father, asked for a penance, and never relapsed. The *Rāmacaritamanāsa* of Tulasīdāsa, which he began to read and to love, was preparing him for a personal relationship with his God. After graduation from high school Gandhi entered Samaldas College in Bhavnagar to study law. He found his studies too demanding and returned home without quite knowing what to do with himself. A friend suggested to go to England. For an orthodox

Hindu that was something unheard of. His mother categorically refused to give her permission. Later she relented under the condition that Mohandas would assure her by way of an oath not to eat meat, not to drink liquor, and not to touch any woman. Mohandas first thought of becoming a medical doctor. Here, again, Hindu taboos interfered. His brother made it clear to him that as a Vaiṣṇava he was not to have anything to do with corpses. His caste declared him impure and outcaste because of his "travels across the dark ocean." Mohandas kept his vows and realized his plans. Difficult as life in England was, he completed his law studies with honors and came in touch with many persons who influenced his thinking decisively. He was introduced to Madame Blavatsky and Mrs. Annie Besant, the founder-leaders of the Theosophical Society. He read, for the first time, the Bhagavadgītā, in a translation by Edwin Arnold. His roommate, Dr. Josia Oldfield, a vegetarian like Gandhi, wanted to convert him to Christianity and took him to Sunday sermons at the major churches. During a strike of longshoremen in 1899 he, together with a friend, visited Cardinal Mannings to express his appreciation for the help he had given to the strikers.

Gandhi became fond of England and the English, and later in life he would say that his sojourn in London taught him to make a distinction between the British colonial government, which he detested, and the English people, whom he loved.[4]

YEARS OF DECISION

After his exams at the Bar, Gandhi did not waste one day before returning to India. He was not interested in traveling through Europe, as did most of his compatriots, who had absolved their studies in England. Arriving in Rajkot in 1891, he underwent the purification ceremony prescribed by his caste-*pañcāyat,* paid his penance, and was fully accepted again. In his own home he began "reforming": he introduced oatmeal and cocoa for breakfast, insisted on European-style dress. He made the acquaintance of a young Jain, whose religiosity deeply impressed him. He debut as a lawyer was not very encouraging. When asked to defend a client in a minor legal matter, he lost his nerve and asked his client to look for another lawyer. He applied for the position of high school teacher, but he lacked the required papers. He finally earned a living by preparing resumés and petitions for other people. In 1893 he signed a contract with Abdullah and Co. to represent the firm in a major case in South Africa.

For the first time Gandhi faced racial discrimination. He was a "coolie lawyer," not accepted by the white ruling class. A minor episode turned into a major personal event. Gandhi was on the way from Durban to Pretoria. A white man entered the first class compartment and demanded that the "colored" copassenger leave. The conductor asked Gandhi to move into a second class compartment. Gandhi refused. He rather preferred to spend the night in an uncomfortable waiting room, than to forgo the right to a first class compartment, for which he had a valid ticket. "My active non-violence dates from this point in time," Gandhi later commented.[5]

Gandhi's interest in religion led him to make the acquaintance of Dr. Baker, who maintained a private chapel and supplied him with Christian literature. Gandhi also read the Quran. But the most profound impression was made by the reading of Tolstoy's *The Kingdom of God Is Within You*. Tolstoy's way of interpreting the Bible became Gandhi's own, and Gandhi henceforth considered Tolstoy his guru.

Originally Gandhi had planned to stay in South Africa for only a few months. It turned out to be almost seventeen years. Interest in Abdullah and Co.'s legal affairs receded more and more into the background. Gandhi became involved in the concerns of his fellow Indians, who, as a colored minority, were exposed to a great deal of oppression and injustice. He opened a legal practice in Pretoria and soon became the moral leader of the Indian community in South Africa.

A short visit to India enabled him to participate in the 1901 All-India Congress in Bombay and travel throughout India. His utterances about conditions in South Africa angered South African politicians.

A telling incident in his private life took place that same year. His son Manilal fell severely ill. The physician prescribed a diet of eggs and boullion. Gandhi did not allow this. His vegetarianism had become part of his religion. He rather risked the life of his son than breaking his own principles.[6]

After returning to South Africa in late 1902 he had to face the anger of the white population which felt slighted by Gandhi's remarks in India.

He read books by Vivekananda and Tagore and memorized the Bhagavadgītā. He considered adopting the Gītā notions of *aparigraha* and *samabhāva*. He let his life insurance run out and told his brother that henceforth he would not send any more money to India, but would distribute all his surplus income to the Indian community in South Africa. He began simplifying his own life and experimenting with all kinds of diets and nature cures.

Ruskin's *Unto This Last* became the second "key book" of his life. He drew three conclusions from it. First, that the well-being of the individual was contained in the well-being of all. Second, that the work of a lawyer had the same value as that of a barber, insofar as all have the same right to earn their living through their work. Third, that the life of manual labor, that is, the life of peasants and artisans, was the most desirable life.[7]

Moving from theory to praxis he established the Phoenix Settlement, to which he transferred the editorial offices of his recently founded *Indian Opinion*.[8] An international group of ideal-socialists began work in the desertlike wastelands. Every settler received a hut and an acre of land. Gandhi was against the use of machines. The aim of self-sufficiency was to be reached by an utmost restriction of wants. All had to work in the fields, all had to collaborate in producing the *Indian Opinion*. Gandhi continued meanwhile his legal practice and had a large clientele: his honesty and conscientiousness were widely appreciated. To the poor he gave free legal advice.

In his home he continued to reform. At 6:30 A.M. all male members of the household had to get up to grind wheat. Bread was made in the home. Gandhi walked to his office, a distance of 6 miles. On the way to and from the office his children had to accompany him: he taught them Gujarati. He did not send them to school. He edited a "health guide," incorporating elements of his philosophy of life and began to contemplate taking vows of voluntary poverty and chastity, as preparation for unconditional service of India.[9]

THE BEGINNING OF *SATYĀGRAHA*

When the South African government passed a law demanding that all Indians be registered and fingerprinted, Gandhi called for passive resistance. It was the occasion when the term *satyāgraha* was coined, which would circumscribe Gandhi's entire future life. *Satyāgraha*, Gandhi explained, was the strength born of truth, love, and nonviolence.[10] *Satyāgraha* was more than passive resistance, it was action in the awareness of having truth on one's side and the belief that truth will prevail in the end. When the government arrested 155 *satyāgrahis* on January 29, 1908, Gandhi exhorted all to strictly follow the prison regulations: they were not law breakers but truth defenders. He used his time in prison to study religious scriptures. Mornings he was reading the Gītā, afternoons the Quran, in the evenings he instructed a Chinese fellow inmate in the Bible.

Gandhi's second spell in prison followed his appeal to the Indians to burn their registration papers. Prison became his "university": he began an extensive reading program in religion, political science, economics and sociology. He was not dejected at all, on the contrary he praised his time in jail and thought that it was the greatest blessing to be imprisoned for the sake of the well-being of his country and his religion.

In London in 1909 he met with the radical youth wing of the congress. They celebrated Dinghra who shortly before had killed Lord Curzon, Britain's viceroy in India, like a national hero. Gandhi condemned the act and advised nonviolence. He studied Britain's India policy and wrote his famous *Hind Swarāj*, containing some of his basic principles.[11] He believed in a real meeting of East and West, but he wholeheartedly condemned modern civilization and technology. Modern medicine was particularly abhorrent to him. He admonished India to unlearn everything she had learned from the West. He referred to the ancient sages as the true teachers of life for India and stated categorically that a mere exchange of government would not be an improvement of the situation.

Gandhi began to become known in India. Gokhale, the great old man of the congress movement, praised Gandhi on his visit to South Africa.[12] When Herrman Kallenbach, a German architect, in 1910 Gandhi offered his extensive ranch for the *satyāgraha* movement, Gandhi accepted and began his large-scale experiment of communal living with his "Tolstoj Farm." The ideological basis was a kind of idealistic naturalistic communism. The daily routine was structured along the prison regulations of Pretoria. The needs of everyone were reduced to the essentials. The aim was total self-sufficiency. Things that could not be produced locally were supposed not to be required. All worked in the fields and attended the religious devotions of all religions represented on the farm. Only nature cures were allowed. All had to practice some handicraft. Kallenbach had learned sandal making in a German Trappist monastery: he taught this art to Gandhi and Gandhi handed it on.

Gandhi developed his own system of education for the children on the farm. Mornings they had to work in the fields, afternoon they had to study. There were no textbooks. Gandhi's endeavor was to transmit education of the heart and mind. He personally taught religion using as text his *Niti Dharma or Ethical Religion.* In 1910, Gandhi closed his legal practice and moved with his whole family to Tolstoj Farm. In 1912, he took a vow renouncing all private property. At the outbreak of World War I Gandhi traveled with his family to England. He volunteered for the medical corps, but his physical condition made him ineligible.

January 9, 1915, Gandhi returned to India for good. He received a hero's welcome but Gokhale asked him to observe a year of silence: he should travel throughout India and familiarize himself with the situation, before appearing in public. Gandhi agreed.

The same year he founded his Satyāgraha Āshram in Wardha, not far from Ahmedabad in Gujarat. It was to be the place to educate perfect servants for the *satyāgraha* movement on a national level. He divided the ashram population into managers, candidates and students. All managers had to work in the fields out of solidarity with the Indian country people. Indian languages were taught. Children were admitted at age 4 and had to undergo 10 years of schooling in religion, agriculture, weaving, literature, Sanskrit, Hindī, and a Dravidian language. Dress and food were spartan. There was no holiday and no vacation. For three months each year the students had to walk through India.

The first serious ashram crisis happened when a family of untouchables asked for membership. The donors, who had so far supported the ashram, withdrew their financial help. Gandhi indicated that he was willing to move the whole ashram into the untouchable quarters of Ahmedabad. Other supporters emerged and the Satyāgraha Āshram became the focus of Gandhi's activities in the next few years.

RULES FOR AN IDEAL LIFE

In his ashram rules Gandhi expressed the entire program of his life, the fruits of his "experiments with truth." Throughout his further life he strove to realize what he had put down in that small booklet. The *Ashram Observances in Action*[13] contain eleven observances, seven activities, and some remarks about the acceptance of applicants. "The first and foremost vow is that of truth." Truth was the cornerstone of Gandhi's religion; he was proud to have reversed the statement "God Is Truth" into "Truth Is God." Truthfulness was to be the basis on which independent India was to be built. Devotees of truth are not supposed to deviate from truth, not even for the sake of a seeming advantage for the country. Throughout his life Gandhi called himself a seeker after truth, never claiming to have found it, but insisting that he had found a way to truth which he was determined to go.[14] One of the preconditions for finding truth was self-effacement: Gandhi called it "making oneself a zero" or to "drown oneself in the infinite ocean of life."[15] This notion of truth excludes an escape from social and political responsibilities. Gandhi could not find his *mokṣa* in a Himālayan hermitage. He had to engage in ceaseless work, as Kṛṣṇa in the Bhagavadgītā had told Arjuna. No wonder that the Gītā played such a central role in his thought—a gospel of action, a doctrine of *niṣkāma karma,* cooperation with the process of world deliverance. Gandhi called his life "experiments with truth." In the light of what was said before we can say: experiments with God. He felt "like an earthen vessel in the hands of his creator"; for him even the smallest act gained immense importance as a stage to God realization. For him the independence of India was part of the Truth for which he was willing to give his life. "Only a free India can worship the true God."

The second principle upon which Gandhi founded his life and his institution was *ahiṃsā,* non-violence. It is complementary to truth, the only way to truth. *Ahiṃsā,* Gandhi explains, is not only nonkilling; it means active love, a love that extends to all living things from the smallest insect to the greatest human. Someone who follows that law cannot be angry with even the most evil of persons, but must love her, wish her well, and serve her. While loving the evildoer, one must hate the evil done. *Ahiṃsā* is the only means to reach self-realization. Nonviolence in the negative sense, as practiced in noncooperation and civil disobedience, became the most powerful weapon in the freedom struggle. It is the weapon of truth. In the last analysis, *ahiṃsā,* like *satya,* is not our doing but it is God's activity in a human, it is the elimination of the egotistical violent element in human nature. *Ahiṃsā,* Gandhi repeats, is not cowardice, it presupposes the ability to fight and constitutes a conscious renunciation of violence. "*Ahiṃsā* without fearlessness is impossible."[16] Gandhi proved his point throughout his life. He walked into dangerous situations, consciously and knowingly, that others would have run away from. He was not deterred by threats of death in situations of communal rioting and did not break his routine of his evening prayer meetings in Delhi's Birla House, even after first attempts on his life had been made and he had premonitions of death.

The third vow Gandhi took and wanted his followers to adopt was that of *brahmacarya,* sexual continence. Gandhi believed that *satya* and *ahiṃsā* could be observed only by people who lived a celibate life in thought, word, and action, as the ancient Indian ideal had suggested. Similarly, his fellow workers had to abstain from all intoxicating drinks, tobacco, drugs, and everything designed to stimulate the senses. He considered his own practice of fasting the culmination of this vow of abstention.[17]

Gandhi's dramatic public "fasts to death" became legendary in his own time and made him, possibly, better known in the West than anything else he did or said. Gandhi used fasting both as a weapon against colonialism and as a means for self-purification. He claimed to have undertaken his big fasts in response to a call from God. For him, fasting was an essential part of religion.[18] Fasting, of course, is an integral part of the Vaiṣṇava tradition, in which he had grown up. Gandhi goes much further both in the extent of fasting and in the importance attributed to it. Fasting presupposes unlimited faith in God. When his first public *swadeshi* movement in 1921 lead to severe rioting in Bombay by Hindus against Muslims, Christians, and Parsis, Gandhi decided to fast "in order to obtain further credit from God."[19] He was prepared to die in his fast, if that was to be God's will. Or to be transformed into a more suitable instrument of God's will. His last fast was undertaken in January 1948, shortly before his death, in response to the large-scale Hindu-Muslim communal rioting following the partition of India. He believed in the redeeming and transforming effects of self-imposed suffering; fasting unto death was the most perfect form of *ahiṃsā*.

Although Gandhi personalized and modernized the "vows" of *satya, ahiṃsā*, and *brahmacarya*, they are easily recognizable as part of the age-old *yama-niyama* ethics of Hinduism. Gandhi adopted the rest of it, too, in his vows of *asteya*, nonstealing, and *aparigraha*, non-possession, and added bodily labor as his own precept for the India of his time. On his extensive travels through India, Gandhi saw not only the abject poverty in which a great majority of his countrymen lived in the villages, but he also noticed their—often enforced—idleness throughout much of the year. He insisted on "bread labor": all should contribute, through their own manual work, to their physical upkeep, and nobody should exploit others. He insisted on reducing wants to a minimum and asking oneself with regard to any material possession whether it was really necessary. He understood bodily work as a means to realize *asteya* and *aparigraha*. In India, where most housework is done by servants and menial employees, and manual work is considered degrading by the socially higher classes, Gandhi's message of manual labor certainly sounded revolutionary. The universal obligation of bread labor found a uniquely Gandhian expression in the *cakra,* the spinning wheel, which for some time was even used as an emblem in the Indian flag. When pondering possibilities of providing additional work and income to the largely underemployed rural population, Gandhi struck upon the spinning wheel. Hand spinning and weaving had been widespread activities in India's villages before the import of cheap, machine-made cloth from England ruined these indigenous industries. Gandhi not only led agitations against imports of foreign cloth—he held large bonfires of such fabrics in major cities—he also offered a workable substitute. Almost a hundred years of interruption of the local textile manufacture had made it difficult to reactivate it on a large scale. By chance someone brought Gandhi an old handmade spinning wheel, which, with some improvement, was distributed throughout the villages. Handlooms were repaired and brought back into production. Gandhi insisted that all members of congress had to devote at least half an hour each day to spinning, and they had to wear only handspun and handwoven cloth (*khadi*). The "Gandhi cap" has remained a symbol of congress membership to this very day. Many from the upper classes protested against Gandhi's "primitivism," but he insisted that India's leaders had not only to lead by words, but also to demonstrate solidarity with the concerns of the masses in a visible way. From the early 1930s on, Gandhi would rarely be seen without his spinning wheel, which he praised as his "wish-fulfilling tree" and the instrument of salvation for India.[20] In his spinning wheel Gandhi saw the confluence of *ahiṃsā,* bread labor, and *swarāj,* independence. For him it also symbolized God, who, as he said, can appear to a hungry person only in the form of bread. Independence was meaningless for the masses, if it did not also bring with it increased employment and income.

ADDRESSING UNTOUCHABILITY

Untouchability, which seemed so inextricably connected with Hinduism, Gandhi maintained, was wholly irreligious.[21] He demanded that his fellow workers take a vow to eradicate untouchability. To show his respect for the *aspṛha,* the untouchables, Gandhi called them *Harijan,* "People of God." He gave equal status to the untouchables in his ashram and thereby created dilemmata for many orthodox Hindus. Paradoxically Gandhi did not attempt to abolish caste, as some nineteenth century reformers had done. He believed in the importance of the *varṇāśrama-dharma*. In his opinion this was an occupational, not a personal division of society, and as such beneficial to humanity. Untouchability he rejected as being against *ahiṃsā*; as far as the distinctions of *āśramas* was concerned, all his fellow ashramites who had taken the vows, were deemed to be *saṃnyāsis*.

Gandhi undertook fasts to achieve the opening of temples to the untouchables—but he also defended Hinduism. When Dr. Ambedkar, himself one of the outcastes and the leader of the Depressed Classes Conference, recommended in 1935 the severance of all untouchables from Hinduism and the adoption of another religion (at first he was not sure whether he should choose Christianity or Buddhism, but finally decided in favor of Buddhism, because it was an indigenous religion), Gandhi was quite upset. He commented that *varṇāśrama-dharma* was a natural law and that Dr. Ambedkar had unfairly attacked the very essence of Hinduism. Religion, Gandhi argued, is not like a piece of garment that one can change at will. Religion is an essential part of our selves, more essential even than the body.[22]

Gandhi acquainted himself early on with the scriptures and doctrines of various major religious traditions and intended to develop his Satyāgraha Āshram into a multireligious community. Through his study and contact with believers from different backgrounds he had come to the conviction that all major religions of the world were revelations of truth; fragmentary, human, imperfect, but to be respected for what they offered. He admonished his coworkers to show equal respect to all religions; there was no need to proselytize, but also no reason to reject any religion. Religions, he said, are different paths that converge on one point; it does not matter which way we go as long as we reach the goal. There are, basically, as many religions as there are individuals.[23] This position also allowed him to profess his loyalty to the Hindu tradition, while criticizing certain historic expressions of it.

He loved the Hindu tradition in spite of its flaws, because he was connected with it through his whole existence. In spite of his admiration for the Sermon on the Mount, ultimately the Bhagavadgītā and Tulsidas's *Rāmacaritamānasa* inspired him most. Time and again he affirmed his belief in karma, in rebirth, his faith in the *avatāras* and the *guru-paramparā*. It was from a deep understanding of, and sympathy for, Hinduism that he condemned untouchability and other inhumane practices historically connected with Hinduism. Although faithfully undergoing religious rites he chastised the greed of the *paṇḍas* and the sloth of *pūjāris*.

RELIGION-INSPIRED ECONOMICS AND ECOLOGY

Gandhi was a thoroughgoing pragmatist, in spite of his otherworldly idealism. He knew that the cornerstone of India's independence was its economy. In prison he studied economists and drew his own conclusions from their writings. Although he advocated limitation of wants and self-limitation in the use of material goods, he never glorified abject poverty or destitution. Traveling third class by railway through India, walking to remote villages, and sharing shelter with ordinary people, he learned firsthand about India's economic problems. The spinning wheel was one response, a response that he considered important and effective. As a member of congress and its sometime president, he also developed more elaborate plans, such as the "Constructive Programme" of 1945, which he wanted to be accepted as the basic document for India's economic development after independence. He believed that the ideal society was the village community. He envisaged an India consisting of 500,000 self-sufficient villages, grounded in *satya* and *ahiṃsā*, supportive of each other and the whole. The metaphor he used was that of an "oceanic circle,"[24] over against the commonly used pyramid of power. He visualized the country structured in concentric circles, with the individual as center. The individual, however, would be willing to sacrifice itself for the sake of the village, the village for the sake of the village cluster, the village cluster for the sake of the country. The larger unit would not use its power to oppress the smaller unit, and the smaller unit would not take undue advantage of the larger.

Gandhi knew about the utopian character of his model, but he argued that it had incomparable value as an idea, similar to the Euclidean point that has no physical existence but is crucially important for all geometry. His ideal future India would be a community of economically equal citizens. Appalled by the gulf that separated the very rich from the masses of the very poor, he implored the former to lower their living standard for the sake of the latter. He feared that a bloody revolution might bring about later what the élite was unwilling to do now.[25] Gandhi advocated the idea of trusteeship: it might be difficult to put into practice, but, he said, "that is true of non-violence as a whole." As far as material needs were concerned he pleaded to "give to everyone according to his needs." When reminded that Karl Marx had used the same formula he remarked that he would not mind calling himself a *socialist* or a *communist,* and he accused those who called themselves *Communists* and *Socialists* of not knowing the true meaning of these terms. For Gandhi *socialism* meant "the incarnation of *satya* and *ahiṃsā*"[26] and *communism* was "to reduce oneself to the level of the poorest of all." And that, he said, he had tried for half a century; so he could call himself a model communist. He never refused help from the "capitalists" and defended them against unjust attacks. The bottom-line of his economics was: all land belongs to God and has been given to humans in trusteeship; all should have what they need, nobody should own more.

From early on, Gandhi showed an almost irrational aversion to machines. The most important reason for this attitude was that, with machines, a subhuman element invades human life. Manual work, which machines were invented to make easier, was for Gandhi not an unpleasant necessity but a religious duty, the fulfilment of a divine command, and the principal means to find truth. His economics was not based on maximizing productivity and profit, but on full employment (in the literal sense of the word), even at the cost of a decline in productivity. He had no sympathy for the leisure-time society of the Socialists, and Soviet Russia rather repelled him. He called it a madness to produce labor-saving machines and then to throw millions out of work. The highest consideration must be the human person and a machine should not lead to a stunting of humanity.[27] Gandhi refused to define the aim of economics as "achievement of the highest possible good for the highest possible number": it had to be the highest good for all. He demonstrated what he meant through his life: he identified with the poorest by not possessing more or using more than what the poorest have. In his famous "Talisman"[28] he recommended to all politicians to visualize the face of the poorest and weakest human beings they had seen in their life and then to ask themselves whether the intended action was of any use for them. As he saw it, industrial mass production is the reason for the worldwide economic crises. Industrial mass production is based in principle on the exploitation of the weaker members of society. Gandhi wanted to replace it through a production *by* the masses. Everyone should participate equally in the growth of national wealth.

Gandhi saw enough of the reality of Indian villages to be aware of the need to improve them. He did not hesitate to call the average North Indian village a "dung heap" and scolded his compatriots for their lack of sense of cleanliness and hygiene.[29] He emphasized the need for sanitation and wanted to see *bhaṅgis* and *dhobis*, traditionally the lowest of castes, elevated to the highest rank, because of the importance of their work for the well-being of society. He insisted that in his ashram everybody take turns to clean the latrines and do all the work required to keep the place clean.

MAHĀTMĀ—THE GREAT SOUL

Gandhi certainly was a practically minded person, a skilful politician, a man concerned with the well-being of his fellow humans and constantly responding to challenges of a very down-to-earth kind. Nevertheless, all his restless activity was motivated by his religion and its ultimate aim was not the welfare state but Rām Rājya, the Kingdom of God.[30] It is important, in the face of present day Indian Rām Rājya politics, to note that Rām Rājya for Gandhi was not the quasi-totalitarian rule of a right-wing Hindu political party, but "the rule of justice" and the "realization of God." He never separated the personal aim of reaching the vision of God from his public activities of transforming India into a truly human society. At several occasions he said that "*satyāgraha* is a religious movement, a process of progressive purification and penance." The India that Gandhi visualized was a holy land that had purified itself through suffering and made itself acceptable to God. One of his most mature maxims, uttered only months before his assassination, engulfed by a sea of tragedy after the partition, reveals his heart best: "By my fetters I can fly, by my worries I can love, by my tears I can walk and by my cross I can enter the heart of humanity. Let me praise my cross, O God."[31]

30 Hindu Nationalist Politics and Hinduism as a World Religion

> Slowly, but surely, like a juggernaut gaining angry momentum, a palpable, resurgent, united and increasingly militant movement of Hindu revivalism—*Hindu Jagaran*—is sweeping across the land. Frenzied in pace, frenetic in character, the religious and communal combat vehicle is free-wheeling across the collective Hindu consciousness . . .
>
> —*India Today* 31 May 1986[1]

The whole world watched with fascination and horror the demolition of the Babri Masjid on December 6, 1992, by thousands of Hindu political activists and the subsequent large-scale rioting, burning, and looting in dozens of India's major cities. For decades the West used to stare at the growth of communism in India as the greatest threat to democracy, but it finally awoke to the reality of a far more serious challenge from the right, that of Hindu extremism, by now well organized and powerful and well within reach of success. The "militant revivalism" of Hinduism has been coming for long. It was not taken seriously by most Westernized Indians and all but ignored by most foreign observers.[2]

Traditional Hinduism, as described in this survey, consisting of a great number of quite independent and more often than not conflicting religions and philosophies, cannot possibly provide an ideology for Hindu party politics. The nineteenth century Hindu Renaissance, too, has spawned all kinds of new understandings of Hinduism, from a humanistic, universalistic, tolerant, and generous religiosity to exclusivist, sectarian, and narrow-minded fundamentalism. The political Hinduism of our age requires a unified, denominational understanding of Hinduism, something that so far has not existed but is obviously taking shape in our time.

Traditional Hinduism had always a political dimension, too, a consequence of its holistic nature, which did not divide life into a religious and a secular sphere. Dharma comprises all aspects of life. In the nineteenth century, under the influence of European nationalism, Hindus turned nationalist, too.

Terms like *Holy Mother India* were not meaningless rhetoric for Hindus but signified a living reality, which every Hindu was called upon to defend, protect, and foster. Bankim Chandra Chatterjee, the great Bengali novelist, whose *Ānandamaṭha* depicted the 1770 *Saṃnyasi* uprising as a national war of liberation from foreign rule, made his patriotic ascetics sing a hymn to Mother India, which for some time became the national anthem of the freedom movement and which Hindu activists today want to reintroduce, the *"Bande Mātarām,"* "Mother, I bow to thee," in which India is identified with the Goddess:

> With many strengths who are mighty and stored,
> To thee I call, Mother and Lord!
> Thou who savest, arise and save! . . .
> Thou art wisdom, thou art law,
> Thou our heart, our soul, our breath,
> Thou the love divine, the awe
> In our hearts that conquers death.
> Thine the strength that nerves the arm,
> Thine the beauty, thine the charm.
> Every image made divine
> In our temples is but thine.
> Thou art Durgā, Lady and Queen,
> With her hands that strike and her swords of sheen,
> Thou art Lakshmi Lotus-throned,
> And the Muse a hundred-toned.
> Pure and Perfect without peer,
> Mother, lend thine ear.[3]

Another Bengali, Sri Aurobindo Ghose, who first fought for India's political independence in a terrorist band, had according to his own testimony, a vision of Kṛṣṇa through which he was made to understand that his life work was to be for the restoration of the true dharma, that is, Hinduism. Bal Gangadhar Tilak and many others undertook their political agitation against the British *rāj* as a duty imposed on them by their religion; their aim was the restoration of Hindu India on the socio-political level.[4] The most radical advocates of the restoration of Hindu dharma on the socio-political level today are the many groups and parties that developed out of the Ārya Samāj, the "Āryan society" of Swāmi Dāyānanda Saraswatī briefly described previously.

THE RADICAL HINDU POLITICAL MOVEMENTS ON A NATIONAL LEVEL

In 1909 Pandit Mohan Malaviya, who became later the first vice-chancellor of Benares Hindu University, founded together with other leading Ārya-Samājists the Hindū Mahā-sabhā, which soon developed into a right-wing militant Hindu political party. It has remained one of the national parties based on a narrow definition of Hindu nationhood. Their Election Manifesto read:

> Hindustan is the land of the Hindus from time immemorial. The *Hindū Mahāsabhā* believes that Hindus have a right to live in peace as Hindus, to legislate, to rule, to govern themselves in accordance with Hindu genius and ideals and establish by all lawful and legal means a Hindu state based on Hindu Culture and Tradition, so that Hindu ideology and way of life should have a homeland of its own. The cardinal creed of the *Hindū Mahāsabhā* is:
>
> 1. Loyalty to the unity and integrity of Hindustan.
> 2. The *Hindū Mahāsabhā* reiterates once again that it is pledged to the re-establishment of *Akhaṇḍ Bhārat* by all legitimate means.
> 3. The *Hindū Mahāsabhā* again reiterates its clarion call, as given by Vīr Savarkar as far back as 1938: "Hinduize Politics and Militarize Hinduism."[5]

The referred-to Vīr Savarkar (1883–1966), the greatest theoretician of the Hindū Mahāsabhā, fought in countless speeches and publications for a violent liberation of India under the Hindu banner from everything foreign, and a complete restoration of Hindu ideas and Hindu society. India's independence from British rule in 1947 was not enough for him, he bitterly opposed Nehru's secular state concept and continued agitating for the total Hinduization of India (which earned him long spells of house arrest in his Bombay-Matunga home). In his essay "Hindutva" he developed the outlines of the new Hindu India. He distinguished between *Hindu-dharma*, Hinduism as a religion, which is divided into countless *saṃpradayas* and *Hindutva*, Hindudom as the unifying socio-cultural background of all Hindus.[6]

One of the members of the Hindū Mahāsabhā, K. V. Hedgewar (1890–1940), a medical doctor who never practiced medicine, in 1925 founded the Rāṣṭrīya Svayam-sevak Saṅgh (R.S.S.). He was afraid of Muslim influence over the Indian National Congress. The R.S.S., strictly organized from the very beginning, is the most powerful and most controversial Hindu organization of today: it claims to be a cultural organization and is not registered as a political party.

Nathuram Godse, Gandhi's murderer, was a member of the R.S.S., which also had been held responsible for a great deal of the communal slaughter around the time or partition.[7] Nehru's reaction to Godse's crime was swift and decisive: he banned the R.S.S. and jailed tens of thousands of its members. About a year later the ban was lifted and the leaders were freed. Apparently the movement had friends in high places and so it was declared that no direct involvement of the R.S.S. in Gandhi's death could be proved.

The events connected with partition that had brought great suffering to many millions of Indians, were perceived by the Hindus in India as inflicting more than an equal share of sacrifice on the Hindus. Differences over Muslim-Hindu policies brought about several breakaways from the monolithic Congress party from 1948 onward.

Events in East Bengal in early 1950 lead to the formation of the Jana Sangh party, which had a clearly pro-Hindu and anti-Muslim orientation.[8] Millions of Hindus had fled from East Bengal to West Bengal telling about forcible eviction, Muslim brutalities, and large-scale repression. The conciliatory talks between Nehru and Liaquat Ali were considered inadequate by a number of politicians in West Bengal and at the Center. The major figures involved were Shyamaprasad Mookerjea (minister for industries and supplies), John Mathai (finance minister), and K. C. Neogy, who resigned from the Union cabinet. They proposed their own set of conditions for Pakistan to agree to and, while ostensibly promoting the cause of the Hindus in Pakistan, articulated also an alternative approach to Indian internal and external politics.

The new party called itself Bhāratīya Jana Saṅgh, in Bengal it first appeared under its English name People's Party of India. Although its origins were connected with dissatisfaction with the existing congress Nehru government's policies, the founders of the Jana Sangh pointed out, correctly, that it did not just constitute a breakaway congress faction.

As Deendayal Upadhyāya wrote:

> The Jana Sangh was founded as an all-India party on 21 October 1951. It was not a disgruntled, dissident or discredited group of Congressmen who formed the nucleus of the party, as is the case with all other political parties. . . . Its inspiration came from those who basically differed from the Congress outlook and policies. It was an expression of the nascent nationalism. It was felt that the ruling party had failed to harness the enthusiasm created by freedom to the task of realization of the great potentialities of the country. It was because of their anxiety to make Bhārat a carbon-copy of the West, that they have ignored and neglected the best in Bhāratīya life and ideals. The Jana Sangh predicted that the *Abhāratīya* and unrealistic approach to the national problems by the party in power would create more complications than solve any. Its forebodings have come true.[9]

The leading light in the early years was Shyamprasad Mookerjea. A man with a distinguished academic record and an early involvement in Bengal politics, he joined the Hindū Mahāsabhā in 1937. In 1946 Nehru offered him a cabinet position. Mookerjea was one of five non-Congress-members of the fourteen member cabinet. Dr. Mookerjea disagreed with the Hindū Mahāsabhā on many issues and demanded, after the assassination of Mahātmā Gandhi, that it either withdraw from political activities altogether or shed its communal Hindu character. The Hindū Mahāsabhā had not been very successful in the 1946 elections anyhow. Eventually Dr. Mookerjea left the Hindū Mahāsabhā and also resigned from the Nehru cabinet in 1950 over the Bengal issue. He established links with the R.S.S. leaders Vasantrao Oak and Balraj Madhok. He tried to persuade the R.S.S. to become a political party. The R.S.S. leadership had rejected such an idea since its foundation: the R.S.S. had wider aims. The Jana Sangh won considerable support in some state elections and became powerful enough on the national level to attract the attention and vituperation of both Congress and leftist parties as being "fascist," "totalitarian," and so forth. Apart from its overall view to Indianize-Hinduize Indian politics it kept pleading for a reunification of India, the introduction of Hindī as national language, the recognition of Israel, and the ban of cow slaughter.[10] It merged with a number of other parties (among others the anti-Indira Gandhi wing of the Congress party) to form the Janata party, which after the resignation of Indira Gandhi in 1977 won elections in a landslide victory.

The coalition that was Janata was shaky from the very beginning. Its lack of initiative and its increasing internal quarrels, largely about the relations of former Jana Sangh members with the R.S.S., created widespread disappointment. Eventually a split occurred, and this brought about the downfall of the Janata government with a return to power of Indira Gandhi's Congress. A further split occurred in March 1980 and again in April 1980, when the former Jana Sangh group formed a new party called the Bhāratīya Janata party (BJP). The leadership was taken over (again) by A. B. Vajpayee, who had been external affairs minister under the Janata government. In a speech on April 6, 1980, he had declared: "We are proud of our association with the R.S.S." Lately he was quoted as saying to be disillusioned with the new party as well.[11] With L. K. Advani's popular rhetoric and organisational skills, the BJP became a nationalist movement attracting worldwide attention through such highly visible events as the *Rāma-sila-yātrā*, a "pilgrimage" through India to collect bricks for a new Rāmā temple in Ayodhyā in 1991; an *Ekta-yātrā*, terminating in Śrīnagar-Kashmir in early 1992 at the height of the state's crisis; and finally the destruction of the Babri Masjid in December 1992. The BJP is clearly poised to take over the leadership of the country and is forging alliances both at the state and the union levels.[12]

Deen Dayal Upadhyāya, Atal Bihari Vajpayee, Lal Krishna Advani, Nanaji Deshmukh, Balraj Madhok, Lal Hansraj Gupta, men who shaped national politics in the 1960s and 1970s were all prominent activists of the R.S.S. The R.S.S. spawned a great number of other front organizations like the Bhāratīya Mazdūr Sabhā, a trade union, the Akhil Bhāratīya Vidyārthi Pariṣad, a students' union; and the Viśva Hindū Pariṣad (VHP), a religious organization (founded in 1964), and others, which attempt to articulate a kind of universal Hinduism that would embrace different sects and at the same time possess a basic common creed and common practice.[13]

It is not always clear where the borderline between R.S.S. and V.H.P. passes, if there is one to begin with. Both organizations boast thousands of centers all over India, millions of members, and both are extremely active on behalf of *Hindū Jagaran* (Hindu Awakening).[14] They organize processions, meetings, festivities, and they work toward bridging the differences between different Hindu denominations in the interest of a united and politically strong Hinduism. Membership figures mentioned are impressive. So are the violent confrontations. One of the immediate aims of the Viśva Hindū Pariṣad after the Ayodhyā victory, was to repossess the areas of the Kṛṣṇa Janmabhumī temple in Mathurā and of the Viśvanāth Temple in Banaras, two of the holiest places of Hinduism, which were (partially) occupied and desecrated by the Muslims in the Middle Ages.

Partly cooperating and partly competing with these organizations are others devoted to the same goal of Hindu awakening and Hindu political power: the Virāt Hindū Sammelan, the Hindū Samājotsav, Bajrang Dal, for example. There can be no doubt that the major role in the Hindu revival has been played for quite some time by the R.S.S.

The training of the R.S.S. members is rigorous and purposeful: bodily exercises and indoctrination sessions have to be attended by all members daily for at least an hour. The leaders are usually unmarried and unsalaried, and they devote all their time and energy to the movement.[15]

M. S. Golwalkar, the successor to K. V. Hedgewar, who died in 1973, early in his career wrote *Bunch of Thoughts*, in which he systematically and openly laid out the ideology and the policies of the R.S.S. He quite frankly declared Muslims, Christians, and Communists (in that order) the major enemies of India and promised that they would not be citizens of a Hindu India shaped according to R.S.S. principles. According to Golwarkar the Hindu nation has been given the divine mandate to spiritualize the world, and this mandate has fallen on the R.S.S. in our time. With genuinely religious fervor Golwarkar exhorts his followers to do their utmost for the reestablishment of this Hindu order not only in India but worldwide. Thus he writes: "The R.S.S. has resolved to fulfill that age old national mission by forging, as the first step, the present-day scattered elements of the Hindu Society into an organised and invincible force both on the plane of the Spirit and on the plane of material life. Verily this is the one real practical world-mission if ever there was one."[16]

After Golwalkar's death Madhukar Dattatreya, known as Balasaheb Deoras (also a bachelor and a member of the R.S.S. since his twelfth year) became *Sarsaṅghachalak*, the supreme leader of the R.S.S. He echoes Savarkar when stating: "We do believe in the one-culture and one-nation Hindu *rāṣṭra*. But our definition of Hindu is not limited to any particular kind of faith. Our definition of Hindu includes those who believe in the one-culture and one-nation theory of this country. They can all form part of the *Hindu-rāṣṭra*. So by Hindu we do not mean any particular type of faith. We use the word Hindu in a broader sense."[17]

Many Indians, who subscribe to the idea of a secular democratic state, with equal rights for all its members, regardless of race, creed, or sex, consider the R.S.S. to be a threat to this state—the biggest and most serious threat considering its membership (upwards of 5 million) and the caliber of its organization. While the R.S.S. and its front organizations may be the most visible manifestation of extremist and radical political Hinduism on the national level, it is not the only one. Thus, Swāmi Karpartriji Maharaj founded in the late forties the Rām Rājya Pariṣad (Kingdom of God party), which also contended in national elections, objecting to Nehru's secular democracy.[18] It is not very powerful but it has attracted also a number of swāmis who campaign on its behalf for seats in the *Lok Sabhā*.

REGIONAL HINDU POLITICAL MOVEMENTS

In the 1960s numerous regional organizations developed in India with the aim to either establish language- or religion-based separate states or to protect the natives of a particular state from the competition of out-of-state immigrants. Regional interests and Hindu interests very often overlap. They are meanwhile too numerous to be dealt with in the context of this book.[19] The example of one—the earliest, most active, and exclusive Hindu organization of this type—may suffice to make the point.[20]

The Shiv Sena (Shivaji's army) was founded in 1966 in Bombay by Bal Thakkeray, a former cartoonist for a local paper. It was to protect the rights and jobs of Mahārāṣṭrians, especially in Bombay, a metropolis with large contingents of Indians from all parts of the country. Thakkeray demanded, among other things, that 80 percent of government jobs be reserved for native Mahārāṣṭrians. By 1969 it had become powerful enough to organize a general strike in Bombay, paralyzing the entire huge city for three days, burning buses and trains, and terrorizing non-Mahārāṣṭrians. Many South Indian coffee shops were burned down, many non-Mahārāṣṭrian businesses were vandalized. Not long afterward the Shiv Sena won the majority of seats in Bombay's municipal election and became a major factor in Mahārāṣṭrian state politics.[21] Hindu interests and regional interests overlap in the Shiv Sena: although the organization is purely Hindu, it demonstrated hostility to all non-Mahārāṣṭrians, Hindu as well as non-Hindu. During the past few years the Shiv Sena has expanded to other Indian states, especially to Uttar Pradeś and Punjab. It claims to have hundreds of thousands of followers there.

The Shiv Sena may have arisen as a rightist Hindu movement counterbalancing leftist forces, but its rise has occasioned the emergence of a great number of regional communal "defense organizations." A Muslim Sena and a Christian Sena emerged to protect the interests of these minorities. It is often difficult to arrange the *senas* within the Indian political spectrum (Kanada Sena, Gopala Sena, Tamil Army, Lachit Sena, Bhim Sena, etc.). Although many of them may not have a significant following and may not have more than local importance, they certainly have helped to polarize the Indian political scene and to weaken whatever sense of unity on the basis of a common Indianness had developed over the years. Although not all of them are Hindu, several of them are increasingly becoming the instruments of politically active and often extreme Hinduism, which throughout history has considered regional loyalties of greater importance than all-Indian interests.

POLITICAL HINDUISM ON A SECTARIAN BASIS

The Ānand Mārg (Path of Bliss) was founded in 1955 by Anand Murti, alias P. R. Sarkar, who, after several stints with newspapers, had found employment in the railways in Jamalpur-Bihar. For his followers Anand Murti is "the great Preceptor, the harbinger of a new civilization and the loving guru." He was born in 1921 and claims to be the third incarnation of God after Śiva and Kṛṣṇa. The movement has many front organizations, including a national political party, the Proutist Block of India. It claimed some years ago to have 2,000 centers and 5 million members. Its declared aim is to "establish the dictatorship of Baba." The Ānand Mārg was linked to a number of acts of violence in India and abroad, and P. R. Sarkar was eventually arrested when his wife denounced him to the police as responsible for thirty-five murders, mostly of former Ānandmārgis who had become disloyal to the movement. Although the number of followers is not large enough to make any impact on the Indian political scene, the acts of violence perpetrated by some of its members abroad and in India aroused the Indian public.[22]

HINDU COMMUNALISM

In its forty-five years of independence India has so far successfully upheld its ideal of a secular democracy on the national level. This did not prevent extremist political Hindu groups from putting pressure on non-Hindu minorities in a number of states like Madhya Pradesh, Uttar Pradesh, Bihar, and Orissa. Although documents such as the Niyogi report purport to attack only foreign Christian missionaries, the Indian Christians rightly interpreted it as an attack on Christianity in India. Again, whereas India was at war with Pakistan, and not Hindus with Muslims, in the several wars that eventually lead to the establishment of Bangladesh, during these wars Muslims did experience harassment from fanaticized Hindus as "enemies of India." The potential for violence that political Hinduism possesses translated at numerous occasions in the past forty years into provocations of Muslims and subsequent large scale rioting along communal lines.[23]

"Communalism" is, of course, not only a Hindu problem.[24] It is a vast and complex phenomenon with which many social and political scientists have dealt and that seems to develop ever new forms, although its basic structure remains the same. Moin Shankar, an Indian political scientist calls communalism "the most intractable problem of the Indian polity and society." It is, he says, "a many faced phenomenon with diverse causes and reveals itself in difficult (sic) forms under different sets of circumstances." His own view is that "under the mask of religion, culture and tradition the communal leaders have been aiming at protecting the interests of the lower middle class and urban intelligentsia."[25]

All are agreed that religious identity is a major factor in communalism and that it constitutes a misapplication of religious principles. For several decades it appeared as if communalism were largely a Hindu-Muslim problem. Lately the Sikh communalists have raised their voices and the regional chauvinisms that find expression in the various *senas* described previously are not only promoting intrareligious but also intraregional hatred.

Many analysts interpret the increasing communal wave as caused by a weakening of central power.[26] That may be so, but it does not explain much either. The Indian socio-political landscape is still forming. The most pressing economic needs having been satisfied (a cause that provided a certain measure of cohesion among all groups) and national independence having been achieved (another cause that united people in spite of differences), the process of normalization of life includes the development of political factions and societal groups that have to arrange themselves vis-à-vis each other on matters other than nationality and bare survival.

It was a symbol of things to come to observe at the celebrations marking the fortieth anniversary of India's Independence in Delhi, on August 15, 1987, a group of people described as a "revolutionary Hindu movement" protesting loudly against Rajiv Gandhi and his concept of a secularist India. "Hindus will be like lions, and they will dominate the country" one of their representatives declared.

Meanwhile so much has happened to make that threat sound like a prophecy. The radical right wing Hindu parties and their supporting movements are riding from success to success, and even major failures, such as the inability of their leaders to control the outbreaks of violence last winter and the ban imposed by the government following these events, seem not to diminish their growing power. The dream of K. B. Hedgewar, the founder of the RSS, whose one hundreth anniversay was recently celebrated[27] seems closer to fulfillment than ever.

The parallels evoked between Hindutva and the rule of dharma under the great Indian rulers of the past and the arguments used to convince the populace of the need for a Hindu India are, however, flawed. The kind of symbiosis that existed in classical India between traditional monarchies and traditional Hinduism was of a different kind than today's intertwining of party politics and an ideologized Hinduism. The responsibility of the traditional Indian king extended to all his subjects, and he was held responsible for their well-being regardless of sectarian affiliation. Likewise, traditional Hinduism took a rather liberal view of doctrinal and ritual matters and was focused primarily on ethical concerns. Political parties as well as denominational religions have partisan concerns. The mix of modern party politics and denominational religions can lead to rather fatal consequences, as one could observe repeatedly in our century in several countries. Almost invariably, the outcome is a dictatorial, intolerant, narrow-minded, and highly arbitrary kind of regime. In and through it, both government and religion will become corrupted. Government, instead of focusing on the needs of the people, will concentrate on matters of ideology and party discipline. Religion, instead of acting as the repository of the moral conscience of the people, will become part of the oppressive system itself and sell its soul for the sake of power.

A PRELIMINARY ASSESSMENT

A long history of foreign invasions and occupation has given an extra edge to political Hinduism: it almost always contains an element of rejection of foreign institutions, customs, and authorities. Considering the high sophistication of traditional Indian thought also in the area of government—the detailed provisions made for the bearers of political authority from the ancient *smṛtis* onward—it is understandable that traditional Hindus want to see these provisions once more in place. Such a suggestion gains even more weight when one compares a glorified Indian past with a disenchanting and problematic Indian present.

Political Hinduism is not a homogenous "movement." It is the result of a reinterpretation of Hinduism along many different lines. Neither are all Hindus agreed that Hinduism or its professional representatives ought to be involved in power politics at all. The traditional *yatidharma*, as explained before, forbids involvement of *saṃnyasis* in political or economic affairs. There are many voices in today's India who demand a separation of religion and state and many view the influence of Hindu authorities on party politics with disapproval. Although *Hinduism Today*[28] proudly presents "The Holy Men in India's New Parliament" and expects them to "re-establish the supremacy of moral values in both politics and society and work for the betterment of the lot of the poor and the downtrodden in the country,"[29] others resent the substitution of spirituality by party politics and influence pandering. As a visitor to Rishikesh expressed it: "You come here for getting as close to *nirvāṇa* as you can and end up being lectured on today's petty politics."[30]

Political Hinduism is right wing. Its major support comes from landowners and industrialists, shopowners, high school and college teachers, students, and small entrepreneurs. The potential power of the Hindu political parties, however, lies not only in the as yet pervasive traditionalism and obscurantism of the large masses (especially in rural and small-town India) but also in the correct perception of a widespread lack of social, ethical and personal values in Western-style party politics. Indians, who have become aware of the value vacuum of the formal democratic process frequently fall back on Hinduism (often somewhat modernized, desectarianized, and enlightened in Sarvepalli Radhakrishnan's way) as the only acceptable basis: Hinduism, after all, is indigenous, it has shaped Indian society and mentality for thousands of years, it is flexible and, in the opinion of most Hindus, far superior in its philosophy to any other religion or philosophy.

The standard Western sociological and economic investigation that leads to the compilation of statistics of election results, distribution of incomes, family size, and so on, leaves out important factors. It seems to presuppose tacitly U.S. society and politics as the standard model that contains all the relevant parameters. It also seems to presuppose that developments can go only in one direction; namely, the direction of what the West calls *modernity*. One indication that things are still different in India is the widespread and frequent large-scale defections from parties, the "crossing over" of large groups of elected representatives from one party to another, the splitting of existing parties, and the formation of new ones. Personal loyalties have priority over party tradition, personal rifts override party discipline. Matters of conviction and principle (however questionable and shallow) very easily win out against an economic or voting calculus.

Contrary to the commonly held belief that ideological parties are obsolete and that modern politics boils down to a distribution of shares in the economy of a given county, we are clearly in for a new wave of ideological politics on all levels.[31] Issues with highly emotional content become anew the focus of world and national politics. The peace issues are one of them, reunification of divided nations (the favorite recipe for peace in the 1940s and 1950s) is another. Language issues become another source of political ferment. In the process, the structures of political parties, built upon the rationalization of societal needs, seem to become irrelevant. Grassroots movements, cutting across the classical political spectrum, mobilizing people who would never join an existing political party, arise and become decisive. Grassroots movements are usually not wholly spontaneous; they develop out of issues that for a long time had been neglected by the official parties but were cultivated by interest groups.

All these elements are present in political Hinduism. By declaring its contempt for the institution of Western-style political parties it attracts all those who find the spectacle of party bickering and horse trading distasteful. By promoting Akhaṇḍ Bhārat, undivided India, it appeals not only to those who have suffered directly under the partition and its continued aftereffects but also to all those for whom Mother India is a reality.[32] And they are many. By its emphasis on Indianization it again appeals to vast numbers who feel that the present elite is too Western oriented and forgetful of India's own cultural and spiritual heritage. And, last not least, by emphasizing Hindudom, it speaks to many shades of religiosity and nationalism alive in present-day India.[33]

The majority of Indian political scientists and sociologists are Marxist oriented. They try to find emerging "classes" in India as the major political agents and class struggle (of sorts) as the key to political dynamics. This may be too simple a solution—and too Western a view, too. Of course there are "new classes," of course there is "class-struggle" (there always was), but the Indian socio-political scene has other dimensions, too, not covered by these categories.

The Indian Freedom Movement was not a class struggle; political Hinduism is not a matter of class, although some of the above interpreters try to make it out as a reactionary middle-class movement. The age-old fascination with renunciation, selfless service, worship of an absolute incarnate in a person, a place, a tradition is still alive. It was alive enough to attract hundreds of dedicated coworkers to Gandhi, who had renounced all property, title, and class affiliation. It is alive in the R.S.S., which demands from its leaders rigorous self-control, renunciation of private property, pleasure, and status and not only insists on classlessness but also on castelessness.

Political Hinduism cannot be understood by applying either a Western party democratic gauge or a Marxist socialist pattern. Its potential has much to do with the temper of Hinduism, which was able throughout the ages to rally people around causes that were perceived to be of transcendent importance and in whose pursuit ordinary human values and considerations had to be abandoned. Whether one considers this good or bad will depend on one's standpoint. The fact remains, however, and a student of Indian politics will be able to ignore this only to his or her own detriment.

HINDUISM AS A WORLD RELIGION

The picture of Hindu communalism and narrowly focused Hindu politics has to be balanced by pointing toward the profound ambivalence of present-day Hinduism.

Side by side with the most intense nationalistic fervor shown by Hindus as pointed out previously there is a rejection of the "Western" concept of nation-state in the writings of such spokesmen of modern Hinduism like Rabindranath Tagore, Aurobindo Ghose, and Sarvepalli Radhakrishnan.

Alongside the reaffirmation of the *varṇāśramadharma* as the basis of India are also statements from representatives of orthodoxy and political Hinduism that advocate a casteless and classless society. The wholesale condemnation of modernization and secularization by some is counterbalanced by the advocacy of a militarily strong and industrially modern India by others.

Although there had been Hindu resistance all along against all changes introduced in society and legislation, it must also be pointed out that virtually all the progressive moves have been initiated by Hindus, too. Parallel to, and in stark contrast with, the tendency to provincialize and sectarianize Hinduism, there are strong countermoves to universalize and spiritualize Hinduism and regard it as the home of all genuine religiosity.

Hinduism has brought forth in the modern era not only a Dāyānanda and a Tilak, but also a Mahātmā Gandhi and a Sarvepalli Radhakrishnan, an Aurobindo Ghose and a Krishnamurti, true citizens of the world and prophets of a universal religion. What we see happening with Hinduism today may be the formation of a truly new world religion. Hinduism, of course, is a world religion already on account of the large number of its adherents. But its strong ties to the geographic entity India and the social structure of native castes has prevented it from reaching out into the world at large. Also its internal dissensions, its uncertainty with regard to its own essentials, and its history of sectarianism has worked against its status as a truly universal religion.

All this is changing. Hinduism has produced high-profile exponents in our century who downplayed sectarianism, emphasized the common foundations of all its branches and modernized and revitalized Hinduism. Hinduism has proven much more open than any other religion to new ideas, scientific thought, and social experimentation. Many beliefs, basic to Hinduism and initially strange to the West like reincarnation, polydevatism, meditation, and guruship have found worldwide acceptance. Also Hinduism's traditional fuzziness with regard to doctrinal boundaries is becoming a fairly universal feature of religion worldwide. Its living tradition of Yoga and methods of interiorization give it an edge over other traditional religions that stress the absolute authority of an official or the ultimate truth of a scripture.

Hinduism is organizing itself; it is articulating its own essentials; it is modernizing; and it is carried by a great many people with strong faith. It would not be surprising to find Hinduism the dominant religion of the twenty-first century. It would be a religion that doctrinally is less clear-cut than mainstream Christianity, politically less determined than Islam, ethically less heroic than Buddhism, but it would offer something to everybody, it would delight by its richness and depth, it would address people at a depth that has not been reached for a long time by other religions or by the prevailing ideologies. It will appear idealistic to those who look for idealism, pragmatic to the pragmatists, spiritual to the seekers, sensual to the here-and-now generation. Hinduism, by virtue of its lack of an ideology and its reliance on intuition, will appear to be much more plausible than those religions whose doctrinal positions petrified a thousand years ago or whose social structures remain governed by tribal mores.

That is how an open-minded scholarly Hindu like A. S. Altekar sees it, too: "Hindu religion, philosophy and social structure are nothing but the records of a glorious and instructive struggle of the human mind to free itself from limitations that become meaningless in the course of time, and to attain to more and more glorious heights that are revealed by man's ever expanding vision. There is no doubt that Hinduism will become once more a great world force, the moment this consciousness becomes a part and parcel of the modern Hindu mind and begins to mold and influence its activities in the different spheres of life."[34]

Hinduism will spread not so much through the gurus and swāmis, who attracted a certain number of people looking for a new commitment and a quasi-monastic life-style, but it will spread mainly through the work of intellectuals and writers, who have found certain Hindu ideas convincing and who identify with them as their personal beliefs. A fair number of leading physicists and biologists have found parallels between modern science and Hindu ideas. An increasing number of creative scientists will come from a Hindu background and will consciously and unconsciously blend their scientific and their religious ideas. All of us may be already much more Hindu than we think. Various strands of Hinduism have provided much of the substance of the "New Age" thinking and Hinduism may take up "New Age" ideas much more readily than any other historic tradition.

Although initially, for the sake of avoiding a customary misidentification, the difference between Hinduism and what is called *religion* in the West had to be stressed, we now have to virtually reverse that position. Many people in the West come to realize more and more that organized and denominationalized Christianity (called *Churchianity* by Hindus) does not even represent the essence of Christianity, let alone that of religion, a new, broader, and looser understanding of religion is emerging that approaches the Hindu notion of dharma. It recognizes, on the one hand, the impossibility of dogmatizing what is beyond human grasp and understanding, and it realizes, on the other hand, that "religion," in order to be genuine, must inform all aspects of life, not only a church routine.

Hinduism, both in the past and in the present, had and has its shortcomings. Nobody can overlook these. But it also had always enough vitality and genuine spiritual substance to outweight its deficiencies. Its openness to reality, its experimental and experiental character, its genuine insights and its authentic sages are a guarantee for its continued growth and relevance.

Chronology

According to a recent report,[1] A. K. Sharma, of the Archeological Survey of India, unearthed remains of a paleolithic settlement in Northern India "extending over 400 km,[2] dated 1.2 million years ago or even earlier." Palaeolithic sites in Tamiḷnādu and Punjāb are dated at ca. 470,000 B.C.E. The so-called Soan culture (with different phases)[2] flourished between 400,000 and 200,000 B.C.E. Excavations in Mehrgarh in 1974 unearthed remains of a neolithic culture dating back to the eighth millennium B.C.E. The area was continuously inhabited for several thousands of years. Other settlements, representing early phases of the Indus civilization, date back to ca. 5500 B.C.E.[3] The Indus civilization reached its peak between 2700–1700 B.C.E. It did not die suddenly but slowly faded out, and elements of it entered later riverine cultures along the Ganges and Narbada.

It is becoming ever more evident that there is no single-track prehistoric or proto-historic development in South Asia but that a variety of different cultures coexisted in this large area and developed at different paces and in different directions. Thus, cultural developments in the Indus region (Indus civilization), were paralleled by developments in the area of Gujarāt (Dwarka, Kṛṣṇa dynasty), Delhi[4] (Pāṇḍava–Kaurava clans), Eastern India[5] (Ayodhyā, Rāma dynasty). The "parallel histories" of these different populations show some common elements but even more distinctive features. Only at a relatively late period was a systematic attempt made to extend Vedic culture through most of India;[6] even then leaving out large areas in the interior, inhabited by a number of populous tribes. The formerly widely held notion that the invasion of the Āryans, the Vedic Indians, brought a sudden and violent end to the Indus civilization has been all but abandoned. "Harappan culture did *not* fall, die, or come to a more or less abrupt end . . . many, but not all Indus settlements were abandoned, not destroyed."[7]

India's traditional chronology, supported by astronomical calculations,[8] provides precise dates for prehistoric events also. Thus the creation of the present world is dated at 1,972,947,101 B.C.E. and the beginning of the Kali-yuga at 3102 B.C.E., the date of the end of the Bhārata War according to one school. Scholars accepting the historicity of the Purāṇic materials[9] take this also to be the date of Manu. Rāmacandra is said to have flourished around 1950 B.C.E. and Kṛṣṇa around 1400 B.C.E. According to this school, that would also be the date for the Bhārata War.

According to C. Sengupta,[10] July 25, 3928 B.C.E., is the date of the earliest solar eclipse mentioned in the Ṛgveda. He set Kṛṣṇa's birthdate on July 21, 2501, B.C.E. and the date of the Bhārata War on 2449 B.C.E. S. B. Roy, using astronomical observations recorded in the Ṛgveda, and working with the list of Purāṇic kings and *ṛṣis* as established by Pargiter, arrived at a fairly precise dating of most of the major events of early Indian history.[11] By cross referencing Indian events and names with exactly dated events and names in Babylonia and Persia, he appears to provide a fairly good foundation for his dates. He states that Max Müller, who most earlier Western scholars followed in dating Vedic literature and events of early Indian history, had based his calculations only "on the ghost story of *Kathāsaritasāgara* composed in about 1200 A.D., i.e. nearly 3,500 years after the event." Max Müller, in fact, based his conjectures on the by then fairly well-established dates of the life of Buddha. Assuming that the Upaniṣads were pre-Buddhist and conjecturing that it would take about 2 centuries for each of the four parts of the Veda to develop, he arrived at 1200 B.C.E. as the date of the composition of the Ṛgveda. No archeological evidence was then available, but even without it, some younger contemporary scholars like M. Winternitz, C. Bloomfield, and others challenged these dates and gave a much greater age to the Ṛgveda, as did most Indian scholars. Max Müller's conjecture was also predicated on the suppositions that the Indians and Iranians had once formed one single people, inhabiting the area of Northern Iran or Southern Russia, and that they split up around 1500 B.C.E. Indologists of that time had to be careful not to challenge the presumed higher age established for the biblical Patriarchs.

S. B. Roy also assumed that certain events mentioned in the Ṛgveda took place in Iran where the Vedic Indians had lived before the invasion of India. He provides a list of basic dates according to "high chronology" and "low chronology."

Manu Vaivasvata, the first of the kings in the Purāṇic list, was born in 3167 B.C.E. according to the high chronology (h.c.) and in 2851 B.C.E. according to the low chronology (l.c.). On the assumption that Bhārata (no. 44 in the Purāṇic list) was a contemporary of Sargon of Accad, his birthdate would either be 2393 B.C.E. (h.c.) or 2077

B.C.E. (l.c.). The major portion of the Vedic hymns was composed at the time of Viśvamitra I (2609 B.C.E. h.c., 2293 B.C.E. l.c.), whereas the invasion of India took place under the Divodāsa dynasty (2051–1961 B.C.E. h.c., 1735–1645 B.C.E. l.c.). The Āryans then spread throughout Northern India in the next five centuries. The Bhārata battle took place in 1424 B.C.E. (h.c.) or 1088 B.C.E. (l.c.). The early Upaniṣads were composed 1450–1350 B.C.E. (h.c.) or 1100–1000 B.C.E. (l.c.). Vedāṅga and Sūtra literature is assumed to be of similar age. The *Aṣṭadhyāyī* of Pāṇini was composed in 1320 B.C.E. (h.c.) or 1000 B.C.E. (l.c.). By the end of the eighth century B.C.E. Sanskrit ceased as a spoken tongue.

Many of these dates appear surprisingly high compared to the dates found in most Indological literature. Although it may be premature to endorse S. B. Roy's chronology without further study, it should be kept in mind that the chronology suggested by Max Müller is based on very shaky ground indeed.

Geological evidence suggests that the Sarasvatī (Ghaggar-Hakra River) dried out around 1900 B.C.E., well within the period established beyond doubt for the flourishing of the Indus civilization. Because the majority of settlements mentioned in the Ṛgveda, as well as a great many sites connected with the Indus civilization, are situated on the banks of the Sarasvatī,[12] the conclusion appears plausible, that the "Vedic Indians" were in the Indian heartlands by the second millenium B.C.E. and that they did not invade and destroy the Indus civilization in 1500 B.C.E. as had been assumed. S. C. Kak estimates that the population of North India was around 24 million at that time, and he rightly points out that it is not imaginable that such a vast number of people could have migrated into Northern India in one major wave.

As regard the date of composition of the Vedic Saṃhitās there is as yet a wide difference of opinion among modern scholars. Leaving aside Dāyānanda Saraswatī's claims of prehistoric antiquity for the Vedas, there is still a large divergence: P. V. Kane assumes that the bulk of the Saṃhitās, Brāhmaṇas and Upaniṣads was composed between 4000 and 1000 B.C.E. and thinks that some hymns of Ṛgveda and Atharvaveda, parts of the *Taittirīya Saṃhitā* and *Brāhmaṇa* go back to the time before 4000 B.C.E. B. G. Tilak arrives at 4500 B.C.E. as the date of the Vedas, M. Winternitz at 2500 B.C.E., and C. Bloomfield at 2000 B.C.E. Indian chronology reaches comparatively firmer ground with the life of Gautama Buddha, whose traditional dates and the dates as established by Western scholarship differ by only about half a century. From then on numerous dated

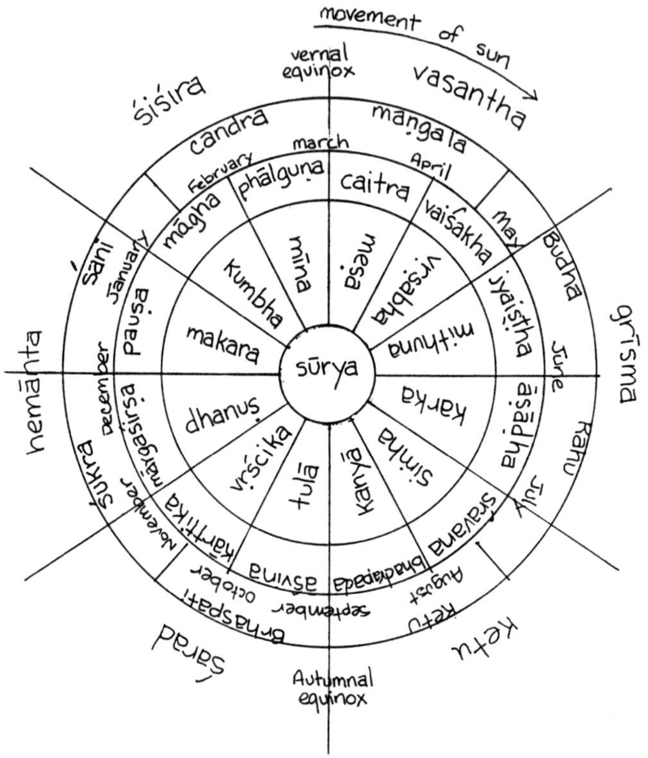

Figure 1 The Hindu calendar

Inner circle: signs of the zodiac (solar)

Second circle: names of months (lunar-solar)

Third circle: corresponding months of Julian Calendar; Planets

Outer circle: names of seasons

NB: The coincidence of the vernal equinox and the beginning of month *caitra meṣa,* upon which the calendar has been based in the sixth century C.E., has since moved, due to an inexact calcuation.

The days of the week are

ravivāra	=	Sunday (day of the sun)
somavāra	=	Monday (day of the moon)
maṅgalavāra	=	Tuesday (day of Mars)
budhavāra	=	Wednesday (day of Mercury)
guruvāra	=	Thursday (day of Jupiter)
śukravāra	=	Friday (day of Venus)
śanivāra	=	Saturday (day of Saturn)

The names of the fifteen moon-days in each half month are

1. *prathamā*	9. *navamī*
2. *dvitīyā*	10. *daśamī*
3. *tṛtīyā*	11. *ekādaśī*
4. *caturthī*	12. *dvadaśī*
5. *pañcamī*	13. *trayodaśī*
6. *ṣaṣṭhī*	14. *caturdaśī*
7. *saptamī*	15. *pañcadaśī*
8. *aṣṭamī*	(a) in *śuklapakṣa*: *pūrṇimā* (full moon)
	(b) in *kṛṣṇapakṣa*: *amāvāsyā*, *darśa* (new moon)

inscriptions and monuments ensure a fairly commonly accepted chronology.

Indian scholars who do not use the Western (Gregorian) calendar have several other systems of dating. The most common are *saṃvat* (beginning 57 B.C.E.) and *śaka* (beginning 78 C.E.).[13] Figure 1 shows the Hindu calendar used today.

On the basis of the more recent research, based on archeology and astronomy, the following chronology can be tentatively[14] established:

ca. 6500 B.C.E.	Mehrgarh: first city cultures in Northwest South Asia, coexisting with earlier (8000 B.C.E.) village cultures. Multiethnic pattern of settlement.
ca. 4000 B.C.E.	Some of the groups settled in Northwest South Asia compose and collect hymns, embodying their knowledge of the universe (Veda). Some others practice early forms of Yoga, akin to Shamanism. Some continue ancestral Himalayan traditions of Śiva worship. Others develop early forms of asceticism, later to be known as Jainism.
ca. 3500 B.C.E.	Early Harappan civilization. Cities with multiethnic populations. Maritime trade with Mesopotamia, possibly also with Egypt.
ca. 3100 B.C.E.	Traditional dates for the "Great Flood" and Manu Vaivasvata.

ca. 3000–2750 B.C.E.	Traditional date for Yayāti period.
ca. 2750–2550 B.C.E.	Traditional date for Mandhātri period.
ca. 2700–1500 B.C.E.	Mature Indus civilization. Urban-rural tensions, reflected in portions of the Ṛgveda.
ca. 2350–1950 B.C.E.	Traditional date for Rāmacandra period.
ca. 1900 B.C.E.	Drying out of Saraswatī. Major tectonic changes, causing large migrations toward the East and desertion of the Indus Valley by the majority of its inhabitants. Age of Rāmāyaṇa.
ca. 1500–500 B.C.E.	Major Upaniṣads, development of early Sāṁkhya, early *Pūrva Mīmāṃsā.*
ca. 1400 B.C.E.	Great Bhārata War—age of Kṛṣṇa. Early version of Mahābhārata.
ca. 1200 B.C.E.	Early śūtra literature. Consolidation of Vedic civilization; *Manusmṛti.*
624–544 B.C.E.	Life of Gautama Buddha according to traditional Śrī Laṅka reckoning (563–483 according to most Western scholars).
527 B.C.E.	End of Mahāvīra's earthly life according to Jain tradition.
518 B.C.E.	Persian invasion under Skylax and conquest of the Indian satrapy for Darius I.
ca. 500 B.C.E.–500 C.E.	Composition of *Śrauta Sūtras, Gṛhya Sūtras, Dharma Sūtras,* Vedāṅgas; the basis of the orthodox systems; composition of the epics and the original Purāṇas.
ca. 500–200 B.C.E.	Composition of the Bhagavadgītā (according to P. V. Kane; others date it ca. 100 B.C.E.–100 C.E.).
ca. 500–200 B.C.E.	Bādarāyaṇa's *Vedānta Sūtra* (according to P. V. Kane)
ca. 490–458 B.C.E.	Reign of Ajātaśatru, king of Magadha.
ca. 400 B.C.E.	Pāṇini's *Aṣṭādhyāyī* (Grammar).
ca. 400–200 B.C.E.	Jaimini's *Pūrvamīmāṃsā Sūtra.*
327–325 B.C.E.	Alexander of Macedonia's invasion of India.
ca. 322–298 B.C.E.	Reign of Candragupta of Magadha.
ca. 300 B.C.E.	Megasthenes, Greek ambassador to Magadha.
ca. 300 B.C.E.	Kauṭilīya's *Ārthaśāstra* (according to some scholars: 100 C.E.) Gautama's *Nyāya Sūtra,* and Kaṇāda's *Vaiśeṣika Sūtra.*

ca. 273–237 B.C.E.	Reign of Aśoka.
ca. 200 B.C.E.–100 C.E.	Manusmṛti.
ca. 200 B.C.E.–100 C.E.	Invasions of Śūṅgas, Iranians, Śākas, and Kuśānas, who founded kingdoms in India.
ca. 200 B.C.E.–200 C.E.	Peak period of Buddhist and Jain influence.
ca. 150 B.C.E.–100 C.E.	Patañjali's *Mahābhāṣya.*
ca. 115 B.C.E.	Besnagar inscription of Heliodorus with a mention of Kṛṣṇa worship.
ca. 100 B.C.E.–500 C.E.	Patañjali's *Yoga Sūtra.*
ca. 100 B.C.E.–100 C.E.	Upavarṣa's Commentary to *Pūrvamīmāṃsā Sūtra* and *Vedānta Sūtra* (according to P. V. Kane).
ca. 100 B.C.E.–400 C.E.	*Śābara-bhāṣya* on Jaimini śūtras.
ca. 100 B.C.E.–800 C.E.	Composition of *Tirukkuṛal.*
ca. 100 B.C.E.	Early Mathurā sculpture; images of gods in temples.
ca. 25 B.C.E.	Indian Embassy to Emperor Augustus of Rome.
ca. 50 C.E.	First documentation of images of gods with several pairs of arms.
ca. 10	Indian Embassy to Emperor Trajan of Rome.
ca. 100–500	Expansion of Hinduism in South-East Asia.
ca. 100–200	*Yājñavalkyasmṛti.*
ca. 100–300	*Viṣṇudharma Sūtra.*
ca. 100–400	*Nāradasmṛti.*
ca. 200–500	Composition of *Viṣṇu Purāṇa.*
ca. 250–325	*Sāṁkhya Kārikā* of Īśvarakṛṣṇa.
ca. 300–600	Composition of some of the older Purāṇas in their present form.
ca. 300–888	Pallava rulers in South India (Kāñcīpuram).
ca. 319–415	Gupta Empire of Mathurā
ca. 400–500	Vatsyāyana's *Kāma Sūtra*
ca. 400	Composition of *Harivaṃśa Purāṇa, Ahirbudhnya Saṃhitā.* Age of Kalidāsa, the greatest Indian dramatist. Spread of Vaiṣṇavism, especially Kṛṣṇa cult. Beginning of Tantricism.
ca. 400–500	Vyāsa's *Yoga-bhāṣya.*
ca. 450–500	Huna invasions.
ca. 500	*Devī-māhātmaya* (in *Mārkaṇḍeya Purāṇa*). Spread of Śāktism into larger areas.

ca. 500–800	Composition of *Kūrma Purāṇa.*
547	Kosmas Indikopleustes travels to India.
ca. 600–650	Poet Bāṇa, author of *Kādāṃbarī* and *Harṣacaritā.*
ca. 600–800	Peak of Pāñcarātra Vaiṣṇavism.
ca. 600–900	Late (metrical) *smṛtis*; composition of *Agni Purāṇa* and *Garuḍa Purāṇa.*
after 600	Strong development of Vedānta.
ca. 600–800	Brahmanical renaissance; successful fight against strongly Tāntric Buddhism.
ca. 640	King Harṣa of Kanauj sends embassy to China.
ca. 650–1200	Several independent kingdoms in Western, Central, East, and South India.
ca. 650–700	Life of Kumārila Bhaṭṭa and Maṇikkavācakar.
since ca. 700	Prevalence of *bhakti* religions.
ca. 700–750	Gauḍapāda, author of a *kārikā* on the *Māṇḍukya Upaniṣad* and Paramaguru of Śaṅkarācārya.
since ca. 700	Flourishing of Kāśmīr Śaivism.
ca. 788–820	Life of Śaṅkarācārya.
ca 800–900	Composition of the *Bhāgavata Purāṇa* in its present form; *Śukra-nīti-sāra.*
ca. 800–1250	Chola dynasty in Tamiḷnādu.
ca. 815–840	Life of Āṇṭāḷ.
ca. 825–900	Medāthiti, writer of a commentary on *Manusmṛti.*
ca. 900	Udāyana's *Nyāyakusumañjalī.*
ca. 900–1100	*Śiva Purāṇa*; Śaivite Tantricism in Indonesia.
ca. 900–1100	Composition of *Yogavāsiṣṭha Rāmāyana* and *Bhaktisūtra.*
999–1026	Mahmud of Ghazni repeatedly raids India.
1026	Muslims loot temple of Somnāth.
1025–1137	Life of Rāmānuja.
ca. 1100	Buddhism virtually extinct in India; life of Abhinavagupta; composition of Hindu Tantras.

ca. 1100–1400	Composition of *Śākta Upaniṣads*; rise of Vīraśaivism in South India.
ca. 1150–1160	Composition of Kalhana's *Rājataraṅginī*, recording the history of Kāśmīr.
ca. 1150	*Śrīkaṇṭha-bhāṣya*; building of Jagannāth temple at Pūrī.
ca. 1197–1276	Life of Madhvācārya.
ca. 1250	Beginning of *Śaiva-siddhānta*; building of sun temple in Konāraka.
1211–1236	Reign of Iltutmish, first sultan of Delhi; beginning of Muslim rule over large parts of India.
ca. 1216–1327	Rule of Pāṇḍyas at Madurai; foundation of the famous Mīnākṣī and Śiva temple of Madurai.
ca. 1275–1675	Jñāneśvara of Mahārāṣṭra and other *bhakti* mystics.
1288	Marco Polo at Kalyan.
ca. 1300–1386	Life of Sāyaṇa, famous commentator of the Vedic Saṃhitās and Brāhmaṇas.
1327	Muslims loot temple at Śrīraṅgam.
ca. 1333	Ibn Battuta's travels in India.
ca. 1340	Life of Mādhava, author of *Sarvadarśana-saṅgraha* and *Pañcadaśī*.
1336–1565	Kingdom of Vijāyanāgara, last Hindu empire in India extending as far as Malaysia, Indonesia, and the Philippines.
ca. 1350–1610	Vīraśaivism as the state religion of Mysore.
ca. 1350–1650	Composition of many works of the Pūrva-mīmāṃsakas.
ca. 1360	Life of Vedāntadeśika.
ca. 1400–1470	Life of Rāmānanda.
ca. 1420	Life of Mīrābāī.
1440–1518	Life of Kabīr.
ca. 1449–1568	Life of Śaṅkaradeva, great Vaiṣṇava preacher in Assam.
ca. 1475–1531	Life of Vallabha.
ca. 1469	Birth of Gurū Nanak, founder of Sikhism.
ca. 1485–1533	Life of Caitanya.

1498	Vasco da Gama, after having rounded the Cape of Good Hope, lands on the Malabar coast.
ca. 1500	Composition of *Adhyātma Rāmāyaṇa* and Sadānanda's *Vedāntasāra.*
ca. 1500–1800	Peak of Durgā worship in Bengal.
ca. 1500–1600	Life of Sūrdās of Agra.
ca. 1550	Life of Brahmānanda Giri, author of a famous commentary on Śaṅkara's *Śarīraka-bhāṣya.*
1510	Portuguese occupy Goa.
ca. 1526–1757	Moghul rule in India, destruction of most Hindu temples in North and Central India.
ca. 1532–1623	Life of Tulasīdāsa.
ca. 1542	The Jesuit missionary Francis Xavier lands in Goa.
ca. 1548–1598	Life of Ekanātha.
1580	Akbar the Great invites some Jesuit missionaries from Goa to his court for religious discussions.
ca. 1585	Life of Harivaṃśa, founder of the Rādhā-Vallabhis.
1608–1649	Life of Tukārāma.
1608–1681	Life of Rāmdās.
1610–1640	Composition of Mitramiśra's *Vīramitrodaya,* famous digests of the *dharma-śāstras.*
ca. 1630	Composition of Śrīnivāsadāsa's *Yatīndra-matadīpikā.*
1631	Death of Mumtaz, in whose honor Shah Jahan built the famous Tāj Mahal of Agra.
1651	The East India Company opens first factory on the Hugli (Bengal).
1657	Dārā Shikóh translates the Upaniṣads into Persian.
1661	Bombay becomes a British possession.
1664	Śivajī declares himself king of Mahārāṣṭra.
1675	Foundation of the French colony of Pondichéry.
ca. 1670–1750	Life of Nagojībhaṭṭa, author of numerous works on grammar, *dharma-śāstra,* yoga, and so forth.

1690	Foundation of Calcutta through East India Company (Fort St. George).
ca. 1700–1800	Life of Baladeva, author of *Govinda-bhāṣya*.
ca. 1750	Composition of the (reformist) *Mahānirvāṇatantra*.
1757	Battle of Plassey; Clive is master of India.
1784	Asiatic Society founded in Calcutta by Sir William Jones.
1818	Defeat of the last Maratha Peshwa.
1828	Rām Mohan Roy founds Brahma Samāj.
1829	Law against *satī*.
1829–1837	Suppression of the *thags*.
1834–1886	Life of Ramakrishna Paramahaṃsa.
1835	Introduction of English school system in India.
1842–1901	Life of M. D. Ranade, great social reformer.
1857	The so-called Mutiny ("First Indian War of Independence" in more recent history books).
1858	The British Crown takes over the administration of India from the East India Company.
1875	Foundation of Ārya Samāj by Swāmi Dāyānanda Sarasvatī.
1885	Foundation of Indian National Congress in Bombay.
1913	Nobel prize in literature for Rabindranath Tagore.
1920	Mahātmā Gandhi begins first all-India civil disobedience movement.
1942	Foundation of Rāṣṭrīa Svayamsevak Saṅgh.
1947	Partition of India and creation of the Indian Union and Pakistan as independent nations.
1948	Assassination of Mahātmā Gandhi; foundation of Rām Rājya Pariṣad; Pandit Nehru prime minister of the Indian Union; Śrī Cakravarti Rajagopalacari appointed governor general.
1950	India declared a republic within the Commonwealth; acceptance of the Constitu-

	tion; death of Śrī Aurobindo Ghose and Ramaṇa Mahārṣi.
1951	Beginning of the first Five Year Plan; inauguration of the Bhudan movement; foundation of the Bhāratīya Jana Sangh
1955	The Hindu Marriage Act passed in Parliament.
1956	Reorganization of states (provinces) according to linguistic principles; inauguration of the second Five Year Plan.
1961	Goa, Damao, and Diu, Portuguese colonies in India, liberated in a military action.
1962	Dr. Rajendra Prasad, the first president of the republic of India (since 1950), dies; Dr. Sarvepalli Radhakrishnan, vice-president, succeeds him; Chinese attack on India.
1964	Death of Jawaharlal Nehru; Lal Bahadur Sastri succeds as prime minister.
1965	Conflict with Pakistan (West).
1966	Tashkent Conference and death of Lal Bahadur Sastri; Indira Gandhi succeeds as prime minister.
1967	In the general elections Congress looses most of the state governments to coalitions of rightist parties; unprecedented droughts precipitate severe crisis.
1971	India takes action against West Pakistan in the East Bengal issue and is instrumental in creating independent Bangladesh
1975	Indira Gandhi wins overwhelming victory in the general elections. In the wake of massive demonstrations by the opposition parties, the president of India, at the request of Prime Minister Indira Gandhi, declares a national emergency and the suspension of many civil rights. Mass arrests of opposition leaders, censorship of newspapers, promulgation of a twenty-point program, and so on.
1977	As a result of free elections Indira Gandhi's government is replaced by a Janata government, a coalition of a num-

	ber of political parties with a wide spectrum; Morarji Desai, aged 80, a member of the Old Congress, heads the government as prime minister and minister for foreign affairs.
1979	Resignation of Morarji Desai as prime minister; Indira Gandhi wins election with a landslide victory.
1984	Sikh agitation for an independent Khalistan; central governemnt forcefully evicts Sikh extremists from Golden Temple in Amritsar-Punjāb; Indira Gandhi assassinated by two of her Sikh guards.
1985	Rajiv Gandhi, Indira's oldest son, elected prime Minister.
1991	Rajiv Gandhi assassinated by Tamil extremist
1992	Hindu agitation on behalf of temple on Rāmā's presumed birthplace in Ayodhyā culminating in destruction of Babri-Masjid and major communal riots in many Indian cities.

Map of India showing present state bounderies

Map of India showing major ancient and holy places

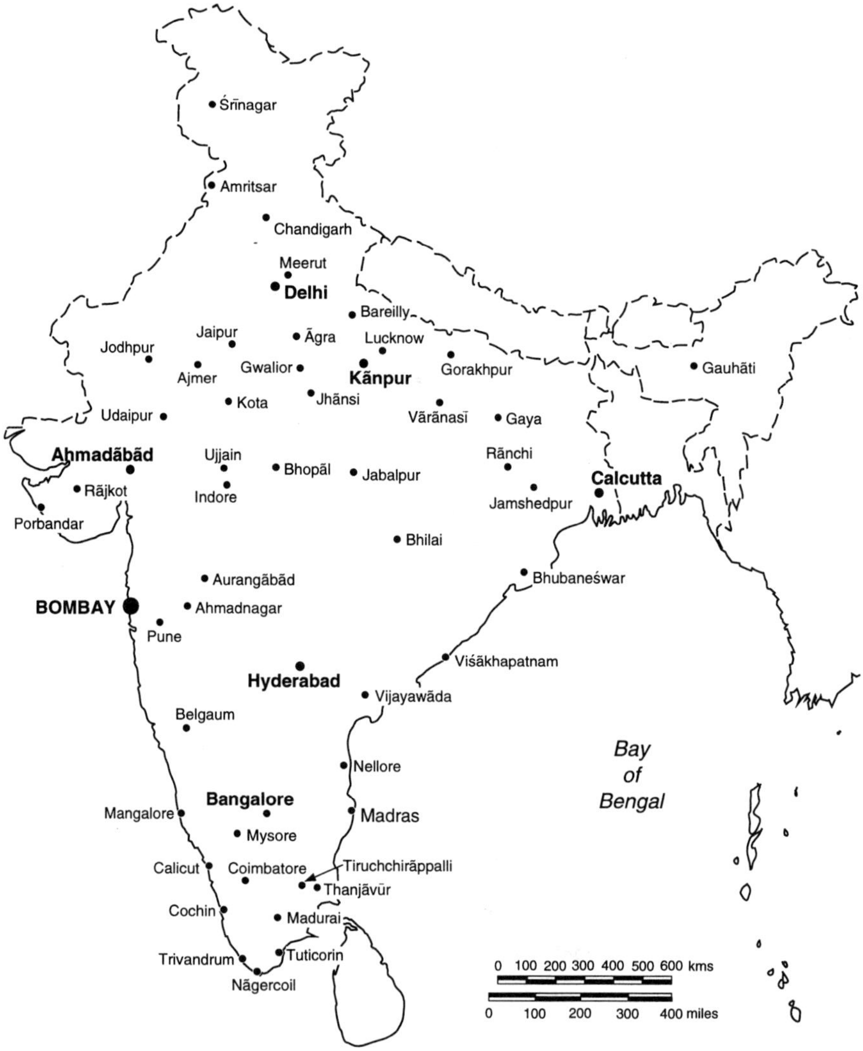

Map of India showing major modern urban centers

Notes

INTRODUCTION

1. W. Crooke, *The Popular Religion and Folklore of Northern India* (Oxford: Oxford University Press, 1896; reprint Delhi: Munshiram Manoharlal 1968), vol. I, p. 1.

2. According to the census of India 1991, India's population on March 1, 1991, was estimated at 843,930,861. *India News*, no. 4 (1991). Annual growth estimated at 35 million.

3. "Deanglicizing Asian Academia," *Hinduism Today* (July 1991): 27.

4. Cf. W. Halbfass, "Indien und die Geschichtsschreibung der Philosophie," *Philosophische Rundschau* 23, nos. 1–2: 104–131.

5. L. Dumont, "A Fundamental Problem," in *Religion/Politics and History in India* (The Hague: Mouton, 1970) [Ecole Pratique des Hautes Etudes; Sorbonne, VIe section: sciences économiques et sociales: Le Monde d'Outre-Mer-Passè et Présent" Première Série, Etudes XXXXIV], p. 160.

6. Malati J. Shendge, an Indian scholar who also had studied in the West, made a strong plea for "The Interdisciplinary Approach in Indian Studies," *ABORI* 63 (1982): 63–98.

7. Agehananda Bharati, a Western scholar who spent years in India, noted in a paper entitled "Psychological Approaches to Indian Studies: More Cons Than Pros" (*Indian Review* 1, no. 1 [1978]: 71–75): "I strongly believe that psychological models are infertile and quite inadequate for Indian studies, particularly for antiquarian research."

8. L. Dumont, "A Fundamental Problem," p. 161. The emphases are L. Dumont's.

9. In 1991 the University of California at Berkeley established its first chair for Tamil, as part of its flourishing Indian Studies Program: *Hinduism Today* (November 1991): 28. Some years ago a group of young North American scholars formed a Brāj-Society that focuses on the study of mediaeval and modern vernacular expression of North Indian Vaiṣṇavism.

10. K. Klostermaier, *In the Paradise of Kṛṣṇa* (Philadelphia: Westminster 1971) and "Remembering Vrindaban," in *Vignettes of Vrindaban*, ed. A. McDowall and A. Sharma (New Delhi: Books and Books, 1987), eds., pp. 45–61.

11. K. Klostermaier, "Hinduism in Bombay," *Religion* 1, no. 2 (1972).

12. According to the 1981 census of India, Hindus constituted 82. 64 percent of the population, Muslims 11. 43 percent and Christians 2. 43 percent.

13. See Alexandra George, *Social Ferment in India* (London: Athlone Press 1986), Chapter 9: "The tribes of India," pp. 233–55. Also, Nirmal Minz, "Anthropology and the Deprived," *Religion and Society* 32, no. 4 (1985): 3–19.

14. 14. George, ibid. "The Scheduled Castes," pp. 202–32. An interesting document shedding light on the life of an untouchable community is the so-called Kahar Chronicle by Tarashankar Banerjea. See Raja Kanta Ray, "The Kahar Chronicle," *Modern Asian Studies* 21, no. 4 (1987): 711–49.

15. R. Inden, "Orientalist Constructions of India," *Modern Asian Studies* 20, no. 3 (1986): 401–46.

1. INDIA AND THE WEST

1. G. W. F. Hegel, *Vorlesungen über die Philosophie der Weltgeschichte*, ed. G. Larsson (Hamburg, 1968, my translation), vol. 2, p. 344.

2. See R. C. Majumdar, *The Classical Accounts of India* (Calcutta: K. L. Mukhopadhyay, 1960) for translations of all passages relating to India found in Diodorus, Herodotus, Megasthenes, Arrian, Strabo, Quintus, Justin, Plutarch, Pliny, Ptolemy and others. W. Halbfass, *Indien und Europa: Perspektiven ihrer geistigen Begegnung* (Basel and Stuttgart: Schwabe and Co., 1981) English translation: *India and Europe: An Essay in Understanding* (Albany: State University of New York Press, 1988) offers a great deal of material relevant to this chapter. See also J. Schwab, *Le Renaissance Orientale* (1950; English translation: *The Oriental Rénaissance: Europe's Rediscovery of India and the East, 1680–1880*, trans. G. Patterson-Black and V. Reinking [New York: Columbia University Press, 1984]).

3. Plutarch, *Life of Alexander*, Chapter 64. The standard work on this period is W. W. Tarn, *The Greeks in Bactria and India* (Cambridge: Cambridge University Press, 1951; reprint 1966).

4. Diodorus Siculus, *Historical Library*, vol. 17, p. 107.

5. Alisaunder, *Alexander: Alexander and Dindimus*, ed. W. W. Skeat (Early English Text Society, Extra Series No. 31, 1876; reprint Oxford: Oxford University Press, 1930), Latin text pp. 10ff., my translation.

6. I. K. K. Menon, "Kerala's Early Foreign Contacts," *Indian and Foreign Review* (15 July 1980): 13f.

7. A famous Pāli work, *Milindapañha,* whose historical character is still a matter of dispute among scholars, describes questions to the Buddhist sage Nāgasena by Menander of Sagala in Northwestern India. English translation by T. W. Rhys Davids, *The Questions of King Milinda,* Sacred Books of the East, vols. 25 and 26 (Oxford: Oxford University Press, 1890).

8. 8. For details, see J. Schwartzberg (ed.), *Historical Areas of South Asia,* 2d ed. (Oxford: Oxford University Press, 1992): p. 117: "Campaign and Empire of Alexander the Great" and "India as Known to Early Greeks."

9. For more details, see: E. Benz, *Indische Einflüsse auf die frühchristliche Theologie* (Mainz: Mainzer Akademie der Wissenschaften, 1951).

10. A great many interesting articles on this subject are contained in R. Baine Harris (ed.), *Neoplatonism and Indian Thought: Studies in Neoplatonism Ancient and Modern,* vol. 2 (International Society for Neoplatonic Studies, Norfolk, Virginia, Albany: SUNY Press, 1982). See also E. Elintoff, "Pyrrho and India" *Phronesis,* no. 1, (1980): 88–108. An attempt to prove the independent origin of Greek philosophy against the arguments of those who assume Indian influence was undertaken by H. J. Krämer, *Der Ursprung der Geistmetaphysik,* 2d ed. (Amsterdam: B. R. Bruner, 1967).

11. For more details, see J. Filliozat, *Les rélations extèrieures de l'Inde,* vol. 1. *Les échanges de l'Inde et de l'Empire Romain aux premiérs siécles de l'ere chretienne*; vol. 2. *La doctrine brahmanique a Rome au IIleme siécle* (Pondichery: Institut Français d'Indologie, 1956).

12. The legend itself is of uncertain age. It found its expression in Nicolas Novotitch's *Life of Issa,* which is supposed to be the translation of a manuscript in a Tibetan monastery containing the life story of Jesus. Quite a few Indians have accepted it. See for instance Pundit Shunker Nath, *Christ: Who and What He Was*: Part 1. *Christ a Hindu Disciple, nay a Buddhist Saint*: Part 2. *Christ a Pure Vedantist* (Calcutta: Dayamoy Printing Works, 1927–1928).

13. Tertullian, *Apologia versus gentes,* in *Migne Patrologia Latina,* vol. 1, pp. 1080ff.

14. *Migne Patrologia Latina,* vol. 17, pp. 1167ff.

15. Evidence of lively exchange between India and the Arab countries is collected in J. Duncan M. Derett's paper, "Greece and India again: the Jaimini-Aśvamedha, the Alexander Romance and the Gospels," *ZRGG,* 22, no. 1 (1970): 19–44.

16. Edward C. Sachau, trans. *Alberuni's India: An Account of the Religion, Philosophy, Literature, Geography, Chronology, Astronomy, Customs, Laws and Astrology of India About* A.D. *1030,* Trübner's Oriental Series (reprint Delhi: S. Chand and Co., 1964).

16. R. E. Latham (trans.), *The Travels of Marco Polo* (Harmondsworth: Penguin Classics, 1958) on India, see 233–68. See also Heimo Rau, "The Image of India in European Antiquity and the Middle Ages," in *India and the West: Proceedings of a Seminar Dedicated to the Memory of Hermann Goetz,* ed. J. Deppert (New Delhi: Manohar, 1983), pp. 197–208.

18. One of the most interesting accounts of South Indian Hinduism in the early eighteenth century is the recently discovered work by the Lutheran missionary Bartholomaeus Ziegenbalg (1682–1719) *Traktat vom Malabarischen Heidentum* (1711), which was never published. See Hans-Werner Gensichen, "Abominable Heathenism—A Rediscovered Tract by Bartholomaeus Ziegenbalg," *Indian Church History Review* 1, no. 1 (1967): 29–40. The work of Abbé Dubois (1770–1848) *Hindu Manners, Customs and Ceremonies,* first published by the East India Company in 1816 has become a classic in its own right and has been reprinted many times by the Oxford University Press.

19. G. H. R. Tillotson, "The Indian Travels of William Hodges," *JRAS,* series 3, vol. 2, no. 3 (1992): 377–98.

20. Ibid., pp. 378f.

21. W. Leifer, *Indien und die Deutschen: 500 Jahre Begegnung und Partnerschaft* (Tübingen und Basel: Horst Erdman Verlag, 1969). Gita Dharampal compiled a bibliography of early German writing about India: "Frühe deutsche Indien-Berichte (1477–1750)," *ZDMG* 134, no. 2 (1984): 23–67. In 1989, Brill published a fascimile of a Sanskrit grammar by Heinrich Roth S. J (1620–1668) claimed to be "the first Sanskrit Grammar composed by a Western author" by the editors A. Camps and J.-C. Muller.

22. *Systema Brahmanicum* (Rome, 1792); *Reise nach Ostindien* (Berlin, 1798).

23. P. J. Marshall (ed.). *The British Discovery of Hinduism in the Eighteenth Century,* The European Understanding of India Series (Cambridge: Cambridge University Press, 1970).

24. 24. For more detail see G. H. Hampton, *Oriental Jones: A Biography of Sir William Jones 1746–1794* (Bombay: Asia Publishing House, 1964) and *The Life and Mind of Oriental Jones: Sir William Jones, the Father of Modern Linguistics* (Cambridge: Cambridge University Press, 1990).

25. *Asiatic Researches* 8: 369–476. For details on the *Ezour Vedam,* used as a source for Indian traditions by Voltaire, see M. Winternitz, *Geschichte der indischen Literatur,* vol. 1, p. 12 n. 1 (1905; reprint Stuttgart: K. F. Kohler Verlag, 1968).

26. A brief history of French Indology is given in P. S. Filliozat's paper "The French Institute of Indology in Pondichery," *WZKSA* 28 (1984):

133–47. A major contribution to Indian studies was also made by Russian and Polish scholars. In Russia especially, the study of Indian languages is flourishing today. Italian, Dutch, Belgian, and Finnish scholarship in Indian studies is alive too—to a lesser degree perhaps in Spain and Latin American from where, however, some very good work has come out recently. V. Stache Rosen, *German Indologists* (New Delhi: Max Müller Bhavan, 1990).

27. At the age of 25 he wrote his epoch-making work: *Über das Conjugationsystem der Sanskrit Sprache in Vergleichung mit jenen der griechischen, lateinischen, persischen und germanischen Sprache. Nebst Episoden des Ramajan und Mahabharat in genau metrischen Übersetzungen aus dem Originaltexte und einigen Abschnitten aus den Vedas.* F. Staal *A Reader on the Sanskrit Grammarians* (Cambridge, Mass.: M. I. T. Press, 1972), has assembled many valuable documents and comments on the history of Western Sanskrit scholarship.

28. The first complete translation of the Bible into Sanskrit was published by W. Carey from Serampore between 1808 and 1818; it was later improved upon by W. Yates and J. Wenger. For further details, see J. S. M. Hooper, *Bible Translation in India, Pakistan, Ceylon,* 2d ed. revised by W. J. Culshaw (Oxford: Oxford University Press, 1963).

29. The *Sanskrit Wörterbuch* together with *Nachträge* has been reprinted by Motilal Banarsidass in 1991.

30. Published originally by Oxford University Press and reprinted several times by other publishers recently, the Sacred Books of the East have not yet been replaced as a standard work, although such series as Sacred Books of the Buddhists, Sacred Books of the Jains, and Sacred Books of the Hindus, offer a large number of text translations in the designated areas.

31. For more complete information consult P. J. Chinmulgund and V. V. Mirashi (eds.), *Review of Indological Research in Last Seventy-Five Years* (Poona: Bharatiya Charitrakosha Mandal, 1967). G. Bougard-Levin and A. Vigasin, *The Image of India: The Study of Ancient Indian Civilisation in the USSR* (Moscow: Progress Publishers, 1984). Hajme Nakamura, "Indian Studies in Japan," in *Indian Studies Abroad* (New York: Asia, 1964).

32. Hindu scholars like R. G. Bhandarkar, S. N. Dasgupta, S. Radhakrishnan, T. M. P. Mahadevan, and T. R. V. Murti, to name just a few, spent considerable time lecturing in the West.

33. For more details, see Dale Riepe, *The Philosophy of India and Its Impact on American Thought* (Springfield, Ill.: Charles C. Thomas, 1970). See also C. T. Jackson, *The Oriental Religions and American Thought, Nineteenth-Century Explorations* (Westport, Conn.: Greenwood Press, 1981).

34. The journal *East and West* published by the University of Hawaii has remained one of the principal instruments for the continued discussion of the conferences' issues.

35. Dale Riepe, *The Philosophy of India*, pp. 275f: "If the American empire meets with the fate of the British, if Americans cannot resolve their life-and-death struggle with the intelligent use of technology, if the alienation in American society cannot be alleviated, then a new attitude may gradually replace the 300 year reign of optimism. Such eventualities may lead to more philosophers turning to contemplation, meditation and increased poring over the Hindu and Buddhist scriptures."

36. Ibid.

37. The case is well stated by Malati J. Shendge in her essay "The Interdisciplinary Approach to Indian Studies," *ABORI* 62 (1982): 63–98.

38. Ananda Coomaraswamy, *The Transformation of Nature in Art* (New York: Dover, 1956), p. 4.

39. *Indian and Western Philosophy: A Study in Contrasts* (London: Allen and Unwin, 1937); *Facets of Indian Thought* (London: Allen and Unwin, 1964).

40. *Philosophies of India*, ed. J. Campbell (Princeton, N.J.: Bollingen Foundation, 1951); *Myths and Symbols in Indian Art and Civilization*, 4th ed. (New York: Harper and Row, 1963).

41. *Nāma-Rūpa and Dharma-Rūpa: Origin and Aspects of an Ancient Indian Conception* (Calcutta: University of Calcutta, 1943).

42. *Introduction génerale a l'étude des doctrines hindoues*, 5th ed. (Paris: Les editions Véga, 1964).

43. *The Hindu Temple* (Calcutta: University of Calcutta, 1946); *The Presence of Ûiva* (Princeton, N.J.: Princeton University Press, 1981).

44. *Asceticism and Eroticism in the Mythology of Ûiva* (London: Oxford University Press, 1973); *The Origins of Evil in Hindu Mythology* (Berkeley: University of California Press, 1976).

45. For those who need a proof the case is convincingly stated in Jaideva Singh's edition and translation of the *Pratyābhijnāhṛdayam* in the numerous references to the earlier translation of the text by K. F. Leidecker.

2. THE HISTORY AND DEVELOPMENT OF HINDUISM

1. Jawaharlal Nehru, *The Discovery of India* (London: Meridian Books, 1960), p. 55.

2. J. C. Heesterman, *The Inner Conflict of Tradition* (Chicago: University of Chicago Press, 1985), 2.

3. The greatest authority in Indian archaeology and prehistory today is H. D. Sankalia, who, in addition to numerous reports on his own excavations and papers in learned journals, has written two general books for wider circles: *Indian Archaeology Today* (New York: Asia Publishing House 1962); and *The Prehistory and Protohistory of India and Pakistan* (Poona: Deccan College Postgraduate and Research Institute, 1974). D. D. Kosambi draws very interesting connections between prehistoric, tribal and present popular Indian culture in his two major works: *An Introduction to the Study of Indian History* (Bombay: Popular Book Depot, 1956); and *Myth and Reality: Studies in the Formation of Indian Culture* (Bombay: Popular Book Depot, 1961). Still of some interest, B. Hronzny, *Über die älteste Völkerwanderung und über das Problem der Proto-indischen Zivilisation* (Prague: Orientalisches Institut, 1939). See also S. K. Chatterji, "Contributions from Different Language-Culture Groups," in *The Cultural Heritage of India* (CHI), H. Bhattacharya, general ed., 2d ed. (Calcutta: Ramakrishna Mission Institute of Culture, 1958), vol. 1, pp. 76–90; N. K. Bose and D. Sen, "The Stone Age in India," ibid., pp. 93–109. The most recent standard work on the subject is B. Allchin and R. Allchin, *The Rise of Civilization in India and Pakistan* (Cambridge: Cambridge University Press, 1982). See also the maps and texts relating to archeology in *HASA*.

4. One of the most comprehensive treatments of the position of tribal cultures in India is provided by Alexandra George, *The Social Ferment in India*, Chapter 9, "The Tribes of India," pp. 235–55 (London and Atlantic Highlands, N.J.: Athlone Press, 1986).

5. First reported by Sir J. Marshall in his *Mohenjo Daro and the Indus Civilization* 3 vols. (London: University of Oxford Press, 1931). For more recent work consult V. N. Mishra, "Prehistory and Protohistory," in *Review of Indological Research in Last Seventy-Five Years*, ed. P. J. Chinmulgund and V. V. Mirashi (Poona: Bharatiya Charitrakosha Mandal, 1967), pp. 353–415, with detailed bibliography. For a short account, M. Wheeler, *The Indus Civilization* (London: Cambridge University Press, 1962); and S. Piggott, *Prehistoric India* (Baltimore: Penguin Books, 1950). For recent specialist literature see *HASA*.

6. See K. A. Nilakantha Sastri, *The History and Culture of the Tamils* (Calcutta: Firma K. L. Mukhopadhyay, 1964); S. K. Aiyangar, *Some Contributions of South India to Indian Culture* (Calcutta: Calcutta University, 1942). T. Balakrishnan Nayar, *The Problem of Dravidian Origins—A Linguistic, Anthropological and Archeological Approach* (Madras: University of Madras, 1977).

7. R. C. Majumdar (general ed.), *The Vedic Age*, vol. 1 of *The History*

and Culture of the Indian People (HCIP), 4th ed. (Bombay: Bharatiya Vidya Bhavan, 1965). Also, C. Kunhan Raja, "Vedic Culture," ibid., pp. 199–220.

8. *An Introduction to the Study of Indian History,* p. 20.

9. Swami Bharati Krishna Tirtha, *Sanātana Dharma* (Bombay: Bharatiya Vidya Bhavan, 1964), pp. 8–38, gives various interesting meanings of this term. *Dharmank* [in Hindi] (Gorakhpur: Gita Press, 1966) contains contributions by all four living Śaṅkarācāryas on the topic of *Sanātana Dharma. Viśva Hindu* (special issue, January 1966), has contributions in English and Hindī by leading Hindus on the topic "What Is Hinduism?"

10. *Essentials of Hinduism* (Allahabad: The Leader, no date). In the Preface we are informed: "The articles collected together in this volume appeared originally as a symposium in the columns of the *Leader* in Allahabad. They have been brought under one cover in the hope that an authoritative declaration as to the Essentials of Hinduism by leading Hindus may be read with interest."

11. "Essentials of Hindutva," in *Samagra Savarkar Wangmaya, Hindu Rastra Darshan,* vol. 6, p. 64 (Poona: Maharashtra Prantik Hindusabha, 1964).

12. *Bunch of Thoughts* (Bangalore: Vikrama Prakashan, 1966), p. 47.

13. *Viśva Hindū Viśeṣānk* [English and Hindi sections] (Bombay: World Council of Hindus, 1966).

14. Kosambi, *An Introduction to the Study of Indian History,* pp. 20f.

15. The most complete representation and summary of research is found in E. Neumayer, *Prehistoric Indian Rock Paintings* (Delhi: Oxford University Press, 1983). Attempts at interpretation are made by Kapila Vatsyayan in an Essay "Prehistoric Paintings," *Sangeet Natak, Journal of the Sangeet Natak Akademi* (October–December 1981): 5–18.

16. B. G. Tilak suggested that they came from the northern polar region and migrated into India as early as 6000 B.C.E. F. E. Pargiter, a great purānic scholar, identifying the vedic Āryans with the purānic Ailas, thinks that they originally came into India about 2050 B.C.E. from the Mid-Himālāyas and first settled in the area of Prāyāga, from where they started their expansion toward the Northwest.

17. See the report by Raj Chengappa, "The Himalayas: Startling Discoveries," in *India Today* (15 March 1993), pp. 90–101, describing the work of geologists such as K. K. Sharma, T. N. Bagati, A. C. Nanada, Arvind Jain, K. S. Valdiya, and Harsh Gupta.

18. S. C. Kak, "Astronomy of the Vedic Altar," *Vistas in Astronomy* 36

(1993): 1–26; and "The Astronomy of the Vedic Altar and the Âgveda," *Mankind Quarterly* 33, no. 1 (1992): 43–55.

19. Subhash C. Kak, "On the Chronology of Ancient India," *Indian Journal of History of Science* 22, no. 3 (1987): 222–234; quote, 231.

20. *Gods, Sages and Kings: Vedic Secrets of Ancient Civilization* (Salt Lake City, Utah: Passages Press, 1991).

21. K. A. Nilakantha Sastri, *The History and Culture of the Tamils*, pp. 5f. A convenient summary of research concerning Indian prehistory can be found in C. Maloney's *Peoples of South Asia* (New York: Holt, Rinehart and Winston, 1974) Chapter 4, "Prehistory" (pp. 63–80) and Chapter 5, "The Rise of Village and Urban Life" (pp. 81–113).

22. Dev Raj, *L'ésclavage dans l'Inde ancienne d'après les textes Palis et Sanskrits* (Pondichery: Institute Français d'Indologie, 1957).

23. See S. N. Dasgupta, *History of Indian Philosophy* (1922; reprint, Cambridge: Cambridge University Press, 1963), vol. 1, pp. 10ff: "Even at this day all the obligatory duties of the Hindus at birth, marriage, death etc. are performed according to the old Vedic ritual. The prayers that a Brahmin now says three times a day are the same selections of Vedic verses as were used as prayer verses two or three thousand years ago. . . . Even at this day there are persons who bestow immense sums of money for the performance and teaching of Vedic sacrifices and rituals."

24. See R. C. Majumdar: "Colonial and Cultural Expansion," in *The Age of Imperial Kanauj HCIP*, vol. 4, pp. 412–53; *The Classical Age, HCIP*, vol. 3, pp. 642–55; *The Age of Imperial Unity HCIP*, vol. 2, pp. 634–58; *The Struggle for Empire, HCIP*, vol. 5, pp. 730–74. R. C. Majumdar, *Hindu Colonies in the Far East*, 2d ed. (Calcutta: Firma K. L. Mukhopadhyay, 1963). Somewhat more daring reconstructions of history may be found in works like Swami Sankarananda's *Hindu States of Sumeria, When India Ruled the West*, no. 1 (Calcutta: Firma K. L. Mukhopadyay, 1962); and Chaman Lal's *Hindu America* (Bombay: Bharatiya Vidya Bhavan, 1960).

25. See R. C. Majumdar, H. C. Raychaudhuri, and K. Datta, *An Advanced History of India* (London: Macmillan, 1960), pp. 199–210.

26. "The Chola King Koluttunga I, a Śaiva, put out the eyes of Mahāpurṇa and Kureśa, the Vaiṣṇava disciples of Rāmānuja, who refused to be converted to Śaivism" (Dasgupta, *History of Indian Philosophy*, vol. 5, p. 45). F. Kingsbury and G. E. Philips (trans.), *Hymns of the Tamil Saivite Saints* (Calcutta: Association Press, 1921), pp. 10f: "The cause [Sambandhar] loved suffered a severe blow when the great King of Madura, with many of his subjects, went over to the Jaina religion. The queen consort and her prime minister remained faithful to Śaivism and sent for Sambandhar. The

lonely saint faced a vast multitude of Jains in the royal presence, conquered them with arguments and reconverted the king. Eight thousand of the stubborn Jains, with Sambandhar's consent, were impaled alive . . . "

27. In the *Bhāgavata-Purāṇa* those who do not follow Kṛṣṇa are called *dogs*, etc.

28. They come out very markedly in the different *senas* that have developed over the past years in India. See "The Private Armies," and "Secret Societies," *The Illustrated Weekly of India* 91, no. 11 (15 March 1970) and "Secret Societies," *Seminar 151* (March 1972).

29. N. K. Bose, "The Geographical Background of Indian Culture," *CHI*, vol. 1, pp. 3–15. The best work on physical geography is O. H. K. Spate, *India and Pakistan; A General and Regional Geography*, 3d ed. (London: Methuen, 1960).

30. See *Tīrthānk* (*Kalyāṇ*) [in Hindi] (Gorakhpur: Gītā Press, 1957). The most popular may be Brājbhumī, the land connected with Kṛṣṇa's birth and youthful exploits. See K. Klostermaier *In the Paradise of Kṛṣṇa* (Philadelphia: Westminster, 1971).

31. See the beautifully illustrated report on a voyage along the Ganges by John J. Putnam in *National Geographic Magazine* (October 1971): 445–83.

32. O. Viennot, *Le culte de l'arbre dans l'Inde ancienne* (Paris: Presses universitaire de France, 1954).

33. The ideas of men like Swami Vivekananda, Sri Aurobindo, B. G. Tilak, and others are represented in V. P. Varma, *Modern Indian Political Thought*, 4th ed. (Agra: Laksmi Narain Agrawala, 1968).

34. (Bombay: Asia Publishing House, 1968), pp. 9ff.

35. Kushwant Singh offers a striking proof for this in his *India: A Mirror for Its Monsters and Monstrosities* (Bombay: Pearl Books, 1969). After describing the fanatical behavior of certain religious leaders which finally led to Delhi's "Bloody Monday" on November 7, 1967, he continues: "I left the sands of the Jumna and drove to the home of my friend Cyrus Jhabwalla, a Parsi architect, and his novelist wife Ruth, who is Jewish. There were other friends present. I was among my own type—Anglicized Indian sahibs. I narrated my experiences of the day. We defied our traditions. We drank Scotch. We ate beef sandwiches ('Not-so-holy-cow; imported beef', explained my host. Someone stretched his hand across the table: 'Ruth, can I have one of your kosher pork sausages, please?'). And so it went on until we felt we had liquidated all the *sadhus* and freed our countrymen of the Hindus' silly food fads. Then our host spoilt it all with a short speech: 'Listen, chaps! When the chips are down, you know very well that however

Westernized the Indian and whatever religion he may have or not have, whenever he eats beef he has a sense of guilt—a teeny-weeny bit of a bad conscience. And not one Indian will bandy words with a *sadhu* for fear of arousing his wrath. It is like our attitude to *sati*. We condemn it but we cannot help admiring a woman who becomes a *sati*. These things have been with us for over 4000 years. They are in our blood and in our bones. We cannot fight them with reason. They are stronger than reason" (p. 126).

36. *The Times of India* reported on 11 December 1965 about an appeal made by Dr. S. Radhakrishnan to the Hindu Visva Dharma Sammelan then in session at Delhi: "The President emphasised that all roads lead to the same God. Men of religion should not quarrel about the road one should take. There was nothing sectarian or dogmatic about Hindu philosophy." See also Dr. S. Radhakrishnan's last work: *Religion in a Changing World* (London: Allen and Unwin, 1967).

37. J. B. Segal. "White and Black Jews at Cochin, the Story of a Controversy," *JRAS* no. 2 (1983): 228–52. See also B. J. Israel, *The Bene Israel of India, Some Studies* (Bombay: Orient Longman 1984); T. A. Timberg (ed.), *Jews in India* (New York: Advent Books, 1986).

38. The most scholarly account of the interaction between early Christianity and Hinduism is found in Stephen Neill, *A History of Christianity in India: The Beginnings to A.D. 1707* (Cambridge: Cambridge University Press, 1984). For an Indian Christian view, see A. M. Mundaden, *The Traditions of St. Thomas Christians* (Bangalore: Dharmaram Studies, 1972).

39. See literature quoted in Chinmulgund and Mirashi, *Review of Indological Research*, pp. 601ff.

40. J. Duncan M. Derret, "Greece and India: The Milindapañha, the Alexander Romance and the Gospels," *ZRGG* 19 (1967): 33–64.

41. See A. M. Mundaden, *St. Thomas Christians and the Portuguese* (Bangalore: Dharmaram Studies, 1970).

42. See for instance the examples quoted in M. M. Thomas, *The Acknowledged Christ of the Indian Renaissance* (London: SCM Press, 1969), and Stanley J. Samartha, *Hindus vor dem universalen Christus* (Stuttgart: Evangelisches Verlagswerk, 1970).

43. See R. Boyd, *An Introduction to Indian Christian Theology*, 2d ed. (Madras: Christian Literature Society, 1977).

3. HINDU *DHARMA*: ORTHODOXY AND HERESY IN HINDUISM

1. "The word *dharm* in Hindī has an almost totally identical application to that of the English word 'religion' which has, of course, an enormous

semantic spread, and it would seem highly probable that the English word and concept is the major determinant factor in the Hindī usage." S. Weightman and S. M. Pandey, "*Dharm* and *Kartavy* in Modern Hindī" in W. D. O'Flaherty and J. D. M. Derret (eds.), *The Concept of Duty in Southeast Asia* (New Delhi: Vikas, 1978), p. 223. The same authors also point out that the word *mat* (literally, "thought," "doctrine") is equally common and used like the word *dharma: "Hindūdharm" = "Hindūmat."*

2. In Gautama's *Nyāya-Sūtra, dharma* is "a specific property of an object."

3. Pandit Dinanath Śarma, "Sanātana Dharma," *Kalyan* [in Hindī] 40, no. 1 (1966): 238–41.

4. *HDhS,* vol. 1, p. 1.

5. *Manusmṛti,* II, 6; see also *Yajñavalkyasmṛti,* vol. 1, p. 7.

6. *Manusmṛti,* II, 9.

7. Ibid., II, 11.

8. J. C. Heesterman, "On the Origin of the Nāstika," *WZKSA* 12, no. 13 (1968–69): 171–85.

9. *Manusmṛti,* II, 17–24.

10. Ibid., I, 111–18.

11. "Sanātan dharm hi sarvabhaum dharm yā mānav dharm hai," in *Dharmāṇk* (Kalyān) 30, no. 1 (January 1966): Gorakhpur, 242–49 [Hindī], my own translation.

12. Bhagavadgītā, III, 35.

13. *Manusmṛti,* VIII, 15.

14. W. D. O'Flaherty in her introduction to *The Concept of Duty in South Asia,* pp. xiiiff., comments on the essentially indefinable character of *dharma* and the clash between existing definitions. She also points out that *dharma* and *adharma* are correlative, that *devas* only appear where there are demons and that "*dharma* is a problem rather than a concept, vague, indeterminable . . . an ambiguous concept."

15. P. V. Kane in his monumental *History of Dharmaśāstra* refers to over 2000 books!

16. The informative essay on "Use and Misuse of the Dharma" by A. Kunst in *The Concept of Duty in Southeast Asia,* pp. 3–17, shows some of the development.

17. "The Concept of Duty in Ancient Indian Jurisprudence: The Problem of Ascertainment," in *The Concept of Duty in Southeast Asia*, pp. 18–65.

18. From *Gautama's Nyāyasūtras with Vātsyāyana Bhāṣya*, ed. and trans. Ganganatha Jha, 2 vols. (Poona: Oriental Book Depot, 1939).

19. *Yoga Sūtras* II, 30–32.

20. Vaikunthavāsi Śrī Bābu Sādhucaranprasād, *Dharmaśāstrasaṁgraha* (Bombay: Sri Venkateśvar stim Mudranayantra laya, 1913), a digest of Hindu law for parctical use, with selections from forty-six *smṛtis* according to topics, gives a good idea of the range of *dharmaśāstra*.

21. The best known and best documented case is that of Raja Ram Mohan Roy, who successfully fought for the abolition of *satī*.

22. "Hinduism: A Static Structure or a Dynamic Force?" in *Nehru Abhinandan Granth* (Calcutta: N. A. G. Committee, 1949), pp. 421–25. The author was formerly head of the Department of Ancient Indian History and Culture, Banares Hindu University.

23. "Moral Foundations of Indian Society," in ibid., 464–69. The author is the editor of the multivolume *Dharmakośa* (Wai: Dharmakośa Maṇḍala, 1937–1961) and one of the most outstanding paṇḍits of contemporary India.

24. Apart from the countless instances one encounters in daily life in India itself, Indian dailies quite frequently carry "letters to the editor" with massive complaints like the following from *Times of India* (8 March 1968): "At the national integration conference held at Delhi in September last a code of conduct was prescribed to be observed by political leaders. The code required them not to exploit communal and caste feelings for political purposes. Hardly six months later, during the recent general elections, one saw in Poona the sorry spectacle of the code of conduct being flagrantly violated by the political leaders in general and the congress leaders in particular. In each of the six constituencies in Poona the congress candidate nominated was of the same caste that was in overwhelming majority in that particular constituency. The election speeches of the leaders conveyed the impression that they were totally unaware of the existence of the code of conduct. Every candidate openly preached caste hatred and exhorted the electorate to vote for him as he belonged to their caste. Perhaps never before were caste and communal feelings so deeply aroused as they were during the recent general elections in Poona" (V. D. Mahajan).

Another reader complained that "even after twenty years of freedom untouchability in the villages is still as virulent as ever. The social justice said to have been one to the Scheduled Castes and Tribes has just not been adequate" (Raja Sekhara Rao).

25. "Sādhana," *RS* 16, no. 2 (1969): 36–50.

26. The most complete and systematic description is to be found in Rāmdās Gaur, *Hindutva* [Hindī] (Banaras: Visvaprasad Gupta, samvat 1995). H. H. Wilson's *Religious Sects of the Hindus* (originally published in 1861; reprint, Calcutta: Punthi Pustak, 1958) is incomplete, unsystematic and in quite a few instances incorrect.

27. G. S. Ghurye, *Indian Sādhus,* 2d ed. (Bombay: Popular Prakashan, 1964), pp. 110ff and 177ff. The latest major incident occurred in Hardwar in spring 1986.

28. *Liṅga Purāṇa* I, 107, 41f.

29. We have to interpret some of these as a reaction against persecution on the part of non-Vaiṣṇavas such as Citrasena, who at the instigation of Śaiva monks prohibited the worship of Viṣṇu in his realm, ordered his officers to persecute the Vaiṣṇavas, and had the images of Viṣṇu thrown into the ocean. See R. C. Hazra, *Studies in the Upapurāṇas* (Calcutta: Sanskrit College, 1963), vol. 2, pp. 262f.

30. W. O'Flaherty "The Origin of Heresy in Hindu Mythology," *HR* 10 (1971): 271–333; S. N. Dasgupta, *HIPh,* vol. 3, p. 19. See *Kūrma Purāṇa,* Chapter 15.

31. For a more extensive treatment of this topic, see K. Klostermaier, "Hindu Views of Buddhism," in R. Amore (ed.), *Canadian Contributions to Buddhist Studies* (Waterloo, Ont.: Wilfrid Laurier University Press, 1980), pp. 60–82.

32. See *HCIP,* Majumdar, general ed., vol. 3, p. 437; S. N. Dasgupta, *HIPh,* vol. 5, p. 45; M. Winternitz, *Geschichte der Indischen Literatur,* vol. 3, pp. 426ff; Alkondavilli Govindacharya, *The Divine Wisdom of the Draviḍa Saints* (Madras: C. N. Press, 1902), pp. 78f.

33. *Viṣṇu Purāṇa,* III, 18, 15ff. (Gorakhpur: Gītā Press, 1954). My translation.

34. P. V. Kane, *HDhS,* vol. 2, part 2, pp. 716f.

35. Nārāyaṇa Bhaṭṭa's *Maṇimañjarī* as summarized by S. N. Dasgupta, *HIPh,* vol. 4, p. 52.

36. The English translation by E. B. Cowell and A. E. Gough is incomplete, it leaves out the last chatper on Advaita Vedanta.

37. *Brahma Sūtra Bhāṣya* I, 1, 2: Thibaut's translation part I, 15.

38. W. Ruben, *Materialismus im Leben des Alten Indien,* Acta Orientalia 13 (Leiden: Brill, 1935); Dale Riepe describes himself in *The Philosophy*

of India and Its Impact on American Thought (Springfield, Ill.: Charles C. Thomas, 1970) as "interested in the naturalistic and materialsitic philosophy in India" mentioning his dissertation on *The Naturalistic Tradition of Indian Thought.* In India M. N. Roy (*Materialism,* 2d ed., written in 1934, published 1940; reprint Calcutta: Renaissance Publishers, 1951) who on his way towards Radical Humanism, via Marxism-Leninism, drew attention to the often underplayed materialistic stream of the Indian tradition.

39. II, 4, 12.

40. *Sarvadarśanasaṁgraha* I.

41. This has been proposed for example, by Raymond Panikkar in *Kerygma und Indien: Zur heilsgeschichtlichen Problematik der christlichen Begegnung mit Indien* (Hamburg: Evangelischer Verlag, 1967), pp. 84f.

42. They also claim quite often personal infallibility!

43. See "Holy War in India," *Newsweek* (21 December 1992): 46–47.

44. "No Holds Barred Battle," *India Today* (15 March 1987): 56f.

45. *India Today* (15 April 1993): 36.

4. REVELATION AND SCRIPTURE IN HINDUISM

1. Those who have no opportunity to observe the actual recitation of a Hindu scripture may get an idea of it from the description given in "Procedure of Reciting *Śrīmad Bhāgavata,*" *Kalyāṇa Kalpatāru* 18, no. 1 (August 1952): 6–8. The details given therein apply (with appropriate modification) to other scriptures, too.

2. Almost all the important popular scriptures have been supplied with a *Māhātmya,* a praise of the greatness (of the work concerned) that contains profuse descriptions of promises attached to the reading of the scripture.

3. See e.g. K. Sivaraman, "The Word as a Category of Revelation," in *Revelation in Indian Thought, A Festschrift in Honour of Professor T. R. V. Murti,* ed. H. Coward and K. Sivaraman (Emeryville, Calif.: Dharma Publishing, 1977), pp. 45–64.

4. Some interesting details are mentioned by A. Esteller in "The Quest for the Original *Ṛgveda,*" *Annals of the Bhandarkar Oriental Research Institute* (ABORI) 50 (1969): 1–40; and "The *Ṛgveda Samhitā* as a 'Palimpsest'," *Indian Antiquary* (third series) 4, no. 1 (January 1967): 1–23.

5. The *guru-paraṁparā,* the succession of teachers, had to be memorized by each student as legitimation of his knowledge. In *Bṛhadaraṇyaka*

Upaniṣad IV, 6 sixty links of this chain of tradition are mentioned, going back through mythical figures to Brahmā, the creator himself, who revealed it.

6. P. V. Kane, *HDhS*, vol. 1 (1930), pp. 70–75.

7. See G. Srinivasa Murti's introduction to *Śrī Pancarātra Rakṣa of Śrī Vedānta Deśika*, ed. M. D. Aiyangar and T. Venugopalacharya (Madras: Adyar Library, 1942), pp. ixx–xii.

8. The most exhaustive account is given in J. Gonda, *Vedic Literature (Saṃhitās and Brāhmaṇas)*, History of Indian Literature, vol. 1 (Wiesbaden: Harrassowitz, 1975). On the Vedic schools, see L. Renou, *Les écoles védiques et la formation du Veda* (Paris: Adrien Maisonneuve, 1947).

9. For annotated text, see T. Aufrecht, *Die Hymnen des Rgveda*, 2d ed. (Bonn: A. Marcus, 1877); and *Ṛgveda with the Commentary of Sāyaṇa*, ed. M. Müller, 6 vols. (London, 1892; reprint Banaras: Chowkhambha Sanskrit Office, 1966). The best complete translation is H. F. Geldner's *Ṛgveda deutsch*, 5 vols (Cambridge, Mass.: Harvard University Press, 1951–57). A complete English translation is by R. T. H. Griffith, *Hymns of the Ṛgveda*, 4th ed., 2 vols (reprint Banaras: Chowkhambha Sanskrit Office, 1963).

10. For text, see Ram Sarma Acarya, *Sāmaveda*, 2d ed. (Bareilly: Sanskrit Samsthana, 1962). For a translation, see T. R. H. Griffith, *Hymns of the Sāmaveda* (reprint Banaras: Chowkhambha Sanskrit Office, 1963).

11. For the text, see A. Weber, *Yajurveda Vajasaneyasaṃhitā*, 2 vols (Berlin: Dümmler, 1871 ff.). For translation, see T. R. H. Griffith, *Hymns of the Yajurveda* (reprint Banaras: Chowkhambha Sanskrit Office, 1957).

12. For the text, see R. Roth and W. D. Whitney, *The Atharvaveda Saṃhitā* (Berlin: Dümmler, 1856). For a translation, see W. D. Whitney, *Atharvaveda Saṃhitā*, 2 vols. Harvard Oriental Series (1902; reprint Banaras: Chowkhambha Sanskrit Office, 1962).

13. L. Renou, *Vedic India* (Calcutta: Susil Gupta, 1957).

14. Ramdas Gaur, *Hindutva* [Hindī], pp. 81ff.

15. For the text, see Pandurang Jawaji, *Śikṣādivedaṣadangāni* (loose leaf) (Bombay: Nirṇaya Sagar Press, 1934).

16. In later times, all these auxiliary sciences developed into independent scholarly disciplines, each with a voluminous literature of its own.

17. Max Müller edited and translated *Śaunaka's Ṛgvedapratiśākhya* (Leipzig, 1856).

18. J. Gonda, *Vedic Literature*, p. 43.

19. I, 6, 3, 10. The story and the precise wording of the fatal formula are often repeated in the epics and Purāṇas.

20. For details see Gonda, *Vedic Literature,* Chapter 8; "The Brāhmaṇas."

21. As for instance in the *Bṛhadāraṇyaka Upaniṣad.* On Āraṇyakas see Gonda, *Vedic Literature,* Chapter 9.

22. For the text, see W. C. Sastri Pancikar (ed.). *One Hundred and Eight Upaniṣads,* 4th ed. (Bombay: Nirṇaya Sagar Press, 1932). Most of these have been translated in several volumes in the Adyar Library Series. A good English translation of the major early Upaniṣads with Sanskrit text and copious notes is in S. Radhakrishnan, *The Principal Upaniṣads* (London: Allen and Unwin, 1953; numerous reprints).

23. Thus a *Ramakrishna Upaniṣad* has been published by the Ramakrishna Mission. Dhanjibhai Fakirbhai, an Indian Christian, recently composed a *Khristopaniṣad* (Bangalore: The Christian Institute for the Study of Religion, 1965).

24. For details consult L. Renou, *Vedic India,* pp. 50f.

25. One of the most important Vaiṣṇava Saṁhitās is the *Ahirbudhnyasaṃhitā,* edited in 2 vols. by M. D. Ramanujacarya (2d ed., ed. V. Krishnamacharya) (Adyar: Adyar Library, 1966). No translation is available in any Western language. An important Śaivite Āgama is the *Ajitāgama,* 2 vols., ed. N. R. Bhatt (Pondichery: Institute Français d'Indologie Pondichery 1964–67), no translation is available in any Western language. An important Śākta Tantra is the *Tripurarāhasyam,* Swami Sanatanadevaji Maharaja (ed.) [*Jñānakhaṇḍa* only] (Banaras: Chowkhamba Sanskrit Series, 1967; English translation by A. U. Vasaveda (Banaras: Chowkhamba Sanskrit Office, 1965).

26. F. O. Schrader, *Introduction to the Pañcarātra and the Ahirbudhnya Saṃhitā* (Adyar: Adyar Library 1916). Quite useful also the brief introduction by Jean Filliozat, "Les Āgamas çivaites," in *Rauravāgama,* ed. N. R. Bhatt (Pondichery: Institut Français d'Indologie, 1961). Lately F. H. Daniel Smith has done extensive research in the literature (largely still in manuscript) of Vaiṣṇava āgamas.

27. *Śrī Pāñcarātra Rakṣa of Śrī Vedānta Deśika* critically edited with notes and variant readings by Pdt. M. Duraiswami Aiyangar and Pdt. T. Venugopalacharya, with an introduction by G. Srinivasa Murti (Adyar: Adyar Library, 1942).

28. See "Purāṇas and Their Authority in Religious Matters," *Kalyāṇa Kalpatāru* 18, no. 1 (August 1952): 5f.

29. For details consult L. Renou, *Vedic India,* pp. 41ff. Texts and translations are too numerous to be mentioned here; this type of literature has been extensively studied by nineteenth century European Indologists. For a fairly representative section of translated texts, see *Sacred Books of the East* (*SBE*) vols. 29 and 30. The most complete treatment is found in Jan Gonda, *The Ritual Sūtras* (vol. 1, fasc. 2 of A History of Indian Literature. Wiesbaden: Harassowitz, 1977).

30. The unquestioned authority in this field was P. V. Kane, with his seven volume *History of Dharmaśāstra,* which offers an unrivalled wealth of details about works, their authors, and materials pertaining to *smṛti.* The major Western authorities in this field are Duncan M. Derrett, professor of Oriental Law at the School of African and Oriental Studies in London, and Ludo Rocher, professor of Indian Studies at the University of Pennsylvania.

31. For the text, see J. Jolly, *Mānava Dharma Śāstra* (London: 1887); English translation by G. Bühler, *The Laws of Manu, SBE,* vol. 25. Many editions with commentaries are available now.

32. For a brief discussion of historical problems related to it, see Kane, *HDhS,* pp. 79–85 as well as G. Bühler's introduction to his translation, ibid.

33. See Kane, *HDhS,* pp. 60–70.

34. Rāmdās Gaur, *Hindutva,* p. 755.

35. The greatest authority on Purāṇas was R. C. Hazra, who wrote numerous books and papers on Purāṇas and *Upapurāṇas.* See his two contributions on Purāṇas and *Upapurāṇas* in *CHI,* vol. 2, pp. 240–86. The latest comprehensive work on the subject is L. Rocher, *The Puraṇas, HIL* vol. 3, fasc. 3 (Wiesbaden: Otto Harrassowitz, 1986).

36. Kane, *HDhS,* vol. 5, pp. 973–80, with ample references to original sources.

37. See A. D. Pusalker, "Puranic Studies" in *Review of Indological Research in the Last Seventy-Five Years,* pp. 689–773.

38. Its main texts are the *Nyāya-sūtras* by Gautama. More about it in Chapter 25.

39. H. G. Coward (ed.), *Studies in Indian Thought. Collected Papers of Prof. T. R. V. Murti* (Delhi: Motilal Banarsidass, 1983), pp. 357–76. See also "Revelation and Reason" in ibid., pp. 57–71.

40. Ibid., p. viii.

41. Ganganatha Jha, *Pūrva-Mīmāṃsā in Its Sources* (Banaras: Benares Hindu University, 1942), p. 146. A very good recent study of this

issue is Othmar Gächter, *Hermeneutics and Language in Pūrvamīmāṃsā: A Study in Śābara Bhāṣya* (Delhi: Motilal Banarsidass, 1983).

42. Mādhava, *Sarvadarśanasaṁgraha*, XIII, 6. An excellent introduction to this school is provided by Harold G. Coward in *Sphoṭa Theory of Language* (Delhi: Motilal Banarsidass 1980). See Coward's *Bhartṛhari*, Twayne World Authors Series (Boston: Twayne Publishers, 1976).

43. Mādhava, ibid., XIII, 13. Pāṇini is supposed to have been inspired by Śiva.

44. There are numerous editions, e.g., by Devaprakasa Patanjala Sastri (Delhi: Motilal Banarsidass, 1954). A complete English translation (with text and notes) was done by Srisa Chandra Vasu, 2 vols (reprint Delhi: Motilal Banarsidass, 1961).

45. V. S. Agrawala, *India as Known to Pāṇini*, 2d ed. (Banaras: Prithvi Prakasan, 1963), p. 3: "Pāṇini, unlike Sakatāyana did not carry to extremes the theory of treating all nouns as verbal derivatives, but also recognized the formation of fortuitous words in the languages for which no certain derivation could be vouchsafed."

46. A complete edition of Patañjali's *Mahābhaṣya* with Kayyaṭa's and several other glosses is published in ten vols. by Haryāṇa Sāhitya Samsthān, in Gurukul Jhajjar (Rohtak), 1961. Parts have been translated into various European languages.

47. K. A. Nilakanta Sastri, *The Culture and History of the Tamils* (Calcutta: Firma K. L. Mukhopadhyay, 1964), p. 10.

48. *Devanāgarī* is the name of the characters in which Sanskrit is usually written, though in various parts of the country also other characters have been used.

49. J. Gonda, *Vedic Literature*, p. 57.

50. According to Jan Gonda (*Vedic Literature*, p. 61), Langlois and Wilson, who were early translators of the entire Ṛgveda, "suffered much under the defect that they were based on the (not always correctly understood) commentary of Sāyaṇa." Ludwig's translation is called "stiff and abrupt" and Grassman's is a "wholly inadequate Germanisation." Griffith's translation is defective, too—he apparently put too much reliance on Sāyaṇa. Geldner "missed the exact meaning of many words." Renou "had to leave his translation unfinished." Roth and Kaegi had believed in an unambiguous uniform translation.

51. J. Gonda, *Vedic Literature*, p. 62.

52. R. N. Dandekar, *Some Aspects of the History of Hinduism* (Poona: University of Bangalore, 1967), p. 136.

53. Madhav M. Deshpande, "Changing Conceptions of the Veda: From Speech-Acts to Magical Sounds," *Adyar Library Bulletin* (1990): 1–41; quote, 4.

54. Ibid., p. 8.

55. RV 3, 55.

56. RV 10. 71. 5.

57. 57. RV 8,100. 11.

58. *LSU Magazine* (21 March 1993): 9. See also S. C. Kak, "The Structure of the Ṛgveda" *Indian Journal of History of Science* 28 (2) 1993, 71–79; "Astronomy of the Vedic Altars," *Vistas in Astronomy,* vol. 36 (1993), 117–40; "Planetary Periods from the Rgvedic Code," *The Mankind Quarterly,* vol. 33 (4) (1993), 433–42.

59. Deshpande, "Changing Conceptions of the Veda," p. 38. That the texts of the Veda are still the object of intense study by Hindu scholars is proven not only by numerous publications on the Vedas that appear every year but also by research institutions such as the Jhajhar Gurukul in Rohtak or the Vaidik Saṁśodan Saṁsthān in Poona. Much of Western Indological scholarship is still focused on Vedic studies. An "International Foundation for Vedic Education" has been recently founded in the United States that is holding an International Veda Conference attended by top researchers in the field. An Atharva Veda Conference was held in July 1993 in New York.

60. The famous *Vāk-Sukta* in Ṛgveda X, 125. The tenth book of the Ṛgveda is considered to be its most recent part.

61. J. Woodroffe, *Introduction to Tantra Śāstra* (Madras: Ganesh and Co., 1963).

62. II, 23, 3.

63. *Taittirīya Upaniṣad I,* 8.

64. *Māṇḍukya Upaniṣad.*

65. *Skandapurāṇa,* Viṣṇukhaṇḍa XVI, 30ff.

66. *Times of India* (9 October 1963).

67. See also H. Coward and W. Goa, *Mantra* (Chambersburg, Pa.: Anima Publications, 1991).

68. S. K. Belvalkar, *Shree Gopal Basu Malik Lectures on Vedānta Philosophy* (Poona: Bilvakunja, 1929). The individual *śākhas* try to expurgate the contradictions in their literatures. The existing *Brahmasūtra* is essentially a (Sāmavedi) Chāndogya Sūtra with later revisions and additions.

5. *ITIHĀSA* AND *PURĀṆA:* THE HEART OF HINDUISM

1. For general orientation, see M. Winternitz, "The Popular Epics and the Puranas," *A History of Indian Literature,* vol. 1, Part 2 (Calcutta: University of Calcutta, 1963). Among modern Western studies of the Mahābhārata the following stand out: B. A. van Nooten, *The Mahābhārata* (New York: Twayne Publishers, 1971); A. Hiltebeitel, *The Ritual of Battle: Krishna in the Mahābhārata* (Ithaca, N.Y.: Cornell University Press, 1976). Among older studies, E. W. Hopkins, *The Great Epic of India* (New York: 1901; reprint Calcutta: Punthi Pustak, 1969); and H. Oldenberg, *Das Mahābhārata* (Göttingen: Vandenhoeck and Ruprecht, 1922) are still often referred to. On the *Rāmāyaṇa,* H. Jacobi's *Das Rāmāyaṇa* (originally published Bonn: 1893, new ed. with foreword by E. Frauwallner and additional literature, Darmstadt: Wissenschaftliche Buchgesellschaft, 1970) is still indispensable. A new English translation of the *Rāmāyaṇa, Critical Edition* has begun to appear (Princeton, N.J.: Princeton University Press, 1984). Goldman's Introduction to the first volume, *Bālakāṇda* (pp. 3–59) deals both with the history of the *Rāmāyaṇa* text and the literature connected with it.

2. For details, consult P. J. Chinmulgund and V. V. Mirashi (eds.), *Review of Indological Research in the Last Seventy-Five Years* (Poona: Bharatiya Charitrakosha Mandal, 1967); pp. 670ff., as well as V. S. Sukhtankar, "Introduction," in *Critical Edition, Mahābhārata* (Poona: Bhandarkar Oriental Research Institute, 1933), *Ādiparvan,* i–cx and G. H. Bhatt, "Introduction" in *Rāmāyaṇa, Critical Edition* (Baroda: Oriental Institute, 1960) Bālakāṇḍa, xiii–xxxv, i–xviii. See also S. M. Katre, *Introduction to Textual Criticism,* with an appendix by P. K. Gode (Poona: Deccan College, 1954).

3. Vishnu S. Sukthankar writes in his "Prolegomena to the Critical Edition of the *Mahābhārata,*" in ibid., vol. 1 *Ādiparvan*: "Next to the Vedas [the Mahābhārata] is the most valuable product of the entire literature of ancient India, so rich in notable works. Venerable for its very antiquity, it is one of the most inspiring monuments of the world and an inexhaustible mine for the investigation of the religion, mythology, legend, philosophy, law, custom, and political and social institutions of ancient India" (p. iii).

4. N. Sen, "The Influence of the Epics on Indian Life and Literature," in *CHI,* vol. 2, p. 117. For details of the immense influence on drama, poetry, fine arts in India and in the whole of Southeast Asia, see this paper as well as B. R. Chatterjee, "The *Rāmāyaṇa* and the *Mahābhārata* in South-East Asia," in ibid., pp. 119ff.

5. H. Raychaudhuri, "The *Mahābhārata*: Some Aspects of its Culture," in *CHI,* vol. 2, pp. 71ff. See also J. L. Fitzgerald, "The Great Epic of India as

Religious Rhetoric: A Fresh Look at the *Mahābhārata*," *Journal of the American Academy of Religion* (*JAAR*) 51, no. 4 (1986): 611–29.

6. The names connected with the former theory are Larssen, Sorenson, Winternitz, and Meyer; with the latter, especially J. Dahlmann. About the theories and their criticism, cf. A. D. Pusalker, "The *Mahābhārata*: Its History and Character," in *CHI*, vol. 2, pp. 51ff. See also Fitzgerald, "The Great Epic," pp. 611–30.

7. *Mahābhārata, Critical Edition with Pratika Index*, 28 vols. (Poona: Bhandarkar Oriental Research Institute, 19233–1972). Several vulgate editions are available, e.g., one in four volumes from the Gītāpress in Gorakhpur.

8. I, 1, 50. See also M. Mehta, "The Problem of the Double Introduction to the Mahābhārata," *JAOS* 93, no. 4 (1973): 547–50.

9. The Bhandarkar Oriental Research Institute has published a critical edition in two volumes. A vulgate edition is available from several publishers, among others from Gītāpress, Gorakhpur (n.d.), with Hindī translation (The same publisher has also brought out a vulgate edition of the entire Mahābhārata in four volumes with a *Nāmānukramāṇikā*).

10. *Yad ihāsti tad anyatra yad nehāsti na tat kva cit.*

11. In *Mahābhāratātparyanirṇaya*

12. V. S. Sukhtankar, *On the Meaning of the Mahābhārata* (Bombay: Asiatic Society, 1957), pp. 128ff.

13. A complete English translation of the Mahābhārata was prepared by Pratap Chandra Roy toward the end of the last century; it has been republished in twelve volumes by Oriental Publishing Co., Calcutta in the late 1950s. A new English translation, following the critical edition was begun by A. van Buitenen (Chicago: University of Chicago Press, 1973–1978); so far three volumes have appeared. C. Rajagopalachari has published a one-volume rendering of some of the most important stories of the *Mahābhārata* (Bombay: Bharatiya Vidya Bhavan, 1958), which has become very popular.

14. *Āraṇyakaparvan*, Chapters 295–98 condensed.

15. The present introduction to the Rāma story contains the story of Vālmīki, who according to legend started out as a brigand, was converted into a Rāmabhakta, and did penance for his sins in a forest by keeping seated in meditation even while ants began building up an anthill (Sanskrit: *vālmīka*) around his body, covering it completely.

16. *Jātaka* 461; about *Rāmāyaṇa* criticism, see A. D. Pusalker, "The

Rāmāyaṇa: Its History and Character," CHI, vol. 2, pp. 14ff. C. Bulcke, *Rāmakathā* [Hindī] (Prāyāg: Hindī Pariṣad Viśvavidyālaya, 1950).

17. See G. H. Bhatt's "Introduction," in *Mahābhārata, Critical Edition.*

18. In the *Hindustan Times* (29 July 1972), a note appeared saying that the original manuscript of the *Rāmacaritamanasa* had been found in the house of a Pathan landlord in Mahilābad, U.P., near Lucknow. There are countless editions of this work in India. The Gītāpress brought out the full text with an English translation in 1968.

19. See A. D. Pusalker, *Studies in Epics and Purāṇas of India* (Bombay: Bharatiya Vidya Bhavan, 1955), pp. 174ff.

20. The Oriental Institute of Baroda has published the *Rāmāyaṇa, Critical Edition,* in seven volumes (1960–1975). Vulgate editions are numerous and easily available, e.g., from the Gītāpress.

21. Pusalker, "The *Rāmāyaṇa,*" pp. 27f.

22. R. T. H. Griffith has brought out a complete English translation of the *Rāmāyaṇa of Vālmīki* in verse (Banaras, 1915; reprint Banaras: Chowkhamba Sanskrit Studies No. 29, 1963). A prose translation, together with the Sanskrit text began to appear from Gītāpress, Gorakhpur, *Kalyāṇa Kalpataru,* in 1960; so far ten fascicles have come out (up to VII, 41). C. Rajagopalachari has summarized the stories of the *Rāmāyaṇa* in one volume (Bombay: Bharatiya Vidya Bhavan, 1962), which also has become very popular. A new English translation of the critical edition has begun to appear from Princeton University Press 1984ff.

23. *Bālakāṇḍa,* Chapter 67.

24. Laṅka is often identified with Śrī Laṅka; scholars are in disagreement, however, about the identity of Laṅka, and many are inclined to look for it not far from eastern Central India, where the rest of the Rāma story takes place.

25. *Uttarakāṇḍa,* 111, 21f.

26. See A. P. Karmarkar, "Religion and Philosophy of the Epics," in *CHI,* vol. 2, pp. 80ff.

27. Thus Swami Dayananda Sarasvati, the founder of the *Ārya Samāj.*

28. In 1986, as part of the multivolume *History of Indian Literature,* ed. Jan Gonda. Ludo Rocher wrote a monograph on the Purāṇas, which for many years to come will be the most authoritative study of the subject. It would be meaningless to attempt to summarize the work here. It goes into

the history of Purāṇa studies, the question of the number of Purāṇas, the controversies surrounding the division between *Mahāpurāṇas* and *Upapurāṇas*, the debate about the "Ur-Purāṇa" and eventually lists all Purāṇas, giving a short summary, indicating text editions, translations, and studies. For all the details concerning either the Purāṇas themselves or scholarship about them the reader is referred to this work.

29. R. C. Hazra, "The Purāṇas," in *CHI*, vol. 2, pp. 240f.

30. *Atharva Veda*, XI, 7, 24; *Bṛhadāraṇyaka Upaniṣad* IV, 5, 11 etc.

31. R. C. Hazra, "The Purāṇas."

32. Sixth century C.E.

33. See F. E. Pargiter, *Ancient Indian Historial Tradition* (Oxford: Oxford University Press, 1922; reprint Delhi: Motilal Banarsidass, 1962).

34. See Preface, in ibid. Criticized by P. V. Kane, *HDhS*, vol. 5, part 2, pp. 850ff.

35. M. A. Mehendale, "Purāṇas," in *HCIP*, vol. 3, p. 296.

36. Thus the *Devībhāgavata Purāṇa* of the Śāktas claims to be the real *Bhāgavata Purāṇa* and is accepted as such by the Śāktas. See C. Mackenzie Brown, "The Origin and Transmission of the Two *Bhāgavata Purāṇas*: A Canonical and Theological Dilemma," *JAAR* 51, no. 4 (1983): 551–67.

37. As does the *Bhaviṣya Purāṇa*, which claims to be an ancient prophetical book about the future (*bhaviṣya*).

38. All *Mahāpurāṇas* have been printed, most of them by several publishers; Motilal Banarsidass has started a fifty volume series, Ancient Indian Tradition and Mythology, which aims at providing a complete translation of all the *Mahapurāṇas*. So far thirty-six volumes have appeared, including *Śiva, Liṅga, Bhāgavata, Garuḍa, Kūrma, Brahmāṇḍa, Agni, Varāha, Brahmā Purāṇas*. Older translations are available of the *Markandeya*, the *Bhāgavata, Matsya*, the *Viṣṇu*, the *Agni* and the *Garuḍa Purāṇas*. For the *Upapurāṇas* consult R. C. Hazra, *Studies in the Upapurāṇas*, 2 vols. (Calcutta: Sanskrit College, 1958) 63; and L. Rocher, "The Purāṇas."

39. *Viṣṇu Purāṇa* VI, 8, 40ff.

40. *Skanda Purāṇa*, Viṣṇukhaṇḍa Margaśirṣamāhātmya XVI, 30ff.

41. *Newsweek* (21 September 1987), pp. 74ff., reviewed a performance of Peter Brook's *The Mahābhārata*, a nine-hour-long recreation of the Indian epic. He and his coworkers had been preparing this modern dramatization for twelve years. *India Today* (15 February 1987): 84, reported:

"Britain's most influential body—the Inner London Education Authority is to stage a £100,000 spectacular based on the *Rāmāyaṇa* to be performed by school children in London's Battersea Park in June this year." *India Today* (30 April 1987), under the title "Ramayan: Divine Sensation," reported the unexpected success of a current TV dramatization of the *Rāmāyaṇa* in India. The TV version of the *Rāmāyaṇa*, circulating also in the Hindu diaspora had the consequence that a great many Hindus living in the West were requesting a Hindī-cum-English version of the *Rāmcaritmānas*. Motilal Banarsidass brought out a sumptuous edition that found wide acceptance abroad. *SEMINAR* devoted its Jan. 89 (no. 353) issue to analyzing "The Rāmāyaṇa Syndrome."

6. THE BHAGAVADGĪTĀ

1. E. J. Sharpe, *The Universal Gita: Western Images of the Bhagavadgītā*, A Bicentenary Survey (Lasalle, Ill.: Open Court, 1985). R. Minor (ed.), *Modern Indian Interpretation of the Bhagavadgītā* (Albany: State University of New York Press, 1986). Arvind Sharma, author of *The Hindu Gītā: Ancient and Classical Interpretations of the Bhagavadgītā* (Lasalle, Ill.: Open Court, 1986) is also the founder-editor of the *Journal of Bhagavadgītā Studies*, now in its sixteenth year.

2. The Mahābhārata contains also an *Aṇugītā* and many of the Purāṇas have Gītās, summarizing in a popular form their main ideas.

3. A Kashmirian text of the Gītā with quite considerable variants has been discovered about fifty years ago. The *Mahābhārata, Critical Edition* vol. 7, *Bhīṣmaparvan* (Poona: Bhandarkar Oriental Research Institute, 1947), pp. 114–18 with the critical notes (pp. 769–86) contains a wealth of precise information about the text and the commentaries as well as major studies on the *Bhagavadgītā*.

4. Bombay: Bharatiya Vidya Bhavan, 1965.

5. Ibid., pp. 83f.

6. *Die Bhagavadgītā*, 2d ed. (Leipzig: H. Haessel, 1921), p. 32.

7. N. C. Chaudhuri, *Hinduism* (London: Chatto and Windus, 1979), however, accepts the *Gītā*'s dependence on Christian ideas.

8. S. Buddhiraja, *The Bhagavadgita: A Study* (Madras: Ganesh and Co., 1927).

9. English translation, in two vols. (Reprint, Poona: Tilak Bros., 1935).

10. Mahadev Desai, *The Gītā According to Gandhi* (Ahmedabad: Navajivan, 1946).

11. Sri Aurobindo, *Essays on the Gītā* (Pondichery: Sri Aurobindo Ashram, 1928).

12. S. Radhakrishnan, *The Bhagavadgītā* (London: Allen and Unwin, 1948).

13. S. K. Belvalkar, "Vedānta in the *Bhagavadgītā*," in *Shree Gopal Basu Malik Lectures on Vedānta Philosophy* (Poona: Bilvakunja, 1929).

14. Ibid., pp. 118f., slightly revised.

15. Quoted in M. Winternitz, *A History of Indian Literature*, vol. 1, part 2 (Calcutta: University of Calcutta, 1963), p. 375.

16. W. M. Callewaert and S. Hemraj, *Bhagavadgītānuvāda: A Study in Transcultural Translation* (Ranchi: Sathya Bharati Publication, 1983).

17. The term is *adhikāra*, qualification or prerequisite.

18. Despite the often advocated spirit of tolerance in the Gītā, the teaching is solidly Kṛṣṇaitic and would not admit that any other religion would yield the same results.

19. *Bhagavadgītā* (*B.G.*) IX, 4–8.

20. Ibid., 16–19.

21. Ibid., 26–34, condensed.

22. The titles given at the end of the chapters are not found in many manuscripts, and in those in which they are found, they are not uniform; the critical edition leaves them out.

23. *BG* XI, 3.

24. *BG* XVIII, 51–55.

25. *BG* XVIII, 64–66; the term is *pāpa*, the Vedic technical word for sin, not evil in the general sense as Radhakrishnan translates.

26. Thomas McCarthy in the Introduction (p. xxv) to his translation of Jürgen Habermas, *The Theory of Communicative Action*, vol. l. *Reason and the Rationalization of Society* (Boston: Beacon Press, 1984), p. 4: "Sociology became the science of crisis par excellence; it concerned itself above all with the anomic aspects of the dissolution of traditional social systems and the development of modern ones."

27. Heiner Kipphardt, "In the Matter of Robert J. Oppenheimer," *Stücke*, vol. 1, p. 309.

28. Published in the *Indian and Foreign Review* (1 March 1981): 27.

7. THE WORLD OF THE HINDU

1. The best work on the subject is still A. A. Macdonell's *Vedic Mythol-*

ogy, originally published in 1897 in the *Encyclopedia of Indo-Aryan Research*, ed. G. Bühler, vol. 3, part 1 a (reprint Banaras: Indological Bookhouse, 1963). See also R. N. Dandekar, "Vṛtrahā Indra," *ABORI* 30, no. 1 (1951): 1–55. On creation myths in general, see D. Maclagan, *Creation Myths: Man's Introduction to the World* (London: Thames and Hudson, 1977). See also F. B. J. Kuiper, *Ancient Indian Cosmogony*, essays selected and introduced by John Irwin (New Delhi: Vikas, 1983).

2. *Ṛgveda* I, 185.

3. S. Kramrisch, "The Triple Structure of Creation in the *ṚgVeda*," *HR* 2, no. 1 (1962): 141.

4. *Ṛgveda* X, 82.

5. Ibid., verse 2, 3, 7.

6. *Ṛgveda* X, 90.

7. Ibid., verse 16.

8. *Ṛgveda* X, 129.

9. Kramrisch, "The Triple Structure," p. 147.

10. *Bṛhadāraṇyaka Upaniṣad* I, 1, 4

11. *Kaṭha Upaniṣad* 3, 10f.; *Ṛgveda* X, 121, 1; *Manusmṛti* I, 9.

12. *Manas* cannot be exactly translated, the nearest concept is the mediaeval *sensus communis*, the coordinating faculty of the senses, not intellect itself.

13. *Ahaṁkāra* is sometimes translated "egoism" (G. Bühler, repeated by M. Eliade, *From Primitives to Zen* [New York: Harper and Row, 1967], p. 112) which gives a wrong idea.

14. *Manusmṛti* I, 1ff.

15. Ibid., I, 64f.

16. Ibid., 65–74.

17. Ibid., 81–86.

18. The best work on the subject is S. M. Ali, *The Geography of the Purāṇas* (New Delhi: People's Publishing House 1966), which offers exhaustive references to the sources, and many serious suggestions concerning the identity of ancient names with contemporary geography.

19. Ibid., p. 32 and Figure 2.

20. *Viṣṇu Purāṇa* II, 4 and many parallels in other Purāṇas.

21. One *yojana* is approximately nine miles.

22. *Viṣṇu Purāṇa*, II, 2, and parallels.

23. Ibid., II, 3, and parallels.

24. Ibid., II, 3, 24–26.

25. The account is taken from a Vaiṣṇava scripture.

26. *Viṣṇu Purāṇa* II, 4, 87.

27. Ibid., verse 98.

28. Ibid., II, 5–8.

29. Ibid., II, 5, 5.

30. Ibid., verses 13ff.

31. Ibid., II, 7, 11.

32. Ibid., verses 15ff.

33. Ibid., II, 7, 22ff.

34. Concerning the discussion of this date see P. V. Kane, *HDhS*, vol. 5 part 1, pp. 648f (Poona: Bhandarkar Oriental Research Institute, 1962).

35. A. D. Pusalker, "Historical Traditions," in *HCIP*, vol. 1, pp. 271–333.

36. According to Puranic accounts the Creator produced before the present creation several kinds of creatures, who, because produced from Brahmā's mind in meditation, did not multiply themselves. He created "mind-born sons, like Himself," the nine Brahmārṣis, celebrated in Indian mythology—all absorbed in meditation and without desire of progeny. Brahmā's anger produced Rudra, half male and half female, who began multiplying into various beings. Finally, he created Manu Svayambhu "born of, and identical with his original self," and the female part of himself he constituted as Satarupa. *Viṣṇu Purāṇa* I, 7.

37. *Viṣṇu Purāṇa* I, 13, and parallels.

38. *Śatapatha Brāhmaṇa* I, 8, 1, 1–6, seems to be the oldest account. Also *Bhāgavata Purāṇa* VIII, 24ff.

39. To forestall a popular confusion, Kali-yuga comes from *kali*, "strife, fight" and has nothing to do with Kālī, "The Black One," the name of Devī, the Goddess in her terrible form.

40. See *Viṣṇu Purāṇa* IV, 21ff., and parallels.

41. Ibid., IV, 20.

42. Ibid., IV, 24 128ff.

43. Ibid., verses 1121ff.

44. The representatives of the Ārya Samāj have been most prominent in this regard.

45. In a talk given on December 10, 1965.

46. For details of this notion, see P. Hacker, *Vivarta: Studien zur Geschichte der illusionistischen Kosmologie und Erkenntnistheorie der Inder* (Wiesbaden: Akademie der Wissenschaften Mainz, 1953).

47. See his "Astronomy of the Vedic Altar," in *Vistas of Astronomy* vol. 36 (1993) (the author graciously provided me with his manuscript before publication).

48. B. Datta and A. N. Singh, *History of Hindu Mathematics: A Source Book* (2 parts) (Bombay, Calcutta, and New Delhi: Asia Publishing House, 1962).

49. *The Positive Sciences of the Ancient Hindus* (reprint, Delhi: Motilal Banarsidass, 1958).

50. "Naturalism and Science in Ancient India" in D. P. Singhal, *India and World Civilisation*, vol. 1 (East Lansing: Michigan State University Press, 1969).

51. "The World Made of Sound: Whitehead and Pythagorean Harmonics in the Context of Veda and the Science of Mantra," *Journal of Dharma*, 17, no. 3 (1992): 233–66.

8. THE MANY GODS AND THE ONE GOD OF HINDUISM

1. For example, A. A. Macdonell, *Vedic Mythology* (reprint Banaras: Indological Bookhouse, 1963).

2. K. Bhattacharya, *Studies in Philosophy* (Calcutta: Progressive Publishers, 1956), vol. 1, p. 35, connects the *devatas* with Plato's *ideas* and the concept of *universalia ante rem*. Through *upāsana* ("worship") one ascends from the concrete individual things to their *adhyātma* ("spiritual") and *adibhūta* ("primaeval") aspect, their absoluteness. *Devata* would correspond to the *noumenon* of Kant.

3. R. N. Dandekar, "God in Hindu Thought," lecture held at Bharatiya Vidya Bhavan (13 January 1968).

4. See the research of A. Esteller, e.g., "The Quest for the Original *Ṛgveda*," *ABORI* 50 (1969): 1–40.

5. R. N. Dandekar, "Vṛtrahā Indra," *ABORI* 30, no. 1 (1951): 1–55. The etymology of Indra is not clear as yet. A. A. Macdonell derives it from *indu*, "drop" (*A History of Sanscrit Literature*, 2d ed. [reprint Delhi: Motilal Banarsidass, 1961], p. 44); J. Gonda from *intoi*, "pushing" (*Die Religionen Indiens* [Stuttgart: Kohlhammer, 1960], vol. 1, p. 60); R. N. Dandekar from *indu*, bringing it in connection with "virile power" ("Vṛtrahā Indra," ibid.); S. S. Sastri connects it with *in*, *inva*, "to rule," and *ina*, "sun," "lord," ("Vṛṣakapi," *Bhāratīya Vidyā* 10: 159). A very thorough and insightful study of Indra is provided by Hertha Krick, "Der Vaniṣṭusava und Indras Offenbarung," *WZKSA* 19 (1975): 25–74.

6. Dandekar, "Vṛtrahā Indra."

7. It is important to note that the Vedic *devas* are in constant conflict with the *asuras*, the demons, and that their high position is due precisely to their power to subjugate the hostile forces. In this context H. von Stietencron's essay "Dämonen und Gegengötter: Überlegungen zur Typologie von Antagonismen," *Saeculum* 34, nos. 3–4 (1983): 372–83.

8. The exact number is 1028 (divided into ten *maṇḍalas*), from which eleven Vālakhilya hymns are usually subtracted, because neither the great Sāyaṇa (fourteenth century) had commented upon them nor are they mentioned in the list (considered authoritative) ascribed to Śaunaka.

9. *Ṛgveda* I, 164, 46.

10. *Ṛgveda* II, 12. From R. H. T. Griffith's trans (with modifications), *Hymns of the Ṛgveda*, 4th ed., 2 vols. (Banaras: Chowkhamba Sanskrit Office, 1963).

11. There are still remnants of Indra worship in some parts of India. See e.g., G. C. Tripathi, "Das Indradhvaja-Fest in Orissa. Die Überreste der Indra-Verehrung in Ostindien," *ZDMG* Supplement 3, no. 2 (1977).

12. *Ṛgveda* I, 1.

13. *Ṛgveda* I, 35.

14. For example, *Ṛgveda* VII, 86.

15. Vol. 1, *Varuṇa und die Wasser* (Göttingen: Vandenhoek and Ruprecht, 1951); vol. 2, *Varuṇa und das Ṛta* (Göttingen: Vandenhoek and Ruprecht, 1959).

16. *Bṛhadāraṇyaka Upaniṣad* III, 9, 1, 9.

17. *Viṣṇu Purāṇa* I, 2, 66f.: "The only God, *Janardana* takes the designation Brahmā, Viṣṇu and Śiva accordingly as he creates, preserves or

destroys. Viṣṇu as creator creates himself, as preserver preserves himself, as destroyer, destroys himself at the end of all things."

18. Thus the celebrated Maheśa (Śiva) *mūrti* in the main cave of Gharapurī (Elephanta). See S. Kramrisch, "The Image of Mahādeva in the Cave Temple on Elephanta Island," *Ancient India* 2 (1946): 4–8.

19. According to this legend, Viṣṇu and Brahmā had been disputing about their supremacy when a huge fiery column appeared before them. To find out about its nature, Viṣṇu, in the form of a boar, dived down to find its lower end; and Brahmā, in the form of a swan, flew up to discover its upper extremity. After some time they met again. Viṣṇu admitted that he had not found an end, Brahmā asserted that he had found the upper end and was hence greater than Viṣṇu and therefore the universal Lord. Just then the sides of the column opened and out stepped Śiva, the infinite, praising Viṣṇu for his truthfulness and establishing him second to Himself, severely chiding Brahmā for his lie and condemning him to remain without worship henceforth.

20. *Ṛgveda* III, 62, 10.

21. *Kūrma Purāṇa* 20.

22. R. C. Hazra, *Studies in the Upapurāṇas* (Calcutta: Sanskrit College, 1958), vol. 1, p. 29f. H. von Stietencron has assembled much interesting information on sun worship in India and its possible connection with Iran in his monograph on Sūrya, *Indische Sonnenpriester: Sāmba und die Śakasdiśpīya Brāhmana* (Wiesbaden: Otto Harrassowitz, 1966).

23. See Sir Mortimer Wheeler, *The Indus Civilization* (Cambridge: Cambridge University Press, 1953).

24. Ibid., pp. 83 and 95. He speaks of a "likelihood that both Śiva and Liṅga worship have been inherited by the Hindus from the Harappans."

25. S. K. Chatterji, "Race Movements and Prehistoric Culture," *HCIP*, pp. 164ff.; See also C. V. Narayana Ayyar, *Origin and Early History of Śaivism in South India* (Madras: University of Madras, 1936), p. 10.

26. A. D. Pusalker, "Aryan Settlements in India," *HCIP*, vol. 1, pp. 258ff.

27. Chatterji, "Race Movements and Prehistoric Culture."

28. *Yajurveda Vajasaneyasaṁhitā*, Chapter 16.

29. *Śvetāśvatara Upaniṣad*, VI, 1.

30. *Mahābhārata Śāntiparvan* 274 and Appendix I, 8; *Droṇaparvan* 201, 64–68; and *Sauptikaparvan* 18.

31. The myth is told in both the epics and most of the Purāṇas. The oldest version is probably in *Vāyu Purāṇa* I, 30.

32. For example, *Vālmīki Rāmāyaṇa* I, 45.

33. See V. Paranjoti, *Śaiva Siddhānta*, 2d ed. (London: Luzac, 1964), pp. 54ff.

34. See A. Coomaraswamy, *The Dance of Śiva* (Bombay: Asia Publishing House, 1948), p. 83.

35. *Śiva Purāṇa Śatarudrasaṁhitā* 3.

36. Ibid., *Umāsaṁhitā*.

37. Ibid., *Rudrasaṁhitā Sātikhaṇḍa* 38, 34.

38. A whole *Liṅga Purāṇa* is devoted to this.

39. See the collection of hymns with English translation, F. Kingsbury and G. E. Philips, trans., *Hymns of the Tamil Saivite Saints* (Calcutta: Association Press, 1921).

40. *Śatapatha Brāhmana* I, 1, 2, 13; I, 9, 3, 9; III, 6, 3, 3.

41. Chatterji, "Race Movements and Prehistoric Culture," p. 165.

42. See D. M. Srinivasan (ed.), *Mathurā: The Cultural Heritage* (New Delhi: American Institute of Indian Studies, 1989).

43. See A. D. Pusalker, "Historicity of Kṛṣṇa," in *Studies in Epics and Puranas* (Bombay: Bharatiya Vidya Bhavan, 1955), pp. 49–81.

44. On the underlying theoretical basis of the *avatāra* doctrine, see P. Hacker, "Zur Entwicklung der Avatāralehre," *WZKSA* 4 (1960): 47–70.

45. The *Viṣṇusahasranāma* is contained in the Mahābhārata and in all Vaiṣṇava Purāṇas and has been printed separately many times. It has also been commented upon by several authorities.

46. See N. Macnicol, *Psalms of the Maratha Saints* (Calcutta: Association Press, 1919). There are countless collections of such hymns in Indian vernaculars, most of them as yet untranslated.

47. E. Neuman, *An Analysis of the Archetype The Great Mother* (Princeton, N.J.: Princeton University Press, 1955), pp. 120ff.

48. R. C. Hazra, *Studies in the Upapurāṇas,* vol. 2, p. 16.

49. H. Whitehead, *The Village Gods of South India,* 2d ed. (Calcutta: Association Press, 1921), p. 11.

50. *Mahābhārata, Sauptikaparvan* 8, 64ff., describes a vision of "Death-Night in her embodied form" just before the great war begins!

51. A. P. Karmarkar, *The Religions of India* (Lonavla: Mira Publishing House, 1950), p. 99.

52. H. von Stietencron, *Gaṅgā und Yamunā* (Wiesbaden: Otto Harrassowitz, 1972).

53. Examples are found in A. Daniélou, *Hindu Polytheism* (London: Routledge and Kegan Paul, 1964), pp. 350ff.

54. Ibid., pp. 291ff.

55. *Viṣṇu Purāṇa* I, 8ff.; *Śiva Purāṇa; Rudrasaṁhitā* III.

56. See J. Gonda, "The Historical Background of the Name Satya Assigned to the Highest Being," *ABORI* 48–49 (1968): 83–93.

57. On this whole issue, see K. Klostermaier, *Mythologies and Philosophies of Salvation in the Theistic Traditions of India* (Waterloo, Ont.: Wilfrid Laurier University Press, 1984).

9. THE PATH OF WORKS: *KARMAMĀRGA*

1. A brief analysis is given by L. A. Ravi Varma, "Rituals of Worship," in *CHI*, vol. 4, pp. 445–63.

2. This is done with reference to *Manusmṛti* VI, 35f.

3. *Ṛgveda* X, 90.

4. A. A. Macdonell, "Vedic Religion," in *Encyclopedia of Religion and Ethics*, 3rd ed., ed. E. Hastings, 1954), vol. 12, pp. 601–18.

5. About the technical aspects of the *yajña*, see P. V. Kane, *HDhS*, vol. 2 (part 2), pp. 983ff.

6. *Taittirīya Saṃhitā* I, 8, 4, 1.

7. See the informative article by N. Wyatt "*Aśvamedha* and *Puruṣamedha* in Ancient India," *Religion* (1989): 1–11.

8. See F. M. Smith "Financing the Vedic Ritual. The Mūlādhyāyapariśiṣṭa of Kātyāyana," *WZKS*, 32 (1988): 63–75.

9. In the same report we read: "In the West, people talk of peace; they hold an atom bomb in one hand and a peace-dove in the other. Thus peace was destroyed. But in the East the guiding principle is *pañca śila*, which has its deep roots in the moral and spiritual tradition of the East. This is the true way to peace."

10. *Blitz* (11 April 1970) reported that the Brahmin who was hired to do it died through electrocution, while performing, the *yajña*.

11. F. Staal, *AGNI: The Vedic Ritual of the Fire Altar*, 2 vols. with many plates (Berkeley: University of California Press, 1983).

12. F. Staal has dealt with Vedic ritual by itself and in a comparative fashion in many other important publications, e.g. *The Science of Ritual* (Poona: Deccan Institute 1982); "The Meaninglessness of Ritual," *Numen* 26 (1979): 2–22; "The Sound of Religion," *Numen* 33 (1986): 33–64. 185–224. See also his "Exchange with a Reviewer of *Agni*," *JAS* 46, no. 1 (1987): 105–10.

13. *Chāndogya Upaniṣad* V, 3–10 contains the *pañcāgni vidyā*.

14. See C. M. Carstairs, *The Twice-Born* (London: Hogarth Press, 1957), which describes in meticulous detail the rituals performed by a Brahmin family in Poona.

15. From *Śaiva Upaniṣads*, trans. T. R. Srinivasa Ayyangar and G. Srinivasa Murti (Adyar: Adyar Library, 1953), pp. 165ff.

16. Ibid., pp. 203f.

17. It is quite typical that even a former leader of the Communist Party in Kerala, N. Nambudiripad belonged to the Brahmin caste. In Tamiḷnādu, the Draviḍa Kazhagam (DK), staged a kind of anti-Brahmin revolt.

18. *Manu* II, 176, prescribes already daily *tarpaṇa*.

19. *Caṇḍālas* were the offspring of a Brahmin father and a *śūdra* mother and were considered the lowest in the social hierarchy.

20. In the *Kaṭha-Upaniṣad* Yama, the god of death himself, apologizes to Naciketas, a Brahmin youth who has come to him, for not having served him due to the former's absence.

21. *Taittirīya Upaniṣad* II, 2, 1.

22. *Chāndogya Upaniṣad* VII, 26, 2.

23. Details may be found under the heading *bhojana*, in Kane, *HDhS*, vol. 2, pp. 757–800.

24. Vedic ritual has been a major preoccupation of Western Indology for more than a hundred years. Part of the fascination this type of study held for Western scholars may have to do with the age of the texts concerned—the quest for origins was a widely shared concern of nineteenth century scholarship—as well as with the formalism of the texts themselves:

rituals are designed to bring order into the cosmos, and ritual literature is characterized by the meticulousness with which it regulates every movement and every sound. In that respect it resembles scholarship: it leaves nothing unexplained, leaves nothing to chance, or to the layperson's inexpert handling of things.

Modern scholarship dealing with Vedic sacrifice ranges from early comprehensive reconstructions from texts like J. Schwab's *Das indische Tieropfer* (Erlangen: Deichert, 1886), and Sylvain Lévi's still often referred to *La doctrine du sacrifice dans le Brahmanas* (Paris: 1898; reprint Paris: Presses Universitaires de France, 1966), to specialized studies like those of F. Staal, *Agni*, and J. Gonda's *Vedic Ritual: The Non-solemn Rites* (Amsterdam: North-Holland Publishing, 1980), and J. C. Heesterman's *The Inner Conflict of Tradition: Essays in Indian Ritual, Kingship and Society* (Chicago: University of Chicago Press, 1985). In addition to these the following works are of interest: W. Caland and V. Henry, *L'Agnistoma: description compléte de la forme normals du sacrifice de Soma dans le culte védique*, 2 vols. (Paris: E. Léroux 1906–1907); C. G. Diehl, *Instrument and Purpose: Studies on Rites and Rituals in South India* (Lund: C. W. K. Gleerup 1956); L. Dumont, *Homo hierarchicus: Essai sur le systéme des castes* (Paris: Gallimard, 1966); L. Renou, *The Destiny of the Veda in India* (Delhi: Motilal Banarsidass, 1965); M. Strickman (ed.), *Classical Asian Rituals and the Theory of Ritual* (Berlin: Springer 1986); and Ria Kloppenborg (ed.), *Selected Studies on Ritual in the Indian Religions: Essays to D. J. Hoens*, Studies in History of Religions: Supplements to Numen 45 (Leiden: Brill, 1983). How detailed this kind of study can become is shown in the most recent work of the doyen of European Indology, J. Gonda, *The Ritual Functions and Significance of Grasses in the Religion of the Veda* (Amsterdam: North-Holland Publishing, 1985) with thousands of textual references.

25. Interesting economic details are supplied by D. D. Kosambi, *An Introduction to the Study of Indian History* (Bombay: Popular Book Depot, 1956), pp. 94ff.

26. A. Weber, "Über das Menschenopfer bei den Indern der vedischen Zeit," in *Indische Streifen* (Berlin: 1886), vol. 1, pp. 54–89, has a collection of all the Vedic evidences concerning human sacrifice. See *Aitareya Brāhmaṇa* VII, 13–18; II, 8, VI, 8; *Śatapatha Brāhmaṇa* I, 2, 3, 6; VI, 2, 2, 18, etc.

27. *Bhāgavata Purāṇa* IX, 7, 20, describes a human sacrifice according to a Vedic ritual.

28. See P. E. Dumont, *L'Aśvamedha* (Paris: P. Geuthner, 1927).

29. The last seems to have been performed in the eighteenth century, as described in P. K. Gode's interesting article, "The Aśvamedha Performed

by Sevai Jayasingh of Amber 1699–1744 A.D.," in *Studies in Indian Literary History* (Bombay: Bharatiya Vidya Bhavan, 1954), pp. 292–306.

30. *Aitareya Brāhmaṇa* II, 18. According to the same text, the *medha* went from the goat into the earth and from the earth into rice. "All those animals from which the *medha* had gone [e.g., camel, ass, mule] are unfit to be sacrificed." See also *Śatapatha Brāhmaṇa* I, 2, 3, 6.

31. R. Gordon Wasson: "The Soma of the Rig Veda: What Was It?," *Journal of the American Oriental Society* (*JAOS*) 91, no. 2 (1971): 169–91.

32. *Ṛgveda* VIII, 48, 3.

33. *Bhagavad Gītā* IX, 26f.

34. The ritual is minutely described in the *kriya-pada* of the Āgamas, Samhitas, and Tantras, the most elaborate of the four traditional parts of each of those scriptures.

35. The ritual of the famous Viṣṇu temple at Śrīraṅgam, as detailed in the *Śrīparameśvara Saṃhitā*, ed. Sri Govindacarya (Śrīraṅgam: Kodandarāmasannidhi, 1953), is said to have been revealed to Yamunācārya by Lord Viṣṇu himself. Similarly the ritual of South Indian Śaivite temples, as outlined in the *Somaśaṃbhupaddhatī* with French translation and notes by H. Brunner-Lachaux (Pondichery: Institut Français d'Indologie, 1963), is associated with a Śiva revelation to its author.

36. A good example is R. V. Joshi, *Le Rituel de la dévotion Kṛṣṇaite'* (Pondichery: Institut Français d'Indologie, 1959).

37. The most famous is that of Ajamila, as reported in the *Bhāgavata Purāṇa*.

38. See M. Strickman, *Classical Asian Rituals*. See also A. J. Blasi, "Ritual as a Form of Religious Mentality," *Sociological Analysis* 46, no. 1 (1985): 59–72.

39. See note 9; also J. F. Staal, "Language and Ritual," in *KSBCCV*, part 2, pp. 51–62.

10. PURITY AND MERIT: THE TWIN CONCERNS OF *KARMAMĀRGA*

1. W. Cenkner, *A Tradition of Teachers. Śaṅkara and the Jagadgurus Today* (Delhi: Motilal Banarsidass, 1983), p. 150.

2. The importance of such activities in contemporary India cannot only be gauged from the increasing crowds at such events like the Kumbhamela, attendance of up to 7 million pilgrims, but also by the attention

given it even by a liberal secular news magazine. "Kumbh Mela: Nectar of the Gods, Photofeature by Raghu Rai," *India Today* (15 May 1986), pp. 74–85. See also J. B. Carman and A. Marglin (eds.), *Purity and Auspiciousness in Indian Society* (Leiden: Brill, 1985).

3. P. V. Kane's aforementioned *History of Dharmaśāstra* is an inexhaustible source of information on all aspects of dharma.

4. A good account of it is given in S. K. Maitra, *The Ethics of the Hindus*, 3rd ed. (Calcutta: University of Calcutta, 1963), pp. 81ff.

5. Ibid., p. 83: "Thus for the Nyāya-Vaiśeṣikas righteousness is a quality of the *Ātman* or Self, i.e., is a subjective category to be distinguished from the objective act (*karma*) as well as from any impersonal transcendental category (*apūrva*) which may be generated by it. Nor is it any objective quality of an act which has any such supersensuous category in its aid or support (*apūrvaprakṛtikarmaguṇa*)."

6. Ibid., pp. 117ff.

7. Ibid., p. 119.

8. S. N. Dasgupta, *HIPh* (Cambridge: Cambridge University Press, 1955) vol. 5, p. 134.

9. *Bhagavadgītā* III, 47. *Niṣkāma Karma*, special volume of *Kalyāṇ* 54 (1980) contains over a hundred articles (in Hindi) on this topic.

10. *Bhagavadgītā*, XVI, 21.

11. Jayanta uses the triad *moha* ("delusion"), *rāga* ("attraction"), and *dveṣa* ("aversion"), which materially is exactly the same; he utilizes *lobha* and *krodha* as derivations of *rāga* and *dveṣa*.

12. This is a typical Vaiṣṇava injunction.

13. *Viṣṇu Purāṇa* III, 12.

14. *Cārakasaṃhitā*, ed. T. Yadava Sarma (Bombay: Nirnaya Sagara Press, 1963), pp. 45–51, *Sūtrasthānam* 8.

15. *The Tirukkural* [in Tamil] with translations in English by G. U. Pope, W. H. Drew, J. Lazarus, and F. W. Ellis (Tinnevelly: South India Śaiva Siddhanta Works Publishing Society, 1962), quotations: nos. 72; 101; 156; 160; 203. There is, however, a scholarly opinion, that the author of the *Tirukkural* was a Jain, not a Hindu.

16. For detail see Sādhucaraṇa Prasād, *Dharmaśāstrasaṅgraha Prayaścittas* form Chapter 21, the longest of all. (Bombay: Śrī Venkaṭeśvara Steam Press, 1913)

17. The *Manusmṛti,* as well as other *dharmaśāstras,* are quite up to date as regards protection of the environment: they punish by loss of caste the injuring of living plants, cutting down green trees for firewood, mining and all mechanical engineering that does damage to the environment, etc. See *Manusmṛti* XI, 64f.

18. Ibid., XI, 53. In XII, 54ff. (a later addition perhaps) Manu points out the various animal rebirths persons have to go through in consequence of their sins: "Those who committed *mahāpātakas,* having passed during large numbers of years through dreadful hells, obtain after that the following births: the slayer of a brahmin enters the womb of a dog, a pig, an ass, a camel, a cow, a goat, a sheep, a deer, a bird, a Caṇḍala, a Pukkasa; a brahmin who drinks *sūra* shall enter the bodies of small and large insects, of moths, of birds feeding on ordure . . . the violator of the *guru's* bed enters a hundred times grasses, shrubs and creepers . . . "

19. See *Devībhāgavata Purāṇa* VIII, 22ff.

20. *Manusmṛti* XI, 45f.

21. Ibid., 73–87. Note, however, that this applies only to a Brahmin; a man from a lower caste who kills a Brahmin has no such means available.

22. Ibid., 228–231.

23. Ibid., 31–33.

24. Thus in Viśvanatha Cakravartti, *Bhaktirasāmṛtasindhubindu, JAOS* 1 (1974). For Saivite rules regarding violation of worship, see *Somaśambhupaddhati,* ed. and trans. [French] H. Brunner-Lachaux (Pondichery: Institut Français d'Indologie, 1963–68), vol. I, pp. 102ff. For the means of expiation see *Śaiva-upaniṣads,* ed. A. Mahadeva Sastri (Madras: Adyar Library 1960), trans. T. R. Srinivasa Ayyangar (Madras: Adyar Library 1955), pp. 142 and 149, where *bhasma,* sacred ashes, is praised as the great remover of sins: "This *bhasma* alone is possessed of the special virtue of bestowing the knowledge of Hari and Śaṅkara, of destroying the most heinous sins resulting from the murder of a *brahmana* and the like and of bestowing great power and glory."

11. THE HINDU SACRAMENTS: THE *SAṂSKĀRAS*

1. On *saṃskāras* in general the most exhaustive source is P. V. Kane, *HDhS,* vol. 2, part 1. See also R. B. Pandey, *Hindu Saṃskāras: Socio-Religious Study of the Hindu Sacraments* (Delhi: Motilal Banarsidass, 1969).

2. *Manusmṛti* II, 26.

3. *Dvi-jāti,* twice-born, is the designation of the upper three castes,

Brahmins, Kṣatriyas, and *Vaiśyas,* whose initiation is considered to be a second, spiritual birth.

4. *Manusmṛti* II, 27f.

5. The child gets a "secret name" immediately after birth, which is known only to the parents. *Manusmṛti* II, 30, says that the official name giving should take place "on the tenth or twelfth on a lucky *tithi,* in an auspicious *muhūrta,* under an auspicious constellation."

6. *Viṣṇu Purāṇa* III, 10.

7. *Manusmṛti* II, 33.

8. Hindus calculate their years of life from the day of conception, not from the day of birth. This must be kept in mind when mentioning age. A good study of the implication of *upanayana* is provided by B. K. Smith, "Ritual, Knowledge and Being. Initiation and Veda Study in Ancient India," *Numen* 33, no. 1 (1986): 65–89, with a good bibliography.

9. *Viṣṇu Purāṇa* III, 10, says: "If he does not propose to enter into the married state, he may remain as a student with his teacher, first making a vow to that effect, and employ himself in the service of his guru and the guru's descendants; or he may become at once a hermit or adopt the order of the religious mendicant according to his original determination."

10. *Manusmṛti* III, 20–42, mentions *brahmā, daiva, ārṣa, prājānatya, āsura, gāndharva, rākṣasa,* and *paiśāca* forms of marriage. It explains them and says that some of these are "blamable," though valid, as, e.g., forcible abduction of the bride (*rākṣasa*), seduction (*paiśāca*), love marraige (*gāndharva*), or bride buying (*āsura*).

11. J. Duncan M. Derret, *The Death of a Marriage Law. Epitaph for the Rishis* (Durham, N.C.: Carolina Academic Press, 1978). Derret has written extensively on Hindu law and teaches Oriental Law at the London School of Oriental and African Studies. Among his well-known publications are *Hindu Law, Past and Present* (Calcutta: A. Mukherjee, 1958); *Introduction to Modern Hindu Law* (Calcutta: A. Mukherjee, 1963); *Critique of Modern Hindu Law* (Bombay: H. M. Tripathi, 1970); *History of Indian Law* (Dharmaśāstra) (Leiden: Brill, 1973); *Essays in Classical and Modern Hindu Law,* 4 vols. (Leiden: Brill, 1976–78).

12. *Viṣṇu Purāṇa* III, 10; *Garuḍa Purāṇa* 62f.

13. The most complete source for all details and variations of ritual is again Kane's *HDhS,* vol 2.

14. *Ṛgveda* X, 85, 36.

15. Ursa Major.

16. Manu has, however, also a verse that would weaken this argument, when he says: "Many thousands of *brahmanas* who were chaste from their youth, have gone to heaven without continuing their race" (V, 159).

17. Ibid., III, 56.

18. Ibid., 58f.

19. Ibid., VIII, 68.

20. Ibid., V, 154.

21. Ibid., 150.

22. *Ṛgveda* X, 14–18.

23. For example, *Viṣṇu Purāṇa* III, 13.

24. The *Pretakalpa* of the *Garuḍapurāṇa* contains a wealth of information on beliefs concerning the afterlife.

12. THE PATH OF KNOWLEDGE: *JÑĀNAMĀRGA*

1. *Muktika Upaniṣad* I, 30, 39, gives the list of the acknowledged 108 *Upaniṣads* and their classification with regard to the four Vedas.

2. The Samskṛti Samsthān Bareli (Uttar Pradesh) in 1967 brought out a complete edition of the 108 *Upaniṣads* (with Hindī paraphrase) divided into three volumes entitled *Jñāna Khaṇḍa, Sādhana Khaṇḍa,* and *Brahmā Vidyā Khaṇḍa.*

3. A survey of recent work done in this area is given in P. J. Chinmulgund and V. V. Mirashi (eds.), *Review of Indological Research in the Last Seventy-Five Years* (Poona: Bharatiya Charitrakosha Mandal, 1967), pp. 40ff.

4. This is the chronology given by R. D. Ranade in his excellent and comprehensive study, *A Constructive Survey of Upanishadic Philosophy: Being an Introduction to the Thought of the Upaniṣads* (1926; reprint, Bombay: Bharatiya Vidya Bhavan, 1968).

5. Thus P. V. Kane.

6. Thus, e.g., J. Gonda with the majority of Indologists today.

7. See R. D. Ranade, *A Constructive Survey of Upanishadic Philosophy,* pp. 30–40.

8. *Muṇḍaka* II, 1, 1ff.

9. *Chāndogya* III, 19.

10. *Praśna* IV, 1.

11. *Chāndogya* III, 14.

12. *Bṛhadāraṇyaka* II.

13. *Chāndogya* VII, 17ff.

14. Ellison Banks Findly, "Gārgī at the King's Court: Women and Philosophic Innovation in Ancient India," in *Women, Religion and Social Change*, ed. Y. Y. Haddad and E. B. Findly (Albany: State University of New York Press, 1985), pp. 37–85.

15. For example, *Śvetāśvatara* IX.

16. For example, the *Māṇḍūkya*, which reduced everything to OM.

17. *Bṛhadāraṇyaka* IV, 5, 15.

18. For example *Chāndogya* VIII, 9ff.

19. *Taittirīya* I, 7.

20. Thus Meister Eckhart in one of his sermons: "Why does my eye recognize the sky, and why do not my feet recognize it? Because my eye is more akin to heaven than my feet. Therefore my soul must be divine if it is to recognize God!" The Platonic and the later Stoic philosophy with its idea of cosmic harmony and correspondences between humanity and universe has kept those ideas alive in the West.

21. *Chāndogya* II.

22. *Bṛhadāraṇyaka* I, 2.

23. Ibid., III, 7.

24. *Māṇḍūkya* 3ff.

25. *Muṇḍaka* I, 1, 4ff.

26. Neo-Platonism, possibly under Indian influence, is the one Western intellectual tradition that comes closest to Vedānta. Plotinus, Proclus, Jamblichus, and others too speak of stages of ascent of the soul, of the need to turn inward and dissociate consciousness from the senses.

27. *Īśa* 9.

28. End of *Chāndogya*.

13. *ĀTMAN* AND *BRAHMAN:* SELF AND ALL

1. *Bṛhadāraṇyaka Upaniṣad* III, 8.

2. Ibid., III, 9, 1, 9.

3. *Taittirīya Upaniṣad* II, 1f.

4. *Chāndogya Upaniṣad* VI, 8ff.

5. Ibid., VIII, 7.

6. *Muṇḍaka Upaniṣad* II, 2, 10ff.

7. *Bṛhadāraṇyaka Upaniṣad* I, 4.

8. *Chāndogya Upaniṣad* VI, 8, 7.

9. *Bṛhadāraṇyaka Upaniṣad* II, 5, 19.

10. *Aitareya Upaniṣad* III, 1, 3.

14. KARMA, *VIDYĀ, MOKṢA*: LIBERATION FROM REBIRTH

1. *Bṛhadāraṇyaka Upaniṣad* IV, 4, 1–7.

2. Ibid. , I, 2, 7; III, 2, 10 etc. It should be emphasized that the frightening factor is not so much rebirth but the repeated painful experience of death!

2. *Kaṭha Upaniṣad.*

4. *Muṇḍaka Upaniṣad* III, 1, 10.

5. *Kaṭha Upaniṣad* I, 5ff.

6. This is a reference to the *pañcāgni vidyā,* treated immediately before this passage.

7. *Bṛhadāraṇyaka Upaniṣad* VI, 2, 15; See also *Chāndogya Upaniṣad* V, 10, 5.

8. A comprehensive coverage of the understanding of karma in various schools is given in W. D. O'Flaherty (ed.), *Karma and Rebirth in Classical Indian Traditions* (Berkeley: University of California Press, 1980); and in R. Neufeldt (ed.), *Karma and Rebirth: Post-Classical Developments* (Albany: SUNY Press, 1986).

9. There are other expressions in Sanskrit for *fate,* such as *daiva, bhagya,* or *niyati.*

10. *Muṇḍaka Upaniṣad* I, 2, 7ff.

11. *Chāndogya Upaniṣad* IV, 11, 3.

12. *Muṇḍaka Upaniṣad* Ii, 2, 9.

13. One of the varieties of the Śiva *naṭarāja* image, in which Śiva is

shown with his right leg thrown high up is interpreted as showing how Śiva accepts into himself all the karma of his devotees so as to offer them instant liberation.

14. The term *mukti* occurs only once in the principal Upaniṣads, namely in *Bṛhadāraṇyaka* III, 1, 3. The term *mokṣa* is used several times in the *Maitrī Upaniṣad* VI, 30.

15. S. N. Dasgupta, *HIPh*, vol. I, p. 48.

16. *Muṇḍaka Upaniṣad* III, 2, 6.

17. *Praśna Upaniṣad* IV, 11.

18. *Muṇḍaka Upaniṣad* III, 3, 8f.

19. *Bṛhadāraṇyaka Upaniṣad* III, 8.

20. *Kaṭha Upaniṣad* II, 3, 8f.

21. *Taittirīya Upaniṣad* II, 9.

22. Ibid., I, 2, 1f.

23. *Muṇḍaka Upaniṣad* III, 2, 8.

15. THE PATH OF LOVING DEVOTION: *BHAKTIMĀRGA*

1. The *Śabdakalpadruma* III, 463bf. offers the following etymology under the entry *bhakti*: *Vibhāga* [division, separation] *sevā* [worship, service] and refers to the two roots *bhañj-* (10 U) [to split, to disappoint] and *bhā-* [to serve, to honor].

2. S. N. Dasgupta, *HIPh*, vol. 4, p. 351.

3. That they were not considered as of equal importance even within *bhakta* circles is demonstrated by the fact that they have not been commented upon as extensively as the *Brahmasūtras*. The real textbooks of *bhakti* are the Purāṇas and the special compendia of the various *saṁpradāyas*: Saṃhitās, Āgamas, and Tantras.

4. *Bhaktidarśaṇa*, with Hindī paraphrase, ed. Swami Jñānandaji Maharaj (Bombay: Sake, 1844), pp. 23ff.

5. Swami Tyagisananda (ed.), *Aphorisms on the Gospel of Divine Love or Nārada Bhakti Sūtras*, 5th ed., Sanskrit text with English translation and copious notes (Madras: Ramakrishna Math Mylapore, 1972). The notes offer numerous other definitions and descriptions of *bhakti*.

6. *Bhagavadgītā* XII, 6ff.

7. P. V. Kane, *HDhS*, vol. 5 (part 2), pp. 950f.

8. *Kaṭha Upaniṣad* II, 22; *Muṇḍaka Upaniṣad* III, 2, 3.

9. Another striking instance is offered by the *puruṣa-sūkta,* which contains the Vaiṣṇava cosmogony *in nucleo*: everything owes its existence to a transformation of a part of the body of the *puruṣottama.*

10. A good survey of literature in English on *bhakti* (up to 1975) is provided by Eleanor Zelliot, "The Mediaeval Bhakti Movement in History. An Essay on the Literature in English," in *Hinduism: New Essays in the History of Religions,* ed. B. L. Smith (Leiden: Brill, 1976).

11. In addition to the work referred to in the next note, see D. Gold, *The Lord as Guru: Hindī Sants in the Northern Indian Tradition* (New York: Oxford University Press, 1987); J. S. Hawley, *Sants and Virtues* (Berkeley: University of California Press, 1987).

12. See C. Vaudeville, "*Sant Mat*: Santism as the Universal Path to Sanctity," in *The Sants: Studies in a Devotional Tradition of India,* ed. K. Schour and W. H. McLeod (Delhi, Banaras, Patna, and Madras: Motilal Banarsidass, 1987).

13. *Sad-nām* is the key term in this religion, meaning the most profound revelation of God.

14. C. Vaudeville, "*Sant Mat,*" p. 31.

15. A famous collection is the *Bṛhatstotraratnakara* (Bombay: Sri Venkatesvar Press) containing 224 hymns, in many editions with old illustrations. The Ramakrishna Mission has also brought out small collections of hymns together with translations.

16. *Bhāgavata Purāṇa.*

17. Ibid., VI, 2, 14; XII, 12, 46.

18. Each crore equals 10 million.

19. *Kalyāna Kalpatāru* 18, no. 1 (August 1952): 3f.

20. See *Bhaktirasāmṛtasindhu of Rupa Gosvami,* ed. V. Snataka, trans. Swami Bon Maharaj (Vrindavan: Institute of Oriental Philosophy, 1964), vol. 1, pp. 2, 90f.

21. *Varāha Purāṇa,* Chapter 68.

22. *Padma Purāṇa* IV, 263.

23. *Bhagavadgītā* VII, 15.

24. Tyagisananda, *Aphorisms,* pp. 82f.

25. *Bhāgavata Purāṇa,* VII, 5, 23f.

26. *Rāmānuja's Vedārthasaṁgraha,* ed. and trans. S. S. Raghavchar (Mysore: Ramakrishna Ashrama, 1956), p. 23.

27. See *Sarvadarśanasaṁgraha of Mādhava,* ed. V. S. Abhyankar, 3rd ed. (Poona: B.O.R.I., 1978), Chapter 5, the Pūrṇaprajñā system.

28. An important reference work is S. K. De, *Early History of the Vaiṣṇava Faith and Movement in Bengal* (Calcutta: Firma K. L. Mukhopadhyay, 1961). Recently, possibly under the influence of *bhakti* missions in the West, much scholarly literature devoted to the study of *bhakti* literature has come out. Jayadeva's *Gītāgovinda* received a large amount of attention. See B. Stoler-Miller, *Love Song of the Dark Lord* (New York: Columbia University Press, 1977); G. Kuppuswamy and M. Hariharan (eds.) *Jayadeva and Gītāgovinda: A Study* (Trivandrum: College Book House, 1980), with a contribution by B. Stoler-Miller "Rādhā: Consort of Kṛṣṇa's Vernal Passion," published earlier in *JAOS* 95, no. 4 (1975): 655–71; L. Siegel, *Sacred and Profane Dimensions of Love in Indian Traditions as Exemplified in the Gītāgovinda of Jayadeva* (Oxford: Oxford University Press, 1978). See also Basanti Choudhury, "Love Sentiment and Its Spiritual Implications in Gauḍīa Vaiṣṇavism," in *Bengal Vaiṣṇavism, Orientalism, Society and the Arts,* ed. D. T. O'Connel, South Asia Series Occasional Papers No. 35 (East Lansing: Asian Studies Center, Michigan State University, 1985).

29. See Krishna Chaitanya, *Sanskrit Poetics* (Bombay: Asia Publishing House 1965). See P. V. Kane, *History of Sanskrit Poetics,* 3rd ed. (Delhi: Motilal Banarsidass, 1961), pp. 355ff.; The Rasa School: "*Rasa* primarily means 'taste' or 'flavour' or 'savour' or 'relish' but metaphorically it means 'emotional experience of beauty in poetry and drama'." By contrast Swami Bon Maharaj, *Bhaktirasāmṛtasindhi of Rūpa Goswami,* vol. 1, n.2: "There is no English equivalent for *rasa.* It is a purely spiritual expression which may be explained like this. When the heart is perfectly purified of all the possible dirts of the three *gunas* or attributes of *Māyā,* the Deluding Energy of the Godhead, viz., *rajas, tamas* and *sattva,* and when the unalloyed soul as distinct from the physical body of flesh and blood and the subtle body of mind-intelligence-ego far transcends the realm of imagination and mental thought-world, the fourfold ingredients called *Vibhāva, Anubhāva, Sāttvika-bhāva* and *Sañcari-bhāva* of mellow-sweetness of the sentiment of the innate normal nature of the *cit*-soul combine with *Sthāyībhāva* or permanent and eternal as also unconditional relation that exists between God and the individual soul, in manifold shades and forms, it gives rise to an inexplicably wondrous flow of charm, which is *Rasa.*

30. See Viśvanātha Cakravartti, "*Bhaktirasamrtasindhubindu,*" trans. K. Klostermaier, *JAOS* 94, no. 1 (1974): 96–107.

31. Kṛṣṇadāsa Goswāmi, *Caitanyacaritāmṛta,* Mādhyalīlā XIX and XXII.

32. *Vedāntaratnamañjuṣa* VI.

33. *Sarvadarśanasamgraha of Mādhava,* Chapter 7, "The Paśupata System." An example of what Hindus call the *pagala* (mad-type) of *bhakti* is available in Anne Feldhaus (trans. and annot.), *The Deeds of God in Riddhipur,* with introductory essays by Anne Feldhaus and E. Zelliot (New York: Oxford University Press, 1984).

34. V. A. Devasenapathi, *Śaiva Siddhānta as Expounded in the Śivajñāna Siddhiar and Its Six Commentaries* (Madras: University of Madras, 1960), pp. 250ff. On Śiva *bhakti* in South India, Carl A. Keller, "Aspiration collective et éxperience individuelle dans la bhakti shivaite de l'Inde du sud," *Numen* 31, no. 1 (July 1984): 1–21, with an ample bibliography.

35. Translation from E. J. Thompson and A. M. Spencer, *Bengali Religious Lyrics, Śākta,* The Heritage of India Series No. 47 (Calcutta: Association Press, 1923), p. 60. See also M. Lupsa, *Chants á Kālī de Rāmprasād,* with introduction, trans. and notes (Pondichery: Institut Français d'Indologie, 1967).

36. *Words of Godrealization* (Sarnath: Rama Tirtha Pratisthan, 1956), p. 415.

37. *Paramārtha Sopāna,* ed. R. D. Ranade (Allahabad: Adhyatma Vidya Mandir Sangli, 1954).

38. Tyagisananda, ed., *"Sant Mat,"* pp. 5ff.

16. LORD VIṢṆU AND HIS DEVOTEES

1. *Viṣṇu Purāṇa* I, 19, 64ff.

2. The most complete survey is offered in Rāmdās Gaur, *Hindutva* (Banaras: Viśvaprasad Gupta (Samvat), 1995), Chapter 17, *"Bhāgavata yā vaiṣṇava mata."* The doctrinal side is well covered in S. N. Dasgupta, *HIPh,* vols. 3 and 4.

3. *Ṛgveda* I, 22; I, 154; VII, 100.

4. *Ṛgveda* X, 90.

5. "Śāntiparvan," *Mahābhārata Critical Edition,* vol. 16, Chapter 321ff.

6. *Bhagavadgītā* IV, 7f. One of the most extensive studies was done by Brajendranath Seal, in 1899 under the title *Comparative Studies in Vaish-*

navism and Christianity with an Examination of the Mahābhārata Legend About Nārada's Pilgrimage to Śvetadvīpa and an Introduction on the Historico-Comparative Method. In articles in the *Journal of the Royal Asiatic Society of Bengal* in 1907 J. Kennedy tried to prove Christian influence on the development of Viṣṇu *bhakti*. His claims were refuted by B. D. Basu (trans.), *Bālarāma Vedāntasūtrabhāṣya*, in *Sacred Books of the Hindus*, vol. 5 (Allahabad: Panini Office, 1934), Appendix I: "The Origin of the Bhakti Doctrine." N. Chaudhuri in his *Hinduism* (London: Chatto and Windus, 1979), pp. 256ff, again suggests Christian influence on the development of Krsna *bhakti*.

7. The most comprehensive discussion of the theory of *avātara*-hood may be R. Seemann's "Versuch zu einer Theorie des Avātara. Mensch gewordener Gott oder Gott gewordener Mensch?" *Numen*, 33, no. 1 (July 1986): 90–140.

8. D. C. Sirkar, "Viṣṇu," *Quarterly Journal of the Mythological Society* 25 (1935): 120ff.

9. For details consult, e.g., A. Daniélou, *Hindu Polytheism* (London: Routledge and Kegan Paul, 1964).

10. More about these in K. Klostermaier, *Mythologies*.

11. Ibid., pp. 73ff.

12. *Bhāgavata Purāṇa* VI, 8.

13. A. George, in *Social Ferment in India* (London: Athlone Press, 1986), advances the theory that "The Rāma tradition probably goes much further back into remote layers of pre-Āryan folklore from the days of tribal struggles between Austric groups in the Gangetic valley. The word *Gaṅgā* itself has been identified linguistically with a non-Āryan Austric word signifying merely a "river." All this may account for the seeming paradox whereby the suffix 'Rām', which ought to denote a blue-blooded Kshatriya prince, tends in modern India to be that of the lower castes" (p. 236).

14. *Bālakāṇḍa* I, 1, of the *Adhyātma Rāmāyaṇa*, which probably was written in the fifteenth century. Of great importance, is the *Yogavāsiṣṭha Rāmāyaṇa*, pertaining to the ninth to twelfth centuries, in which the Rāma story serves as frame for the exposition of Advaita Vedānta. The most popular of all books on Rāma, however, is the Hindī *Rāmacaritamānasa* by Tulasīdāsa, praised by Mahātmā Gandhi as "the greatest religious book in the world." See the critical study by C. Bulcke, *Rāmakathā* (Prayāga: Hindī Pariṣad, Viśvavidyālaya, 1950).

15. *India Today* on December 31, 1992, published a special issue under the title "Nation's Shame," detailing the events leading up to and following December 6 and offering editorials warning of a right-wing

takeover. In its January 15, 1993, edition it carried a graphic of a lotus flower (the symbol of the Hindu political parties) casting a shadow in the form of a *swastika.*

16. Literature on Kṛṣṇa by Indian authors fills bibliographies. Critical-historical writing by Western scholars is growing steadily. Most of it is devoted to studying certain aspects of the Kṛṣṇa tradition, such as John Stratton Hawley, *Kṛṣṇa the Butter Thief* (Princeton, N.J.: Princeton University Press, 1983). Many books on Indian art, especially on Indian painting, are dealing with Kṛṣṇa as well; e.g., W. G. Archer, *The Loves of Krishna in Indian Painting and Poetry* (London: Allen and Unwin, 1957).

17. For more detail, see K. Klostermaier, *Mythologies.* See also V. Schneider, "Kṛṣṇas postumer Aufstieg: Zur Frühgeschichte der Bhaktibewegung," *Saeculum* 33 (1982): 38–49.

18. See Charles S. J. White "Kṛṣṇa as Divine Child," *HR* 12, no. 2 (1972): 156–77.

19. See Norvin Hein, "A Revolution in Kṛṣṇaism; The Cult of Gopala," *HR* 26, no. 3 (1986): 296–317.

20. The most thorough attempt to establish the historicity of Kṛṣṇa has been made by A. D. Pusalker. See his "Historicity of Kṛṣṇa," in *Studies in Epics and Purāṇas of India* (Bombay: Bharatiya Vidya Bhavan, 1955), pp. 49–81, and "Traditional History from the Earliest Time to the Accession of Parikshit," in *The Vedic Age,* 4th ed., vol. 1 of *HCIP* (Bombay: Bharatiya Vidya Bhavan, 1965), pp. 271–322. Pusalker places the "Kṛṣṇa Period" ca 1950–1400 B.C. Recent archeological excavations in Dwāraka, the reputed capital city of Kṛṣṇa, are supposed to have confirmed these assumptions.

21. The most complete Kṛṣṇa scripture is the *Bhāgavata Purāṇa.*

22. See K. Klostermaier, *In the Paradise of Kṛṣṇa* (Philadelphia: Westminster Press, 1971).

23. Several recent theses have devoted substantial attention to the position of Śrī, such as E. T. Hardy, *Emotional Kṛṣṇa Bhakti* (London: London School of Oriental and African Studies, 1978); V. Rajagopalan, "The Śrī Vaiṣṇava Understanding of *Bhakti* and *Prapatti*" (Ph.D. thesis, University of Bombay,1978); M. R. Paramesvaran "The Twofold Vedānta of Śrīvaiṣṇavism" (M.A. thesis, University of Manitoba, 1981).

24. See J. A. B. van Buitenen, "The Name Pāñcarātra," *HR* 1, no. 2 (1961): 291–99, with numerous references to other literature.

25. *Yatīndramatadīpikā of Śrīnivāsadāsa,* ed. and trans. Swami Adidevananda (Madras: Ramakrishna Math Mylapore, 1949).

26. III, 26, 12.

27. J. B. Carman in *The Theology of Rāmānuja. An Essay in Interreligious Understanding* (New Haven, Conn. and London: Yale University Press, 1974) deals only with some aspects of Rāmānuja's theology but provides extensive background and full information on the sources of Śrīvaiṣṇavism. A systematic exposition of the thought of Rāmānuja is given in Krishna Datta Bharadwaj, *The Philosophy of Rāmānuja* (New Delhi: Sir Sankar Lall Charitable Trust Society, 1958). The most recent systematic work is J. Lipner, *The Face of Truth* (Cambridge: Cambridge University Press, 1987).

28. *Vedārthasaṁgraha of Rāmānuja,* ed. and trans. S. S. Raghavachar (Mysore: Ramakrishna Ashrama, 1956).

29. *Śrībhāṣya* II, 1, 3.

30. Ibid., II, 3, 41.

31. *Vedārthasaṁgraha* 126; a slightly condensed rendering.

32. *Śrībhāṣya* I, 1, 4.

33. A good comparison of the main points of difference is given in Narasinha Iyengar (ed. and trans.), *Mumukṣupadī of Lokācārya* (Madras: Adyar Library, 1962), Introduction.

34. See B. N. K. Sharma, *Madhva's Teaching in His Own Words* (Bombay: Bhavan's Book University, 1961). A very thorough study of Madhva's theology was recently made by I. Puthiadan, an Indian Jesuit: *Viṣṇu the Ever Free: A Study of the Madhva Concept of God,* Dialogue Series No. 5 (Madurai: Dialogue Publications, 1985). See also literature on Madhva mentioned in Chapter 27.

35. Roma Chaudhuri, "The Nimbārka School of Vedānta," in *CHI,* vol. 3, p. 333.

36. "Life of Vallabha" in S. N. Dasgupta, *HIPh,* vol. 4, pp. 371–72. See also R. Barz, *The Bhakti Sect of Vallabhācārya* (Faridabad: Thompson Press, 1976); and M. C. Parekh, *Śrī Vallabhācārya: Life, Teachings and Movement* (Rajkot: Sri Bhagavata Dharma Mission, 1943). See also M. V. Joshi, "The Concept of Brahman in Vallabha Vedānta," *JBOI* 22, no. 4 (June 1973): 474–83; and, with a polemical twist, B. S. Yadav, "Vaiṣṇavism on Hans Küng: A Hindu Theology of Religious Pluralism," *Religion and Society,* 27, no. 2 (June 1980): 32–64.

37. M. I. Marfatia, *The Philosophy of Vallabhācārya* (Delhi: Munshiram Manoharlal, 1967), pp. 70–76: "*Puṣṭi* or the Doctrine of Grace."

38. An extensive summary is given in the article "Vallabha" in *ERE,* vol. 12, pp. 580–83, by D. Mackichan. See also J. Gonda, *Die Religionen*

Indiens (Stuttgart: Kohlhammer, 1963), vol. 2, p. 163. Also D. L. Habermann, "On Trial: The Love of Sixteen Thousand Gopees," *HR* 33, no. 1 (1993): 44–70.

39. *History of the Sect of the Maharajas or Vallabhācāryas in Western India* (London, 1865).

40. A good survey of recent English and Hindī literature on Vallabha is provided in J. R. Timm's "Vallabha, Vaiṣṇavism and the Western Hegemony of Indian Thought," *Journal of Dharma*, 14, no. 1 (1989): 6–36.

41. An extensive list of authors and works is given in Dasgupta, *HIPh*, vol. 4, pp. 373–81. Marfatia, *The Philosophy of Vallabhācārya*, provides extensive summaries of many of thse works, pp. 91–314.

42. G. H. Bhatt, "The School of Vallabha," *CHI* vol. 3, p. 348. Vallabha also wrote a short commentary on the *Brahmasūtras* under the name of Aṇubhāṣya, presented by S. T. Pathak in the Bombay Sanskrit and Prakrit Series, 1921–26.

43. Bhatt, ibid., p. 348. Vallabha calls his sysstem *śuddhādvaita*, "Pure Non-Dualism."

44. Ibid., p. 356

45. Dasgupta, *HIPh*, vol. 4, p. 355.

46. Bhatt, "The School of Vallabha," p. 357: "One may be constantly angry with the Lord and still get *sāyujya*."

47. Ibid., pp. 354–55.

48. Dasgupta, *HIPh*, vol. 4, p. 349.

49. According to Vallabha *bhakti* is developing in the following seven stages: (1) *bhāva*, (2) *premā*, (3) *prāṇaya*, (4) *sneha*, (5) *rāga*, (6) *anurāga*, (7) *vyasana*.

50. Dasgupta, *HIPh*, vol. 4, p. 356.

51. The best work with substantial translations from sources, is W. Eidlitz, *Krsna-Caitanya, Sein Leben und Seine Lehre*, Stockholm Studies in Comparative Religion 7 (Stockholm: Almquist and Wiksell, 1968). A good historical survey is offered by A. K. Majumdar, *Caitanya: His Life and Doctrine* (Bombay: Bharatiya Vidya Bhavan, 1969). See also J. T. O'Connell "Historicity in the Biographies of Caitanya," *Journal of Vaisnava Studies*, 1, no. 2 (Winter 1993): 102–32.

52. The "*Śīkṣāṣṭaka*" in *Caitanya Caritāmṛta* III, 20, 3–45, is considered to be his own formulation of the essence of Vaiṣṇavism.

53. See K. Klostermaier (trans.) Viśvanāṭha Cakravarti's compendium of Rūpa Goswāmi's opus magnum, *Bhaktirasāmṛtasindhubindu, JAOS* 94, no. 1 (1974): 96–107, including some background to the author and his works. See also K. Klostermaier "A Universe of Feelings," in P. Bilimoria and P. Fenner (eds.), *Religion and Comparative Thought* (Delhi: Sri Satguru Publications, 1989), pp. 123–39; and "Eine indische Wissenschaft der Gefühle" in E. Weber and R. Töpelmann (eds.), *Indien in Deutschland,* Darmstädter Beiträge zum Diskurs über indische Religion, Kultur und Gesellschaft (Frankfurt am Main: Peter Lang, 1990), pp. 137–50, explaining Rūpa's main ideas of *premā* and drawing some parallels. See also N. Delmonico: "Rūpa Gosvāmi: His Life, Family and Early Vrāja Commentators," *JVS* 1, no. 2 (1993): 133–57.

54. *The Vedāntasūtras of Bādarāyana with the Commentary of Bāladeva,* trans. Srisa Candra Vasu Vidyarnava, vol. 5 *SBH* (Allahabad: Panini Office, 1934). See also M. Wright and N. Wright, "Bāladeva Vidyābhuṣana: The Gauḍīya Vedāntist," *JVS* 1, no. 2 (1993): 158–84. For post-Caitanya developments in Gauḍīa Vaiṣṇavism, see J. K. Brzezinski, "Prabodhananda Saraswati: From Banaras to Braj," *BSOAS* 55, no. 1 (1992); 52–75; and "Prabodhananda, Hita Harivaṁśa and the *Rādhārasasudhānidhī,*" *BSOAS* 55, no. 2 (1992): 472–97.

55. See also E. Zelliot, "The Medieval Bhakti Movement in History: An Essay on the Literature in English," in B. L. Smith (ed.), *Hinduism: New Essays in the History of Religions* (Leiden: Brill, 1976), pp. 143–68.

56. For details consult K. Sharma, *Bhakti and the Bhakti Movements* (Delhi: Manoharlal, 1987).

57. Among Indian scholars writing in English on this subject, the names of R. D. Ranade, *Pathway to God in Hindi Literature* (Bombay: Bharatiya Vidya Bhavan, 1959); *Pathway to God in Marāthī Literature* (Bombay: Bharatiya Vidya Bhavan, 1961); *Pathway to God in Kaṇṇaḍa Literature* (Bombay: Bharatiya Vidya Bhavan, 1960); and Bankey Bihari, *Sufis, Mystics and Yogis of India* (Bombay: Bharatiya Vidya Bhavan, 1962); *Bhaktā Mīrā* (Bombay: Bharatiya Vidya Bhavan, 1961), deserve special mention. Also V. Raghavan, *The Great Integrators: The Saint Singers of India* (Delhi: Ministry of Information and Broadcasting, 1966), a good selection of mediaeval religious poetry in translation. Among Western writers C. Vaudeville deserves special credit for her scholarly monographs and translations (in French and English) dealing with Kabīr, Tulasīdāsa, and others. See also M. Neog, *Early History of the Vaiṣṇava Faith and Movement in Assam: Śaṅkaradeva and His Time,* 2d ed. (Delhi: Motilal Banarsidass, 1985).

58. J. S. Hawley has recently brought out a very attractive monograph on Sūrdās with beautifully translated texts: *Sūrdās: Poet, Singer, Saint*

(Seattle: University of Washington Press, 1984). In a further article in the *JVS* 1, no. 2 (1993): 62–78, Hawley examines the question "Why Sūrdās Went Blind," arriving at the conclusion that a spiritual blindness, which Sūrdās attributes to himself, and not a physical blindness, is referred to.

59. See J. S. Hawley, "Author and Authority in the Bhakti Poetry of North India" in *JAS* 47, no. 2 (1988): 269–90.

60. My own translation, following the text in R. D. Ranade's *Paramārtha Sopāna: Sourcebook of Pathway to God in Hindī Literature* (Allahabad: Adhyatma Vidya Mandir Sangli, 1954), p. 2 (part I, Chapter I, no. 1). J. S. Hawley offers a translation in *Sūrdās,* p. 173, which differs quite substantially from mine. He probably followed a different text edition. While not claiming to be as knowledgeable on Sūrdās as Hawley, or as poetically gifted, I decided to give my own translation because it conveys—or so I believe—better the simplicity and earthiness of the original. I have made a number of translations of the texts provided in *Paramārtha Sopāna,* which will be published at some later date in *JVS.*

61. A good contemporary example is Swami Ramdas, *God-Experience* (Bombay: Bharatiya Vidya Bhavan, 1963).

62. Bankey Bihari, *Bhakta Mīrā,* p. 109. More on Mīrā Bhāī in Chapter 23.

17. ŚIVA: THE GRACE AND THE TERROR OF GOD

1. A. K. Rāmānujan, *Speaking of Śiva* (Harmondsworth: Penguin Books, 1973), p. 71.

2. Stotra 53 in *Bṛhatstotraratnakāra* (96f.), ascribed to Vyāsa.

3. Sir Mortimer Wheeler, *The Indus Civilization* (Cambridge: Cambridge University Press, 1953). Doris Srinivasan, "Unhinging Śiva from the Indus Civilization" (*Journal of the Royal Asiatic Society of Great Britain and Ireland* 1 [1984]: 77–89) tries to prove that the *liṅgas* found in remnants of the Indus civilization do not present a case for an origin of Śaivism in that civilization. Tribal-prehistoric origin of *liṅga* worship is widely accepted today.

4. B. K. Ghosh, "The Āryan Problem," in *HCIP,* vol. 1, p. 207. In the oldest ritual texts care is taken not to mention the name of this "terrible god" directly.

5. See *Mahābhārata Śāntiparvan* 274: *Droṇaparvan* 201, 64–82; *Sauptikaparvan* 18; *Vāyu Purāṇa* I, 30; *Śiva Purāṇa, Vāyavīyasaṁhitā* I, 23, and numerous other places.

6. I have developed the argument more fully in "The Original Dakṣa Saga," *Journal of South Asian Literature* 20, no. 1 (1985): 93–107, reprinted in A. Sharma (ed.) *Essays on the Mahābhārata* (Leiden: Brill, 1991), pp. 110–29.

7. T. M. P. Mahadevan, "Śaivism," in *HCIP*, vol. 2, p. 454.

8. Hence, the idea of the *Śiva-avatāras,* which never gained an importance in actual Śiva worship. Among the Vaiṣṇava Purāṇas the *Vāmana Purāṇa* has also Śaivite materials and the *Viṣṇu Purāṇa* explains the origin of the eight Rudras in I, 8.

9. Kumara Gupta (415–455 C.E.) was a Śaiva king. The Huna king Mīhirakula seems to have been Śaiva, as many of his contemporary rulers in Bengal and the Deccan. Mahendra Varman I (600–630), a convert from Jainism, made his capital, Kāñcīpuram, into a stronghold of Śaivism, embellishing it with temples and statues of Śiva.

10. *HCIP*, vol. 4, pp. 10, 300f.

11. *Ṛgveda* I, 114; II, 33; VII, 46.

12. Doris M. Srinivasan, "Vedic Rudra-Śiva," *JAOS* 103, no. 3 (1983): 543–56.

13. *Ṛgveda* 1. 114. 4.

14. *Ṛgveda* 4. 3. 1.

15. D. M. Srinivasan gives interesting specific details concerning Rudra's role in some of these sacrifices and the ritual connected with it.

16. It forms Chapter 16 of the *Yajurveda* according to the *Vajasaneyasaṁhitā*. English translations in J. Eggeling, *Śatapathabrāhmana*, vol. 4 (*SBE* vol. 43), pp. 150ff. and in R. T. H. Griffith, *The Texts of the White Yajurveda*, 3rd ed. (Banaras: E. J. Lazarus, 1957), pp. 168.

17. It forms Chapter 15 of the *Atharvaveda;* trans. W. D. Whitney (HOS, 1902; reprint Banaras: Motilal Banarsidass, 1962), Introduction, pp. 769ff. See also J. W. Hauer, *Der Vrātya: Untersuchungen über die nichtbrahmanische Religion Altindiens* (Stuttgart: Kohlhammer, 1927).

18. *Atharvaveda* XV, 5, 1ff.

19. *Aitareya Brāhmaṇa* I, 3, 9f.

20. Text and translation in S. Radhakrishnan, *The Principal Upaniṣads* (London: Allen and Unwin, 1953), pp. 707–50. As for content and structure see T. Oberlies, "Die Śvetāśvatara Upaniṣad: Eine Studie ihrer Gotteslehre," *WZKS* 32 (1988): 35–62.

21. *Śvetāśvatara Upaniṣad* VI, 11.

22. *Anuśāsanaparvan*, 135.

23. The oldest among the Śaiva Purāṇas is probably the *Vāyu Purāṇa*, which was written before the second century C.E. according to R. C. Hazra *CHI* vol. 2, pp. 240f. The *Śiva Purāṇa*, a very important source for many features of later Śaivism, belongs to the class of *Upapurāṇas*. For more detailed information, consult L. Rocher, *The Purāṇas*.

24. *Śiva Purāṇa, Rudrasaṁhitā Sātīkhanda* 38, 34f.

25. V. Paranjoti, *Śaiva Siddhānta* (London: Luzac, 1954), pp. 53ff.: "The importance attached to the dance of Śiva is due to the fact that it symbolizes in graphic, concrete and dynamic form the religion and philosophy of Śaiva Siddhānta. Hence the dance cannot be understood without the philosophy which it adumbrates in its movements. Love is the motif of the dance; the dance is love in practical form." On Śaivasiddhānta, see also V. A. Devasenapathi, *Śaiva Siddhānta as Expounded in the Śivajñāna Siddhiyār and Its Six Commentaries* (Madras: University of Madras, 1960); and K. Śivaraman, *Śaivism in Philosophical Perspective* (Delhi: Motilal Banarsidass, 1973).

26. *Śiva Purāṇa, Śatarudrasaṁhitā* 1ff, and *Vāyavīyasaṁhita* II, 9.

27. *Śiva Purāṇa, Kotirudrasaṁhitā* 38ff.

28. Several Āgamas have been published recently by the Institut Français d'Indologie in Pondichery, containing the *padas* on *kriyā* (ritual) and *caryā* (mode of life). For example, *Rauravāgama* (with an important introduction by J. Filliozat "Les Āgamas çivaites" in vol. 1), *Mṛgendrāgama, Ajitāgama, Mataṅgaparameśvarāgama,* all ed. N. R. Bhatt.

29. Mādhava, *Sarvadarśanasaṁgraha*, Chapter 6, quoting from the *Gaṇakarikā*, an ancient *Paśupata* textbook.

30. See V. A. Devasenapathi, *Śaiva Siddhānta*.

31. Ibid., p. 192.

32. Ibid., p. 175.

33. Ibid., p. 257.

34. Śrīkaṇṭha *Brahmasūtrabhāṣya* IV, 4, 22. English translation by Roma Chaudhuri, 2 vols. (Calcutta: Pracyavani, 1959–62).

35. Jaideva Singh in his edition and translation of the *Pratyabhijñāhṛdayam* (Delhi: Motilal Banarsidass, 1963) mentions his guru, Laksman Joo, as "practically the sole surviving exponent of this system in Kash-

mir." Recently, however, Gopī Kṛṣṇa, a layman, who describes his own realization more or less according to classical Kāśmīr Śaivism, has brought out a number of publications that might gain more adherents and students to the system. A brief biography of Swāmi Laksman Joo is found in *Hinduism Today* 17, no. 7 (July 1991): 1 and 25: "Last Bhairav Master Will Teach Until Year 2006." Laksman Joo claims to have 60,000 disciples. He recently named a small boy as his successsor.

36. *Śiva Purāṇa, Kailāsasaṁhitā* 17–19.

37. Mādhava, *Sarvadarśanasaṁgraha,* Chapter 8.

38. Quoted in *Pratyabhijñāhṛdayam* by Jaideva Singh, p. 21.

39. See S. C. Nandimath, *A Handbook of Vīraśaivism* (Dharwar: Liṅgayat Educational Association, 1941). A very attractive introduction to Vīraśaivism is provided by A. K. Rāmānujan in *Speaking of Śiva.* As well as artistic renderings in English of numerous *vacanas* (lyrics by Liṅgāyat poet-saints), the book also contains valuable introductions by Rāmānujan and an essay on "Liṅgāyat Culture" by William McCormack.

40. Hayavadana Rao (ed.) (Bangalore: Bangalore Press, 1936). Not all Vīraśaivas, however, accept Srīpati's interpretation.

41. Sri Kumaraswamiji, "*Vīraśaivism,*" in *CHI,* vol. 4, p. 101.

42. Ibid.

43. See S. Satchidanandam Pillai, "The Śaiva Saints of South India," in *CHI,* vol. 4, pp. 339ff. Also C. V. Narayana Ayyar, *Origin and Early History of Śaivism in South India* (Madras: University of Madras, 1936).

44. *Tiruvācakam* VI, 50, Ratna Navaratnam, trans. (Bombay: Bharatiya Vidya Bhavan, 1963), p. 126. The most celebrated complete translation of the *Tiruvācakam* was made by Rev. G. U. Pope in 1900, reprinted 1970 by the University of Madras in a jubilee edition.

45. *Tiruvācakam* XXV, 8–10; ibid., 181.

46. T. M. P. Mahadevan, "Śaivism," in *HCIP,* vol. 3, pp. 433ff.

47. F. Kingsbury and G. E. Philips, *Hymns of the Tamil Śaivite Saints,* The Heritage of India Series (Calcutta: Association Press, 1921), p. 77.

48. T. M. P. Mahadevan, *HCIP,* vol. 5, pp. 458ff.

49. Princeton, N.J.: Princeton University Press, 1981.

50. See the biographical sketch of S. Kramrisch by B. Stoler-Miller in *Exploring India's Sacred Art* (Philadelphia: University of Pennsylvania, 1983), pp. 3–33.

51. Bollingen Series No. 73 (New York: Clark and Way, 1964).

52. In addition to her widely known monograph *Asceticism and Eroticism in the Mythology of Śiva* (London: Oxford University Press, 1973) Wendy O'Flaherty has written a number of scholarly articles on Śiva symbols and myths.

53. As well as the numerous books by Gopī Kṛṣṇa expounding Kuṇḍalinī Yoga the remarkable coproduction of C. F. von Weizsäcker and Gopī Kṛṣṇa, *Biologische Basis religiöser Erfahrung* (Weilheim: Otto Wilhelm Barth Verlag, 1971) deserves mention.

18. DEVĪ: THE DIVINE MOTHER

1. *Devīmāhātmya* I, 75ff (from *Mārkaṇḍeya Purāṇa* 81).

2. John Woodroffe, who, under the pen-name of Arthur Avalon, did much to make the Tantras known in the West, brought out a translation of the *Mahānirvāṇa tantra: The Great Liberation,* 4th ed. (Madras: Ganesh and Co., 1963. For tantric doctrines in general his *Principles of Tantra,* a translation of the *Tantratattva* of Sivacandra Vidyāranya, may be recommended (3rd ed., Madras: Ganesh and Co., 1960). For beginners the *Introduction to Tantra Śāstra* (4th ed., Madras: Ganesh and Co., 1963) provides the explanation of the technical terms. More recent scholarly writing on Tantra includes H. V. Günther, *Yuganādha: The Tantric View of Life* (Banaras: 1952; reprint, Boulder,Colo.: Shambhala, 1976); and A. Bharati, *The Tāntric Tradition* (London: Rider and Co., 1965). See also the richly illustrated volume by Ajit Mookerjee and Madhu Khanna: *The Tantric Way. Art—Science—Ritual* (London: Thames and Hudson, 1977), with bibliography.

3. Sanskrit edition (Banaras: Pandit Pustakalaya, samvat 2016); English trans. Swami Vijñānanda, *SBH.* For a fuller treatment consult R. C. Hazra, *Studies in the Upapurāṇas,* vol. 2. *The Śākta Upapurāṇas* (Calcutta: Sanskrit College, 1963), pp. 1–361.

4. For more details on Devī mythology, Śākta systems and iconography of the goddess, see K. Klostermaier, *Mythologies,* Part IV.

5. R. C. Hazra, *Studies in Upapurāṇas,* pp. 19f.: "The story of Devī's killing of the demon Mahiṣa in a previous *kalpa* and the tradition that whenever Devī kills the demons she has a lion as her mount seem to be based on the aboriginal concept of Devī as a spirit controlling wild beasts. The bell which is said to be carried by Devī might have been originally meant for scaring away wild beasts." See also H. Whitehead, *The Village Gods of South India,* The Religious Life of India Series (Calcutta: Association Press, 1921).

6. The most recent comprehensive study is by H. von Stietencron, "Die Göttin Durgā Mahiṣāsuramārdini: Mythos, Darstellung und geschichtliche Rolle bei der Hinduisierung Indiens," in *Visible Religion, Annual for Religious Iconography*, vol. 2. *Representations of Gods* (Leiden: Brill, 1983), pp. 11–166, with illustrations.

7. *Devīmāhātmya* X, 1ff.

8. See P. V. Kane, *HDhS*, vol. 5 (part 1), pp. 154ff.

9. *Devī Purāṇa* 38.

10. *Devī Bhagavata*; *Śiva Purāṇa Umāsaṁhitā* 28–45.

11. *Kālikā Purāṇa* 15.

12. Śiva without the *i* is *Śava*, a corpse.

13. The five m's are: *maṁsa* (meat), *matsya* (fish), *mudrā* (fried rice), *mada* (intoxicants), and *maithuna* (intercourse).

14. H. D. Bhattacharya, "Tantrik Religion," in *HCIP*, vol. 4, p. 320.

15. Ibid., p. 321.

16. *Mahānirvāṇa Tantra* XVIII, 154ff.

17. See D. N. Bose: *Tantras: Their Philosophy and Occult Secrets* (Calcutta: Oriental Publishing Co., 1956), Chapter 10, "Tantric Symbols and Practices," explains a number of basic *yantras*.

18. For details see R. Fonseca, "Constructive Geometry and the Sri-Cakra Diagram," *Religion*, 16, no. 1 (1986): 33–49. A very professional study of Devī iconography is Om Prakash Misra's *Mother Goddess in Central India* (Delhi: Agam Kala Prakashan, 1985).

19. See John Woodroff, *Introduction to Tantra Śāstra*, pp. 42ff.

20. *Kālikā Purāṇa*, Chapter 14, is called the *rudhirādhyāya* or *blood chapter*. A. P. Kamarkar, "Religion and Philosophy in the Epics" in *CHI*, cites many historical instances of human sacrifices in honor of Kālī. Volunteers were offered every Friday at the Kālī temple in Tanjore up to the nineteenth century. The head of the victims was placed on a golden plate before Kālī, the lungs were cooked and eaten by Kandra Yogis, the royal family ate rice cooked in the blood of the victim.

21. D. C. Sirkar, *Śākta Pīthas*, rev. ed (Delhi: Motilal Banarsidass, n.d.).

22. Beni Kanta Kakati, *The Mother Goddess Kāmākhyā* (Gauhati: Lawyers Book Stall, 1948). The snake-goddess Manasā is widely worshipped especially in South India.

23. See Maryla Falk, *Nāma-Rūpa and Dharma-Rūpa; Origin and Aspects of an Ancient Indian Conception* (Calcutta: University of Calcutta, 1943), pp. 2ff.

24. *Tripurā Rahasya, Jñānakāṇḍa*, trans. A. U. Vasavada (Banaras: Chowkhamba, 1965), pp. 156f.

25. Ibid.

26. A description of *Vāmācāri* practices is given in H. Wilson, *Religious Sects of the Hindus* (Reprint Calcutta: Punthi Pustak, 1958), pp. 142f. He also gives the translation of the *Śakti Sudhāna*.

27. V. S. Agrawala, "Mother Earth," in: *Nehru Abhinandan Granth* (Calcutta: Nehru Abhinandan Granth Committee 1949), pp. 490ff.

28. Some of the recent books are D. R. Kinsley, *The Sword and the Flute: Kālī and Kṛṣṇa, Dark Visions of the Terrible and the Sublime in Hindu Mythology* (Berkeley: University of California Press, 1975); C. M. Brown, *God as Mother: A Feminine Theology in India* (Hartford, Conn.: Claude Stark, 1974); D. Jacobsen and S. Wadley (eds.), *Women in India: Two Perspectives* (Delhi: Manohar Book Service, 1974); J. S. Hawley and D. M. Wulff (eds.), *The Divine Consort: Rādhā and the Goddesses of India* (Berkeley: University of California Press, 1982); L. E. Gatwood, *Devī and the Spouse Goddess: Women, Sexuality and Marriage in India* (Delhi: Manohar, 1985).

29. Sanjukta Gupta and Richard Gombrich, "Kings, Power and the Goddess," *South Asia Research*, 6, no. 2 (November 1986): 127.

30. *BLITZ* reported on its first page in its April 11, 1970 edition: "Tantrik priest dies half-way through *havan* to kill Indira."

19. MUDALVAN, MURUGAN, MĀL: THE GREAT GODS OF THE TAMILS

1. On Agastya see the entry in John Dowson, *A Classical Dictionary of Hindu Mythology*, 10th ed. (London: Routledge and Kegan Paul, 1961), pp. 4ff, which provides the major references for Agastya in Ṛgveda, Mahābhārata, and Rāmāyaṇa and specifically says: "The name of Agastya holds a great place in Tamil literature, and he is venerated in the south as the first teacher of science and literature to the primitive Dravidian tribes." The authority of Dr. Caldwell is cited who thinks that "we shall not greatly err in placing the era of Agastya in the seventh, or at least in the sixth century B.C.." See also information on the Agastaya tradition in vol. 2 of *HCIP*, pp. 290ff.

2. *Encyclopedia of Religion*, ed. M. Eliade, vol. 12, p. 260b.

3. On dates concerning the *Saṅgam* (*Cankam*), see *HCIP* vol. 2, pp.

291ff, and K. A. Nilakanta Sastri, *The Culture and History of the Tamils* (Calcutta: Firma K. L. Mukhopadhyay, 1964), pp. 127ff. See also C. Jesudason and H. Jesudason, *A History of Tamil Literature,* Heritage of India Series (Calcutta: YMCA Publishing House, 1961). The most recent comprehensive history of Tamil literature is K. V. Zvelebil, *The Smile of Murugan* (Leiden: Brill, 1973).

4. N. Chaudhuri, *Hinduism* (London: Chatto and Windus, 1979), pp. 64f.

5. T. Burrow, *The Sanskrit Language,* 2d ed. (London: Faber and Faber, 1965).

6. Together, these areas comprise about 150 million people.

7. For details, see K. K. Pillai, *A Social History of the Tamils,* 2d ed. (Madras: University of Madras, 1973), vol. 1, Chapter 3, "Pre-History"; and F. W. Clothey, *The Many Faces of Murukan* (The Hague: Mouton, 1978). See also maps of prehistoric sites in South India in *HASA,* plates II, 1 and 2.

8. See the instructive article by F. W. Clothey "Tamil Religion," in *Encyclopedia of Religions,* ed. M. Eliade, vol. 12, pp. 260ff.

9. K. K. Pillai, *A Social History of the Tamils,* pp. 480ff.

10. C. Śivaramamurti, *South Indian Bronzes* (New Delhi: Lalit Kala Akademi, 1963)

11. K. K. Pillai, *A Social History of the Tamils,* p. 476, referring to Bruce Foote.

12. Ibid., p. 477.

13. See D. D. Shulman, *Tamil Temple Myths* (Princeton, N.J.: Princeton University Press, 1980). See also B. Oguibenine, "Cosmic Tree in Vedic and Tamil Mythology: Contrastive Analysis," *Journal of Indo-European Studies* 12, nos. 3–4 (1984): 367–74; G. Kuppuswamy and M. Hariharan, "Bhajana Tradition in South India," *Sangeet Natak* 64–65 (April–September 1982): 32–50. Significant differences between Northern and Southern interpretations of common religious symbols exist also in other areas.

14. K. Klostermaier, "The Original Dakṣa Saga," *Journal of South Indian Literature* 20, no. 1 (1985): 93–107.

15. K. K. Pillai, *A Social History of the Tamils,,* pp. 488ff.

16. Ibid., p. 489. The Tamil name of Kṛṣṇa is Kannan.

17. Ibid., p. 492 with references to Tamil sources.

18. Ibid.

19. K. Zvelebil, *Tiru Murugan* (Madras: International Institute of Tamil Studies, 1982).

20. K. K. Pillai, *A Social History of the Tamils,*, p. 484.

21. Ibid.

22. Ibid., p. 485. See also D. Handelman, "Myths of Murugan: Asymmetry and Hierarchy in a South Indian Puranic Cosmology," *HR* 27, no. 2 (1987): 133–70.

23. Ibid.

24. Ibid., pp. 487f.

25. See also F. W. Clothey, *The Many Faces of Murukan,* vol. 10, pp. 160–61.

26. Ibid., p. 497.

27. A peculiarity of Tamilnāḍu are the *Nadukal* (memorial stones) and *Vīrakal* (hero stones) that were erected with religious solemnity to commemorate especially warriors who had died in battle.

28. This division goes back to the *Tolkappiam,* an ancient Tamil grammar and reputedly the oldest document of Tamil literature ascribed to the second century B.C.E.

29. See K. K. Pillai, *A Social History of the Tamils,*, pp. 504ff.

30. Ibid. with references to Tamil sources.

31. Ibid. Pillai emphasises that during these sacrifices live animals were sacrificed, a practice that continues to this day in certain forms of Śiva worship.

32. See also F. A. Presler, "The Structure and Consequences of Temple Policy in Tamiḷnādu, 1967–81," *Pacific Affairs* (Summer 1983): 232–46. See also "Priestly Protest," *India Today* (15 December 1986): 111, reporting on an agitation in Andhra Pradeś against the abolition of hereditary priesthood and the demand for training of temple priests.

33. See K. K. Pillai, "The Non-Brahmin Movement in South India" in S. P. Sen (ed.), *Social Contents of Indian Religious Reform Movements* (Calcutta: Institute of Historical Studies 1978), pp. 411–25. See also C. A. Ryerson "'Meaning and Modernization in Tamil Nadu: Tamil Nationalism and Religious Culture," *Religion and Society,* 17, no. 4 (1970): 1–16.

34. See also K. V. Zvelebil "Some Tamil Folklore Texts," *JRAS,* no. 2 (1989): 290–303.

35. *Tirukkural,* Chapter 38, p. 9 (380). G. U. Pope's translation.

36. K. K. Pillai, *A Social History of the Tamils,* pp. 524ff.

37. Ibid., p. 426.

38. H. Whitehead, *The Village Gods of South India,* Religious Life of India Series (Calcutta: Association Press, 1921), with illustrations.

39. The author obtained a chart from his Madras landlord who was not only a modern, educated, successful industrialist but also a staunch believer in rahu kālam, during which time he refused to conduct any business.

40. K. Nilakanta Sastri, *The Culture and History of the Tamils,* pp. 108ff, believes that many of the accounts of religious persecution in Tamiḷnādu are exaggerated. But there is no doubt that violence did occur and that the various religious communities denounced each other.

41. N. K. Sastri reports that "even now Madurai conducts an annual festival in the temple commemorating the incredible impalement of eight thousand Jainas at the instance of the gentle boy saint" (ibid., p. 110).

42. Bombay: Bharatiya Vidya, 1961. See also F. W. Clothey, "Tamil Religions," *ER,* vol. 12, pp. 260b–268a, with bibliography.

43. See F. Kingsbury and G. E. Philips (trans.), *Hymns of the Tamil Śaivite Saints,* Heritage of India Series (Calcutta: Association Press, 1921), pp. 10–33.

44. Ibid., p. 25.

45. Bankey Bihari, *Minstrels of God,* vol. 1 (Bombay: Bharatiya Vidya Bhavan, 1956), pp. 118–27. More on Āṇṭāl in Chapter 23.

46. See literature mentioned in Chapter 17 (notes 35–37) and A. K. Rāmānujan, *Speaking of Śiva* (Harmondsworth: Penguin Classics 1973).

47. Ibid., p. 88 (Basavanna No. 820).

48. From my own observations. See also P. V. Jagadisa Ayyar, *South Indian Festivities* (reprint New Delhi: Asian Educational Services, 1982), for other Tamilian festivals such as Bhopi Pandigai, and Sankrānti.

20. THE DIVINE PRESENCE IN SPACE AND TIME: *MŪRTI, TĪRTHA, KĀLA*

1. "Essentials of Hindutva," *Hindu Rāṣṭra Darshan* (Poona: Maharastra Prantik Hindu Sabha, 1964), vol. 6, p. 74.

2. See *HASA,* pp. 264–65.

3. For details see J. N. Banerjea, *The Development of Hindu Iconography*, 2d ed. (Calcutta: University of Calcutta, 1956), Chapters 1–6.

4. See N. R. Roy's in *HCIP*, vol. 2, pp. 506ff.

5. See H. Zimmer, *The Art of Indian Asia* (New York: Bollingen Foundation, 1955), vol. 1, 259ff; plates on pp. 268ff.

6. As, e.g., the famous group of temples at Belur, Mysore.

7. Lively accounts are found in H. M. Elliot and J. Dowson (eds.), *The History of India as Told by Its Own Historians: The Muhammadan Period*, 8 vols. (reprint Allahabad: Kitāb Mahal, 1964). Some doubt has been expressed as to the truth of these reports, whose writers evidently wanted to impress their readers.

8. J. P. Waghorne and N. Cutler (eds.), *Gods of Flesh/Gods of Stone: The Embodiment of Divinity in India* (Chambersburg, Pa.: Anima Publications, 1985).

9. A concise and comprehensive description of the technicalities of *mūrtis* can be found in "Ikonographie des Hinduismus" in V. Möller, *Götter und Mythen des indischen Subkontinents*, vol. 5 of H. W. Haussig (ed.), *Wörterbuch der Mythologie* (Stuttgart: Klett-Cotta, 1972), pp. 86–112. Contains good bibliography of primary and secondary sources.

10. See J. N. Banerjea, *The Development of Hindu Iconography*, Chapter 8. A seminal work is S. Kramrisch, *Indian Sculpture* (originally 1933; reprint Delhi: Motilal Banarsidass, 1981). Of great interest is also H. Zimmer, *Kunstform und Yoga im indischen Kultbild* (Berlin: Frankfurter Verlagsanstalt, 1926).

11. K. Vasudeva Sastri and N. B. Gadre (eds.), Tanjore Sarasvati Mahal Series No. 85 (1958). Two complete manuals of Hindu architecture are available in Western language translations: *Manasāra*, trans. P. K. Acharya (1934; reprint New Delhi: Motilal Banarsidass, 1980) and *Māyāmata* 3 vols., ed. and trans. B. Dagens (Pondichery: Institut Français d'Indologie, 1970–76).

12. For details see T. Bhattacharya, *The Canons of Indian Art*, 2d ed. (Calcutta: Firma K. L. Mukhopadhay, 1963), Chapters 14–20.

13. Special works give rules for restoration of images and special rites for the reconsecration.

14. That is, milk, curds, *ghī*, dung, and urine.

15. *Bṛhatsaṁhitā of Varahamihira*, published with a Hindī translation by Paṇḍit Acutyānanda Jhā Śarmaṇā, Chaukhambha Vidyābhavan Sanskṛt Granthamālā No. 49 (Banaras: Chowkhambha, 1959), Chapter 60, slightly condensed.

16. The ritual of Viṣṇu worship as followed at Śrīraṅgam is described in *Śrī Parameśvara Saṃhitā* (Śrīraṅgam: Kodandarāmasannidhi, 1953). A very detailed study, with illustrations, of Kṛṣṇa worship in the Caitanyite tradition, relying mainly on the *Haribhaktivilāsa* by Gopāla Bhaṭṭa, the authoritative work for it, is R. V. Joshi, *Le Rituel de la dévotion Kṛṣṇaite* (Pondichery: Institut Français d'Indologie, 1959).

17. See N. Ramesan, *Temples and Legends of Andhra Pradesh* (Bombay: Bharatiya Vidya Bhavan, 1962), pp. 70ff.

18. One such complete manual detailing the daily ritual in South Indian Śiva temples is available in a French translation: H. Brunner-Lachaux (ed. and trans.), *Somaśambhupaddhatī*, 3 vols. (Pondichery: Institut Français d'Indologie, 1963–72).

19. The technical expression for this is *nyāsa,* see R. V. Joshi, *Le Rituel*, pp. 87ff.

20. *Bhāgavata Purāṇa* XI, 27, 20ff.

21. One of the earliest such government appointed boards was established to regulate the affairs of one of the most famous and richest temples in India, the *Tirupati Devasthānam*.

22. The merit of having pioneered this study goes to Stella Kramrisch who, in the early 1920s made the first attempt to study Hindu temples with the aid of ancient manuscripts on architecture. See her opus magnum, *The Hindu Temple*, 2 vols. (Calcutta: University of Calcutta Press, 1946). Barbara Stoler-Miller has selected and edited essays by S. Kramrisch, covering a span of almost fifty years and touching upon virtually all aspects of Hindu art, under the title *Exploring India's Sacred Art* (Philadelphia: University of Pennsylvania Press, 1983). The book also contains a brief biography of Kramrisch and a full bibliography. Much recent work has been done by the Indologist-architect M. W. Meister. He is editor of the *Encylopedia of Indian Temple Architecture* and author of several important articles in scholarly journals such as "Maṇḍala and Practice in Nāgara Architecture in North India," *JAOS* 99 (1979): 204–19; "Measurement and Proportion in Hindu Architecture" *Interdisciplinary Science Review* 10 (1985): 248–58. See also his informative article "Hindu Temples," in *ER*, vol. 10, pp. 368–73.

23. S. Kramrisch, *The Hindu Temple*, vol. 1, p. 97.

24. For an interpretation see A. Volwahsen, *Living Architecture: Indian* (New York: Grosset and Dunlap 1969), pp. 43ff.

25. S. Kramrisch, *The Hindu Temple*, vol. 1, p. 97.

26. A very informative article dealing with this issue is R. Kulkarni's

"Vāstupādamaṇḍala," *JOIB* 28, nos. 3–4 (March–June 1979): 107–38 with many diagrams and tables.

27. The most perfect application of this scheme can be seen in the city of Jaipur. On city planning in general the *Viśvakarma Vāstuśāstra,* an authoritative work, can be consulted. The most systematic work is D. Schlingloff, *Die altindische Stadt* (Wiesbaden: Harrassowitz, 1969).

28. The details of the calculation are given in A. Volwahsen, *Living Architecture,* pp. 50–55.

29. Ibid., p. 51.

30. See O. Fischer, *Die Kunst Indiens* (Berlin: Propyläen, 1928), plates pp. 253f.

31. B. Rowland, *The Art and Architecture of India* (Baltimore: Penguin Books, 1967), plate 112.

32. Ibid., plates 101 and 118.

33. The placing of the capstone on top of such a tall structure was a marvelous engineering feat of the time. According to tradition a 4 mile long ramp was built upon which it was inched up. A different theory is held by some Western authors. See A. Volwahsen, *The Hindu Temple,* pp. 180f and B. Rowland, ibid., plate 121b.

34. See A. Volwahsen, ibid. p. 145.

35. See B. Rowland, *The Art and Architecture of India,* plate 103a.

36. See ibid.,plate 106.

37. Ibid., plate 104.

38. See ibid., plate 124.

39. See ibid., plate 120a.

40. See B. Rowland, ibid., Chapters 15–17. Also J. C. Harle, *The Art and Architecture of the Indian Subcontinent* (Harmondsworth: Penguin Books, 1987). Much fascinating detail on the technicalities of temple building, the tools used and the organization of the trades employed can be gathered from A. Boner, S. R. Sarma, and R. P. Das, *New Light on the Sun Temple of Konārkā: Four Unpublished Manuscripts Relating to Construction History and Ritual of This Temple* (Banaras: Chowkhambha Sanskrit Series Office, 1972). The work also contains reproductions of the late-mediaeval palmleaf manuscripts with the complete "blueprint" of the temple and appropriate annotations.

41. D. L. Eck, *Darśan: Seeing the Divine Image in India,* 2d ed. (Chambersburg, Pa.: Anima Books, 1985).

42. For details consult P. V. Kane, *HDhS.*, vol. 5 (part 1), pp. 463ff.

43. *Maitrī Upaniṣad,* VI, 14ff.

44. P. V. Kane, *HDhS,* vol. 5 (part 1), pp. 253–462 offers a list of *vratas* containing more than a thousand individual feasts and observances.

45. *Dharmayuga* brought out an issue dedicated to this feast on August 30, 1964; see also P. V. Kane, *HDhS,* vol. 5 (part 1), pp. 124ff.

46. For details see P. V. Kane, ibid., pp. 154–187.

47. For details see Kane, ibid., pp. 227f. *The Illustrated Weekly of India* brought out a special *Mahāśivarātrī* issue 87, no. 8 (February 20, 1966). See also the very detailed and interesting study by J. B. Long, "Festival of Repentance: A Study of Mahāśivarātrī," *JBOI* 22, nos. 1–2 (1972): 15–38.

48. The Gītāpress brought out a special volume *Tīrthāṅka* [in Hindī] in 1956, describing thousands of *tīrthas* on more than 700 pages with numerous illustrations. See also M. Jha (ed.), *Dimensions of Pilgrimage* (New Delhi: Inter-Indian Publication, 1985). R. Salomon (ed. and trans.), *The Bridge to the Three Holy Cities, The Samāyāna-Praghataka of Nārāyana Bhaṭṭa's Triṣthalisetu* (Delhi: Motilal Banarsidass, 1985). See also E. A. Morinis, *Pilgrimage in the Hindu Tradition: A Case Study of West Bengal,* South Asian Studies Series (New York and New Delhi: Oxford University, 1984).

49. The *Padma Purāṇa* contains a great number of *tīrtha māhātmyas,* as also the *Matsya* and *Agni.* The *Padma Purāṇa* has a long *khaṇḍa* in honor of Kāsī, perhaps the *sthāla purāṇa* itself.

50. 50. An interesting essay about a trip from the source of the Ganges to her entering the sea is J. J. Putnam and R. Singh, "The Ganges, River of Faith," *National Geographic* (October 71): 445–83.

51. See H. von Stietencron, "Suicide as a Religious Institution," *Bharatiya Vidya* 27 (1967): 7–24.

52. *Kalyāna Kalpataru,* 39, no. 12 (March 1966).

53. See L. B. Havell, *Benares, The Sacred City: Sketches of Hindu Life and Religion,* 2d ed. (London, 1905). Also Diana Eck, *Benares, the City of Light* (Princeton, N.J.: Princeton University Press, 1983). Valuable information also in P. V. Kane, *HDhS,* vol. 4, pp. 618–42.

54. Quite instructive are the two special issues Homage to Vārāṇasī brought out by the *Illustrated Weekly of India* 85, nos. 6 and 7 (9 and 16 February 1984) with numerous illustrations.

55. *Varanasi at a Glance*, a souvenir issued on the eve of the XXIV session of All India Oriental Conference, October 1968 (Banaras: Varanaseya Sanskrit Vishwavidyalaya), p. 17.

56. See the section "*Tīrthayātra*" in Kane, *HDhS* vol. 4, pp. 552–827 including a list of *tīrthas* over 100 pages long with thousands of names and indications of further information. A visit to a *Kumbhamelā*, which is held in turn every three years in Allahābad (Prayāga), Hardwār, Ujjain, and Nāsik, gives a good impression of the fervor with which also today millions of Hindus engage in *tīrtha-yātra* and the observance of holy times. See also the report on the *Kumbhamelā* in Hardwar in 1986 in *India Today*, (15 May 1986): 74–85.

57. Good information on the history of Tirupati (and other major centers) in N. Ramesan, *Temples and Legends of Andhra Pradesh* (Bombay: Bharatiya Vidya Bhavan, 1962), pp. 56–69.

58. For a great amount of detail on the architecture of these places, see M. W. Meister, and M. A. Dhaky (eds.), *Encyclopedia of Indian Temple Architecture*, vol. 1. *South India* (New Delhi: American Institute of Indian Studies, 1983).

59. See C. J. Fuller, *Servants of the Goddess: The Priests of a South Indian Temple* (Cambridge: Cambridge University Press, 1984); W. P. Harman, *The Sacred Marriage of a Hindu Goddess* (Bloomington: Indiana University Press, 1989); S. Padmanabhan, *Temples of South India* (Nagercoil: K. Pathipaggam, 1977); D. D. Shulman, *Tamil Temple Myths: Sacrifice and Divine Marriage in the South Indian Tradition* (Princeton, N.J.: Princeton University Press, 1980).

60. V. N. Hari Rao has not only written a monograph on *The Śrīraṅgam Temple: Art and Architecture* (Tirupati: Śrī Venkateśvara University, 1967) but has also translated *Koil Olugu: The Chronicle of the Śrīraṅgam Temple* (Madras: Rochouse and Sons, 1961), which provides insight into the vicissitudes of this famous place of pilgrimage.

61. For details see F. W. Clothey "Pilgrimage Centers in the Tamil Culture of Murukan," *JAAR* 40 (1972): 79–95.

62. For details see K. R. Vaidyanathan, *Śrī Krishna the Lord of Guruvayūr* (Bombay: Bharatiya Vidya Bhavan, 1977).

21. THE HINDU SOCIAL ORDER: *CATURVARṆĀŚRAMADHARMA*

1. The word *caste* is usually derived from the Portuguese *casta*, "race, species, lineage." It serves as a rather inadequate translation for two Indian words: *varṇa* (originally "color") the four "original divisions of

humankind" into *brahmins, kṣatriyas, vaiśyas,* and *śūdras,* and *jāti* (originally "birth"), of which there exist over 3000. Each *varṇa* is divided into a great many *jātis,* which are among themselves again hierarchically ordered, although not uniformly so over India.

2. L. Dumont, *Religion, Politics and History in India: Collected Papers in Indian Sociology* (The Hague: Mouton, 1970), p. 38 n. 10.

3. J. H. Hutton, *Caste in India: Its Nature, Function and Origins,* 3rd ed. (1946; reprint, Oxford: Oxford University Press, 1961).

4. *Homo Hierarchicus,* English translation (Chicago: University of Chicago Press 1970). A very valuable work is also P. H. Prabhu's *Hindu Social Organization: A Study in Socio-Psychological and Ideological Foundations,* 4th ed. (Bombay: Popular Prakashan, 1963). Very worthwhile is the work of an Indian anthropologist, Irawati Karve, *Hindu Society: An Interpretation* (Poona: Deshmukh Prakashan, 1961), highlighting especially the great diversity of Indian society and its customs in the various parts of India.

5. "Orientalist Constructions of India," *Modern Asian Studies* 20, no. 3 (1986): 401–46. Inden writes: "Indological discourse, I argue, holds (or simply assumes) that the essence of Indian civilization is just the opposite of the West's. It is the irrational (but rationalizable) institution of 'caste' and the Indological religion that accompanies it, Hinduism. Human agency in India is displaced by Indological discourse not onto a reified State or Market but onto a substantialized caste" (p. 402). Although I agree with much of Inden's criticism of "orientalist constructions of India" it should be made clear that caste is essential and has been understood as such not only by Indologists but by Indians themselves, high and low.

6. *Ṛgveda* X, 190.

7. Dagmar Gräfin Bernstorff, "Das Kastensystem im Wandel," in *Indien in Deutschland,* ed. E. Weber and R. Töpelman (Frankfurt am Main: Peter Lang, 1990), pp. 29–51.

8. An important issue became the question of intercaste marriages and the position of the "mixed castes." See *Manusmṛti* X, 6–73.

9. Apart from encyclopedic works like E. Thurston and K. Rangachari, *Tribes and Castes of South India,* 4 vols. (Madras: Government Press, 1929), and parallels in other parts of India, village or regional studies like M. N. Srinivas, *Religion and Society Among the Coorgs of South India* (Oxford: Oxford University Press, 1952), and books inspired by this seminal work give a good idea of the actual working of caste.

10. *Article 17*: "Untouchability is abolished and its practice in any form is forbidden. The enforcement of any disability arising out of Untouchability shall be an offence punishable in accordance with law."

11. The story is told in the Anuśānaparvan of the Mahābhārata. See the comments of the editor of the *Mahābhārata Critical Edition,* vol. 18, p. lviii.

12. "The Conception of Kingship in Ancient India," in *Religion, Politics, and History in India,* pp. 62f.

13. Dumont refers here to G. Dumézil's *Mitra-Varuṇa* (Paris, 1940), and A. M. Hocart's *Les Castes* (Paris, 1939; trans., New York: Russell, 1950).

14. See Arvind Sharma, *The Puruṣārthas: A Study in Hindu Axiology* (East Lansing: Asian Studies Center, Michigan State University, 1982). See also C. Malamoud, "On the ṛhetoric and Semantics of Puruśārtha," in *Way of Life,* ed. T. N. Madan (Delhi: Vikas Publishing House, 1982), pp. 33–52.

15. A rich source of information on these matters is P. V. Kane, *HDhS,* vol. 2 (part 2).

16. "Hinduism," in W. Theodore de Bary (general ed.), *Sources of Indian Tradition* (reprint New York: Columbia University Press, 1958), vol. 1, pp. 200–361.

17. "Another Path," *SEMINAR* 17 (January 1961): 41.

18. For an overall view see U. N. Ghosal, *A History of Indian Political Ideas: The Ancient Period and the Period of Transition to the Middle Ages* (Oxford: Oxford University Press, 1959). For the question of Brahmanic vs. *Kṣatriya* views, see the excellent article by R. M. Dandekar, "Ancient Indian Polity," *Indo-Asian Culture* 11, no. 4 (April 1963): 323–32.

19. *Manusmṛti* I, 98–101.

20. See especially *Bhagavadgītā,* III, 35.

21. Sacred Kingship in India and in other cultures has been the topic of a recent Congress of the International Association for the History of Religion. See *Numen* supplement no. 4, with C. M. Edsman's introductory essay, "Zum sakralen Königtum in der Forschung der letzten hundert Jahre," pp. 3–17. Important essays on this topic by M. Biardeau, R. Inden, and A. C. Mayer are also contained in T. N. Madan (ed.), *Way of Life. King, Householder, Renouncer. Essays in Honour of Louis Dumont* (Delhi: Vikas Publishing House, 1982). The relationship between kingship and local temple cults is explored by R. Inden, "Hierarchies of Kings in Early Mediaeval India" in this work (pp. 99–125); and S. Gupta and R. Gombrich "Kings, Power and the Goddess," *South Asia Research* 6, no. 2 (November 1986): 123–38.

22. The term is *daṇḍa,* literally a stick, an instrument of punishment as which the scepter has to be understood throughout in this tradition.

23. The term is *kheda,* meaning "exhaustion"; other Mss. have *dhainya.*

24. *Śāntiparvan* 59, 12ff.

25. *Viṣṇu Purāṇa* I, 13; *Bhāgavata Purāṇa* IV, 14.

26. According to brahmanical lore the *vaiśyas* originated from the thigh, the *kṣatrias* from the arms of the *puruṣa.*

27. *Viṣṇu Purāṇa* I, 13, 61–63.

28. One of the best examples is the *Rājadharma* section in the *Mahābhārata Śāntiparvan* 1–128.

29. See *Kauṭilīya Arthaśāstra,* ed. and trans. R. P. Kangle, three parts (Bombay: University of Bombay, 1960–61), containing the critical text, a translation and a study. See also U. N. Ghosal, "Kautilīya," in *Encyclopedia of Social Sciences* (1953), vol. 3, pp. 473ff.

30. The difference between the Kautilīyan idea of kingship and European absolutism is explored in N. P. Sil, "Political Morality vs. Political Necessity: Kauṭilya and Machiavelli Revisited," *Journal of Asian History* 19, no. 2 (1985): 101–42.

31. The *Arthaśāstra* concludes with the maxim: "What mankind lives by that is *artha,* the science that deals with the means of conquering and possessing the earth is *arthaśāstra.*"

32. *Jāti* is derived from *jā-*, being born and is usually translated as "subcaste." In fact the *jātis* determine the real place of the Hindu in society because every *varṇa* has within itself a hierarchy of *jātis.*

33. Bombay: Asia Publishing House, 1968.

34. Which he defines not necessarily as Westernization, as he shows when he writes: "Modernity, in that sense, is not new; it is a recurring historical force, a recurring opportunity 'which, taken at the flood, leads on to fortune, omitted, all the voyage of your life is bound in shallows and miseries'. Ultimately, we today are striving for the most strategic thing in our time, a new identity for ourselves and for the world. It is no less than an identity with the spirit of the age, the fulfillment of a new *karma,* and here the responsibility has lain squarely on the elites of history. (p. 4).

35. See, e.g., the *prayaścittas* for killing a cow and for killing a *caṇḍāla.*

36. The following letter to the editor of the *Times of India* (Bombay, 20 March 1968) on "Harijan's Plight" by Rajaram P. Mukane from Thana is quite telling: "... millions of untouchables in this country continue to suffer shameful humiliations twenty years after independence. Almost every aspect of our life is infested with casteism and communalism. The Chief Minister of Andhra Pradesh disclosed in the Assembly last week that a Harijan youth was roasted alive on a charge of theft. The committee on untouchability constituted by the Union Government recently revealed that three untouchables were shot dead by caste Hindus for growing their moustaches upwards instead of downward, in keeping with the local Hindu tradition, and that an untouchable youth was killed in Mysore for walking along the street wearing chappals. Everyone remembers how in Maharastra three Harijan women were stripped naked and made to walk before the public on the roads. These are not isolated incidents. Such atrocities are perpetrated everywhere in our country due to the virus of casteism and untouchability, although the practice of the latter has been banned by law. The law against untouchability is almost inoperative because of the indifferent attitude of the so-called upper caste Hindus holding key positions. For Hinduism the cow and other such things seem to occupy a more significant position than human dignity." More recent examples of injustices committed against the former outcastes can be found in A. George, *Social Ferment in India* (London: Athlone Press, 1986), Chapter 7, "The Scheduled Castes," pp. 202ff.

37. See B. R. Ambedkar, *What Congress and Gandhi Have Done to the Untouchables*, 2d ed. (Bombay: Thacker and Co., 1946).

22. THE PROFESSIONAL RELIGIOUS: *SAṂNYĀSA*

1. *Manusmṛti*, X, 74ff.

2. Ibid., VI, 37 threatens those with hell who take *samnyāsa* without having begotten a son and performed the proper rites. See also *Viṣṇusmṛti* V, 13.

3. Some of the works that could be mentioned in this context are I. C. Oman, *The Mystics, Ascetics and Saints of India*(1903; reprint Delhi: Oriental Publisheres, 1973); H. H. Wilson, *Religious Sects of the Hindus*, first published in *Asiatick Researches* 16 (1828) and 17 (1832) (reprint Calcutta: Punthi Pustak, 1958); S. Chattophadyaya, *The Evolution of Theistic Sects in Ancient India* (Calcutta: Progressive Publishers, 1962); G. S. Ghurye, *Indian Sādhus*, 2d ed. (Bombay: Asia Publishing House, 1964).

4. *Mahābhārata, Anuśāsanaparvan* 141.

5. The *śikhā*, also called *choṭī*, is the little wisp of hair left at the place of the *brahmārandra*, the place where according to Vedic belief, the *ātman*

leaves the body. It is never cut, while the rest of the head is shaved ritually quite often. It is, even today, a sign of Brahmanic orthodoxy and is cut off only if someone takes *samnyāsa*, whereby he technically ceases to belong to the community that observes dharma.

6. *Paramahaṃsa Upaniṣad*, condensed rendering from *108 Upaniṣadé, Brahmā Vidyā Khaṇḍa*, No. 33, 526ff.

7. A classical text relating to *samnyāsa* has recently been translated into English. P. Olivelle (ed. and trans.), *Vasudevāśrama's Yatidharmaprakāśa. A Treatise on World Renunciation*. 2 vols. (Vienna: De Nobili Research Library, 1977). Also P. Olivelle, *Renunciation in Hinduism: A Mediaeval Debate*, 2 vols. (Vienna: Institute for Indology, University of Vienna, 1986–87).

8. *Yatidharmasaṅgraha of Viśveśvarasarasvatī*, ed. V. G. Apte (Poona: Ānandāśrama, 1928), 154.

9. *Vedārthasaṁgraha* no. 251.

10. An early example is *Bṛhadāraṇyaka Upaniṣad* II, 6, mentioning fifty-eight generations of gurus ending with "Parameṣṭhin from Brahman." Later sectarian sūtras carry lengthy lists of names, too.

11. *Upadeśasahasrī* No. 6.

12. For many details concerning the legal aspects of *samnyāsa*, see P. V. Kane, *HDhS*, vol. 2 (part 2), pp. 933ff.

13. Rāmdās Gaur, *Hindutva* [Hindī] (Banaras: Visvaprasad Gupta, samvat 1995), "*saṃpradāya khaṇḍa*," Chapters 67–75.

14. On the life and work of Śaṅkara and the order founded by him, see W. Cenkner: *A Tradition of Teachers. Śaṅkara and the Jagadgurus Today* (Delhi: Motilal Banarsidass, 1983). See also Yoshitsugu Sawai, "Śaṅkara's Theology of Samnyāsa," *JIPh* 14 (1986): 371–87.

15. Also other ancient establishments claim to be founded by Śaṅkarācārya and to possess his *guru paramparā*, expressed in the title *jagadguru* and Śaṅkarācārya given to the resident chief ascetic. See e.g., T. M. P. Mahadevan, *The Sage of Kanchi* (Secunderabad: Sri Kanchi Kamakothi Śaṅkara Mandir, 1967) describing the life of Śrī Jagadguru Śaṅkarācārya of Kāmakothi Pīṭha, His Holiness Śrī Chandrasekharendra Sarasvatī on the completion of sixty years of spiritual rulership as the sixty-eighth Head of the Pitha.

Śaṅkara is supposed to have founded a great many other *āśrams* like the Summeru and Paduka Mathas at Vāraṇāsī and the Vadakkāri Madaur and Naduvilai Madaur in Kerala. Their *guru paraṁparā* is disputed. A reader who has made a special study of the succession of the Śaṅkara *maṭhas* informed me that today the *samnyāsi* names ending in Pūrī, Sāgara, Āśrama, Giri, Vāna, or Pārvata are rare and the most frequently used are Bhāratī, Tīrtha, and Sarasvatī. He mentioned that all the orders today greet each other or sign documents with the words *Iti Nārāyaṇasmaraṇam* or *Nārāyaṇasmṛtiḥ*. He also provided me with several pages of arguments, concluding that the Kamakothi Pitha at Kanchipuram is not one of the four original *maṭhas* founded by Śaṅkara and that a 1979 meeting of the four undisputed *maṭhas* (called Chaturamnyāya Sammelan) did not mention Kāmakothi Pīṭha (letter by S. Vidyasankar, July 21, 1992).

16. To enhance their prestige non-Śaṅkarite *sādhus* as, e.g., the Neo-Caitanyites, also adopt these titles.

17. See S. G. Ghurye, *Indian Sādhus,* Chapter 6.

18. W. Cenkner, *A Tradition of Teachers,* p. 134.

19. Ghurye, *Indian Sādhus,* Chapter 10.

20. See T. M. P. Mahadevan, in *HCIP,* vol. 5, p. 458. See also H. H. Wilson, *Religious Sects of the Hindus,* pp. 131ff and 142ff. Rāmānuja, *Śrībhāṣya,* II, 2,36; S. G. Ghurye, *Indian Sadhūs,* pp. 48ff.

21. This group, founded in the early seventeenth century with centers in Banaras, Gazipur, and Jaunpur, is classified as *sudhārak* (reformist) in Rāmdās Gaur, *Hindutva,* p. 739. The traditional Aghoris are unapproachable to outsiders.

22. A. S. Raman, "Homage to Varanasi," *Illustrated Weekly of India* 85, nos. 6–7.

23. For a full-length monograph, see A. K. Banerjea, *The Philosophy of Gorakhnāth* (Gorakhpur: Mahant Dig Vijai Nath Trust, Gorakhnath Temple, 1962).

24. In addition to the information offered by Rāmdās Gaur, see H. H. Wilson, *Religious Sects of the Hindus,* pp. 148f.

25. Pandit Śrīnarāyan Śāstri Khiste, "Śrīvidyā," in *Kalyāṇa Devībhāgavatam Aṅgka* (Gorakhpur: Gītā Press, 1960): pp. 689–96.

26. Rāmdās Gaur, *Hindutva,* pp. 730f.

27. W. S. Deming, *Rāmdās and the Rāmdāsis,* Religious Life of India Series (Oxford: Oxford University Press, 1928).

28. In addition to the text editions, translations, and works mentioned by C. Vaudeville in *Kabīr Granthavālī* (*Doha*) (Pondichery: Institut Français d'Indologie, 1957), G. H. Westcott, *Kabīr and the Kabīr Panth* (1907; reprint Calcutta: YMCA Press, 1953), is still recommended.

29. Details in Rāmdās Gaur, *Hindutva,* pp. 735ff.

30. Karpātrijī Mahārāj, *Rāmrājya aur Marksvād* [in Hindī] (Gorakhpur: Gītā Press, 1964).

31. It was interesting to see the comments and reports in the dailies and weeklies of India in the days following the incident, especially the rather interesting opposite versions offered by the left-wing *Blitz* and the right-wing *Organiser.*

32. See the Hindū Viśva Pariṣad publication, *Viśva Hindū,* started in Bombay in 1964, with a special edition in January 1966, on occasion of a conference at the *Kumbha Melā* at Allahabad.

33. See K. Klostermaier, "Vaiṣṇavism and Politics: The New Dharma of Brāj?" *JVS* 1,no. 1 (1992): 166–82 describing a meeting with Swāmi Vāmadeva and the present secretary general of the organization, Swāmi Muktānanda. As appendix to the article is offered a translation of a Hindī pamphlet containing the goals and demands of the movement.

34. As the Delhi paper *Pioneer* reports in its March 3, 1993, issue, the Sant Samiti appears to gain importance in the Hindu-extremist agītātion in India. Since the Viśva Hindū Pariṣad, the Rāṣṭrīya Swayamsevak Sangh, and the Bajrang Dal, who had been implicated in the Ayodhyā debacle and its aftermath, were banned, the Sant Samiti under the direction of Swāmi Vāmadeva through frequently held *sant sammelans* (gatherings of *sādhus*) has taken up the task to continue the movement to "liberate" the major temple sites at Kāśī, Mathurā, and Delhi. "In their scheme of things the campaign is expected to peak around Rām Nāvamī in April. A nine-day *anuṣṭhān* would be organised near the controversial site in Ayodhyā."

35. D. D. Kosambi has critically edited *The Epigrams Attributed to Bhartṛhari Including the Three Centuries,* Singhi Jain Series No. 23 (Bombay: Bharatiya Vidya Bhavan, 1948. The Advaita Āśrama Calcutta has brought out the text with translation of the *Vairāgya Śatakam* (1963) according to the rather heavily interpolated "vulgate" text. The extract here is from nos. 2–7 and 99–100.

36. Madhava Ashish, "The *Sādhu* in Our Life," *SEMINAR* 200 (April 1976): 12–18.

23. *STRĪDHARMA*: THE POSITION OF WOMEN IN HINDUISM

1. R. K. Prabhu and U. R. Rao (eds.) *The Mind of Mahatma Gandhi* (Ahmedabad: Navajivan Publishing House, 1967), p. 296.

2. Minoti Bhattacharyya, "Hindu Religion and Women's Rights', *RS* 35, no. 1 (March 1988): 52–61.

3. *Ṛgveda* V, 28.

4. *Ṛgveda* VIII, 91, 1; I, 117, 7; X, 40, 1; X, 145, 16.

5. See also E. B. Findly, "Gargī at the King's Court: Women and Philosophic Innovation in Ancient India," in Y. Y. Haddad and E. B. Findly (eds.), *Women, Religion and Social Change* (Albany: State University of New York Press, 1985), pp. 37–58.

6. *Ṛgveda* I, 116, 16.

7. *Ṛgveda* I, 48, 1. 14–15.

8. *Ṛgveda* X, 125. 3. 4. 5.

9. *Ṛgveda* V, 84.

10. A convenient collection of all *smṛti* references to *strīdharma* is provided in Sadhu Charan Prasad, *Dharmaśāstrasaṅgraha* [Sanskrit and Hindī] (Bombay: Venkatesvar Steam Press, 1913): Section 13, 209–22.

11. See *Manusmṛti* 5, 150–156; *Vyāsasmṛti* 2, 18–20.

12. *Manusmṛti* 2, 66–67.

13. *Manusmṛti* 5, 150–56. *Atrismṛti* 13, 3–137, goes one step further: like *śudras*, it says, women "fall" (i.e., they commit a sinful act) if they practice *japa, tapasya, saṃnyāsa, mantra-sādhana,* or *devapūjā.*

14. *Manusmṛti* 9, 2–11.

15. See *Yājñavalkyasmṛti* 1, 70–82, for specifics, also *Manusmṛti* 11, 177–78.

16. *Manusmṛti* 9, 12ff.

17. *Vyāsasmṛti* 2, 18–40.

18. *Angirasasmṛti* 35–38.

19. See also *Vyāsasmṛti* 2, 38–40.

20. *Dakṣasmṛti* 213.

21. In the *smṛtis, svayamvara* was the course of action to be taken if a father failed to find a husband for his daughter five years after she attained puberty.

22. A. K. Majumdar, *Caitanya: His Life and Doctrine* (Bombay: Bharatiya Vidya Bhavan, 1969), p. 290.

23. N. Chaudhuri, *Hinduism* (London: Chatto and Windus, 1979), 286.

24. The most recent monograph of Āṇṭāl (also spelled Aṇḍal), containing a complete translation of her *Tiruppāvai* and her *Nācciyār Tirumoli* (with notes) in contemporary, idiomatic English is Vidya Deheja's, *Āṇṭāl and Her Path of Love* (Albany: State University of New York Press, 1990). The book also has a good bibliography on Āḷvārs.

25. See also D. Hudson, "Āṇṭāl Āḷvār: A Developing Hagiography," *JVS* 1, no. 2 (1993): 27–61.

26. A good traditional account of Mirābāī's legend together with a reproduction in the original languages of many of her poems, and translations into English of a few of these, is found in Bankey Bihari, *Bhakta Mīrā* (Bombay: Bharatiya Vidya Bhavan, 1961). See also W. M. Callewaert, "The 'Earliest' Song of Mīrā (1503–1546)," *JOIB* 39, nos. 3–4 (1990): 239–53, with a good bibliography of editions of Mirābāī's songs.

27. See "Sri Ānandamayī" by Stephen (Umananda) Quong in *Hinduism Today* (September and October 1992): 7.

28. *Young India* (15 September 1921).

29. *Young India* (21 October 1926).

30. For detail and present-day discussion see A. Sharma, *Satī* (Delhi: Motilal Banarsidass, 1989.

31. K. Klostermaier, "The Original Dakṣa Saga" in A. Sharma (ed.), *Essays on the Mahābhārata*, Brill's Indological Library Vol. 1 (Leiden: Brill, 1991), pp. 110–29.

32. G. H. R. Tillotson, "The Indian Travels of William Hodges," *JRAS*, Series 3, vol. 2, no. 3 (1992): 377–98.

33. *Pacific Affairs* 61, no. 3 (Fall 1988): 465–85.

34. Ibid., p. 483.

24. HINDU STRUCTURES OF THOUGHT: THE *ṢAḌDARŚANAS*

1. *Manusmṛti* II, 114 (Bühler's translation SBE XXV).

2. *Manusmṛti* II, 156.

3. *Manusmṛti* II, 171.

4. Some interesting details are presented in a lighthearted manner by Kuppuswami Sastri in a contribution to "The Library Movement" under the title "*Kośavan ācāryah*" (i.e., one who has a library is a teacher, or: a teacher is one how has a library). Reprinted in S. S. Janaki (ed.), *Kuppuswamy Sastri Birth Centenary Commemoration Volume*, Part 1 (Madras:

Kuppuswami Research Institute, 1981). This claim is also supported by the information on the scholastic engagement of the Śaṅkarācāryas past and present, in W. Cenkner, *A Tradition of Teachers*, esp. Chapter 4, "The Teaching Heritage after Śaṅkara," pp. 84–106.

5. A popular maxim is *Svadeśe pūjyate rājā vidvān sarvatra pūjyate*, that is, although a king is honored in his own realm (only), a scholar is honored everywhere.

6. The many (thirty-two) different *vidyās* mentioned in the Upaniṣads can be seen as the beginning of different school traditions of Hinduism.

7. *Vādavāda*, a study of different viewpoints and polemics became an integral part of traditional Indian learning. As T. R. V. Murti says: "polemic (*parapakṣanirākaraṇa*) is an integral part of each system" ("The Rise of the Philosophical Schools," *CHI*, vol. 3, p. 32).

8. The text used as motto for this chapter provides the rationale for Śaṅkara to develop his extensive commentary on the *Brahmasūtra*.

9. Not only are a number of highly philosophical *stotras* ascribed to Śaṅkarācārya, hymns to different deities recited by ordinary Hindus in their daily worship, also the vernacular religious poetry of such favorites of contemporary Hindus like Tulasīdāsa, Kabīr, Sūrdāsa, Tūkarām, and others are highly speculative.

10. *Manusmṛti* II, 11.

11. *Tantravārttika* I, 3, 4.

12. S. Radhakrishnan mentions in *Indian Philosophy* (London: Allen and Unwin, 1948), vol. 2, p. 20 n. 4, that Bhīmācārya in his *Nyāyakośa* included Sāṁkhya and Advaita Vedānta under the *nāstika*, i.e., unorthodox systems. He specifically quotes the sentence *Māyāvādivedānti api nāstika eva paryavasāna sampadyate* ("In the end also the Vedāntin holding the opinion of illusionism [*māyāvāda*] turns out to be a *nāstika*, i.e., a nonbeliever in the Veda"). This sentence is not found in the fourth edition, revised by V. S. Abhyankar (Poona: Bhandarkar Oriental Research Institute, 1978).

13. *Brahmasūtrabhāṣya* I, 1, 5.

14. S. Radhakrishnan, *Indian Philosophy*, vol. 2, 19.

15. Ibid., pp. 20f.

16. Ibid., p. 24: "The six systems agree on certain essentials." In a footnote Radhakrishnan quotes Max Müller, who, with reference to Vijñānabhikṣu, who, in the fourteenth century, had attempted to bring about a

unified *darśana* had stated "that there is behind the variety of the six systems a common fund of what may be called national or popular philosophy, a large *manasa* lake of philosophical thought and language far away in the distant North and in the distant past, from which each thinker was allowed to draw for his own purposes." Max Müller, *The Six Systems of Indian Philosophy* (reprint, Banaras: Chowkhambha, 1962), p. xvii. Radhakrishnan made a bold statement of the unity of Hindu philosophy in his popular *The Hindu View of Life* (New York: Macmillan, 1962).

17. The term *darśana* has been common in India since the second century. Before that the term *anvīkṣikī*, later restricted to 'logic' seems to have served. This issue is competently discussed by W. Halbfass in "Indien und die Geschichtsschreibung der Philosophie" *Philosophische Rundschau* 23 (1976):104–31.

18. Therefore the commentaries on Gaṅgeśa's *Tattvacintāmaṇi* were called *Didhiti, Gaṅgadhārī, Kārṣikā, Candrakālā, Nakṣatramālikā*, etc. See R. Thangasami Sarma, *Darśanamañjarī*, part 1 (Madras: University of Madras, 1985), pp. 64f.

19. The abovementioned author uses the titles *Nyāya, Vyākāraṇa, Vedānta, Śiromaṇī*, showing that he is qualified in logic, grammar, and Vedānta.

20. Thus K. H. Potter, in his otherwise indispensable and much valued *The Encyclopedia of Indian Philosophy*, restricts selections of text extracts to those portions that have a parallel in contemporary analytic Western philosophy.

21. K. Potter has assembled a very extensive *Bibliography of Indian Philosophies* (Delhi: Motilal Banarsidass, 1970), with additions published in *JIPh*. For professionals the as yet incomplete *New Catalogus Catalogorum*, appearing from the University of Madras (thirteen volumes so far), is the most valuable bibliographic resource, listing not only published editions and translations but also manuscripts and their location.

22. The text has been published several times (e.g., Poona: Bhandarkar Oriental Research Institute) and was translated into English, without *Śaṅkaradarśana*, more than a century ago by Cowell and Gough. This translation has been reprinted many times.

23. See Kuppuswami Sastri's Introduction to his *Primer of Indian Logic* (Madras: Kuppuswami Research Institute, 1932; reprints 1951, 1961), reprinted in *KSVCCV*, vol. 1, pp. 104–18. 22

24. Ibid., p. 104.

25. D. Krishna et al. (eds.), *Saṃvāda: A Dialogue Between Two Philosophical Traditions* (Delhi: Indian Council of Philosophical Research 1991).

25. HINDU LOGIC AND PHYSICS: *NYĀYA-VAIŚEṢIKA*

1. S. N. Dasgupta, *History of Indian Philosophy* (Cambridge: Cambridge University Press, 1961), vol. 1, p. 282.

2. See the evidence offered by S. N. Dasgupta, ibid.

3. It has only been preserved in a Chinese translation; this has been edited and translated and commented upon by H. Ui (1917; reprint, Banaras: Chowkhambha Sanskrit Series, 1962).

4. The best known may be the *Bhāṣāpariccheda* with *Siddhānta Muktavalī by Viśvanātha Nyāyapañcānana*, trans. Swami Madhavananda (Calcutta: Advaita Ashrama, 21954).

5. K. Sastri, "Nyāya-Vaiśeṣika—Origin and Development," Introduction to Kuppuswami Sastri, *Primer of Indian Logic*, reprinted in *KSBCCV*, p. 104.

6. In addition to sections on Nyāya and Vaiśeṣika in the major handbooks on Indian philosophy (as well as the English language works by S. N. Dasgupta and S. Radhakrishnan, also the French works by Renou and Filliozat as well as Biardeau and Siauve, the German works by P. Deussen and E. Frauwallner, and the Sanskrit survey by Thiru Thanghasamy deserve consultation), the following specialized works will be found useful for more advanced students: D. H. H. Ingalls, *Materials for the Study of Navya-Nyāya Logic*, Harvard Oriental Series No. 40 (Cambridge, Mass.: Harvard University Press, 1968); B. K. Matilal, *The Navya Nyāya Doctrine of Negation*, Harvard Oriental Series No. 46 (Cambridge, Mass.: Harvard Univesrity Press, 1972); S. C. Chatterjee, *The Nyāya Theory of Knowledge*, 3rd ed. (Calcutta: University of Calcutta, 31965); V. Mishra, *The Conception of Matter According to Nyāya-Vaiśeṣika* (Allahabad, 1936; reprint, Delhi: Gian Publications, 1983). Some important and very informative essays on Nyāya-Vaiśeṣika in S. K. Maitra, *Fundamental Questions of Indian Metaphysics and Logic* (Calcutta: Chuckervertty, Chatterjee and Co., 1956).

W. Halbfass, *On Being and What There Is*, subtitled *Classical Vaisesika and the History of Indian Ontology* (Albany: State University of New York Press, 1992), offers not only an up-to-date description of Vaiśeṣika research but also an incisive comparative study of ontology in the Greek and Indian contexts.

An indispensable source is Sati Chandra Vidyabhusana, *A History of Indian Logic* (1920; reprint, Delhi: Motilal Banarsidass, 1971). The most authentic representation of *Nyāya* and *Vaiśeṣika*, historically and doctrinally, is found in R. Thangaswami Sarma, *Darśanamañjarī*, part 1 [Sanskrit] (Madras: University of Madras, 1985), which not only contains abundant information on the literature of *Nyāya* and *Vaiśeṣika* and their authors but also has many charts and diagrams illustrating the interconnection of works and concepts.

7. Early writers used the word *Nyāya* as a synonym with *Mīmāṁsā*.

8. *Arthaśāstra* 2, 30, a text often referred to in this connection. So far I have not seen reference made to *Viṣṇu Purāṇa* I, 9, 121, which has the same enumeration of sciences. In this text the Goddess (after churning the Milk Ocean) is addressed as the embodiment of all knowledge (*vidyā*) specifically of *anvīkṣikī, trayī, vārtā,* and *daṇḍanīti*.

9. Kuppuswami Sastri, "Nyāya-Vaiśeṣika," p. 107.

10. *Vaiśeṣikardarśana,* ed. Anatalal Thakur (Darbhanga: Mithila Institute, 1957), trans. N. Sinha (Allahabad: Panini Office, 1911).

11. W. Halbfass in an excursus "The Concept of Viśeṣa and the name of the Vaiśeṣika System" in *On Being,* pp. 269–75, offers alternative suggestions.

12. *Padārthadharmasaṅgraha* No. 156, trans. Ganganatha Jha (Allahabad: Lazarus, 1916).

13. Dasgupta, *HIPh,* vol. 1, p. 363.

14. These "nine things" are: *buddhi, sukha, duḥkha, icchā, dveṣa, prayatna, dharma, adharma, and saṃskāra.*

15. *Nyāyasūtra* with *Vātsyāyana Bhāṣya,* ed., trans. and commentator Ganganatha Jha, 2 vols. (Poona: Oriental Book Agency, 1939).

16. *Maṇikaṇa, A Navya-Nyāya Manual,* ed. and trans. E. R. Sreekrishna Sarma (Adyar: Adyar Library and Research Center, 1960), Introduction, p. xvii.

17. *Nyāya Sūtra* I, 1, 22.

18. Ibid., IV, 1, 66.

19. For details see G. Chemparathy, *An Indian Rational Theology. Introduction to Udayana's Nyāyakusumañjalī* (Vienna: Indological Institute of the University of Vienna, 1972).

20. Udayanācārya's *Nyāyakusumañjalī,* with the commentary of Haridasa Bhattacarya, trans. E. B. Cowell (Calcutta: 1864).

21. *Nyāya-bhāṣya* IV, 1, 21f.

22. *Tarkabhāṣa of Keṣava Miśra,* ed. and trans. Ganganatha Jha (Poona: Oriental Book Agency, 1949).

26. HINDU PSYCHOLOGY AND METAPHYSICS: *SĀṀKHYA-YOGA*

1. The best known text of *Haṭhayoga* is the *Haṭhayogapradīpikā by Svātmārāma Yogīndra* (Adyar: Theosophical Publishing House, 1933).

2. See Chapter 23.

3. For example, *Bhāgavata Purāṇa* II, 25, 13ff.; III, 28.

4. A. B. Keith, *The Sāṁkhya System*, The Heritage of India Series (Calcutta: YMCA Publishing House, 21949), p. 18. The most comprehensive recent study of *Sāṁkhya* is G. J. Larsen, *Classical Sāṁkhya* (Delhi: Motilal Banarsidass, 1969). See also H. Bakker, "On the Origin of the Sāṁkhya Psychology" in: *WZKSA* 26 (1982): 117–48, with an extensive bibliography. G. J. Larsen makes an important point in his essay "The Format of Technical Philosophical Writing in Ancient India: Inadequacies of Conventional Translations" *Philosophy East and West*, 30, no. 3 (1980): 375–80. Comprehensive information on the development of *Sāṁkhya* is contained in E. Frauwallner, *Geschichte der Indischen Philosophie* (Salzburg: Otto Müller Verlag, 1953), vol. 1, pp. 228ff and 472ff.

5. Dasgupta, *HIPh*, vol. 1, p. 264.

6. *Bhāgavata Purāṇa* III, 28.

7. The best edition and translation with ample comments is that by S. S. Suryanarayana Sastri (Madras: University of Madras, 1948). Also *Sāṁkhya Kārikā of Mahāmuni Śrī Īśvarakṛṣṇa* with the commentary *Sārabodhinī* of Paṇḍit Śivanārāyana Śāstrī and *Sāṅkhya Tattvakaumudī of Vācaspati Miśra* (Bombay: Nirnaya Sagar Press, 1940).

8. *Sāṁkhyadarśana*, ed. Pyarelal Prabhu Dayal (Bombay: Nirnaya Sagar Press, 1943); trans. J. R. Ballantyne (London: 1885).

9. Edited and translated under the title *The Yoga Upaniṣads* (Adyar: Adyar Library, 1920 and 1952).

10. A good edition is that by Swāmī Vijñāna Āśrama (Ajmer: Sri Madanlal Laksminivas Chandak, 1961). A complete English translation of the Patañjala *Yogasūtra* with Vyāsa's *Bhāṣya* and Vācaśpati Miśra's *Tattva Vaiśāradī* has been done by J. H. Woods in the Harvard Oriental Series no. 17 (Cambridge, Mass.: Harvard University Press, 1914). Students may find useful I. K. Taimni *The Science of Yoga*, 3rd ed. (Wheaton, Ill.: Theosophical Publishing House, 1972); it offers the text and the translation of the *Yogasūtra* and a good running commentary that avoids the technicalities of the classical commentaries. Valuable recent treatments of Yoga are S. N. Dasgupta, *Yoga as Philosophy and Religion* (1924; reprint

Delhi: Motilal Banarsidass, 1973); J. W. Hauer, *Der Yoga als Heilsweg* (Stuttgart: W. Kohlhammer, 1932); G. Feuerstein, *The Philosophy of Classical Yoga* (Manchester: University of Manchester Press, 1982); G. M. Koelman, *Pātañjala Yoga. From Related Ego to Absolute Self* (Poona: Papal Athenaeum, 1970). Special problems connected with *Sāṁkhya-Yoga* are addressed in these recent papers: Swami Ranganathananda, "The Science of Consciousness in the Light of Vedānta and Yoga" *Prabuddha Bhārata* (June 1982): 257–63; Mohan Singh, "Yoga and Yoga Symbolism" *Symbolon: Jahrbuch für Symbolforschung,* 2 (1959): 121–143; S. Bhattacharya "The Concept of *Bideha* and *Prakṛti-Laya* in the Sāṁkhya-Yoga System" *ABORI* 48–49 (1968): 305–12; C. T. Kenghe, "The Problem of the Pratyayasarga in Sāṁkhya and Its Relation with Yoga" *ABORI* 48–49 (1968): 365–73; K. Werner, "Religious Practice and Yoga in the Time of the Vedas, Upaniṣads and Early Buddhism" *ABORI* 56 (1975): 179–94; G. Oberhammer, "Das Transzendenzverständnis des Sāṁkhyistischen Yoga als Strukturprinzip seiner Mystik" in G. Oberhammer (ed.), *Transzendenzerfahrung, vollzugshorizont des Heils* (Vienna: De Nobili Research Library, 1978), pp. 15–28; idem "Die Gotteserfahrung in der yogischen Meditation" in W. Strolz and S. Ueda (eds.), *Offenbarung als Heilserfahrung im Christentum, Hinduismus und Buddhismus* (Freiburg, Basel, and Vienna: Herder, 1982), pp. 146–66; M. Eliade *Yoga: Immortality and Freedom* (Princeton, N.J.: Princeton University Press, 1958; 2d ed., 1969) has become a classic in its own right: it not only describes Pātañjala Yoga, but compares it to other phenomena and has an exhaustive bibliography of works up to 1964. Controversial new ideas on classical Yoga are advanced in G. Oberhammer, *Strukturen Yogischer Meditation* (Vienna: Österreichische Akademie der Wissenschaften, 1977).

11. *Tejobindu Upaniṣad,* VI, 107.

12. P. Hacker, "Śaṅkara der Yogin und Śaṅkara der Advaitin: Einige Beobachtungen" *WZKSA* 12–13 (1968): 119–48. A full translation of the work has been made by James Legget, published in 1990.

13. *Sāṁkhya Karika,* 1.

14. This is the traditional interpretation given to *duhkhatraya.*

15. *Sāṁkhya Kārikā,* 2.

16. Ibid., 18.

17. Ibid., 8.

18. Ibid., 63.

19. Ibid., 67.

20. *Yogasūtra* I, 5ff.

21. Ibid., I, 23ff.

22. Ibid., II, 5f.

23. According to *Haṭhayoga* the *utthita padmāsana* confers superhuman vision and cures troubles of the respiratory tract; *sūpta padmāsana* cures illnesses of the digestive organs, *bhadrāsana* activates the mind, *dhastricāsana* regulates body temperature, cures fever, and purifies the blood, *guptāṅgāsana* cures venereal diseases, etc. There are centers in India, like the Yoga Research Institute at Lonavla, in which medical research is done on the effects of yoga on body and mind.

24. *Yogasūtra* II, 54.

25. Ibid., III, 1–3.

26. Ibid., III, 16ff.

27. Ibid., IV, 34: *puruṣārthaśūnyānām guṇānām pratiprasavaḥ / kaivalyam svarūpapratiṣṭhā vā citiśaktiriti.*

28. These notions find a surprising parallel in contemporary scientific thought. See I. Prigogine, *Order out of Chaos* (New York: Bantam Books, 1948).

27. HINDU THEOLOGY, OLD AND NEW: *PŪRVA MĪMĀṂSĀ AND VEDĀNTA*

1. B. G. Apte (ed.), *Śābarabhāṣya,* 6 vols. (Pune, Ānandāśrama, 1931–34); English trans. Ganganatha Jha, 3 vols., Gaekwad Oriental Series (Baroda: Oriental Institute, 1933–36; reprint 1973–74).

2. Prabhākara Miśra wrote a voluminous subcommentary to the *Śābarabhāṣya* called *Bṛhatī,* ed. S. K. Ramanatha Sastri, 3 vols. (Madras: University of Madras, 1931). Kumārila Bhaṭṭa wrote the famous *Ślokavārtika,* another subcommentary on the first part of it, as well as the *Tantravārttika* and the *Tupṭīkā,* subcommentaries on the later parts. S. K. Ramanatha Sastri, ed (Madras, 1940). Ganganatha Jha has complete English translations of the *Ślokavārtika* (Calcutta: Asiatic Society, 1907) and of the *Tantravārtika* (Calcutta 1924; reprint Delhi: Śrī Satguru Publications, 1983, 2 vols.).

3. Dasgupta, *HIPh,* vol. 1, p. 371. Concerning the influence of *Mīmāṃsā,* the very useful book by Ganganatha Jha, *Pūrva Mīmāṃsā in Its Sources* (Banaras: Banaras Hindu University, 1942), Chapter 33, has some interesting things to say. An important source for Mīmāṃsā studies is the seven volume *Mīmāṃsākośa,* ed. Kevalanda Sarasvati (Wai Dharmakośamandala, 1952–1966).

4. As W. Cenkner in *A Tradition of Teachers*, reports, the study of *Mīmāṃsā* is one of the subjects which students in the schools associated with the present Śaṅkaramaṭhas have to take. See also F. Staal (ed.), *A Reader on the Sanskrit Grammarians* (Cambridge, Mass.: MIT, 1972), and K. Kunjunni Raja, *Indian Theories of Meaning* (Adyar: The Adyar Library, 1963).

5. *Jaimini Sūtras* I, 1, 2: *codanalakṣano'artho dharmaḥ*.

6. Ibid., I, 2, 1.

7. *Sābara Bhāṣya* I, 1, 22: "There can be no creator of this relation because no soul is cognized as such by any of the means of cognition. If there had been such a creator, he could not have been forgotten." See also *Ślokavārttika*, XVI, 41ff.

8. Ganganatha Jha, *Pūrvamīmāṃsā in Its Sources*, pp. 178ff.

9. *Jaimini Sūtras* Vi, 1, 6ff.

10. Ganganatha Jha, *Pūrva Mīmāṃsā*, pp. 264f.

11. *Jaimini Sūtras* IV, 3, 15.

12. *Śabara Bhāṣya* on VI, 1, 1.

13. *Nyāyaratnakara*: "Liberation must consist in the destruction of the present body and the non-production of the future body." Quoted by G. Jha, *Pūrva Mīmāṃsā*, p. 38.

14. *Prakāraṇapañcikā, Tattvāloka*, p. 156.

15. O. Gächter, *Hermeneutics and Language in Pūrvamīmāṃsā, A Study in Śābara Bhāṣya* (Delhi: Motilal Banarsidass, 1983), with bibliographic references to both Eastern and Western authors.

16. H. G. Coward, *The Sphoṭa Theory of Language. A Philosophical Analysis* (Delhi: Motilal Banarsidass, 1980), with extensive bibliography. The complete text has been edited by K. V. Abhyankar and Acharya V. P. Limaye, University of Poona Sanskrit and Prakrit Series (Poona: University of Poona, 1965).

17. Rāmdās Gaur, *Hindutva*, p. 589.

18. According to S. K. Belvalkar (*Shree Gopal Basu Malik Lectures on Vedānta Philosophy* (Poona: Bilvakunja, 1929), Part 1, Chapter 4, "Vedānta in the Brahmasūtras"(142), Jaimini, the author of the *Mīmāṃsāsūtra* wrote a *Śarīrakasūtra*, which sought to harmonize the teaching of the *Sāmaveda Upaniṣads*, particularly the *Chāndogya Upaniṣad*, and this *sūtra* was incorporated within, and forms the main part of the present text of the *Brahmasūtra*.

19. The ten recognized *Vedāntācāryas* are Śaṅkara, Rāmānuja, Madhva, Vallabha, Bhāskara, Yadavaprakāśa, Keśava, Nīlakaṇṭha, Vijñānabhiksu, and Baladeva. They are the founders of separate branches of Vedānta philosophy. There are several comparative studies of the different schools of Vedānta such as V. S. Ghate, *The Vedānta* (Poona: Oriental Book Agency, 1926; reprint 1960); O. Lacombe, *L'absolu sélon le Vedānta* (Paris: Geuthner, 1957; reprint 1973). See also B. N. K. Sharma, *A Comparative Study of Ten Commentaries on the Brahmasūtras* (Delhi: Motilal Banarsidass, 1984).

20. See Rāmdās Gaur, *Hindutva,* pp. 591ff.

21. Other commentaries interpret Vedānta in the light of sectarian dogma under the names of *Dvaitādvaita* (Nimbārka), *Śuddhādvaita* (Vallabha), *Acintyabhedābheda* (Baladeva), etc.

22. A complete list with a critical analysis is given in S. K. Belvarkar, *Shree Gopal Basu Malik Lectures,* pp. 218ff. See also R. T. Vyas, "Roots of Śaṅkara's Thought" *JBOI* 32, nos. 1–2 (September–December 1982): 35–49.

23. Swami Nikhilananda has an English paraphrase of the *Maṇḍukyopaniṣad with Gauḍapāda's Kārikā and Śaṅkara's Commentary,* 4th ed. (Mysore: Ramakrishna Ashram, 1955). See also T. Vetter, "Die Gauḍapadīya-Kārikās: Zur Entstehung und zur Bedeutung von [A]dvaita," *WZKSA* 22 (1978): 95–131.

24. For example, *Maitrī Upaniṣad* VI, 15; *Muṇḍaka* II, 2, 8.

25. Contained in H. R. Bhagavat (ed.), *Minor Works of Śrī Śaṅkarācārya,* Poona Oriental Series No. 8 (Poona: Oriental Book Agency, 1952), pp. 374–402.

26. Several complete English translations of the *Śaṅkarabhāṣya* are available: G. Thibaut (*SBE,* vols. 34 and 38); Swami Gambhirananda (Calcutta: Advaita Ashrama, 1965) makes use of some major classical commentaries; P. Deussen's German translation is still of importance. Out of the numerous publications dealing with Śaṅkara and his Advaita Vedānta a few may be mentioned: S. G. Mudgal, *Advaita of Śaṅkara: A Reappraisal* (Impact of Buddhism and Sāṁkhya on Śaṅkara's Thought) (Delhi: Motilal Banarsidass, 1975). Haripada Chakraborti, "Śaṅkarācārya" in *Asceticism in Ancient India* (Calcutta: Punthi Pustak, 1973); D. N. Lorenzen, "The Life of Śaṅkarācārya" in F. Clothey and J. B. Long (eds.), *Experiencing Śiva* (Columbia, Mo.: South Asia Books, 1983); P. Hacker, "Eigentümlichkeiten der Lehre und Terminologie Śaṅkaras: *Avidyā, Nāmarūpa, Māyā, Īśvara,*" ZDMG 100 (1950): 246–86; idem. *Vivarta: Studien zur Geschichte der illusionistischen Kosmologie und Erkenntnistheorie der Inder* (Wiesbaden: Akademie der Wissenschaften Mainz, 1953); E. Deutsch, *Advaita Vedānta:*

A Philosophical Reconstruction (Honolulu: University of Hawaii, 1969); and E. Deutsch and J. A. B. van Buitenen (eds.), *A Source Book of Advaita Vedānta* (Honolulu: University of Hawaii, 1971). See also, R. V. Das, *Introduction to Śaṅkara* (Calcutta: Firma K. L. M. Mukhopadhyay, 1968); K. S. Murty, *Revelation and Reason in Advaita Vedānta* (Waltair: Waltair University, 1961). Authoritative and important studies on various aspects of Advaita Vedānta are also contained in the essays by S. K. Maitra, *Fundamental Questions of Indian Metaphysics and Logic* (Calcutta: Chuckerverrty, Chatterjee and Co., 1959–61); and H. G. Coward (ed.), *Studies in Indian Thought. Collected Papers of Prof. T. R. V. Murti* (Delhi: Motilal Banarsidass, 1984). The most exhaustive survey of the source literature for Advaita Vedānta is R. Thangaswami, *A Bibliographical Survey of Advaita Vedānta Literature* [Sanskrit] (Madras: University of Madras, 1980).

27. Sureśvara in his *Naiṣkarmyasiddhi* refers to Śaṅkara as "the source of pure knowledge . . . and of illumination"; he calls him "omniscient," "the guru of gurus," and compares him to Śiva himself. Śaṅkara, as is well known, is one of the names of Śiva. The *Naiṣkarmyasiddhi* has been edited and translated by K. K. Venkatachari (Adyar: Adyar Library, 1982). For Sureśvara's teaching and his relationship to Śaṅkara see the Introduction to R. Balasubramanian (ed. and trans.), *The Taittirīyopaniṣad Bhāṣya-Vārtika of Sureśvara,* 2d ed. (Madras: The Radhakrishnan Institute for the Advanced Study of Philosophy, University of Madras, 1984).

28. A. Nataraja Aiyer and S. Lakshminarasimha Sastri, the authors of *The Traditional Age of Śrī Śaṅkarāchārya and the Maths* (Madras: Private Publication, 1962), not only provide the lists of all the successors to Śaṅkarācārya, relying on eminent scholars who "have already proved that the date of Śaṅkara is 509–477 B.C." (Preface), but also bring excerpts from court cases initiated in our century in order to settle the claims of candidates and countercandidates to some *gaddis* (headships of *maṭhas*).

29. For biographical details see M. Yamunacarya, *Rāmānuja's Teachings in His Own Words* (Bombay: Bharatiya Vidya Bhavan, 1963), pp. 1–39; also J. B. Carman, *The Theology of Rāmānuja. An Essay in Interreligious Understanding,* Yale Publications in Religion 18 (New Haven, Conn., and London: Yale University Press, 1974), Chapter 2, "Rāmānuja's Life."

30. See Krishna Datta Bharadwaj, *The Philosophy of Rāmānuja* (New Delhi: Sir Sankar Lall Charitable Trust Society, 1958); Arvind Sharma, *Viśiṣṭādvaita Vedānta: A Study* (New Delhi: Heritage Press, 1978).

31. R. Balasubramanian, a contemporary Indian scholar, formerly head of the S. Radhakrishnan Institute for the Advanced Study in Philosophy at the University of Madras, which under T. M. P. Mahadevan's leadership had become the leading modern scholarly centre for Advaita, responds to this criticism in *Some Problems in the Epistemology and Metaphysics of*

Rāmānuja, Professor L. Venkataraman Endowment Lectures 1975–76 (Madras: University of Madras, 1978). See also J. Grimes, *The Seven Great Untenables (sapta-vidhā anupapatti)* (Delhi: Motilal Banarsidass, 1990).

32. S. N. Dasgupta, *HIPh*, vol. 3, p. 471.

33. This is the last verse of the *Vedāntasūtra* meaning "no return, on account of the scripture words."

34. In English see *Rāmānujabhāṣya*, trans. G. Thibaut, in SBE, vol. 48, p. 1904. The text edition used is *Śrī Bhagavad Rāmānuja Granthamāla*, ed. P. B. Annangaracharya Swami (Kanchipuram: Granthamala Office, 1956).

35. For details see B. N. K. Sarma, *Madhva's Teachings in His Own Words* (Bombay: Bharatiya Vidya Bhavan, 1961), pp. 1–26, and also the major works of the same author: *Philosophy of Śrī Madhvācārya* (Bombay: Bharativa Vidya Bhavan, 1962); *A History of the Dvaita School of Vedānta and Its Literature*, 2 vols. (Bombay: Bookseller Publishing Co., 1960–61). A very thorough work is S. Siauve, *La doctrine de Madhva* (Pondichery: Institut Français d'Indologie, 1968).

36. Text and French translation with introduction and notes in S. Siauve, *La voie vers la connaissance de Dieu sélon l'Aṇuvyākhyāna de Madhva* (Pondichery: Institut Français d'Indologie, 1957).

37. *Aṇuvyākhyāna*, 13.

38. *Mahānārāyāṇopaniṣad* 1f.

39. R. Raghavendracharya (ed.) *Madhva Brahmasūtrabhāṣya with several commentaries*, 4 vols. (Mysore: Government Branch Press, 1922); S. S. Rau (trans.), *Madhva's Commentary on the Brahmasūtras* (Madras: Thompson and Co., 1904).

40. Swami Nikhilananda (ed. and trans.), *Ātmatbodha*, 2d ed. (Mylapore: Ramakrishna Math, 1962); Swami Jagadananda (ed. and trans.), *Upadeśasahasrī* (Madras: Ramakrishna Math, 1961); Swami Madhavananda (ed. and trans.), *Vivekacudāmaṇi* (Calcutta: Ramakrishna Math, 71966).

41. Swami Nikhilananda (ed. and trans.), *Vedāntasara* (Calcutta: Ramakrishna Math, 1959).

42. Swami Swahananda (ed. and trans.), *The Pañcadaśī* (Madras: Ramakrishna Math, 1967). Vidyāraṇya is supposed to be identical with Mādhavācārya, the author of the famous *Sarvadarśanasaṁgraha*, and head of the Śṛngerī Maṭh from 1377 to 1386. In India, *Vedāntasāgara* [Hindī] by Swami Nīścaldās of the nineteenth century enjoys a very great reputation. A Sanskrit version of this work has also been published.

43. S. S. Suryanarayana Sastri (ed., trans., and commentator), *Vedāntaparibhāṣa* (Adyar: Adyar Library, 1942).

44. S. S. Raghavacar (ed. and trans.), *Vedārthasaṅgraha* (Mysore: Ramakrishna Math, 1956).

45. Swami Adidevananda (ed. and trans.), *Yatīndramatadīpikā* (Mylapore: Ramakrishna Math, 1949).

46. V. Krishnamacarya (ed. and trans.), *Vedāntakarikāvalī* (Adyar: Adyar Library 1950).

47. P. Nagaraja Rao (ed. and trans.), *Vādāvalī* (Adyar: Adyar Library, 1943).

28. HINDU REFORMS AND REFORMERS

1. S. Radhakrishnan, *My Search for Truth* (Agra: Agrawala, 1946), pp. 6f.

2. I am thinking specifically of the "Nātha movements," such as the Gorakhnātha and the Kabīr Panth, the Sikh community founded by Gurū Nanak, and similar groups. See G. H. Wescott, *Kabīr and the Kabīrpanth* (Calcutta: Susil Gupta, 1953); M. A. Macauliffe, *The Sikh Religion: Its Gurus, Sacred Writings and Authors*, 6 vols. (Oxford: Oxford University Press; reprinted in 3 vols., Delhi: S. Chand, 1963); and more recent works by H. McLeod.

3. In "Hinduism a Static Structure or a Dynamic Force" in *Nehru Abhinandan Granth* (Calcutta: Nehru Abhinandan Granth Committee, 1949), A. S. Altekar, a highly repected scholar, wrote: "It was an evil day when the non-official change-sanctioning authority, the *Daśāvara pariṣad* of the *Smṛti* was replaced by a government department presided over by the Minister for Religion. For, when Hindu rule came to an end by the thirteenth century, this department also disappeared, and during the last 600 years Hinduism has remained more or less static. With no authoritative and intelligent agency to guide him, the average Hindu believes that religious beliefs, philosophical theories and social practices, current in the twelfth century, are of hoary antiquity, it is his conviction that they are all sanctioned by the scriptures (which he does not understand), and that to depart from them is unpardonable sin" (pp. 421f).

4. Second edition (Madras: Christian Literary Society for India, 1900).

5. Ibid., p. 12.

6. Ibid., pp. 40ff. See also C. T. Jackson, *The Oriental Religions and American Thought* (Westport, Conn.: Greenwood Press, 1981), Chapter 5, "The Missionary View."

7. The first major study was J. N. Farquar, *Modern Religious Movements in India* (Oxford: Oxford University Press, 1914). Since then countless studies have been produced by Indian and foreign scholars. See N. S. Sarma, *Hindu Renaissance* (Banaras: Banaras Hindu University, 1944).

8. *Complete Works of Swami Vivekananda,* 8 vols. (Calcutta: Advaita Ashrama, 1970–1971), vol. 3, p. 151.

9. Ibid., vol. 5, p. 152.

10. The most recent work is S. C. Crawford, *Ram Mohan Roy: Social, Political and Religious Reform in Nineteenth Century India* (New York: Paragon House, 1987). As a source still indispensable is M. C. Parekh, *The Brahmo Samāj* (Calcutta: Brahmo Samaj, 1922).

11. A party of orthodox Brahmins, in an attempt to get the law rescinded traveled to London to state their case; Ram Mohan Roy also journeyed there, dying in Birmingham in 1833.

12. Important contemporary documents are collected in J. K. Majumdar, *Raja Rammohun Roy and Progressive Movements in India,* vol. 1. *A Selection from Records (1775–1845)* (Calcutta: Brahmo Mission Press, n. d.), p. 19, reproduces the list of names who voted for and against the abolition of *satī.*

13. The cover story of *India Today* (15 June 1986): 26–33, "Female Infanticide: Born to Die." Also child marriages are still quite common in India as a feature article, "Wedding of the Dolls" (pp. 74–77) in the same magazine demonstrates.

14. See. M. C. Parekh, *The Brahmo Samāj.*

15. The text with English translation by Hem Chandra Sarkar appeared as a Centenary Edition (Calcutta: Brahmo Samāj, 1928).

16. See. M. C. Parekh, *Brahmarṣi Keshub Chander Sen* (Rajkot: Oriental Christ House, 1926).

17. See Lala Lajpat Rai, *The Ārya Samāj* (London: Longmans, 1932). Major work on Dayānanda Saraswatī and the Ārya Samāj has recently been done by J. Jordens whose findings are apt to revise the prevailing impressions. Dāyānanda's main work is *Satyārtha Prakāśa,* published first in the Āryan-era year of 1972949060 and reprinted many times (English translation Allahabad: Kal Press, 1947).

18. D. G. Tendulkar, *Mahatma,* 8 vols. (Bombay: V. K. Jhaveri, 1951–1958), with numerous illustrations; Suresh Ram, *Vinoba and His Mission,* 3rd ed. (Banaras: Akhil Bharata Sarva Seva Sangh, Rajghat, 1962).

19. *Young India* (6 October 1921).

20. Ibid.

21. Modhi Prasad, *A Gandhian Patriarch. A political and spiritual biography of Kaka Kalelkar,* Foreword by Lal Bahadur Shastri (Bombay: Popular Prakashan, 1965), p. 21.

22. The source of all books about Ramakrishna is the voluminous *Gospel of Ramakrishna,* an English rendering of the transcript of all the utterances of Ramakrishna over many years. See Swami Nirvedananda, "Sri Ramakrishna and Spiritual Renaissance," in *CHI,* vol. 4, pp. 653–728, published by this institute. There is a large amount of literature informing about the main figures of the Ramakrishna Mission and its activities published by this movement.

23. *Complete Works,* vol. 3, p. 139.

24. Ibid., vol. 3, pp. 27–29.

25. The Sri Aurobindo Ashram Pondichery is bringing out all the writings of Śrī Aurobindo and informs through numerous magazines, films, and so on, also about its present activities.

26. For the works of S. Radhakrishnan see the Bibliography. An informative survey together with an autobiographical sketch is given in: P. Schilpp (ed.), *The Philosophy of Sarvepalli Radhakrishnan* (New York: Tudor Publishing Company, 1952). His son, the historian S. Gopal, wrote a biography that is intimate as well as scholarly, *Radhakrishnan: A Biography* (New Delhi: Oxford University Press, 1989).

27. *Bunch of Thoughts,* p. 123.

28. *The Collected Works of Śrī Ramana Maharsi,* 8 vols., ed. A. Osborne (New York: S. Weiser, 1959). A. Osborne, *Ramaṇa Maharṣi and the Path of Self-Knowledge,* 2d ed. (Bombay: Jaico, 1962). See also *Śrī Maharṣi: A Short Lifesketch,* 4th ed., with many photographs (Tiruvannamalai: Ramanashramam, 41965).

29. Swami Sivananda published a large number of books and tracts at Sivananda Publication League, Sivanandanagar. About him, see the brief biography of his successor, Swami Cidananda, *Light Fountain* (Rishikesh: Divine Light Society, 1967), and K. S. Ramaswami Sastri, *Śivānanda: The Modern World Prophet* (Rishikesh: Divine Life Society, 1953).

30. The numerous and often reprinted books by Jiddu Krishnamurti are transcripts of his public addresses and questions and answers noted down by his numerous followers. One of the most popular is his *The First and Last Freedom* with a Foreword by Aldous Huxley (London: V. Gollancz,

1967). One of the last, *The Awakening of Intelligence* (New York: Avon Books, 1976), contains a by now famous interview with physicist David Bohm. About him see Pupul Jayakar, *J. Krishnamurti: A Biography* (Delhi: Penguin India, 1987).

31. See C. Das Gupta, *Mother as Revealed to Me* (Banaras: Shree Shree Anandamayi Sangha, 1954).

32. See *Autobiography of a Yogi* (Bombay: Jaico, 1960) and the magazines of the Yoga Fellowship.

33. Martin Eban (ed.), *Maharishi the Guru. The Story of Maharishi Mahesh Yogi* (Bombay: Pearl Publications, 1968). See also the numerous periodical publications of this movement.

34. See *Back to Godhead,* the magazine of the Hare Krishna movement, which gives several times in each issue complete lists of the works of the founder guru.

35. His works have been collected under the title *Wanderings in the Himalayas* (Madras: Ganesh, 1960).

36. See his twelve-volume commentary on the Bhagavadgītā and his monthly publication, *Tapovan Prasād,* as well as the pamphlets issued in connection with the Sandeepany Sadhananlaya.

37. See *Satya Sāī Speaks,* 6 vols. (Kadugodi: Śrī Sathya Sai Education and Publications Foundation, 1974–75).

38. H. Sunder Rao, "The Two Babas" *Illustrated Weekly of India* (21 November 1965).

39. "Call to Revive Hinduism: Viswa Sammelan," *Times of India* (10 December 1977).

40. See M. N. Roy, *Materialism,* 2d ed. (Calcutta: Renaissance Publishers, 1951). In the Foreword to the second edition he wrote: "Since this book was written in 1934 and first published in 1940 religious revivalism has gained ground in philosophical thought. Mystic and irrationalistic tendencies have become more and more pronounced even in social philosophy and political theories. These developments are the symptoms of an intellectual crisis." See also his *New Humanism,* 2d ed. (Calcutta: Renaissance Publishers, 1953).

41. P. C. Chatterji, *Secular Values for Secular India* (Delhi: Lola Chatterji, 1986).

42. *Illustrated Weekly of India* (5 February 1965). It must be kept in mind that this English language weekly does not necessarily reflect the opinion of the traditional non-English-speaking Hindus.

43. *SEMINAR* 64 (December 1964).

44. S. K. Haldar, *SEMINAR* 64 (December 1964): 20ff.

45. J. Duncan M. Derret, *The Death of a Marriage Law. Epitaph for the Rishis* (reprint, New Delhi: Vikas, 1978). A. S. Altekar (see note 3) blames the opposition on a misunderstanding: "This utter and pitiable ignorance of the real nature of Hinduism is at the root of the amazing opposition which measures like the Hindu Code have evoked in the recent past even in educated circles. . . . Our ancient *rishis* never expected that the rules that they had laid down would be regarded as binding for ever by their descendants. They themselves have pointed out the necessity of making periodical changes in them." Altekar refers here to *Manusmṛti* IV, 60. One of the major symptoms of "secularism" in India is the rapidly increasing divorce rate. See *India Today* (31 December 1986), "Divorce Getting Common" 86–93. The New Hindu Marriage Act also allows Hindu women to file for divorce and expect alimony from their former husbands.

46. As Peter Robb, "The Challenge of Gau Mata: British Policy and Religious Change in India, 1880–1916" *Modern Asian Studies* 20, no. 2 (1986): 285–319, has shown, the agītātion against cow slaughter, which is a major political issue in today's India, has a rather long history.

47. V. K. Sinha, "Secularization," *SEMINAR* 269 (January 1982): 37–40.

48. T. N. Madan, "Secularism in Its Place" *JAS* 64, no. 4 (1987): 747–759.

49. See also P. C. Upadhaya, "The Politics of Indian Secularism," *Modern Asian Studies* 26, no. 4 (1992): 815–53.

50. See, e.g., the article "Nice People, Nasty Mood" by Madhu Jain, in *India Today* (15 February 1993): 72–73.

51. Some more on this in K. Klostermaier, "Truth and Tolerance in Contemporary Hinduism," in E. Furcha (ed.) *Papers from the 1990 Symposium on Truth and Tolerance* (Montreal: McGill University, 1990), pp. 125–49.

29. MAHĀTMĀ GANDHI: A TWENTIETH-CENTURY KARMAYOGI

1. Einstein made this comment at the occasion of Mahātmā Gandhi's sixtieth birthday in 1939. Published in *Albert Einstein: Ideas and Opinions* (New York: Crown Publishers, 1985), pp. 77f.

2. The best and most detailed Gandhi biography to date is D. G. Ten-

dulkar's eight volumes *Mahātmā: Life and Work of Mohandas Karamchand Gandhi* (Bombay: V. K. Javeri, 1951–54; 2d ed., 1989) with a Preface by Pandit Nehru.

3. Several editions from Navajivan Publishing House, the literary heir of Gandhi's writings. M. K. Gandhi, *An Autobiography, or The Story of My Experiments with Truth,* translated from the original Gujarati by Mahadev Desai (London: Penguin Books, 1982).

4. *Mahātmā,* vol. 1, p. 39.

5. Ibid. , p. 44.

6. Ibid. , p. 71.

7. *Autobiography,* p. 365.

8. See *Mahātmā,* vol. 1, pp. 75–78.

9. *A Guide to Health* (Madras, 1930), p. 3: "The relation between the body and the mind is so intimate that, if either of them got out of order, the whole system would suffer. Hence it follows that a pure character is the foundation of health in the real sense of the term, and we may say that all evil thoughts and evil passions are but different forms of disease."

10. *Mahātmā,* vol. 1, p. 103.

11. *Hind Swarāj or Indian Home Rule* appeared, first serialized in *Indian Opinion,* then as a separate booklet (Bombay. 1910); edition used (Navajivan, 1944).

12. Gokhale on Gandhi: "A purer, a nobler, a braver, and a more exalted spirit has never moved on this earth" *Mahātmā,* vol. 1, p. 137.

13. Quoted according to the Navajivan edition, 1955.

14. *Mahātmā,* vol. 2, p. 99.

15. *Young India* (31 December 1931).

16. *Young India* (4 November 1926).

17. *To the Students,* p. 46.

18. *Young India* (25 September 1924).

19. *Mahātmā,* vol. 2, p. 92.

20. *Mahātmā,* vol. 2, p. 347.

21. *To the Students,* p. 47.

22. *Mahātmā,* vol. 4, pp. 50ff.

23. *To the Students.*

24. *Harijan* (28 July 1946).

25. *Constructive Program,* p. 13.

26. *Harijan* (20 July 1947): "*Satyāgraha* can rid society of all evils, political, economic and moral."

27. Preface to the English edition of *Hind Swarāj,* 1938.

28. Facsimile of Gandhi's own handwriting of the "Talisman" in *Mahātmā,* vol. 8.

29. *Constructive Program,* p. 12.

30. *Young India* (4 May 1921).

31. *Harijan* (3 October 1947).

30. HINDU NATIONALIST POLITICS AND HINDUISM AS A WORLD RELIGION

1. Cover story *India Today* (31 May 1986): 76–85.

2. There are notable exceptions. Journals like *SEMINAR* have long warned of "Hindu Fascism," and several scholars have studied the development of right-wing political Hinduism.

3. An extract (in translation) from *Ānanadamaṭha* with the full text of the *Bande Mātarām* is provided in W. T. de Bary (general ed.), *Sources of Indian Tradition* (New York and London: Columbia University Press, 1958), vol. 2, pp. 156ff. The Akhil Bhāratiya Sant Samiti, an organization of *sādhus* in support of Hindu political parties, founded in 1989 by Swāmi Vāmadeva, advocates the readoption of the "*Bande Mātarām*" as the national anthem of India, because it considers the "*Janaganamana,*" the present anthem "a manifestation of slave-mentality . . . since it was sung at the welcoming ceremony of King George V in India." See K. K. Klostermaier's translation of the manifesto of the Sant Samiti in *JVS,* 1, no. 1 (1992): 176–79.

4. See M. J. Harvey, "The Secular as Sacred? The Religio-Political Rationalization of B. G. Tilak" *Modern Asian Studies* 20, no. 2 (1986): 321–31.

5. The full text of the manifesto is reproduced in M. Pattabhiram (ed.), *General Elections in India 1967. An Exhaustive Study of Main Political Trends* (Bombay: Allied Publishers, 1967), pp. 217ff.

6. Samagra Savarkar Wangmaya, *Hindū Rāṣṭra Darśan,* 6 vols. (Poona: Maharastra Prantik Hindu Sabha, 1964).

7. A very well-researched account of the background of N. Godse and the events up to and including Gandhi's assassination is given in L. Collins and D. Lapierre, *Freedom at Midnight* (New York: Simon and Shuster, 1975; reprint New York: Avon Books, 1980).

8. M. A. Jhangiani, *Jana Sangh and Swatantra: A Profile of the Rightist Parties in India* (Bombay: Manaktalas, 1967). Also see V. P. Varma, *Modern Indian Political Thought*, 4th ed. (Agra: L. N. Agrawala, 1968); and S. Ghose, *Modern Indian Political Thought* (New Delhi: Allied Publishers, 1984).

9. Quoted in M. A. Jhangiani, ibid., p. 10.

10. See the "election manifesto" in Pattabhiram, *General Elections in India in 1967*, pp. 204ff.; also Deendayal Upadhyaya, "Jana sangh" *SEMINAR* 89 (January 1967): 34–37; and "A Democratic Alternative" *SEMINAR* 80 (April 1966): 21–24.

11. See K. Saxena, "The Janata Party Politics in Uttar Pradesh (1977–79)," *Indian Political Science Review* (July 1983): 172–87. The vindictiveness of the Janata government vis-à-vis the former Congress leaders is quite vividly described in Chapter 15 of the biography of the former President of India, *Giani Zail Singh*, by Surinder Singh Johar (New Delhi: Gaurav Publishing House, 1984).

12. *India Today* (15 February 1993): 59–63.

13. The *Viśva Hindū Pariṣad* publishes a monthly *Hindū Viśva*. In a special issue, brought out before the Prayaga Sammelan, January 1966, a number of prominent leaders spelled out the essence of the movement in Hindī and English articles: e.g., S. S. Apte, "Visva Hindu Parisad. Confluence of Hindu Society" *Hindū Viśva* (January 1966): 87–89.

14. The article in *India Today* quoted at the beginning of this chapter calls the Viśva Hindū Pariṣad "the intellectual arm of the R.S.S., with a million dedicated workers in 2500 branches all over India."

15. Information on the origin and structure of the R.S.S. is contained in literature mentioned in note 7. *SEMINAR* 151(March 1972) had a major article on the R.S.S. by D. R. Goyal and provided a fairly extensive bibliography pp. 40f. More recent publications are referred to in P. Dixit, "Hindu Nationalism" *SEMINAR* 216(August 1977): 27–36. *The Illustrated Weekly of India's* cover story on its March 12, 1978, was "How Powerful Is the R.S.S. ?" It also carried an interview with Balasaheb Deoras. The R.S.S. publishes a weekly magazine, *The Organiser*. See also C. P. Barthwal, "Rashtriya Swayamsevak Sangh: Origin, Structure and Ideology" *Indian Political Science Review* (December 1983): 23–37. "Open Offensive" *India Today* (30 June, 1989): 58–61, claims that the R.S.S. has over 25, 000

branches in almost 20, 000 cities and villages with about 2 million activists and 5 million members.

16. *Bunch of Thoughts* (Bangalore: Vikrama Prakashan, 1966), Chapter 1, "Our World Mission" pp. 9f.

17. *Illustrated Weekly of India* (12 March 1978): 11. See also L. Rattanani and Y. Ghimire's recent report on the R.S.S. "Manning All Battle Stations" *India Today* (15 January 1993): 55.

18. His principles are laid down in *Rām Rājya aura Marxvāda* (Gorakhpur: Gītā Press, 1956).

19. See K. P. Karunakaran, "Regionalism." *SEMINAR* 87 (November 1966): 21–25.

20. *The Illustrated Weekly of India* devoted its March 15, 1970, issue to the theme "Private Armies." Meanwhile much has been written on them.

21. See, e.g., A. George, *Social Ferment in India* (London: Athlone Press, 1986); also K. K. Gangadharan, "Shiv Sena" *SEMINAR* 151 (March 1972): 26–32.

22. N. K. Singh, "Ānandmārg," *SEMINAR* 151 (March 1972): 21–25, with bibliography. Also see "Ānand Mārg's Lust for Blood" *Illustrated Weekly of India* (30 October 1977).

23. P. C. Chaterji, "Secularism: Problems and Prospects" Chapter 7 in *Secular Values for Secular India* (New Delhi: Lala Chatterji, 1986), gives a fairly detailed account of some of the major recent communal riots and their genesis. See also S. P. Aiyar, *The Politics of Mass Violence in India* (Bombay: Manaktalas, 1967).

24. Louis Dumont, in a very incisive study, "Nationalism and Communalism" in *Religion, Politics and History in India* (The Hague: Mouton, 1970), pp. 89–110, operates with a definition of communalism provided by W. C. Smith in *Modern Islam in India*, 3rd ed. (Lahore: Mohammed Ashraf, 1963), p. 185, as "that ideology which emphasizes as the social, political and economic unit the group of adherents of each religion, and emphasizes the distinction, even the antagonism, between such groups." "Communalism" is, in a certain sense, a specifically Indian phenomenon; large enough to make sure that the routine Western sociology and political science approach to Indian society is inadequate. Nirmal Mukarji, "The Hindu Problem" *SEMINAR* 269 (January 1982): 37–40.

25. Moin Shankar, "Social Roots of Communalism" *RS*, 31, no. 4 (1984): 24–44.

26. Ajit Roy, "Communalism—Its Political Roots" *RS* 31, no. 4 (1984): 14–23. Ajit Roy is editor of *Marxist Review*.

27. "RSS Open Offensive," *India Today* (30 June 1989): 58–61.

28. Volume 13, no. 12 (December 1991): 1 and 4.

29. See also "Swamis in Politics," *Hinduism Today* 13, no. 7 (July 1991): 25–26.

30. "Pilgrim's Protest" *India Today* (15 March 1993): 74–76.

31. Upadhyaya, "A Democratic Alternative," p. 23: "Ideology-based parties and policy-oriented politics are desirable, for they alone can sublimate politics and distinguish it from the game of self-aggrandizing power-hunting . . . an education of the people on an ideological and programmatic basis is necessary so that they are freed of casteism, communalism and regionalism."

32. See, "One-Nation Challenge" *India Today* (15 February 1993): 15.

33. See, "Nice People, Nasty Mood," *India Today* (15 February 1993): 72–73.

34. A. S. Altekar, "Hinduism; A Static Structure or a Dynamic Force," p. 425.

CHRONOLOGY

1. *MLBD Newsletter* (January 1993): 7.

2. See H. D. Sankalia, "Paleolithic, Neolithic and Copper Ages" in *HCIP*, vol. 1, pp. 125–42. Major archeological research has been reported by B. Allchin and F. R. Allchin, *The Rise of Civilization in India and Pakistan* (Cambridge: Cambridge University Press, 1982); G. C. Possehl (ed.), *Harappan Civilisation: A Contemporary Perspective* (Warminster: Aris and Philips, 1982). For locations of Stone Age archeological sites in India see *HASA* plate II, p. 1; Neolithicum and Chalcolithicum plate II, 2 with reproductions of characteristic artefacts and appropriate text information, pp. 263–66. For a map of locations of Harappan and other contemporary South Asian cultures, see *HASA* plate II, p. 3, and text pp. 266f.

3. J. F. Jarrige, "Die frühesten Kulturen in Pakistan und ihre Entwicklung" in Philipp von Zabern (ed.), *Vergessene Städte am Indus, Frühe Kulturen in Pakistan vom 8. bis zum 2. Jahrtausend* (Mainz: Verlag Philipp von Zabern, 1987), pp. 50–66; See also G. Quivron "Die neolithische Siedlung von Mehrgarh," ibid., pp. 67–73.

4. *HASA* map "India as Revealed in the Mahābhārata," Plate III A. 2, pp. 164f., text and bibliography, p. 266.

5. Ibid., "India as Revealed in the Rāmāyaṇa." Plate III A. 1, p. 164, text and bibliography, p. 266.

6. Ibid., "Vedic India," Plate III A, pp. 162ff, text and literature, p. 266.

7. J. G. Shaffer, "Prehistory" in "Addenda and Corrigenda" *HASA*, p. 265a.

8. See P. C. Sengupta, *Ancient Indian Chronology*, illustrating some of the most important astronomical methods (Calcutta: University of Calcutta, 1947). See also S. C. Kak, "The Indus Tradition and the Indo-Aryans" *The Mankind Quarterly* 32, no. 3 (1992): 195–213.

9. See A. D. Pusalker, "Historical Traditions," in *HCIP*, vol. 1, pp. 271–336. F. E. Pargiter, *Ancient Indian Historical Tradition* (reprint Delhi: Motilal Banarsidass, 1962), starting from Purāṇic records takes a notably different departure and assumes that the Āryans entered India from the mid-ranges of the Himālayas and settled around Banaras ca. 2300 B.C.E. before spreading westward and eastward, so that the decline of the Indus civilization would not have any causal connection with the Āryan invasion.

10. *Ancient Indian Chronology*, pp. 101f.

11. S. B. Roy, "Chronological Infrastructure of Indian Protohistory" *Journal of the Bihar Research Society* 58 (1972): 44–78; and "Chronological Framework of Indian Protohistory—The Lower Limit," *JOIB* 32, nos. 3–4 (1983): 254–74.

12. M. R. Mughal, "Recent Archeological Research in the Cholistan Desert," in G. Possehl (ed.), *Harappan Civilization. A Contemporary Perspective*. See also the map of Vedic India in *HASA*, plaate II, p. 2.

13. About these and other eras used in India, see L. Renou and Jean Filliozat (eds.), *L'Inde Classique*, vol. 2 (Paris and Hanoi: Imprimerie National, 1953), Appendix 3, "Notions de chronologie," pp. 720–38.

14. See also *HASA*, the folding map "A Chronology of South Asia Third Millennium to 1975" and "1975–1990" showing development in various areas in five parallel columns. Also "Timeline of Hinduism: A Chronological Account of Hinduism from 400,000 B.C.E." *Hinduism Today*, insert (November 1991).

Glossary

abhāva	Nonperception (in the Nyāya system); nonbeing (in the Vaiśeṣika system).
abhaya	Fearlessness; in iconology, *abhaya mudrā* is the hand pose of a deity, inspiring confidence and trust.
abhiniveśa	Desire; in the yoga system, instinctive craving for life.
abhiṣeka	Anointment, part of installation ceremony of a king and an image of the deity.
abhyāsa	Exercise, practice, exertion.
abhyudaya	Rise of sun or other heavenly bodies; festival.
ācamana	Rinsing of mouth with water before worship and before meals.
acara	Immobile (used as an attribute of the Supreme Being).
ācārya	Master (also used as equivalent to M.A.).
acetana	Without consciousness (used as attribute of matter).
acintya	Beyond intellectual understanding.
ādāna	Taking away.
adbhuta	Marvellous, miraculous.
adharma	Unrighteousness, evil.
adhidaivata	Presiding deity.
adhikāra	Qualification (especially of students of religion).
adhikāraṇa	Section of a textbook.
adhiyajña	Principal sacrifice.
adhyāsa	Superimposition; misidentification.
adhyātma	Supreme; spiritual; relating to the Supreme Being.
adhyāya	Chapter (of a treatise).
aditi	Vedic Goddess, "Mother Earth," mother of *ādityas*.
ādivāsī	Original inhabitants; appellation adopted by the tribals of India.
adṛṣṭa	Invisible; important technical term in the Nyāya and Vaiśeṣika systems as well as in linguistic speculation.

advaita	Nonduality; name of a school of Vedānta.
ādya prakṛti	Primeval matter.
āgama	Source, beginning; name of a class of writings considered as revealed by the Śaivas.
aghora	Horrible; name of a sect of Śaivites.
agni	Fire; one of the foremost Vedic gods.
agnicayana	A particular kind of Vedic fire sacrifice.
agnihotra	A Vedic fire sacrifice.
agniṣṭoma	Fire sacrifice.
ahaṁkāra	Principle of individuation; egotism.
ahiṃsā	Not killing; nonviolence.
ahita	Improper, unwholesome, not propitious.
aiśvarya	Lordliness.
aja	Unborn (masc.); attribute of the Supreme Being; billygoat.
ajā	Unborn (fem.), attribute of primordial matter; nannygoat.
akala	Without parts; attribute of Supreme Being.
akāma	Without desire.
ākāśa	Ether (one of the five elements of India cosmology); space.
ākhyāna bhāga	Narrative part of a sacred text.
akhāḍā	Place of assembly; proper noun for establishments of some sects.
akhila	Undivided; complete.
akṛti	Uncreated; eternal principle underlying words.
akṣara	Imperishable; syllable (letter); name of Supreme Being.
alaṁkāra	Ornament; technical term for ornate literature.
amara	Immortal.
amarṣa	Impatience; anger; passion.
aṃbikā	Mother; Mother Goddess.
amṛta	Nectar; draught of immortality.
aṃśa	Part, fragment.
anādhāra	Without support.
anādi	Without beginning; eternal.
ānanda	Bliss; used as last part of the proper name of many *samnyāsis*.
ananta	Without end; proper name of the world snake upon which Viṣṇu rests.
aṇava	Veil; congenital ignorance concerning the ultimate; stain.

aṅga	Member, constituent part, for example, of a major work.
aṇimā	Smallness; in Yoga the faculty to diminish one's size.
aniruddha	Free, without hindrance; proper name of one of the *vyūhas* of Viṣṇu.
anitya	Not permanent; transient.
añjali	A handful (e.g., of flowers).
aṅkuśa	Goad; one of the divine weapons.
anna	Food, especially rice; formerly, sixteenth part of a rupee.
anṛta	Against the (moral) law.
anta	End, death.
antarātman	Conscience.
antaryāmin	The 'inner ruler', the Supreme Being as present in the heart (literally understood).
antyeṣṭi	Last rites.
aṇu	Atom.
anubhava	Experience.
anugraha	Attraction; grace of God.
anumāna	Inference.
apara	Unsurpassed; attribute of the Supreme Being.
aparādha	Fault, sin.
aparādha kṣamāpañca	Prayer for forgiveness of faults.
aparigraha	Without having (and wanting) possessions.
aparokṣa	Immediate, present.
apas	Water.
apāśraya	Supportless.
apauruṣeya	Not human-made; technical term to describe the supernatural origin of the Veda in the Mīmāṃsā system.
āpsara	Nymph.
apūrva	Technical term in the Mīmāṃsā system to denote the not-yet realized effect of a sacrifice.
araṇya	Forest.
arcā	Rites of worship of an image.
arcāvātāra	Image of God, who took on this form to become an object of worship for the devotees.

ardha	Half.
ardhanārīśvara	Figurative representation of Śiva, in which one half shows a male figure, the other half a female one.
arghya	Water to rinse hands before worship or before meals.
arjuna	Bright; proper name of the hero of the Bhagavadgītā.
arka	Sun.
artha	Object; meaning; wealth.
arthāpatti	Inference, presumption.
ārya	Noble (man); self-designation of the Āryans.
asaṃbaddha	Unfettered; incoherent (talk).
āsana	Seat, sitting posture.
asat	Not true; "not real."
āśīrvāda	(Ritual) blessing.
āsmitā	Egoism; abstract noun from *asmi*, "I am."
aspṛha	Without desire.
āśrama	Hermitage; stage in life; proper name of a group of *saṁnyāsis*.
aṣṭāgraha	A certain constellation of sun, moon, earth, and the five major planets.
aṣṭāvaraṇa	Eight concealing (clouding) veils of the Self.
asteya	Not stealing.
āstika	Someone who accepts the authority of the Veda; orthodox.
aśubha	Inauspicious.
asuras	Demons; class of superhuman beings.
asūyā	Indignation; envy, jealousy.
aśvamedha	Horse sacrifice.
aśvatha	A tree (*ficus sacra*).
aśvins	Vedic gods, a pair of brothers; in astronomy, Castor and Pollux.
ātmakūṭa	Self-deceit.
ātman	Self.
ātmanastuṣṭi	Contentment.
audarya	Being in the womb.
audārya	Generosity.
āvāhana	Invitation of the deity at worship.
avatāra	Descent (of god in a bodily form).
avidyā	Ignorance (of reality).
avyakta	Unmanifest.

āyurveda	Traditional Indian medicine; literally, "life knowledge."
bābā(jī)	"Little Father"; affectionate nickname for ascetics.
bala	Strength, power.
bandha	Bondage.
bhadra	Well, happy; blessing.
bhāga	Luck, fortune.
bhagavan	Lord; most general title of god.
bhāī [Hindī]	Brother; most common appellation.
bhajana	Devotional recitation.
bhakti	Love, devotion.
bhasma	(Sacred) ashes.
bhāṣya	Commentary.
bhāva	Condition; emotion; nature.
bhaviṣya	Future.
bhaya	Fear, terror.
bheda	Difference.
bhikṣu	Mendicant; proper name of Buddhist monks.
bhoga	Enjoyment.
bhū, bhūmī	Earth; proper name of Viṣṇu's second consort.
bhukti	Enjoyment.
bhūta	A being, a spirit.
bibhatsa	Trembling.
bīja	Seed.
binḍu	Crescent.
brahmā	(Personal) creator god.
brahmacari	Student; celibate.
brahmacarya	First period in life, celibate studenthood.
brahmaloka	World of Brahmā; highest abode.
brahman	(Impersonal) absolute.
Brāhmaṇa	Member of the highest caste; class of ritual texts.
brahmārandra	The place from which the soul departs at death (the backside of the cranium).
buddhi	Intelligence; in the Sāṁkhya system name of the first product of the union of *puruṣa* and *prakṛti*.
caitanya	Spirit, consciousness, also proper name for the Supreme; proper name of a Bengali saint of the sixteenth century.
caitta	Consciousness.
cakra	Circle, disc; centers in body; one of Visnu's weapons; discus.
cakravarti	Universal ruler.

caṇḍa	Moon; silver.
candāla	Wild; bad; proper name of lowest caste; outcaste.
caṇḍana	Sandalwood.
caṇḍī	Fierce woman; proper name of Devī.
capāti	Bread; flat unleavened wheat breads.
carita	Biography.
caryā	Activity; mode of behavior.
caturmukha	Four faced; proper name of Brahmā.
caturvarṇāśrama	The four *varṇas* ("castes") and stages of life.
chāyā	Shadow.
choṭī	The wisp of hair left on the top of the head.
cit	Consciousness; spirit.
citta	thought.
daitya	A goblin, a slave, a demon.
dakṣiṇa	Sacrificial fees.
dakṣiṇācāra	Right-handed path.
dāna	Gift; charity.
darśana	View; audience; theory; philosophical system.
dāsa	Servant; often part of proper name.
daśanāmi	Ten named; proper name of a religious order.
dasyu	Slave; name for non-Āryan in Ṛgveda.
dayā	Compassion.
deva, devatā	Divine (superior) being.
devayāna	Path of the gods.
devī	Goddess.
dhairya	Firmness.
dhāma	Area; body.
dhāraṇa	Support.
dharma	"law," religion, support, and so forth.
dharmaśāstras	Lawbook.
dharmakṣetra	"The field of righteousness."
dhatṛ	Giver; proper name for God.
dhātu	Root (in grammar).
dhṛti	Firmness.
dhūpa	Incense.
dhyāna	Meditation; concentration in Yoga.
digvijaya	Conquest of the four quarters; appella-

	tion of the successful competition of a religious teacher.
dīkṣā	Initiation.
dīpa	Lamp.
dohā	A couplet in Hindī poetics.
dravya	Substance; material (for sacrifice).
droha	Malice.
duḥkha	Sorrow, suffering.
dvaita	Duality; name of a school of Vedānta.
dvaitādvaita vivarjita	Beyond duality and nonduality.
dvandva	Pair of opposites (hot-cold, etc.).
Dvāpara-yuga	Second era of each *kalpa*.
dveṣa	Hatred.
dvijati	Twice born; appellation of the three upper castes whose initiation is considered a second birth.
dvīpa	Island; continent.
dyaus	Resplendent; sky; Vedic high god.
ekādaśī	Eleventh day (of each half-month); sacred to Vaiṣṇavas.
ekāgratā	One-pointedness, single-mindedness.
ekoddiṣṭa	Funeral ceremony for one deceased.
ekaśṛṅga	One horn (unicorn); the fish descent (of Viṣṇu) with one horn, on which Manu fastened his raft and thus was saved in the great flood.
gaddi	Throne, seat, headship (as of a *maṭha*).
gambhīrya	Serenity; seriousness.
gandharva	Celestial musician.
Gaṇeśa	Lord of the celestial armies; elephant-headed son of Śiva and Parvati.
garbha	Womb; *garbha-gṛha;* innermost sanctuary of the temples.
garuḍa	Viṣṇu's vehicle; gryphius.
gāyatrī	The Vedic formula that a Brahmin is supposed to recite thrice a day.
ghāṭ(a)	Steps; especially flight of steps leading to a river.
ghī	Liquified butter.
gopī	Milkmaid.
gopura	Towerlike structure over entrance into (South) Indian temple compounds.

gośālā	Old-age home for cows, maintained for religious reasons.
gosvāmi	Lord of cows; title for high-ranking Vaiṣṇavas of certain communities.
gotra	Stable; family, descent.
grantha	(Sacred) book; an ancient Indian script.
gṛhasta	House father, male head of household.
gṛhastya	Second stage in the life of a Hindu (as householder).
gṛhyasūtras	Scriptures setting down the rituals to be performed in the home.
guṇa	Quality.
guru	Elder; spiritual master; teacher in general.
gurukula	School according to the ancient Indian pattern.
hala	Plough.
halāhala	Poison churned up from the Milk Ocean, consumed by Śiva to save the world.
hara	Literally, the one who takes away; name of Śiva.
hari	Literally, the yellowish green one; name of Viṣṇu.
harṣa	Joy.
hasyā	Laughter.
haṭhayoga	Literally, forced or violent Yoga; physical exercises.
hetu	Cause.
hiṃsā	Violence, killing.
Hindutva	"Hindudom," Hinduism as cultural and political, over against "Hindu dharma," as a religious concept.
hiraṇyagarbha	Literally, golden womb; in cosmology the first being.
hita	Beneficial, good.
hitavācana	Well-intentioned speaking.
hlādinī	Enjoyment.
holi	Popular festival (India carnival); New Year.
homa	Fire oblation.
hotṛ	Class of Vedic priests.
hṛdaya	Heart; core of something.
icchā	Wish, desire.
iḍā	Name of one of the main vessels in the body according to traditional Indian physiology.
indriya	Sense organs.

īrṣyā	Envy, jealousy.
iṣṭa	Preferred, wished for; *iṣṭa-deva,* the god of one's choice.
īśvara	Lord; God.
itihāsa	History; technical term for the epics; historical proof.
jāgarita	Waking consciousness.
jagat	World; for example, *jagadguru* is the world preceptor.
jāl(a)	Net (symbol for the world entangling the spirit).
jana sangha	Literally, people, community; name of (rightist) political party.
janëu	Sacred thread worn by the three upper castes.
japa	Repetition of the name of God or a *mantra* .
jātakarma	Rites performed at time of birth.
jātī	Birth; race, family, "subcaste."
jaya	Victory; also as greeting; "hail."
jīva(-ātman)	Life; individual living being.
jñāna	Knowledge; *jñānaniṣṭha* is the state of being firmly and irrevocably established in ultimate knowledge.
jñāni	A knower (of the absolute).
jyotiṣa	One of the auxiliary sciences of the Veda, astronomy and astrology.
jyotiṣṭoma	A seasonal sacrifice for the departed.
kaivalya	"Aloneness"; ultimate aim of Yoga.
kāla	Time; black color; fate; death.
kālamukha	Black mouth; name of Śiva; name of a Śaivite sect.
Kālī	The "black one"; name of the terrible form of the goddess.
Kali-yuga	Age of strife; last period in each world era (*kalpa*).
kalki	The future (last) *avatāra* of Viṣṇu in the form of a white horse.
kalpa	World era, day of Brahmā (432 million years); ritual; one of the auxiliary sciences of Veda, for example, *kalpasūtras* is the texts describing sacrificial rituals.
kāma	Desire, lust, love; name of god of love.
kāmadhenu	"Wish-fulfilling cow."
kāṇḍa	Part (of a text).

kāpalī	Literally, one with a skull; name of followers of certain Śaivite groups.
kāraṇa	Cause; title of the Supreme Being; God.
karma	Work; action; result of an action.
karyā	Worship of an image through various acts.
kaṣṭa	Evil; wrong; harsh.
kaupina	Small stip of cloth to cover the private parts; the only garment worn by many ascetics.
kavi	Poet, wise man, omniscient.
khadga	Sword.
khila-bhāga	Supplement (of texts).
kīrtaṇa	Congregational religious singing.
kleśa	Suffering; pain.
kośa	Sheath; cover; treasury; lexicon.
kriyā	Activity; skill; exercises.
krodha	Anger.
kṛpā	Favor; grace.
Kṛṣṇa	Black; proper name of the most famous *avatāra* of Viṣṇu.
Kṛta-yuga	The first age in each world era; the golden age.
kṣamā	Forgiveness.
kṣaṇa	Moment; shortest time measure.
kṣatriya	Warrior; the second caste.
kṣetra	Field; also metaphorical.
Kubera	God of wealth, king of the *yakṣas*, friend of Śiva.
kuṃbha	Water pot; astronomically, sign of Aquarius.
kumbha-melā	A great gathering at specific holy places every twelfth year.
kuṇḍalinī	Serpent; in Tantricism, life energy.
kūrma	Tortoise; one of the *avatāras* of Viṣṇu.
kuśa	A kind of grass required in Vedic rites.
lajjā	Modesty; shame.
lakṣaṇa	Characteristic; attribute; sign.
līlā	Play.
liṅga	Characteristic sign; subtle nature; phallic symbol of Śiva.
lobha	Greed.
loka	World; sphere; for example, *loka-nāṭha* is the Lord of the world.
lokasaṅgraha	Universal welfare.
mada	Intoxication; dementia.
Mādhava	Sweet like honey (*madhu*); proper name of

	Kṛṣṇa; proper name of several famous philosophers.
madhurasa	Literally, honey sentiment; highest love and affection.
madhuvidyā	Literally, honey knowledge; see, Upaniṣads.
mahā	Great.
mahant(a)	Head of a monastic establishment.
maharṣi	Great sage; honorific title.
mahat	Great; in the Sāṁkhya system, first evolute (intellect).
mahātmā	Great soul; honorofic title.
Maheśvara	Great lord; proper name of Śiva.
mahiṣa	Buffalo; proper name of a demon killed by Devī.
maithuna	Copulation; pair; astronomically, Gemini.
makara	Crocodile; alligator.
mala	Stain.
mālā	Garland; chain; "rosary" of beads.
maṃsa	Meat.
māna	Pride; idea, concept; honor.
manas	Mind.
mānasa	Mind born.
mānava	Relating to Manu; human, for example, *mānavadharma* is the laws given by Manu; laws valid for the entire humankind.
maṇḍala	Circle; section of Ṛgveda.
maṇḍapa	Covered hall; tent.
mandira	Palace; temple.
maṅgala	Auspicious, lucky.
maṅgala-śloka	An opening verse or prayer of a text to ensure that the undertaking is auspicious.
maṇi	Jewel.
mantra	Word, formula (especially from scriptures).
Manu	Ancestor of humankind.
manvantara	An age of one (of fourteen) Manu (432 million years); according to Hindu tradition we live now in the seventh *manvantara* (seven more are to follow before the end).
mārga	Way; street; especially in metaphor, path of salvation.
mārjāra	Cat.
markaṭa	Monkey.
marut	Wind; wind god.

maṭha	Monastic establishment.
mātsara	Jealous; selfish.
matsya	Fish.
māyā	Fiction, illusion.
melā	Fair, assembly.
mīmāṃsā	Inquisition; system; proper name of one *darśana*.
mithyā	Futile; false.
mleccha	"Barbarian" somebody who does not belong to Hindu culture.
moha	Delusion.
mokṣa	Liberation.
mṛtyu	Death.
mudrā	(Hand) pose.
muhūrta	Thirtieth part of day, about 45 minutes, "hour."
mukta	One who is liberated; for example, *jīvan-mukta* is one liberated while still living in the body.
mukti	Liberation; for example, *mukti-dātā* is the giver of liberation.
mūla	Root; *mūla-prakṛti* is primary matter.
mūla-bera	The firmly installed image in a temple.
mūla-saṃhitā	Original text.
Mulayahan	Name of demon, personification of evil, subdued by Śiva.
mumukṣutva	Desire for liberation.
muni	Literally one who keeps silence; ascetic; "monk."
mūñja	A kind of grass.
mūrti	Literally, embodiment; figure; image.
muśala	Hammer.
nāda	(Loud) sound.
nāḍī	(Body) vessel, nerve.
nāga	Superior being; snake; naked, heretic.
nagna	Naked.
naivedya	Food offered to the image of God (prepared under certain conditions to ensure its purity).
nāmakīrtana	Congregational singing whereby the name of God is repeated.
nāma-rūpa	Name and form; individuality.
namaskāra	Greeting in a spirit of worship.
nandi	Śiva's vehicle; a bull.
naraka	Hell.
Nāsadīya	Title of a famous Ṛgvedic hymn beginning with *nāsad* ("there was not").

nāstika	Heretic; someone who denies the authority of the Veda.
nāstikya	Irreligiosity.
naṭarāja	Kind of dance, title of Śiva.
nāṭha	Lord; for example, Viśvanaṭha is the Lord of the Universe.
nigama	Veda; authoritative scripture.
nigamana	Quotation (from Veda); in logic, deduction, conclusion.
nīla	Dark blue, for example, *Śiva nīlakaṇṭha* is Śiva with a dark-blue throat.
nimeṣa	Moment (shortest measure of time).
nimitta	Cause.
nirguṇa	Without qualities or attributes.
nirukta	Classical work of etymology.
niṣkala	Without part; undivided, complete.
niṣkāma	Without desire; for example, *niṣkāma karma* is action done without selfish motive.
nīti	"Ethics" rules for life.
nitya	Eternal.
nivṛtti	Withdrawal.
niyama	(Negative) commandment.
nṛsinha	Man-lion; one of the *avatāras* of Viṣṇu.
nyāya	Rule, method; motto; logic; syllogism.
pada	Foot; verse.
pāda	Part of a text.
padārtha	Category (in Vaiśeṣika system).
padma	Lotus.
pādya	Water for washing feet in ritual.
pañca	Five; for example, *pañcāgni* is five fires.
pañcāṅga	The traditional Indian calendar.
pañcagavya	The five products of the cow.
pāñcarātra	Branch of Vaiṣṇavism.
pañcatantra	Famous collection of allegorical animal stories.
pañcāyat(a)	"Council of five" the traditional caste or village authority.
pañcāyātana-pūjā	Worship of five gods.
panda	Pale; proper name of father of the Pāṇḍavas.
paṇḍa	Family Brahmin who performs the traditional rituals.
paṇḍit(a)	Learned man; honorific title.

pantha	Path, way; for example, *Kabīr-pantha* is the religious sect founded by Kabir.
pāpa	Sin.
para	Beyond; supreme; liberation.
paradravyābhīpsā	Desiring another's property.
paradroha	Injurious in speech or deed.
paramārthika	That which concerns ultimate reality.
paraṃparā	Tradition.
paraśurāma	Rāma with the battleaxe; one of the *avatāras* of Viṣṇu.
paricaraṇa	Attenting; rendering service.
parikrama	Circumambulation.
paritrāṇa	Deliverance.
paruṣa	Harsh speech.
Pārvatī	"Daughter of the mountains"; name of Śiva's consort.
pāśa	Fetter.
pāṣaṇḍa	Heretic; unbeliever; hypocrite.
paśu	Animal; cattle; in Śaivasiddhānta: unliberated men.
paśupati	Lord of the animals; name of Śiva.
patra	"Leaf," scripture, scroll.
pattiśa	Spear.
pāvana	Purifying; holy; fire.
pavitra	Ritually pure; holy.
phala	Fruit; result of an action.
piṇḍa	Small ball of rice that is offered to ancestors oblation.
piṅgalā	One of the major vessels in the body.
piśāca	Imp; ogre.
pitāmahā	Grandfather, often used as proper name of Brahmā.
pitṛ	Ancestor, forefather; *pitṛyāna* is the path of the ancestor.
plakṣa	A tree (*ficus Indica*).
prabhā	Splendor.
pradākṣinā	Respect shown through certain actions.
pradhāna	Head; source; in Sāṁkhya system, ground from which everything develops.
prajāpati	Lord of creatures; creator.
prakāśa	Splendor.
prakṛti	Matter; nature.

pralaya	Dissolution of the world.
pramāda	Error.
pramāṇa	Logical proof; means of cognition.
prāṇa	Life breath.
prāṇava	The mantra OM.
prāṇayama	Breath control.
prārabdha	Remained (or karma of former births).
prārthana	Prayer.
prasthāna trayī	Triad of authorities (Upaniṣads, Bhagavadgītā, Brahmasūtras).
pratibiṃba	Reflection; mirror image.
pratijñā	Recognition; proposition.
pratisarga	Dissolution of the universe.
pratisiddha maithuna	Unlawful liaison.
pratyabhijñā	Recognition.
pratyakṣa	Immediate (sense) perception.
pravṛtti	Inclination; active liberation.
prayaścitta	Atonement (through certain prescribed acts).
prayatna	Effort.
premā	Love; used as technical term for spiritual love.
preta	Soul of a deceased who has not (yet) received offerings.
prīti	Amity; love.
priyavācana	Gentle of speech.
pṛthivī	Earth.
pūjā	Worship.
punarjanma	Rebirth.
punarmṛtyu	Redeath.
puṇḍarīkākṣa	Lotus eyed.
puṇya	Merit.
pura	Fort.
purāṇa	Old; proper name of class of authoritative scriptures.
pūrṇimā	Full moon.
purohita	Class of Vedic priests.
puruṣa	Man; person; supreme being; spirit.
puruṣārtha	Aim of human life.
puruṣottama	Supreme person.
puṣpa	Flower.
puṣṭimārga	Special form of *bhakti*, "way of grace."

putra	Son.
rāga	Passion; in music; basic tune.
rāgānuga bhakti	"Passionate love"; special form of *bhakti.*
rājanīti	Statecraft.
rajas	Excitement; one of the basic three *guṇas.*
rājayoga	"Royal way"; name of Patañjali's Yoga system.
rajñī	Splendor.
rakṣasa	Goblin.
raktāṃbara	Red clothed, a name for Buddhist monks.
Rāma	Main hero of the Rāmāyaṇa; general name for God.
rāmarājya	Rāma's rule; "kingdom of God."
rasa	Juice; sentiment.
rathamelā	Chariot feast.
rati	Pleasure; proper name of consort of god of Love.
ratna	Jewel; pearl; often used as honorific title.
ratrī	Night.
romāñcā	Horripilation; gooseflesh; enthusiasm.
ṛk	Hymn.
ṛṣi	Seer; wise man.
ṛta	(Vedic) law of the world (moral and cosmic).
ṛtvik	Class of Vedic priests.
Rudra	Reddish; name of Vedic god; name of Śiva especially in his frightful aspect.
rudrākṣa	"Rudra's eye"; rough-round seed of an Indian shrub, used in garlands of Śaivites.
Rukminī	Kṛṣṇa's spouse.
śabda	Sound; word; scriptural authority.
saccidānanda	The Supreme Being (being, consciousness, bliss).
sadācāra	Morality; good behavior.
ṣaḍdarśana	The six orthodox systems.
sādhana	Means (to gain liberation).
sādhaka	One who practices a *sādhana..*
sādhāraṇa dharma	Common law; religion common to humankind.
sādhu	"Holy man"; mendicant.
sādhvī	A female ascetic.

sāgara	Sea; great mass of things.
saguṇa	With qualities; for example, *saguṇa brahman* is Brahman with attributes.
sahajā	Natural; inborn.
sahāmārga	One of the practices of Śaivasiddhānta.
śākhā	Branch; a school of thought of practice.
sākṣātkāra	Bodily vision of the supreme.
sākṣī	Witness; the Supreme as present in humans.
śākta	Follower of Śakti cult.
Śakti	Power; name of Śiva's consort.
śālagrāma	Ammonite; symbol under which Viṣṇu is present.
sālokya	Sharing the same world; one of the stages of liberation.
samādhī	Deep concentration; death; memorial.
sāman	Vedic tune.
sāmānya	Equality; category in Vaiśeṣika.
samāvāya	Similarity.
samāveśa	Togetherness.
saṃbhoga	Enjoyment.
saṃdhyā	Twilight; dusk and dawn; prayers recited at dawn.
saṃdhyā-bhāṣā	Words with double meaning.
saṃhitā	Collection; name of class of authoritative scriptures.
samīpa	Nearness; stage of liberation.
samjñā	Understanding.
sāṁkhya	Figure, number; proper name of philosophical system.
saṁkīrtana	Congregational singing.
samnyāsa	Renunciation.
samnyāsi	Ascetic, homeless mendicant.
sampat	Wealth.
saṃpradāya	A religious order or sect.
saṃsāra	World; connoting constant cyclic change.
saṃskāra	Rites; "sacraments."
saṃskṛtam	Artfully composed, refined, name of old Indian high language.
samyama	Concentration.
sanātana dharma	Eternal law; "Hinduism."
śaṅkha	Conch shell.

sanmārga	"The true way"; highest stage in *Śaivasiddhānta.*
sanskṛti	Culture.
śānta	Sentiment of peacefulness.
santāpa	Heat; compunction; atonement.
śanti	Peace.
santoṣa	Contentment.
śaraṇāgatī	Seeking refuge.
sarga	Creation; emanation.
sāraṅga	Bowstring.
śarīra	Body.
sārūpa	Of equal form.
sarvauṣadi	Mixture of all (healing) herbs.
śāstra	Doctrine; treatise.
śāstri	One who knows the traditional doctrine; B.A.
sat	Being, truth.
satī	"Faithful," wife who (voluntarily) dies with deceased husband.
śatasahasrasaṃhitā	Collection of 100,000 verses; proper name for the Mahābhārata.
satsaṅg	"Gathering of the righteous," religious meeting.
sattva	Being; nature; virtue; one of the three *guṇas.*
satya	Truth; reality.
śauca	Purity.
saulabhya	Benevolence.
sauśilya	Kindness.
śava	Corpse; Śiva with out *i* (*śakti*) is *śava.*
savitṛ	Sun god.
sāyujya	Togetherness.
śeṣa	The endless, immortal world serpent upon which Viṣṇu rests.
sevā	Service.
siddha	Accomplished; saint.
siddhi	Accomplishment; in Yoga, extraordinary faculties.
śikhā	Tuft on the crown of the head.
śikhara	Spirelike elevation over central sanctuary.
śīksā	Instruction.

śīla	Good behavior; morality.
śirīṣa	A tree (acacia).
Sītā	Furrow; proper name of Rāma's consort.
śloka	Double verse.
smāsana	Cremation ground.
smṛti	What has been committed to memory; proper name for a certain class of scriptures.
snāna	(Ritual) bath.
śoka	Sorrow.
Soma	Intoxicating drink used in Vedic sacrifices.
spaṇḍaśāstra	Part of Kāśmīr Śaivism; treatise of vibrations.
sphoṭa	Boil; idea; connection between letter and meaning.
spṛha	Worldliness.
śraddhā	Faith.
śrāddha	Last rites.
śrautasūtras	Ritual texts dealing with public Vedic sacrifices.
śravaṇa	Listening to the recitation of religious texts.
Śrī	Fortune; proper name of Viṣṇu's consort; Sir.
śrīvatsa	Mark on Viṣṇu's body signifying Lakṣmī's presence.
śṛṅgāra	Feeling of erotic love.
ṣṛṣthi	Creation; emanation.
śruti	What has been revealed and heard.
steya	Stealing.
sthūla	Gross material.
stithi	Maintenance.
stotra	Hymn in praise of God.
strīdhāna	Marriage.
śubha	Auspicious.
sūcanā	Calumny.
śuddha	Pure.
śuddhi	Ritual of purification (for readmission into caste).
śukha	Bright.
sūkṣma	Subtle.
sūkta	Vedic hymn.
sūnā	Activity (or place) where life is harmed.
śuṇya	Zero; nothing; emptiness.
sura	Divine being.
surā	Intoxicating drink.
Sūrya	Sun.

suṣumnā	One of the main vessels in the body.
suṣupti	Dreamless deep sleep.
sūta	Bard; charioteer.
sūtra	Aphoristic textbook; thread.
svadharma	One's own duties.
svādhyāya	Study of Vedic texts.
svāhā	Invocation at offering to *devas*.
svapna	Dream.
svarga	Heaven.
svārtha	Self-contained.
svāstika	Sign of auspiciousness.
svatantra	Free.
svayambhu	Being of itself; name for Supreme Being.
swāmī	Lord; today usually "Reverend."
Śyāma	Black; name of Kṛṣṇa.
tamas	Darkness; dullness; one of the three *guṇas*.
tantra	Loom; system of practices; main branch of Hinduism.
tapas	Heat; energy.
tapasvi	Ascetic; one who has accumulated much merit through self-mortification.
tarka	Logic; debate.
tarpaṇa	Offering of water to ancestors.
tat	That; name of the Supreme Being.
tatetat	This is that; identity of Self and Supreme.
tattva	Principle; nature; reality, element.
tejas	Splendor; light; heat.
ṭīkā	Subcommentary.
tīlaka	Mark on forehead.
tirobhāva	Disappearance.
ṭippaṇī	Gloss.
tīrtha	Fording place; place of pilgrimage (on holy river).
tīrthayātra	Pilgrimage.
tiru	(Tamil) holy; for example, *tiru-kuṛaḷ* is the Tamilveda.
tithi	Moon day.
traividyā	Knowledge of the three Vedas.
Treta-yuga	Third world age.
Trilocana	Three-eyed; name of Śiva.
tri-loka	The three worlds.
trimārga	Literally, "three ways"; the collective name for the paths of works, devotion, knowledge.

tripuṇḍra	Śiva's trident; sign of the forehead.
triśaṇku	Name of a constellation halfway between heaven and earth; name of a mythical king of Ayodhyā.
tristhalī	The three most important places of pilgrimage, viz., Prayāga (Allahābad), Kāśī (Banaras), and Gāyā.
trivarga	The triad of dharma, *artha, kāma.*
tṛṣṇa	Thirst; greed for life.
tulasī	A small tree (holy basil), sacred to Viṣṇu.
turīya	The fourth; designation of highest stage of consciousness.
turyātīta	Beyond the fourth; highest stage in some Hindu schools who claim to transcend the Vedāntic *turīya.*
tyāgi	Renouncer; ascetic.
udāhāraṇa	Example, illustration; part of Nyāya syllogism.
udbhava	Appearance.
uḍambara	Indian fig tree, sacred to Śiva.
udyama	Exertion; rising or lifting up.
upadeśa	Advice; religious instruction.
upādhi	Attribute; title; deceit.
Upagītā	"Lesser Gītā."
upamāna	Analogy.
upaṃśū	Prayer uttered in a whisper.
upanayana	Initiation; investiture with sacred thread.
upāṅga	Auxiliary sciences or texts to Vedāṅgas.
Upaniṣad	Class of authoritative scriptures; secret doctrine.
Upapurāṇa	Lesser Purāṇa.
upāsana	Worship.
upavāsa	(Religious) fasting.
ūrdhva	Upward.
utsava bera	Processional image.
vācika	Audibly uttered.
vahana	Conveyance.
vaicitriya	Manifoldness; distraction.
vaidhi-bhakti	Devotion expression itself through ritual worship.
vaikuṇṭha	Viṣṇu's heaven.
vairāgi(ṇī)	Ascetic (fem.).
vairāgya	Renunciation.
vaiśeṣika	Name of a philosophical system.
vaiśya	Member of third caste; businessman, artisan.

vajra	Diamond; thunderbolt.
vāk	Voice; word.
vālmīka	An anthill.
vāmācāra	Left-handed way (in Tantra).
vāmana	Dwarf; one of the *avatāras* of Viṣṇu.
vaṃśa	Genealogy.
vānaprastha	Forest dweller; third stage in a Brahmin's life.
varāha	Boar; one of the *avatāras* of Viṣṇu.
varṇāśramadharma	Social system of Hindu based on a partition into four classes and four stages of life.
vāstuvidyā	Architecture.
vaṭa	The fig tree.
vātsalya	Love toward a child.
vāyu	Wind; wind god.
veda	Knowledge; sacred knowledge: revelation; scripture.
vedāṅga	Limb of Veda; auxiliary sciences.
Vedānta	End of Veda; Upaniṣads; name of a system.
vedī	Altar for Vedic sacrifices.
vibhava	Emanation.
vibhuti	Supernatural power.
videha	Without a body.
vidhi	Ritual.
vidyā	Knowledge.
vijñānamaya	Made of knowledge.
vinaya	Discipline.
vipra	Brahmin.
vīra	Hero.
virajā	Purity.
virāṭ	First product of Brahman; universe.
vīrya	Heroism.
viṣāda	Despair.
viśeṣa	Propriety.
viśiṣṭa	Qualification.
viśvarūpa	All form.
vitarka	Debate; logical argument.
viveka	Discrimination.
vrata	Vow; celebration.
vrātya	Mendicant; class of people; Supreme Being.
vṛddhi	Growth.

vṛtti	Being; condition; fluctuation; activity, means of subsistence.
vyākaraṇa	Grammar.
vyakta	Manifest; revealed.
vyāpāra	Function.
vyāsa	Arranger; proper name of Vedic sage credited with the compilation of the Vedas, the Mahābhārata and the Purāṇas.
vyavahāra	Livelihood; the world of senses.
vyūha	Part; special manifestation of Viṣṇu.
yajña	Vedic sacrifice.
yajñopavīta	Sacred thread.
yajus	Rites.
yakṣa	Goblin; tree spirit.
yama	God of the netherworld; restraint (yoga).
yantra	Machine; meditational device.
yatanīya	Something to be accomplished.
yati	Wandering ascetic.
yatidharma	Rules for ascetics.
yātrā	Pilgrimage.
Yoga	Yoke; name of a system.
yojana	"Mile" (either four, five, or nine miles).
yoni	Source; womb.
yuga	World era.

Abbreviations Used

ABORI	*Annals of the Bhandarkar Oriental Institute* (Poona)
BSOAS	*Bulletin of the School of Oriental and African Studies* (London)
CHI	*The Cultural Heritage of India* (general ed., H. Bhattacharya)
ERE	*Encyclopedia of Religion and Ethics (ed. J. Hastings)*
HASA	*Historical Atlas of South Asia* (ed. J. Schwarzberg, 2d ed.)
HCIP	*The History and Culture of the Indian People* (general ed., R. C. Majumdar)
HDhS	*History of Dharmaśāstra* (P. V. Kane)
HIL	*A History of Indian Literature* (ed. Jan Gonda)
HIPh	*History of Indian Philosophy* (S. N. Dasgupta)
HOS	*Harvard Oriental Series* (Cambridge, Mass.)
HR	*History of Religion* (Chicago)
IFR	*Indian and Foreign Review*
JAAR	*Journal of the American Academy of Religion*
JAOS	*Journal of the American Oriental Society* (New Haven)
JAS	*Journal of the Asian Society* (Ann Arbor)
JBRS	*Journal of the Bihar Research Society* (Patna)
JIPH	*Journal of Indian Philosophy*
JOIB	*Journal of the Oriental Institute* (Baroda)
JRAS	*Journal of the Royal Asiatic Society*
JVS	*Journal of Vaiṣṇava Studies*
KSBCCV	*Kuppuswami Sastri Birth Centenary Commemoration Volume* (Madras: Kuppuswami Research Institute)
RS	*Religion and Society* (Bangalore, Delhi)
SBE	*Sacred Books of the East* (Oxford University Press)
SBH	*Sacred Books of the Hindus* (Allahabad: Panini Office)
WZKSA	*Wiener Zeitschrift für die Kunde Südasiens*
ZDMG	*Zeitschrift der Deutschen Morgenländischen Gesellschaft*
ZRGG	*Zeitschrift für Religions- und Geistesgeschichte*

Bibliography

Abbot, J. E. (ed. and trans.). The Poet Saints of Mahārāṣṭra, 12 vols., Poona: Scottish Mission Industries, 1926–41.

Abhyankar, V. S (ed.) *Nyāyakośa* by Bhīmācārya, Poona: Bhandarkar Oriental Research Institute, 1978.

Agni Purāṇa. Poona: Anandashram, 1957

Agni Purāṇa, trans. M. N. Dutt, 2 vols. Reprint Banaras: Chowkhambha, 1967.

Agrawal, D. P. "The Technology of the Indus Civilization. " In *Indian Archeology, New Perspectives*, ed. R. K. Sharma, pp. 83–91. Delhi: Agam Kala Prakashan, 1982.

Agrawala, V. S. *India as Known to Pāṇini*, 2d ed. Banaras: Prithvi Prakasan, 1963.

———. *Matsya-Purāṇa: A Study*. Banaras: All-India Kashiraj Trust, 1963.

———. "Mother Earth." In *Nehru Abhinandan Granth*, pp. 490ff. Calcutta: Nehru Abhinandan Granth Committee, 1949.

Ahirbudhnyasaṃhitā, 2 vols., ed. M. D. Rāmānujacarya; 2d ed., ed. V. Krishnamacharya. Adyar: Adyar Library, 1966.

Aiyangar, S. K. *Some Contributions of South India to Indian Culture*. Calcutta: Calcutta University, 1942.

Aiyar, C. P. Ramaswamy. *Fundamentals of Hindu Faith and Culture*. Trivandrum: Government Press, 1944.

Aiyar, S. P. *The Politics of Mass Violence in India*. Bombay: Manaktalas 1967.

Aiyer, A. N. and S. L. Shastri. *The Traditional Age of Śrī Śaṅkarāchārya and the Maths*. Madras: private publication, 1962.

Aiyer, V. G. Ramakrishna. *The Economy of a South Indian Temple*, Annamalai: Annamalai University, 1946.

Ajitagama, ed. N. R. Bhatt, 2 vols. Pondichery: Institut Français d'Indologie, 1964–67.

Ali, S. *The Congress Ideology and Programme*. New Delhi: People's Publishing House, 1958.

Ali, S. M. *The Geography of the Purāṇas*. New Delhi: People's Publishing House, 1966.

Alisaunder. *Alexander: Alexander and Dindimus*, ed. W. W. Skeat, Latin text. Early English Text Society, Extra Series No. 31, 1876; reprint Oxford: Oxford University Press, 1930.

Allchin, B., and R. Allchin. *The Rise of Civilization in India and Pakistan.* Cambridge: Cambridge University Press, 1982.

Alper, H. P. "Siva and the Ubiquity of Consciousness." *JIPH* (1976): 345–407.

Altekar, A.D. "Hinduism, A Static Structure or a Dynamic Force?" In *Nehru Abhinandan Granth,* pp. 421–25. Calcutta: N.A.G. Committee, 1949.

———. *The Position of Women in Hindu Civilization from Prehistoric Times to the Present Day.* Banaras: Motilal Banarsidass, 1956.

———. *Sources of Hindu Dharma in its Socio-Religious Aspect.* Sholapur: Institute of Public Administration, 1952.

id. *State and Government in Ancient India,* 4th ed. Delhi: Motilal Banarsidass, 1962.

Ambedkar, B. R. *What Congress and Gandhi Have Done to the Untouchables,* 2d ed. Bombay: Thacker and Co., 1946.

Amore, R. C., and L. D. Shinn. *Lustful Maidens and Ascetic Kings: Buddhist and Hindu Stories of Life.* New York: Oxford University Press, 1981.

Anand, M. R. *The Hindu View of Art.* Bombay: Popular, 1957.

———. *Coolie.* Bombay: Katub, 1957.

———. *Untouchable.* Bombay: Jaico, 1956.

Sri Anandamurti. *Anandamarga,* 2d ed. Anandanagar: private publication, 1967.

Ancient Indian Tradition and Mythology (English translation of all the *Mahapuranas*), 50 vols. Delhi: Motilal Banarsidass, n.d.

Anderson, W. K., and S. D. Dhamle. *The Brotherhood in Saffron: The Rāṣṭrīya Swayamesevak Sangh and Hindu Revivalism.* Boulder Colo.: Westview Press, 1987.

Animananda, B. *The Blade: Life and Work of Brahmabhandav Upadhyaya.* Calcutta: Roy and Son, n.d.

Aṇuvākhyāna of Madhva. Bombay: Nirnaya Sagara Press, S. S. Rao, trans., 2d ed. Tirupati: 1936.

Aparokṣānubhūti of Śaṅkarācārya, trans. Swami Vimuktananda, 2d ed. Calcutta: Ramakrishna Math, 1955.

Appadorai, A. *Economic Conditions in Southern India 1000—1500 A.D.* , 2 vols. Madras: University of Madras, 1936.

Apte, S. S. "Viśva Hindu Pariṣad. Confluence of Hindu Society." *Hindū Viśva* (January 1966): 87–89.

Apte, V. M. *Ṛgvedic Mantras in Their Ritual Setting in the Gṛhyasūtras.* Poona: Deccan College Research Institute, 1950.

Arapura, J. G. *Hermeneutical Essays on Vedāntic Topics.* Delhi: Motilal Banarsidass, 1986.

Archer, W. G. *India and Modern Art*. London: Allan and Unwin, 1959.

———. *Indian Miniatures*. Greenwich, Conn.: New York Graphic Society, 1960.

———. *The Loves of Krishna in Indian Painting and Poetry*. London: Allen and Unwin, 1957; reprint, New York: Grove Press, 1957.

Armadio, B. A. "The World Made of Sound: Whitehead and Pythagorean Harmonics in the Context of Veda and the Science of Mantra." *Journal of Dharma* 17, no. 3 (1992): 233–66.

———. *Arthasaṅgraha of Laugākṣi Bhāskara*, trans. D. V. Gokhale. Poona: Oriental Book Agency, 1932.

Ashish, Madhava. "The *Sadhu* in Our Life." *SEMINAR* 200 (April 1976): 12–18.

Athalye, D. *Life of Lokmanya Tilak*. Poona: A. Chiploonkar, 1921.

———. *Neo-Hinduism*. Bombay: Tareporevala, 1932.

Atharvaveda. trans. W. D. Whitney, 2 vols. HOS, 1902; reprint Banaras: Motilal Banarsidass, 1962.

The Atharvaveda Saṃhitā, ed. R. Roth and W. D. Whitney. Berlin: 1856.

Ātmabodha of Śaṅkarācārya, 2d ed., trans. Swami Nikhilananda. Mylapore: Ramakrishna Math, 1962.

Atreya, B. L. *The Philosophy of the Yogavāsiṣṭha*. Adyar: Adyar Library, 1936.

Auboyer, J. *Daily Life in Ancient India from Approximately 200* B.C. to A.D. 700. New York: Macmillan, 1965.

Aufrecht, T. *Die Hymnen des Ṛgveda*, 2d ed. Bonn: A. Marcus, 1877.

Aurobindo, Sri. *Essays on the Gītā*. Pondichery: Sri Aurobindo Ashram, 1928.

Ayrookuzhiel, A. M. Abraham. *The Sacred in Popular Hinduism: An Empirical Study in Chirakkal, North Malabar*. Madras: Christian Literature Society, 1983.

Ayyar, C. V. Narayana. *Origin and Early History of Śaivism in South India*. Madras: University of Madras, 1936.

Ayyar, P. V. Jagadisa. *South Indian Festivities*. Madras: Higginbothams, 1921; reprint, New Delhi: Aslan Educational Services, 1982.

Baden-Powell, B. H. *The Indian Village Community*. Reprint New Haven, Conn.: Yale University Press, 1958.

———. *Land Systems of British India*, 3 vols. Oxford: Oxford University Press, 1892.

Bailey, G. M. "Brahmā, Pṛthu and the Theme of the Earth-Milker in Hindu Mythology." *Indo-Iranian Journal* 23 (1981): 105–16.

———. "Notes on the Worship of Brahmā in Ancient India." *Annali dell' Istituto Orientali di Napoli* 39 (1979): 1–170.

Baird, Robert D. (ed.). *Religion in Modern India.* Delhi: Manohar, 1981.

Bakker, H. "On the Origin of the Sāṁkhya Psychology." *WZKSA* 26 (1982): 117–48.

Bālarāma Vedāntasūtrabhāṣya, trans. B. D. Basu. *Sacred Books of the Hindus,* vol. 5. Allahabad: Panini Office, 1934.

Balasubramanian, R. *Advaita Vedānta.* Madras: University of Madras, 1976.

———. *The Mysticism of Poygai Āḷvār.* Madras: Vedānta Publications, 1976.

———. *Some Problems in the Epistemology and Metaphysics of Rāmānuja.* Professor L. Venkataraman Endowment Lectures 1975–76. Madras: University of Madras, 1978.

——— (ed. and trans.). *The Taittirīyopaniṣad Bhāṣya-Vārtika of Sureśvara,* 2d ed. Madras: Radhakrishnan Institute for the Advanced Study of Philosophy, University of Madras, 1984.

Balasundaram, T. S. *The Golden Anthology of Ancient Tamil Literature,* 3 vols. Madras: South India Śaiva Siddhānta Book Publishing Society, 1959–1960.

Balsara, J. F. *Problems of Rapid Urbanisation in India.* Bombay: Manaktala, 1964.

Banerjea, A. K. *Philosophy of Gorakhnāṭh.* Gorakhpur: Mahant Dig Vijai Nath Trust, Gorakhnath Temple, 1962.

Banerjea, J. N. *The Development of Hindu Iconography,* 2d ed. Calcutta: University of Calcutta, 1956.

Banerjea, S. C. *Dharma Sūtras: A Study of Their Origin and Development.* Calcutta: Punthi Pustak, 1962.

Banerjee, G. N. *Hellenism in Ancient India.* Delhi: Munshi Ram Manoharlal, 1961.

Banerjee, N. V. *The Spirit of Indian Philosophy.* New Delhi: Arnold-Heinemann, 1958.

Barthwal, C. P. "Rashtriya Swayamsevak Sangh: Origin, Structure and Ideology." *Indian Political Science Review* (December 1983): 23–37.

Barua, B. M. *History of Pre-Buddhistic Indian Philosophy.* Calcutta: Calcutta University, 1921.

de Bary, W. T. (general ed.). *Sources of Indian Tradition.* New York: Columbia University Press, 1958.

Barz, R. *The Bhakti Sect of Vallabhācārya.* Faridabad: Thompson Press, 1976.

——— and M. Thiel-Horstmann (eds.). *Living Texts from India*. Wiesbaden: Harrassowitz, 1989.

Basham, A. L. *History and Doctrines of the Ājīvikas*. London: Luzac, 1951.

———. *The Wonder That Was India*. New York: Grove Press, 1959.

Baynes, A. *Indian Ethnography: Castes and Tribes*. London: 1912.

Beal, S. *Si-Yu-Ki: Buddhist Records of the Western World*. London: 1884; reprint Delhi: Oriental Books Reprint Corporation, 1969.

Beals, A. R. *Gopalpur: A South Indian Village*. New York: Holt Rinehart and Winston, 1965.

Beane, W. C. *Myth, Cult and Symbols in Śākta Hinduism: A Study of the Indian Mother Goddess*. Leiden: Brill, 1977.

Bechert, H., and G. von Simson. *Einführung in die Indologie*. Darmstadt: Wissenschaftliche Buchgesellschaft, 1979.

Beck, B (ed.). *Folktales of India*. Chicago: University of Chicago Press, 1987.

Belvalkar, S. K. *Shree Gopal Basu Malik Lectures on Vedānta Philosophy*. Poona: Bilvakunja, 1929.

——— and R. D. Ranade. *History of Indian Philosophy*. vol. 2. *The Creative Period*. vol. 3. *Mysticism in Mahārāṣṭra*. Poona: Bilvakunja, 1927 and 1932.

Bengali Religious Lyrics: Śākta, trans. E. J. Thompson and A. M. Spencer. Calcutta: Association Press, 1923.

Benz, E. *Indische Einflüsse auf die frühchristliche Theologie*. Mainz: Mainzer Akademie der Wissenschaften, 1951.

Bernard, T. *Hatha Yoga*. New York: S. Weiser, 1944.

Bernstorff, D. "Das Kastensystem im Wandel." In *Indien in Deutschland*, ed. E. Weber and R. Töpelman, pp. 29–51. Frankfurt am Main: Peter Lang, 1990.

Berreman, G. D. *Hindus of the Himalāyas*. Berkeley: University of California Press, 1963.

Besant, A. *Hindu Ideals*. Adyar: Theosophical Publishing House, 1904.

———. *Wake up, India*. Adyar: Theosophical Publishing House, 1913.

———. *Theosophy and World Problems*. Adyar: Theosophical Publishing House, 1922.

Beteille, A. *Caste, Class and Power: Changing Patterns of Stratification in a Tanjore Village*. Berkeley: University of California Press, 1965.

———. *Castes, Old and New*. New York: Asia Publishing House, 1969.

Betty, L. Stafford (trans.). *Vādirāja's Refutation of Śaṅkara's Non-Dualism: Clearing the Way for Theism*. Delhi: Motilal Banarsidass, 1978.

Bhagavadgītā, trans. F. Edgerton. Cambridge, Mass.: Harvard University Press, 1944.

Bhagavadgītā, trans. S. Radhakrishnan. London: Allen and Unwin, 1956.

Bhagavadgītā, trans. R. C. Zaehner. Oxford: Oxford University Press, 1969.

Bhagavat, H. R. (ed.). *Minor Works of Sri Śaṅkarācārya*, 2d ed. Poona Oriental Series No. 8. Poona: Oriental Book Agency, 21952.

Bhāgavata Purāṇa, 2 vols., text and trans. Gorakhpur: Gītā-Press, 1952–60.

Bhaktirasāmrtasindhu of Rūpa Goswāmi, ed. Vijendra Snataka. Delhi: Dilli Viśvavidyalaya, 1963; trans. Swami Bon Maharaj, 3 vols. Vrindavan: Institute of Oriental Philosophy, 1964–78.

The Bhāmatī of Vācaspati on Śaṅkara's Brahmasūtrabhāṣya, ed. and trans. S. S. Suryanarayana Sastri and C. Kunhan Raja. Adyar: Theosophical Publishing House, 1933.

Bhandarkar, R. G. *Vaiṣṇavism, Śaivism and Minor Religious Systems*. Reprint Banaras: Indological Book House, 1965.

Bharadwaj, K. D. *The Philosophy of Rāmānuja*. New Delhi: Sir Sankar Lall Charitable Trust Society, 1958.

Bharati, Agehananda (L. Fischer). *The Ochre Robe*. Seattle: University of Washington Press, 1962.

———. "Psychological Approaches to Indian Studies: More Cons Than Pros." *The Indian Review* 1, no. 1 (1978): 71–75.

———. *The Tāntric Tradition*. London: Rider and Company, 1965.

Bhardwaj, Surinder Mohan, *Hindu Places of Pilgrimage in India: A Study in Cultural Geography*. Berkeley: University of California Press, 1973.

Bhartṛhari: Vākyapādīya, ed. K. V. Abhyankar and Acharya V. P. Limaye. University of Poona Sanskrit and Prakrti Series, Poona: University of Poona, 1965.

Bhāṣapariccheda with Siddhānta Muktāvalī of Viśvanātha Nyāyapañcanana, trans. Swami Madhavananda. Calcutta: Advaita Ashrama, 1954.

Bhatt, G. P. *The Epistemology of the Bhaṭṭa School of Pūrva Mīmāṃsā*. Banaras: Chowkhamba, 1954.

Bhattacharji, S. *The Indian Theogony: A Comparative Study of Indian Mythology from the Vedas to the Purāṇas*. Cambridge: Cambridge University Press, 1970.

Bhattacharya, H. (general ed.). *The Cultural Heritage of India*, 2d ed., 4 vols. Calcutta: Ramakrishna Mission Institute of Culture, 1957–62.

Bhattacharya, H. D. "Tantrik Religion." In *HCIP*, vol. 4.

Bhattacharya, K. C. *Studies in Vedāntism*. Calcutta: University of Calcutta, 1909.

———. *Studies in Philosophy*, vol. 1. Calcutta: Progressive Publishers, 1956.

Bhattacharya, S. "The Concept of *Bideha* and *Prakṛti-Laya* in the Sāṃkhya-Yoga System." *ABORI* 48–49 (1968): 305–12.

Bhattacharya, T. *The Canons of Indian Art: A Study of Vāstuvidyā*, 2d ed. Calcutta: Firma K. L. Mukhopadhyay, 1963.

———. *The Cult of Brahmā*. Patna: C. Bhatacarya, 1957.

Bhattacharyya, M. "Hindu Religion and Women's Rights." *Religion and Society* 35, no. 1 (1988): 52–61.

Bhattacharyya, N. N. *History of the Tantric Religion*. Delhi: Manohar, 1982.

Bhattojī-Dīkṣita: Siddhānta Kaumudī, ed. and trans. Srisa Candra Vasu, 2 vols. Reprint Delhi: Motilal Banarsidass, 196.

Bhave, V. *Bhoodan-Yajña*. Ahmedabad: Navajivan, 1954.

———. *Sarvodaya and Communism*. Tanjore: Sarvodaya Prachuralaya, 1957.

Biardeau, M. *Théorie de la connaissance et philosophie de la parole dans le brāhmaṇisme classique*. Paris: Mouton, 1964.

Bihari, B. *Minstrels of God*, 2 vols. Bombay: Bharatiya Vidya Bhavan, 1956.

———. *Bhaktā Mīrā*. Bombay: Bharatiya Vidya Bhavan, 1961.

———. *Sufis, Mystics and Yogis of India*. Bombay: Bharatiya Vidya Bhavan, 1962.

Bishop, D. H. (ed.). *Indian Thought: An Introduction*. New York: John Wiley and Sons, 1975.

——— (ed.), *Thinkers of the Indian Renaissance*. New York: Wiley Eastern, 1982.

Blasi, A. J. "Ritual as a Form of Religious Mentality." *Sociological Analysis* 46, no. 1 (1985): 59–72.

Bloomfield, M. *The Religion of the Veda*. New York: G. B. Putnam's, 1908.

———. *Vedic Concordance*. Reprint Delhi: Motilal Banarsidass, n.d.

Bolle, K. W. trans. *The Bhagavadgītā, a New Translation*. Berkeley: University of California Press, 1979.

Boner, A., S. R. Sarma, and R. P. Das. *New Light on the Sun Temple of Konārak: Four Unpublished Manuscripts Relating to Construction History and Ritual of This Temple*. Banaras: Chowkhambha Sanskrit Series Office, 1972.

Bougard-Levin, G., and A. Vigasin. *The Image of India: The Study of*

Ancient Indian Civilization in the USSR. Moscow: Progress Publishers, 1984.

Bose, D. N. *Tantras: Their Philosophy and Occult Secrets*, 3rd ed. Calcutta: Oriental Publishing Co., 1956.

Bose, N. K. "The Geographical Background of Indian Culture." In *CHI*, vol. 1, pp. 3–16.

———. *Peasant Life in India: A Study in Indian Unity and Diversity*. Calcutta: Anthropological Survey of India, 1961.

Bose, N. K., and D. Sen. "The Stone Age in India." In *CHI*, vol. 1, 2d ed., pp. 93–109.

Boyd, R. *An Introduction to Indian Christian Theology*, 2d ed. Madras: Christian Literature Society, 1977.

Brahma, N. K. *Philosophy of Hindu Sadhāna*. London: Trübner, 1932.

Brecher, M. *Nehru: A Political Biography*, London: Oxford University Press, 1959.

Bṛhaddevatā, ed. and trans. A. A. Macdonell. Reprint Delhi: Motilal Banarsidass, 1965.

Bṛhati, Prabhākara Miśra's Sub-Commentary to the Śābarabhāṣya, ed. S. K. Ramanatha Sastri, 3 vols. Madras: University of Madras, 1931–.

Bṛhatsaṃhitā of Varāhamihira, ed. and Hindī trans. Pandit Acutyananda Jha Sarmana. Banaras: Chowkhamba, 1959.

Briggs, G. W. *The Chamars*. Calcutta: Association Press, 1920.

———. *Gorakhanātha and Kānphaṭa Yogis*. Calcutta: Association Press, 1938.

Brown, C. M. *God as Mother: A Feminine Theology in India: An Historical and Theological Study of the Brahmavaivarta Purāṇa*. Hartford, Vt: Claude Stark, 1974.

———. "The Origin and Transmission of the Two *Bhāgavata Purāṇas*: A Canonical and Theological Dilemma." *JAAR* 51, no. 4 (1983): 551–67.

Brown, L. W. *The Indian Christians of St. Thomas*. London: Cambridge University Press, 1956.

Brown, P. *Indian Painting*. Calcutta: YMCA Publishing House, 1960.

———. *Indian Architecture*, 4th ed., 2 vols. Bombay: Taraporevala, 1964.

Brown, W. N. *Man in the Universe: Some Continuities in Indian Thought*, Berkeley: University of California Press, 1966.

———. *The United States and India and Pakistan*. Cambridge: Harvard University Press, 1963.

———. *India and Indology: Selected Articles*, ed. Rosane Rocher. Delhi: Motilal Banarsidass, 1978.

Brunton, P. *Maharṣi and His Message*. London: Rider and Co., 1952.

Buck, H. M., and G. E. Yocum (eds.). *Structural Approaches to South Indian Studies*. Chambersburg, Pa.: Wilson Books, 1974.

Buddhiraja, S. *The Bhagavadgītā: A Study*. Madras: Ganesh and Co., 1927.

Bühler, G. (ed.). *Encyclopedia of Indo-Aryan Research*. 1897; reprint Banaras: Indological Bookhouse, 1963.

———. *The Sacred Laws of the Āryas*. In SBE, vols. 2 and 14. Reprint Delhi: Motilal Banarsidass, 1964.

van Buitenen, J. A. B. *Tales of Ancient India*. New York: Bantam Books, 1961.

———. "The Name Pāñcarātra." *HR* 1, no. 2 (1961): 291–99.

———. *Rāmānuja on the Bhagavadgītā*. Delhi: Motilal Banarsidass, 1965.

Bulcke, C. *Rāmakathā* [Hindī]. Prayag: Hindī Parisad Viśvavidyalaya, 1950.

Burrow, T. *The Sanskrit Language*. London: Faber and Faber, 1965.

Bussabarger, R. F. and B. D. Robins. *The Everyday Art of India*. New York: Dover Publications, 1968.

Caitanya, K. *A New History of Sanskrit Literature*. Calcutta, 1964.

Caitanyacaritāmṛta of Kṛṣṇadāsa Goswāmi (ed. and trans., 2d ed.) London: 1922.

Śrī Caitanyacaritāmṛtam, trans. S. K. Chaudhuri, 3 vols., 2d ed. Calcutta: Gaudia-Math, 1959.

Cakravartti, Viśvanatha. "*Baktirasāmṛtasindhubindu*," trans. K. Klostermaier. *JAOS* 1 (1974): 96–107.

Caland, W., and V. Henry. *L'Agnistoma: description complète de la forme normals du sacrifice de Soma dans le culte. védique*, 2 vols. Paris: E. Léroux, 1906–1907.

Callewaert, W. M., and S. Hemrai. *Bhagavadgītānuvāda: A Study in Transcultural Translation*. Ranchi: Sathya Bharati Publication, 1983.

Campbell, A. *The Heart of India*. New York: Alfred A. Knopf, 1958.

Candidasa, B. *Singing the Glory of Lord Krishna*, trans. M. H. Klaiman. Chico, Calif.: Scholars Press, 1984.

Cārakasaṃhitā, ed. T. Yadava Sarma, 3rd ed. Bombay: Nirnaya Sagara Press, 1933.

Carman, J. B. *The Theology of Rāmānuja. An Essay in Interreligious Understanding*. New Haven, Conn., and London: Yale University Press, 1974.

——— and A. Marglin (eds.) *Purity and Auspiciousness in Indian Society*. Leiden: Brill, 1985.

Carpenter, J. E. *Theism in Mediaeval India*. London: Constable and Co., 1921.

Carstairs, G. M. *The Twice-Born.* London: Hogarth Press, 1957.

Cenkner, W. *A Tradition of Teachers: Śaṅkara and the Jagadgurus Today.* Delhi: Motilal Banarsidass, 1983.

Chaitanya, Krishna. *Sanskrit Poetics.* Bombay: Asia Publishing House, 1965.

Chakladar, H. C. *Social Life in Ancient India,* 2d ed. Calcutta: Greater India Society, 1954.

Chakraborti, Haripada. "Śaṅkarācārya." In *Asceticism in Ancient India.* Calcutta: Punthi Pustak, 1973.

Chakravarti, C. *Tantras: Studies on Their Religion and Literature.* Calcutta: Punthi Pustak, 1963.

Chakravarti, S. C. *The Philosophy of the Upaniṣads.* Calcutta: University of Calcutta, 1935.

Chand, T. *Influence of Islam on Indian Culture.* Allahabad: The Indian Press, 1963.

Chandavarkar, B. D. *A Manual of Hindu Ethics,* 3rd ed. Poona: Oriental Book Agency, 1965.

Chatterjee, B. R. "The *Rāmāyaṇa* and the *Mahābhārata* in South-East Asia." In *CHI,* vol. 2, pp. 119ff.

Chatterjee, M. *Gandhi's Religious Thought.* South Bend, Ind.: University of Notre Dame Press, 1983.

Chatterjee, S. *The Nyāya Theory of Knowledge,* 3rd ed. Calcutta: University of Calcutta, 1965.

Chatterji, C. *Hindu Realism.* Allahabad: The Indian Press, 1952.

Chatterji, P. C. *Secular Values for Secular India.* New Delhi: Lola Chatterji, 1986.

Chatterji, S., and D. M. Datta. *An Introduction to Indian Philosophy,* 7th ed. Calcutta: University of Calcutta, 1968.

Chatterji, S. K. "Contributions from Different Language-Culture Groups." In *CHI* vol. 1, pp. 76–90.

———. *Languages and Literatures of Modern India.* Calcutta, 1963.

———. "Race Movements and Prehistoric Culture." In *HCIP,* vol. 1, 164ff.

Chattopadhyaya, S. *Reflections on the Tantras.* Delhi: Motilal Banarsidass, 1978.

———. *Some Early Dynasties of South India.* Delhi: Motilal Banarsidass, 1974.

Chattopadyaya, S. *The Evolution of Theistic Sects in Ancient India.* Calcutta: Progressive Publishers, 1962.

Chaudhuri, N. C. *Autobiography of an Unknown Indian.* London: Macmillan, 1951.

———. *The Continent of Circe*. Bombay: Jaico, 1966.

———. *The Intellectual in India*. New Delhi: Vir Publishing House, 1967.

———. *Hinduism*. London: Chatto and Windus, 1979.

Chaudhuri, R. "The Niṃbārka School of Vedānta." In *CHI*, vol. 3, pp. 333ff.

———. *Doctrine of Śrīkaṇṭha*, 2 vols. Calcutta: Pracyavani, 1959–1960.

Chemparathy, G. *An Indian Rational Theology. Introduction to Udayana's Nyāyakusumañjalī*. Vienna: De Nobili Research Library, 1972.

Chengappa, Raj. "The Himalayas: Startling Discoveries." *India Today* (15 March 1993), pp. 90–101.

Chethimattam, J. B. *Consciousness and Reality. An Indian Approach to Metaphysics*. Bangalore: Dharmaram Publications, 1967

——— (ed.). *Unique and Universal: Fundamental Problems of an Indian Theology*. Bangalore: Dharmaram Publications, 1972.

Chinmulgund, P. J., and V. V. Mirashi (eds.). *Review of Indological Research in the Last Seventy-Five Years*. Poona: Bharatiya Charitrakosha Mandal, 1967.

Choudhuri, D. C. Roy. *Temples and Legends of Bihar*. Bombay: Bharatiya Vidya Bhavan, 1965.

Choudhury, B. "Love Sentiment and Its Spiritual Implications in Gauḍīa Vaiṣṇavism." In *Bengal Vaiṣṇavism, Orientalism, Society and the Arts*, ed. D. T. O'Connel. South Asia Series Occasional Papers No. 35, East Lansing: Asian Studies Center, Michigan State Universtiy, 1985.

Cidananda, Swami. *Light Fountain*. Rishikesh: Divine Light Society, 1967.

Clothey, F. W. *The Many Faces of Murukan: The History and Meaning of a South Indian God*. Religion and Society No. 6, The Hague: Mouton, 1978.

———. "Tamil Religion," *Encyclopedia of Religions*, ed. M. Eliade, vol. 12, pp. 260ff.

———. "Pilgrimage Centers in the Tamil Cultus of Murukan." *JAAR*, 40 (1972): 79–95.

——— and J. B. Lond (eds.) *Experiencing Śiva*, Columbia Mo.: South Asian Books, 1983.

Coburn, T. B. *Devī Mahatmya: The Crystallization of the Goddess Tradition*. Delhi: Motilal Banarsidass, 1984.

Cohn, B. *India: The Social Anthropology of a Civilization*. Englewood Cliffs, N.J.: Prentice-Hall, 1971.

Colebrook, T. "On the Vedas, or Sacred Writings of the Hindus." *Asiatic Researches* 8: 369–476.

Collins, L., and D. Lapierre. *Freedom at Midnight*. New York: Simon and Shuster 1975, reprint, New York: Avon Books, 1980.

Coomaraswamy, A. *The Dance of Śiva*, 3rd ed. Bombay: Asia Publishing House, 1956.

———. *History of Indian and Indonesian Art*. Reprint New York: Dover, 1965.

———. *The Transformation of Nature in Art*. Reprint New York: Dover Publications, 1956.

Coomaraswamy, A, and Sister Nivedita. *Myths of the Hindus and Buddhists*. Reprint New York: Dover Publications, 1967.

Cormack, M. L. *She Who Rides a Peacock: Indian Students and Social Change*. New York: Praeger Books, 1962.

Courtright, P. B. *Ganeśa: Lord of Obstacles, Lord of Beginnings*. New York: Oxford University Press, 1985.

Coward, H. G. *Bhartṛhari*. Boston: Twayne Publishers, 1976.

———. *Jung and Eastern Thought*. Albany: State University of New York Press, 1985.

———. *The Sphoṭa Theory of Language: A Philosophical Analysis*. Delhi: Motilal Banarsidass, 1980.

——— (ed.). *"Language" in Indian Philosophy and Religion*, SR Supplements. Waterloo, Ont.: Wilfrid Laurier University Press, 1978.

——— (ed.). *Studies in Indian Thought. Collected Papers of Prof. T. R. V. Murti*. Delhi: Motilal Banarsidass, 1983.

——— and W. Goa. *Mantra*. Chambersburg, Pa.: Anima Publications, 1991.

Crawford, S. C. *The Evolution of Hindu Ethical Ideals*, rev. ed. Honolulu: University of Hawaii Press, 1982.

———. *Ram Mohan Roy: Social, Political and Religious Reform in Nineteenth Century India*. New York: Paragon House, 1987.

Creel, A. B. *Dharma in Hindu Ethics*. Columbia, Mo.: South Asia Books, 1977.

Cronin, V. A. *Pearl to India: The Life of Roberto de Nobili*. London: Darton, Longman and Todd, 1966.

Crooke, W. *The Popular Religion and Folklore in Northern India*, 2 vols. Oxford: Oxford University Press, 1896; reprint Delhi: Munshiram Manoharla, 1968.

Cunningham, A. *Ancient Geography of India*. Calcutta: Archeological Survey of India, 1924.

Cuttat, J. A. *Encounter of Religions*. New York: Desclee and Co., 1962.

Dandekar, R. N. "Ancient Indian Polity." *Indo-Asia Culture*, 11, no. 4 (April 1963): 323–32.

———. *Some Aspects of the History of Hinduism*. Poona: University of Bangalore, 1967.

———. *Universe in Hindu Thought*. Bangalore: University of Bangalore, 1972.

———. *Vedic Bibliography*. vol. 1, Bombay: Karnatak Publishing House, 1946; vol. 2, Poona: University of Poona, 1967.

———. "Vṛtrahā Indra." *ABORI* 30, no. 1 (1951): 1–55.

Daniélou, A. *Hindu Polytheism*. London: Rutledge and Kegan Paul, 1964.

———. *Yoga: The Method of Re-Integration*. New York: University Books, 1956.

Danielson, H. (trans.). *Adiśeṣa: The Essence of Supreme Truth (Paramārthasāra)*. Nisaba, Religious Texts Translation Series, Leiden: Brill, 1980.

Das, B. *Kṛṣṇa: A Study in the Theory of Avatāras*. Bombay: Bharatiya Vidya Bhavan, 1962.

Das, R. V. *Introduction to Śaṅkara*. Calcutta: Firma K.L.M. Mukhopadhyay, 1968.

Daśapadārtha Śāstra, ed. and trans. H. Ui. 1917; reprint, Banaras: Chowkhambha Sanskrit Series, 1962.

Das Gupta, C. *Mother as Revealed to Me*. Banaras: Shree Shree Anandamayi Sangha, 1954.

Dasgupta, S. H. *Obscure Religious Cults*, 2d ed. Calcutta: Firma K. L. Mukhopadhyay, 1962.

Dasgupta, S. N. *Development of Moral Philosophy in India*. Bombay: 1961.

———. *Hindu Mysticism*. New York: 1960.

———. *History of Indian Philosophy*, 5 vols., 3d ed. Cambridge: Cambridge University Press, 1961–1962.

———. *Natural Science of the Ancient Hindus*. Delhi: 1986.

———. *A Study of Patañjali*. Calcutta: 1930.

———. *Yoga as Philosophy and Religion*. 1924; reprint Delhi: Motilal Banarsidass, 1973.

Dass, A. C. "The Origin of Brahmanical Image Worship and the Icono-Genic Properties in *Ṛg Veda*." *JOIB* 34, nos. 1–2 (1984): 1–11.

Datta, B. and A. N. Singh. *History of Hindu Mathematics: A Source Book* (2 parts). Bombay, Calcutta, and New Delhi: Asia Publishing House, 1962.

Dave, J. H. *Immortal India*, 4 parts, 2d ed. Bombay: Bharatiya Vidya Bhavan, 1959–1962.

Davis, K. *The Population of India and Pakistan*. Princeton, N.J.: Princeton University Press, 1951.

Day, T. P. *The Conception of Punishment in Early Indian Literature*. Waterloo, Ont.: Wilfrid Laurier University Press, 1982.

De, S. K. *Early History of the Vaiṣṇava Faith and Movement in Bengal*, 2d ed. Calcutta: Firma K. L. Mukhopadhyay, 21961.

———. *Sanskrit Poetics as a Study of Aesthetic*. Berkeley: University of California Press, 1963.

Deheja, V. *Āṇṭāl and Her Path of Love*. Albany: State University of New York Press, 1990.

Deming, W. S. *Rāmdās and Rāmdāsis*. The Religious Life of India Series, Oxford: Oxford University Press, 1928.

Derrett, J. D. M. *Critique of Modern Hindu Law*. Bombay: H. M. Tripathi, 1970.

———. *The Death of a Marriage Law: Epitaph for the Rishis*. Durham, N.C.: Carolina Academic Press, 1978.

———. *Essays in Classical and Modern Hindu Law*, 4 vols. Leiden: Brill, 1976–1978.

———. "Greece and India: The Milindapañha, the Alexander-Romance and the Gospels." *ZRGG* 19 (1967): 33–64.

———. "Greece and India Again: The Jaimini-Aśvamedha, the Alexander Romance and the Gospels." *ZRGG* 22, no. 1 (1970): 19–44.

———. *Hindu Law Past and Present*. Calcutta: A. Mukherjee, 1957.

———. *History of Indian Law (Dharmaśāstra)*. Leiden: Brill, 1973.

———. *Introduction to Modern Hindu Law*. Calcutta: A. Mukherjee, 1963.

Desai, M. *The Gītā According to Gandhi*. Amhedabad: Navajivan, 1946.

Deshpande, M. M. "Changing Conceptions of the Veda: From Speech-Acts to Magical Sounds." *Adyar Library Bulletin* (1990): 1–41.

Deussen, P. *The Philosophy of the Upaniṣads*. 1905; reprint New York: Dover Publications, 1966.

———. *The Philosophy of the Veda*. Edinburgh: Clark, 1908.

Deutsch, E. *Advaita Vedānta: A Philosophical Reconstruction*. Honolulu: University of Hawaii, 1969.

——— and J. A. B. van Buitenen (eds.). *A Source Book of Advaita Vedānta*. Honolulu: University of Hawaii, 1971.

Devanandan, P. D. *The Concept of Māyā*. Calcutta: YMCA Publishing House, 1954.

Devasenapathi, V. A. *Śaiva Siddhānta as Expounded in the Śivajñāna Siddhiyar and Its Six Commentaries*. Madras: University of Madras, 1960.

Devī-Bhāgavata Purāṇa (Banaras: Swami Vijnananda 1962), trans. Pandit Pustakalaya, 2 vols. in SBH. Allahabad: Panini Office, 1923.

Dharampal, Gītā. "Frühe deutsche Indien Berichte (1477–1750)." *ZDMG* 134, no. 2 (1984): 23–67.

Dharmaśāstrasaṅgraha [ed. Sādhu Charan Prasad]. Bombay: Sri Venkatesvar Press, 1970 [samvat].

Dhatta, A. K. *Bhaktiyoga*. Bombay: Bharatiya Vidya Bhavan, 1959.

Dhavamony, M. *Classical Hinduism*. Rome: Universita Gregoriana Editrice, 1982.

———. *Love of God According to Śaiva Siddhānta: A Study in the Mysticism and Theology of Śaivism*. Oxford: Clarendon Press, 1971.

Dhingra, B. *Asia Through Asian Eyes*. Bombay: Asia Publishing House, 1959.

Diehl, C. G. *Instrument and Purpose: Studies on Rites and Rituals in South India*. Lund: C. W. K. Gleerup, 1956.

Diksitar, V. R. *Studies in Tamil Literature and History*. London: Luzac, 1930.

Dimmit, C., and J. A. B. van Buitenen (eds. and trans.). *Classical Hindu Mythology: A Reader in the Sanskrit Purāṇas*. Philadelphia: Temple University Press, 1978.

Dimock, E. C. (trans.). *The Thief of Love: Bengali Tales*. Chicago: University of Chicago Press, 1963.

Dixit, P. "Hindu Nationalism" *SEMINAR* 216 (August 1977): 27–36.

Doctrine of Śrīkaṇṭha, trans. R. Chaudhuri, 2 vols. Calcutta, 1959f.

Dowson, J. *A Classical Dictionary of Hindu Mythology and Religion, Geography, History and Literature*. London: Routledge and Kegan Paul, 1961.

Drekmeier, C. *Kingship and Community in Early India*. Stanford, Calif.: Stanford University Press, 1962.

Dube, S. C. *India's Changing Villages*. London: Routledge and Kegan Paul, 1958.

———. *Indian Villages*. New York: Harper and Row, 1967.

Dubois, Abbé. *Hindu Manners, Customs and Ceremonies*, 4d ed. Oxford: Oxford University Press, 1959.

Dumont, L. "A Fundamental Problem." In *Religion, Politics and History in India*. The Hague: Mouton, 1970. [Ecole Pratique des Hautes Etudes; Sorbonne, VIe section: sciences économiques et sociales: "Le Monde d'Outre-Mer-Passè et Présent" Première Série, Etudes XXXXIV.]

———. *Religion, Politics and History in India: Collected Papers in Indian Sociology*. The Hague: Mouton, 1970.

———. *Homo Hierarchicus: Essai sur le systéme des castes*. Paris: Gallimard 1966; English translation Chicago: University of Chicago Press, 1970.

Dumont, P. E. *L'Aśvamedha*. Paris: Geuthner, 1927.

Dutt, P. R. *India Today and Tomorrow*. Delhi: People's Publishing House, 1955.

Dutt, R. C. *Economic History of India 1757–1900* 2 vols. Reprint Delhi: Publications Division, Govt. of India, 1960.

Dutt, S. *Buddhist Monks and Monasteries in India: Their History and Their Contribution to Indian Culture*. London: Allen and Unwin, 1962.

Eban, Martin (ed.). *Maharishi the Guru. The Story of Maharishi Mahesh Yogi*. Bombay: Pearl Publications, 1968.

Eck, D. L. *Banaras: City of Light*. Princeton, N.J.: Princeton University Press, 1983.

———. *Darśan: Seeing the Divine Image in India*, 2d ed. Chambersburg, Pa.: Anima Books, 1985.

Edsman, C. M. "Zum sakralen Königtum in der Forschung der letzten hundert Jahre." *Numen* Supplement no. 4: 3–17.

Edwardes, S. M., and H. O. O. Garrett. *Mughal Rule in India*. Reprint Delhi: S. Chand, 1962.

Eidlitz, W. *Krsna-Caitanya, Sein Leben und Seine Lehre*. Stockholm Studies in Comparative Religion 7, Stockholm: Almquist and Wiksell, 1968.

Einstein, A. *Ideas and Opinions*. New York: Crown Publishers, 1985.

Eisenstadt, S. N., R. Kahane, and D. Shulman (eds.). *Orthodoxy, Heterodoxy and Dissent in India*. Leiden: Walter de Gruyter, 1984.

Elder, J. W. (ed.). *Lectures in Indian Civilization*. Dubuque, Iowa: Kendall Hunt Publishing Co., 1970.

Eliade, M. *From Primitives to Zen*. New York: Harper and Row, 1967.

———. *Yoga: Immortality and Freedom*, 2d ed. Bollingen Series 41. Princeton, N.J.: Princeton University Press, 1969.

Elintoff, E. "Pyrrho and India." *Phronesis* no. 1 (1980): 88–108.

Elliot, H. M., and J. Dowson. *The History of India as Told by Its Own Historians: The Mohammedan Period*, 8 vols. Reprint Allahabad: Kitāb Kahal, 1964.

Elkman, S. M. *Jiva Goswami's Tattvasandarbha*. Delhi: Motilal Banarsidass, 1986.

Elmore, W. R. "Dravidian Gods in Modern Hinduism." *University Studies* 15, no. 1 (January 1915).

Elwin, V. *The Religion of an Indian Tribe*. London: Oxford University Press, 1955.

Erikson, E. H. *Gandhi's Truth*. New York: W. W. Norton, 1970.

Essentials of Hinduism, Allahabad: The Leader, n.d.

Esteller, A. "The Quest for the Original *Ṛgveda*." *ABORI* 507 (1969): 1–40.

———. "The *Ṛgveda Saṁhitā* as a 'Palimpsest'." *Indian Antiquary* (third series), 4, no. 1 (January 1967): 1–23.

Fakirbhai, D. *Khristopaniṣad*. Bangalore: The Christian Institute for the Study of Religion, 1966.

Falk, H. "Die Legende von Sunaḥṣepa vor ihrem rituellen Hintergrund." *ZDMG* 134, no. 1 (1984): 115–35.

Falk, M. *Nāma-Rūpa and Dharma-Rūpa; Origin and Aspects of an Ancient Indian Conception*. Calcutta: University of Calcutta, 1943.

Farquar, J. N. *Modern Religious Movements in India*. Oxford: Oxford University Press, 1914; reprint Banaras: 1967.

———. *An Outline of the Religious Literature of India*. Reprint Banaras: Motilal Banarsidass, 1967.

Feldhaus, A. (trans. and annotator). *The Deeds of God in Ṛiddhipur*. New York: Oxford University Press, 1984.

Fergusson, J. *Tree and Serpent Worship*. London: W. H. Allen, 1868.

Feuerstein, G. *The Philosophy of Classical Yoga*. Manchester: University of Manchester Press, 1982.

———. *Encyclopedic Dictionary of Yoga*. New York: Paragon House, 1990.

——— and J. Miller. *Yoga and Beyond: Essays in Indian Philosophy*. New York: Schocken Books, 1972.

Filliozat, J. "Les Āgamas Civaites." Introduction in *Rauravagama*, ed. R. Bhatt. Pondichery: Institut Français d'Indologie, 1961.

———. *The Classical Doctrine of Indian Medicine: Its Origins and Its Greek Parallels*, trans. D. R. Chanama. Delhi: Munshiram Manoharlal, 1964.

———. "The French Institute of Indology in Pondichéry." *WZKSA* 28 (1984): 133–47.

———. *Les rélations extèrieures de l'Inde*, 2 vols. Pondichery: Institut Français d'Indologie, 1956.

Findly, E. B. "Gārgī at the King's Court: Women and Philosophic Innovation in Ancient India" In *Women, Religion and Social Change*, pp. 37–85, ed. V. V. Haddad and E. B. Findley. Albany: State University of New York Press, 1985.

Fischer, L. *The Life of Mahātmā Gandhi*. Reprint Bombay: Bharatiya Vidya Bhavan, 1959.

Fitzgerald, J. L. "The Great Epic of India as Religious Rhetoric. A Fresh Look at the Mahābhārata." *JAAR* 51, no. 4 (1986): 611–30.

Fonseca, R. "Constructive Geometry and the Sri-Cakra Diagram." *Religion* 16, no. 1 (1986): 33–49.

Frauwallner, E. *Geschichte der Indischen Philosophie,*. 2 vols. Salzburg: Otto Müller Verlag, 1953.

———. *History of Indian Philosophy,* V. M. Bedekar, trans., 2 vols. Delhi: Motilal Banarsidass, 1983–1984.

Frawley, David. *Gods, Sages and Kings: Vedic Secrets of Ancient Civilization.* Salt Lake City: Passage Press, 1991.

Frekmeier, C. *Kingship and Community in Early India.* Stanford: Stanford University Press, 1962.

French, H. W., and A. Sharma. *Religious Ferment in Modern India.* New York: St. Martin's Press, 1981.

Frykenberg, R. E. (ed.). *Land Control and Social Structure in Indian History.* Madison: University of Wisconsin Press, 1969.

Fuller, C. J. *Servants of the Goddess: The Priests of a South Indian Temple.* Cambridge: Cambridge University Press, 1984.

———. *The Camphor Flame: Popular Hinduism and Society in India.* Princeton, N.J.: Princeton University Press, 1992.

Gächter, O. *Hermeneutics and Language in Pūrvamīmāṁsā, A Study in Śābara Bhāṣya.* Delhi: Motilal Banarsidass, 1983.

Gandhi, M. K. *Collected Works.* 90 vols. Delhi: Government of India, 1958–1984.

———. *An Autobiography,* London: Penguin Books, 1982.

Gangadharan, K. K. "Shiv Sena." *SEMINAR* 151 (March 1972): 26–32.

Gangadharan, N. *Liṅgapurāṇa: A Study.* Delhi: Ajanta Books International, 1980.

Garbe, B. *Die Bhagavadgītā,* 2d ed. Leipzig: H. Haessel, 1921.

Gatwood, L. E. *Devī and the Spouse Goddess: Women, Sexuality and Marriage in India.* Delhi: Manohar, 1985.

Gaur, R. *Hindutva* [Hindī]. Banaras: Visvaprasad Gupta, 1995 (samvat).

Gaur, R. C. *Excavations in Atranjikhera. Early Civilization of the Upper Ganga Basin.* Delhi: Archeological Survey of India, 1983.

Gautama's Nyāyasūtras with Vātsyāyana Bhāṣya, Sanskrit ed. and English trans. Ganganatha Jha, 2 vols. Poona: Oriental Book Depot, 1939.

Gayal, S. R. *A History of the Imperial Guptas.* Allahabad: Kitab Mahal, 1967.

Gazetteer of India. Reprint, 4 vols., Delhi: Ministry for Information and Braodcasting, 1965.

Gelberg, S. J. (ed.). *Hare Krishna, Hare Krishna: Five Distinguished Schol-*

ars on the Krishna Movement in the West*. New York: Grove Press, 1983.

Geldner, H. F. *Ṛgveda deutsch*, 5 vols. Cambridge, Mass.: Harvard University Press, 1955–1957 (English translation in progress).

Gensichen, H. W. "Abominable Heathenism—Ā Rediscovered Tract by Bartholomaeus Ziegenbalg." *Indian Church History Review* 1, no. 1 (1967): 29–40.

George, A. *Social Ferment in India*. London: Athlone Press, 1986.

Getty, A. *Gaṇeśa*. Oxford: Oxford University Press, 1936.

Ghate, V. S. *The Vedānta*. Poona: Oriental Book Agency, 1926; reprint, 1960.

Gheraṇḍasaṃhitā, trans. S. C. Vasu. Allahabad: Panini Office, 1914.

Ghose, A. *Sri Aurobindo*. Birth Centenary Library, 30 vols. Pondichery: Śrī Aurobindo Ashram, 1972–1975.

Ghose, S. K. *Lord Gaurāṅga*. Bombay: 1961

———. *Modern Indian Political Thought*. New Delhi: Allied Publishers, 1984.

Ghosh, B. K. "The Āryan Problem." In *HCIP*, vol. 1, pp. 205–21.

———. "The Origin of the Indo-Āryans." In *CHI*, vol. 1, pp. 129–43.

Ghoshal, U. N. *A History of Indian Political Ideas: The Ancient Period and the Period of Transition to the Middle Ages*, 3rd ed. Oxford: Oxford University Press, 1959.

———. "Kauṭilīya." *Encyclopedia of Social Sciences*, 10th ed., 1953, vol. 3, pp. 473ff.

Ghurye, G. S. *Caste, Class and Occupation*, 3rd ed. Bombay: Popular Book Depot, 1961.

———. *Gods and Men*. Bombay: Popular Book Depot, 1962.

———. *Indian Sādhus*, 2d ed. Bombay: Popular Prakashan, 1964.

Gibb, H. A. R. (ed.). *Ibn Battuta: Travels in Asia and Africa*, 2d ed. London: Routledge and Kegan Paul, 1957.

Glucklich, A. "Karma and Pollution in the Dharmaśāstra." *JOIB* 35, nos. 1–2 (1985): 49–60.

Gode, P. K. "The Aśvamedha Performed by Sevai Jayasingh of Amber 1699–1744 A.D.." In *Studies in Indian Literary History*, pp. 292–306. Bombay: Bharatiya Vidya Bhavan, 1954.

Godman, D (ed.). *Be as You Are: The Teachings of Ramaṇa Maharṣi*. Boston: Arkana, 1985.

Goetz, H. *The Art of India*. New York: Crown Publishers, 1964.

Gold, D. *The Lord as Guru: Hindī Sants in the Northern Indian Tradition.* New York: Oxford University Press, 1987.

Goldman, Robert P. (trans.). *The Rāmāyana of Vālmīki: An Epic of Ancient India.* Vol. 1. *Balakanda.* Princeton, N.J.: Princeton University Press, 1984.

Golwalkar, M. S. *A Bunch of Thoughts,* 2d ed. Bangalore: Vikrama Prakashan, 1966.

Gonda, J. *Aspects of Early Viṣṇuism.* Utrecht: 1954. Reprint Delhi: Motilal Banarsidass, 1965.

———. "The Historical Background of the Name Satya Assigned to the Highest Being." *ABORI* 48–49 (1968): 83–93.

———. *Die Religionen Indiens,* 2 vols. Stuttgart: Kohlhammer, 1960–1963.

———. *The Ritual Functions and Significance of Grasses in the Religion of the Veda.* Amsterdam: North-Holland Publishing, 1985.

———. *The Ritual Sūtras.* In *HIL,* vol. 1, fasc. 2. Wiesbaden: Harrrassowitz, 1977.

———. *Vedic Literature (Saṃhitās and Brāhmaṇas).* In *HIL,* vol. 1, fasc. 1. Wiesbaden: Harrrassowitz, 1975.

———. *Vedic Ritual: The Non-solemn Rites.* Amsterdam: North-Holland Publishing, 1980.

———. *The Indra Hymns of the Ṛgveda.* Leiden: Brill, 1989.

Gopal, R. *British Rule in India: An Assessment.* New York: Asia Publishing House, 1963.

———. *Indian Muslims.* New York: 1959.

Gopi, Krishna. *The Biological Basis of Religion and Genius,* Religious Perspectives, New York: Harper and Row, 1972.

Gordon, D. H. *The Prehistoric Background of Indian Culture.* Bombay: N. M. Tripathi, 1960.

Goudriaan, T. *Māyā Divine and Human: A Study of Magic and Its Religious Foundations in Sanskrit Texts, with Particular Attention to a Fragment on Viṣṇu's Māyā Preserved in Bali.* Delhi: Motilal Banarsidass, 1978.

Govindacharya, A. *The Divine Wisdom of the Dravida Saints,* Madras: C. N. Press, 1902.

———. *The Life of Rāmānuja.* Madras: C. N. Press, 1906.

Griffith, R. T. H. *The Texts of the White Yajurveda,* 3rd ed. Banaras: Lazarus, 1957.

——— (trans.). *Hymns of the Ṛgveda,* 4th ed. 2 vols. Reprint Banaras: 1963.

——— (trans.). *Hymns of the Yajurveda* Reprint Banaras: Chowkhambha Sanskrit Office, 1957.

Grihyasūtras, trans. H. Oldenberg and F. Muller. In *SBE*, vols. 29 and 30.

Griswold, H. D. *Religion of the Rigveda*. Delhi: Motilal Banarsidass, n.d.

Growse, F. S. *Mathura: A District Memoir*. Reprint New Delhi: Asian Education Services, 1979.

Guénon, Rene. *Introduction génerale a l'étude des doctrines hindoues*, 5th ed. Paris: Les editions Vega, 1964.

Günther, H. V. *Yuganādha: The Tantric View of Life*. Banaras, 1952; reprint Boulder, Colo.: Shambhala, 1976.

Gupta, S., and R. Gombrich. "Kings, Power and the Goddess." *South Asia Research* 6, no. 2 (1986): 123–38.

Gupta, S., D. J. Hoens, and T. Goudriaan. *Hindu Tantrism. Handbuch der Orientalistik*, general ed. B. Spuler. Leiden: Brill, 1979.

Gyana, S. G. *Agni Purāṇa: A Study*, 2d ed. Banaras: Chowkhamba, 1966.

Habermann, D. L. "On Trial: The Love of Sixteen Thousand Gopees." *HR* 33, no. 1 (1993), 44–70.

Hacker, P. "Eigentümlichkeiten der Lehre und Terminologie Śaṅkaras: *Avidyā, Nāmarūpa, Māyā, Īśvara*." *ZDMG* 100 (1950): 246–86.

———. "Śaṅkara der Yogin und Śaṅkara der Advaitin: Einige Beobachtungen." *WZKSA* 12–13 (1968): 119–48.

———. *Vivarta: Studien zur Geschichte der illusionistischen Kosmologie und Erkenntnistheorie der Inder*, Wiesbaden: Akademie der Wissenschaften Mainz, 1953.

———. "Zur Entwicklung der Avatāralehre." *WZKSA* 4 (1960): 47–70.

Halbfass, W. "Indien und die Geschichtsschreibung der Philosophie." *Philosophische Rundschau* 23, nos. 1–2 (1976): 104–31.

———. *India and Europe: An Essay in Understanding*. Albany: State University of New York Press, 1988.

———. *Indien und Europa: Perspektiven ihrer geistigen Begegnung*, Basel and Stuttgart: Schwabe and Co., 1981.

———. *On Being and What There Is: Classical Vaisesika and the History of Indian Ontology*. Albany: State University of New York Press, 1992.

Hampton, G. H. *The Life and Mind of Oriental Jones: Sir William Jones, the Father of Modern Linguistics*. Cambridge: Cambridge University Press, 1990.

———. *Oriental Jones: A Biography of Sir William Jones 1746–1794*. Bombay: Asia Publishing House, 1964.

Handelman, D., "Myths of Murugan: Asymmetry and Hierarchy in a South Indian Puranic Cosmology." *History of Religions* 27, no. 2 (1987):133–70.

Hardgrave, R. L. *The Dravidian Movement*. Bombay: Popular Prakashan, 1965.

Hardy, E. T. *Viraha Bhakti* Delhi: Oxford University Press, 1983.

Harle, J. C. *The Art and Architecture of the Indian Subcontinent*. Harmondsworth: Penguin Books, 1987.

Harper, E. B. (ed.). *Religion in South Asia*. Seattle: University of Washington Press, 1964.

Harper, M. H. *Gurus, Swāmis, and Avatāras: Spiritual Masters and Their American Disciples*. Philadelphia: Westminster Press, 1972.

Harris, I. C. *Radhakrishnan: The Profile of a Universalist*. Columbia, Mo.: South Asia Books, 1982.

Harris, R. B. (ed.). *Neoplatonism and Indian Thought: Studies in Neoplatonism Ancient and Modern*, vol. 2. Albany: SUNY Press, 1982.

Harrison, S. S. *India: The Most Dangerous Decade*. Oxford: Oxford University Press, 1960.

Harvey, M. J. "The Secular as Sacred? The Religio-Political Rationalization of B. G. Tilak." *Modern Asian Studies* 20, no. 2 (1986): 321–31.

Hathayogapradīpikā by Svātmarāma Yogīndra, 2d ed., trans. Srinivasa Iyengar. Adyar: Theosophical Publishing House, 21933.

Hauer, J. W. *Der Vrātya: Untersuchungen über die nichtbrahmanische Religion Altindiens*. Stuttgart: Kohlhammer, 1927.

———. *Der Yoga als Heilsweg*. Stuttgart: W. Kohlhammer, 1932.

Havell, E. B. *Banaras, The Sacred City: Sketches of Hindu Life and Religion*. London: W. Thacker and Co., 1905.

Hawley, J. S. *Kṛṣṇa, the Butter Thief*. Princeton, N.J.: Princeton University Press, 1983.

———. *At Play with Krishna: Prilgrimage Dramas from Brindāvan*. Princeton, N.J.: Princeton University Press, 1981.

———. *Saints and Virtues*. Berkeley: University of California Press, 1987.

———. *Sūrdās: Poet, Singer, Saint*. Seattle: University of Washington Press, 1984.

———. "Why Sūrdās Went Blind." *Journal of Vaisnava Studies*, 1, no. 2 (1993): 62–78.

———. "Author and Authority in the Bhakti Poetry of North India." *JAS* 47, no. 2 (1988):269–90.

Hawley, J. S., and D. M. Wulff (eds.). *The Divine Consort: Radha and the Goddesses of India*. Berkeley: University of California Press, 1982.

Hazra, R. C. "The Purāṇas." In *CHI*, vol. 2, pp. 240ff.

———. *Studies in the Purāṇic Records of Hindu Rites and Customs*. Dacca: University of Dacca, 1940; reprint Delhi: 1968.

———. *Studies in the Upapurāṇas*, 2 vols. Calcutta: Sanskrit College, 1958–63.

Hedayetullah, M. *Kabir: The Apostle of Hindu-Muslim Unity*. Delhi: Motilal Banarsidass, 1978.

Heesterman, J. C. *The Inner Conflict of Tradition: Essays in Indian Ritual, Kingship and Society*. Chicago: University of Chicago Press, 1985.

———. "On the Origin of the Nāstika." *WZKSA* 12, no. 13 (1968–69): 171–85.

Hegel, G. W. F. *Vorlesungen über die Philosophie der Weltgeschichte*, vol. 2, ed. G. Larsson. Hamburg, 1968.

Heimann, B. *Facets of Indian Thought*. London: Allen and Unwin, 1964.

———. *Indian and Western Philosophy: A Study in Contrasts*. London: Allen and Unwin, 1937.

Heimsath, C. H. *Indian Nationalism and Hindu Social Reform*. Princeton, N.J.: Princeton University Press, 1968.

Hein, N. *The Miracle Plays of Mathura*. New Haven, Conn.: Yale University Press, 1972.

———. "A Revolution in Kṛṣṇaism: The Cult of Gopāla." *HR* 26, no. 3 (1986): 296–317.

Hellman, S. *Rādhā: Diary of a Woman's Search*. Porthill: Timeless Books, 1981.

Hiltebeitel, A. *The Ritual of Battle: Krishna in the Mahābhārata*. Ithaca, N.Y.: Cornell University Press, 1976.

Hiriyanna, M. *Outlines of Indian Philosophy*, 4th ed. London: George Allen and Unwin, 1958.

———. *Indian Conception of Values*. Mysore: Kavyalaya Publishers, 1975.

Hocart, A. M. *Caste: A Comparative Study*. New York: Russell, 1950.

Holland, B. (compiler). *Popular Hinduism and Hindu Mythology: An Annotated Bibliography*. Westport, Conn.: Greenwood Press, 1979.

Hooper, J. S. M. *Bible Translation in India, Pakistan and Ceylon*, 2d ed., revised by W. J. Culshaw. Oxford: Oxford University Press, 1963.

———. *Hymns of the Āḷvārs*. Calcutta: Association Press, 1929.

Hopkins, E. W. *Epic Mythology*. Strassbourg: Trübner, 1915.

———. *Ethics of India*. New Haven, Conn.: Yale University Press, 1924.

———. *The Great Epic of India*. New York: 1901; reprint Calcutta: Punthi Pustak, 1969.

Hopkins, T. J. *The Hindu Religious Tradition*. Belmont, Calif.: Dickenson, 1971.

Hronzny, B. *Über die älteste Völkerwanderung und über das Problem der Proto-indischen Zivilisation*. Prague: Orientalisches Institut, 1939.

Hudson, D. "Āṇṭāl Āḷvār: A Developing Hagiography." *Journal of Vaiṣṇava Studies* 1, no. 2 (1993): 27–61.

Hume, R. (trans.) *Principal Upaniṣads*. Oxford: Oxford University Press, 1921.

Hunashal, S. M. *The Vīraśaiva Social Philosophy*. Raichur: Amaravani Printing Press, 1957.

Hutton, J. H. *Caste in India: Its Nature, Function and Origins*, 3rd ed. Oxford: Oxford University Press, 1961.

Inden, R. "Hierarchies of Kings in Early Mediaeval India." In *Way of Life, King, Householder, Renouncer. Essays in Honour of Louis Dumont*, ed. T. N. Madan, pp. 99–125. Delhi: Vikas Publishing House, 1982.

———. "Orientalist Constructions of India." *Modern Asian Studies* 20, no. 3 (1986): 401–46.

Indich, W. M. *Consciousness in Advaita Vedānta*. Delhi: Motilal Banarsidass, 1980.

Indradeva, S. "Cultural Interaction Between Ancient India and Iran" *Diogenes* 111 (1980): 83–109.

Ingalls, D. H. H. *Materials for the Study of Navya-Nyāya Logic*. Harvard Oriental Series No. 40, Cambridge, Mass.: Harvard University Press, 1968.

Ions, V. *Indian Mythology*. London: Paul Haymlyn, 1967.

Isaacs, H. R. *India's Ex-Untouchables*. New York: John Day, 1965.

Isacco, E. and A. L. Dallapiccola (eds.). *Krishna, the Divine Lover: Myth and Legend Through Indian Art*. Boston: Serindia Publications and David R. Godine, 1982.

Israel, B. J. *The Bene Israel of India, Some Studies*. Bombay: Orient Longman, 1984.

Iyengar, N. (ed. and trans.). *Mumukṣapadī of Lokācārya*. Madras: Adyar Library, 1962.

Iyer, L. K. Anantakrishna. *The Mysore Tribes and Castes*. 4 vols. Mysore: Mysore University, 1928–1935.

Iyer, M. K. Venkatarama. *Adviata Vedānta*. Bombay: Asia Publishing House, 1964.

Jacobi, H. *Das Rāmāyaṇa*. Bonn: 1893; rev. ed. Darmstadt: Wissenschaftliche Buchgesellschaft, 1970.

Jacobsen, D., and S. Wadley (eds.). *Women in India: Two Perspectives*. Delhi: Manohar Book Service, 1974.

Jackson, C. T. *The Oriental Religions and American Thought. Nineteenth-Century Explorations*. Westport, Conn.: Greenwood Press, 1981.

Jaimini's Mīmāṃsāsūtra with Śābara's Commentary and Notes, trans. Ganganatha Jha, 3 vols., Gaekwad Oriental Series, Baroda: 1933–36; reprint Oriental Institute, 1973–1974.

Janaki, S. S (ed.) *Kuppuswamy Sastri Birth Centenary Commemoration Volume.* 2 parts. Madsras: Kusspuswamy Sastri Research Institute, 1981.

Jarrige, J. F. "Die frühesten Kulturen in Pakistan und ihre Entwicklung." In *Vergessene Städte am Indus: Frühe Kulturen in Pakistan vom 8. bis yum 2. Jahrtausend,* P. von Zabern (ed.). Mainz: Verlag P. von Zabern, 1987.

Jarrell, H. R. *International Yoga Bibliography, 1950–1980.* Metuchen: Scarecrow Press, n.d.

Jayakar, P. *J. Krishnamurthi: A Biography*. Delhi: Penguin India, 1987.

Jayaswal, K. P. *Hindu Polity,* 4th ed. Bangalore: Bangalore Press, 1967.

Jesudason, C., and S. H. Jesudason. *A History of Tamil Literature.* Heritage of India Series, Calcutta: Y. M. C. A. Publishing House, 1961.

Jha, G. *Pūrva Mīmāṃsā in Its Sources.* Banaras: Benares Hindu University, 1942: reprint Delhi: 1981.

Jha, M. (ed.). *Dimensions of Pilgrimage.* New Delhi: Inter-Indian Publications, 1985.

Jhangiani, M. A. *Jana Sangh and Swatantra: A Profile of the Rightist Parties in India.* Bombay: Manaktalas, 1967.

Jindal, K. B. *A History of Hindī Literature.* Allahabad: Kitab Mahal, 1955.

Johar, S. S. *Giani Zail Singh.* New Delhi: Gaurav Publishing House, 1984.

Johnson, Clive (ed.). *Vedānta: An Anthology of Hindu Scripture, Commentary, and Poetry.* New York: Harper and Row, 1971.

Johnston, E. H. *Early Sāṁkhya.* Delhi: Motilal Banarsidass, 1969.

Jolly, J. *Hindu Law and Custom.* Calcutta: Greater India Society, 1928.

Joshi, L. S. "Moral Foundations of Indian Society." In *Nehru Abhinandan Granth,* pp. 464–69. Calcutta: Nehru Abhinandan Granth Committee, 1949.

Joshi, M. V. "The Concept of Brahman in Vallabha Vedānta." *JBOI* 22, no. 4 (June 1973): 474–83.

Joshi, R. V. *Le Rituel de la dévotion Kṛṣṇaite.* Pondichery: Institut Français d'Indologie 1959.

Kak, S. C. "Astronomy of the Vedic Altar." *Vistas in Astronomy* 36 (1993): 1–26.

———. "The Astronomy of the Vedic Altar and the Ṛgveda." *Mankind Quarterly* 33, no. 1 (Fall 1992): 43–55.

———. "On the Chronology of Ancient India." *Indian Journal of History of Science*

22, no. 3 (1987): 222–34.

———. "The Indus Tradition and the Indo-Aryans." *The Mankind Quarterly* 32, no. 3 (1992): 195–213.

Kakati, B. K. *The Mother Goddess Kāmākhyā*. Gauhati: Lawyers' Book Stall, 1948.

Kale, M. R. *A Higher Sanskrit Grammar*. Reprint Delhi: Motilal Banarsidass, 1961.

Kane, P. V. *History of Dharmaśāstra,* 5 vols. (7 parts), Poona: Bhandarkar Oriental Research Institute, 1930–1962.

———. *History of Sanskrit Poetics,* 3rd ed. Delhi: Motilal Banarsidass, 1961.

Kapadia, K. M. *Marriage and Family in India,* 2d ed. Oxford: Oxford University Press, 1959.

Karmarkar, A. P. "Religion and Philosophy of the Epics." In *CHI*, vol. 2, pp. 80ff.

———. *The Religions of India*. Lonavla: Mira Publishing House, 1950.

Karpatriji Maharaj, Swami. *Rāmrājya aura Marksvāda* [in Hindī]. Gorakhpur: Gītā Press, 1964.

Karunakaran, K. P. "Regionalism." *SEMINAR* 87 (November 1966): 21–25.

Karve, I. *Hindu Society: An Interpretation*. Poona: Deshmukh Prakashan, 1961.

———. *Kinship Organisation in India*. New York: Asia Publishing House, 1965.

Katre, S. M. *Introduction to Textual Criticism*. Poona: Deccan College, 1954.

Kauṭilīya's Arthaśāstra, ed. and trans. R. P. Kangle, three parts. Bombay: University of Bombay, 1960–1961.

Kaylor, R. D. "The Concept of Grace in the Hymns of Nammāḷvār." *JAAR* 44 (1976): 649–60.

Keay, F. E. *Hindī Literature,* 3rd ed. Calcutta: YMCA Publishing House, 1960.

———. *Kabīr and His Followers*. London: 1931.

Keith, A. B. *The Age of the Ṛgveda*. Cambridge, Mass.: Harvard University Press, 1922.

———. *A History of Sanskrit Literature*. London: Oxford University Press, 1920.

———. *Indian Logic and Atomism*. Oxford: Clarendon Press, 1921.

———. *The Karma Mīmāṃsā*. Calcutta: Association Press, 1921.

———. *The Religion and Philosophy of the Veda and Upaniṣads*, Cambridge, Mass.: Harvard University Press, 1925.

———. *The Sāṁkhya System*, Heritage of India Series. Calcutta: YMCA Publishing House, 1949.

———. *The Sanskrit Drama*. Reprint Oxford: Oxford University Press, 1924.

Keller, C. A. "Aspiration collective et éxperience individuelle dans la bhakti shivaite de l'Inde du sud." *Numen* 31, no. 1 (July 1984): 1–21.

Kenghe, C. T. "The Problem of Pratyayasarga in Sāṁkhya and Its Relation to Yoga." *ABORI* 48–49 (1968): 365–73.

Kennedy, M. T. *The Chaitanya Movement*. Calcutta: Association Press, 1925.

Khiste, Pandit S. S. "Śrīvidyā." In *Kalyāṇa Devībhāgavatam Aṅgka*, pp. 689–96. Gorakhpur: Gītā Press, 1960.

Kingsbury, F., and G. E. Philips (trans.). *Hymns of the Tamil Śaivite Saints*. Calcutta: Association Press, 1921.

Kinsley, D. *Hindu Goddesses*, Berkeley: University of California Press, 1986.

———. *Hinduism: A Cultural Perspective*. Englewood Cliffs, N.J.: Prentice-Hall, 1982.

———. *The Sword and the Flute: Kālī and Kṛṣṇa, Dark Visions of the Terrible and the Sublime in Hindu Mythology*. Berkeley, University of California Press, 1975.

Kirfel, W. D. *Purāṇa Pañcalakṣana*. Banaras: Motilal Banarsidass, 1963.

Klaiman, M. H. (trans.). "Singing the Glory of Lord Krishna." In *The Śrī Kṛṣṇa Kīrtana of Baru Cāṇḍīdāsa*. Chico, Calif.: Scholars Press, n.d.

Klimkeit, H. J. *Der politische Hinduismus, Indische Denker zwischen religiöser Reform und politischem Erwachen*. Wiesbaden: Harrassowitz, 1984.

Kloppenborg, R. (ed.). *Selected Studies on Ritual in the Indian Religions: Essays to D. J. Hoens*. Supplements to *Numen* 45. Leiden: Brill, 1983.

Klostermaier, K. "Hindu Views of Buddhism." In *Canadian Contributions to Buddhist Studies*, ed. R. Amore, pp. 60–82. Waterloo, Ont.: Wilfred Laurier University Press, 1980.

———. "Hinduism in Bombay." *Religion* [U. K.] 1, no. 2 (1972): 83–91.

———. *Hinduismus*. Cologne: Bachem, 1965.

———. *In the Paradise of Kṛṣṇa*. Philadelphia: Westminster Press, 1971.

———. *Mythologies and Philosophies of Salvation in the Theistic Traditions of India*. Waterloo, Ont.: Wilfred Laurier University Press, 1984.

———. "The Original Dakṣa Saga." *Journal of South Asian Literature* 20, no. 1 (1985): 93–107.

———. "*Sādhana.*" *Religion and Society* 16, no. 2 (1969): 36–50.

———. "Vaiṣṇavism and Politics." *JVS* 1, no. 1 (1992): 166–82.

Knipe, D. M. *In the Image of Fire: Vedic Experiences of Heat.* Delhi: Motilal Banarsidass, 1975.

———. *Hinduism: Experiments in the Sacred.* San Francisco: Harper, 1991.

Koelman, G. M. *Pātañjala Yoga. From Related Ego to Absolute Self.* Poona: Papal Athenaeum, 1970.

Koestler, A. *The Lotus and the Robot.* New York: Harper and Row, 1961.

Kölver, B. "Stages in the Evolution of a World Picture" *Numen* 32, no. 2: 131–168.

van Kooij, K. R. "Protective Covering (*Kavaca*)." In *Selected Studies on Ritual in the Indian Religions,* ed. R. Kloppenburg, pp. 118–129. Leiden: Brill, 1983.

Kopf, D. *The Brahmo Samāj and the Shaping of the Modern Indian Mind.* Princeton, N.J.: Princeton University Press, 1979.

Kosambi, D. D. (ed.). *The Epigrams Attributed to Bhartṛhari Including the Three Centuries,* Singhi Jain Series, Bombay: Bharatiya Vidya Bhavan, 1948.

———. *An Introduction to the Study of Indian History.* Bombay: Popular Book Depot, 1956.

———. *Myth and Reality: Studies in the Formation of Indian Culture.* Bombay: Popular Prakashan, 1962.

Kothari, R. *Caste in Indian Politics.* New Delhi: Orient Longman, 1970.

Krämer, H. J. *Der Ursprung der Geistmetaphysik,* 2d ed. Amsterdam: B. R. Bruner, 1967.

Kramrish, S. *The Art of India: Traditions of Indian Sculpture, Painting and Architecture.* London: Phaidon, 1954.

———. *The Hindu Temple,* 2 vols. Calcutta: University of Calcutta 1946; reprint Delhi: Motilal Banarsidass, 1977.

———. "The Image of Mahādeva in the Cave Temple on Elephanta Island." *Ancient India* 2 (1946): 4–8.

———. *Indian Sculpture.* 1933; reprint Delhi: Motilal Banarsidass, 1981.

———. *The Presence of Śiva,* Princeton, N.J.: Princeton University Press, 1981.

———. "The Triple Structure of Creation in the *ṚgVeda.*" *HR* 2, nos. 1–2 (1962): 140–75, 256–85.

Krick, H. "Der Vaniṣṭusava und Indras Offenbarung." *WZKSA* 19 (1975): 25–74.

Krishna, G. *The Awakening of Kuṇḍalinī*. New York: E. P. Dutton, 1975.

Krishnamurti, J. *The Awakening of Intelligence*. New York: Avon Books, 1976.

———. *The First and Last Freedom*. London: V. Gollancz, 1967 [1954].

Kṛṣṇakarṇamṛta of Līlāsūka, ed. and trans. M. A. Acharya. Madras: V. Ramaswamy Sastrulu, 1958.

Kulkarni, R. "Vāstupadamaṇḍala." *JOIB* 28, nos. 3–4 (March–June 1979): 107–38.

Kumar, G. D. "The Ethnic Components of the Builders of the Indus Civilization and the Advent of the Aryans." *Journal of Indo-European Studies* 1, no. 1 (1973): 66–80.

Kumarappa, B. *The Hindu Conception of the Deity*. London: Luzac, 1934.

Kumari, V. (trans.). *The Nīlamata Purāṇa*. Srinagar: J and K Academy of Art, Culture and Language, 1968.

Kuppuswamy, B. *Dharma and Society: A Study in Social Values*. Columbia, Mo.: South Asia Books, 1977.

Kuppuswamy, G., and M. Hariharan. "Bhajana Tradition in South India." *Sangeet Natak* 64–65 (April–September 1982): 32–50.

——— (eds.). *Jayadeva and Gītāgovinda: A Study*. Trivandrum: College Book House, 1980.

Lacombe, O. *L'absolu sélon le Vedānta*. Paris: Geuthner, 1957; reprint 1966.

Laghusiddhāntakaumudī of Vāradarāja, ed. and trans. J. R. Ballantyne. Reprint Delhi: Motilal Banarsidass, 1961.

Lal, B. B. "The Indus Script: Some Observations Based on Archaeology." *JRAS*, no. 2 (1975): 173–209.

———. "Reading the Indus Script." *IFR* (15 April 1983): 33–36.

Lal, C. *Hindu America*. Bombay: Bharatiya Vidya Bhavan, 1960.

Lal, K. *Holy Cities of India*. Delhi: Asia Press, 1961.

Lamb, B. P. *India: A World in Transition*, 3rd ed. New York: Praeger Books, 1968.

Lannoy, R. *The Speaking Tree*. Oxford: Oxford University Press, 1971.

Larson, G. J. "The *Bhagavad-Gītā* as Cross-Cultural Process: Toward an Analysis of the Social Locations of a Religious Text." *JAAR*, 43 (1975): 651–69.

———. *Classical Sāṁkhya*, 2d ed. Delhi: Motilal Banarsidass, 1969.

———. "The Format of Technical Philosophical Writing in ancient India:

Inadequacies of Conventional Translations." *Philosophy East and West* 30, no. 3 (1980): 375–80.

Latham, R. E. (trans.). *The Travels of Marco Polo.* Harmondsworth: Penguin Classics, 1958.

Laws of Manu, trans. G. Bühler. In *SBE,* vol. 25.

Legget, T (trans.). *The Complete Commentary by Śaṅkara on the Yoga Sūtras: A Full Translation of the Newly Discovered Text.* London: Kegan Paul, 1990.

Leifer, W. *Indien und die Deutschen: 500 Jahre Begegnung und Partnerschaft,* Tübingen and Basel: Horst Erdmann Verlag, 1969.

LeMay, R. *The Culture of South-East Asia: The Heritage of India.* London: Allen and Unwin, 1954.

Lester, R. C. *Rāmānuja on the Yoga.* Madras: The Adyar Library and Research Centre, 1976.

Lévi, S. *La doctrine du sacrifice dans le Brāhmaṇas.* Paris: 1898; reprint Paris: Presses Universitaires de France, 1966.

Liebert, G. *Iconographic Dictionary of the Indian Religions: Hinduism, Buddhism, Jainism.* Leiden: Brill, 1976.

Long, J. B. "Festival of Repentance: A Study of Mahaśivarātrī." *JBOI* 22, no. 1–2 (September–December 1972): 15–38.

Lorenzen, D. N. *The Kāpālikas and Kālamukhas: Two Lost Śaivite Sects.* Berkeley: University of California Press, 1972.

———. "The Life of Śaṅkarācārya." In *Experiencing Śiva,* ed. F. Clothey and J. B. Long. Columbia, Mo.: South Asia Books, 1983.

Lott, E. J. *God and the Universe in the Vedāntic Theology of Rāmānuja: A Study in His Use of the Self-Body Analogy.* Madras: Ramanuja Research Society, 1976.

Lueders, H. *Varuna,* vol. 1, *Varuṇa und das Ṛta.* Göttingen: Vanderhoek and Ruprecht, 1959.

Lupsa, M. *Chants á Kālī de Rāmprasād.* Pondichery: Institut Français d'Indologie, 1967.

Lütt, Jürgen, *Hindu-Nationalismus in Uttar Prades̀ 1867–1900.* Stuttgart: Ernst Klett Verlag, 1970.

Macauliffe, M. A. *The Sikh Religion: Its Gurus, Sacred Writings and Authors,* 3 vols. Reprint Delhi: S. Chand, 1963.

Macdonnell, A. A. *A History of Sanskrit Literature,* 2d ed. Reprint Delhi: Motilal Banarsidass, 1961.

———. *Vedic Mythology.* Reprint Banaras: Indological Bookhouse, 1963.

———. "Vedic Religion." In *Encyclopedia of Religion and Ethics,* 3rd ed., ed. E. Hastings, 1954, vol. 12, 601–18.

——— and A. B. Keith. *Vedic Index of Names and Subjects,* 2 vols. Reprint Delhi: Motilal Banarsidass, 1958.

Maclagan, D. *Creation Myths: Man's Introduction to the World.* London: Thames and Hudson, 1977.

Macnicol, N. *Indian Theism.* London: Oxford University Press, 1915.

———. *Psalms of the Maratha Saints,* Heritage of India Series. Calcutta: Association Press, 1919.

Madan, T. N. (ed.). *Way of Life. King, Householder, Renouncer. Essays in Honor of Louis Dumont.* Delhi: Vikas Publishing House, 1982.

———. "Secularism in Its Place" *JAS* 64, no. 4 (1987):747–59.

——— and G. Sarana. *Indian Anthropology,* New York: Asia Publishing House, 1962.

Mahābhārata (short summary), ed. C. Rajagopalachari, Bombay: Bharatiya Vidya Bhavan, 1958.

Mahābhārata, trans. P. C. Roy. Calcutta: 1884–96; several reprints, Calcutta: Oriental (without date).

Mahābhārata, Books 1–5, trans. J. A. B. van Buitenen. 3 vols. Chicago: Chicago University Press, 1973–1978.

Mahābhārata, Critical Edition, with Pratika-Index, 28 vols. Poona: Bhandarkar Oriental Research Institute, 1933–1972.

Mahadevan, T. M. P. *Outline of Hinduism,* 2d ed. Bombay: Cetana, 1960.

———. *Ramaṇa Maharṣi and His Philosophy of Existence.* Annamalai: 1951.

———. *The Sage of Kanchi.* Secunderabad: Sri Kanch Kamakothi Sankara Mandir,1967.

———. "Śaivism." In *HCIP,* vol. 2, pp. 433ff.

———. *Ten Saints of India.* Bombay: Bharatiya Vidya Bhavan, 1961.

——— (ed. and trans.). *Hymns of Śaṅkara.* Madras: 1970.

Mahadevananda, Swami (trans.). *Devotional Songs of Narsi Mehta.* Delhi: Motilal Banarsidass, 1985.

Maitra, S. K. *The Ethics of the Hindus,* 3rd ed. Calcutta: University of Calcutta, 1963.

———. *Fundamental Questions of Indian Metaphysics and Logics,* 2 vols. Calcutta: Chuckervertty, Chatterjee and Co., 1956–1961.

Maitra, S. *An Introduction to the Philosophy of Śrī Aurobindo,* 2d ed. Banaras: Banaras Hindu University, 1945.

Majumdar, A. K. *Caitanya: His Life and Doctrine.* Bombay: Bharatiya Vidya Bhavan, 1969.

Majumdar, D. N. *Caste and Communication in an Indian Village,* 3rd ed. Bombay: Asia Publishing House, 1962.

———. *Races and Cultures of India.* Bombay: Asia Publishing House, 1964.

Majumdar, J. K. *Raja Rammohan Roy and Progressive Movements in India, volume I. A Selection from Records (1774–1845).* Calcutta: Brahmo Mission Press, n.d.

Majumdar, R. C. *The Classical Accounts of India.* Calcutta: Firma K. L. Mukhopadhyay, 1960.

———. *Hindu Colonies in the Far East,* 2d ed. Calcutta: Firma K. L. Mukhopadhyay, 1963.

——— (general ed.). *The History and Culture of the Indian People.* Bombay: Bharatiya Vidya Bhavan, 1945–1978.

———, H. C. Raychaudhuri, and K. Datta. *An Advanced History of India,* 3d ed. London: Macmillan, 1965.

Malamoud, C. "On the Rhetoric and Semantics of Purusartha." In *Way of Life,* ed. T. N. Madan. Delhi: Vikas Publishing House, 33–52.

Maloney, C. *Peoples of South Asia.* New York: Holt, Rhinehart and Winston, 1974.

Mānameyodaya, trans. C. Kunhan Raja. Adyar: Theosophical Publishing House, 1933.

Manasāra, trans. P. K. Acharya. 1934; reprint New Delhi: Motilal Banarsidass, 1980.

Mānava Dharma Sastra, trans. J. Jolly. London: 1887.

Mānava Śrauta Sūtra, trans. J. M. van Gelder. New Delhi: International Academy of Indian Culture, 1963.

Māṇḍukyopaniṣad with Gauḍapāda's Kārikā and Śaṅkara's Commentary, 4th ed., trans. Swami Nihkilananda. Mysore: Ramakrishna Ashram, 1955.

Manickam, V. S. *The Tamil Concept of Love.* Madras: South Indian Śaiva Siddhānta Works Publishing Society, 1962.

Maṇikana, A Navya-Nyāya Manual, ed. and trans. E. R. Sreekrishna Sarma. Adyar: Adyar Library, 1960.

Marfatia, M. I. *The Philosophy of Vallabhācārya.* Delhi: Munshiram Manoharlal, 1967

Mārkaṇḍeya Purāṇa. Bombay: Venkatesvar Steam Press, 1910; trans. F. E. Pargiter, reprint Delhi: Indological Book House, 1969.

Marriott, McKim (ed.). *Village India: Studies in the Little Community.* Chicago: University of Chicago Press, 1963.

Marshall, J. *Mohenjo Daro and the Indus Civilization,* 3 vols. London: University of Oxford Press, 1931.

Marshall, P. J. (ed.). *The British Discovery of Hinduism in the Eighteenth Century.* European Understanding of India Series, Cambridge: Cambridge University Press, 1971.

Masani, M. R. *The Communist Party of India.* London: Derek Versdroyle, 1954.

Mate, M. S. *Temples and Legends of Maharastra.* Bombay: Bharatiya Vidya Bhavan, 1962.

Mathur, S. K. *Caste and Ritual in a Malwa Village.* New York: Asia Publishing House, 1964.

Matilal, B. K. *Logic, Language and Reality.* Delhi: Motilal Banarsidass, 1985.

———. *The Navya Nyāya Doctrine of Negation.* Harvard Oriental Series No. 46. Cambridge, Mass.: Harvard University Press, 1972.

Māyāmata, French trans. B. Dagens, 2 vols. Pondichery: Institut Français d'Indologie, 1970–1976.

Mayer, A. C. *Caste and Kinship in Central India: A Village and Its Religion.* Berkeley: University of California Press, 1965.

McDowall, A., and A. Sharma (eds.). *Vignettes of Vrindāban.* New Delhi: Books and Books, 1987.

McKenzie, J. *Hindu Ehtics.* Oxford: Oxford University Press, 1922.

Meenaksisundaram, T. P. *A History of Tamil Literature.* Annamalainagar: Annamalai University, 1965.

Mehendale, M. A. "Purāṇas." In *HCIP,* vol. 3, pp. 291–99.

Mehta, M. "The Evolution of the Suparna Saga in the *Mahābhārata.*" *JOIB* 1971: 41–65.

———. "The Problem of the Double Introduction to the *Mahābhārata.*" *JAOS* 93, no. 4 (1973): 547–50.

Meister, M. W. "Hindu Temples." In *Encyclopedia of Religion,* ed. M. Eliade, vol. 10, pp. 368–73.

———. "Maṇḍala and Practice in Nāgara Architecture in North India." *JAOS* 99 (1979): 204–19.

———. "Measurement and Proportion in Hindu Architecture." *Interdisciplinary Science Reviews* 10 (1985): 248–58.

——— and M. A. Dhaky (eds.) *Encyclopedia of Indian Temple Architecture,* vol. 1. *South India.* New Delhi: American Institute of Indian Studies, 1983.

——— (ed.) *Discourses on Śiva.* Philadelphia: University of Pennsylvania Press, 1984.

Menon, I. K. K. "Kerala's Early Foreign Contacts." *IFR* (15 July 1980): 13f.

Miller, D. M., and D. C. Wertz. *Hindu Monastic Life: The Monks and Monasteries of Bhubaneswar.* Montreal: McGill-Queen's University Press, 1976.

Mīmāṃsākosa, ed. Kevalananda Sarasvati, seven vols. Wai: Dharmakosamandala, 1952–1966.

Mīmāṃsāparibhāsa of Kṛṣṇa Yajvan, ed. and trans. Swami Madhavanand. Belur Math: The Ramakrishna Mission Sarada Pitha, 1948.

Minor Lawbooks, trans. J. Jolly. In *SBE,* vol. 33.

Minor, R. (ed.). *Modern Indian Interpretation of the Bhagavadgītā.* Albany: State University of New York Press, 1986.

———. *Bhagavad-Gītā: An Exegetical Commentary.* Columbia, Mo.: South Asia Books, 1982.

Minz, N. "Anthropology and the Deprived." *Religion and Society* 32, no. 4 (1985): 3–19.

Mishra, V. *The Conception of Matter According to Nyāya–Vaiśeṣika.* Reprint Delhi: Gian Publications, 1983.

———. *Hinduism and Economic Growth.* Oxford: Oxford University Press, 1963.

———. "Prehistory and Protohistory." In *Review of Indological Research in Last Seventy-Five Years,* ed. P. J. Chinmulgund and V. V. Mirashi, pp. 353–415. Poona: Bharatiya Charitra Kosha Mandal, 1967.

Miśra, O. P. *Mother Goddess in Central India.* Delhi: Agam Kala Prakashan, 1985.

Mitra, A. M. *India as Seen in the Bṛihatsaṃhitā of Varāhamihira.* Delhi: Motilal Banarsidass, n.d.

Moddie, A. D. *The Brahmanical Culture and Modernity.* Bombay: Asia Publishing House, 1968.

Mollat, M. "The Importance of Maritime Traffic to Cultural Contacts in the Indian Ocean." *Diogenes* 3 (1980): 1–18.

Möller, V. *Götter und Mythen des indischen Subkontinents,* vol. 5 of H. W. Haussig (ed.), *Wörterbuch der Mythologie.* Stuttgart: Klett-Cotta, 1972

Mookerjee, A., and M. Khanna. *The Tantric Way: Art—Science—Ritual.* London: Thames and Hudson, 1977.

Morinis, E. A. *Pilgrimage in the Hindu Tradition: A Case Study of West Bengal,* South Asian Studies Series, New York and New Delhi: Oxford University Press, 1984.

Morris-Jones, W. H. *The Government and Politics of India.* London: Hutchinson University Library, 1964.

Mudgal, S. G. *Advaita of Śaṅkara: A Reappraisal*. Delhi: Motilal Banarsidass, 1975.

Mughal, M. R. "Recent Archeological Research in the Cholistan Desert." In *Harappan Civilisation*, ed. G. Possehl. Warminster: Aris and Phillips, 1982.

Mukarji, N. "The Hindu Problem." *SEMINAR* 269 (January 1982): 37–40.

Müller, M. (ed.). *Ṛgveda with the Commentary of Śayaṇa*, 2d ed., 4 vols. London: 1892; reprint: Banaras: Chowkhambha Sanskrit Office, 1966.

———. *The Six Systems of Indian Philosophy*. Reprint Banaras: Chowkhamba, 1962.

Mundaden, A. M. *St. Thomas Christians and the Portuguese*. Bangalore: Dharmaram Studies, 1970.

———. *The Traditions of St. Thomas Christians*. Bangalore: Dharmaram Studies, 1972.

Murti, G. S. "Introduction." In *Śrī Pāñcarātra Raksa of Śrī Vedānta Deśika*, ed. M. D. Aiyangar and T. Venugopalacharya. Madras: Adyar Library, 1942.

Murti, T. R. V. "The Rise of the Philosophical Schools." In *CHI*, vol. 3, p. 32.

Murty, K. S. *Revelation and Reason in Advaita Vedānta*. Waltair: Waltair University, 1959.

Nagendra, D. *Indian Literature*. Agra: Lakshmi Narain Agarwal, 1959.

Nair, K. *Blossoms in the Dust*, 2d ed. London: Duckworth, 1962.

Naiṣkarmyasiddhi, ed. and trans. K. K. Venkatachari. Adyar: Adyar Library, 1982.

Nakamura, H. "Indian Studies in Japan." In *Indian Studies Abroad*. New York: Asia, 1964.

Nāḷadiyār, trans. G. U. Pope. Oxford: Oxford University Press, 1893.

Nandimath, S. C. *Handbook of Viraśaism*. Dharwar: Lingayat Educational Association, 1941.

Nārada Bhakti Sūtras: Aphorisms on the Gospel of Divine Love, 3rd ed., trans. Swami Tyagisananda. Mylapore: Ramakrishna Math, 1955.

Narayan, J. *From Socialism to Sarvodaya*. Kashi: Sarva Seva Sangh Prakashan, n.d.

Nath, P. S. *Christ: Who and What He Was*: Part 1. *Christ a Hindu Disciple, Nay a Buddhist Saint*; Part 2. *Christ a Pure Vedāntist*. Calcutta: Calcutta Dayamoy Printing Works, 1927–1928.

Nayar, T. B. *The Problem of Dravidian Origins—A Linguistic, Anthropological and Archeological Approach*. Madras: University of Madras, 1977.

Neevel, W. G., Jr. *Yamuna's Vedānta and Pāñcarātra: Integrating the Classical and the Popular*. Chico, Calif.: Scholars Press, 1977.

Nehru, J. *Autobiography*. London 1936; Indian ed., New Delhi: Allied Publishers, 1962.

———. *The Discovery of India*. London, 1946; reprint Meridian Books, 1960.

Neill, S. *A History of Christianity in India: The Beginnings to A.D. 1707*. Cambridge: Cambridge University Press, 1984.

Neog, M. *Early History of the Vaiṣṇava Faith and Movement in Assam: Śaṅkaradeva and His Time*, 2d ed. Delhi: Motilal Banarsidass, 1985.

Neufeldt, R. F. *Max Müller and the Ṛg-Veda: A Study of Its Role in His Work and Thought*. Columbia, Mo.: South Asia Books, 1980.

——— (ed.). *Karma and Rebirth: Post-Classical Developments*. Albany: State University of New York Press, 1986.

Neuman, E. *An Analysis of the Archetype The Great Mother*, trans. R. Manheim. Princeton, N.J.: Princeton University Press, 1955.

Neumayer, E. *Prehistoric India Rock Paintings*. Delhi: Oxford University Press, 1983.

de Nicolás, A. T. *Avatāra: The Humanization of Philosophy Through the Bhagavad Gītā*. New York: Nicholas Hays, 1976.

Swami Nikhilananda (trans.). *Gospel of Śrī Ramakrishna*. Calcutta: 1930.

Nimbārka. Vedānta Parijāta Saurabha and Vedānta Kausthubha of Śrīnivāsa, trans. R. Bose. 3 vols. Calcutta: Royal Asiatic Society of Bengal, 1940–1943.

Nirvedananda, Swami. "Sri Ramakrishna and Spiritual Renaissance." In *CHI*, vol. 4, pp. 653–728.

Nooten, B. A. van. *The Mahābhārata*. New York: Twayne Publishing, 1971.

Nyāyakrsnmañjalī of Udayana, ed. and trans. E. G. Cowell. Calcutta: 1864.

Oberhammer, G. "Die Gotteserfahrung in der yogischen Meditation." In *Offenbarung als Heilserfahrung im Christentum, Hinduismus and Buddhismus*, eds. W. Strolz and S. Ueda, pp. 146–66. Freiburg, Basel, and Vienna: Herder, 1982.

———. *Strukturen Yogischer Meditation*, Vienna: Österreichische Akademie der Wissenschaften, 1977.

———. "Das Transzendenzverständis des Sāmkhyistischen Yoga als Strukturprinzip seiner Mystik." In *Transzendenzerfahrung, vollzugshorizont des Heils*, ed. G. Oberhammer, pp. 15–28. Vienna: De Nobili Research Library, 1978.

O'Flaherty, W. D. *Asceticism and Eroticism in the Mythology of Śiva*. London: Oxford University Press, 1973.

———. *The Origins of Evil in Hindu Mythology*. Berkeley: University of California Press, 1976.

———. "The Origin of Heresy in Hindu Mythology." *HR* 10 (May 1971): 271–333.

———. *Śiva: The Erotic Ascetic*. New York: Oxford University Press, 1981.

——— (ed.). *Karma and Rebirth in Classical Indian Traditions*. Berkeley: University of California Press, 1980.

——— and J. D. M. Derret (eds.). *The Concept of Duty on Southeast Asia*. New Delhi: Vikas, 1978.

Oguibenine, B. "Cosmic Tree in Vedic and Tamil Mythology: Contrastive Analysis." *Journal of Indo-European Studies* 12, no. 3–4 (1984): 367–74.

Oldenberg, H. *Das Mahābhārata*. Göttingen: Vandenhoeck and Ruprecht, 1922.

Olivelle, P. (ed. and trans.). *Vasudevāśrama's Yatidharmaprakāśa. A Treatise on World Renunciation*, 2 vols. Vienna: De Nobili Library, 1977.

———. "Contributions to the Semantic History of Saṃnyāsa." *JAOS* 101 (1981): 265–74.

———. *Renunciation in Hinduism: A Mediaeval Debate*. 2 vols. Vienna: Institute of Indology University of Vienna, 1986–87

O'Malley, L. S. *Popular Hinduism: The Religion of the Masses*. Oxford: Oxford University Press, 1941.

Oman, I. C. *The Mystics, Ascetics and Saints of India*. Reprint Delhi: Oriental Publishers, 1973.

O'Neil, L. T. *Māyā in Śaṅkara: Measuring the Immeasurable*. Delhi: Motilal Banarsidass, 1980.

Osborne, A. *Ramaṇa Maharshi and the Path of Self-Knowledge*, 2d ed. Bombay: Jaico, 1962.

——— (ed.). *The Collected Works of Ramaṇa Maharshi*. New York: S. Weiser, 1959.

Ostor, A. *The Play of the Gods: Locality, Ideology, Structure and Time in the Festivals of a Bengali Town*. Chicago: University of Chicago Press, 1980.

Otto, R. *Mysticism East and West*. New York: Macmillan, 1957.

Overstreet, L., and M. Windmiller. *Communism in India*. Berkeley: University of California Press, 1959.

Pañcadaśī of Vidyāraṇya, ed. and trans. Swami Swahananda. Madras: Ramakrishna Math, 1967.

Pāñcarātra Rakṣa of Śrī Vedānta Deśika, critical eds. M. Duraiswami Aiyanjar and T. Venugopalacharya, with notes and variant readings, introduction by G. Srinivasa Murti. Adyar: Adyar Library, 1942.

Pañcatantra, trans. A. W. Ryder. Reprint Bombay: Jaico, 1962.

Pañcaviṃśa Brāhmaṇa, trans. W. Caland. Calcutta: Asiatic Society of Bengal, 1931.

Pancikar, W. C. (ed.). *One Hundred and Eight Upaniṣads,* 4th ed. Bombay: Nirnaya Sagar Press, 1932.

Pandey, R. B. *Hindu Saṃskāras: Socio-Religious Study of the Hindu Sacraments,* 2d ed. Banaras: Motilal Banarsidass, 1969.

Pandeya, L. P. *Sun Worship in Ancient India.* Delhi: Motilal Banarsidass, 1972.

Panikkar, W. C. Sastri (ed.). *One Hundred and Eight Upaniṣads.* Bombay: Nirnaya Sagar Press, 1932.

Panikkar, K. M. *Asia and Western Dominance.* London: Allen and Unwin, 31955.

———. *Geographical Factors in Indian History.* Bombay: Bharatiya Vidya Bhavan, 1955.

———. *Hindu Society at Cross Roads.* Bombay: Asia Publishing House, 1956.

———. *Hinduism and the Modern World.* Bombay: Bharatiya Vidya Bhavan, 1956.

———. *A Survey of Indian History.* Bombay: Asia Publishing House, 1947.

Pannikkar, R. *Kerygma und Indien: Zur heilsgeschichtlichen Problematik der christlichen Begegnung mit Indien.* Hamburg: Evangelischer Verlag, 1967.

——— (ed. and trans.). *The Vedic Experience: Mantramañjarī—An Anthology of the Vedas for Modern Man and Contemporary Celebration.* Berkeley: University of California Press, 1977.

Pāṇini's Aṣṭādhyāyī, ed. Sastri, Devaprakasa Pātañjala. Delhi: Motilal Banarsidass, 1954.

Pāṇini's Aṣṭādhyāyī, ed. and trans. Srisa Candra Vasu, 2 vols. Reprint Delhi: Motilal Banarsidass, 1961.

Paramārtha Sopāna, ed. R. D. Ranade. Allahabad: Adhyatma Vidya Mandir Sangli, 1954.

Paramesvaran, M. R. "The Twofold Vedānta of Śrīvaisnavism." M.A. thesis, University of Manitoba, 1981.

Paranjoti, V. *Śaiva Siddhānta,* 2d ed. London: Luzac, 1954.

Pareckh, M. C. *Brahmarshi Keshub Chander Sen.* Rajkot: Oriental Christ House, 1926.

———. *The Brahmo Samāj*. Calcutta: Brahmo Samaj, 1922.

———. *A Hindu's Portrait of Jesus Christ*. Rajkot: Sri Bhagavata Dharma Mission, 1953.

———. *Śrī Swāmi Nārāyana*. Rajkot: Sri Bhagavata Dharma Mission, 1936.

———. *Sri Vallabhācārya*. Rajkot: Sri Bhagavata Dharma Mission, 1936.

Pargiter, F. E. *Ancient Indian Historical Tradition*. Reprint Delhi: Motilal Banarsidass, 1962.

———. *The Purāṇa Text of the Dynasties of the Kaliage*. Oxford: Oxford University Press, 1913.

Parpola, A. *The Sky Garment: A Study of the Harappan Religion and the Relation to the Mesopotamian and later Indian Religions*. Helsinki: Finnish Oriental Society, 1985.

Parvathamma, C. *Politics and Religion*. New Delhi: Sterling Publishers, 1971.

Patañjali Mahābhāṣya, ed. Vedavrata Snataka, 10 vols. Gurukul Jhajjar (Rohtak): Haryana Sahitya Samsthan, 1961–1964.

Patañjali's Yogasūtra, ed. and trans. Swami Vijnana Asrama. Ajmer: Śrī Madanlal Laksminivas Chandak, 1961.

Pathak, P. V. "Tectonic Upheavals in the Indus Region and Some Rgvedic Hymns." *ABORI* 64 (1983): 227–32.

Patil, D. R. *Cultural History of Vāyu Purāṇa*. Delhi: Motilal Banarsidass, n.d.

Pattabhiram, M. (ed.). *General Elections In India 1967. An Exhaustive Study of Main Political Trends*. Bombay: Allied Publishers, 1967.

Payne, A. A. *The Śāktas*. Calcutta: YMCA Publishing House, 1933.

Pereira, J. (ed.). *Hindu Theology: A Reader*. Garden City, N.Y.: Doubleday, 1976.

Piggott, S. *Prehistoric India*. Baltimore: Penguin Books, 1961.

Pillai, G. S. *Introduction and History of Śaiva Siddhānta*. Annamalai: Annamalai University, 1948.

Pillai, K. K. "The Caste System in Tamil Nadu." *Journal of the Madras University* 49, no. 2 (1977): 1–89.

———. *A Social History of the Tamils*, 2d ed., vol. 1. Madras: University of Madras, 1973.

Pillai, S. S. "The Śaiva Saints of South India." In *CHI*, vol. 4, pp. 339ff.

Podgorski, F. R. *Hinduism: A Beautiful Mosaic*. South Bend, Ind.: Foundations Press of Notre Dame, 1983.

Popley, H. A. *The Music of India*. Calcutta: YMCA Publishing House, 1950.

Possehl, G. C. (ed.). *Harappan Civilisation: A Contemporary Perspective.* Warminster: Aris and Philips, 1982.

Potter, K. *Bibliography of Indian Philosophies.* Delhi: Motilal Banarsidass, 1970.

———. *Presuppositions of India's Philosophies.* Englewood Cliffs, N.J.: Prentice-Hall, 1963.

——— (gen. ed.). *The Encyclopedia of Indian Philosophies.* Banaras: Motilal Banarsidass, 1970–.

Powell-Price, J. C. *A History of India.* London: T. Nelson, 1955.

Prabhananda, Swami. "Who Gave the Name Ramakrishna and When?" *The Vedānta Kesari* 74 (1987): 107–12.

Prabhu, P. H. *Hindu Social Organisation: A Study in Socio-Psychological and Ideological Foundations,* 4th ed. Bombay: Popular Prakashan, 1963.

Prabhu, R. K. and U. R. Rao (eds.). *The Mind of Mahātmā Gandhi.* Ahmedabad: Navajivan Publishing House, 1967

Prabhupada, A. C. Bhaktivedanta Swami, *Śrī Caitanya-Caritāmṛta of Kṛṣṇadāsa Kavirāja Gosvāmi: Antya-līlā,* vol. 7. New York: Bhaktivedanta Book Trust, 1975.

Prakash, O. *Political Ideas in the Purāṇas.* Allahabad: Panchanda Publications, 1977.

Prasad, M. *Kaka Kalekor: A Gandhian Patriarch.* Bombay: Popular Prakashan, 1965.

Pratyābhijñāhṛdayam, ed. and trans. Jaideva Singh. Delhi: Motilal Banarsidass, 1963.

Presler, F. A. "The Structure and Consequences of Temple Policy in Tamiḷnādu, 1967–81." *Pacific Affairs* (Summer 1983): 232–46.

Pusalker, A.D. "Aryan Settlements in India." In *HCIP,* vol. 1, pp. 245–67.

———. "Historical Traditions." In *HCIP,* vol. 1, pp. 271–336.

———. "Historicity of Kṛṣṇa." In *Studies in Epics and Purāṇas of India,* pp. 49–81. Bombay: Bharatiya Vidya Bhavan, 1955.

———. "The Indus Valley Civilization." In *HCIP,* vol. 1. pp. 172–202.

———. "The *Mahābhārata*: Its History and Character." In *CHI,* vol. 2, pp. 51ff.

———. "Puranic Studies" *Review of Indological Research in the Last Seventy-Five Years,* ed. P. J. Chinmulgund and V. V. Mirashi (Poona: Bharatiya Charitra Kosha Mandal, 1967), pp. 689–773.

———. "The *Rāmāyaṇa*: Its History and Character." In *CHI,* vol. 2, pp. 14ff.

———. *Studies in Epics and Purāṇas of India*. Bombay: Bharatiya Vidya Bhavan, 1955.

———. "Traditional History from the Earliest Time to the Accession of Parikshit." In *The Vedic Age*, vol. 1 of *HCIP*, pp. 271–322.

Puthiadan, I. *Viṣṇu the Ever Free: A Study of the Madhva Concept of God*. Dialogue Series No. 5. Madurai: Dialogue Publications, 1985.

Putnam, J. J., with photography by Raghubir Singh. "The Ganges, River of Faith." *National Geographic Magazine* (October 1971): 445–83.

Radhakrishnan, S. *The Bhagavadgītā*. London: Allen and Unwin, 1948.

———. *The Brahmasūtra*. London: Allen and Unwin, 1961.

———. *Eastern Religions and Western Thought*. New York: Oxford University Press, 1964.

———. *The Hindu View of Life*. New York: Macmillan, 1962.

———. *Indian Philosophy*, 2d ed., 2 vols. London: Allen and Unwin, 1948.

———. *My Search for Truth*. Agra: Agrawala, 1946.

———. *The Principal Upaniṣads*. London: Allen and Unwin, 1953.

———. *Religion and Society*. London: Allen and Unwin, 1947.

———. *Religion in a Changing World*. London: Allen and Unwin, 1967.

——— and C. A. Moore. *A Sourcebook in Indian Philosophy*. Princeton, N.J.: Princeton University Press, 1957.

Raghavacendra, R. (ed.). *Madhva Brahmasūtrabhāṣya with Several Commentaries*, 4 vols. Mysore: Government Branch Press, 1922.

Raghavan, V. *The Great Integrators: The Saint Singers of India*. Delhi: Ministry of Information and Broadcasting, 1966.

———. *The Indian Heritage*. Bangalore: Indian Institute of Culture, 1956.

Rai, L. *The Ārya Samāj*. London: Longmann, 1932.

Raj, D. *L'ésclavage dans l'Inde ancienne d'après les textes Palis et Sanskrits*. Pondichery: Institut Français d'Indologie, 1957.

Raja, C. K. "Vedic Culture." In *CHI*, vol. 1, pp. 199–220.

Raja, K. K. *Indian Theories of Meaning*. Adyar: The Adyar Library and Research Centre, 1963.

Rajagopalachari, R. C. *Hinduism: Doctrine and Way of Life*. Bombay: Bharatiya Vidya Bhavan, 1959.

Rajagopalan, V. "The Śrī Vaiṣṇava Understanding of *Bhakti* and *Prapatti*." Ph.D. thesis, University of Bombay, 1978.

Raju, P. T. *The Philosophical Traditions of India*. London: Allen and Unwin, 1971.

———. *Idealistic Thought of India*. London: Allen and Unwin, 1953.

———. *Structural Depths of Indian Thought.* Albany: State University of New York Press, 1985.

Ram, S. *Vinoba and his Mission,* 3rd ed. Banaras: Akhil Bharata Sarva Seva Sangh, Rajghat, 1962.

Rāmacaritamānasa by Tulsīdās. Gorakhpur, Gītāpress, 1968.

Śrī Bhagavad Rāmānuja Granthamālā, ed. P. B. Annangaracharya Awami. Kanchipuram: Granthamala Office, 1956.

Rāmānuja's Vedārthasaṅgraha, ed. and trans. S. S. Raghavachar. Mysore: Ramakrishna Ashrama, 1956.

Ramanujan, A. K. (trans.). *Speaking of Śiva.* Harmondsworth: Penguin Books, 1973.

Rāmāyaṇa (brief summary), ed.C. Rajagopalachari, 4th ed. Bombay: Bharatiya Vidya Bhavan, 1962.

The Rāmāyaṇa, trans. M. N. Dutt, 3 vols. Reprint Calcutta: Oriental Publishing Co., 1960.

Rāmāyaṇa of Vālmīki, trans. R. T. H. Griffith, 3d ed. Banaras: Chowkhamba, 1963.

Rāmāyaṇa, Critical Edition, 7 vols. Baroda: Oriental Institute, 1960–1975.

Rāmdās, Swami. *God-Experience.* Bombay: Bharatiya Vidya Bhavan, 1963.

Ramesan, R. *Temples and Legends of Andhra Pradesh.* Bombay: Bharatiya Vidya Bhavan, 1962.

Ranade, R. D. *Bhagavadgītā as a Philosophy of God-Realization, Being a Clue Through the Labyrinth of Modern Interpretations,* 2d ed. Bombay: Bharatiya Vidya Bhavan, 1965.

———. *A Constructive Survey of Upaniṣadic Philosophy.* Reprint Bombay: Bharatiya Vidya Bhavan, 1968.

———. *Pathway to God in Hindī Literature.* Bombay: Bharatiya Vidya Bhavan, 1959.

———. *Pathway to God in Kaṇṇaḍa Literature.* Bombay: Bharatiya Vidya Bhavan, 1960.

———. *Pathway to God in Marāthī Literature.* Bombay: Bharatiya Vidya Bhavan, 1961.

Ranganathananda, Swami. "The Science of Consciousness in the Light of Vedānta and Yoga." *Prabuddha Bharata* (June 1982): 257–63.

Rao, H. S. "The Two Bābās" *Illustrated Weekly of India* (21 November 1965).

Rao, S. R. "Deciphering the Indus Valley Script." *Indian and Foreign Review* (15 November 1979): 13–18.

———. *The Decipherment of the Indus Script.* Bombay: Asia Publishing House, 1982.

———. "Krishna's Dwarka." *Indian and Foreign Review* (15 March 1980): 15–19.

Rao, T. A. G. *Elements of Hindu Iconography*, 4 vols. Reprint New York: Paragon, 1968.

Rapson, E. I. (general ed.). *Cambridge History of India*, 6 vols. Reprint Delhi: S. Chand, 1964.

Rau, C. V. Sankar, *A Glossary of Philosophical Terms* [Sanskrit–English]. Madras: University of Madras, 1941.

Rau, H. "The Image of India in European Antiquity and the Middle Ages." In *India and the West: Proceedings of a Seminar Dedicated to the Memory of Hermann Goetz*, ed. J. Deppert, pp. 197–208. New Delhi: Manohar 1983.

Rau, S. S. (trans.). *Madhva's Commentary on the Bhahmasūtras*. Madras: Thompson and Co., 1904.

Ray, R. K. "The Kahar Chronicle." *Modern Asian Studies* 21, no. 4 (1987): 711–49.

Raychaudhuri, H. "The *Mahābhārata*: Some Aspects of its Culture." In *CHI*, vol. 2, pp. 71ff.

Reddy, Y. G. "The Svargabrahma Temple of Alampur: Iconographical Study" *Journal of Indian History* 55, nos. 1–2 (1977): 103–17.

Renou, L. *Le déstin du Veda dans l'Inde*. Paris: Adrien Maisouneuve, 1960.

———. *The Destiny of the Veda in India*. Delhi: Motilal Banarsidass, 1965.

———. *Les écoles védiques et la formation du Veda*. Paris: Adrien Maisouneuve, 1947.

———. *Hinduism*. New York: Washington Square Press, 1964.

———. *Indian Literature*. New York: Praeger Books, 1965.

———. *Religions of Ancient India*. London: Athlone Press, 1953.

———. *Vedic India*. Calcutta: Sunil Gupta, 1957.

——— and J. Filliozat (eds.). *L'Inde Classique*, 2 vols. Paris and Hanoi: Imprimerie Nationale, 1953.

Rhys Davids, T. W. *The Questions of King Milinda*. *SBE*, vols. 25 and 26. Oxford: Oxford University Press, 1890.

Rice, E. P. *Kanarese Literature*. Calcutta: Association Press, 1921.

Riepe, D. *The Naturalistic Tradition in Indian Thought*. Seattle: University of Washington Press, 1961.

———. *The Philosophy of India and Its Impact on American Thought*. Springfield, Ill.: Charles C. Thomas, 1970.

Risley, H. H. *The Peoples of India*, 2d ed. London: W. Thacker, 1915.

Robb, P. "The Challenge of Gau Mata: British Policy and Religious Change in India, 1880–1916." *Modern Asian Studies* 20, no. 2 (1986): 285–319.

Robins, R. H. "The Evolution of Historical Linguistics." *JRAS,* no. 1 (1986): 5–20.

Rocher, L. *The Purāṇas.* In *HIL,* vol. 2, p. 3. Wiesbaden: Harrassowitz, 1986.

Ross, A. D. *The Hindu Family in Its Urban Setting.* Toronto: University of Toronto Press, 1962.

Rowland, B. *The Art and Architecture of India: Buddhist, Hindu, Jain,* 2d ed. Baltimore: Penguin Books, 1967.

Roy, A. "Communalism—Its Political Roots." *Religion and Society,* 31, no. 4 (1984): 14–23.

Roy, D. K., and J. Devi. *Kumbha: India's Ageless Festival.* Bombay: Bharatiya Vidya Bhavan, 1955.

Roy, M. N. *India's Message.* Calcutta: Renaissance Publishers, 1950.

———. *Materialism,* 2d ed. Calcutta: Renaissance Publishers, 1951.

———. *New Humanism,* 2d ed. Calcutta: Renaissance Publishers, 1953.

Roy, S. B. "Chronological Framework of Indian Protohistory—The Lower Limit." *JOIB* 32, nos. 3–4 (March–June 1983): 254–74.

———. "Chronological Infrastructure of Indian Protohistory." *JBRS* 32 (1972): 44–78.

Ruben, W. *Materialismus im Leben des Alten Indien,* Acta Orientalis 13, Leiden: Brill, 1935.

Rudolph, L. I., and S. H. Rudolph. *The Modernity of Tradition.* Chicago: Chicago University Press, 1967.

Ruhela, S. P., and D. Robinson (eds.). *Sai Baba and His Message.* Delhi: Vikas, 1976.

Śābarabhāṣya, with contemporary Sanskrit commentary by B. G. Apte, 6 vols. Poona: Ānandāśrama, 1931–1934. Engl. trans. G. Jha, 3 vols. Baroda: Oriental Institute, 1973–74.

Sachau, Edward C. (trans.). *Alberuni's India: An Account of the Religion, Philosophy, Literature, Geography, Chronology, Astronomy, Customs, Laws and Astrology of India About* A.D. *1030.* Trübner's Oriental Series. Reprint Delhi: S. Chand and Co., 1964.

Sadhu Caran Prasad, Vaikunthavasi Śrī Babu. *Dharmaśāstrasaṅgraha.* Bombay: Sri Venkateśvar Stim Mudranayantralaya, 1913.

Sai Baba (Sri Sathya). *Satya Sai Speaks,* 7 vols. Kadugodi: Śrī Sathya Sai Education and Publication Foundation, 1972–76.

Sakare, M. R. *History and Philosophy of the Liṅgāyata Religion.* Belgaum: Author, 1942.

Śākta, Vaiṣṇava, Yoga, Śaiva, Sāmanyavedānta, and Minor Upaniṣads. ed. and trans. P. Mahadev Sastri. Adyar: Adyar Library, 1912–1938 (reprints).

Saletore, B. A. *Ancient Indian Political Thought and Institutions.* Bombay: Asia Publishing House, 1963.

Salomon, R. (ed. and trans.). *The Bridge to the Three Holy Cities, The Samāyaṇa-Praghaiṭṭaka of Nārāyaṇa Bhaṭṭ's Triṣṭhalisetu.* Delhi: Motilal Banarsidass, 1985.

Sāmaveda, ed. Ram Sarma Acarya. Bareilly: Samskrit Samsthana, 1962; trans. R. T. H. Griffith, reprint Banaras: Chowkhamba, 1963.

Sāṁkhyakārikā, 4th ed., trans. S. S. Suryanarayana Sastri. Madras: University of Madras, 1948.

Sāṁkhya Kārikā of Mahamuni Śrī Īṣvarakṛṣṇa, with the commentary of Pandit Swanarayana Sastri and *Sāṅkhya Tattvakaumudī of Vācaspati Miśra.* Bombay: Nirnaya Sagar Press, 1940.

Sangani, N. P. "*Sanātan dharm hi sarvabhaum dharm yā mānav dharm hai.*" *Dharmāṅk, Kalyān* 30, no. 1 (1966): 242–49.

Sankalia, H. D. *Indian Archeology Today.* New York: Asia Publishing House, 1962.

———. "Paleolithic, Neolithic and Copper Ages." In *HCIP,* vol. 1, pp. 125–42.

———. *Prehistoric Art in India.* Delhi: Vikas Publishing House, 1978.

———. *The Prehistory and Protohistory of India and Pakistan.* Poona: Deccan college, 1974.

Śaṅkarabhāṣya, trans. Swami Gambhirananda. Calcutta: Advaita Ashrama, 1965.

Sankarananda, Swami. *Hindu States of Sumeria.* Calcutta: Firma K. L. Mukhopadhyay, 1962.

Sankaranarayan, P. *The Call of the Jagadguru.* Madras: Akhila Bharata Śaṅkara Seva Samiti, 1958.

Saṅkhāyana Śrautasūtra, trans. S. W. Caland. Nagpur: The International Academy of Indian Culture, 1953.

Santucci, J. A. *An Outline of Vedic Literature,* Missoula, Mont.: Scholars Press, 1977.

Saraswati, D. *Satyārtha Prakāśa.* Allahabad: Kal Press, 1947.

Sarkar, B. K. *The Positive Background of Hindu Sociology,* 3 vols. In *SBH.* vols. 18, 25, and 32. Allahabad: Panini Press, 1914–37.

Sarkar, S. *The Aboriginal Races of India.* Calcutta: Bookland, 1954.

Sarma, D. S. *Hinduism Through the Ages,* rev. ed. Bombay: Bharatiya Vidya Bhavan, 1958.

———. *The Renaissance of Hinduism*. Banaras: 1958.

———. "Sanātana Dharma." *Kalyān* 40, no. 1 (1966): 238–41.

Sarma, N. S. *Hindu Renaissance*. Banaras: Banaras Hindu University, 1944.

Sarma, R. T. *Darśanamañjarī*, part 1. Madras: University of Madras, 1985.

Sarvadarśanasaṁgraha of Mādhava, 3rd ed., ed. V. S. Abhyankar. Poona: Bhandarkar Oriental Research Institute, 1978; trans. E. B. Cowell and A. E. Gough (incomplete), 1892; reprint Banaras: Chowkhamba, 1960.

Sastri, G. *A Study in the Dialectics of Sphoṭa*. Delhi: Motilal Banarsidass, 1981.

Sastri, K. A. Nilakantha. *The Colas*, 3 vols. Madras: University of Madras, 1935.

———. *The Culture and History of the Tamils*. Calcutta: Firma K. L. Mukhopadhyay, 1964.

———. *History of South India*. Madras: Oxford University Press, 1955.

Sastri, K. S. Ramaswami. *Śivananda: The Modern World Prophet*. Rishikesh: Divine Light Society, 1953.

Sastri, K. "Kośavan ācāryah." Reprinted in *Kuppusamy Sastri Birth Centenary Commemoration Volume*, ed. S. S. Janaki. Madras: Kuppuswami Research Institute, 1981, Part 1.

———. "Nyāya-Vaiśeṣika—Origin and Development." Introduction to K. Sastri, *Primer of Indian Logic*, 1932; reprinted in *Kuppuswami Birth Centenary Commemoratioin Volume*, ed. S. S. Janaki. Madras: Kuppuswami Research Institute, 1981.

Sastri, P. D. *The Doctrine of Māyā in Vedānta*. London: 1911.

Sastry, R. A. (trans.). *Viṣṇusahasranāma: With the Bhāṣya of Śrī Saṁkarācārya*. Adyar Library General Series, Adyar: Adyar Library and Research Centre, 1980.

Satapatha Brāhmaṇa, ed. and trans. J. Eggeling, 5 vols. In *SBE*, vols. 12, 26, 41, 43, and 44.

Savarkar, V. "Essentials of Hindutva." In *Samagra Savarkar Wangmaya, Hindu Rāṣṭra Darshan*, vol. 6. Poona: Maharashtra Prantik Hindusabha, 1964.

Sawai, Yoshitsugu. "Śaṅkaras Theology of Samnyāsa." *Journal of Indian Philosophy* 14 (1986): pp. 371–87.

Saxena, K. "The Janata Party Politics in Uttar Pradesh (1977–79)." *Indian Political Science Review* (July 1983): 172–87.

Scharfe, H. *The State in Indian Tradition*. Leiden: Brill, 1989.

Schilpp, P. A. (ed.). *The Philosophy of Sarvepalli Radhakrishnan*. New York: Tudor Publishing Co., 1952.

Schlingloff, D. *Die altindische Stadt*. Wiesbaden: Harrassowitz, 1969.

Schneider, U. "Kṛṣṇa's postumer Aufstieg: Zur Frühgeschichte der Bhaktibewegung." *Saeculum* 33, no. 1 (1982): 38–49.

Schour, K., and W. H. McLeod (eds.). *The Sants: Studies in a Devotional Tradition of India*. Delhi, Banaras, Patna, and Madras: Motilal Banarsidass, 1987.

Schrader, F. O. *Introduction to the Pāñcarātra and the Ahirbudhnya Saṃhitā*. Adyar: Adyar Library and Research Centre, 1916.

Schwab, J. *Das indische Tieropfer*. Erlangen: Deichert, 1886.

———. *Le Rénaissance Orientale*, 1950. English translation: *The Oriental Renaissance: Europe's Rediscovery of India and the East, 1680–1880*, trans. G. Patterson-Black and V. Reinking. New York: Columbia University Press, 1984.

Schwartzberg, J. E. (ed.). *Historical Atlas of India*, 2d ed. Chicago: University of Chicago Press, 1990.

Seal, A. *The Emergence of Indian Nationalism*. Cambridge: 1968.

Seal, B. N. *Comparative Studies in Vaishnavism and Christianity with an Examination of the Mahābhārata Legend About Nārada's Pilgrimage to Śvetadvīpa and an Introduction on the Historico-Comparative Method*. Calcutta: Private publication, 1899.

———. *The Positive Sciences of the Hindus*. Reprint Delhi: Motilal Banarsidass, 1958.

"Secret Societies" *SEMINAR* 151 (March 1972).

Seemann, R. "Versuch zu einer Theorie des Avatāra. Mensch gewordener Gott oder Gott gewordener Mensch?" *Numen* 33, no. 1 (1986): 90–140.

Segal, J. G. "White and Black Jews at Cochin, the Story of a Controversy." *JRAS*, no. 2 (1983): 228–52.

Segal, R. *The Crisis of India*. Harmondsworth: Penguin, 1965.

Sen, N. "The Influence of the Epics on Indian Life and Literature." In *CHI*, vol. 2, p. 117.

Sen, S. P. *Social Contents of Indian Religious Reform Movements*. Calcutta: Institute of Historical Studies, 1978.

Sengupta, N. C. *Evolution of Ancient Indian Law*. London: Probsthain, 1953.

Sengupta, P. C. *Ancient Indian Chronology*. Calcutta: University of Calcutta, 1947.

Shankar, M. "Social Roots of Communalism." *RS* 31, no. 4 (1984): 24–44.

Sharma, A. *The Hindu Gītā: Ancient and Classical Interpretations of the Bhagavadgītā*. LaSalle, Ill.: Open Court, 1986.

———. *The Puruṣārthas: A Study in Hindu Axiology*. East Lansing: Asian Studies Center, Michigan State University, 1982.

———. *Viśiṣṭādvaita Vedānta: A Study*. New Delhi: Heritage Press, 1978.

Sharma, B. N. K. *A Comparative Study of Ten Commentaries on the Brahmasūtras*. Delhi: Motilal Banarsidass, 1984.

———. *A History of Dvaita School of Vedānta and Its Literature*, 2 vols. Bombay: Booksellers Publishing Co., 1960–1961.

———. *Madhva's Teaching in His Own Words*. Bombay: Bhavatiya Vidya Bharan, 1961.

———. *Philosophy of Śrī Madhvācārya*. Bombay: Bharatiya Vidya Bhavan, 1962.

Sharma, H. D. *Brahmanical Asceticism*. Poona: Oriental Book Agency, 1939.

Sharma, R. K. (ed.). *Indian Archeology. New Perspectives*. Delhi: Agam Kala Prakashan, 1982.

Sharma, R. S. *Śūdras in Ancient India*. Delhi: Motilal Banarsidass, 1958.

Sharma, S. R. *Swami Rama Tirtha*. Bombay: Vidya Bhavan, 1961.

Sharpe, E. J. *The Univeral Gītā: Western Images of the Bhagavadgītā*, A Bicentenary Survey. La Salle, Ill.: Open Court, 1985.

Shastri, A. M. *India as Seen in the Bṛhatsaṃhitā of Varāhamihira*. Delhi: Motilal Banarsidass, 1969.

Shastri, D. R. *Short History of Indian Materialism*. Calcutta: The Book Company, 1930.

Shendge, M. J. "The Interdisciplinary Approach to Indian Studies." *ABORI* 63 (1982): 63–98.

———. *The Civilized Demons: The Harappans in Ṛgveda*. New Delhi: Abhinav, 1977

Sheth, N. *The Divinity of Krishna*. Delhi: Munshiram Manoharlal Publishers, 1984.

Shils, E. A. *The Intellectual Between Tradition and Modernity: The Indian Situation*. The Hague: Mouton, 1961.

Shinn, L. D. *The Dark Lord: Cult Images and the Hare Krishnas in America*. Philadelphia: Westminster, 1987.

Shourie, A. *Hinduism: Essence and Consequence—A Study of the Upaniṣads, the Gītā and the Brahma-Sūtras*. New Delhi: Vikas Publishing House, 1980.

Shulman, D. D. *Tamil Temple Myths: Sacrifice and Divine Marriage in the South Indian Śaiva Tradition*. Princeton, N.J.: Princeton University Press, 1980.

Siauve, S. *La doctrine de Madhva*. Pondichery: Institut Français d'Indologie, 1968.

———. *La voie vers la connaissance de Dieu sélon l'Aṇuvyākhyāna de Madhva*. Pondichery: Institut Français d'Indologie, 1957.

Siegel, L. *Fires of Love—Waters of Peace: Passion and Renunciation in Indian Culture*. Honolulu: University of Hawaii Press, 1983.

———. *Sacred and Profane Dimensions of Love in Indian Traditions as Exemplified in the Gītāgovinda of Jayadeva*. Oxford: Oxford University Press, 1978.

Śikṣadivedaṣadaṅgāṇi, ed. Pandurang Jawaji. Bombay: Venkatesvara Steam Press, 1934.

Sil, N. P. "Political Morality vs. Political Necessity: Kauṭilya and Machiavelli Revisited." *Journal of Asian History* 19, no. 2 (1985): 101–42.

Singer, M. (ed.). *Krishna: Myths, Rites and Attitudes*. Chicago: University of Chicago Press, 1969.

——— (ed.). *Traditional India: Structure and Change*. Philadelphia: American Folklore Society, 1959.

Singh, K. *India: A Mirror for Its Monsters and Monstrosities*. Bombay: Pearl Books, 1970.

Singh, M. "Yoga and Yoga Symbolism." *Symbolon: Jahrbuch für Symbolforschung*, 2 (1959): 121–43.

Singh, N. K. "Anandmarg." *SEMINAR* 151 (March 1972): 21–25.

Singh, S. *Vedāntadeśika*. Banaras: Chowkhamba, 1958.

Singhal, D. P. *India and World Civilization*. East Lansing: Michigan State University Press, 1969.

———. "Naturalism and Science in Ancient India." In *India and World Civilisations*, vol. 1, 1969.

Sinha, J. *History of Indian Philosophy*, 2 vols. Calcutta: Sinha Publishing House, 1956–1961.

———. *Indian Psychology*, 2 vols. Calcutta: Sinha Publishing House, 1958–1960.

———. *Indian Realism*. London: K. Paul, French, Trübner and Co., 1938.

Sinha, P. N. *A Study of the Bhāgavata Purāṇa*, 2d ed. Madras: Theosophical Society, 1950.

Sirkar, D. C. *The Śākta Pīṭhas*, rev. ed. Delhi: Motilal Banarsidass, 1948.

———. "Viṣṇu." *Quarterly Journal of the Mythological Society* 25 (1935): 120ff.

Śivapadasundaram, S. *The Śaivaschool of Hinduism*. London: Allen and Unwin, 1934.

Śiva-Purāṇa. Banaras: Pandit Pustakalaya, 1962; trans. J. L. Shastri, 4 vols. Delhi: Motilal Banarsidass, 1970–1971.

Śivaramamurti, C. *South Indian Bronzes*. New Delhi: lalitkala Akademi, 1963.

Śivaraman, K. *Śaivism in Philosophical Perspective*. Delhi: Motilal Banarsidass, 1973.

———. "The Word as a Category of Revelation." In *Revelation in Indian Thought, A Festschrift in Honour of Professor T. R. V. Murti*, ed. H. Coward and K. Śivaraman, pp. 45–64. Emeryville, Calif.: Dharma Publishing, 1977.

Śivasaṃhitā, trans. S. C. Vasu. Allahabad: Panini Office, 1923.

Ślokavārtika of Kumārila Bhaṭṭa with the Commentary Nyāyaratnakāra of Parthasarathi Miśra, trans. Ganganatha Jha (Calcutta: Asiatic Society, 1907), ed. Swami Drankasa Sastri (Banaras: Tara Publications, 1978).

Smart, N. *Doctrine and Argument in Indian Philosophy*. London: Allen and Unwin, 1964.

Smith, B. D. (ed.). *Hinduism: New Essays on the History of Religions*. Leiden: Brill, 1976.

Smith, B. K. "Ritual, Knowledge, and Being: Initiation and Veda Study in Ancient India." *Numen* 33, no. 1 (1986): 65–89.

Smith, B. L. (ed.). *Religion and the Legitimation of Power in South Asia*. International Studies in Sociology and Social Anthropology, Leiden: Brill, 1978.

Smith, D. E. *India as a Secular State*. Princeton, N.J.: Princeton University Press, 1967.

Smith, F. M. "Financing the Vedic Ritual. The Mūlādhyāyapariśiṣṭa of Kātyāyana." *WZKS* 32 (1989): 63–75.

Smith, V. *History of India*. Oxford: Oxford University Press, 1955.

Smith, W. C. *Modern Islam in India*, 3rd ed. Lahore: Mohammed Ashraf, 1963.

Somaśaṃbhupaddhatī, ed. French trans. and notator H. Brunner-Lachaux, 2 vols. Pondichery: Institut Français d'Indologie, 1963–1968.

Sorenson, M. *Index of Subjects in the Mahābhārata*. Reprint Delhi: Motilal Banarsidass, 1962.

Spate, O. H. K. *India and Pakistan: A General and Regional Geography*. London: Methusen, 1967.

Spellman, J. W. *Political Theory of Ancient India*. New York: Oxford University Press, 1964.

Srinivas, M. N. *Caste and Ohter Essays*. Reprint, Bombay: Asia Publishing House, 1965.

———. *India's Villages*. Bombay: Asia Publishing House, 1960.

———. *Religion and Society Among the Coorgs of South India*, 2d ed. Bombay: Asia Publishing House, 21965.

Srinivasacari, P. *The Philosophy of Viśiṣṭādvaita*. Adyar: Theosophical Society, 1946.

Srinivasan, D. "Unhinging Śiva from the Indus Civilization." *JRAS* 1 (1984): 77–89.

Srinivasan, D. M (ed.). *Mathurā: The Cultural Heritage*. New Delhi: American Institute of Indian Studies, 1989.

Śrīparameśvara Saṃhitā, ed. Sri Govindacarya. Srirangam: Kodandaramasannidhi, 1953.

Śrīpati's Śrīkara Bhāṣya, ed. Hayavadana Rao. Bangalore: 1936.

Staal, J. F. *Advaita and Neoplatonism*. Madras: University of Madras, 1961.

———. *AGNI: The Vedic Ritual of the Fire Altar*, 2 vols. Berkeley: University of California Press, 1983.

———. "Exchange with a reviewer of *Agni*." *JAS* 46, no. 1 (1987): 105–10.

———. "Language and Ritual." In *Kuppuswamy Sastri Birth Centenary Commemoration Volume*, part 2, pp. 51–62. Madras: Kuppuswami Research Institute, 1985.

———. "The Meaninglessness of Ritual." *Numen* 26 (1979): 2–22.

———. *The Science of Ritual*. Poona: Deccan Institute, 1982.

———. "The Sound of Religion." *Numen* 33 (1986): 33–64, 185–224.

——— (ed.). *A Reader on the Sanskrit Grammarians*. Cambridge, Mass.: MIT Press, 1972.

Stevenson, M. *The Rites of the Twice Born*. Oxford: Oxford University Press, 1920.

von Stietencron, H. "Dämonen und Gegengötter: Überlegungen zur Typologie von Antagonismen." *Saeculum* 34, nos. 3–4 (1983): 372–83.

———. "Die Göttin Durgā Mahiṣāsuramārdinī: Mythos, Darstellung und geschichtliche Rolle bei der Hinduisierung Indiens." In *Visible Religion, Annual for Religious Iconography*, vol. 23, pp. 11–166. Leiden: Brill, 1983.

———. *Gaṅgā und Yamunā*. Wiesbaden: Otto Harrassowitz, 1972.

———. *Indische Sonnenpriester: Samba und die Śākasdiśpīya Brāhmaṇa*. Wiesbaden: Otto Harrassowitz, 1966.

———. "Suicide as a Religious Institution." *Bharatiya Vidya* 27 (1967): 7–24.

Stoler-Miller, B. *Love Song of the Dark Lord*. New York: Columbia University Press, 1977.

———. "Rādhā: Consort of Kṛṣṇa's Vernal Passion." *JAOS* 95, no. 4 (1975): 655–71.

———. "Stella Kramrisch: A Biographical Essay." In *Exploring India's Sacred Art*, ed. B. Stoler-Miller, pp. 3–33. Philadelphia: University of Pennsylvania, 1983.

Strickman, M. (ed.). *Classical Asian Rituals and the Theory of Ritual*. Berlin: Springer, 1986.

Subbarao, B. *The Personality of India*. Baroda: University of Baroda, 1959.

Śukra Nītisāra, trans. B. K. Sarkar, 2d ed. Allahabad: Panini Office, 1923.

Sukthankar, V. S. *On the Meaning of the Mahābhārata*. Bombay: Asiatic Society, 1957.

Sundaram, P. K. *Advaita Epistemology*. Madras: University of Madras, 1968.

Swarup, B. *Theory of Indian Music*, 2d ed. Allahabad: Swamy Brothers, 1958.

Tagore, R. *Sādhanā*. Calcutta: Macmillan, 1950.

———. *Creative Unity*. Calcutta: Macmillan, 1959.

Taimni, I. K. *The Science of Yoga*. Wheaton, Ill.: Theosophical Publishing House, 1972.

Talbot, P., and S. L. Poplai. *India and America: A Study of Their Religions*. New York: Harper and Row, 1959.

Tandon, P. *Punjabi Century*. Berkeley: University of California, 1968.

Taposwami Majaraj, Swami. *Wanderings in the Himalayas*, Madras: Ganesh, 1960.

Tarkabhāṣa of Keśava Miśra, 2d ed., ed. and trans. G. Jha. Poona: Oriental Book Agency, 1949.

Tarn, W. W. *The Greeks in Bactria and India*. Cambridge: Cambridge University Press, 1951; reprint 1966.

Tendulkar, D. G. *Mahātmā: Life and Work of M. K. Gandhi*, 8 vols. Bombay: V. K. Jhaveri, 1951–1958.

Thangaswami, R. *A Bibliographical Survey of Advaita Vedānta Literature* [Sanskrit]. Madras: University of Madras, 1980.

———. *Darśanamañjarī*. Madras: University of Madras, 1985.

Thapar, R. *A History of India*, 2 vols. Baltimore: Penguin Books. 1966.

———. *India in Transition*. Bombay: Asia Publishing House, 1956.

Thomas, P. *Epics, Myths and Legends of India*. Bombay: Taraporevala, 1961.

———. *Hindu Religion, Custom and Manners*. Bombay: 1961.

Thompson, E. J., and A. M. Spencer. *Bengali Religious Lyrics, Śākta*. Calcutta: Association Press, 1923.

Thurston, E., and K. Rangachari. *Tribes and Castes of South India*, 4 vols. Madras: Government Press, 1929.

Tilak, B. G. *The Arctic Home in the Vedas*. Reprint Poona: Tilak Bros., 1956.

———. *Gītā-Rahasya*, 2 vols. Reprint Poona: Tilak Bros., 1956.

———. *Orion, or Researches into the Antiquity of the Veda*. Bombay: Sagoon, 1893. Reprint Poona: Tilak Bros., 1955.

———. *Vedic Chronology*. Poona: 1909.

Tillotson, G. H. R. "The Indian Travels of William Hodges." *JRAS*, series 3, vol. 2, no. 3 (1992): 377–98.

Timberg, T. A. (ed.). *Jews in India*. New York: Advent Books, 1986.

Timm, J. R. "Vallabha, Vaiṣṇavism and the Western Hegemony of Indian Thought" *Journal of Dharma* 14, no. 1 (1989): 6–36.

Tirtha, Swami B. K. *Sanātana Dharma*. Bombay: Bharatiya Vidya Bhavan, 1964.

The Tirukkural [Tamil], trans. G. U. Pope, W. H. Drew, J. Lazarus and F. W. Ellis. Tinnelvelly: South India Śaiva Siddhānta Works Publishing Society, 1962.

Tiruvācagam, ed. and trans. G. U. Pope. 1900; reprint Madras: University of Madras, 1970.

Tiruvācakam, trans. Ratna Navaratnam. Bombay: Bharatiya Vidya Bhavan, 1963.

Tod, J. *Annals and Antiquities of Rajasthan*, ed. William Crooke, 3 vols. Delhi: Motilal Banarsidass, n.d.

Tripurā Rahasya, trans. A. U. Vasavada. Banaras: Chowkhamba, 1965.

Tripurārahasyam, ed. Swami Sanatanadevaji Maharaja. Banaras: Chowkhamba, 1967.

Trivedi, M. M. "Citsukha's View on Self-Luminosity." *JIPh*, 15 (1987): 115–23.

Tyagisananda, Swami (ed.). *Aphorismms on the Gospel of Divine Love or Nārada Bhakti Sūtras*, 5th ed. Madras: Ramakrishna Math, Mylapore, 1972.

Underhill, M. M. *The Hindu Religious Year*. Calcutta: Association Press, 1921.

Upadeśasahasrī of Śaṅkarācārya, 3rd ed., ed. and trans. Swami Jagadananda. Madras: Ramakrishna Math, 1962.

Upadhyaya, D. "A Democratic Alternative." *SEMINAR* 80 (April 1966): 21–24.

———. "Jana Sangh." *SEMINAR* 89 (January 1967): 34–37.

Upadhyaya, K. D. *Studies in Indian Folk Culture*. Calcutta: Indian Publications, 1964.

Upadhye, P. M. "Manusmṛti—Its Relevance in Modern India." In *JOIB* 35, no. 1–2 (1985): 43–48.

Vadāvalī of Nagoji Bhaṭṭa, ed. and trans. Nagaraja Rao. Adyar: Adyar Library, 1943.

Vaidyanathan, K. R. *Śrī Krishna, the Lord of Guruvayūr*. Bombay: Bharatiya Vidya Bhavan, 1977.

Vaiśeṣikardarśana, ed. and trans. Anantalal Thakur. Darbhanga: Mithila Institute, 1957.

Vaiśeṣikasūtras of Kanāḍa, trans. N. Sinha. Allahabad: Panini Office, 1911.

Varma, K. C. "The Iron Age, the Veda and the Historical Urbanization." In *Indian Archeology, New Perspectives*, ed. R. K. Sharma, pp. 155–83. New Delhi: Indian Archeological Survey, 1982.

Varma, L. A. Ravi, "Rituals of Worship." In *CHI*, vol. 4, pp. 445–63.

Varma, V. P. *Modern Indian Political Thought*, 4th ed. Agra: Laksmi Narain Agarwala, 1968.

Vasudevāśrama: Yatidharmaprakāśa. A Treatise on World Renunciation. ed. and trans. P. Olivelle, 2 vols. Vienna: De Nobili Research Library, 1977.

Vatsyayan, K. "Prehistoric Paintings." *Sangeet Natak, Journal of the Sangeet NatakAkademi* 66 (October–December): 5–18.

Vaudeville, C. *Kabīr Granthavalī* (Doha). Pondichery: Institut Français d'Indologie, 1957.

Vedāntakarikāvalī of Venkatācārya. ed. and trans. V. Krisnamacarya. Adyar: Adyar Library, 1950.

Vedāntaparibhāṣa by Dharmarāja. Sastri ed. and trans. S. S. Suryanarayana. Adyar: Adyar Library, 1942.

Vedāntasāra of Sādānanda Yogīndra, 4th ed., ed. and trans. Swami Nikhilananda. Calcutta: Ramakrishna Math, 1959.

Vedāntasūtras with the Commentary of Baladeva, trans. S. C. Vasu Vidyaranava, 2d ed. In *SBH*. Allahabad: Panini Office, 21934.

Vedāntasūtras with the Commentary of Madhva, 2d ed. trans. S. S. Rao. Tirupati: Śrī Vyasa Press, 1936.

Vedāntasūtras with Rāmānuja's Commentary, trans. G. Thibaut. In *SBE*, vol. 48.

Vedāntasūtras with Śaṅkarācārya's Commentary, trans. G. Thibaut, 2 vols. In *SBE*, vols. 34 and 38.

Vedārthasaṁgraha of Rāmānuja, ed. and trans. S. S. Ragavacar. Mysore: Ramakrishna Ashrama, 1956.

Vetter, T. "Die Gaudapadīya-Kārikās: Zur Entstehung und zur Bedeutung von [A]dvaita." *WZKSA* 22 (1978): 95–131.

Vidyabhusana, S. C. *A History of Indian Logic*. Calcutta: University of Calcutta, 1921.

Vidyarthi, L. P. *Aspects of Religion in Indian Society*. Meerut: Vednat Nath Rammath, 1962.

Vidyarthi, P. B. *Knowledge, Self and God in Rāmānuja*. New Delhi: Motilal Banarsidass, 1978.

Viennot, O. *Le culte de l'arbre dans l'Inde ancienne*. Paris: Presses Universitaire de France, 1954.

Viṣṇu Purāṇa, trans. H. H. Wilson. Reprint Calcutta: Punthi Pustak, 1961.

Viśva Hindū Viśeṣāṅk. Bombay: World Council of Hindus, 1966.

Viśvakarma Vāstuśāstra, ed. K. Vasudeva Sastri and N. B. Gadre. Tanjore Sarasvati Mahal Series No. 85, 1958.

Vivekacudāmaṇi of Śaṅkarācārya, 7th ed., ed. and trans. Swami Madhavananda. Calcutta: Ramakrishna Math, 1966.

Vivekananda, Swami. *Complete Works of Swami Vivekananda*, 8 vols. Calcutta: Advaita Ashrama, 1970–1971.

Vogel, J. P. *Indian Serpent Lore*. London: Probsthain, 1926.

Volwahsen, A. *Living Architecture: Indian*. New York: Grosset and Dunlap, 1969.

Vyas, K. C. *The Social Renaissance in India*. Bombay: Asia Publishing House, 1957.

Vyas, R. T. "Roots of Śaṅkara's Thought." *JOIB* 32, nos. 1–2 (September–December 1982): 35–49.

Vyas, S. N. *India in the Rāmāyaṇa Age*. Delhi: Atura Ram and Sons, 1967.

Waghorne, J. P. and N. Cutler (ed.). *Gods of Flesh/Gods of Stone: The Embodiment of Divinity in India*. Chambersburg, Pa.: Anima Publications, 1985.

Walker, B. *The Hindu World: An Encyclopedic Survey of Hinduism*, 2 vols. New York: Praeger Books, 1968.

Warder, A. K. *Outline of Indian Philosophy*. Delhi: Motilal Banarsidass, 1968.

Wasson, R. G. "The Soma of the Rig Veda: What Was It?" *JAOS* 91, no. 2 (1971): 169–91.

Weber, A. "Über das Menschenopfer bei den Indern der vedischen Zeit." *Indische Streifen*, vol. 1, pp. 54–89. Berlin: Nicolai, 1886.

Weber, M. *The Religion of India: The Sociology of Hinduism and Buddhism*. Reprint New York: Free Press, 1967.

Weiss, B. "Meditations in the Myth of Savitri." *JAAR* 53, no. 2: 259–70.

von Weizsäcker, C. F. V., and Gopi Kṛṣṇa. *Biologische Basis religiöser Erfahrung*. Weilheim: Otto Wilhelm Barth Verlag, 1971.

Welborn, G., and G. E. Yocum (eds.). *Religious Festivals in South India and Śrī Lanka*, Delhi: Manohar, 1985.

Werner, K. "A Note on Karma and Rebirth in the Vedas" *Hinduism* 83 (1978): 1–4.

———. "Religious Practice and Yoga in the Time of the Vedas, Upaniṣads and Early Buddhism." *ABORI* 56 (1975): 179–94.

———. "The Vedic Concept of Human Personality and Its Destiny." *JIPh* 5 (1978): 275–89.

Westcott, G. H. *Kabīr and the Kabīr Panth*, 2d ed. Reprint Calcutta: Susil Gupta, 21953.

Whaling, F. *The Rise of the Religious Significance of Rāma*. Delhi: Motilal Banarsidass, 1980.

Wheeler, M. *The Indus Civilization*. Cambridge: Cambridge University Press, 1953.

Wheelock, W. T. "Patterns of Mantra Use in a Vedic Ritual." *Numen* 32, no. 2 (1986): 169–93.

White, S. J. "Kṛṣṇa as Divine Child." *HR* 12, no. 2 (1972): 156–77.

Whitehead, H. *The Village Gods of South India*, 2d ed. Religious Life of India Series. Calcutta: Association Press, 1921.

Williams, R. B. *A New Face of Hinduism: The Swaminarayan Religion*. Cambridge: Cambridge University Press, 1984.

Wilson, H. H. *Essays and Lectures on the Religion of the Hindus*, 2 vols. London: Trübner, 1962.

———. *Religious Sects of the Hindus*. 1861; reprint Calcutta: Punthi Pustak, 1958.

Winternitz, M. *Geschichte der indischen Literatur*, vol. 1, 1905, reprint Stuttgart, K. F. Kohler Verlag, 1968. English translation: *A History of Indian Literature*, trans. S. Ketkar and H. Kohn, 3 vols. Reprint Calcutta: University of Calcutta, 1927–1967.

Wiser, W. H. *Behind Mud Walls 1930–60*. Berkeley: University of California, 1963.

———. *The Hindu Jajmani System*. Lucknow: Lucknow Publishing House, 1958.

Woodroffe, J (Arthur Avalon). *Introduction to Tantra Śāstra*, 4th ed. Madras: Ganesh and Co., 1963.

———. *Mahānirvāṇatantra: The Great Liberation*, 4th ed. Madras: Ganesh and Co., 1963.

———. *Principles of Tantra*, 3rd ed. Madras: Ganesh and Co., 1960.

Woods, J. H. trans. *Patañjali's Yogasūtra, with Vyāsa's Bhāṣya and Vācaspati Miśra's Tattva Vaisāradi*, Harvard Oriental Series no. 17. Cambridge, Mass.: Harvard University Press, 1914.

Wyatt, N. "*Aśvamedha* and *Puruṣamedha* in Ancient India." *Religion* (1989): 1–11.

Yadav, B. S. "Vaiṣṇavism on Hans Küng: A Hindu Theology of Religious Pluralism." *Religion and Society* 27, no. 2 (June 1980): 32–64.

Yajurveda Vājasaneyasaṃhitā, ed. A. Weber, 2 vols. Leipzig: Indische Studien, 1871–1872.

Yamunacarya, M. *Rāmānuja's Teachings in His Own Words*. Bombay: Bharatiya Vidya Bhavan, 1963.

Yatidharmasaṅgraha of Viśveśvarasaraswatī, ed. V. G. Apte. Poona: Ānandāśrama, 1928.

Yatīndramatadīpikā of Śrīnivāsadāsa, ed. and trans. Swami Adidevananda. Madras: Ramakrishna Math, Mylapore 1949.

Yatiswarananda, Swami. *The Divine Life*. Mylapore: 1964.

——— (ed.). *Universal Prayers*. Mylapore: Ramakrishna Math, 1956.

Yocum, G. E. "The Goddess in a Tamil Śaiva Devotional Text, Manikkavacakar's Tiruvacakam." *JAAR* supplement 45 (1977): 367–88.

———. *Hymns to the Dancing Śiva: A Study of Manikkavacakar's Tiruvacakam*. Columbia, Mo.: South Asia Books, 1982.

———. "Shrines, Shamanism, and Love Poetry: Elements in the Emergence of Popular Tamil Bhakti." *JAAR*, 41 (1973): 3–17.

Yogananda, P. *Autobiography of a Yogi*. Bombay: Jaico, 1960.

Yogavaśiṣṭha Rāmāyaṇa, trans. D. N. Bose, 2 vols. Calcutta: Oriental Publishing Co., 1958.

Young, K., and A. Sharma. *Images of the Feminine—Mythic, Philosophic and Human—in the Buddhist, Hindu and Islamic Traditions: A Biography of Women in India*. Chico: New Horizons Press, 1974.

Young, R. F. *Resistant Hinduism: Sanskrit Sources on Anti-Christian Apologetics in Early Nineteenth-Century India*. Vienna: Indologisches Institut der Universität Wien, 1981.

Younger, P. "A Temple Festival of Mariyamman." *JAAR*, 48 (1980): 493–517.

———. *Introduction to Indian Religious Thought*. Philadelphia: Westminster Press, 1972.

Zaehner, H. *Hinduism*. Oxford: Oxford University Press, 1962.

Zelliot, E. "The Mediaeval Bhakti Movement in History. An Essay on the Literature in English." In *Hinduism: New Essays in the History of Religions*, ed. B. L. Smith. Leiden: Brill, 1976.

Zimmer, H. *The Art of Indian Asia*, 2 vols. New York: Bollingen Foundation, 1955.

———. *Artistic Form and Yoga in the Sacred Images of India*, trans. Gerald Chapple and James B. Lawson. Princeton, N.J.: Princeton University Press, 1984.

———. *The King and the Corpse*. New York: Pantheon Books, 1947.

———. *Myths and Symbols in Indian Art and Civilization*, 4th ed. New York: Harper and Row, 1963.

———. *Philosophies of India*, ed. J. Campbell. Princeton: Bollingen Foundation, 1951.

Zvelebil, K. *Tiru Murugan*. Madras: International Institute of Tamil Studies, 1982.

INDEX

abhāva, 73, 415
Abhinavagupta, 271, 484
abhiniveśa, 402
abhiṣeka, 90
Abhyankar, K. V., 575
Abhyankar, V. S., 537, 569
ācamanīya, 163
Acarya, Ram Sarma, 508
ācāryā, 362
ācāryāṇī, 362
Acharya, P. K., 554
action, 105, 106
Acutyaprekṣa, 60
ādāna, 268
adbhuta, 229
adharma: threefold, 53, 85; rise of, 105; apportioned by Brahmā, 124; not found in the Lord, 395
adhidaivata, 76
adhikāra, 271, 348
adhiyajña, 76
adhyāsa, 415, 419
adhyātma, 76; *adhyātma vidyā*, 392; *Adhyātma Rāmāyaṇa*, 244, 486, 539
Ādi Granth, 356
Ādi Samāj, 435
Adidevananda, Swami, 540, 579
Ādiśaṅkara, 351. See also: Śaṅkara, Śaṅkarācārya.
Aditi, 134
ādivāsīs, 8, 31, 34, 335
adṛṣṭa, 387, 389, 390, 392, 395
adultery, 178, 363
Advaita, 63, 249, 413, 419; Advaita Vedānta, 60, 228, 377, 380, 413 ff, 440, 539; Advaitins, 422
Advani, Lal Krishna, 466
ādyaprakṛti, 291
Āgamas, 39, 69, 70, 163, 168, 270, 273, 289, 435, 546
Agastya, 294, 550; Agastyam, 294
Aghoris, 353, 564
Agni, 96, 114, 116, 131, 133, 134, 158, 163, 190, 270; *Agni Purāṇa*, 96, 484; *agnicayana*, 158; *agnihotra*, 363; *agniṣṭoma*, 161, 179
Agrawala, V. S., 95, 293, 511, 550
agriculture, 125
aham brahmāsmi, 210, 350
ahaṁkāra, 116, 400, 519
ahiṃsa, 351, 403, 454, 457, 458, 459
Ahirbudhnya Saṃhita, 483
Ahirs, 245
Aikṣvāka dynasty, 125
Aila dynasty, 125, 500
air, 197, 206
aiśvarya, 248
Aitareya Brāhmaṇa, 212, 266, 527, 528, 545; *Aitareya Upaniṣad*, 194, 534
Aiyangar, M. Duraiswami, 509
Aiyangar, S. K., 499
Aiyar, S. P., 587
Aiyer, A. Nataraja, 577
Ajamila, 226, 528
Ajantā, 7
Ajataśatru, 482
ajñā, 293; *ajñā cakra*, 288; *ajñādhāra*, 293
ākāśa, 197, 206, 390, 391
Akbar, 46, 97, 258, 370, 486
akhāḍās, 351, 353
Akhaṇḍ Bhārat, 463, 473
Akhil Bhāratīya Sādhu Samāj, 357
Akhil Bharatīya Sant Samitī, 358, 585
Akhil Bharatīya Vidyārthi Pariṣad, 466

akhilarasāmṛta mūrti, 229
Akkad, 147
akṛti, 74
akṣobhya, 288
Alberuni, 20
Alexander the Great, 17, 482; Alexander romance, 18
Alexandria, 18, 100
Ali, S. M., 519
Allahābad, 329
Allchin, B., 499, 588
Allchin, F., 499, 588
alphabet, 286, 287, 289
Alsdorf, L., 137
alsmgiving, 216
Altekar, A. S., 54, 475, 579, 583, 588
Āḷvārs, 223, 246, 251, 301, 304
Amarakanṭaka, 354
Amarakośa, 95
Amarnāth, 315
Aṃbā, 283
Ambedkar, B. R., 9, 344, 457, 562
Aṃbikā, 281
Ambrose of Milan, 19
aṃbu, 123
American Oriental Society, 24
Amore, R., 506
amṛta, 127, 141, 166
amṛta manthana, 128
anahaṭ-śabda, 259
anahaṭa cakra, 288
ānanda, 195, 207, 271, 350
Ānandagiri, 351
Ānandamaṭha, 462
ānandamaya, 207
Ananadamayi Ma, 356, 371, 442
Ananda Tirtha, 352, 422
Ānand Mārg, 469
Ānand Mūrti, 469
ananta, 122
aṇava, 269, 268, 271
ancestors, 190, 192
ancient Egypt, 18
Andhaka, 266
Aṇḍakaṭaha, 119
Andrews, Rev., 448
Aṅgāraka, 123
anger, 256, 403
Aṅgirasasmṛti, 566
aṇima, 207
animals, 152, 299, 552; animal sacrifice; 45, 165, 166, 267; animal rebirths, 530; animal worship, 149
Aniruddha, 248
anna, 164, 206; *annarasamaya*, 206
Annadurai, C. N., 300
anṛta, 125
Anṭāl, 224, 302, 304, 368, 567, 484
antar-ātman, 246, 248, 251, 266, 419, 423
Anti-Brahmin movements, 299
Antoninus Pius, 19
antyeṣṭi, 189
aṇu, 392, 389
Anugītā, 517
anugraha, 268, 326
anumāna, 73, 393
anurāga, 542
Aṇuvyākhyāna, 423, 578
anvīkṣikī, 383, 569, 571
Apalā, 361
apara jñāna, 200
aparādha kṣamā pañca stotra, 65
aparigraha, 403, 450, 455
apāśraya, 95
apauruṣeya, 380, 409
aphorisms, 196
Apollonius of Tyana, 19
apophatic method, 196
Appar, 268, 274
Appaya Dīkṣita, 351
appearance, 198
aprakṛta-śarīra, 248
āpsaras, 116
Apte, B. G., 574
Apte, S. S., 586
Apte, V. G., 563
apūrva, 168, 170, 215, 409, 410, 529. See also: *Mīmāṃsā*.

Arabs, 20, 46
Āraṇya, 350
Āraṇyakāṇḍa, 91
Āraṇyakaparvan, 87
āraṇyakas, 67, 193
arcana, 230; *arcāvatāra*, 246, 248, 315
Archer, W. G., 540
Ardhamagadhī, 6
arghya, 163
Aristotle, 18
Arjuna, 82, 85, 87, 88, 103, 105, 107, 167
Armadio, B. A., 129
Arnold, E., 449
ārṣa, 531
artha, 95, 159, 336, 337, 340, 342, 364, 561; *artha-maṇḍapa*, 321; *arthāpatti*, 73; *Ārthaśāstra*, 338, 341, 482, 571; *arthavāda*, 67, 410
Arthapañcaka, 315
Aruṇācala, 43
Arundhatī, 188
Aruṇi, 195
Arur, 304
Ārya Samāj, 32, 63, 186, 435, 462, 487, 580
Āryan origins, 96
Āryandā, 265
Āryans, 34, 76, 132, 147, 479, 500, 589; Aryanization, 295f; Āryavārta, 294
āsana, 163, 403
asat, 106, 114, 115
asceticism, 19, 269, 275
ashes, 268
Ashish, Madhava 565
Ashram Observances in Action, 453
Asiatic Society of Bengal, 22, 487
āśīrvāda, 172, 185
Asmarāthya, 411
āsmitā, 402
Aśoka, 341, 483
aspṛha, 456
Āśrama, 350
Āśrama, Swāmi Vijñāna, 572
āśramas, 185, 337, 378, 385, 457
Aṣṭādhyāyī, 74, 479, 482
aṣṭāgraha, 155, 157
aṣṭamūrti, 268
aṣṭāvaraṇa, 273
asteya, 403, 455
āstika, 50, 62, 380
astrologer, 185; astrology, 96, 325. See also *jyotisi.*
asuras, 208, 241, 531; *asura* power, 131
aśvamedha, 97, 157, 166, 525, 527
asymmetry, 114
Atala, 122
Atharva Veda, 67, 78, 94, 163, 181, 266, 479, 516, 545
atheism, 177. See also: *nāstika.*
Athens, 19
athiti, 164
Atiśūdras, 223
Ātmabodha, 425, 578
ātmakūta, 173
ātman, 79, 104, 105, 106, 115, 173, 200, 204 ff, 212, 213, 271, 388, 389, 391, 392, 394, 413, 415, 416, 417, 423; *ātmanastuṣṭi*, 50; *ātmanivedana*, 231, 255
atom bomb, 109, 110
atoms, 390, 391; atomism, 389
atonement, 152, 178f, 179, 180
Atreya, 350, 411
Atri, 361
Atrismṛti, 566
attachment, 267
Attenborough, Sir Richard, 447
audārya, 288
audhas, 248
Audulomi, 350, 411
Aufrecht, T., 508
aughara, 354
Augustus, 18, 19
AUM, 79. See also: OM.
Aurangzeb, 356

Aurobindo Ghose, 101, 278, 293, 371, 356, 438, 462, 474, 475, 488, 518
auspicious, 161; auspicious time, 167; auspicious qualities, 420; auspicious-inauspicious, 162, 170, 187, 301
austerities, 179, 262, 268, 274
avahana, 163
Avalon, Arthur, 548. See also: Woodroff, John.
avatāras, 41, 43, 45, 52, 58, 90, 145, 149, 225, 240, 248, 251, 365, 423, 457, 539
Avesta, 34
avidyā, 392, 389, 402, 415, 416, 419, 421
Avimuktā, 330
avyakta, 289; *avyakta mūrti*, 106
ayam ātma brahman, 210, 350
Ayodhyā, 89, 90, 91, 92, 125, 146, 180, 244, 353, 358, 367, 446, 477, 489, 565
Ayurveda, 67, 440
ayus, 206
Ayyangar, T. R. Srinivasa, 530
Ayyar, C. V. Narayana, 523
Ayyar, P. V. Jagadisa, 553

Baba Avadhut Bhagavat Ram, 354
Baba Kinnaram, 354
Babri Masjid, 461, 466, 489
Babylonia, 147, 478
backbiting, 234
Bādarāyaṇa, 196
Bādarī, 350, 411
baddhas, 419
Badrīnāth, 350
Bagati, T. N., 500
bahūdakas, 347
Bahvici, 362
Bajrang Dal, 467, 565
Bakker, H., 572
bala, 248
Bāladeva, 297, 487, 543, 576
Baladeva Vidyabhusana, 258
Bālakāṇḍa, 90
Bālarāma, 146, 244, 297
Balasubramanian, R., 577
Bali, 145, 228, 240, 326
Bāna, 484
Bande Mātarām, 358, 462
bandha-gṛha, 326
Banerjea, A. K., 564
Banerjea, J. N., 554
bara sthāna, 353
barley, 180
Barthwal, C. P., 586
Barz, R., 541
Basava / Basavanna, 261, 273, 305
Basu, B. D., 539
beauty, 228, 237, 298, 419
Belur, 323
Belvalkar, S. K., 102, 512, 518, 575, 576
Benares, 96, 261, 262, 353, 557
Benares Hindu University, 463
Bene Israel, 45
Bengal Vaiṣṇavism, 223
Benz, E., 495
Bernstorff, D., 334, 559
Besant, Annie, 330, 440, 449
Bhadrakālī, 283
bhadrāsana, 574
Bhadravarṣa, 120
bhāg, 44
Bhagavadgītā, 14, 21, 24, 41, 51, 65, 66, 71, 99, 140, 145, 150, 167, 173, 174, 182, 222, 228, 241, 245, 251, 339, 423, 446, 449, 450, 454, 457, 482, 504, 517, 528, 536, 560
Bhagavadgītānuvāda, 102
bhagavan, 138, 419, 420
Bhagavat, H. R., 576
Bhāgavata, 79, 96
Bhāgavata Māhātmya, 97
Bhāgavata Purāṇa, 41, 70, 97, 145, 166, 229, 244, 249, 254, 255, 256, 257, 258, 294, 297, 304, 316, 349, 356, 399, 412, 423, 484, 502, 527, 536, 537, 539, 540, 555, 561, 572

Bhāgavata Saṃpradāya, 356
Bhāgavatism, 60, 145, 240, 245
bhagya, 534
Bhairava, 140, 245
bhajan, 145, 189, 258, 259, 379, 446; *bhajan-āśramas*, 236; *bhajānanda*, 256
bhakta, 108, 216
bhakti, 47, 62, 102, 107, 108, 145, 157, 167, 252, 257, 273, 278, 370, 425, 484, 535, 536; degrees of, 228; steps of, 229; grades of, 232; *bhakti* movement 368; Bhakti Vedānta, 260; *bhaktimārga*, 49, 151, 192, 221 ff; *Bhaktisūtras*, 222, 228
Bhaktivedanta, Swami, 29, 260, 358, 442
Bhandarkar Oriental Research Institute, 514
Bhandarkar, R. G., 497
bhaṅgi, 292, 460
Bharadwaj, K. D., 541, 577
Bharata (Rama's brother), 82, 90–93
Bhārata (Early form of *Mahābhārata*), 83
Bharata (son of Ṛsabḥa), 340, 478
Bhārata (India), 340, 465; Bhārat-Mātā, 43
Bhārata war, 126, 478, 479, 482
Bhārata varṣa, 118, 121, 123
Bharatī, 350
Bharati, Agehananda, 493, 548
Bhāratīya Jana Sangh, 337, 464, 488
Bhāratīya Janata Party (BJP), 466
Bhāratīya Mazdūr Sabhā, 466
Bhāratīya Vidyā Bhavan, 443
Bhārgava, 89; Bhārgavas, 84
Bhartṛhari, 74, 358, 411, 412, 565
Bhartṛmitra, 412
Bhartṛprapañca, 412
Bhāruci, 412
Bharva, 266
Bhāskara, 576
bhasma, 160, 530; *Bhasmajabala Upaniṣad*, 160
bhāṣya(s), 80, 382, 411, 425
Bhatt, G. H., 513, 515, 542
Bhatt, N. R., 509
Bhaṭṭa, Gopala, 555
Bhaṭṭa, Kumārila, 574
Bhattacharya, K., 521
Bhattacharya, S., 573
Bhattacharya, T., 554
Bhattacharyya, Minoti, 361, 565
bhava, 140, 265, 266, 542
bhavana-bhakti, 232
Bhaviṣya Purāṇa, 96, 516
bhaya, 125
bhayanakā, 229
bhedābheda, 270
Bhīma, 86, 87, 88
Bhīmadevī, 282
Bhimbetka, 34
Bhīṣma, 85, 108; *Bhīsma Parvan*, 99, 102
Bhoja, 399
bhojana, 164. See also: food.
Bhojraj, 369, 370
Brahmā saṃpradāya, 352
Bhramaradevī, 282
Bhṛgu, 84
Bhubaneśvara, 319, 321
Bhudan movement, 488
bhukti, 291
Bhur, 123; Bhurloka, 122
bhūtas, 59; *bhutādi*, 123; *bhūtayajña*, 159
Bhuvarloka, 122, 123
Biardeau, M., 570
bibhatsa, 229
Bihari, Bankey, 543, 544, 553, 567
bīja-mantra, 286, 288
Billimoria, P., 543
Bilvamaṅgala, 257
biṃba-pratibiṃba, 254
biṇḍu, 289
Birla temples, 324

birth, 185, 262
Biṣpalā, 362
Black Jews, 45
Blasi, A. J., 528
Blavatsky, Madame, 449
bliss, 213, 217, 234, 237, 262, 271
Bloomfield, C., 478, 479
boar, 241
Boden professorship, 23
Bodhāyana, 249, 412
Bodhgāyā, 329
bodhisattvas, 145
body, 204, 208, 209, 216, 248, 249, 286, 292, 305, 394, 417, 419; body of Viṣṇu, 127, 419, 423
Bohm, D., 582
Bombay, 7, 18, 46, 487
Bon Maharaj, Swami, 535, 537
bondage, 254, 257, 267, 268, 283, 291
Boner, A., 556
Bopp, Franz, 22
Bose, N. K., 499, 502
Bose, D. N., 549
Böthlingk, Otto, 23
Bougard-Levin, G., 497
bow of Rudra, 90
bow and arrows, 281
Boyd, R., 503
Brahmā, 94, 107, 116, 124, 138, 139, 143, 162, 203, 213, 239, 261, 267, 279, 283, 317, 336, 523, 531; *brahmaloka*, 123, 203, 215; *Brahmā Purāṇa*, 96
brahmavidyā, 201
brahmayajñā, 159
brahmacarya, 178, 336, 337, 345, 403, 412, 454; *brahmacari*, 185, 186
Brahmadatta, 412
brahman, 74, 76, 137, 138, 156, 195, 204 ff, 289, 317, 347, 349, 411, 412, 413, 415, 419, 420, 422, 425; *brahman nirguṇa*, 415, 416; *brahman saguṇa*, 415, 419;
brahman enquiry, 41
Brāhmaṇahatyā, 176
Brahmananda Giri, 486
Brahmānandī, 412
Brāhmaṇas, 67, 69, 96, 145, 166, 193, 409, 479
brahmāṇḍa, 121, 123; *Brahmāṇḍa Purāṇa*, 95
Brahmanical Culture, 44
brahmārandra, 562
Brahmārṣis, 520
Brahmasūtra, 60, 80, 66, 196, 216, 249, 251, 255, 257, 408, 411, 423; *Brahmasūtrabhāṣya*, 377
brahmavādinī, 362
Brahmavaivarta Purāṇa, 96
Brahmavarta, 50
Brahmeśvara temple, 321
brahmins, 18, 19, 39, 114, 334, 336, 338, 378; duties, 162 ff
Brahmo Dharma, 434
Brahmo Samāj, 434, 487
Brāja, 257
Brājbhūmi, 245
branding, 352
bread labor, 456
breath control, 234, 402
Bṛhadāraṇyaka Upaniṣad, 61, 69, 94, 104, 115, 130, 137, 194, 195, 210, 211, 212, 213, 507, 508, 516, 533, 534, 535, 563
Bṛhadīśvara temple, 3212
Bṛhaspati, 61, 228; *Bṛhaspativāra*, 325
Bṛhati, 574
Bṛhatsaṃhitā, 313, 554
Broach, 19, 354
Brown, C. M., 516, 550
Brunner-Lachaux, H., 528, 530, 555
Brzezinski, J. K., 543
Bucci Venkataraya, 426
Buddha, 58, 146, 166, 228, 241, 429
buddhi, 85, 124, 394, 400
Buddhirāja, S. 517
Buddhism, 9, 25, 32, 39, 45, 61, 228,

301, 350, 379, 389, 398, 419, 429, 438, 484
Buddhists, 8, 19, 32, 50, 57, 59, 60, 169, 196, 274, 388, 394, 415, 422; Buddhist missionaries, 18
budha, 123, 125; *Budhavāra*, 325
buffalo, 291; buffalo demon, 279
Bühler, G., 519
Bulcke, C., 515, 539
bull, 143, 276
Bunch of Thoughts, 467
burning ghats, 353
Burnouf, Eugéne, 23, 75
Burrow, T., 295, 551

Caitanya, Mahāprabhu, 223, 236, 246, 257, 352, 367, 485, 542; *Caitanya-caritāmṛta*, 232; Caitanyites, 380
caitanya (consciousness), 271, 377, 417
caitta, 377
cakra, 229, 248, 254, 323, 352, 456
cakras, 285, 288
Cakravarti, Viśvanātha, 543
cakṣus, 125, 210
Caland, W., 527
calendar, 480
Callewaert, W., 102, 518, 567
Cālukyas, 323
camphor, 301
Cānakya, 341
Candra, 279
caṇḍālas, 163, 364, 526, 561. See also: caste, outcastes.
Caṇḍhamadanā, 283
caṇḍana, 163
Caṇḍīdāsa, 257
Candragupta, 335, 341, 362, 482
Candrakānta, 389
Caracalla, 19
Cārakasaṃhitā, 175, 529
Cāraṇadāsis, 356
Carey, W., 22, 497
Carman, J. B., 529, 541, 577
Carstairs, C. M., 526
Cārvākas, 58, 60, 61, 169, 228
caryā, 268
caste, 224, 333f, 431, 443, 457, 530, 558, 559; loss of, 380; rights, 343; ranking, 335; duties, 338
castelessness, 176
cat school, 254
catursaṃpradāya nāgas, 353
caturaṇukas, 390
caturāśrama, 337
caturvarga, 336, 337
caturvarṇāśrama, 51, 55, 71; *caturvarṇāśramadharma*, 106, 333 ff
cauḍa, 183, 185
Cenkner, W., 528, 563, 564, 565, 575
Census of India, 493, 494
cetana, 417
Chaitanya, K., 537
Chakraborti, H., 576
Chanda, 67
Chāṇḍogya Upaniṣad, 78, 194, 195, 197, 204, 207, 526, 532–534
Chatterji, P. C., 443, 582, 587
Chatterjee, Bankim Chandra, 462
Chatterjee, B. R., 513
Chatterjee, S. C., 570
Chatterji, S. K., 499, 528
Chattophadyaya, S., 562
Chaudhuri, N. C., 295, 368, 517, 539, 551, 566
Chaudhuri, Roma 541, 546
chāyā, 139
Chemparathy, G., 571
Chengappa, Raj, 500
Chera, 299
Chézy, A. L., 22
children, 152, 189, 224; child marriages, 580
Chinmulgund, P. J., 497, 499, 513, 532
Chipko movement, 8
Chitor, 369
Cholas, 296, 297, 299, 484
choṭī, 562

Choudhury, Basanti, 537
Christians in India 8; missionaries, 20, 22; influence, 46
chronology, 477 ff
Cidambaram, 121, 143, 296, 331
Cidananda, Swami, 581
Cinmayananda, Swami, 357, 442
cit, 268, 377
citra nāḍī, 288
citta-śakti, 406
citta-vṛtti-nirodha, 402
city building, 125
civil marriage, 187
Classical Antiquity, 17
Claudius, 19
Clive, 487
Clothey, F. W., 294, 551, 552, 553, 558
Cokamela, 224
Colebrook, Thomas, 22
Collins, L., 586
Columbus, Cristopher, 20
commensality, 335
communalism, 469 ff, 587
communism, 461
companionship, 232
Comparative Religion, 23
compassion, 252, 402
concentration, 193
conception, 183
confession, 179
Congress, 465
conscience, 50
consciousness, 200, 204, 210, 211, 213, 217, 271, 291, 377, 415, 417, 420. See also: *cit, caitanya.*
consorts of gods, 365
Constructive Programme, 458
contentment, 402
continuity of culture, 33
Coomaraswamy, Ananda, 27, 498, 524
corpse, 190
cosmography, 117
cosmology, 195, 205
cosmos, 317
cow, 137, 176, 561; cow dung, 190; cow slaughter, 583
Coward, H. G., 510, 511, 512, 575, 577
Cowell, E. B., 506, 571
Cranganore, 18
Crawford, S. C., 580
creation, 71, 116, 141, 147, 246, 248, 278, 395, 419, 477; creation and destruction, 117; creation myths, 112, 127; creator, 112, 138, 150, 419
cremation, 183, 189, 190, 191, 349; cremation grounds, 354
criminal code, 179
crisis, 109
Crooke, W., 1, 493
crows 163,, 191
cruelty, 285
cult, 483
Curzon, Lord, 452
Cutler, N., 554

D. A. V. University, 436
Dadhisāgara, 119
Dadu Panth, 356
Dadyac, 195
Dagens, B., 554
daily rites, 59
daityas, 58, 122
daiva, 248, 531, 534
Dakṣa, 141, 263, 283, 297, 372; *Dakṣasmṛti*, 364, 566
dakṣina, 157, 163, 187; *dakṣinācāra*, 285
Dakṣineśvara, 292
dāl, 180
Dalit, 344
Damodāra, 248
dāna, 95, 117, 180, 391
Dānavas, 122
dance, 267; dancing, 268
daṇḍa, 341, 561; *daṇḍanīti*, 571
Dandekar, R. N., 76, 131, 337, 511, 519, 521, 522, 560

Daniell, Thomas and William, 21
Daniélou, A., 275, 525, 539
Danish Lutherans, 47
Dara Shikoh, 21, 486
darkness, 201, 211, 212, 278
darśanas, 323, 382, 569
Das, R. P., 556
Das, R. V., 577
dāsa, 185, 353; *dāsamārga*, 234
Daśanāmis, 60, 346, 349, 350, 351, 413; *Daśanāmi nāgas*, 351
Daśapadārtha Śāstra, 387, 391
Daśapadārthi, 389
Daśaratha Jātaka, 89
Daśāśvamedha ghāṭ, 166
Daśāvara pariṣad, 54, 579
daśāvatāras, 241. See also: *avatāras*, Viṣṇu.
Dasgupta, S. N., 384, 398, 409, 419, 497, 501, 506, 529, 535, 541, 542, 570, 571, 572, 574, 578
Dassera, 93, 327
Dāsya, 231
Dasyus, 34, 133
Datta, 225; Datta saṃpradāya, 356
Datta, B., 521
Datta, K., 501
Dattatreya, Madhukar, 467
day, 213; day and night of Brahmā, 117
Dayal, Pyarelal Prabhu, 572
Dayananda, 350, 475
Dayananda Saraswati, Swami, 435
de Bary, W. Theodore, 560
De, S. K., 537
death, 177, 189, 190, 198, 209, 212, 213, 216, 217, 262, 265, 330, 412; deathlessness, 208, 217
debates, 379, 383
decoding of the *Ṛgveda*, 77
Delhi, 86, 375, 477
deliverance, 141, 150
Delmonico, N., 543
delusion, 269, 278, 403
Deming, W. S., 564
Democritus, 390
demons, 262
Deorala, 372
Deoras, Balasaheb, 467, 586
depressed classes, 102; Depressed Classes Conference, 457. See also: *Dalit*.
Derret, J. D. M., 52, 495, 503, 504, 531, 583
Desai, Mahadev, 448, 517
Desai, Morarji, 489
Deshmukh, N., 466
Deshpande, M. M., 78, 512
desire, 232, 269, 359, 394, 404, 416; desire for heaven, 409
destroyer, 138, 150
destruction, 116, 141, 147
Deussen, P., 570, 576
Deutsch, E., 576
Dev, Swami Niranjan, 443
Devanāgarī, 511
Devapi, 127
devas, 56, 107, 130, 138, 157, 160, 162, 183, 194, 208, 213, 311; *devayajña*, 159, 163; *devayāna*, 21
Devasenapathi, V. A., 538, 546
Devī, 139, 152, 206, 225, 227, 278 ff; Devī worship, 147; Devī *bhakti*, 234; Devī *bhaktas*, 225; Devī *avatāras*, 283; *Devī Bhāgavata Purāṇa*, 81, 279, 365, 516, 530, 549; *Devī Purāṇa*, 283, 549; *Devīmāhātmya*, 279, 483; Devīsthāna, 289; *Devīsūkta*, 362
devotion, 106, 168, 221, 249, 275, 416. See also: *bhakti*.
dhainya, 288, 561
Dhaky, M. A., 558
Dhanuṣveda, 67
Dharampal, Gita, 496
dhāraṇa, 403, 405
dharma, 14, 49, 84, 85, 88, 95, 105, 124, 127, 157, 159, 185, 219, 241, 337, 338, 339, 340, 364, 388, 395,

dharma (continued)
409, 416, 462, 471, 476, 503; *dharma-adharma*, 116, 117, 128, 392; *dharmarājya*, 245; *dharmaśāstra*, 52, 71, 333, 341; *dharmaśālas*, 164; *Dharmasūtras*, 71, 435, 482
Dharmarāja, 426
dhastricāsana, 574
dhobis, 460
dhṛti, 288
Dhṛtarāṣṭra, 85, 86
Dhruva, 123
dhūpa, 163
dhyāna, 116, 288, 403, 405
dialectics, 196
dice, 86
Diehl, C. G.
diet, 404
digpāla, 318
Digambara, 18
digvijaya, 60, 196
dīkṣā, 80, 191, 269, 285, 349
Dindimus, 18
Dinghra, 452
Diogenes, 19
Dionysos, 19
dīpa, 163
Dī(pā)valī, 327
discipline, 211, 336
discrimination, 219, 403, 416
discus, 281
disputations, 388
Divine body, 107, 246
Divine Child, 245
Divine Life Society, 440
Divine Name, 226
Divine qualities, 248
Divodāsa dynasty, 479
divorce, 187, 375, 583
Dixit, P., 586
domestic rites, 163
donkey, 186
dowry, 372; dowry murder, 374, 361; Dowry Prohibition Act, 375
Dowson, J., 550, 554
Draupadī, 85, 86, 87, 187, 365 ff
Draviḍa, 139, 147, 153; Draviḍa style of temples, 320
Draviḍa Kazhagam, 339
Draviḍa Munnetra Kazhagam, 300
Draviḍa Prabandham, 419
Dravidians, 38, 295; Dravidian culture, 31; Dravidian association, 300; Draviḍanādu, 300
dravya, 157
dream, 208, 412; dream-state, 199; dreamless sleep, 209
Drew, W. H., 529
Drona, 108
Dṛṣadvatī, 50
dṛṣṭa, 389
drugs, 177
du Perron, Anquetil, 21
Dubois, Abbé, 496
Duff, Alexander, 22
duḥkha, 125; *duḥkhānta*, 267
Dumézil, G., 336, 560
Dumont, L., 4, 5, 333, 336, 527, 559, 587
Dumont, P. E., 527
Duncan, J., 330
Durgā, 147, 236, 281, 282, 365, 430, 462; Durgā worship, 486; Durgā Mahiṣāsuramārdiṇī, 549; Durgāpūjā, 149, 278, 282, 313, 327
Duryodhana, 85, 86
duties, 51, 64, 106, 173, 338
Dvaita Vedānta, 254, 413, 422 ff; *dvaitādvaita vivarjita*, 291
dvandvas, 216, 403
Dvāpara yuga, 117
dvaras, 353
dveśa, 402, 529
dvijati, 335, 530
Dvijanatha, Swami, 357
dvīpas, 118, 163
dvyāṇukas, 390, 395
Dwāraka, 36, 103, 350, 477

earth, 114, 123, 147, 188, 190, 206, 210, 241, 279, 388
East India Company, 433, 487
East-West Philosophers' Conference, 25
Eban, M., 582
Eck, Diana, 556, 557
Eckhart, Meister, 533
economy, 458
Edgerton, F., 24
Edsman, C. M., 560
Eggeling, J., 545
egotism, 234
Egypt, 38
Eidlitz, W., 542
Einstein, Albert, 43, 447, 583
ekadaṇḍi, 343, 422
ekāgratā, 288, 402
Ekanāṭha, 146, 486
Ekānti Vaiṣṇavas, 422
Ekaśriṅga, 241
ekoddiṣṭa, 192
Ektāyātrā, 466
elements of sovereignty, 341
elephant, 298, 315
Elephanta, 7
Eliade, M., 519, 573
Elintoff, E., 495
Elliot, H. M., 554
Ellis, F. W., 529
Ellorā, 321
emancipation, 118, 391
Emerson, Ralph Waldo, 23
emotions, 228
emptiness, 417
environment, 530
epics, 2, 39
epidemics, 291
epistemology, 393, 409
equality of women, 372
equanimity, 395
error, 395
Esteller, A., 507, 522
eternal, 317
ether, 123, 197
ethics, 110, 112, 172, 219, 342; ethical standards, 172
etiquette, 174
etymology, 196
evil, 85, 141, 416, 421; evil spirits, 282
exile, 86
existence of God, 409
experience, 259
Ezour Vedam, 22

faith, 64, 234, 455
Falk, Maryla, 27, 550
falsehood, 234
family-religion, 255
farmers, 334
Farquar, J. N., 580
fasting, 56, 180; fasts to death, 455
fatalism, 44
fate, 216, 300
female infanticide, 431, 580
Fenner, P., 543
festivals, 324 ff, 431
Feuerstein, G., 573
field, 108
fifth caste, 343
fifth Veda, 81
Filliozat, J., 495, 496, 509, 546, 570, 589
Findly, E. B., 533, 566
fire, 123, 197, 206, 209, 288, 311, 388; fire ordeal, 92; fire sacrifice, 34. See also: Agni, *agnicayana*.
Fischer, O., 556
fish, 165, 241
Fitzgerald, J. L., 513, 514
five 'm', 285
five-faced, 262
flood, 241
Fonseca, R., 549
food, 164 f, 185, 206, 215, 273; food taboos, 165. See also: *bhojana*.
forbearance, 258
forgiveness, 252
form, 249
Frauwallner, E., 513, 570, 572

Frawley, David, 38, 39
free will, 216
freedom, 193, 213, 268, 291, 298, 391
Freud, S., 43
friendliness, 402
full moon, 325
Fuller, C. J., 558
fullness, 203
Furcha, E., 583

Gabhastimat, 122
Gächter, O., 511, 575
gada, 248
Gadre, N. B., 554
Gaṇapati, 356
Gaṇḍaka river, 249
Gandhamandana, 120
gāndharva (form of marriage), 531
Gandharvas, 105, 116, 213; *Gandharvaveda*, 67
Gandhi, Indira, 158, 293, 465, 488, 489
Gandhi, Mahātmā, 47, 101, 149, 164, 182, 343, 344, 361, 371, 436, 443, 446, 447, 465, 475, 487
Gandhi, Manilal, 450
Gandhi, Rajiv, 470, 489
Gaṇeśa, 3, 72, 149, 225; Gaṇeśa caturthi, 326
Gaṅgā/Ganges, 120, 147, 166, 191, 225, 241, 261, 283, 288, 328, 477, 539
Gangadharan, K. K., 587
Gaṅgeśa, 393
Garbe, 100
garbhagṛha, 314, 319
Gargī, 195, 205
garlic, 165
Garuḍa, 19, 96, 116, 146, 262; *Garuḍa Purāṇa*, 484, 531
garuḍa-stambha, 321
Garutman, 132
Gatwood, L. E., 550
Gauḍapada, 412, 413, 484
Gauḍīa Vaiṣṇavism, 229, 257
Gaur, Ramdas, 506, 508, 510, 538, 563, 565, 575, 576
Gaurī, 188, 261, 282
Gautama Buddha, 149, 339, 347, 479, 482
Gautama, 227, 388, 482, 510
Gāyā, 96, 180, 329
gāyatrī mantra, 139, 160, 161, 186
Geldner, K. F., 75, 508, 511
Gensichen, W., 496
George, A., 494, 499, 539, 562, 587
ghana-patha, 68
Ghate, V. S., 576
ghī, 146, 188
Ghoṣā, 361
Ghosal, U. N., 560, 561
Ghose, S., 586
Ghosh, B. K., 544
ghosts, 189, 191, 192, 301
Ghurye, G. S., 506, 562, 564
gifts, 162, 180, 215
Giri, 350
Giridhāra, 260
Girijā, 262
Girirāja, 257
Gītā-Rahasya, 101
Gītāgovinda, 245, 257, 367, 537
Goa, 47
Goa, W., 512
goat, 166, 291, 298
goblins, 301
God, 423, 456. See also: Brahmā, Viṣṇu, Śiva.
Goddess, 147, 234, 278, 362, 365
Gode, P. K., 513, 527
Godse, Nathuram, 464
Goetz, H., 496
Gokhale, 452, 453, 584
Gokula, 245
Gold, D., 536
Golden Age of India, 39
Golden Temple, 329
Goldmann, R. P., 513
Goloka, 146
Golwalkar, M. S., 32, 440, 467

Gombrich, R., 293, 550, 560
Gonda, J., 75, 508, 509, 510, 511, 515, 522, 525, 527, 532, 541
good and evil, 53, 85, 128, 173, 213, 215, 216, 270
goodness, 237
Gopal, S., 581
Gopāla Bhaṭṭa, 257
Gopījanavallabha, 256
gopīs, 228, 245, 256, 353
gopura, 320, 331
Gorakhnātha, 354
gośalas, 353
Gospel of Ramakrishna, 581
Goswami, K., 538
Gough, A. E., 506
Govardhana, 245
Govinda, 146, 245, 248
Govinda Bhāṣya, 258, 487
Govinda Bhagavatpada, 412
Govindacarya, Alkondavilli, 528
grace, 150, 167, 213, 216, 223, 228, 234, 252, 254, 255, 256, 261, 268, 270, 274, 326, 328, 396, 423, 442
grammarians, 74, 77, 410
Grassman, 511
Great Epics, 81
Great Flood, 125, 481
Great Mantra, 226
Great Mother, 147
Great Sayings, 210
Great War, 86, 366
Greece, 18; Greek philosophy, 19; Greek Sophists, 18
greed, 403. See also: *lobha*.
gṛhastya, 337, 345
Gṛhya Sūtras, 71, 482
Griffith, R. H. T., 508, 511, 515, 522, 545
Grimes, J., 578
gross body, 213. See also: *sthūla śarīra*.
ground, 106; ground of being, 197
Gudimally, 143
Guénon, René, 27
guest, 164
guilt, 152
Gujarātī, 6
guṇas, 116, 400, 406
Günther, H. V., 548
Gupta, 39, 126, 185, 293; Gupta empire 483; Gupta restoration, 45
Gupta, C. Das, 582
Gupta, Harsh, 500
Gupta, Kumara, 545
Gupta, Lal Hansraj, 466
Gupta, S., 550, 560
guptāṅgāsana, 574
guru, 152, 221, 224, 236, 237, 251, 252, 254, 268, 285, 346, 348, 349; *guru paraṃpara*, 194, 202, 349, 351, 411, 457, 507; *guruseva*, 363; *guruvaṅganagāma*, 177; *gurukulas*, 186, 436
Gurū Nanak, 46, 485
Guruji, Balyogeshwar, 29
Gurukul, Jhajhar, 512

Habermann, D. L., 542
Habermas, Jürgen, 518
Hacker, P., 521, 524, 573, 576
Haddad, Y. Y., 533
hair, 190
hala, 248
Halbfass, W., 493, 494, 569, 570, 571
Haldar, S. K., 583
Hamilton, Alexander, 22
Hampton, G. H., 496
Haṃsa avatāra, 352
hamsas, 347
Handelman, D., 552
Hanuman, 82, 92, 149; Hanumansetu, 92
Hanxleden, J. E., 21
happiness, 402
Hara, 140, 266. See also: Śiva.
Harappa, 34, 38, 39, 481, 588
Hardwar/Haridvāra, 180, 263, 328
Hardy, E. T., 540

Hare Krishna Movement, 223, 352
Hari, 125, 146, 168, 236, 237, 254, 259, 266, 423. See also: Viṣṇu.
Haribhaktirasāmṛtasindhu, 257
Haribhaktivilāsa, 257, 555
Hariharan, M., 537, 551
Harijans, 8, 177, 344, 456
Hariras, 259
Haritā, 66
Haritāsmṛti, 362
Harivaṃśa Purāṇa, 84, 483, 486
Harivarṣa, 120
Harman, W. P., 558
Harris, R. Baine, 495
harṣa, 269, 484
Harṣacarita, 484
Harvey, M. J., 585
Hastinapura, 86
Hastings, Warren, 21
hasyā, 229, 288
Haṭha Yoga, 351, 397, 403
Haṭhayogapradīpikā, 572
Hauer, J. W., 573, 545
Haussig, H. W., 554
Havell, L. B., 557
Hawley, J. S., 536, 540, 543, 544, 550
Hazra, R. C., 94, 95, 506, 510, 516, 523, 524, 546, 548
Halebid, 323
health, 175, 282
heart, 210, 212
heaven, 114, 156, 188, 191, 193, 216, 268, 392. See also: svarga.
Hedgewar, K. V., 464, 467, 471
heedlessness, 251
Heesterman, J. C., 30, 499, 527
Hegel, G. W. F., 17, 494
Heimann, Betty, 27
Hein, Norvin, 540
Heliodorus, 483
hells, 122, 178, 188, 191, 227, 268. See also: *nārakas*.
Hemakuṭa, 120
Hemraj, Shilanand, 102, 518
henotheism, 130
Henry, V., 527
Heracles, 19
heresy, 49
hetu, 95, 394
Himālaya, 41, 120, 283
Hiṃsā, 125; *hiṃsā-ahiṃsā*, 116
Hind Swarāj, 452, 584
Hindī, 6
Hindu Code, 54
Hindu extremism, 461
Hindū Jagaran, 52, 461, 466
Hindū Mahāsabhā, 32, 63, 357, 463, 464, 465
Hindu Marriage Act, 187, 455, 488
Hindu Renaissance, 182, 432 ff
Hindū Samajotsav, 467
Hindu University, 330
Hindū Viśva Dharma Sammelan, 503
Hindū Viśva Pariṣad, 357
Hindudharma, 32
Hinduism Today, 472
Hindutva, 32, 63, 182, 463, 471
Hiranmaya, 120
Hiraṇyakaśipu, 241
Hiriyanna, M., 384
history, 96; historical pessimism, 117
Hita Harivaṃśa, 543
hita-ahita, 173
Hitopadeśa, 21
hlādinī-śakti, 232
Hocart, A. M., 336, 560
Hodges, W., 20, 374, 496
Holi, 327
Holikā, 328
holiness, 181, 182
Holtzmann, 100
holy places, 96
homas, 183
Homer, 19
Hooper, J. S. M., 497
Hopkins, E. W., 24, 100, 513
horoscope, 326
hospitality, 163

hotar, 134
householder, 156, 157, 159
Hronzny, B., 499
Hṛśikeśa, 248
Hudson, D., 567
human rights, 343
human sacrifice, 166, 267, 275, 289, 549
human skull, 354
Humboldt, Wilhelm von, 102
Hume, Robert Ernest, 24
humility, 232, 258
hunger, 198
Hutton, J. H., 333, 559
Huxley, Aldous, 581
hygiene, 159
hymns, 416
hypocrisy, 444

icchā, 116
Idā, 288
ideal social order, 156
ignorance, 201, 212, 216, 267
Ikṣurasasāmudra, 119
Īkṣvāku, 105, 125
Ila, 125
Ilā, 125
Illakumi, 298
illumination, 259
illusion, 147, 258, 267
Iltutmish, 485
images, 163, 221, 224, 229, 249, 311, 483; image of God, 248; image worship, 96, 246, 433. See also: *mūrti, mūrtipūjā.*
immortality, 106, 193, 198, 208, 210, 212, 213, 217
impurity, 364
inaction, 105
incarnation, 237. See also: *avatāra*
Inden, R., 333, 494, 560
Indian constitution, 344
Indian National Congress, 487
individuality, 116
individuation, 400
Indo-European, 38
Indo-Greek, 18
Indonesia, 39
Indra, 68, 114, 132, 133, 134, 147, 166, 205, 208, 209, 245, 279, 282, 297, 299, 326; Indra's heaven, 87, 122; Indra *bhakti*, 222
Indra-Agni, 293
Indragopa, 248
Indrāṇī, 361
Indraprāṣṭa, 86
Indravilā, 297
Indus, 588; Indus civilization, 31, 34, 139, 147, 262, 312, 477, 482; Indus script, 38. See also: Harappa, Mohenjo daro.
infanticide, 182, 434
Ingalls, D. H. H., 570
initiation, 79, 236
injustice, 85
Inner Controller, 249
insects, 163, 215
insight, 207, 379
Institut Français d'Indologie, 546
intermarriage, 335
International Foundation for Vedic Education, 512
International Society for Krishna Consciousness (ISKCON), 29, 260, 358
International Transcendental Meditation Society, 442
interpretation, 75, 76
Iran, 478
īśa, 138, 533. See also: *īśvara.*
Īśa(vasya) Upaniṣad, 194, 201
Iśāna, 266, 267
Islam, 47, 429, 436
Israel, B. J., 503
iṣṭa devata, 149, 151, 159, 163, 225, 286, 403
iṣṭi, 167
īśvara, 137, 138, 168, 246, 248, 288, 390, 392, 395, 396, 402, 409, 417, 415, 419, 423; *īśvara praṇidhāna*, 402, 403

Īśvara Kṛṣṇa, 399, 483
Īśvara Muni, 251
itihāsa, 71, 81
Iyengar, Narasinha, 541

Jackson, C. T., 497, 579
Jacobi, H., 513
Jacobsen, D., 550
jaḍapatha, 68
jagamohan, 321
jagadgurus, 170, 351
Jagadananda, Swami, 578
Jagannatha Puri, 350
jagaritasthāna, 199
Jagjivandas, R., 356
Jaimini, 228, 482, 575; *Jaimini Sūtras*, 409, 575. See also: *Mīmāṃsā Sūtras*.
Jains, 8, 18, 32, 50, 59, 60, 254, 274, 302, 422, 449, 501; Jainism, 32, 39, 45, 61, 301, 379, 419, 429
Jain, A., 500
Jain, M., 583
Jaivali, 195
Jaipaul, Rikhi, 110
jāl, 44
Jalasāgara, 119
Jaṃbudvīpa, 118, 119, 120
Jana Sangh, 357, 464, 465. See also: Bhāratīya Jana Sangh.
Janaloka, 123
Janaka of Videha, 90
Janaki, S. S., 567
Janaloka, 122
Janata Party, 465. See also: Bhāratīya Jānata Party.
janëu, 160, 185, 186
japa, 56, 161, 168, 180, 226, 227, 236, 267, 285, 566
Jarrige, J. F., 588
jātakarma, 183
Jatayu, 92
jātī, 334, 561
Jawaji, P., 508
Jayadeva, 245, 257, 367
Jayadratha, 108
Jayakar, Pupul, 581
Jayanta, 174
Jayantī, 283
Jesudason, C., 551
Jesudason, H., 551
Jesus, 19, 149
Jews, 8, 45
Jha, Ganganatha, 510, 571, 574, 575
Jha, M., 557
Jhangiani, M. A, . 586
Jīna Mahāvīra, 149, 347
jīvas, 95, 140, 251, 254, 273, 317, 419
jīvanmukta, 217, 219, 395; *jīvanmukti*, 269, 270
jīvātman, 85, 248, 397, 412, 417, 422, 423
jñāna, 102, 108, 199, 248, 391, 425; *jñāna niṣṭha*, 269; *jñāna-kāṇḍa*, 69, 156, 408; *jñānamārga*, 49, 151, 152, 192, 193 ff; *jñānamaya*, 289
Jñānasambhandar, 268
Jñāneśvara, 356, 485
Johar, S. S., 586
joint family, 363
Jolly, J., 510
Jones, Sir William, 21, 487, 496
Joo, Laksman, 546
Jordens, J., 580
Joshi, Laxman Shastri, 54
Joshi, M. V., 541
Joshi, R. V., 528, 555
jungle, 86
Jupiter, 123
justice, 85
Justice Party, 300
Jyoti Maṭha, 350
jyotiṣṭoma, 62
jyotirliṅga, 143
jyotiṣa, 67; *jyotiṣi*, 325

Kabīr, 46, 223, 224, 225, 236, 259, 356, 485; Kabīr Panth, 356
Kādāmbarī, 484
Kaegi, 511

Kaikeyī, 90, 91, 93, 366
Kailāsa, 43, 123, 143; Kailāsa temple, 321; Kailāsanāthadevaram, 331
kairos, 326
kaivalya, 402, 404, 406
Kak, S. C., 36, 38, 39, 77, 129, 479, 500, 501, 512, 589
Kakati, B. K., 549
Kakṣivant, 361
kāla, 116, 190, 213, 281, 311f, 325. See also: time
Kalahasti, 315
Kālamukhas, 275, 353
Kalanos, 18
Kālapī, 362
Kālaratrī, 283
Kalelkar, Kaka, 581
Kali yuga, 87, 97, 117, 126, 146, 228, 285, 328, 338, 477, 520; life in, 126
Kālī, 236, 244, 292, 549; Kālī-Śakti, 288
Kālīdāsa, 483
Kālikā Purāṇa, 283, 289, 549
Kālikā, 283
Kālika Pīṭha, 350
Kalki, 127, 146, 244
Kallenbach, H., 452
kalpa, 67, 106, 123
Kalpasūtras, 71
Kalyān, 6
kāma, 95, 114, 213, 336, 337, 339, 364; *kāma-kāla*, 289; *Kamasūtra*, 483
Kāmākhyā, 291, 549
Kāmakothi Pīṭha, 564
Kāmar, 147, 289
Kāmeśvarī, 291
Kaṇāda, 227, 387, 482
Kanakhala, 297, 263
Kañcanībhūmī,119
Kāñcīpuram, 331
Kaṇḍarpa, 266; *kaṇḍarpa-vāyu*, 288
kaṇḍu, 297
Kane, P. V., 50, 222, 479, 482, 504, 506, 508, 510, 516, 520, 529, 530, 536, 537, 557, 558, 560, 563
Kangle, R. P., 561
Kangri Gurukula, 436
Kannan, 551
Kāṇphata, 354
Kapālikas, 275, 353
Kapila, 146, 228, 241, 398, 399
Karan Singh, 64
kāraṇa, 267
karma, 102, 168, 212 ff, 248, 259, 268, 271, 335, 399, 402, 535; *karmakāṇḍa*, 69, 156, 408; *karmamārga*, 49, 151, 152, 155 ff, 192
Karmarkar, A. P., 515, 525, 549
Karṇa, 108
Kārpātikas, 60
Karpatriji Maharaj, 357, 468, 565
karsevaks, 244
Kārṣṇa, 350
Kārṣṇajinī, 411
karuṇa, 229
Karunakaran, K. P., 587
Karve, Irawati, 559
kārya, 267
Kasakṛtsna, 411
Kāśī, 126, 155, 180, 328, 329. See also: Benaras, Vārāṇasī.
Kaśmīr Śaivism, 271, 275, 277, 385, 484
kāṣṭā, 116
Kaśyapa, 411
Kaṭha Upaniṣad, 194, 213, 223, 526, 534, 535
Kathāsaritasāgara, 478
Kathī, 362
Katre, S. M., 513
Kātyāyana, 57, 157
Kaula, 285
kaupina, 347, 349
Kauravas, 83, 85, 86, 103, 366
Kauśala Aśvalāyana, 195
Kauśalyā, 90

Kauśītaki, 195; *Kauśītaki Upaniṣad*, 194
Kauṭilīya, 341, 378, 482; *Kauṭilīya Ārthaśāstra*, 388
Kautsa, 77
Kauveri (river), 331, 332
kavi, 131
Kedarnāth, 294
Keith, A. B., 572
Kena Upaniṣad, 194, 211
Kenghe, C. T., 573
Kennedy, J., 539
Keśava, 146, 248, 576
Keśava Miśra, 396, 571
Keṭumāla, 120
kevala, 269
khadga, 248
khadi, 456
Khajurāho, 321
Khalistān, 8
Khandarīya Mahādeva temple, 321
Khanna, Madhu, 548
kheda, 561
khila-bhāga, 84
Khiste, Pandit Srinarayan Sastri, 564
Khristopaniṣad, 509
killing, 176, 178
Kiṃpuruṣa, 120
kings, 157, 334; kingship, 339
Kingsbury, F., 501, 524, 547, 553
Kingsley, B., 447
Kinnaras, 137
Kinsley, D. R., 550
Kipphardt, H., 109, 518
kīrtaṇ(a), 145, 230, 257
kleśas, 402
Kloppenborg, Ria, 527
Klostermaier, K., 494, 493, 502, 506, 525, 537, 539, 540, 548, 543, 551, 565, 567, 583, 585
knower of the field, 108
knowledge, 99, 200, 206, 212, 232, 234, 269, 379, 391, 394, 395, 401, 415, 423, 425
Koelman, G. M., 573
Koil Olugu, 558
Koluttunga I, 501
Konārka, 323, 485
Kośala, 126
Kosambi, D. D., 499, 500, 527, 565
Kosmas Indikopleustes, 484
Koṭai, 368
Kotravai, 298
krama-patha, 68
Krämer, H. J., 495
Kramrisch, S., 27, 113, 115, 275, 519, 523, 547, 555
Krauñcadvīpa, 119
Krick, Hertha, 522
Krishna, D., 569
Krishnamacarya, V., 579
Krishnamurti, Jiddu, 440, 475, 581
kriyā, 124, 268
krodha, 116, 174, 229, 403
kṛpā, 288
Kṛṣṇa, 19, 36, 82, 83, 85, 102, 103, 104, 105, 107, 145, 167, 146, 182, 222, 225, 228; 229, 232, 236, 244, 245, 257, 266, 297, 353, 369, 454, 469, 478, 482, 524, 540; Kṛṣṇa period, 126, 452, 482; Kṛṣṇa *jayanti,* 326; Kṛṣṇa *janma-bhūmī,* 466; historicity of Kṛṣṇa, 540
Kṛṣṇa (river), 331
Kṛṣṇa, Gopi, 277, 547, 548
Kṛṣṇakarṇāmṛta, 257
Kṛṣṇa-pakṣa, 325
Kṛṣṇa Prem, 358
Kṛta yuga, 117, 127
Krypto-Buddhists, 415
kṣamāprārthana, 10
kṣatriyas, 39, 114, 176, 241, 334, 338, 339; *kṣatriya dharma*, 104
Kṣīrasāgara, 119
Kubera, 137, 279
Kuiper, F. B. J., 519
Kulācāra, 285
Kulkarni, R., 555

Kumārila Bhaṭṭa, 380, 409, 484
Kumbha Melā, 33, 57, 347, 528
Kuṇḍalinī, 271, 273, 287, 288, 289, 292, 397
Kunst, A., 504
Kuntī, 88
Kuppuswamy, G., 537, 551
Kureśa, 501
Kuriñchi, 299
kūrma, 146, 241; *Kūrma Purāṇa*, 96, 484, 523
Kurukṣetra, 283, 329
kuśa, 134
Kuśadvīpa, 120
Kuśānas, 483
kuṭicakas, 347

laborers, 334
Lacombe, O., 576
lakṣana, 422
Lakṣmaṇa, 82, 90, 91, 92, 366
Lakṣmī, 124, 298, 462
Lakulin/Lakuliṣa, 263, 267
Lal, Chaman, 501
Lāldāsī Panth, 356
landscape, 41
Langlois, 511
language, 74, 473
Laṅka, 92, 515
Lanman, C. R., 24
Lapierre, D., 586
Larsen, G. J., 572
Larssen, C., 25, 514
Latham, R. E., 496
Latin, 47
Lavaṇasamudra, 119
Lazarus, J., 529
Leifer, W., 496
lepers, 163, 354; leprosy, 175, 178
Lessing, 18
Lévi, Sylvain, 527
Liaquat Ali, 464
liberation, 147, 151, 212 ff, 249, 258, 262, 267, 269, 283, 283, 287, 389, 394, 329, 402, 410, 416, 417, 423. See also: *mokṣa, mukti.*
life, 198, 305, 330; life force, 289; life stages, 336
light, 212, 213, 234, 279
lightning, 210, 215
līlā, 44, 141, 237, 367, 423
Limaye, Acharya V. P., 575
line of tradition, 63. See also: *paraṃpara.*
liṅga, 139, 140, 143, 213, 262, 267, 273, 304, 314, 327, 330, 348; *liṅga-śarīra*, 266; *liṅgodbhāva*, 143 ; *Liṅga Purāṇa*, 56, 57, 506
Liṅgāyats, 265, 304
linguistic analysis, 388
Lipner, J., 541
lobha, 174, 339, 403, 529
local traditions, 41
logic, 384, 387, 388, 393
Lok Sabhā, 468
lokasaṅgraha, 105
Lokacarya Pillai, 254, 542
Lokāloka, 121; Lokālokaśaila, 119
Lokāyata, 60, 61, 417
Lomaharsana, 95
Long, J. B., 576
Lopamudra, 356
Lord, 138, 140, 181, 395, 398, 419; Lord of thieves, 140, 265
Lorenzen, D. N., 576
Lorinser, R., 100
loṭha, 160, 258, 423
love marriage, 187
Lüders, H., 137
Ludwig, 511
Lunar dynasty, 125

Macauliffe, M. A., 579
Macdonell, A. A., 518, 521, 525
machines, 459
Mackichan, D., 541
Maclagan, D., 519
Macnicol, N., 524
macrocosm-microcosm, 198, 204, 400
mada, 269, 549
Madan, T. N., 445, 560, 583

Mādhava, 60, 61, 267, 383, 511, 578
Madhavananda, Swami, 578
Madhok, Balraj, 465, 466
madhurasa, 232
madhuvidyā, 195
Madhusūdana, 248
Madhva, 59, 60, 84, 229, 248, 254, 352, 380, 413, 422, 420, 485, 541, 576, 578
Madhyadeśa, 43
Madras, 7, 46, 143
Mādrī, 88, 89
Madurai, 7, 296, 301, 331, 485
Magadha, 18, 126
maghavān, 132
mahāyajña, 158
mahāmāyā, 291
mahāpātakas, 176, 530; *mahāpātakasaṃsarga*, 177
mahāvākyas, 210, 421
Mahabalipuram, 18, 321
Mahābhārata, 14, 72, 81, 82, 118, 139, 140, 145, 147, 162, 180, 187, 223, 240, 263, 266, 338, 339, 347, 353, 365, 399, 410, 423, 425, 430, 482, 513
Mahābhāṣya, 77, 411, 483
Mahādeva, 266
Mahadevan, T. M. P., 302, 305, 497, 547, 563, 564, 577
Mahānarayaṇopaniṣad, 578
Mahānirvāṇa Tantra, 291, 487, 549
Mahāprabhu, 257
Mahāpurāṇas, 72, 81, 94, 96, 516
Mahāpūrṇa, 501
Māhār, 9
Mahārāja case, 254
Maharloka, 122, 123
Mahaśaṅkha mālā, 285
mahāsiddhānta, 421
Mahāśivarātri, 557
mahat, 116, 123, 400, 402
Mahātala, 122
Mahatma Party, 436
mahātmyas, 97, 180, 328
Mahāvīra, 132, 166, 429, 482
Mahāyāṇa, 283
Mahāyogi, 262, 273
Mahesh Yogi Maharishi, 29, 358, 442
Maheśvara, 140
Mahiṣāsura, 147, 279, 281
Mahmud of Ghazni, 484
Mahrattas, 335
maintenance, 147
maithuna, 549
Maitra, S. K., 529, 570
Maitri, 195; *Maitri Upaniṣad*, 194, 325, 535, 557, 576
Majumdar, A. K., 367
Majumdar, J. K., 542, 566, 580
Majumdar, R. C., 494, 501
Majumdar, R. D., 499
Māl, 294 ff
mālā, 139, 161
Malamound, C., 560
Malaviya, Pandit Mohan, 463
Mālayās, 283
malice, 234
Maloney, C., 501
Malwa, 18
Malyavata, 120
maṃsa, 549
mana, 131
Manabhau, 356
manana, 425
manas, 116, 210, 213, 391, 392, 394, 519; *manas-cakra*, 288; *mānasa japa*, 180
Mānasā, 283, 549
mānava dharma, 51
Mandal Commission, 9
Maṇḍana Miśra, 351, 429
maṇḍapa, 320
Maṇḍara mountain, 241
Mandhātri period, 125, 482
Māṇḍukya Upaniṣad, 79, 194, 199, 512, 533; *Māṇḍukya Upaniṣad Kārikā*, 413
Maṅgalā, 283

maṅgalaśloka, 65
Maṅgalavāra, 325
Maṇikana, 571
Maṇikarṇikā ghaṭ, 330
Manikkavacakar, 268, 274, 302, 484
Manimat, 59
manipura, 288
Manmatha, 356
manomaya, 206
Manoravatāranam, 125
Mantharā, 90
mantras, 56, 68, 78, 79, 80, 157, 159, 234, 237, 286, 316, 349; *mantrapuṣpa*, 163
Manu, 51, 71, 105, 115, 125, 126, 139, 178, 179, 181, 183, 185, 186, 189, 241, 245, 334, 336, 363, 378, 430, 478, 530, 532; *Manusmṛti*, 22, 49, 50, 71, 116, 117, 300, 338, 435, 482, 483, 504, 519, 525, 530, 531, 559, 560, 561, 562, 566, 568; Manu Svayambhuva, 124; Manu Vaivasvata, 125, 478, 481; Manvantara, 95, 117
manuṣa, 248
manuṣya-yajña, 159, 163
Mar Thoma Christians, 46
Marathī, 6
Marco Polo, 20, 485
Marfatia, M. I., 541, 542
mārga, 49, 152, 397
Marglin, A., 529
Margosa, 301
Mariammā, 301
Marica, 91
Maridan, 299
Mārkandeya Purāṇa, 96, 279, 483
marriage, 186, 326, 337, 363; ritual, 187; of trees, 41
Mars, 123
Marshall, P. J., 496, 499
Maruts, 134, 170
Marwad, 369
Marx, Karl, 43, 459
mata, 143
maṭha, 60, 350
Mathai, John, 464
Mathurā, 96, 146, 180, 245, 245, 312, 326, 524; sculpture, 483
Maticandra, 389
Matilal, B. K., 570
matriarchy, 364
Mātrikās, 283
Matsya, 96, 125, 146, 241, 549; *Matsya Purāṇa*, 96, 330
matted locks, 261
matter, 286, 400
Maurya, 335
māyā, 44, 125, 127, 147, 268, 271, 273, 291, *māyā-moha*, 58
Mayer, A. C., 560
Māyaṉ/Māyavaṉ/Māyon, 297, 299
McCarthy, Th., 518
McCormack, W., 547
McDowall, A., 493
McLeod, W. H., 536, 579
meat eating, 45, 165
Medatithi, 484
medha, 166, 528
medicine, 175
meditation, 267, 403, 412, 475
Mediterranean, 18
megaliths, 295
Megasthenes, 145, 263, 362, 482
Mehendale, M. A., 516
Mehrgarh, 477, 481, 588
Mehta, M., 514
Meister, M. W., 555, 558
melās, 56
Melkote, 419
Menon, I. K. K., 494
menstruation, 364
merchants, 334
Mercury, 123, 267
mercy, 252
merit, 164, 170, 171, 252, 326, 328, 391; of reading, 97
Mesopotamia, 38
metaphysics, 397

metempsychosis, 19
Mettapur Narayana Bhattatiripad, 332
Meyer, 514
Meykaṇḍa, 268
Milindapañha, 495
milk, 180, 191
Milk Ocean, 118, 141, 241
Mīmāṃsā, 78, 141, 383, 384, 385, 380, 408; *Mīmāṃsā Sūtra*, 408; Mīmāṃsākas, 60, 66, 215. See also: *Pūrva Mīmāṃsā*
Mīnākṣi temple, 296, 331, 485
mind, 377, 388, 391, 394
Minor, R., 517
Minz, Nirmal, 494
Mīrābāī, 224, 236, 259, 260, 368, 369f, 485, 567
miracles, 245
Mirashi, V. V., 497, 499, 513, 532
misery, 399
Mishra, V. N., 499
Mishra, V., 570
Misra, O. P., 549
Miśra, Prabhākara, 574
Miśra, Vacāspati, 572
mithyā-jñāna, 395
Mitra, 133, 134
mlecchas, 21, 51, 127, 216
Moddie, A. D., 44
modern Indian languages, 5
modernity, 54, 472, 562; modernity vs. tradition, 342
Moghuls, 486
moha, 174, 269, 339, 403, 529; *moha māyā*, 227
Mohammadabad, 329
Mohenjodaro, 34, 39, 398
mokṣa, 95, 155, 171, 212 ff, 217, 219, 256, 336, 337, 391, 392, 393, 394, 410, 416, 421, 535
Möller, V., 554
money, 162
Monier-Williams, M., 23
monkey school, 254
monogamy, 187
monotheism, 130
Mookerjea, Shyamprasad, 464, 465
Mookerjee, Ajit, 548
moon, 114, 123, 209, 210, 215, 261, 268, 288, 299
Moore, Charles A., 25
Moral Imperative, 173
morality, 219
Morinis, E. A., 557
mortification, 224
mother(s), 278 ff, 370; mother goddess, 312; Mother Earth, 134, 293; Mother India, 473
Mount Meru, 118, 119, 120
mṛduta, 288
mṛtyu 125, 190; *mṛtyu-samskāra*, 189; *mṛtyuñjaya*, 267; *mṛtyuñjaya-kāvaca*, 143
Mudalvan, 294 ff
Mudgal, S. G., 576
mudgara, 248
mudrā, 286, 293, 316, 549
Mughal Empire, 427
Mughal, M. R., 589
muhūrta, 116, 157, 326
Mukarji, Nirmal, 587
mukhaśāla, 321
mukta, 410, 419
Muktananda, Swami, 565
mukti, 95, 217, 291, 425, 535; *mukti-dātā*, 251; mukti-triveni, 288
Muktikā Upaniṣad, 532
mūlabera, 323
mūladhāra, 288
Mūlādhyāya-pariśiṣṭa, 157
mūlaprakṛti, 291
Mūlasaṃhitā, 95
Mullai, 299
Müller, F. M., 23, 25, 34, 36, 75, 130, 478, 479, 508, 596
Mundaden, A. M., 503
Muṇḍaka Upaniṣad, 194, 200, 209, 223, 532–53, 576

muñja, 183, 186, 378
Munshi, K. M., 443
mūrti, 157, 163, 249, 311 ff; *mūrti pūjā*, 258, 315, 323
Murti, G. S., 70, 508
Murti, T. R. V., 73, 305, 497, 510, 568, 577
Murty, K. S., 577
Murugan, 294 ff, 332
muśala, 248
Muslims, 7, 31, 447
mustard seed, 301
Muyālahan, 141
Muziris, 18
mythology, 96
myths, 196

Nabhaji, 356
nabhas, 123
Naciketas, 213
nadas, 116, 289
nāḍis, 288
Nadukal, 552
Nāgapañcami, 327
Nāgarastyle, 321
nāgas, 107, 122
Nāgasena, 18
Nagojibhaṭṭa, 486
nails, 190
Naimiṣa forest, 83
Naiṣadha, 120
Naiṣkārmyasiddhi, 577
naistika brahmacari, 186
naivedya, 163
Naiyāyikās, 60
Nakamura, H., 497
Nakula, 87, 88, 89
nāma, 225; *nāma japa*, 227, 258. See also: name.
Nāmadeva, 356
nāmaskāra, 163
Nambudiripad, N., 526
Nambudiris, 343
name, 181, 226, 229, 259; name of God, 216, 236; name-giving, 185
Nammalvar, 251, 302
Nanada, A. C., 500
Nanda, 224, 283; Nanda empire, 126
Nanda, Gulzarilal, 357
nandi, 143
Nandimath, S. C., 547
Nāra, 240
Nārada, 122, 195, 222, 228, 237, 240
Nāradīya Purāṇa, 96
nārakas, 122
Narasiṃha, 146
Narasimhavarman, 321
Narasiṃha saṃpradāya, 356
Nārāyana, 145, 146, 226, 240, 240, 261; *Nārāyana kāvaca*, 244; *Nārāyanīyam*, 100, 240, 332
Narbadā/Narmadā, 96, 354, 477
nāsadīya sūkta, 113, 114
nāstikas, 50, 62, 380, 381, 504, 569
nāṭa-mandira, 312
Nāṭarāja, 141, 267
Nath, Pundit Shunker, 495
nāṭha, 579
Nāṭha Muni, 251
Nāṭhapanthis, 354
nationalism, 43, 54
nature worship, 299
navarātrī, 327
Navaratnam, Ratna, 547
Navya-Nyāya, 392 ff
Nayanmars, 223, 265, 268, 273, 301, 304
Nayar, 343
Nayar, T. Balakrishnan, 499
nectar, 259
Neduvel, 298
Nehru, Jawaharlal, 30, 43, 149, 443, 463, 464, 465, 487, 488, 498
Neill, S., 503
Neo-Platonism, 533
Neog, M., 543
Neogy, K. C., 464
Neolithic, 297
netherworlds, 122

neti neti, 201, 211
Neufeldt, R., 534
Neuman, E., 524
Neumayer, E., 500
New Age, 476
new ethics, 54
new moon, 167, 325
Neydal, 299
nidhidhyāsana, 425
Nigama, 289
nigamana, 394
nigraha, 326
Nikhilananda, Swami, 576, 578
Nikṛti, 125
Nīla, 120
Nīlagrīva, 265
Nīlakaṇṭha, 140, 265, 270, 576
Nīmavats, 352
Niṃbārka, 254, 352, 541
nirālambanā purī, 288
nirguṇa, 206; *nirguṇa bhakti*, 225; *nirguna brahman*, 379, 419
nirriti, 115
Nirukta, 67, 77
Nirvedananda, Swami, 581
Niṣāda, 125, 340
Niścaldas, Swami, 578
niṣkāma karma, 106, 173, 216, 454, 529
Nitala, 122
nīti, 84, 342
Nīti Dharma, 453
nitya, 389; *nitya karma*, 216; *nitya līlā*, 256; *nityamuktas*, 419
nimeṣa, 116
nivṛtti, 236
niyama, 403
niyati, 534
non-violence, 252. See also: *ahiṃsā*.
noose, 281
Nordheimer, I., 24
Novotitch, N., 495
Nṛsinha, 241, 327
Nyāya-Vaiśeṣika, 74, 387 ff
Nyāgrodha, 121, 208
nyāsa, 66, 73, 227, 287, 383, 384, 387 ff, 420
Nyāya Sūtras, 388, 392, 482, 571
Nyāyakośa, 569
Nyāyakusumañjalī, 395, 484, 571
Nyāyaratnakāra, 575

O'Connell, J. T., 537, 542
O'Flaherty, W. D., 277, 504, 506, 534, 548
Oak, Vasantrao, 465
Oberhammer, G., 573
Oberlies, T., 545
occupation, 162
oceanic circle, 458
Oguibenine, B., 551
old age, 216, 217, 262
Oldenberg, H., 100, 513
Oldfield, Josia, 449
Olivelle, P., 563
OM, 78, 106, 203, 236, 288, 402. See also: AUM.
Oman, I. C., 562
one, 198, 204, 212; oneness, 206
onion, 165
Oppenheimer, J. Robert, 109
Oriental Institute of Baroda, 515
Orientalism, 10
origins, 30; origin of the world, 113, 197
orthodoxy, 49, 63
orthopraxy, 63
Osborne, A., 581
Otto, R., 100
outcastes, 8, 163, 308, 343, 335, 364

pādapatha, 68
padārtha, 74
Padārthadharmasaṅgraha, 389, 571
Padma Purāṇa, 96, 227, 230, 536, 557
padmagarbha, 319
Padmanābha, 248
Padmanabhan, S., 558
Padmapada, 351

pādya, 163
pagala, 538
painlessness, 391
paiśāca, 531
Pakistan, 7, 464, 487
Palani, 298
Paleolithic, 477
Pali, 61
Pallavas, 39, 331, 483
pañca mahāyajñas, 159, 183
pañca mahākāras, 285 f
pañca bheda, 423
pañcabhūta liṅga, 315
pañcācāra, 273
Pañcadaśī, 426
pañcāgni vidyā, 195, 198, 534
pañcalakṣana, 95
pañcāṅga, 162, 167
Pāñcarātra, 19, 114, 240, 246, 251, 380, 484; *Pāñcarātra Āgamas*, 249; *Pāñcarātra Saṁhitās*, 423
pañcāyat, 63, 181
pancāyātana-pūjā, 59, 139
Pancikar, W. C. Sastri, 509
Pāṇḍavas, 83, 86, 103, 365
Pandey, S. M., 504
Pandharpur, 356
Paṇḍu, 85
Pandy, R. B., 530
Pandyas, 485
Panikkar, R., 507
Pāṇini, 74, 145, 263, 397, 479, 482, 511
pāpātama, 174
para jñāna, 200
para, 246
Parabrahman, 246
Parainām̄i saṃpradāya, 356
paramahaṃsa, 289, 347, 348
Paramahaṃsa Upaniṣad, 347, 563
paramakula, 288
paramāṇus, 390
paramātman, 85, 116, 397
Paramesvaran, M. R., 540
Paranjoti, V., 524, 546
Parāśara, 83, 251
Paraśiva, 273, 288
Parāśurāma, 146, 241; Parāśurāma period, 125
Paravasudeva, 246
Parekh, M. C., 541, 580
parental love, 232
Pargiter, F. E., 96, 478, 500, 514, 589
paria, 343
Parīkṣit, 126
Parliament of Religions, 437
Parsis, 8
Parsons, T., 333
Pārvata, 350
Pārvatī, 139, 146, 291
pāśa, 248, 267, 268; *pāśajñāna*, 269
pāsaṇḍa, 59
pāśu, 267, 268; *pāśujñāna*, 269
Pāśupata, 60, 227, 380; Pāśupatas, 60, 234, 263, 267, 353
Pāśupatasūtra, 267
Pāśupati, 140, 262, 265, 266
Pātāla, 122
Patañjali, 53, 75, 106, 274, 397, 403, 306, 411, 484
Path of Knowledge, 193 ff
Path of Devotion, 221 ff
Path of Works, 155 ff
paṭhaśālas, 379, 385
pati, 268; *patijñāna*, 269
patience, 258
patita, 255
patriarchal religion, 375
Pattabhiram, M., 585, 586
Pattadakal, 321
paṭṭiśa, 248
Pauravas, 126
peace, 266
peacock, 298; peacock feathers, 354
penances, 186, 178 ff. See also: *prayaścittas*.
Pennai, 275
pentads, 197
Periyar, 300
Persia, 478

Peshwas, 487
phalaśloka, 97
Philips, G. E., 501, 524, 547, 553
philosophy, 381, 384
physics, 387
Piggott, S., 499
pilgrimage, 166, 168, 171, 172, 180, 216, 289, 328, 431, 557
Pillai, K. K., 298, 551, 552, 553
Pillai, S. S., 547
piṇḍas, 191, 329
Piṅgalā, 281
piśācas, 116, 191
Pischel, R., 75
pitāmahā, 139
pitṛs, 160, 162, 183, 190, 192, 213, 239, 311; *pitṛyajña*, 159; *pitṛyāna*, 213
pity, 285
Plakṣadvīpa, 119
planets, 122, 123
Plassey, 487
Plato, 19
poison, 292, 370
pole star, 188
Political Hinduism, 472
polyandry, 187, 365
polytheism, 14, 130
Pondichéry, 371, 486
Pongal, 305
Pope, G. U., 529, 547
Portuguese, 47, 486
Possehl, G., 588, 589
Potter, K. H., 569
power, 130, 134, 157, 249, 445
Prabandham, 251
prabhā, 139
Prabhākara, 409
Prabhu, P. H., 559
Prabhu, R. K., 565
Prabodhananda Saraswati, 543
pracanna bauddha, 380
prācārya, 413
pradakṣina, 163; *pradakṣina patha*, 319
pradhāna, 124, 381, 406; *pradhāna-puruṣa*, 123
Pradyumna, 248
Prahlāda, 241, 228, 327
prajānātya, 531
Prajāpati, 116, 166, 203, 208, 209, 213, 241, 279, 325; Prajapatiloka, 205
prajñānam brahman, 210, 350
Prajñātīrtha, 59
prakāra, 320
prakāraṇas, 425
Prakrit, 5
prakṛti, 106, 115, 140, 147, 249, 286, 398 ff, 407, 419, 422, 423
Pralamba, 244
pralaya, 392
pramāda, 395
pramāṇa, 66, 73, 393
prāṇa, 138, 195, 198, 210, 404, 213; *prāṇamaya*, 206; *prāṇayama*, 56, 179, 190, 403, 404
prāṇava, 78, 288. See also: OM
prāṇaya, 542
prapatti, 229, 252
prārabdha, 269
Prasad, Rajendra, 488
Prasad, Modhi, 581
prasāda, 323
Praśāstapāda, 389, 390
Praśna Upaniṣad, 194, 195, 533, 535
prasthāna trayī, 66, 413
pratijñā, 394
Pratiśākhyas, 68
pratisarga, 95
pratiṣṭhāpana, 313
Pratyābhijñā, 60, 271
pratyāhāra, 403, 404
pratyakṣa, 73, 393
pravṛtti, 172, 236, 394
Prayāga, 155, 180, 328, 329, 352
prayaścittas, 176, 178, 363, 529, 561. See also: penance
precedence, 57

predestination, 254
prehistoric cave paintings, 34
premā, 222, 232, 256, 542
preserver, 138, 150
Presler, F. A., 552
preta, 189, 191, 192
Prigogine, I., 574
Priyavrata, 124
probation, 349
Prosper of Aquitania, 19
protection, 141
Protestant, 47
Proto-Āryans, 34
Proutist Block of India, 469
Pṛthu, 118, 125, 340
pṛth(i)vī, 118, 147, 340, 342; *pṛthvī maṇḍala*, 288
Pṛthvī-Dyaus, 112, 128
psycho-analyzing, 3
psychology, 397
pūjā, 156, 157, 163, 165, 171, 229, 260, 367, 431; implements for, 235; *pūjāri*, 172
pumān, 124
punarmṛtyu, 213
Punjab, 8, 140
puṇya, 164, 166, 168, 2161
Purāṇas, 2, 14, 39, 70, 71, 73, 81, 94, 117, 124, 126, 147, 163, 180, 181, 191, 216, 267, 279, 329, 338, 339, 364, 410, 419, 425, 431, 435, 482, 516
pure love, 232
Puri, 350
purity, 170, 171, 182, 252, 258, 348
pūrṇam, 203
Pūrṇaprajñā, 352, 422. See also: Madhva
purohit, 134
Pururavas, 125
puruṣa, 113, 115, 206, 209, 212, 215, 271, 286, 398, 400, 401, 402, 406; *puruṣa sūkta*, 94, 113, 116, 334, 536; *puruṣamedha*, 166, 525; *puruṣa-prakṛti*, 108, 128
puruṣārthas, 95, 128, 336, 337, 363, 560
Puruṣottama, 146, 213, 252, 420, 421
Puruṣottamācārya, 232
Pūrva Mīmāṃsā, 69, 74, 155, 168, 228, 408 ff, 420, 482. See also: Mīmāṃsā; *Pūrvamīmāṃsā Sūtra*, 482
pūrvavat, 394
Pusalker, A. D., 125, 510, 514, 515, 520, 523, 524, 540, 589
Puṣan, 190
Puṣkara, 96
Puṣkaradvīpa, 119, 121
puṣpa, 163
puṣṭi, 255; *puṣṭimārga*, 254, 255, 352
Puthiadan, I., 541
Putnam, John J., 502, 557
putra, 188
Pythagoras, 19, 129, 389

Queen Hatsheput, 18
Quivron, G., 588
Quong, Stephen (Umananda), 567
Quran, 450, 452

R. S. S., 32, 33, 64, 244, 440, 464, 467, 471, 474, 586. See also: Rāṣṭrīya Svayamsevak Sangh.
Rādhā, 145, 245, 246, 367, 368, 370, 550; Rādhā-Kṛṣṇa, 353, 367
Radhakrishnan, S., 43, 45, 47, 101, 127, 381, 305, 384, 417, 429, 438, 446, 472, 474, 475, 488, 497, 503, 509, 518, 545, 569, 570, 579, 581
Rādhāvallabhis, 486
rāga, 269, 402, 542; *rāgānuga-bhakti*, 232
Raghavachar, S. S., 537, 541, 579
Raghavan, V., 543
Raghavendracharya, R., 578
rahu kālam, 301, 553
Rai, Lala Lajpat, 580
Raidās, 224

Raj, Dev, 501
rāja, 132, 340; *rājadharma*, 340, 561; *rājaguhya*, 106; *rājanīti*, 342; *rājasuya*, 299; rājavidyā, 106
Rāja Yoga, 397
Raja, C. Kunhan, 500
Raja, K. Kunjunni, 575
Rajagopalacari, Cakravarti, 487, 515
Rajagopalan, V., 540
rajas, 400, 419; *rajasik*, 165
Rajasthan, 36
Rājataraṅginī, 485
rajñī, 139
Rakhi bandhan, 326
rakṣa, 95; *rakṣaka*, 251
rākṣasa (form of marriage), 531
rākṣasas, 91
Raktadantā, 282
raktāmbarā, 58
Ram, Suresh, 580
Rāma, 3, 82, 89, 90, 91, 92, 93, 145, 225, 236, 241, 244, 336, 352, 372, 539; Rāma bhaktas, 228; *Rām(a)līlā*, 93; *Rām(a)rājya*, 460; Rām(a) Rājya Pariṣad, 357, 468, 487; Rām(a)śila, 244; Rāmaśilayātrā, 466
Rāma Tīrtha, 236, 267
Rāmacandra, 146, 478; Rāmacandra period, 126, 482
Rām(a)carit(a)mānas(a), 6, 89, 448, 457, 515, 539
Rām(a)dās(a) Swami, 356, 486, 544; Rāmādāsis 356
Ramakrishna, Paramahaṃsa, 292, 302, 365, 437, 487; Ramakrishna Mission, 337 ff, 358; *Ramakrishna Upaniṣad*, 509
Raman, A. S., 564
Ramana Maharṣi, 302, 440, 581
Rāmānanda, 352, 485
Rāmānuja, 127, 229, 249, 251, 252, 348, 352, 379, 412, 413, 417, 420, 422, 426, 501, 541, 575, 577; Rāmānuja *saṃpradāya*, 60, 352
Ramanujacarya, M. C., 509
Ramanujan, A. K., 544, 553
Ramaswami Naickker, E. V., 300
Ramaswami, K. S., 581
Rāmavata saṃpradāya, 356
Ramayaka, 120
Rāmāyaṇa, 6, 14, 41, 72, 88, 89, 93, 140, 145, 149, 162, 223, 263, 266, 366, 425, 430, 513, 588; *Rāmāyaṇa* age, 482
Ramesan, N., 555, 558
Rameśvaran, 92
Ramesvarananda, Swami, 357
Ramprasad, 223, 234
Rām(a)ras(a), 259
Ranade, M. D., 487
Ranade, R. D., 100, 532, 538, 543, 544
Rangachari, K., 559
Ranganathananda, Swami, 573
Rann of Kutch, 36
Rao, Hayavadana, 547
Rao, H. S., 582
Rao, P. Nagaraja, 579
Rao, U. R., 565
Rao, V. N. Hari, 558
rasa, 229, 537; *rasa* school, 537; *ras(a)līlā*, 238
Raseśvara, 60
Rāṣṭrīya Svayamsevak Sangh, 63, 464, 487, 565. See also: R. S. S.
ratha, 324
rati, 116
Rau, H., 496
Raurava, 122
Rāvaṇa, 82, 91, 92, 93
Ravivāra, 325
Ray, Raja Kanta, 494
Raychaudhuri, H. C., 501, 513
rayī, 195
real, 204, 212; reality 198, 211, 259, 348, 358
realization, 426

rebirth, 106, 178, 181, 191, 197, 212 ff, 213, 329, 389, 394, 457, 475
recitation, 65
redeemer, 251
redemption, 161
reformers 429
reforms, 430 f
Rege, M. P., 385
regicide, 339
religious persecutions, 301
Renou, L., 33, 510, 527, 570, 589
renouncer, 345
renunciation, 258, 288, 308, 474
repentance, 179
resentment, 256
revelation, 13, 63, 65, 66, 72, 74, 79, 107, 149, 380, 417, 457
Ṛgveda, 23, 34, 36, 39, 67, 75, 94, 112, 116, 132, 131, 134, 139, 145, 166, 170, 188, 222, 240, 265, 295, 362, 398, 423, 478, 479, 482, 511, 519, 522, 523, 525, 538, 545, 559, 566
rice, 180
Richards, Mira, 371
riddles, 195
Riepe, D., 497, 498, 506
right belief, 57
righteousness, 53, 226, 173
rites of passage, 152, 186
ritual, 155, 169, 171, 193, 216, 232, 257, 267, 268, 269, 273, 334, 423, 432, 443, 528, 555
rivers, 328
ṛk, 188
Robb, P., 583
Rocher, L., 95, 510, 515, 516, 546
Roman emperors, 19
romañcā, 288
Rome, 18
Rosen, S. J., 260
Rosen, V. Stache, 497
Roth, R., 23, 75
Roth, H., 496, 511
Rowland, B., 556
Roy, Ajit, 587
Roy, M. N., 443, 507, 582
Roy, N. R., 554
Roy, Pratap Chandra, 514
Roy, Raja Ram Mohan, 47, 182, 433, 487, 505, 580
Roy, S. B., 478, 589
Ṛṣabha, 340
ṛṣis, 36, 107, 131, 134, 138, 160, 162, 163, 183, 194, 347
ṛta, 115, 134, 137, 206
ṛtu, 134
Ruben, W., 506
Rudra, 239, 263, 265, 266, 267, 275, 353, 520; Rudra *saṃpradāya*, 352
rudrākṣa, 143, 273, 354; *rudrākṣa mālā*, 161
Rūpa Goswāmi, 257, 367
Ruskin, 451
Ryerson, C. A., 552

S. V. Museum on Temple Art, 331
Śabara, 410; *Śābarabhāśya*, 408, 411, 483, 574
śabda, 73, 74, 227, 390, 393, 394; *śabda* body, 286; *śabdabrahman*, 78
Śānti, 124
saccidānanda, 415, 423
Sachau, E. C., 495
sacraments, 183
sacred ashes, 160
Sacred Books of the East, 23
sacred geography, 311 ff
sacred kingship, 569
sacred knowledge, 378
sacred thread, 185, 186
sacrifice, 69, 113, 114, 134, 156, 165, 167, 185, 195, 311, 409, 552
Sadnām, 536
sadācāra, 50
Sadananda, 351, 425
Sadāśiva, 268
ṣaḍdarśanas, 377 ff
sādhaka, 346, 348

sādhana, 49, 55, 236, 346, 347, 402; *sādhanabhakti*, 232
Sadhāraṇa Brahmo Samāj, 431
sadhāraṇadharma, 172
sādhu, 55, 64, 177, 191, 346, 358
Sadhu Charan Prasad, 566, 529
sādhvī, 346
sādhya, 346
Sāgara, 350
sage, 108, 172
saguṇa brahman, 379, 419
Sahādeva, 87
sahāmārga, 234
sahasranāma, 149, 227
śahnai, 161
saiddha, 248
saint, 62, 2199
Śaiva Advaita, 271
Śaiva Āgamas, 140, 141, 267
Śaiva Purāṇas, 140, 143
Śaiva Siddhānta, 141, 227, 234, 263, 268, 275, 485, 546; Saiva Siddhanta Mission, 277
Śaiva Vedānta, 270
Śaivaguru, 265
Śaivas, 32, 41, 60, 67, 161, 419
Śaivism, 5, 41, 49, 57, 60, 69, 140, 501
śaka, 481
Śakadvīpa, 119
sakala, 269
Sākambharī, 282
Śakas, 483
Sakatāyana, 511
śakhas, 381
sakhya 231
sākṣātkāra, 236, 259
śakṣī, 423
Śākta Pīṭhas, 283, 289
Śākta Upaniṣads, 485
Śāktas, 32, 41, 67, 225
śakti, 141, 146, 248, 271, 273, 278, 369; *śakti nipata*, 371; *śaktirūpi*, 116; *śaktipatā*, 271
śaktis, 316
Śāktism, 49, 57, 69, 146, 147, 365, 483
Śaktiviśiṣṭādvaita, 273
Sākya mountains, 283
śālagrāma, 249
Salisbury, E. E., 24
Śālmaladvīpa, 119
Salomon, R., 557
salt, 178
Salt Ocean, 118, 120
salvation, 2, 62, 168, 251, 175, 178 365, 384, 388, 393, 398, 419. See also: *mokṣa, mukti.*
sāma, 188
sāmabhāva, 450
samādhi, 191, 262, 354, 402, 403, 405, 406
sāmānyato dṛṣṭa, 394
Samartha, S. J., 503
Sāmaveda, 67, 116
samaveśa, 271
Sambandhar, 274, 302, 501
saṃdhyā, 161, 348; *saṃdhyābhāṣa*, 289
saṃhitās, 39, 67, 69, 163, 193, 435
samjñā, 139
saṃkalpa, 328
Saṃkarṣaṇa, 248
Sāṁkhya, 115, 116, 128, 227, 241, 249, 380, 397 ff, 412, 420, 482
Sāṁkhyakārikā, 50, 60, 102, 104, 106, 108, 399, 572, 573
Sāṁkhyasūtra, 399
saṁkirtaṇ(a), 236, 258, 260. See also: *kīrtaṇa.*
saṃnyāsa, 55, 64, 102, 237, 254, 308, 337, 445 ff, 562
saṃnyāsi, 50, 156, 162, 164, 189, 191, 328, 457; *saṃnyāsi* revolt, 357, 462
sampat, 288
saṃpradāyas, 49, 55, 57, 63, 64, 143, 346, 350
samsāra, 251, 257, 268, 271, 415, 416

saṃskāras, 51, 152, 172, 183, 202, 335, 348, 363, 435
Saṃskṛti Samsthān Bareli, 532
samvāda, 385
samvat, 481
samyama, 405
Sanaiścara, 283
Sanāndana, 123
Sanatanadevaji, Maharaja, 509
sanātana dharma, 31, 32, 51, 380, 435, 443; sanātanists, 66
Sanātkumāra, 195
Sandeepany Sadhanalaya, 442
Śāṇḍilya, 195, 222
Saṅgam age, 297
Sangani, N. P., 51
Śani,, 123; *Śanivāra*, 325
Sankalia, H. D., 499, 588
Śaṅkara, 31, 60, 127, 128, 196, 228, 275, 302, 345, 349, 353, 377, 379, 399, 411, 413, 416, 420–425, 429, 484, 576, 577; *Śaṅkarabhāṣya*, 576; Śaṅkarācāryas, 59, 170, 265, 346, 351, 563
Śaṅkaradeva, 485
Śaṅkara Miśra, 389
Śaṅkarananda, Swami, 501
śaṅkha, 248
sanmārga, 234
Sanskrit, 6, 21, 153; Sanskrit philology, 5; Sanskrit grammar, 77
Sanskrit University, 330
Sanskritisation, 8, 139, 295
sant, 346, *sant sādhana*, 225; *sant* tradition 223 f; Sant Samitī, 565
śānta, 229
Śānti, 84
santoṣa, 403
saptavidhā anupapatti, 578
Śārada Pīṭha, 350
śaraṇa, 109; *śaraṇāgati*, 229
Sarasvatī (goddess), 50, 88, 430
Sarasvatī (river), 36, 329, 479, 482
Sarasvatī (order), 350
Sarasvati, Kevalanda, 574
Sarasvati, Swami Dayananda, 515
sarga, 95
Śarīrakabhāṣya, 413
Sarkar, Hem Chandra, 580
Sarkar, P. R., 469
Śarma (name of brahmin), 185
Sarma, B. N. K., 578
Sarma, E. R. S., 571
Sarma, N. S., 580
Sarma, Pandit Dinanath, 504
Sarma, R. Thangasami, 569, 570
Sarma, S. K., 393
Sarma, S. R. 556
Sarmana, Pandit Acutyananda Jha, 554
śārṅga, 248
Sarsanghachalak, 467
Sarva, 140, 265, 267
Sarvadarśanasaṁgraha, 383
sarveśvara, 420
Śaṣṭitantra, 399
śāstrārtha, 385
śāstras, 156, 174
Sastri, A. Mahadeva, 530
Sastri, Devaprakasa Patanjala, 511
Sastri, K., 570
Sastri, K. A. Nilakantha, 499, 501, 511, 551, 553
Sastri, Kuppuswami, 384, 387, 388, 567, 569
Sastri, Lal Bahadur, 488
Sastri, S. K. Ramanatha, 574
Sastri, S. Lakshminarasimha, 577
Sastri, S. S. Suryanarayana, 572, 579
sat, 106, 114, 115, 210, 268
sat-cit-ānanda, 246. See also: *saccidānanda*.
Śatadhanu, 59
Satajit, 118
Śatākṣī, 282
Śatapatha Brāhmaṇa, 68, 69, 77, 94, 266, 527, 528
Śatarudriya, 140, 265

Śatarūpa, 520
śatasāhasrī saṃhitā, 83
satguru, 225
satī, 182, 283, 361, 372, 374, 434, 487, 503; *satī* memorials 372, 373
satputramārga, 234
Śatrughna, 90, 91, 93
satsaṅg, 62, 225
sattva, 400, 419; *sattvaguṇa*, 108; sattvik food, 165
Saturn, 123
satya, 206, 208, 403, 458, 459, 525
satyāgraha, 451, 452, 460; Satyāgraha Āshram, 453, 457
Satyaloka, 122, 123
Satyanāmis, 356
Satyaprajñā, 59
Satyārtha Prakāśa, 435, 580
Satya Sāī Bābā, 356, 442
satyasya satya, 211
Satyavatī, 83
śauca, 403
Śaunaka, 83
Saura Purāṇas, 139
śava, 283
Savarkar, V. D., 32, 311, 463
savior, 132, 245; Saviour God, 132
Savitṛ, 134, 139, 186
Sawai, Yoshitsugu, 563
Saxena, K., 586
Sāyana, 75, 485, 511
scheduled castes, 9. See also: *Dalit*, outcastes.
Schilpp, P., 581
Schlegel, August von, 102
Schlingloff, D., 556
Schneider, V., 540
Schopenhauer, Arthur, 21
Schour, K., 536
Schrader, F. O., 70, 509
Schrödinger, E., 384
Schwab, J., 494, 527
Schwartzberg, J., 495
scripture, 65, 398
Seal, B. N., 129, 538
Second birth, 185
secularism, 443, 445, 446, 583, 587
secularists, 443
Seemann, R., 539
Segal, J. B., 503
self, 199, 202, 204 ff, 403; self-awareness, 217; self-consciousness, 352, 423; self-control, 258; self-discovery, 199; self-immolation, 189; self-interest, 237; self-mortification, 171; self-surrender, 229, 252, 255, 423
Sen, D., 499
Sen, Keshub Chandra, 47, 434
Sen, N., 513
Sen, S. P. 552
senas, 46
Sengupta, P. C., 478, 589
Serampore, 437
service, 64, 221, 474. See also: *seva*.
servitude, 232
śeṣa, 122, 123, 246, 249, 261, 321
sesame seeds, 190
śeṣavat, 394
seva, 181, 221, 237, 255, 257
seven *ṛṣis*, 113, 123, 188
sexual continence, 186
Sey, 298
Seyon, 299
Shaffer, J. G., 589
Shamasastri, R., 341
Shankar, Moin, 470, 587
Sharma, A., 493, 517, 545, 560, 567, 577
Sharma, A. K., 477
Sharma, B. N. K., 500, 541
Sharma, K., 543
Sharma, K. K., 500
Sharpe, E. J., 517
sheaths, 213
Shendge, Malati J., 493, 498
Shiv Sena, 468
Shulman, D. D., 551, 558
Siauve, S., 570, 578

Śibi, 140
siddha, 346
siddhāntācāra, 285
siddhis, 286, 404, 406
Siegel, L., 537
śikha, 186, 347, 348, 562
śikhara, 321
Sikhs, 8, 32, 46, 67
Śīkṣaṣṭaka, 542
Sil, N. P., 561
śila, 391
silence, 56, 196, 202
sin, 152, 160, 161, 164, 176 ff, 177, 181, 183, 186, 217, 219, 252, 262, 330, 403; against name, 181, 227; against service, 181
sincerity, 252, 258
Singh, A. N., 521
Singh, Giani Zail, 586
Singh, Jaideva, 498
Singh, Kushwant, 502
Singh, Mohan, 573
Singh, N. K., 587
Singh, R., 557
Singhal, D. P., 521
Sinha, N., 571
Sinha, V. K., 445, 583
Sirkar, D. C., 539, 549
Sītā, 82, 90, 91, 92, 93, 228, 244, 352, 353, 365 ff, 366, 368, 372; Sītā-Rāma, 353
Śītalā, 283
Śiva, 19, 41, 56, 138, 139, 152, 168, 188, 206, 225, 227, 229, 261 ff, 353, 359, 372, 430, 469, 577; Śiva Nīlakaṇṭha, 141; Śiva Paśupati, 139; Śiva *avatāras*, 141, 267, 268; Śiva *ardhanārī*, 141, 291; Śiva Mahāyogi, 139; Śiva Nāṭaraja, 296; Śiva Trimukha, 139; Śiva *bhagats*, 263; Śiva *bhaktas*, 225; Śiva *bhakti*, 234, 430; Śiva *japa*, 143; Śivaloka, 123, 270, 271; *Śiva Purāṇa*, 96, 263, 271, 297, 484, 524, 546; Śivarātrī, 267, 327, 435; Śiva-Vedānta, 266
Śiva Āgamas, 263
Śiva Paśūpati seal, 38
Śiva-Śakti, 292
Śiva-Viṣṇu, 293
Śivajī, 486
Śivajñānabodha, 268
Sivananda, 356, 440, 581
Sivaramamurti, C., 551
Sivaraman, K., 507, 546
Śivāṣṭamūrti, 141
Śivasthāna, 289
śivatva, 269
Skanda Purāṇa, 96, 298
sky, 114, 122
Skylax, 482
slavery, 39
sleep, 199, 412
Ślokavārtika, 574
smallpox, 283, 301
smaraṇa, 230
smārta, 350, 72, 161
smāsana, 190
Smith, B. K., 531
Smith, B. L., 536, 543
Smith, F. H. Daniel, 509
Smith, F. M., 525
Smith, W. C., 587
smṛti, 50, 66, 71, 84, 96, 348, 409, 419, 421, 471, 484
snake, 298, 291, 299, 315, 370
snānīya, 163
Snataka, V., 536
sneha, 542
śobhya, 140
social justice, 53; social order, 52, 333 ff; social reforms, 273; social reformers, 342
socialism, 337, 459
śoka, 125
Solar Dynasty, 125
Soma, 133, 134, 165–167, 215; Somacakra, 288; Soma hymns, 166

Soma-Rudra, 265
Somavāra, 325
Somnāth, 484
Somnāthpur, 323
son, 188
Sopāra, 18
Sørenson, 514
sorrow, 220
śoṣa, 269
soul of all, 249
sound, 259, 390
South Indian languages, 5
space, 197, 311, 391
Spaṇḍaśāstra, 271
Spate, O. H. K., 502
speech, 78
Spencer, A. M., 538
sphoṭa, 74, 575; *sphoṭavāda*, 411
spinning wheel, 456
spirit, 286, 400
spiritual experience, 381
spirituality, 195
splendor, 249
sraddhā (last rites), 62, 95, 188, 189, 191, 192, 380
śrāddha (faith), 124, 206, 216
śrauta, 157; *Śrautasūtras*, 71, 165, 482
śravaṇa, 230, 425
Śrī, 146, 246, 249, 252, 282, 286, 299.
Śrī Haridāsī *saṃpradāya*, 356
Śrī Laṅka, 18
Śrī Nāthajī, 257
Śrī Parameśvara Saṃhitā, 555
Śrī Rādhā vallabhis, 356
Śrī *saṃpradāya*, 352
Śrī sanātani *saṃpradāya*, 356
Śrī Swāmi Nārāyanī *saṃpradāya*, 356
Śrī Vaiṣṇavism, 232, 246, 252, 332, 352, 541
Śrībhāṣya, 419 251
Śrīdhāra, 248
Śrīkaṇṭha, 270, 546; *Śrīkaṇṭha-bhāṣya*, 485
Śrīkāra Bhāṣya, 273
Śrīmad Bhāgavata Māhātmya, 79
Śrīnagar, 385
Srinivasan, D. M., 524, 544, 545
Srinivasan, D. N., 265
Śrīnivāsadāsa, 426
Srinivas, M. N., 8, 559
Śrīpati, 273, 348
Śrīraṅgam, 249, 251, 296, 301, 304, 311, 320, 351, 352, 369, 417, 485, 528, 555
śrīvatsa, 246; Srivilliputtur, 368
ṣṛṅgāra, 229
Ṣṛṅgavan, 120
Ṣṛṅgerī, 350
śrota, 210
sṛṣṭi, 268
śruti, 66, 94, 172, 193, 421, 497, 526, 527, 575
Staal, F., 158, 169, 528
staff, 349
stars, 210
stealing, 177
Stein, Dorothy, 375
steya, 177
Sthāla Purāṇas, 96, 315
sthaṇḍila maṇḍala, 320
Sthānu, 267
sthiti, 268
sthūla śarīra, 213
Stietencron, H. von, 522, 523, 525, 549
Stoler-Miller, B., 537, 547, 555
stotraratnas, 225
straw, 266
strīdharma, 189, 361 ff
Strickman, M., 528
Strolz, W., 573
study, 352, 376; of scriptures, 56
Subrahmania, 298
substitution, 157
subtle body, 191, 213. See also: *sūkṣma śarīra*.
Sudalaimāḍan, 297

sudhārak(a), 356, 564
śūdras, 39, 107, 114, 176, 177, 223, 334, 336, 410
suffering, 220
suicide, 329
Śukadeva, 356
sukha-duḥkha, 173
Sukhtankar, V. S., 513, 514
śukla-pakṣa, 325
Śukra, 123; *Śukranītisāra*, 484
Śukravāra, 325
sūkṣma śarīra, 191, 213. See also: subtle body
Sumitrā, 90
sun, 114, 123, 137, 140, 205, 209, 210, 215, 268, 288, 289, 299; sun of darkness, 289. See also: Sūrya.
Sundaramūrti, 268, 269, 274, 302
Sundarapāṇḍya, 412
Śūṅgas, 483
śūṇya, 417; *śūṇyatā*, 415; Śūṇyavādins, 394
superimposition, 415. See also: *adhyāsā*
supreme reality, 249
Supreme God, 213
śupta padmāsana, 574
sura-asura, 128
surāpāna, 177
Sūrasamudra, 119
Sūrdās, 223, 258, 259, 486, 543
Sureśvara, 577
Śurpaṇakhī, 91
Sūrsagar, 258
Sūrya, 116, 137, 139, 225, 279, 281, 356. See also: sun
Suṣumnā, 288
suṣupti, 199
Sutalā, 122
sūtras, 71, 80, 382, 479
svadharma, 51, 64, 110, 172, 335, 338
svādhiṣṭhāna, 288
svādhyāya, 162, 183, 378, 402, 403
Śvapaca, Ṛṣi, 224
svapna-sthāna, 199
svarga, 193, 392, 410; Svar, 123
Svarloka, 122
svarūpānanda, 256
svāstika, 122
svatantra sādhus, 346
svayaṃbhu bhagavān, 165
svayaṃbhu liṅgas, 314
svayaṃvara, 366, 566
svayaṃvyakta, 248; *svayaṃvyakta mūrtis*, 313
Śveta, 120
Śvetadvīpa, 240
Śvetaketu, 207
Śvetāśvatara Upaniṣad, 140, 194, 223, 266, 275, 523, 533, 545, 546
Swadeshi movement, 455
Swahananda, Swami, 578
Swami, P. B. Annangaracharya, 578
swarāj, 456
sword, 281
Śyāma, 245
śyaṃbhu liṅga, 288
syllogism, elements of, 394
Syrian, 47

taboos, 190
Tagore, Debendranath, 434
Tagore, Rabindranath, 434, 450, 474, 487
Taimni, I. K., 572
Taittirīya Brāhmaṇa, 479; *Taittirīya Saṃhita*, 479, 525; *Taittirīya Upaniṣad*, 193, 194, 219, 256, 512, 526, 533, 534, 535
tamas, 398, 400, 419; *tāmasa-śāstras*; 227; *tāmasik*, 165
tāṃbūla, 163
Tamil, 6, 153
Tamilnāḍu, 39, 147, 153, 234, 262, 294 ff
Tamils, 39
taṇḍava, 141, 331
Tanjore, 296, 319, 321, 549
Taṅka, 412

Tansen, 370
Tantras, 147, 279, 283 ff, 484, 548; Tantricism, 483; Tantrikas, 356
Tantravārttika, 568, 574
tapas, 55, 56, 114, 116, 171, 179, 216, 366, 378, 402, 566; *tapasvīn*, 56
Tapoloka, 122, 123
Taposwami, Maharaj, 442
Taprobane, 18
Tārā, 283, 285
tarkaśāstra, 392, 396
Tarkabhāṣa, 571
Tarn, W. W., 494
tarparṇa, 107, 160, 162, 526
tat tvam asi, 208, 350, 421
Tattvacintāmani, 393
tattvajñāna, 392
Taxila, 46
teacher, 378
Tehri Garhwal, 187
tejas, 248
Tejobindo Upaniṣad, 399
temples, 168, 221, 311f, 317 ff, 431, 443; temple architecture, 249
temporality, 416
Tendulkar, D. G., 580, 584
Teṅgalai, 252
terracottas, 147
terror, 261
Tertullian, 19, 495
thags, 289, 487
Thakkeray, Bal, 468
Thaku, Anantalal, 571
Thaneśvar, 96
Thar desert, 36
theology, 381, 384, 408
Theosophical Society, 449
theosophy, 442
Thibaut, G., 576, 578
Thomas (Apostle), 46
Thomas, M. M., 503
Thompson, E. J., 538
Thoreau, Henry David, 23
three-eyed, 261
Thurston, E., 559
tiger skin, 261
tīkās, 382, 425
Tilak, B. G., 101, 182, 462, 475, 479, 500
tilaka, 190, 323
Tillotson, G. H. R., 496, 567
Timberg, T. A., 503
time, 107, 190, 213, 311, 317, 325, 388, 391; divisions of, 116
Timm, J. R., 542
ṭippaṇis, 382, 425
tirobhava, 268
tīrtha, 8, 95, 171, 191, 311 ff, 328, 350; *tirthayātrā*, 180
Tirtha, Swami Bharati Krishna, 500
Tiru, 298
Tiruchirapalli, 249
Tirukkural, 175, 294, 300, 483, 529, 553
Tirumāl, 297
Tirumular, 274
Tirunavukkarasu, 143, 302
Tirupati, 7, 304, 331, 385, 558; Tirupati Devasthānam, 555
Tiruttani, 332
Tiruvācakam, 274, 302
tithi, 167, 325
Tolkappiam, 75, 552
Tolstoy, 450, Tolstoy Farm, 450
tomato, 165
Töpelman, R., 543, 555
toraṇas, 313
tortoise, 241
totemism, 145
tradition, 30, 66, 85, 380
traditional pandits, 385
traividyā, 183
Trajan, 483
Transcendental Meditation Society, 29, 358
translation, 27
transmigration, 19, 34, 71. See also: rebirth, *punarmṛtyu*.

trayī, 571
trees, 299
Tretayuga, 117
triguṇa, 108, 128
triloka, 113, 128
trimārga, 49
tribals, 539; tribal population, 39; tribal religions, 140; tribal gods, 263. See also: *ādivāsis*.
trident, 261, 281, 351
Trika, 271
trimūrti, 138, 268
Tripathi, G. C., 522
tripuṇḍra, 160
Tripura, 161, 266, 292; *Tripurā Rāhasya*, 291
Triśaṅku, 444
tristhalī, 329
trivarga, 83
Trivikrama, 248
Tṛṣṇa, 125
trusteeship, 458
truth, 150, 173, 196, 202, 209, 219, 234, 237, 274, 380, 392, 453, 459
truthfulness, 175, 258, 402
tryaṇukas, 390
tubers, 180
Tukārām(a), 223, 236, 356, 486
tulasī, 41, 161, 249
Tul(a)sīdās(a), 89, 223, 228, 448, 486, 539
Tupṭīka, 574
tur(ī)ya, 79, 199, 200, 210, 211, 273; *tūryātīta*, 273
Tvastṛ, 68
twice born, 51, 183, 335, 336. See also: *dvija*.
tyāga, 157
tyāgi, 353
Tyagisananda, Swami 535

udaharaṇa, 394
Udāyana, 484
udbhava, 268
Uddālaka, 195, 210
Uḍipī, 351, 422
Udumbara, 41
Ueda, S., 573
Ui, H., 570
Ujjain, 283
Ujjaiṇī, 180, 283
Ujjvala Nīlāmaṇi, 367
Ūl/Ūl Vinai, 300
ultimate freedom, 2
Umā, 147, 266, 270, 283
unborn, 198
understanding, 4
universe, 239,, 246,, 262,, 278,, 282
unreal, 212
unreality, 416
unrighteousness, 53, 267
untouchability, 344, 456, 457, 559
untouchables, 224, 453, 562
untruth, 416
upapātakas, 176
upadeśa, 349
Upadeśasahasrī, 425, 563
upadhyāya, 362
Upadhyaya, Deendayal, 337, 464, 466, 586
Upadhyaya, P. C., 583, 588
upamāna, 73, 393, 394
upaṃṣu japa, 180
upanaya, 394
upanayana 185, 192, 202, 336, 363
Upaniṣads, 66, 67, 69, 80, 115, 125, 164, 171, 193, 249, 270, 285, 349, 379, 398, 411, 419, 421, 423, 435, 478, 479, 482, 545
Upapurāṇas, 72, 96, 279
Upavarṣa, 412, 483
upavāsa, 180
Upavedas, 67
Ur-Gītā, 100
Ur-Mahābhārata, 83
Ur-Purāṇa, 73
Ur-Rāmāyaṇa, 90
Uṣas, 362
utsava, 336; *utsava bera*, 323
Uttānapāda, 124
Uttara Kuru, 120

Uttara Mīmāṃsā, 420. See also: Vedānta.
utthita padmāsana, 574

vāc, 76
Vācaknavī, 362
Vācaspati Miśra, 351
vācika japa, 180
Vaḍagalai, 252
Vādavāda, 568
vahana, 146
vahni, 123
Vaibhrajas, 123
vaicitriya, 269
Vaideha, 283
vaidhibhakti, 232
Vaidik dharma, 14; Vaidik Samṣodan, 512
Vaidyanathan, K. R., 558
Vaikuṇṭha, 123, 146, 236, 246
vairāgi(nī)s, 346, 352
vairāgya, 288; *Vairāgya śatakam*, 358
Vairocana, 208
Vaiśaṃpayana, 83
Vaiśeṣika, 60, 227, 383, 387 ff, 412; *Vaiśeṣika Sūtras*, 387, 482; *Vaiśeṣikardarśana*, 571
Vaiṣṇavas, 32, 41, 67, 140, 161, 165, 181, 352; Vaiṣṇavism, 5, 41, 46, 49, 57, 69, 483; Vaiṣṇava *nāgas*, 351; *Vaiṣṇava Saṃhitās*, 145; Vaiṣṇava Sāṁkhya, 249; Vaiṣṇava Vedānta, 251 ff, 417
vaiśyas, 39, 107, 114, 176, 334, 338
Vajpayee, A. B., 466
vāk, 147, 362; *Vāksūkta*, 76, 512
Vākyapādīya, 411
Vāla, 133
Valdiya, K. S., 500
Valiyon, 279
Vallabha, 221, 254 ff, 352, 485, 541, 576
Vālmīki, 89, 514; *Vālmīki Rāmāyaṇa*, 244 ff. See also: *Rāmāyaṇa*.
value vacuum, 472
vāmācāra, 285, 292
Vāmadeva, 195, 358, 565, 585
Vāmana, 96, 146, 240, 248; Vāmana dvadaśī, 327; *Vāmana Purāṇa*, 96
vaṃśa, 95; *vaṃśānucarita*, 95
van Buitenen, J. A. B., 514, 540, 577
van Nooten, B. A., 513
Vana, 350
vānaprastha, 337, 345
vandana, 231
Varāha, 96, 146, 241; *Varāha Purāṇa*, 96, 227, 536
Vārāṇasī, 329, 330
Vārkarīs, 356
Varma (name of Kṣatriyas), 185
Varma, L. A. Ravi, 525
Varma, V. P., 502, 586
Varman, Mahendra, 545
varṇa, 76, 334, 336
varṇaśrama dharma, 110, 172, 255, 443, 457, 474
vārta 341, 571
Varuṇa, 132, 134, 137, 188, 279, 281, 299; *Varuṇabhakti*, 222
vasant, 327
Vasavada, A. U., 509, 550
Vasco da Gama, 20, 486
vastra, 163
vāstupuruṣa, 317; *vāstupuruṣa maṇḍala*, 318; *vāstuśāstra*, 313, 317
Vasu, 279
Vasu, Srisa Chandra, 511
Vasudeva, 19, 239, 248
Vāsudeva Kṛṣṇa, 145, 240, 244, 554
Vatsyayan, Kapila, 500
Vātsyāyana, 53, 483
Vaudeville, C., 223 f, 225, 536, 543, 564
Vāyu, 46, 60, 114, 116, 123, 254, 315, 423; *Vāyu Purāṇa*, 73, 95,

546
Veda, 13, 22, 23, 61, 128, 162, 181, 185, 200, 209, 263, 378, 380, 381, 395, 409, 419, 425, 430, 435, 437, 446, 491; *vedarakṣa*, 77; *Vedāṅgas*, 67, 186, 200, 325, 479, 482; Vedavyāsa, 411
Vedānta, 24, 69, 80, 193, 203, 350, 398, 408 ff, 484; *Vedāntasūtra*, 180, 196, 350, 411, 482. See also: *Brahmasūtra*; schools of Vedānta, 412 ff; Vedāntācāryas, 413, 576
Vedāntadeśika, 253, 485
Vedāntakarikāvalī, 426
Vedāntaparibhāṣa, 426
Vedāntasāra, 425, 486
Vedārthasaṅgraha, 251, 426
vedī, 311
Vedic Concordance 24; Vedic civilisation, 38; Vedic sacrifices 39, 299. See also: *yajñas*; Vedic recitation, 68; Vedic religion, 31, 435; Vedic mathematics, 129; Vedic *saṃhitās*, 479; Vedic exegesis, 409; Vedic culture, 477; Vedic ritual, 526
vegetarianism, 45, 165
Veḷ/Velan, 298
Vena, 125, 339, 340
Vendan, 299
Venkatachari, K. K., 577
Vennainallur, 275
Venugopalacharya, T., 509
Venus, 123
Veriyadal, 298
Vesara style, 323
Vetter, T., 576
vibhava, 246, 248
Vibhiṣāna, 228
vibhuti, 402, 404, 406; *vibhutivistarayoga*, 107
vices, 53, 174
Vicitravīrya, 85
vidhi, 267
Vidhyas, 283
Vidura, 85
vidyā, 151, 212 ff, 216, 268, 282, 291, 411, 416; vidyas, 568
Vidya, Deheja, 567
Vidyābhūṣana, Satis Chandra, 570
Vidyāpati, 257
Vidyāraṇya, 351, 426, 578
Vidyarnava, Srisa Candra Vasu, 543
Viennot, O., 502
Vigasin, A., 497
Vijayanāgara, 485
Vijñānabhikṣu, 576
Vijñānanda, Swami, 548
vijñānamaya, 206
Vijñānavāda, 377
Vikra, 56, 57
vikṛtis, 77
villages, 459; village cults, 147; village community, 458
Vimalā Pīṭha, 350
vin, 145
vinaya, 288
Vindhya mountains, 125, 283; Vindhyavāsi, 282
violence, 234; see also: himsa
Vīraśaivas, 4, 189, 273, 353, 485, 547
Virāj, 113, 116
virajā, 270, 339
Virajananda Saraswati, Swami, 435
Virakal, 552
Vīramitrodaya, 313, 486
Virāṭ Hindū Sammelan, 467
Virāṭ Hindū Samāj, 64
Virāṭa, 86
virtues, 53, 416
Virupakṣa temple, 321
vīrya, 229, 248
viṣāda, 269
viśeṣa, 390, 391, 571
viśiṣṭa, 419
Viśiṣṭādvaita, 413, 417 ff

Viṣṇu, 41, 56, 58, 62, 90, 93, 96, 108, 120, 122, 138, 139, 143, 145, 152, 181, 206, 225, 226, 239ff, 248, 249, 261, 267, 279, 283, 297, 348, 352, 368, 419, 423, 425, 430, 523, 528; *Viṣṇu Purāṇa*, 58, 70, 95, 112, 124, 145, 174, 183, 239, 251, 428, 506, 520, 522, 525, 529, 531, 532, 538, 561, 571; Viṣṇu trivikrama, 145, 240; Viṣṇu *bhaktas*, 191, 225; Viṣṇu *avatāras*, 241; Viṣṇu *bhakti*, 222, 430; Viṣṇuloka, 123, 270, 271; Viṣṇuśakti, 124
Viṣṇucitta, 368, 369
Viṣṇudharmasūtra, 483
Viṣṇugupta, 341
Viṣṇusahasranāma, 524
Viṣṇusmṛti, 71, 562
Viṣṇuswami, 254
viśuddha cakra, 288
Viśva Hindū Pariṣad, 33, 466, 565, 586
Viśva Hindū Sammelan, 127
viśvarūpa, 266; *viśvarūpa darśana*, 107
Viśvakarma, 113
Viśvakarma Vāstuśāstra, 313, 556
Viśvamitra, 76, 336, 479
Viśvanātha, 261, 262; Viśvanāth(a) temple, 330, 466
Viśvanātha Cakravartti, 530
Viśvara, 362
Vitala, 122
Viṭṭal, 356
Vivādārnavasetu, 21
vivaha, 186, 192. See also: marriage
Vivasvān, 105
viveka, 403, 406
Vivekacudāmaṇī, 578
Vivekananda, Swami, 43, 47, 350, 432, 437f, 450
Volwahsen, A., 555, 556
vratas, 95, 183, 347, 448
Vrindāban, 7, 121, 146, 245, 257, 369
Vṛṣṇi, 145
Vṛtra, 132
vṛtti, 95, 382
Vyākaraṇa, 67
vyāpāra, 173
Vyas, R. T., 576
Vyāsa, 72, 83, 94, 363, 364, 399, 483; *Vyāsasmṛti*, 566; Vyāsāśrama, 422
vyāsana, 256, 542
vyavahāra-paramārtha, 128
vyūhas, 246, 248, 423

Wadley, S., 550
Waghorne, J. P., 554
war, 104; war dances, 298; warriors, 334
Wasson, R. G., 528
water, 116, 123, 160, 163, 190, 191, 197, 205, 206, 273, 283, 349, 388
Weber, A., 100, 508, 527
Weber, E., 543, 559
Weber, M., 333
Weightman, S., 504
Weizsäcker, C. F. von, 277,, 384,, 548
Werner, K., 573
Wescott, G. H., 564, 579
Wessdin, J. P., 21
Weyl, H., 384
wheat, 180
Wheeler, Sir Mortimer, 499, 523, 544
White Yajurveda, 69
White, Charles S. J., 540
Whitehead, H., 129, 524, 553, 548
Whitney, W. D. 508, 545
widows, 189, 374, 431
Wilkins, C., 21, 102
Wilson, H. H., 23, 434, 506, 511, 550, 562, 564
wind, 205
Winternitz, M. 478, 479, 496, 513, 514, 518

wisdom, 106, 249. See also: *vidyā*
women, 102, 107, 152, 185, 188, 189, 215, 255, 259, 308, 361 ff, 410, 431, 550; women philosopher, 195; women's duty 363; women's rights 375
Woodroff, John, 512, 548, 549
Woods, J. H., 24, 572
word, 74, 78, 147
world egg, 115, 119, 121, 123
worldrulers, 124
worldview, 112
worship, 107, 162, 163, 168, 221, 248, 255, 269, 278, 289, 316, 323 332, 431. See also: *pūjā*
Wright, M., 543
Wright, N., 543
writing, 77
Wulff, D. M., 550
Wyatt, N., 525

Yadav, B. S., 541
Yādavaprakāśa, 576
Yādavas, 145
yajñas, 38, 39, 67, 77, 105, 114, 116, 155–158, 165, 183, 213, 294, 334, 372
Yajñavālkya, 130, 137, 195, 205, 362; *Yajñavālkyasmṛti*, 71, 483, 566
yajñopavita, 160, 163, 185
Yajurveda, 67, 116, 140, 265, 523, 545
yajus, 94
yakṣas, 75, 87, 116, 122, 137
Yale, 24
yama-niyama, 53, 403, 455
Yama, 88, 97, 139, 190, 267, 279, 526
Yamī, 139
Yamunā, 147, 191, 225, 288, 329
Yamunācārya, 251, 528
Yamunacarya, M., 577
yantras, 149, 286, 286, 321
Yāska, 77
yatanīyaśarīra, 191
yatidharma, 348, 471; *Yatidharmasaṅgraha*, 563
Yatīndramatadīpikā, 426, 486
Yayāti period, 125, 482
yoga, 38, 60, 102, 105, 106, 234, 267, 268, 274, 380, 383, 391, 397 ff, 475
Yoga Research Institute, 574
Yogabhāṣya, 483
Yogānanda, Paramahamsa, 350, 442
yogāṅgas, 403
Yogasūtra, 53, 106, 397, 402, 404, 483, 505, 572, 573
Yogavaśiṣṭha Rāmāyaṇa, 539
Yogi Dhirendra Brahmacari, 293
Yogindra, Svatmarama, 572
Yogi(ni)s, 106, 267, 346, 354, 391
yojana, 120
yoni, 291
Yudhiṣṭhira, 86–89

Zabern, P. von, 588
Zelliot, E., 536, 538, 543
Ziegenbalg, B., 496
Zimmer, H., 27, 554
Zoroaster, 149
Zvelebil, K., 552